CLUES

ML2831.S39
SIMPSON, C BRITISH BROADSIDE BALLAD   CC

I CUM 00 0063402 B

W9-BZK-828

The
British Broadside
Ballad
and Its Music

The 1ᵗ Protestant-FLAYL :

A tory thing

An Excellent New SONG.

To the Tune of, *Lacy's Maggot* ; Or, *The Hobby-Horse.*

14ᵗ. Jun⁹. 1682

[1]

LIsten a while, and I'll tell you a Tale
Of a New Device of a *Protestant Flayl,*
With a *Thump, Thump, Thump, a Thump,*
Thump, a Thump, Thump.
This *FLAIL* it was made of the finest wood,
Well lin'd with Lead, and notable good,
For splitting of Bones, and shedding the Bloud
Of all that withstood,
With a Thump, Thump, &c.

[2]

This *Flayl* was invented to thrash the Brain,
And leave behind not the weight of a grain,
With a Thump, &c.
At the handle-end there hung a *Weight,*
That carried within unavoidable Fate,
To take the Monarch a rap in the Pate,
And govern the State,
With a Thump, &c.

[3]

It took its Degree in *Oxford*-Town,
And with the Carpenter went down,
With a Thump, &c.
If any durst his Might oppose,
He had you close, in spight of your Nose,
To carry on clever the *Good Old Cause,*
And down with the Laws,
With a Thump, &c.

[4]

VVith this they threatened to fore-stall
The Church, and give the Bishops a Mawl
With a Thump, &c.
If *King* and *Lords* would not submit
To the *Joyner's* wit whiles the *House* did sit,
If this in the right place did hit,
The Cause it would split,
With a Thump, &c.

[5]   [fast.

Two handfuls of Death, with a Thong hung
By a Zealot who hang'd himself at last,   *Stephen Colledge.*
With a Thump, &c.
VVith a moving head both stiff and stout,
Found by the *Protestant Joyner* out,
To have at the King & the Laws t'other bout,
And turn them both out,
With a Thump, &c.

[6]

Invisibly 'twou'd deal his Blows,
All to maintain the *Good Old Cause,*
With a Thump, &c.
VVou'd *Liberty* and *Freedom* bring
To every thing except the King,
At *Monarchy* it had a fling,
And took its swing,
VVith a Thump, &c.

[7]

This *Flayl* was made of the Newest Fashion,
To heal the Breaches of the Nation,
With a Thump, &c.
If *Faction* any difference bred,
T'twou'd split the Cause in the very Head,
Till *Monarchy* reel'd, and *Loyalty* bled,
And were knock'd in the Head,
With a Thump, &c.

[8]

VVhen any Strife was in the State,
This *Flayl* wou'd end the whole Debate,
With a Thump, &c.
'Gainst *Arbitrary Power of State,*
And *Popery* which the *Zealous* hate,
It wou'd give them such a Rap on the Pate,
They must yield to their Fate,
With a Thump, &c.

[9]

It had a thousand Vertues more,
And had a Salve for every Sore,
With a Thump, &c.
VVith this they thought to have maintain'd,
The *Loyal* Tribe, and *Royalists* braind:
But the *Joyner* was hang'd, and the *Flayl* was
And the Conquest Regain'd,   [Arraign'd
With a Thump, &c.

[10]

May *Tony* and all our Enemies, *E Shaftsbury.*
Meet with no better fate then his,
With a Thump, &c.
May *Charles* still Live to rule the State,
And *York* whom all *Dissenters* hate,
To be reveng'd upon their Pate,
By timely fate,
With a Thump, Thump, Thump a Thump,
Thump, a Thump, Thump.

LONDON: Printed for *A. Banks,* MDCLXXXII.

This broadside contains music of "The Hobby Horse" as well as manuscript notations of price and purchase date in the hand of Narcissus Luttrell, the original owner. Reproduced from the Luttrell-Bindley pamphlets, No. 144, by permission of the Huntington Library, San Marino, California.

The
British Broadside
Ballad
and Its Music

by

CLAUDE M. SIMPSON

CUMBERLAND COUNTY COLLEGE
LIBRARY P.O. BOX 517 VINELAND N.J.

RUTGERS UNIVERSITY PRESS

New Brunswick   *New Jersey*

ML2831
539
Bn
1966

68-4343

Copyright © 1966 by Rutgers, The State University

Library of Congress Catalogue Card Number: 63-16308

Manufactured in the United States of America by Quinn & Boden Company, Inc., Rahway, New Jersey

This book was manufactured with the assistance of a grant from the Ford Foundation.

To
Elizabeth Carrigan Simpson
and
To the Memory of
Hyder Edward Rollins

Contents

Introduction

Until about a century ago, collectors and scholars drew no clear line of demarcation between the orally circulating ballad of tradition and the printed or broadside ballad. Yet the two genres are essentially distinct, even though some traditional ballads and songs found their way into print (many Robin Hood ballads are known to us chiefly from broadsides), and a goodly number of broadside pieces have become traditional.[1] Although Francis J. Child was not the first to concentrate his attentions on the ballad of tradition, his pioneering work, *The English and Scottish Popular Ballads*, 1882–1898, has firmly established the concept of distinction between the two modes of circulation and preservation, and his general denigration of the broadside has furnished much subsequent criticism with a fashionable, if unexamined, point of view.[2]

As a generic term, the word *broadside* designates a single sheet, usually of folio size, printed on one side. Broadsides thus include proclamations, news letters, and other prose pieces; and among poetical broadsides must be included odes, satires, theatrical prologues and epilogues, heroic epistles, elegiac verses, as well as ballads. This being said, we shall ordinarily use the word broadside to mean broadside ballad, recognizing further that the conventional concept of ballad as narrative is often stretched to include pieces predominantly lyric. The broadside, written usually by a hack versifier to a common tune, was sold in bookstalls or fair booths or hawked about cities and towns by street singers (hence the frequent allusions to stall or street ballad). The term *slip ballad* derives from the long, narrow shape frequently encountered after the early

---

[1] G. Malcolm Laws, *American Balladry from British Broadsides*, 1957, lists as traditionally current in North America 290 ballads deriving from British broadsides or songsters. I have treated only those few European analogues which in broadside form were associated with a tune.

[2] Albert B. Friedman, *The Ballad Revival*, 1961, has performed a useful service in showing the influence of both broadside and traditional balladry upon sophisticated poetry. Friedman's study enables us to see in historical context the assumed similarities as well as the distinctions between the two popular genres.

eighteenth century; and the word *garland,* which ordinarily signified a small pamphlet or chapbook containing several ballads,[3] was occasionally used as a synonym for broadside, as in the single piece entitled "The Masquerade Garland."

The broadside ballad was essentially an urban variety of subliterary expression, and London was its undisputed headquarters. Although the production of printers in the Seven Dials district—Pitts, Such, Catnach, and others—achieved astronomical sales during the Victorian age,[4] the most influential period of the broadside ballad was from the beginning of Elizabeth I's reign to about 1700. During its heyday the broadside was printed in black letter and the verses were embellished by one or more pictorial woodcuts, chosen with only the loosest regard for their appropriateness. There were exceptions to this general practice: from the middle of the seventeenth century, political ballads were often printed in roman letter, and, during the final quarter of that century, woodcuts were sometimes replaced or augmented by lines of musical notation.

This is not the place for a history of the broadside ballad.[5] Suffice it to say that before the days of the newspaper and magazine, the broadside was a medium of mass communication whose importance can scarcely be overestimated. It reported such historical events as the coronation of William and Mary or Charles I's escape after the battle of Worcester. It proved invaluable in partisan political propaganda, rising to heights of effectiveness—accompanied often by depths of scurrility—when public interest was focused on the Rump Parliament, the Popish Plot, or the bloodless revolution of 1688. But concern with current events was not limited to affairs of state. Scarcely a criminal of any notoriety was executed without the issuance of a versified account of his crime, his trial, and his good-night to the world. Sensationalism of other sorts abounded, too, as in the Sunday supplements of today's newspapers. Prodigies of nature—monstrous births, rains of frogs, stranded whales—were served up to the credulous, along with warnings of God's judgment to be read into human calamities, whether the subject were a woman swallowed up by a sudden crack in the earth or Dr. Faustus being claimed by the devil. The ballad of "Greensleeves" inspired more than one moral parody, and

[3] Two of the most interesting collections of prose and poetical chapbooks are the seventeenth-century Penny Merriments gathered by Samuel Pepys, and the Penny Histories brought together by Joseph Ritson a century later.

[4] See Charles Hindley, *The Life and Times of James Catnach (Late of Seven Dials), Ballad Monger,* 1878, and William Henderson, *Victorian Street Ballads,* 1937.

[5] For an excellent treatment of its major phase, see Hyder E. Rollins, "The Black-Letter Broadside Ballad," *PMLA,* XXXIV (1919), 258–339. Less thorough but interesting for its discussion of more recent developments is Leslie Shepard, *The Broadside Ballad,* 1962. Branford P. Millar's British Balladry of the Eighteenth Century, unpublished Harvard dissertation, 1946, is an intensive and illuminating study.

the way to virtue was literally spelled out, hornbook fashion, in such an acrostic broadside as "The Virgin's A. B. C."

To offset the doleful ballad there were countless pieces on amatory subjects, exploiting the perennial grotesquerie of the jilted suitor, the shrewish wife, the fumbling husband. Conspicuous among ballads of courtship is the sort made by expanding a short pastoral lyric with its stiffly conventional Strephons and Chloes. The tone becomes earthier when the narrative places Jockey and Jenny against a sketchily synthetic Scotch background. Typically the youth is more interested in giving his lass a green gown than a wedding ring. As time passes, the frank gusto of many such Renaissance and Restoration ballads gives way to a sentimentalized resolution in which timely marriage vows are exchanged or the maid, abandoned and with child, becomes the subject of pathos.

The broadside ballad is both a conditioner and a mirror of popular attitudes. In the period with which we are most concerned the whole gamut is in evidence, from the stern phrases of the Puritan moralist to the bawdy jests of the rude groundling or the cynicism of the rake-about-town. Despite a steady attack by the pious upon indecent plays and ballads, the attention of Licensers of the Press and their paid informers was directed chiefly against sedition and only rarely against the obscene. To some extent the immunity enjoyed by the ballad and the prose pamphlet resulted from the ease with which brief pieces could be printed surreptitiously. But the large number of unlicensed ballads published by well-established syndicates of booksellers would seem to indicate that concealment was only occasionally necessary. Except in the treatment of vital political topics in time of crisis, there was really no significant difference between licensed and unlicensed ballads.[6]

One explanation for the popularity and influence of the broadside is that it was written to music already familiar. The evidence, though it is not uniform, indicates that the ballad writer ordinarily had a specific tune in mind as he began to frame his stanza pattern. The black-letter broadside only exceptionally contained music; instead, a tune direction named the tune or tunes to which the ballad could be sung. "The States-mans Downfal," for instance, had as part of its heading the rubric "Tune of, Hold fast thy Sword and Scepter Charles; or, Russels farewel." Some sheets contained such blind directions as "To a Pleasant New Play-House Tune" or "To a New Northern Tune." And the onset of the eighteenth century saw the gradual disappearance of the tune direction from ballads

---

[6] The records of the Company of Stationers show some three thousand ballads licensed between 1557 and 1709 (see Rollins, *Anal. Index*). As a guess, at least three to five times that number were issued without license or without specific entry in the Stationers' Registers.

old and new, depriving us of the links between printed ballad and singing traditions.[7]

For a brief period at the end of the seventeenth century, a small percentage of broadside sheets included music. Doubtless this development is related to the increasing importance of new stage tunes and the exploitation of theatrical popularity to float new songs and ballads. Whether or not this is the sole explanation, the tunes printed were more likely to be new than old. Unhappily, musical notation was often inaccurate, and almost half the extant exemplars prove to be a meaningless profusion of clef signs, rests, and notes in an impossible musical grammar. A few of these fakes became printer's stock and reappeared with ballad after ballad, like the ubiquitous woodcut of Queen Elizabeth. The fifth volume of Samuel Pepys's collection may serve as an example of late seventeenth-century practice. It is made up almost exclusively of roman-letter ballad sheets, and the 435 pieces include some 156 with musical notation; but more than a hundred of these musical specimens are corrupt and most can be classified as meaningless.[8] We can be grateful for those melodies that are printed with some degree of accuracy on ballad sheets, yet this is one of our slenderest resources, and we must look in other directions to find traces of most of the surviving broadside tunes.

By a fortunate circumstance of taste, sixteenth- and seventeenth-century instrumental pieces often exploited the theme-and-variation form, and such composers as William Byrd, Orlando Gibbons, Thomas Morley, and Dr. John Bull did not disdain to write their "divisions" upon popular song and dance-tunes. The rich keyboard literature, typified by *My Ladye Nevells Booke,* a collection of pieces by Byrd, and *The Fitzwilliam Virginal Book,* a voluminous general anthology, shows widespread indebtedness to street tunes, many of which were used for singing broadsides.[9] Lute tablatures, most of them in manuscript, also contain many pieces by John Dowland, John Johnson, Antony Holborne, Francis Cutting, and others based on broadside tunes.[10] A small amount of similar music

[7] Among other casualties, we must regret the absence of tune directions from versions of such familiar traditional ballads as "Barbara Allen" and "Lord Thomas and Fair Eleanor" which appeared in print during the seventeenth and eighteenth centuries. Lacking such information we cannot determine the continuity, if any, between tunes used then and now.

[8] The corrupt notation on page 206 is reproduced also on broadsides preserved at pages 221, 260, 401, and 403 of the volume.

[9] For a description of the principal keyboard manuscripts and printed collections of the English Renaissance, with inventory of their contents, see the article "Virginal Music" in the fifth edition of *Grove's Dictionary of Music and Musicians* plus Supplement. Thurston Dart, "New Sources of Virginal Music," *Music and Letters,* XXXV (April, 1954), 93–106, offers further addenda.

[10] A good handlist is contained in David Lumsden, "The Sources of English Lute Music (1540–1620)," *Galpin Society Journal,* No. VI (July, 1953), 14–22. Lumsden's unpublished Cambridge dissertation of 1957, under the same title, includes inventories.

for viols or for broken consort has also survived. A general limitation of all this composed music is that we cannot always extract a satisfactory unembellished statement of the thematic air; because ballad tunes were not coupled with ballad verse, natural constraining influences upon tune detail gave way easily before the tendency to virtuoso effects. In some pieces a descant line can be found in an ostinato bass; sometimes no unadorned version of the air is present; occasionally only the final section of a florid piece presents the tune in starkly simple form. This literature of instrumental performance pieces, although serving quite other purposes, remains our best source for such tunes as "Sellenger's Round," "John, Come Kiss Me Now," "The Carman's Whistle," "Fortune My Foe," "The Shaking of the Sheets," and a great many others.

During the Renaissance the relationship between England and the Continent was musically a two-way street. A few broadside tunes came from abroad, e.g., "Chi Passa," "The Spanish Pavan," "Rogero," and, in a later generation, "Farinel's Ground." Likewise English tunes found their way across the Channel and took root, particularly in the Low Countries. The Thysius lute book, a Dutch MS of c. 1600, contains a cosmopolitan repertoire including many song and dance tunes from Britain. More striking perhaps is a group of seventeenth-century Dutch songbooks which printed many English ballad tunes in conjunction with sacred or secular Dutch verses. Of these J. J. Starter's *Friesche Lust-Hof*, 1621, and Adriaen Valerius's *Neder-Landtsche Gedenck-Clanck*, 1626, are representative, while other collections without music contain the names of English tunes familiar enough to be cited for singing.

Another invaluable source of ballad tunes is a collection of country dances with their music, *The Dancing Master*. This popular work, the first edition of which was called *The English Dancing Master*, went through eighteen editions between 1651 and c. 1728 and grew from an original hundred tunes to more than 900 in three fat volumes. It is often a moot point whether a given air represents a ballad tune adapted to dance purposes or vice versa; evidently both processes operated. Moreover, in successive editions one can observe the gradual recasting of melodic lines to convert modal tunes to conventional major or minor.

John Playford, the original publisher of *The Dancing Master*, was the leading purveyor of instruction books which recognized ballad and dance tunes as a cornerstone of the music student's basic repertoire. To him we owe such popular tutors as *Apollo's Banquet for the Treble Violin*, *Musick's Delight on the Cithren*, *Musicks Recreation on the Lyra Viol*, *Musicks Hand-maid* for keyboard instruments, and Thomas Greeting's *Pleasant Companion* for flageolet. Playford's several collections of song, including *Select Musicall Ayres, and Dialogues*, Henry Lawes's *Ayres and Dialogues*, and the variously titled volumes of *Choice Ayres, Songs, & Dialogues*, are of special value because many of their texts were later expanded by hack poets to fill a broadside sheet; in many cases the composed music associated with the original verses was used repeatedly for singing other broadsides. This kind of appropriation became widespread in the last decades of the seventeenth century, when amplified playhouse songs entered the broadside market in wholesale lots. A notable example is Henry Purcell's tune composed for "If love's a sweet passion" in *The Fairy Queen*, 1692, which was used for singing some three dozen street ballads.[11]

Of even greater importance to us than the folio vocal collections is the handful of poetical miscellanies containing music. One such is *A Choice Collection of 180 Loyal Songs*, 1685, made up largely of contemporary political broadside texts, and full of indifferently printed tunes. A larger and more general collection, retrospective of popular tastes, is *Wit and Mirth: or Pills to Purge Melancholy*. Begun as a two-volume anthology in 1699–1700, this work grew to five volumes in several editions published up to 1714. Its final six-volume edition of 1719–1720 was edited by the well-known dramatist, song writer, and singer Thomas D'Urfey. Although *Pills* was not the only work of its kind, it is much the most voluminous, and almost all the 1100 songs are printed with their music. Many pieces are reprints of broadsides, perhaps set up from the sheets themselves, with music added whether it was on the original issues or not. Because it was D'Urfey's common practice to write stage songs to ballad airs, we find his appreciation for this kind of tune reflected throughout the collection. Indeed, the first two volumes of his edition consist entirely of D'Urfey songs. The importance of *Pills* for broadside music lies in the fact that many a ballad tune has been preserved solely in its pages.

The last important storehouse of broadside tunes is the ballad opera. John Gay's *The Beggar's Opera* was a phenomenal success when it appeared in 1728, and, before the rage subsided a generation later, more than a hundred ballad operas had been written. Gay was satirizing operatic convention, among other things, and instead of elaborate arias he punctuated his drama with more than sixty brief songs set to common tunes, most of them derived from broadside literature of the previous age. Gay's little stratagem is a fine indication of the tunes that were still familiar to an eighteenth-century audience. Most of the productions imitating Gay's successful formula were pedestrian, though Henry Fielding, before he turned to fiction, wrote seven ballad operas that require little apology. Fortunately for us, about fifty were printed with their

[11] An indispensable bibliographical guide is Robert Gale Noyes and Roy Lamson, Jr., "Broadside-Ballad Versions of the Songs in Restoration Drama," *Harvard Studies and Notes in Philology and Literature*, XIX (1937), 199–218. Also pertinent is Lamson's "Henry Purcell's Dramatic Songs and the English Broadside Ballad," *PMLA*, LIII (1938), 148–161.

music, and most of the others name the air to which each song text was to be sung. This extensive documentation gives us a vivid insight into tastes at a time when an important transition was occurring, for around the end of the seventeenth century the broadside ballad as a vehicle for singing began to face competition from the single-sheet song. Typically the engraved sheet contained an air with bass, plus another version of the tune in a key suitable for recorder or transverse flute, and a much reduced song text. Here was born the direct ancestor of modern popular sheet music.

Whereas the single-sheet song emphasized music at the expense of text, the broadside's relationship with music became more tenuous as the eighteenth century advanced. Ballad reprints dropped tune directions, and new pieces, as often as not, named no air for singing. The broadside persisted, and in its essentials continues alive today. But the great flowering before 1700 remains the period of its dominance. To it our attentions are chiefly directed in these pages.

The purpose of this book is to relate broadside ballads to the tunes for which they were designed. Some two thousand tune names are associated with broadsides, and from what we know of the way in which tunes acquired multiple titles, it seems fair to assume that about a thousand different airs are implied. Of these, over four hundred have survived, and I undertake to discuss the uses to which each of these tunes has been put.

Inevitably I have built upon the researches of William Chappell, whose *Collection of National English Airs*, 1838–1840, was followed by his major work, *Popular Music of the Olden Time*, 1855–1859. In demonstrating that England had a national music, Chappel assembled a vast quantity of lore, supplementing the accounts of Sir John Hawkins and Charles Burney. The less formal aspects of music centering around song and dance were his particular interest, and in addition to the music itself he ransacked literary sources for evidence of currency and vogue. In an age before the traditional ballad had been sharply defined or systematically collected, he perforce depended chiefly upon written evidence, and as a consequence *Popular Music* is largely devoted to broadside literature. It is here that Chappell made perhaps his most distinctive contribution, although he did not consciously attempt a definitive study. Indeed, he stated that he had dealt inclusively with the broadside only to about 1660, being selective in his discussion of the Restoration and later periods.

Chappell's researches were amazingly thorough, his standard of scholarship exceptional for his day. His *Popular Music* has remained a standard reference tool in its field, despite shortcomings which we can see from our perspective of a century. His book, for all its erudition, was addressed to a general audience and was intended as much for the pianoforte music-rack as for the library shelf. Consequently the criterion of presentability took precedence over antiquarian unconventionality whenever the two were in conflict. Academic harmonic patterns were imposed on popular melodies, ancient modalities suppressed, irregular tunes squared off. When Chappell reprinted song and ballad verse the same standards prevailed, with bowdlerization sometimes indicated by inverted commas, sometimes not. But Chappell should not be judged harshly; if he was limited by the tastes of his age, he often transcended them, and his essential sanity and healthiness of mind deserve respect.

Under the title *Old English Popular Music,* a revision of Chappell's book by H. E. Wooldridge was issued in 1893. Wooldridge was interested chiefly in Renaissance music and provided more nearly accurate transcripts, but only for tunes in the first of his two volumes. He eliminated the few traditional airs which Chappell had printed, omitted virtually all Chappell's attention to the eighteenth century, and systematically abridged the commentary without bringing it up to date. He did draw on a few musical sources not available to Chappell, but otherwise his revision seems less useful than the original and has found only limited favor in the intervening years.

I have not attempted another revision of Chappell's *Popular Music of the Olden Time.* Histories of professional music and musicians now give detailed treatment to Renaissance and baroque periods, viewing them in international perspective and relating music to the other arts and to society, including those special societies of the court and the church. Moreover, the vitality of a musical tradition among the English populace seems no longer a proposition in need of defense, so clearly has it been demonstrated by Chappell and subsequent historians. But that part of Chappell's work which deals with the broadside ballad I have used as a starting point for my own research, retracing his steps, correcting and amplifying him wherever possible in the light of present-day knowledge. In accordance with my aims, I have eliminated discussion of tunes having no broadside relationship, but I have added materially to Chappell's post-1660 coverage, and in all I treat about twice as many broadside tunes as did he.[12] A significant number of new musical sources have been discovered, particularly in manuscripts of the sixteenth and seventeenth cen-

[12] I have consciously ignored a handful of theater tunes whose only broadside connection is with the verses of the dramatic song itself: the verses were printed on a broadside, but the music was not named for singing any other broadside. Typical are two Purcell songs, "Celemene, pray tell me," from Southerne's *Oroonoko* (broadside text, Morgan 39), and "Come let us leave the town," from Settle's *The Fairy Queen* (broadside text, *OPB*, p. 98). The same criterion accounts for my passing over such religious broadsides as are listed and discussed in Susi Jeans, "The Easter Psalms of Christ's Hospital," *Proceedings of the Royal Musical Association,* LXXXVIII (1961–1962), 45–60.

tury; scholarly editions of keyboard and vocal music have incorporated much of these recent findings, but tablatures have received relatively sparse attention. Several important ballad collections unknown to Chappell have subsequently come to light, others have been assembled, and a great migration from private collections to public or university libraries on both sides of the Atlantic has taken place; indeed, except for the collections in London, Oxford, and Cambridge, the location of almost every important gathering of broadside ballads has altered since Chappell wrote. Modern reprints of more than three thousand broadsides (in *BB*, Collmann, *CP, OEB, OPB, PA, PB, PG, RB, SB,* and one or two others) are for the most part highly dependable [13] and obviate the need for swelling these pages in a manner useful in Chappell's age, but the number of yet unreprinted ballads is so large that one wishes those spacious days had not departed, perhaps forever.

Citations of broadsides follow spelling, capitalization, and pointing of the original, but do not reproduce italics, small capitals, or full capitals other than initial letters of words. To facilitate identification I usually quote both title and first line, as well as tune direction and significant details of refrain, where appropriate. This information is usually followed by a parenthetical location reference, cast in one or other of the forms illustrated here:

Ex. 1 (Wood 417 [34], Euing 352)
Ex. 2 (Douce, Euing, Harvard, Roxburghe; reprinted in *RB* VI, 235)

The distinction between these examples is that, if I know of no modern reprint, I give detailed location data for broadside originals (Ex. 1), whereas I merely name the appropriate collections when I can direct the reader to a modern reprint, where full data can usually be found (Ex. 2).[14] In each example, the first collection named is the source from which I have quoted; other copies are not necessarily of the same edition. In the second example the order of parts indicates that the source of the *RB* reprint is the Roxburghe copy.

The dating of ballads by means of printers' and booksellers' imprints has been subject to increasing refinement, thanks to the enterprise of Chappell, Frank Kidson, and the cataloguer of Lord Crawford's collection.[15] I have given greatest weight, however, to the more recent authority

[13] For reservations expressed toward the practices of one editor, see my "Ebsworth and the Roxburghe Ballads," *JAF*, LXI (1948), 337–344.

[14] Ballads in American libraries are often not identified with named collections. Because it is common practice to catalogue each piece separately (especially those antedating 1700), I have merely named the appropriate library, even in contexts requiring full location data.

[15] Paul G. Morrison's *Index of Printers, Publishers and Booksellers* for both *STC*, 1950, and Wing, 1955, must be used with caution inasmuch as his dating of ballad

of R. B. McKerrow *et al.*, *A Dictionary of Printers and Booksellers . . . ,
1557–1640,* 1910, and Henry R. Plomer's continuations for the periods
1641–1667 and 1668–1725, supplemented by the invaluable information
on booksellers' syndicates in Cyprian Blagden's "Notes on the Ballad
Market in the Second Half of the Seventeenth Century," *Studies in Bibliography,* VI (1953–1954), 161–180. For ballad vogue as mirrored by incidental references in plays, I am indebted to the painstaking work in
Andrew J. Walker's unpublished Harvard dissertation of 1934, Popular
Songs and Broadside Ballads in the English Drama, 1559–1642, and I
have often drawn on Alfred Harbage's *Annals of English Drama, 975–
1700,* 1940, in matters of dating and authorship.

I cite musical sources as explicitly as possible, at the risk of repeating
bibliographical information from one article to another. I usually indicate the location of music manuscripts, except for such frequently cited
sources as the Euing lute book (University of Glasgow), the Leyden MS
of 1639, the Agnes Hume MS, the Skene MS, and the Graham transcripts
of the Straloch MS and the Leyden lyra viol MS (National Library of
Scotland), the several Drexel manuscripts and the John Gamble Commonplace Book (New York Public Library), the William Ballet and
Thomas Dallis lute books (Trinity College, Dublin). The Marsh lute
book is in Archbishop Marsh's Library, Dublin. It is to be noted that
the three Dublin MSS are of English origin, as are the several Paris
Conservatoire MSS cited in these pages. The lost Dorothy (*recte* John)
Welde lute book has been rediscovered in the library of Lord Forrester,
where it was formerly known to be; I usually cite it as the Welde Lute
MS. Priscilla Bunbury's Virginal Book is in the library of Mr. Roger
Lancelyn Green of Poulton-Lancelyn, Cheshire.[16]

I have tried to indicate precisely whether verse texts are or are not
accompanied by music. When I note the presence of a tune direction,
I do not thereby imply that musical notation is also present; if such is
the case I say so explicitly. A few tune discussions are headed with
bracketed titles, to indicate my arbitrary assignment of a tune name,
made necessary by the absence of a meaningful tune title on broadsides,
but the music is confidently associated with broadside verse unless otherwise noted.

In transcribing tunes I have usually limited myself to the melodic line,
except that lute tablatures with their precise pitch indications possess

imprints reflects the often superseded approximations in such sources as the Crawford
Catalogue.

[16] For other location details, see the sources cited in notes 9 and 10 above. I regret
that the second volume of John Bull's *Keyboard Music,* ed. Thurston Dart, *Musica
Britannica,* vol. XIX, 1963, was published too late for me to note at appropriate points
the printing of such Bull sets as "Bonny Sweet Robin," "Go from my window," "Bonny
Peg of Ramsey," "The Spanish Pavan," and "Walsingham."

an objective harmonic validity worth preserving, and I have ordinarily rendered fully the statement of a tune as it stands in tablature. I have indicated emendations by brackets within the transcript or by textual remarks beneath it. Where I have corrected mistakes in time values or barring, I have reproduced uncorrected notational elements immediately beneath the emended forms. I have supplied bar-lines for unbarred musical texts having a perceptibly regular pattern of accentuation and have so indicated in a textual note. When I have regularized irregular or incomplete barring, brackets indicate those bar-lines supplied. A few older melodies and a pair of psalm tunes are sufficiently irregular to be presented in their original unbarred form. I have reproduced slurs as they are found in MS or printed sources. Usually indicating groups of two or more notes sung to one syllable, they may exactly fit an initial stanza but not succeeding ones, and rarely is the pattern completely suitable for singing other songs. A comparable problem arises in the frequent need to divide notes to accommodate minor syllabic irregularities from one stanza to another. Musical transcripts, often from nonvocal sources, cannot hope to fit these ever-shifting needs, but the singer emends subconsciously and has always done so.

Finally, when it is possible to choose from among several versions of a tune, I have selected the earliest one which is suitable for singing, aware that these criteria cannot always be objective. Where a tune has undergone significant changes in the course of its vogue, I have not hesitated to print multiple versions.

I express my cordial thanks to the following institutions and governing boards for granting me kind permission to reproduce tunes from manuscripts in their possession: the Folger Shakespeare Library (MS 448.16; MS 1610.1); the New York Public Library (MS Drexel 4257, John Gamble's Commonplace Book; MS Drexel 5612); the Trustees of the British Museum (MS Harl. 7578; MS Add. 4900; MS Add. 10337, Elizabeth Rogers's Virginal Book; MS Add. 11608; MS Add. 15117; MS Add. 17786; MS Add. 18936; MS Add. 23623; MS Add. 24665, Giles Earle's Song Book; MS Add. 30486; MS Add. 32343; MS Add. 38539; MS Add. 38599); the Royal College of Music (MS 1119); the Bodleian Library (MS Ashmole 36–37; MS Mus.b.1; MS Rawl. Poet. 152); the Governing Body of Christ Church, Oxford (Music MS 431; Music MS 437); the University Library, Cambridge (MS Dd.2.11; MS Dd.3.18; MS Dd.4.23; MS Dd.6.48; MS Dd.9.33); the Syndics of the Fitzwilliam Museum, Cambridge (MS 30.G.20); the Warden and Fellows of St. Michael's College, Tenbury Wells, Worcs. (MS 1019); the Trustees of the National Library of Scotland (Adv. MS 5.2.14, the Leyden MS of 1639); the Edinburgh University Library (MS Dc.1.69); the Board of Trinity College, Dublin (MS D.1.21, William Ballet Lute Book; MS D.3.30, Thomas Dallis Lute Book; MS

F.5.13); Bibliothèque du Conservatoire de Musique, Paris (MS Rés. 1185; MS Rés. 1186).

I am most grateful to those libraries which have allowed me to reprint tunes from ballads and single-sheet songs in their possession. I have drawn substantially on the great collections in the British Museum, the Bodleian Library, the Pepysian Library of Magdalene College, Cambridge, the Houghton Library of Harvard University, and the Huntington Library, San Marino, California. I am equally indebted to the William Andrews Clark Memorial Library of the University of California, Los Angeles; the Library of Congress; the Rt. Hon. The Earl of Crawford; the Manchester Public Libraries; and the Feoffees of Chetham's Hospital and Library, Manchester. For permission to use a tune from *The Dublin Virginal Manuscript*, 1954, I express thanks to Professor John Ward, editor of the manuscript, and to Wellesley College, holder of the copyright.

One of my fundamental debts is to my friend and former colleague, Roy Lamson, Jr., whose Harvard dissertation of 1936, English Broadside Ballad Tunes, 1550–1700, is a bibliographical resource of first importance to anyone working in the field. In addition, I am glad to acknowledge the great value of his typescript file, deposited in the Houghton Library, containing bibliographical descriptions of the Harvard black-letter broadsides and many roman-letter pieces of later date. Without Professor Lamson's encouragement and kind cooperation over the years, I should not have had the temerity to undertake the present work.

I have also received invaluable assistance from Prof. John Ward, whose knowledge of Renaissance music is encyclopedic. He has generously supplied me with manuscript materials and has answered many vexing questions; the use to which I have put his important article, "Music for *A Handefull of Pleasant Delites*," *JAMS*, X (1957), 151–180, can be seen on many of my pages.

Like all students of the printed ballad, I have depended heavily upon the superb collections of Harvard's Houghton Library, and have profited from the unfailing kindnesses of Mr. William A. Jackson, Miss Carolyn Jakeman, Mr. William B. Bond, and the special courtesies of Mr. Thomas Matthews. I have been repeatedly welcomed at the Folger Shakespeare Library, and I owe thanks to its director Louis B. Wright for the timely grant of a fellowship, to Miss Dorothy Mason for putting the musical resources of the library freely at my disposal, and to Mr. Giles E. Dawson for special assistance in dating several Renaissance manuscripts. Likewise I am happy to acknowledge the many courtesies of the Huntington Library and particularly wish to record my indebtedness to the late Miss Edythe N. Backus, who shared her minute knowledge of Huntington music in days before the publication of her *Catalogue;* I owe thanks also to Mr. John Pomfret and Miss Mary Isabel Fry for numerous favors. The New York Public Library kindly gave me access to important seventeenth-century music books and manuscripts, and Carleton Sprague Smith, Philip Miller, Sydney Beck, and Mrs. Sirvart Poladian of the Music Division were especially helpful.

Other American libraries and librarians deserving my warmest thanks include the Yale University Library; the Library of Congress; the Pierpont Morgan Library; the William Andrews Clark Memorial Library of the University of California, Los Angeles, and its reference librarian, Mrs. Edna C. Davis; the Music Library of the University of California, Berkeley, and its directors, Mr. Vincent Duckles and Mrs. Harriet Nicewonger; the Stanford University Music Library and Mr. Edward E. Colby, its director; the Vassar College Library; the Ohio State University Libraries and Miss Olga Buth, head of the Music Library; the University of Michigan Libraries; and the Chapin Library of Williams College.

During a year in England and Scotland, I incurred many debts which I am happy to acknowledge. The staff of the British Museum was tirelessly cooperative in unearthing many a fugitive piece and in allowing me unlimited use of its unparalleled broadside ballad and sheet song collections; the privilege of working in the North Library greatly simplified my researches, thanks to the good offices of the late F. Geoffrey Rendall. I single out Arthur G. Hudd of the Museum staff for many favors over the years. Thanks are due also to the Library of the London Society of Antiquaries; the Bodleian and Christ Church libraries, Oxford; the Cambridge University Library and its gracious Secretary Arthur Tillotson; the Pepysian Library of Magdalene College, Cambridge; the Fitzwilliam Library in Cambridge and its librarian Miss Phyllis M. Giles; the Chapter Library of Durham Cathedral; the Manchester Public Libraries; the John Rylands Library of the University of Manchester; the Chetham College Library and its librarian Miss Hilda Lofthouse; St. Michael's College, Tenbury Wells; the National Library of Scotland; the Edinburgh University Library; the Glasgow University Library; the Mitchell Library in Glasgow; and the Dundee Free Library. I am uniquely in the debt of the Rt. Hon. The Earl of Crawford for his kindness in allowing me to inspect his incomparable collection of broadsides and for other personal favors.

To many associates I am indebted for information, encouragement, research assistance, or salutary skepticism. In addition to the late Hyder E. Rollins, the undoubted *magister* of the broadside ballad in our century and my mentor in matters great and small, I should like to thank Richard D. Altick, Matthew J. Bruccoli, Bertrand H. Bronson, Helen S. Culler, Cyrus L. Day, Margaret Dean-Smith, Robert M. Estrich, W. N.

H. Harding, Frederic W. Heimberger, Lucyle Hook, J. Leslie Hotson, William M. Howie, Ruth Hughey, Henry W. Kaufman, Herbert Livingston, Richard B. Looser, Milton O. Percival, Gordon N. Ray, Robert G. Shedd, Helen Smith, Ruth Smith, Hans Sperber, Regina Tanzy, Francis Lee Utley, Harold R. Walley, Everett Walters, Bartlett Jere Whiting, and John Harold Wilson. I owe special gratitude to Joseph B. Carrigan for a host of personal kindnesses extending over many years.

For academic leave, travel, and research assistance I wish to thank Harvard University, which granted me a Dexter Fellowship and provided clerical aid through the Milton and Clark Funds; the Rockefeller Foundation, which granted me a Post-War Fellowship in the Humanities; the United States Department of State, under whose auspices I enjoyed a Fulbright Research Grant at the University of London; and the Graduate School of the Ohio State University, which generously provided research and clerical funds.

Enthusiastically and with no false modesty, I offer my final word of thanks to my wife, whose eyes and hand and brain have been extensions of my own. She had a large share in every stage of this work, so much so that I cannot hope to express an indebtedness that has no end.

CLAUDE M. SIMPSON

Stanford, California

Abbreviations

The following list identifies abbreviations, catchwords, and short titles frequently used in this volume.

Antidote against Melancholy	*An Antidote against Melancholy: Made up in Pills. Compounded of Witty Ballads, Jovial Songs, and Merry Catches*, 1661; 2d ed., 1669. Enlarged as *Wit and Mirth. An Antidote against Melancholy . . .* , 3d ed., 1682; with sixteen additional pages, reissued as *Wit and Mirth. . . . The Third Edition, Enlarged . . .* , 1684. This series is to be distinguished from the songbooks cited under *Pills.*
Apollo's Banquet	*Apollo's Banquet for the Treble Violin*, 1670. (Neither of the two known copies of this edition contains a title page; title and date are here supplied from the entry in Arber's *Term Catalogues*, I, 38.) Copies of the following editions have survived: 5th ed., 1687; 6th ed., 1690 (Second Book, 1691); 7th ed., 1693; 8th ed., *Apollo's Banquet, Newly Reviv'd*, 1701. This popular work had its inception in "The Tunes of the French Dances and other New Tunes for the Treble-Violin," which John Playford published as a supplement to the third edition of *The Dancing Master*, c. 1662 (56 pieces) and 1665 (85 pieces).
Arber, *Term Catalogues*	*The Term Catalogues, 1668–1709 . . .* , ed. Edward Arber, 3 vols., 1903–1906.
Arber, *Transcript*	*A Transcript of the Registers of the Company of Stationers of London, 1554–1640*, ed. Edward Arber, 5 vols., 1875–1894.

Bagford	A collection of ballads assembled by John Bagford (1650–1716) and now in the British Museum. Most of the contents were reprinted in *BB* or (if duplicated in the Roxburghe collection) in *RB*.
BB	*The Bagford Ballads,* ed. J. W. Ebsworth, 2 vols., Ballad Society, 1878.
BM	Library of the British Museum. Usually the abbreviation is followed by press-mark.
BM Huth	A collection of Elizabethan ballads, formerly in the possession of Henry Huth, who allowed them to be reprinted as *Ancient Ballads and Broadsides,* Philobiblon Society, 1867; reissued as *A Collection of Seventy-Nine Black-Letter Ballads and Broadsides,* 1867. The ballads were part of a notable bequest to the BM by Alfred H. Huth in the early years of this century.
BM Luttrell	A collection of broadsides, ballads, pamphlets, &c., in three volumes, formed by Narcissus Luttrell (1657–1732) and now in the BM.
BM Thomason	The so-called Thomason Tracts (which Chappell referred to as the King's Pamphlets since they were presented to the BM by George III) include a number of broadside ballads. See under "Poems" in the index to *Catalogue of the Pamphlets, Books, Newspapers, and Manuscripts Relating to the Civil War, the Commonwealth, and Restoration, Collected by George Thomason, 1640–1661,* 2 vols., 1908.
Bodleian	Bodleian Library, Oxford University.
Booke of New Lessons	*A Booke of New Lessons for the Cithern & Gittern,* 1652. This instrumental tutor, issued by John Playford, was a predecessor of *Musick's Delight on the Cithren,* 1666.
Brooks, "Rump Songs"	H. F. Brooks, "Rump Songs: an Index with Notes," *Oxford Bibliographical Society Proceedings & Papers,* V (1936–1939), 283–304.
California	Music Library of the University of California, Berkeley.
CBEL	*Cambridge Bibliography of English Literature,* 4 vols., 1941; supplement, 1957.

Chappell, *NEA*	William Chappell, *A Collection of National English Airs*, 2 vols., 1838–1840.
Chappell, *OEPM*	William Chappell, *Old English Popular Music*, a revision of *PMOT* by H. E. Wooldridge, 2 vols., 1893. Reissued in photofacsimile reprint, 1961.
Chappell, *PMOT*	William Chappell, *Popular Music of the Olden Time*, 2 vols. [1855–1859]. Part of the edition was titled *The Ballad Literature and Popular Music of the Olden Time*.
Chetham	A miscellaneous collection of seventeenth- and eighteenth-century broadsides and single-sheet songs, presented to the library of Chetham College, Manchester, by J. O. Halliwell-Phillipps. The contents are listed in his *Catalogue of Proclamations, Broadsides, Ballads, and Poems*, 1851.
Child	Francis J. Child, *The English and Scottish Popular Ballads*, 5 vols., 1882–1898. Reissued in photofacsimile reprint, 5 vols. in 3, 1956.
Choyce Drollery	*Choyce Drollery: Songs & Sonnets*, 1656. A reprint, ed. J. W. Ebsworth, 1876, includes also *An Antidote against Melancholy*, 1661, and "extra songs" from *Merry Drollery*, 1661.
Clark	William Andrews Clark Memorial Library, University of California, Los Angeles.
Collier, *Extracts*	*Extracts from the Registers of the Stationers' Company . . . 1557 [–] 1587*, ed. J. P. Collier, Shakespeare Society, 2 vols., 1848–1849.
Collier, *Old Ballads*	*Old Ballads, from Early Printed Copies*, ed. J. P. Collier, Percy Society, 1840.
Collmann	*Ballads and Broadsides, Chiefly of the Elizabethan Period . . . in the Library at Britwell Court*, ed. Herbert L. Collmann, Roxburghe Club, 1912. The broadsides reprinted in this volume are now in the Huntington Library.
Columbia	Library of Columbia University, New York City.
Complete Collection of . . . English and Scotch Songs	*A Complete Collection of Old and New English and Scotch Songs*, 4 vols., 1735–1736. Contains no music.
CP	*Cavalier and Puritan: Ballads and Broadsides . . . , 1640–1660*, ed. Hyder E. Rollins, 1923.

Crawford, Lord	A handsome collection of 1,466 broadsides in possession of the present Earl of Crawford, Balcarres, Scotland. The contents are listed in *Bibliotheca Lindesiana: Catalogue of a Collection of English Ballads of the XVIIth and XVIIIth Centuries,* 1890; reissued in photofacsimile reprint, 1962.
The Dancing Master	This title is used in referring to all editions, including the *editio princeps* which John Playford published as *The English Dancing Master,* 1651. Subsequent editions, all entitled *The Dancing Master,* are as follows: 2d ed., 1652; 3d ed., 1665 (an earlier state, 1657?, contains a supplement of c. 1662); 4th ed., 1670; 5th ed., 1675; 6th ed., 1679; 7th ed., 1686; 8th ed., 1690; 9th ed., 1695 (includes a "Second Part," 1696, 2d ed., 1698); 10th ed., 1698; 11th ed., 1701; 12th ed., 1703; 13th ed., 1706; 14th ed., 1709; 15th ed., 1713; 16th ed., 1716; 17th ed., 1721; 18th ed., c. 1728. A second volume was issued c. 1713; 2d ed., 1714; 3d ed., 1718; 4th ed., 1728. A third volume appeared c. 1719 and again c. 1727. Miss Margaret Dean-Smith's facsimile reprint, *Playford's English Dancing Master 1651,* 1957, includes a descriptive bibliography of all editions, with census of copies known.
Day-Murrie	Cyrus L. Day and Eleanore B. Murrie, *English Song-Books, 1651–1702: A Bibliography with a First-Line Index of Songs,* Bibliographical Society, 1940.
Deloney, *Works,* ed. Mann	*The Works of Thomas Deloney,* ed. F. O. Mann, 1912.
DNB	*Dictionary of National Biography.*
Douce	A four-volume collection of seventeenth- and eighteenth-century broadsides, formerly in the possession of Francis Douce (1757–1834) and now in the Bodleian.
D'Urfey, *Compleat Collection*	Thomas D'Urfey, *A Compleat Collection of Mr. Durfey's Songs and Odes,* 1687.
D'Urfey, *New Collection*	Thomas D'Urfey, *A New Collection of Songs and Poems,* 1683.
Euing	A collection of seventeenth-century broadsides

formerly in the possession of William Euing, now in the library of Glasgow University. The contents are listed in *A Catalogue of an Unique Collection of Ancient English Broadside Ballads,* 1856.

Fitzwilliam Virginal Book — *The Fitzwilliam Virginal Book,* ed. J. A. Fuller Maitland and W. Barclay Squire, 2 vols., Leipzig, 1894–1899; reissued in photofacsimile reprint editions, 1949, 1963. The manuscript here published, long erroneously known as "Queen Elizabeth's Virginal Book," is believed to have been compiled in London Fleet Prison by Francis Tregian, c. 1609–1619. It is preserved in the Fitzwilliam Museum, Cambridge, as Music MS 32.G.29.

Forbes's *Cantus* — *Cantus, Songs and Fancies. To Thre, Foure, or Five Partes, both apt for Voices and Viols. . . .* Aberdene, Printed by Iohn Forbes, 1662; 2d ed., 1666; 3d ed., 1682.

Harvard — Houghton Library, Harvard University.

Huntington — Henry E. Huntington Library and Art Gallery, San Marino, California.

JAF — *Journal of American Folklore.*

JAMS — *Journal of the American Musicological Society.*

JEFDSS — *Journal of the English Folk Dance and Song Society.*

JEGP — *Journal of English and Germanic Philology.*

JFSS — *Journal of the Folk Song Society.*

JIFSS — *Journal of the Irish Folk Song Society.*

Johnson, *Scots Musical Museum* — James Johnson, *The Scots Musical Museum,* 6 vols., 1787–1803. Reprint editions 1839, 1853, with notes by William Stenhouse; photofacsimile reprint of the latter edition, 1962.

Julian Marshall — A large collection of eighteenth-century single-sheet songs formed by Julian Marshall (1836–1903) and now in Harvard.

LC — Library of Congress, Washington, D.C.

Lemon, *Catalogue* — Robert Lemon, *Catalogue of a Collection of Broadsides in the Possession of the Society of Antiquaries,* 1866.

Loyal Songs, 1731 — *A Collection of Loyal Songs Written against the Rump Parliament,* 2 vols., 1731. Reprints pieces from *The Rump,* 1660, and its enlarge-

	ment, *Rump*, 1662. Not related to *120 Loyal Songs* or *180 Loyal Songs*.
Luitboek van Thysius, Het	*Het Luitboek van Thysius*, ed. J. P. N. Land, Amsterdam, 1889. Originally published in *Tijdschrift der Vereeniging voor Noord-Nederlands Muziekgeschiedenis*, I–III (1884–1888). The lute manuscript of c. 1600 here printed is preserved in the University Library, Leyden.
Mackay, *Cavalier Songs*	*The Cavalier Songs and Ballads of England*, ed. Charles Mackay, 1863.
Madden	A large collection of late broadsides and slip songs, formed by Sir Frederic Madden (1801–1873) and now in the Cambridge University Library.
Manchester	A collection of some 130 seventeenth-century ballads preserved in the Manchester Free Reference Library, press-marks 310.D.2 and 310.D.3.
The Merry Musician	*The Merry Musician: Or, A Cure for the Spleen*, 4 vols., 1716–c. 1733. Vol. I contains type-set music (2d ed., 1730); vols. II–IV are engraved, and are conjecturally dated 1728, 1731, and 1733 in *CBEL*. This series is not to be confused with a different work, *The Merry Musician, Or, A Cure for the Spleen*, c. 1729 (Harvard), engraved.
MLN	*Modern Language Notes*.
Morgan	A collection of about 100 seventeenth- and eighteenth-century broadsides in the Pierpont Morgan Library, New York City, shelf-mark E2.45D.
Musicks Hand-maid(e)	*Musicks Hand-maide. Presenting New and Pleasant Lessons for the Virginals or Harpsycon*, 1663; the preface is signed by John Playford. Another edition: *Musicks Hand-maid: New Lessons and Instructions for the Virginals or Harpsychord*, 1678. Henry Playford issued *The Second Part of Musick's Hand-maid . . . for the Virginals, Harpsichord, and Spinet*, 1689.
Musicks Recreation on the Lyra Viol	*Musicks Recreation: on the Lyra Viol*, 1652, with preface by John Playford. Later editions are

	Musicks Recreation on the Viol, Lyraway, 1661, 1669; and *Musicks Recreation on the Viol, Lyra-way,* 2d ed., enlarged, 1682.
My Ladye Nevells Booke	William Byrd, *My Ladye Nevells Booke,* ed. Hilda Andrews, 1926.
NEA	See Chappell, *NEA.*
Nichols, *Progresses of King James*	John Nichols, *The Progresses, Processions, and Magnificent Festivities, of King James the First . . . ,* 4 vols., 1828.
OEB	*Old English Ballads, 1553–1625,* ed. Hyder E. Rollins, 1920.
OEPM	See Chappell, *OEPM.*
Old English Ditties	*Old English Ditties, Selected from W. Chappell's "Popular Music of the Olden Time" . . . New Words Written by J. Oxenford, the Symphonies and Accompaniments by G. A. Macfarren,* 2 vols., c. 1860.
180 Loyal Songs	*A Choice Collection of 180 Loyal Songs . . . To which is added, The Musical Notes to each Song,* 3d ed., 1685. This is the first edition to contain music. *A Collection, Of One Hundred and Eighty Loyal Songs,* 4th ed., 1694, consists of sheets of the 1685 edition with a fresh title page. *Loyal Songs,* 1731, is an independent publication.
120 Loyal Songs	*A Choice Collection of 120 Loyal Songs,* 1684. Contains no music; see the preceding entry.
OPB	*Broadside Ballads of the Restoration Period from the Jersey Collection Known as The Osterley Park Ballads,* ed. F. Burlingame Fawcett, 1930. The pieces reprinted in this volume are now in the BM, press-mark C.39.k.6.
PA	*The Pack of Autolycus,* ed. Hyder E. Rollins, 1927.
Parnassus Biceps	*Parnassus Biceps. Or Severall Choice Pieces of Poetry,* 1656. Preface signed Ab[raham] Wright. Reprint ed. G. Thorn-Drury, 1927.
PB	*The Pepys Ballads,* ed. Hyder E. Rollins, 8 vols., 1929–1932. Reprints 505 broadsides from the Pepys Collection.
Pepys	A collection of some 1,700 sixteenth- and seventeenth-century broadsides, begun by John Sel-

	den and continued by Samuel Pepys, now in the Pepysian Library, Magdalene College, Cambridge.
Pepys Penny Merriments	A collection of chapbooks formed by Samuel Pepys, now in the Pepysian Library, Magdalene College, Cambridge.
Percival, *Walpole Ballads*	*Political Ballads Illustrating the Administration of Sir Robert Walpole,* ed. Milton O. Percival, Oxford Historical and Literary Studies, vol. VIII, 1916.
Percy Collection	Printed and manuscript ballads, inventories, and other materials assembled by Bishop Percy while preparing his *Reliques.* Now in Harvard.
Percy Folio MS	BM MS Add. 27879, published as *Bishop Percy's Folio Manuscript,* ed. J. H. Hales and F. J. Furnivall, 4 vols., 1867–1868.
Percy's *Reliques*	Thomas Percy, *Reliques of Ancient English Poetry,* 1765.
PG	*A Pepysian Garland . . . , 1595–1639,* ed. Hyder E. Rollins, 1922. Reprints 73 broadsides from the Pepys Collection.
Pills	*Wit and Mirth: or Pills to Purge Melancholy,* ed. Thomas D'Urfey, 6 vols., 1719–1720; the first five volumes were also issued as *Songs Compleat, Pleasant and Divertive,* 1719. A page-for-page reprint of a mixed set was issued in 1876, and a photofacsimile of this edition, 6 vols. in 3, appeared in 1959. See Day-Murrie for bibliographical details of editions published between 1699 and 1714.
Plomer	Under this name are subsumed the following related works: Henry R. Plomer, *A Dictionary of the Booksellers and Printers . . . in England . . . from 1641 to 1667,* 1907; R. B. McKerrow *et al., A Dictionary of Printers and Booksellers in England . . . 1557–1640,* 1910; and Henry R. Plomer *et al., A Dictionary of the Printers and Booksellers . . . in England . . . from 1668 to 1725,* 1922.
PMLA	*Publications of the Modern Language Association of America.*
PMOT	See Chappell, *PMOT.*

Ramsay, *Tea-Table Miscellany*	Allan Ramsay, *The Tea-Table Miscellany*, 1723 (Yale). Other copies of this edition are dated 1724. By 1737 the collection had swelled to four volumes, and thereafter the contents were reprinted in various formats. See *CBEL*.
Rawlinson	A collection of 218 black-letter broadside ballads in the Bodleian Library, catalogued as 4to Rawlinson 566.
RB	*The Roxburghe Ballads*, ed. William Chappell and J. W. Ebsworth, 8 vols., Ballad Society, 1871–1899. Reprints, with frequent bowdlerization, almost all the broadsides in the Roxburghe Collection, several hundred from the Pepys Collection, and many pieces from other sources. Pagination anomalies include the addition of single, double, and triple asterisks to designate multiple introductory sequences.
Ritson's Penny Histories	A collection of chapbooks and garlands, formed by Joseph Ritson (1752–1803) and now in Harvard.
Rollins, *Anal. Index*	Hyder E. Rollins, *An Analytical Index to the Ballad-Entries (1557–1709) in the Registers of the Company of Stationers of London*, 1924. Printed also in *SP*, XXI (1924), 1–324.
Roxburghe	A rich collection of almost 1,500 broadsides, the majority in black letter. Begun by Robert Harley, Earl of Oxford (1661–1724), the collection passed through several hands and was greatly enriched by John Ker, third Duke of Roxburghe; it was acquired by the BM in 1845.
SB	*Shirburn Ballads, 1585–1616*, ed. Andrew Clark, 1907. Reprints 80 ballads from a MS in the library of the Earl of Macclesfield, Shirburn Castle, Oxfordshire.
Scots Musical Museum	See Johnson.
Skene MS	The Skene MS, now preserved in the National Library of Scotland as Adv. MS 5.2.15, is substantially reproduced in William Dauney, *Ancient Scotish Melodies*, 1838. Although the date of original compilation is commonly given as the first quarter of the seventeenth

century, I believe it to be more recent by twenty-five to fifty years. The manuscript is an extensive collection of song and dance tunes (many of them not Scottish) in tablature for five-course mandore. Because time values are often lacking in the MS, one can excuse many of the liberties taken in Dauney's transcripts.

SP	*Studies in Philology.*
Stationers' Register	See Rollins, *Anal. Index,* and Arber, *Transcript.*
STC	*A Short-Title Catalogue of Books Printed in England, Scotland, & Ireland . . . , 1475–1640,* compiled by A. W. Pollard and G. R. Redgrave, 1926. Reissued in photographic reprint, 1946.
Taubman, *An Heroick Poem*	Matthew Taubman, *An Heroick Poem . . . With Some choice Songs and Medleyes on the Times,* 1682.
Texas	University of Texas Library, Austin.
Thomson, *Orpheus Caledonius*	*Orpheus Caledonius, or a Collection of the best Scotch Songs set to Musick by W*[*illiam*] *Thomson,* 1725. An enlarged edition: *Orpheus Caledonius: or, a Collection of Scots Songs,* 2 vols., 1733; photofacsimile reprint issued in 1962.
TLS	*The* [London] *Times Literary Supplement.*
Walsh's *Compleat Country Dancing-Master*	*The Compleat Country Dancing-Master,* 1718; another ed., 1731. *The Second Book of the Compleat Country Dancing-Master,* 1719. *The New Country Dancing-Master,* 3d Book, c. 1728. This series, published by J. Walsh or J. Walsh and Joseph Hare, extensively pirated the later editions of the Playford-Young *Dancing Master* volumes.
Wilkins, *Political Ballads*	*Political Ballads of the Seventeenth and Eighteenth Centuries,* ed. William W. Wilkins, 2 vols., 1860.
Williams College	Citations are to a collection of seventeenth- and eighteenth-century ballads formerly in the Huth collection and now in the Chapin Library, Williams College, Williamstown, Mass.
Wing	*Short-Title Catalogue of Books Printed in England, Scotland, Ireland, Wales, and British*

	America . . . , 1641–1700, compiled by Donald G. Wing, 3 vols., 1945–1951.
Wit and Drollery	Sir John Mennes, James Smith, *et al., Wit and Drollery, Jovial Poems,* 1656. Enlarged editions, 1661, 1682.
Wit and Mirth, 1682, 1684	See *Antidote against Melancholy.*
Wit Restor'd	*Wit Restor'd In severall Select Poems,* 1658. Reprinted in Thomas Park, *Musarum Deliciae,* 1817.
Wood	An extensive collection of ballads gathered by Anthony Wood (1632–1695) and now in the Bodleian Library.
Wright, *Political Ballads*	*Political Ballads Published in England during the Commonwealth,* ed. Thomas Wright, Percy Society, 1841.
Wright, *Songs and Ballads*	*Songs and Ballads, with Other Short Poems, Chiefly of the Reign of Philip and Mary,* ed. Thomas Wright, Roxburghe Club, 1860.
Yale	Yale University Library.

Adieu to the Pleasures

and Follies of Love

One of the songs in Shadwell's version of *The Tempest,* 1674, was a pastoral lament beginning "Adieu to the Pleasures and Follies of Love." It was not printed with the play, but its words appeared in *The Several Songs Now in Mode,* 1675; with music by James Hart, it is to be found in a two-leaved pamphlet, *The Ariels Songs in . . . the Tempest,* c. 1675, in *Choice Ayres, Songs & Dialogues,* 1676, p. 73 (Fig. 1), and in *Pills,* 1719–1720, III, 178. An expanded broadside version written by Dr. Walter Pope was entitled "The Musical Shepherdess, or, Dorinda's

Lamentation for the loss of Amintas." Copies of the ballad, in different editions, appear in the Pepys, Wood E.25, Douce, Lord Crawford, BM C.22.f.6, and Roxburghe collections (reprinted in *RB* IV, 462). All copies direct the ballad to be sung to "Amintas farewel" (doubtless internally inspired) or an alternate tune "Digby's Farewell," q.v.

The tune of "Adieu to the Pleasures and Follies of Love" was used for at least one political ballad of the 1680s: "Good News in Bad Times; or, Absaloms Return to David's Bosome," beginning "Adieu to the hopes of the Whigs of the State" (Harvard, Clark [with MS date 30 Nov. 1683], Roxburghe; reprinted in *RB* V, 399).

A later copy of the tune is in Dr. John Leyden's MS Lyra Viol Book (after 1690), No. 58, preserved only in the nineteenth-century transcript by G. F. Graham in the National Library of Scotland.

Ah! Chloris Awake

The history of this tune begins with a broadside first issued probably in the 1670s, "Strephon and Cloris," which is directed to be sung "To a pleasant New Play-house Tune; Or, Love will find out the way." The opening lines are "Ah! [*or* Oh!] Cloris awake,/it is all abroad day" (Lord Crawford, Wood E.25, Roxburghe; reprinted in *RB* VI, 128; later editions in Pepys III, 191, Lord Crawford 7, Euing 344–346, and Douce II, 197ᵛ, III, 82ᵛ). The twelve stanzas of the broadside appear in *Pills* IV, 313, with a florid air (Fig. 2) which is probably the playhouse tune; it fits the words admirably, but, intended for a twelve-line stanza, it requires a repetition of the second quatrain of the eight-line stanzas uniformly associated with the tune. "Love will find out the way" is an independent tune, q.v.

An answer to the original broadside is "The Lamentation of Cloris For the Unkindness of her Shepherd," beginning "My Shepherd's un-kind,/alas, what shall I do?," to the tune of "O Cloris awake" (Pepys,

Lord Crawford, Euing, Harvard, Roxburghe; reprinted in *RB* VI, 131). The tune is named "Strephon and Cloris" in "The Jolly Shepherd, and Jovial Shepherdess," beginning "Alas my dear Celia,/'tis time to complain" (Douce I, 105); and "Awake, Oh my Cloris" in "The Algier Slaves Releasment," beginning "Of a Constant Young Seaman,/a Story I'le tell" (Pepys, Douce, Roxburghe; reprinted in *RB* VI, 447), and in "Whipping Tom," beginning "Give ear to my ditty,/and I will declare" (Pepys IV, 288).

A number of ballads give the tune as "Cloris awake," including two that have apparently not been republished: "The Lamenting Shepherdess: or, The Unkind Shepherd," beginning "Ah! my Cruel Shepheard,/so false and unkind" (Pepys III, 368); and "The Distasted Lovers Downfall," beginning "When Phoebus had run/the three thirds of his course" (Pepys IV, 45). Another piece in the same measure, "The Jovial May-Pole Dancers," beginning "Rowland and Roger,/With Bridget and Mary" (Lord Crawford 1034, BM C.22.f.6 [128], Harvard), seems to be intended for the tune, for its tune direction, "Top and top Gallant," echoes the burden of "A Ship-load of Waggery," beginning "A Ship must have a Steers-man," which is to the tune of "Ah Cloris awake" (Pepys IV, 177, Lord Crawford 1052, Harvard).

"The West Countrey Maids Lamentation For the loss of her Maidenhead," a ballad licensed before 1685 beginning "Long time I lamented,/in sorrow and grief," bears the tune direction "Over Hills and high

Mountains: Or, Cloris Awake" (Douce II, 246). The first tune title, used for a number of ballads near the end of the century, is derived from the opening line of "The Wandring Maiden . . . To an excellent new Tune" (Pepys, Lord Crawford, Bagford; reprinted in *BB* II, 572). A sequel to this ballad exists in two distinct editions, with the title "The Wandring Virgin"; one, which is "the Answer to the wand'ring Maiden," is to the tune "Over Hills and High Mountains" (Lord Crawford, Pepys, Douce, Harvard, Roxburghe; reprinted in *BB* II, 575); the other, with no reference to the original ballad, has the tune direction "Cloris awake, or the loving Chambermaid" (Euing 373, Lord Crawford 1437). "The loving Chamber-Maid" is the title of a ballad beginning "Shut the door after me,/pull off the Boule," which is "To a New Tune" (Lord Crawford, Douce, Euing, Roxburghe; reprinted in *RB* VII, 447). From this complex of associations we cannot deduce much with certainty. "The loving chambermaid" seems to be an independent tune which has not survived. "Over hills and high mountains" and "Ah! Chloris awake" are interchangeable but probably not identical. No music for the former has survived, unless it is to be associated with "Over the mountains and under the waves," the first line of a ballad whose tune is commonly known as "Love will find out the way." [1]

Ah Cruel Bloody Fate

"Ah Cruel Bloody Fate," known also as "Philander," originated as a song in the fifth act of Nathaniel Lee's *Theodosius*, 1680. The music was written by Henry Purcell and was first printed in that year as a supplement to the play. The song was reprinted in *Choice Ayres and Songs,* Third Book, 1681, p. 29 (Fig. 3), in *Wit and Drollery,* 1682, and in all editions of *Pills.* The tune appears in a number of musical instruction books, among them *Musicks Recreation on the Viol, Lyra-way,* 1682; Humphry Salter, *The Genteel Companion . . . for the Recorder,* 1683; Thomas Greeting, *The Pleasant Companion . . . for the Flagelet,* 1683; and *Apollo's Banquet,* 5th ed., 1687.

The stage song was twice expanded into broadside form, one version

[1] Chappell (*PMOT* II, 681–682), finding no music for "Over hills and high mountains," used instead the air "On yonder high mountains," which appears in several ballad operas, and which is strikingly reminiscent of the much older "Love will find out the way."

3

entitled "The faithful Lovers Downfal" (Douce I, 74), the other "The True Lovers Tragedy" (Lord Crawford, Pepys, Harvard, Roxburghe; reprinted in *RB* IV, 38). Both ballads begin "Ah! cruel bloody fate,/ what canst thou now do more?"; the tune in some copies is called "Oh! cruel bloody fate." In 1683 a burlesque broadside appeared, entitled "Dagon's Fall: or, The Whigs Lamentation for the Death of Anthony King of Poland," to the tune of "Philander" (BM, Harvard, Huntington, Yale). The tune title is another name for "Ah cruel bloody fate" and derives from the name of one of the lovers in the original stage song. "Dagon's Fall" was reprinted in *180 Loyal Songs*, 1685 (with music), and in *RB* V, 234. A political broadside of 1684, "The Bully Whig: or, The Poor Whores Lamentation for the Apprehending of Sir Thomas Armstrong," begins also as a parody: "Ah! Cruel Bloody Tom!/ What canst thou hope for more" (Harvard, Clark, BM 1872.a.1, and Bodleian Ashmole G.16 [140]; reprinted in *180 Loyal Songs* and in *RB* V, 482).

Among the numerous other ballads written to this tune, the following may be mentioned: "The Marriners Delight" (Pepys IV, 165) and "The Faithful Mariner" (Pepys IV, 171), both beginning "Farewel my dearest Dear,/for thee and I must part," and one obviously a slight reworking of the other; "The Constant Seaman and his Faithful Love" (Pepys IV, 189), beginning "Farewell my dearest Dear,/for needs I must away"—a similar restatement of a threadbare theme; "A Remedy for Greensickness" (Pepys, Bagford; reprinted in *BB* II, 543), a provocative ballad beginning "A handsom buxom Lass/lay panting in her bed." In all these ballads the tune is referred to as "Philander."

The tune could also be put to religious use, for in *A Cabinet of Choice Jewels*, 1688, it is named for singing "A Carrol for St. Stephens

· 5 ·

Day," as if a tune appropriate to lovers' suicide were equally suitable to accompany a song of the Christmas season.

Despite its earlier popularity, it was used in only one ballad opera: *The Country-Wedding*, 1749, where it is cited as "O cruel, cruel Fate."

An apparent analogue to the tune of "Ah cruel bloody fate" is the music of "The Farmer's Daughter of Merry Wakefield," a single-sheet song beginning "Down in the north country" (BM H.1601 [133], dated 1705?; other editions in BM, Folger, and Harvard; reprinted in *The Merry Musician*, I, 1716). The tunes are somewhat similar in the first four measures but thereafter are unrelated. As "Down in the North Country" it was used in Gay's *The Beggar's Opera*, 1728, and Coffey's *The Merry Cobler*, 1735, and is cited, without the music, in Worsdale's *A Cure for a Scold*, 1735.[1]

A tune called "The merry Milk Maids" in the second volume of *The Dancing Master* (3d ed., 1718; 4th ed., 1728) begins very much like that of "Down in the north country," but after the opening phrase it too has its own melodic and harmonic pattern, and the tune comprises four eight-measure strains. The first two strains, with the same title, are found in one ballad opera, *Momus turn'd Fabulist*, 1729. This air is not related to the "Merry Milkmaids" tune which is also called "Ye Nymphs and Sylvan Gods."

Ah! How Pleasant 'Tis to Love

The Pepys collection (V, 37) preserves a ballad entitled "England's Joy in the merry month of May," to the tune of "Ah! how pleasant 'tis to Love," and beginning "Hark! how sweet the Birds do sing." Music printed on the broadside is actually the tune "Great York has been debarred of late," though it appears meaningless because the two staves of music are in reverse order. It has no connection with "England's Joy."

---

[1] If "Down in the North Country" is considered an offshoot from "Ah cruel bloody fate," it cannot stand in parental relationship to "Within the North Country," which is cited as the tune for Martin Parker's much earlier ballad "Take time while 'tis offer'd" (*RB* II, 555) and for an untitled song beginning "Brave Tamberlain he was/a Shepherd on the Plains" in Richard Climsell, *Cupid's Soliciter of Love*, 1680. The poulter's measure (here 6.6.8.6) of these two pieces does, however, fit the music of "Down in the North Country."

The tune cited on the broadside is by Henry Purcell and is to be found in *The Banquet of Musick*, Second Book, 1688, p. 4 (Fig. 4), and

in *Vinculum Societatis*, Second Book, 1688. The first line of the Purcell song becomes the tune title as found in the Pepys broadside. It was apparently not used with any other ballads.

Aimable Vainqueur

Thomas D'Urfey wrote "A Song to Celia who was forc'd to Marry another Her Lover being Absent," to the tune called "the Aimable Vanqure." It appeared in *The Monthly Masks of Vocal Musick* for March, 1704, and was issued also as a single-sheet song (BM H.1601 [65], Huntington=Fig. 5). It was reprinted in *The Merry Musician*, 1716, I, 256, and in *Pills*, 1719–1720, II, 49. No ballads seem to have been set to the

tune, and in all probability it does not belong properly in a discussion of broadside literature. The tune itself, arranged for harpsichord or spinet, is to be found in *The Second Book of the Ladys Banquet,* 1706, as "Aymable Vainqueur." An imperfect version of the tune, preserved in an eighteenth-century French commonplace book, BM MS Egerton 814, pp. 199–200, is coupled with words beginning "Aimable Danchet" which relate to an untraced *Anchise* by the celebrated opera librettist Antoine Danchet.

Alas, Poor Thing

"Alas, Poor Thing" seems to take its name from the stanza tags of "The Mourning Conquest," a twelve-stanza ballad beginning "As I did walk abroad one time,/I chanced for to see" and to be sung to the tune "A loving Husband will not be unto his Wife unkind." I have not found this tune or any references to it, but the wording suggests the beginning or, more likely, the ending of some ballad. The Pepys (III, 139) and Douce (II, 155ᵛ) texts of "The Mourning Conquest" indicate the author to be S. B. (Samuel Butler?); the Bagford copy (reprinted in *BB* I, 447) is unsigned; and in Rawlinson 35 the imprint is torn away.

A seven-stanza version derived from "The Mourning Conquest" is "A homely Dialogue betwixt a young woman and her sweetheart." It begins "As I was walking forth,/I chanced for to see," and the tune title is given as "Alace poor thing" (Harvard, Roxburghe; reprinted in *RB* VIII, 695). This is in roman letter, without imprint, and is probably later than "The Mourning Conquest." The only music which I can associate with "Alas, poor thing" is found in *The Merry Musician*, 1716, I, 302 (Fig. 6), set to another derivative text beginning "Abroad as I was

walking,/It was my Chance to see." Here some of the eleven stanzas end "Alas poor thing," and the movement of the music fits the ballad texts.

In two other ballads our tune is named along with "Hey, boys, up go we," which is in the same meter: "The Wanton Maidens Choice," beginning "I am a Maid now in my prime,/and fain I would be wed" (Lord Crawford 548, Pepys III, 190), and "The Westminster Frolick," beginning "In Westminster there is a wife,/a very noble dame" (Harvard, BM, Lord Crawford; reprinted in *RB* VIII, 702). In the latter the first tune title appears as "Hey boys slap goes she" and the stanzas usually end "and that spoiles all."

"James and Susan," a poem in *Windsor Drollery*, 1672, and in the thirteenth edition of Richard Johnson's *Golden Garland of Princely Pleasures*, 1690, is probably not to be associated with the tune, for although many of the stanzas end "Alas poor thing," the metrical pattern does not fit the music.

All in a Garden Green

English settings of this tune are preserved in William Ballet's MS Lute Book, p. 56 (Fig. 7), and in the first eight editions of *The Dancing*

Original lyra-viol set is an octave lower.

Master, 1651–1690. A keyboard piece by J. P. Sweelinck, "Unter der Linden grüne," is a set of variations on "All in a Garden Green" (*Werken,* ed. Max Seiffert, 2d ed., I, 1943, No. 63), and Nicolas Vallet's *Tablature de Luth,* 1618–1619, II, 7, names the tune "Onder de Linde-groene." Under the title "All in a Garden green" William Byrd set a different tune in *The Fitzwilliam Virginal Book,* I, 411.

An entry of 1565–1566 in the Stationers' Register licensed William Pekering to publish "All in a garden grene/betwene ij lovers." This is evidently "A merrye new ballad, of a countrye wench and a clowne," beginning "All in a garden greene,/where late I layde me downe," sung "To a fine tune" (*SB,* p. 220). The stanzas of twenty-eight lines are not metrically suited to either of the tunes known as "All in a garden green." [1]

[1] The text which Chappell (*PMOT* I, 111) used with the tune was from "a manuscript volume, in the possession of Mr. Payne Collier." Professor Rollins (*JEGP,* XVIII

A Handefull of Pleasant Delites, 1584 (ed. Rollins, 1924, p. 46), contains a ballad to the tune: "An excellent Song of an outcast Louer," beginning "My fancie did I fixe,/in faithful forme and frame." The four-line stanza in poulter's measure, syllabically 6.6.8.6, will fit the first half of the popular tune; the second half requires five lines but will fit a stanza if the third line of the quatrain be repeated. The first two stanzas of the *Handefull* ballad were copied into Bodleian MS Ashmole 48 (reproduced in *Songs and Ballads,* ed. Thomas Wright, 1860, p. 183); and since this MS was compiled by 1566, Professor Rollins deduces that the *Handefull* ballad was in print by that date and may have been included in the original (lost) 1566 edition of the *Handefull.*[2]

In *Westward for Smelts,* 1620 (ed. Halliwell[-Phillipps], 1848, pp. 7–8), a boatman offers to entertain the western fishwives with song while they are aboard. "They prayed me so to doe, but yet not to cloy their eares with an old fidler's song, as *Riding to Rumford, or, All in a garden greene.*" He agrees to give them instead a new song "which neither punke, fidler, or ballad-singer had ever polluted with their unsavorie breath." But if the ballad was considered passé by 1620, it had clearly not passed out of existence. Some years later the owner of a copy of Slatyer's *Psalmes, or Songs of Sion,* 1642, now in the British Museum, indicated in a manuscript note that "Garden Green" was a suitable alternative tune for singing Psalm 47, beginning "All people clap your hands,/Sing laud unto the Lord," and Psalm 48, beginning "Great is the Lord on hie." The popular tune will fit both verse paraphrases.

All in the Land of Cider

An early eighteenth-century italic-letter broadside, "The Clock and Cushion," beginning "All in the Town of Ailsbury,/The Truth You may rely on," is directed to be sung to the tune of "All in the Land of Cyder" (Lord Crawford 38). This tune takes its name from the opening line of "The Welsh Saint: or, A full and true account of Burning the defiled Bed, at Sir Anthony Crab-Tree's House, in Herefordshire," a song which appeared in *Political Merriment,* 1714, Part II, p. 45. No

[1919], 53) administered the *coup de grâce* to Collier's suspicious manuscript, citing evidence that convicts Collier of "cooking" texts to fit entries in the Stationers' Register.

[2] See his "Concerning Bodleian MS. Ashmole 48," *MLN,* XXXIV (1919), 346, and *Handefull,* 1924, p. 108.

music is printed, but the tune is named as "When first I laid Siege to my Cloris." A song with such a first line (originating in Sedley's play, *Bellamira*, 1687, III, i) is to be found in the 1714 edition of *Pills* V, 212 (1719–1720, VI, 308), with the music (Fig. 8). The same air, untitled,

is used with "All in the land of Cyder" in *The Merry Musician*, 1716, I, 274. Later appearances of this song use the music of "Of noble race was Shinkin," q.v., but it seems likely that the Crawford broadside was intended to be sung to the music associated with "When first I laid Siege to my Cloris."

All Joy to Fair Psyche

This is a stage song from Shadwell's *Psyche*, 1675, Act III, which was expanded into a broadside. As "The Power and Pleasure of Love" it appears with first line and tune title "All joy to fair Psyche (in this happy place)" in Pepys III, 93, Wood E.25 (144), Douce II, 183, and Roxburghe IV, 68; reprinted in *RB* IV, 458. The stage song, with music by Matthew Locke, appears in *Choice Ayres and Songs*, Fourth Book, 1683, p. 40 (Fig. 9).

All You That Love Good Fellows

Perhaps the earliest ballad set to this tune is "The Honour of a London Prentice. Being an Account of his matchless Manhood and brave Adventures, done by him in Turkey, and by what means he married the King's Daughter of the same Country, &c.," beginning "Of a worthy London Prentice,/my purpose is to speak." References in the text to the apprentice's Queen suggest that this is an Elizabethan composition, and the later popularity of the ballad is attested by references to it in seventeenth-century plays. The character Covet in Glapthorne's *Wit in a Constable*, 1640, III, i, names the "London Prentice" as a song he likes, and in the comedy, *The London Chanticleers*, 1659, Scene III, Ditty offers the ballad for sale. "The honour of an appr[entice] of London" was registered in 1656, and all surviving copies of the ballad date from the second half of the seventeenth century or later. Black-letter editions are to be found in the Euing, Lord Crawford, Wood 401, Douce, Bagford, Pepys, and Roxburghe collections (reprinted in *RB* VII, 589). The tune title "All you that are good fellows" in the Wood and Pepys copies gives us a possible link with the John Barleycorn songs noted below.

"The Honour of a London Prentice" was reprinted in the 1714 edition of *Pills* V, 259, with the music; in *A Collection of Old Ballads*, 1723–1725, I, 199; in Ritson, *English Songs*, 1783 (1813, II, 335, music III, 312); and in Charles Mackay, *Songs of the London Prentices and Trades*, Percy Society, 1841, I, 22.

· 13 ·

The music found with "The London Prentice" in *Pills*, 1714, and with an amatory song of the same title in the 1719–1720 edition, VI, 342 can be traced back to Elizabethan times. In the Shirburn MS the tune, called "All those that are good fellowes," appears in its short form (facsimile in *SB*, p. 272) with "A true discou[r]se of the winning of the towne of Berke . . . [i.e., (Rhein)berg] . . . 1601," beginning "That gallant prince, Graue Maurice" (Fig. 10). In *The Fitzwilliam Virginal*

Original is unbarred.

Book I, 57, the music appears as "Nancie" in an arrangement by Thomas Morley. In the Welde MS Lute Book, c. 1600, fol. 7, it is called "Nowells Delighte." Under this title it was taken up by a number of seventeenth-century Dutch songbooks. In J. J. Starter's *Friesche Lust-Hof*, 2d ed., 1621, p. 179 (Fig. 11), it is "Sir Eduward Nouwels delight," and in several others it appears either as "Eduward Nouwels" or, from the first line of a Dutch song coupled with the tune, as "Silvester inde Morgenstond": *Bellerophon*, 1622 (with music in editions of 1633 *et seq.*); *Een Nieu Geuse Liedt-Boeck*, 1645 (reprinted in *Het Geuzenliedboek*, ed. E. T. Kniper, 1924); Jacob van Eyk, *Der Fluyten Lust-Hof*, 1654. A five-voiced instrumental arrangement of the air, without title, is No. 74 in Valentin Haussmann's *Rest von polnischen und andern Täntzen*, 1603 (reprinted in *Denkmäler deutscher Tonkunst*, I ser., XVI, 134, new ed., 1958). As "London Apprentice" it is one of the airs in Charles Coffey's ballad opera, *The Devil to Pay*, 1731. The eighteenth-century 16-measure versions of the air—in *Pills* and *The Devil to Pay*—fit the double ballad stanza of pieces associated with the tune, while earlier music (except

11

Original is unbarred and, though pitched in C, contains key signature of one sharp.

for the *SB* air) contains an additional eight-measure phrase at the end. "The British Grenadiers" clearly descends from this old tune.

Among the ballads naming the tune is the following: "Good Newes from Virginia . . . this present Moneth . . . March, 1623," beginning "No English heart, but heard with griefe,/the massacre here done," to be sung to "All those that be good fellowes" (Public Record Office, London; reprinted in *Virginia Vetusta,* ed. E. D. Neill, 1885, p. 147). Of even earlier origin is "Pride's Fall: Or, A Warning for all English Women, by the Example of a strange Monster lately born in Germany, by a Merchant's proud Wife, at Geneva,"[1] beginning "England's fair dainty dames,/see here the fall of pride," to the tune of "All you that love Goodfellows" (Lord Crawford, Wood 401, Bagford, Chetham, Euing, Pepys, Roxburghe; reprinted in *RB* VIII, 20). The ballad is on Thackeray's list of items in print in 1689, and the black-letter editions date from the second half of the century. A Shirburn MS version, dated 1609 (printed in *SB,* p. 134), has the tune direction "All yow that fathers bee," which allies it with the tune "Dainty come thou to me." The trimeter lines of the ballad fit that lost tune far better than they do the

---

[1] The place-name is properly Jena, as is seen from the Stationers' Register, August 15, 1608, entering the pamphlet from which the ballad was conceived.

music of "All you that love good fellows." To the tune of "England's fair dainty dames," a name inspired by the first line of "Pride's Fall," is "The Court-Miss Converted: Or, A Looking Glass for Ladies," beginning "When Phoebus with his Beams" (Pepys, Lord Crawford, Roxburghe; reprinted in *RB* III, 638). This ballad too is in trimeters and perhaps should also be associated with the music of "Dainty come thou to me."

Another "monster" ballad is "Natures Wonder . . . 1664," to the tune of "London Prentice: Or, Jovial Batchelor," beginning "Come take a view good People all" (Euing, dated Nov. 12, 1664; reprinted in *PA*, p. 139). "A true Relation of one Susan Higges," telling of a murderess whose victim "spat three drops of blood in her face, which never could be washt out," is to the tune of "The worthy London Prentice" and begins "To mourne for my offences" (Roxburghe; reprinted in Evans, *Old Ballads,* 1810, and *RB* II, 633). A late example naming the tune is "The Drapier's Ballad," beginning "Of a worthy Dublin Drapier," Dublin, 1724–1725 (BM 839.m.23 [36]).

No ballads seem to have survived with a first line "All you that love good fellows," to which we might trace the beginning of our tune. Those beginning "All you that are good fellows" have an ambiguous relationship at best. Of three editions of a garland on "The Arraigning and Indicting of Sir John Barleycorn," one in Ritson's collection of Penny Histories, vol. III (Harvard), contains a song which begins, "All you that are good fellows"; it has no tune direction. In another garland bound up in the same volume, the song begins "All you that be good Fellows," and the tune direction is "Old Sir John Barleycorn, or Jack of all Trades." Similar, except for a second tune title, "Tom of all Trades," is the song in a garland among the Pepys Penny Merriments, vol. I (Pepysian Library, Cambridge). Of the tunes "Old Sir John Barleycorn" and "Jack of all Trades" nothing further is known. A ballad entitled "Merry Tom of all Trades" (reprinted in John Ashton, *A Century of Ballads,* 1887, p. 332) is to the tune "Behold the man," whose music has not survived. "An other [Carol] for Christmas day" has a first line and tune title "All you that are good fellows" (*Good and True, Fresh and New, Christmas Carols,* 1642); its metrical pattern is the same as that of "London Prentice," but the opening formula seems so commonplace that one is not inclined to see any necessary connection between the two.

Amaryllis

This tune is to be found among the "Select New Tunes and Jiggs for the Treble-Violin," No. 41 (Fig. 12), at the end of *The Dancing Master*,

3d ed., 1665, and is regularly incorporated into all later editions. It is in *Musick's Delight on the Cithren*, 1666, *Apollo's Banquet*, 1670, Thomas Greeting's *The Pleasant Companion . . . for the Flagelet*, 2d ed., 1673, *Musicks Recreation on the Viol, Lyra-way*, 1682, and Walsh's *Compleat Country Dancing-Master*, 1718. The Greeting set is signed J[ohn?] B[anister?] and repeats the final four-bar phrase; other seventeenth-century versions repeat the initial four-bar strain. Without either repetition we have a twelve-bar tune which fits the six-line stanza usually associated with the tune; with either repetition it will fit those eight-line stanza texts set to it.

The tune evidently takes its name from a pastoral song of Colin and Amarillis beginning "Amarillis told her Swain," sung by Mariane in Thomas Porter's play, *The Villain*, 1663, Act II. The words, inappropriately entitled "A Catch," are reprinted in *Merry Drollery Complete*, 1670, and in *OEPM* II, 12. Porter's song was expanded into a broadside, "The Arcadian Lovers or, Colin and Amarillis . . . To be sung to a Tune of great rarity" (Euing 7, not later than 1665). It begins "Vpon the smooth Arcadian plain," and the playhouse text forms stanzas 4–6 of the broadside.

The first song in *Folly in Print, or, A Book of Rymes*, 1667, is "The

Cotsal Sheapheards. To the Tune of Amarillis told her Swain," beginning "Amarillis why so coy." A ballad by J. P. has the same form of the tune title: "Love in the Blossome: Or, Fancy in the Bud," beginning "One summer evening fresh and fair" (Harvard, Lord Crawford, Roxburghe; reprinted in *RB* VI, 110). The Crawford *Catalogue* conjectures that J. P. might be John Playford, the musician and publisher; our ballad editions are from the 1660s or 1670s, when Playford flourished.

Another ballad by J. P., "The Coy Shepherdess or, Phillis and Amintas," sung to the tune of "Phillis on the new made Hay, or Amarillis," derives its first tune name from the opening line of the ballad (Lord Crawford, Roxburghe; reprinted in *RB* III, 619). The same pair of tune names appears in "Fancy's Freedom. or The true Lovers bliss," beginning "All in the West of England fair," to the tune of "Amarillis, or, Phillis on the new made hay" (Roxburghe; reprinted in *RB* VI, 113).

To the same tune, under still different names, is "The true Lovers Happiness Or, Nothing venture, Nothing have," beginning "O my Dearest come away," to be sung to "Amintas on the new-made Hay, or Loyal Lovers" (Euing, Chetham, Pepys, Douce, Harvard, Rawlinson, Roxburghe; reprinted in *RB* VI, 116). The first tune title involves merely a substitution of names from J.P.'s "Coy Shepherdess"; the second derives from "A new Love-Song, and a true Love-Song" by Thomas Jones, which begins "Loyal Lovers listen well" (Lord Crawford 786 and Douce I, 76ᵛ). Its tune direction, "Collin and Amarillis," is derived from the title of the broadside which expands the original stage song. It will be noted that, though it is given several names, one tune serves all these ballads listed; those thus far named are all in six-line stanzas.[1]

At least two "Amaryllis" ballads are in eight-line stanzas: "The Description of a Town Miss," beginning "You Limber Ladies that appear,/ in diverse kind of dresses" (Pepys III, 57, Lord Crawford 1402, BM C.22.f.6 [109]). A song, "The Angler" (*Merry Drollery Complete*, 1670), is found on broadsides as "The Royal Recreation Of Jovial Anglers," beginning "Of all the Recreations which/attend on humane Nature" (Lord Crawford, Roxburghe; reprinted in *RB* VII, 82). Although the broadside is to be sung to "Amarillis," the text in *Pills*, 1719–1720, III, 126, calls for the tune "my Father was born before me," which fits the eight-line ballad stanza exactly; moreover, the internal rhyme in lines 5 and 7 found in "The Angler" and "The Description of a Town Miss" is also present in songs sung to "My father was born before me," q.v.

---

[1] Another in the same stanza form is "The Virgins Constancy," beginning "Hard hap had I, poor harmless Maid," sung to "Amarillis" in an edition issued after 1665 (Pepys IV, 55). In an earlier issue the tune is named "Loves ride, or, Wert thou more fairer" (Douce II, 272, Lord Crawford 480, Harvard). For a discussion of both tune titles, see "Wert thou . . ."

Amoret and Phyllis

This tune takes its name from the opening line, "As Amoret with Phillis sat," of a song written by Sir Carr Scrope for Sir George Etherege's play *The Man of Mode,* 1676, V, ii. The verses were reprinted in *A New Collection of the Choicest Songs,* 1676, in W. P.'s *The Wits Academy,* 1677, and in such later collections as *The Hive,* 3d ed., 1727, II, 96, and *Vocal Miscellany,* 1734, p. 254. With music by Nicholas Staggins the song appears in *Choice Ayres & Songs,* Second Book, 1679, p. 5 (Fig. 13);

the same melody has the title "When Clori[s] full of" in *Youth's Delight on the Flagelet,* 9th ed., c. 1690. Both versions of the tune fit a nine-line stanza—eight lines of ballad meter with a ninth line repeating the eighth.[1]

The stage song was expanded into a broadside "Amoret and Phillis," with the tune titled "Whilst Amoret &c." (Pepys III, 240, Douce I, 6ᵛ, both editions before 1685). This ballad and the two following have a

[1] New music was written by Dieupart to the poem "Amoret and Phillis" for a revival of Etherege's play about 1715. It continued to be a popular single-sheet song throughout the eighteenth century, with fresh musical settings by Digard and Ramondon. Several editions of an anonymous setting "Sung by Miss Falkner at Marybon Gardens" about 1750 are in BM and Harvard collections. None of these tunes appears to be related to the broadside tradition.

nine-line stanza: "The Soldiers delight, Or the she Voluntier," to the tune of "Amoret and Phillis," beginning "A young man lately lov'd a Lass" (Wood E.25, reprinted in *RB* VII, 732);[2] "The stubborn Lover catcht," beginning "Young Corridon whose stubborn heart" (Pepys III, 382).

Several ballads to this tune do not repeat the final line of each stanza. One is "The healing Balsom of a true Lover," beginning "Phillis my wounded hearts delight" (Pepys, Lord Crawford, BM C.22.f.6, Harvard, Bagford; reprinted in *BB* II, 568). Another is "Loves Conquest, or, Take her in the Humour. . . . To a New Pleasant Tune, Or, Amoret and Phillis," beginning "Young Pheon strove the bliss to taste,/but Strapho [i.e., Sappho] still deny'd" (Douce I, 128). The "New Pleasant Tune" was one by John Banister which became known as "Young Phaon," q.v., and the eight-line stanza is in the meter of "Hy boys up go Wee," which an owner of the Douce sheet has written in as an additional tune direction.[3]

Much the same double identification occurs in "Corydon and Cloris Or, The Wanton Sheepherdess [sic]," an expansion of Rochester's poem beginning "As Cloris full of harmless Thought" (Douce, with MS tune direction "or Hye boys up go we," Roxburghe; reprinted in *RB* VI, 134). Now "Cloris full of harmless thoughts" is a tune title with its own music, though it would seem to derive originally from "Amoret and Phyllis," since the latter tune title is used with this ballad, and we found "Amoret and Phillis" music labeled "When Clori[s] full of" in *Youth's Delight*. Ebsworth (*RB* VI, 133) is only partially correct in equating the two tune titles. The explanation in both cases may be that the poems "Young Phaon . . ." and "As Cloris . . ." became popular enough to inspire their own tunes, to which other ballads in turn were sung. The MS additions of "Hey boys up go we" indicate a popular alternate tune to which the eight-line stanzas could be sung.

[2] This ballad has no relation to the tune "Soldier's Delight," which is in an entirely different rhythm.

[3] The song of which the broadside is an expansion appeared in *The Art of Courtship*, 1686, sig. A8, without music but with the tune direction "Amoret and Phillis." The song was partially reprinted in *Pills*, 1719–1720, IV, 287, with Banister's music.

Andrew and Maudlin

A ballad entitled "The Young-Man's Ramble," beginning "Andrew, Maudlin, Rebecka, and Will," has as its tune title "Andrew and Maudlin" (Pepys III, 47, Wood E.25 [23]). The music to the tune is to be found in *Pills,* 1719–1720, II, 19 (Fig. 14), where it is associated with a

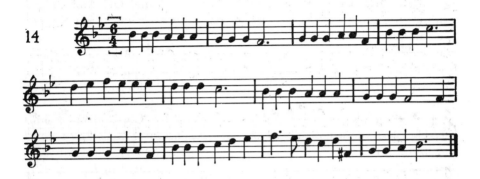

14

song unrelated to "The Young-Man's Ramble" after the first two stanzas. The ballad, a simple account of a boisterous country dance among members of the servant class, is full of titles, proverbial phrases, and tags from other ballads. With trifling variations, the text of the *Pills* song had appeared, without the music, in *Mercurius Democritus,* June 23–30, 1652, p. 99, and in *Wit and Drollery,* 1656, p. 136.

As May in All Her Youthful Dress

The anonymous song beginning "As May in all her youthful Dress," with music by Samuel Akeroyde, appeared in 1685 in *The Theater of Music,* First Book, and was reprinted in the same year in *A Collection of Twenty Four Songs,* sig. A3ᵛ (Fig. 15), and *180 Loyal Songs.* It is found with the music in all editions of *Pills,* 1719–1720, III, 198.[1] The Akeroyde air is also contained in a roman-letter broadside, "Faithful Coridon,"

1 A single-sheet edition of the song published about 1740 under the title of "The Honey-Moon" (BM, Harvard) has a new tune by an anonymous composer.

beginning "Now am I tost on waves of Love" (Wood 417 [135]), licensed by Sir Roger L'Estrange and so not later than 1685. A black-letter edition of the same ballad, without music, is titled "Cupids Conquest: Or, Will the Shepherd, and fair Kate of the Green" (Lord Crawford, Douce, Harvard; reprinted in *RB* VIII, clvii*). It was to be sung to "As I went forth to take the Air: Or, My dearest dear and I must part," both of which derive from "Flora's Farewell," a tune not extant.

"As May in all her youthful dress" is the tune for at least two other ballads. It is called "As May was in her youthful dress" in "The Maidens Moan For the Loss of Her Unkind Lover," beginning "As a Maid was walking in a Grove" (Pepys V, 290, with meaningless music). "The Lovers Invitation: Or, Forsaken Batchelors Complaint" is directed to be sung to "Love in Phantastick Triumph sat; Or, May in all her youthful dress" (Pepys IV, 46). This ballad, whose opening line gives us the first tune title, is an expansion of a song sung in Aphra Behn's tragedy *Abdelazar*, 1677, I, i.[2]

Akeroyde's tune is also named for singing Alexander Brome's song, "Now I'm resolv'd to Love no more," in *The Country Garland*, 1687, and in *Pills* VI, 312. In *A Complete Collection of . . . English and Scotch Songs*, 1735–1736, II, 49, it is named as the tune for the song beginning "When all that lies beneath the sun."

[2] The two-stanza stage song was reprinted in *The Last and Best Edition of New Songs*, 1677, in Mrs. Behn's *Poems upon Several Occasions*, 1684, and in *The Loyal Garland*, 1686, but no music appears to have survived.

At the Foot of a Willow,
or On the Bank of a River

Thomas D'Urfey's "A Song made to a Tune, by the command of a Lady of Quality," beginning "At the foot of a Willow close under the shade," appears with the music in his *New Collection of Songs and Poems*, 1683, p. 1 (Fig. 16). His text had earlier been printed anony-

mously in a poetical miscellany of 1682, *A New Collection Of the Choicest Songs*. In that same year, one of the poems added to the second edition of *Female Poems* [1] begins "On the Bank of a River close under a Shade," and is thereafter almost identical with D'Urfey's two-stanza text. Without further evidence it would be difficult to assign priority to either of the 1682 versions of the song. "On the Bank of a River" is found in *Choice Ayres and Songs*, Fourth Book, 1683, with the same music D'Urfey used; and the tune is called "On the banck of a River" in Humphry Salter's *Genteel Companion . . . for the Recorder*, 1683. The music is also preserved in Fitzwilliam Museum MS 30.G.20, p. 57 (1680s), coupled with words beginning "On ye brink of a river." The poem was reprinted in such eighteenth-century miscellanies as *The Hive*,

[1] The original edition consisted of poems by "Ephelia," i.e., Mrs. Joan Philips; the additions in 1682 are by various authors, but the paraphrase of D'Urfey's poem is anonymous.

3d ed., 1727, II, 15. It appears in Watts's *Musical Miscellany*, 1729–1731, III, 118, with a new musical setting by John Sheeles.

The history of the tune is hazy before D'Urfey appropriated it, but in 1682 Matthew Taubman wrote a political poem "The Healths," beginning "Since Plotting's a Trade, like the rest of the Nation," which he printed with the tune in *An Heroick Poem . . . With Some choice Songs . . . On The Times*, p. 12. In the same year an expansion of the text was published as a broadside, now called "The Loyal Health." No music is on the sheet, but the "Delicate new Tune" is named as "At the Foot of a Willow, close under the Shade" (BM Luttrell II, 96, Bodleian Ashmole G.16 [165], Wood 417 [79] and [111], Huntington [with MS date 13 June 1682], Yale, Harvard; reprinted with a corrupt version of the tune in *180 Loyal Songs*, 1685, p. 179).

The song in *Female Poems* was expanded into a broadside "Loves Triumph over Bashfulness," beginning "On the Banks of a River, close under a shade," sung to "a Pleasant new Play-House Tune" (Lord Crawford, Harvard, Roxburghe; reprinted in *RB* VII, 442). Several broadsides cite the tune as "On the Bank of a River," including "The Night-Walkers; or, The Loyal Huzza," 1682, beginning "The Town is our own,/ when the Streets are all clear" (Lord Crawford, BM C.39.k.6; reprinted in *OPB*, p. 15). Others add older alternative tunes which could be presumed to be more familiar: "Packington's Pound" in "The Oxford Health," beginning "Here's a health to the King and his lawful successors" (Wood E.25, Lord Crawford, Harvard, Roxburghe; reprinted in *RB* V, 37); "Digby's Fare-well" in "A Terror for Traitors" [1683], beginning "You Traytors of England how dare you Conspire" (Roxburghe; reprinted in *RB* V, 329); and "Now now the Fights done" in "The late Duke of Monmouth's Lamentation," beginning "The World is ungrateful/the People deceitful," licensed on July 18, 1685, just three days after Monmouth's execution (BM C.22.f.6, Lord Crawford, Harvard, Pepys; reprinted in *RB* V, 699).[2]

Another name for the tune, "The Loyal Health" (from the title of the broadside version of Taubman's poem), is cited in one edition of "The Pot-Companions," beginning "Come make a good Toast, and stir up the Fire" (Pepys, c. 1691, with meaningless music; reprinted in *PB* VI, 7).[3] The tune direction is "The Loyal Health; or, Why are my Eyes still Flowing" in "An Excellent New Song; or, A True Touch of the

---

[2] This last named ballad has the equivalent of six lines of anapestic tetrameter, in contrast to the usual eight. It can be sung to "On the bank of a river" by eliminating the repetition of the first strain; it fits the other tune unaltered.

[3] The original broadside issue of 1682 contained the tune direction "Thus all the day long we are frolick and gay: Or, We'l teach the little Dogs, &c." (Wood 417 [93]; reprinted without music in *180 Loyal Songs*, 1685, p. 310). The tunes are named from

Times . . . to . . . James the Second," beginning "King James the First was a Gallant King" (Euing; reprinted in *RB* VII, 707; an edition of 1687 in the Library of Congress lists only the first tune; a later edition, ". . . to . . . William the Third," is in BM C.22.f.6 [32] and Harvard).

"On the Banks of a River" was one of the airs called for in Aston's *The Fool's Opera*, c. 1730, a ballad opera for which no music was printed.

Aye, Marry, and Thank You Too

"I marry, and thank you too" is the refrain of a ballad entitled "The Thankful Country Lass," which begins "I met with a Country Lass" (Pepys; reprinted in *Amanda Group of Bagford Poems*, ed. J. W. Ebsworth, 1880, p. 542*).

The musical ramifications of this ballad are complex but lead nowhere. On the Pepys broadside are printed scraps of "Packington's Pound," but that tune does not fit the meter of this ballad. The tune direction given is "I am so sick of Love," for which no music exists: that tune name derives from the first line of "The Young-mans Lamentation" (Pepys; reprinted in *RB* VII, 300), which contains the equally inappropriate music of "Cold and Raw" and the direction that it is to be sung to an "excellent Play-House Tune" not otherwise identified. "I met with a country lass" is itself used as a tune title, but I have found no music for it.

Music for "Aye, marry, and thank you too" does, however, exist. It is earliest to be found in the unpaged *Youth's Delight on the Flagelet*, 9th ed., c. 1690 (Fig. 17); later and somewhat smoother versions appear in two printed ballad operas: *Robin Hood*, 1730, Air 15 (Fig. 18), called "The Bark in Tempest tost," and George Lillo's *Silvia*, 1731, Air 16, entitled "I live in the Town of Lynn." [1] The tune in *Pills*, 1719–1720, V, 59 is quite different except in its rhythmic pattern.

The tenth stanza of "The Thankful Country Lass," beginning "I

successive stanza openings of a song in Shadwell's *The Royal Shepherdess*, 1669, which may be found, with music by John Banister, in *Choice Songs and Ayres*, 1673, p. 13, and in *Pills*, 1719–1720, III, 162.

[1] *Silvia*, which was first produced in 1730, must have been written before *Robin Hood*, for the tune title in the latter is drawn from the first line of the song to "Aye, marry" in the former.

17

Original is a fifth higher.

18

Original time signature is erroneously 6/8.

live in the Town of Lynn,/next door to the Anchor blew," establishes a link with two of the many ballads sung to the tune of "Aye, marry." One of these is "An Answer to I Marry and thank ye too; or, the Lass of Lyn's sorrowfull Lamentation for the Loss of her Maiden-head. To the same Tune," beginning "I am the young Lass of Lyn,/who often said Thank you too" (Pepys V, 245, with meaningless music; reprinted in *Pills* V, 59, in *A Complete Collection of . . . English and Scotch Songs*, 1735–1736, IV, 86, and in *BB* I, 463). This is followed by "The Lass of Lynn's New Joy For finding a Father for her Child. Being a Third Song of Marry and Thank ye too. To the same tune," beginning "Come listen, and hear me tell/the end of a tale so true" (Pepys, Bagford; reprinted in *BB* I, 466).

The following ballads to the tune do not seem to have been reprinted: "The Denying Lady: or, A Travellers Frolick with a Woman that Reply'd no to all Questions," beginning "As I was upon the way" (Pepys V, 248, containing scraps of music to "Hey, boys, up go we"); "A Dialogue Between A Master and his Maid," beginning "Come hither my pretty Sue" (Pepys V, 224, containing music of "Sabina in the dead of night," which will not fit this ballad); "Wanton Will. of Wapping," beginning "A Gardiner brisk and brave" (Pepys V, 251, with meaningless music); "A Looking-Glass for Lascivious Young Men," beginning "An Honest Old Man of late" (Pepys II, 72); "The May Morning Ramble," beginning "Kind Robin he met young Kate" (Pepys IV, 65); "Nell's humble Petition," beginning "There was an old Maid of late" (Pepys III, 79); "The Old Woman's Resolution," beginning "There was an old

Woman then" (Douce II, 170ᵛ, Lord Crawford 1157, Pepys III, 186, Harvard); and "The Young Womens Complaint for Pressing the Old Ones," beginning "Young Women and Maidens all" (Pepys V, 399). All these are of the late seventeenth century, and all except the first three are in black letter—music being almost uniformly limited, as here, to roman-letter ballads.

At least five other ballads to this tune are reprinted in *RB* or *CP*.

The tune "I met with a country lass," for which there is no music, was at least interchangeable with "Aye, marry, and thank you too." A pair of related ballads suggests that we are concerned with alternate names for the same tune: "Hen-peckt Cuckold," beginning "I marry'd a Scolding Wife" (Pepys; reprinted in *RB* VII, 432) is to the first, while "The Wifes Answer to the Hen-peckt Cuckolds Complaint," beginning "My Cuckold tells tales of me" (Pepys; reprinted in *RB* VII, 433) is to the second. Two ballads of 1689 to the tune of "I met with a country lass" employ a burden, as is common with "Aye, marry" pieces, and supply one more point of close kinship linking the two tune names: "The Fright'ned York-shire Damosel," beginning "When first I began to Court" (Pepys V, 250, with meaningless music); and "The Wenching Tanner," beginning "I am but a Servant poor" (Pepys V, 252).

The Baffled Knight

This tune appears as "There was a Knight" in *Youth's Delight on the Flagelet,* 9th ed., c. 1690, and as "There was a Knight was drunk with Wine" in George Lillo's ballad opera *Silvia,* 1731, Air 54 (Fig. 19).

The ballad called "The Lady's Policy; or, The Baffled Knight" is a broadside version of the traditional ballad which is No. 112 in Child's *The English and Scottish Popular Ballads,* 1882–1898, and is but one of many reworkings of the story.[1] The opening line, "There was a Knight was drunk with Wine," establishes the connection with the flageolet and ballad-opera tune; our editions specify "a pleasant New Tune" or lack a tune direction. The Pepys copy is dated 1693 and is followed in the collection by separately issued second and third parts recounting further episodes in which the lady outwits the knight (Pepys V, 169, 170, 171). Later broadside issues add still another adventure and print all four parts on a single sheet (Douce III, 52ᵛ, Roxburghe III, 674; reprinted in *RB* VII, 439; the four-part text in *A Collection of Old Ballads*, 1723–1725, III, 178, is reprinted as Child 112 C). The text in the *Reliques*, 1765, caused Joseph Ritson to note (*Ancient Songs*, p. 159) that "Percy found the subject worthy of his best improvements."

At least three broadsides were sung to the tune of "The Baffled Knight," all of them dating from the last dozen years of the seventeenth century. They are: "The Unconstant Quaker," beginning "In London-town we understand" (Pepys V, 241); "The Victualar's Wifes Kindness to the Jolly Horse-Courser," beginning "You Victualers all I pray attend" (BM C.22.f.6 [202], Lord Crawford 1435, Pepys IV, 114, Harvard); and "The West-Country Lawyer: Or, The Witty Maid's Good Fortune," beginning "A Youthfull Lawyer fine and gay" (Lord Crawford, Harvard, Roxburghe; reprinted in *RB* VII, 428).

Although the old broadside tune is no longer sung, the ballad of "The Baffled Knight" has persisted in tradition down to our own day. For references to British texts and tunes, see Margaret Dean-Smith, *A Guide to English Folk Song Collections*, 1954, s.v. "Blow away the morning dew." Cecil Sharp's numerous recoveries of this song are discussed and in part reprinted by James Reeves, *The Idiom of the People*, 1958, pp. 40–43, 77–81. On current American survivals, most of which are confined to New England, see T. P. Coffin, *The British Traditional Ballad in North America*, rev. ed., 1963, p. 99.

[1] The earliest broadside version is "The politick Maid. Or, A dainty new ditty,/both pleasant and witty:/Wherein you may see,/the maides policie," beginning "There was a Knight was wine-drunke," and to "a pleasant new tune." This ballad by R[ichard] C[limsell] was licensed on May 16, 1637 to its publisher, Thomas Lambert (Roxburghe; reprinted in *RB* II, 281, and Child 112, Appendix). Here the stanza pattern is four lines of ballad meter plus a refrain of four lines, comparable to the octosyllabics of "Yonder comes a courteous Knight," noted below; "The Lady's Policy" contains no refrain. A still earlier text, with music, begins "Yonder comes a courteous Knight" (Thomas Ravenscroft, *Deuteromelia*, 1609; reprinted in *Pills* III, 37, and Child 112 A). A later version in an eight-line stanza without refrain, beginning "There was a Knight and he was young," is in *Pills* V, 112, with a still different tune; words alone are found in *A Complete Collection of . . . English and Scotch Songs*, 1735–1736, I, 68, and Child 112 B.

The Bailiff's Daughter
of Islington

The tune of "The Baily's Daughter of Islington" appears in the anonymous ballad opera *The Jovial Crew,* 1731, Air 12 (Fig. 20).[1] The

broadside giving rise to the tune title is "True Love Requited: Or, The Bailiff's Daughter of Islington. To a North-Country Tune. Or, I have a good old Mother at home," beginning "There was a youth, and a well-belov'd youth/and he was a Esquires Son" (Lord Crawford, Harvard, Chetham, Pepys, Douce [three editions, one substituting "Wife" for "Mother" in the tune title], Roxburghe; reprinted in *RB* VI, 243, in John Ashton's *A Century of Ballads,* 1887, p. 158, and in Child, No. 105). Ritson, *English Songs,* 1783, II, 234, reprints the ballad without tune direction; it was earlier included in Percy's *Reliques.*

The tune of "I have a good old Mother at home" has not survived, though other ballads were written to it, including one by T[homas] L[anfiere], "The Taunton Maids delight, Or, Hey for the honest Woosted-Comber," beginning "You pretty Maids where e're you are" (Lord Crawford 1420, Harvard). Two other ballads may be related to this tune title: "Virginity grown Troublesome," which begins "I have a good old Mother at home" (Lord Crawford, BM C.22.f.6, Harvard, Roxburghe; reprinted in *RB* VI, 246) and its apparent sequel, "Crums of

---

[1] E. F. Rimbault, in Gutch's *Robin Hode,* 1847, II, 434, reprinted as the tune of "The Jolly Pinder of Wakefield" the "Baily's Daughter" music from *The Jovial Crew.* Rimbault did not mention the ballad opera but named as the source of his tune "an old MS. in lute tablature, formerly in the collection of the Rev. Mr. Gostling, of Canterbury." What he called "another copy of this tune" in Cambridge University MS Dd.3.18 is evidently "Wakefilde on a green," fol. 11v, an entirely different air. Its title, coming from the burden of "The Jolly Pinder," probably led Rimbault to an association which the music does not justify.

Comfort For the Youngest Sister," beginning "I have a good old Father at home" (Pepys, Lord Crawford, Douce, Harvard; reprinted in *RB* VI, 248). Both are to be sung to "a pleasant New West-Country Tune" not otherwise identified and are in the same stanza form as "The Bailiff's Daughter." [2]

Child printed only a broadside text of "The Bailiff's Daughter," but the ballad has persisted in tradition into the present generation and has been recovered on both sides of the Atlantic. Among the interesting survivals are five Aberdeenshire tunes preserved in Gavin Greig's *Last Leaves of Traditional Ballads and Ballad Airs,* 1925, p. 84, one of which (1 b) is almost identical with the *Jovial Crew* tune, except for flatted sevenths in the Scotch air.

A good deal of discussion has centered around another tune, which seems to have been first printed in Chappell's *National English Airs,* 1840. It is there identified as "the traditional tune commonly sung all over the country," and Chappell repeated the description in *PMOT* I, 203. Meantime, E. F. Rimbault printed the tune in his *Musical Illustrations of Bishop Percy's Reliques,* 1850, p. 100, saying that he had noted it down in northern England. The Rimbault version became a drawing-room favorite as a result of ballad concerts following the publication of Chappell's *Popular Music;* it was issued as a single song and was reprinted in *Old English Ditties* and other collections. It is not surprising, then, that traditional recoveries should show little textual or musical variation from print (see A. K. Davis, *Traditional Ballads of Virginia,* 1929, pp. 383, 585, and E. H. Linscott, *Folk Songs of Old New England,* 1939, p. 160). Rimbault's connection with the tune has, however, been questioned. He is reported to have confessed that he composed it himself (*JFSS,* VII [1923], 36); moreover, it may have been Rimbault who gave Chappell the tune and reported its general popularity. It is significant that Rimbault in 1838 wrote an operetta on *The Fair Maid of Islington* (unpublished; did it contain the air?). That he may have adapted an extant traditional tune is suggested by the similarity which Miss A. G. Gilchrist has noted between Rimbault's air and a Mixolydian set of "Come mother . . . make up my bed" which she collected in Sussex (*JFSS,* V [1915], 135; see also a Vaughan Williams specimen, III [1909], 304). Her tune is equally reminiscent of an air commonly found with American versions of "The Wife of Usher's Well" (e.g., Sharp-Karpeles, *English Folk-Songs from the Southern Appalachians,* 1932, I, 150–160). A

---

[2] Ebsworth, *RB* VI, 245, reprints "The Good Fellow" from an eighteenth-century copy in Roxburghe III, 657, because of its lines "I have a good old Father at home" (opening of stanza 2) and "I have a good old Mother at home" (opening of stanza 3); but its stanza pattern is incompatible with that of "The Bailiff's Daughter," and no connection between the two seems probable.

Devonshire tune of "A Maid Was I," from Frank Kidson's MSS (*JEFDSS*, III [1936–1939], 51), has an even stronger resemblance to the Rimbault tune. Finally, it should be noted that other traditional tunes for "The Bailiff's Daughter" are encountered oftener than Rimbault's among folksingers. See *JFSS*, VII (1923), 34–36, and H. M. Belden, *Ballads and Songs*, 1940, p. 68, for discussion and references. Bertrand H. Bronson's treatment in *The Traditional Tunes of the Child Ballads*, 1959–   , II, 515ff., is definitive, with all the relevant tunes systematically classified. As we have seen, the broadside history of the ballad has been overshadowed by its persistence as a property of the folk.

Balow

Three distinct tunes are associated with the nursery word "Balow" or "Baloo," and much of the confusion in earlier discussions has resulted from a failure to separate the several tune traditions. Controversy over origins has, as we shall see, aroused nationalistic bias and produced some strangely distorted history as well as angry rebuttal.

Of sixteenth-century origin is "A sweet lullabie" beginning "Come little babe, come silly soule," found in *The Arbor of Amorous Devices*, 1597. This song, which is usually credited to Nicholas Breton (see Hyder E. Rollins's facsimile edition of the *Arbor*, 1936, p. xvi), is in six-line stanzas without tune direction or refrain. A number of late seventeenth-century broadside reprints have survived, entitled "A Lullaby" or "An Excellent Song, Call'd, Lullaby," bearing no tune direction (Pepys, Bagford, Harvard, Roxburghe; reprinted in *RB* II, 525). The poem has often been cited as the "original" of the "Balow" presently to be discussed, but what they share is merely the basic situation in which a deserted mother sings to her babe. The only serious reason for mentioning Breton's lyric is that it has been linked, though on no evidence, with an Elizabethan tune called "Baloo" in William Ballet's MS Lute Book, p. 111, and "Balowe" in Thomas Morley's *First Booke of Consort Lessons*, 1599, 1611, ed. Sydney Beck, 1959, No. 18 (Fig. 21). As Beck has noted, a different tune is associated with Breton's poem in a setting for voice and viols attributed to William Byrd in a New York Public Library MS, Drexel 4180, fol. 50ᵛ (cantus).

More to our purpose is a seventeenth-century broadside, "The New Balow: or, A Wenches Lamentation for the loss of her Sweet-heart," beginning "Balow, my Babe, weep not for me," directed to be sung to

"Balow" (Roxburghe; reprinted in *RB* VI, 577). Since the imprint is shorn from the unique broadside, a close dating of the sheet is impossible, but it may well represent the ballad entered in the Stationers' Register to Margaret Trundle in 1627 as "Balloe my Babe." In any case, the piece seems to be an expansion of early seventeenth-century verses preserved in several manuscript copies. One is in the Percy Folio MS (ed. Hales and Furnivall, III, 522), beginning "Balowe my babe, lye still & sleepe/itt greeues me sore to see thee weepe." The printed broadside contains five of the Percy Folio's seven stanzas, not much changed. Moreover, it should be noted that a distinctive feature of the manuscript poem, i.e., internal rhyme in the fifth line of each stanza, appears in the broadside only in those stanzas paralleled in the manuscript poem, as if the broadside poet were oblivious of that metrical detail. The eight-line stanzas conclude with an elaborate two-line "Balow" refrain.

Two other manuscript texts are analogues of that in Percy's Folio and are especially important because they are coupled with a tune which can also serve for the "New Balow" broadside. A six-stanza version is in John Gamble's Commonplace Book, 1659 (MS Drexel 4257), No. 46 (Fig. 22); and one of four stanzas is in the Elizabeth Rogers Virginal Book (BM MS Add. 10337, fol. 57) among pieces that can be dated in the second half of the seventeenth century. Despite significant differences in detail, these two settings of air with bass render the same complex and artistic tune, with the "Balow" refrain fully indicated, and the musical parallelism in measures 9 and 10 organically related to the rhyming hemistiches of the fifth line in each stanza.

At least one other adaptation of the manuscript song text is found during the seventeenth century. It is "The Forsaken Maid. To the Tune: Of Balloo," beginning "My dearest Baby, prethee sleep,/It grieves me

22 C3i

sore to see thee weep" in *Mock Songs and Joking Poems*, 1675, p. 126 (reprinted in *Amanda Group of Bagford Poems*, ed. J. W. Ebsworth, 1880, p. 477*). Its four stanzas, with an "Ay me, ay me" refrain, fit the "Balow" pattern and without mockery or joking are clearly related to stanzas 1, 3, 2, and 7 of the Percy Folio text. An early imitation with no verbal correspondences is a two-stanza lullaby which Constance sings in Richard Brome's *The Northern Lasse*, 1632, IV, iv, beginning "Peace wayward Barne; O cease thy mone:/Thy farre more wayward Daddy's gone." It contains a "Ballow, Ballow, &c." refrain and exhibits the characteristic fifth-line internal rhyme pattern.

A third cluster of poems, coupled with a distinctive Scotch tune, is in reality another offshoot of the "New Balow" tradition we have just described. Commonly titled "Lady Anne Bothwel's Balow" or "Lady Anne Bothwell's Lament," the thirteen-stanza song beginning "Balow my Boy, ly still and sleep" seems to have appeared first in James Watson's *Choice Collection of . . . Scots Poems*, Part III, 1711, p. 79. By 1733 a slightly variant text with some rearrangement of stanzas had appeared in Allan Ramsay's *Tea-Table Miscellany*, p. 130; and in the same year the text, with air and bass, was printed in W. Thomson's *Orpheus Caledonius*, II, No. 17. It was reprinted in Johnson's *Scots Musical Museum*, 1787–1803, II, 135. Joseph Ritson reprinted the Thomson tune in his *Scotish Songs*, 1794, I, 158, and described his text as Watson's, compared with that in the 1750 *Tea-Table*.

Despite the personalized title of this song, eleven of its stanzas are from the seventeenth-century broadside "The New Balow," their order

shifted about and the language somewhat polished by Ramsay, Scotchified by later editors. Thomson's tune is Scottish, to be sure, and the
song evidently enjoyed popularity in Scotland during the eighteenth
century and afterward. But the Bothwell attribution is a romantic affix,
in view of the almost complete derivation from the English broadside
text. Even Percy in his *Reliques* was influenced by the Bothwell lure,
for in printing the seven-stanza Folio MS song, improved from Ramsay,
he transformed its language into Scots and titled it "Lady Anne Bothwell's Lament. A Scottish Song." Beside Percy, other ballad editors made
a case for Scottish origin through minute sifting of historical particulars;
see, for instance, Robert Chambers, *The Scottish Ballads*, 1829, p. 118,
and William E. Aytoun, *The Ballads of Scotland*, 1858, II, 44. Arrayed
against this kind of patriotic effort is the bibliographical approach of
Chappell, who wrote most of the headnote in Hales and Furnivall's edition of the Percy Folio MS, III, 515ff. Chappell made the appeal to
history irrelevant, but his generally accurate account is marred by his
usual lack of sympathy for Scotch expropriations. Later Ebsworth joined
the fray (*RB* VI, 575ff.), repeating Chappell in matter and manner. In
an effort to bring something fresh to a stale controversy, he made positive claims for the Nicholas Breton "Lullaby" as the original poem from
which the later "Balow" songs were derived—claims which careful textual
comparison does not sustain.

Bara Faustus' Dream

This tune title is to be associated with an elusive broadside "Bar'ra
Faustus' Dream," beginning "When of late I sought my bed,/Sad my
thoughts, I could not slumber," sung "To a Pleasant New Tune." This
ballad is reprinted in *RB* VIII, 596, but Ebsworth does not specify his
source; he dates it as before 1609. Ebsworth also reprints (VIII, 598),
without citation of source, "The Secoud part of Barrow Faustus Dreame.
To a pleasant new tune" (Manchester II, 51). This he dates about 1660;
but the Manchester sheet was printed by A. M., who may have been
Augustine Mathews, active in the ballad trade from 1619 to near the
middle of the century.

Perhaps the earliest musical setting is "Barrow fosters dreame," arranged "violl way" in William Ballet's late sixteenth-century MS Lute
Book, p. 29. Two sets of variations appear in *The Fitzwilliam Virginal*

Book, one by Thomas Tomkins, the other anonymous. Further virginal sets are "Barrow ffaustus" in Paris Conservatoire MS Rés. 1186, fol. 19, and "Barowfostus Dreame" in New York Public Library MS Drexel 5612, p. 160. Philip Rosseter's *Lessons for Consort,* 1609, contains an arrangement by Edmund Kete; and a lute version, called "Chançon angloise," is in Nicolas Vallet, *Tablature de Luth, entitulé Le Secret des Muses,* 1618–1619.

The tune had an amazing currency in seventeenth-century Dutch songbooks, under the title "Phoebus die is lang over de Zee" or some variation of these words (the opening line of an early seventeenth-century Dutch song, perhaps inspired by "Phoebus long over the sea," line 13 of the English ballad). The music is found in J. J. Starter, *Friesche Lust-Hof,* 1621, in A. Valerius's *Neder-Landtsche Gedenck-Clanck,* 1626, and Camphuysen's *Stichtelyche Rymen,* 1647, the two latter with alternate tune names "Engels Bara vastres drom" and "Forsters Droom." Songbooks without music in which "Phoebus . . ." is named as a tune include: *Cupido's Lusthof,* c. 1613, p. 34; *Apollo of Ghesengh der Musen,* 1615, p. 60; G. A. Bredero, *Aendachtigh Liedt-Boeck,* 1622, p. 57; *De Groote Bron Der Minnen,* 1622, p. 10; and several others.[1]

In Richard Johnson's *Golden Garland of Princely Pleasures,* 3d ed., 1620, sig. F8, the song beginning "Come sweet Loue, let sorrow cease" is entitled "The Shepheards Joy. To the tune of Barra Faustus Dreame." The song begins with stanza 5 of "Bar'ra Faustus' Dream"; the three other stanzas of the song text are not to be found in the ballad. Words and music are also in the early seventeenth-century "Airs and Sonnets" section of MS F.5.13, p. 88, Trinity College, Dublin; in the Leyden MS of 1639, fol. 12ᵛ, National Library of Scotland; in University of Edinburgh MS La. III.483, p. 180; and in John Forbes's *Cantus, Songs and Fancies. . . .* 1662, No. 32 (Fig. 23). The tune alone, entitled "Come sueat love lett sorrow cease," is in the unpaged seventh section of the Skene MS.

[1] See F. van Duyse, *Het Oude Nederlandsche Lied,* 1903–1908, II, 1292–1297.

In the BM copy of William Slatyer's *Psalmes, or Songs of Sion*, 1642, a MS note indicates that Psalm 19 could be sung to "Barbara Forster's Dream."

Bartholomew Fair

In *The Dancing Master*, 9th to 16th editions, 1695–1716 (1695, p. 170 = Fig. 24) and in Walsh's *Compleat Country Dancing-Master*, 1718, this

24   

tune appears as "The Whim." But in the seventeenth edition of *The Dancing Master*, 1721, it is called "Bartholomew Fair: Or, The Whim." The tune is thus connected with a late seventeenth-century broadside, "Roger in Amaize, or, The Countrey Mans Ramble through Bartholo-mew-Fair," beginning "Adzooks Ches went the other day to London Town," to the tune of "Dutch Womans Jigg" (Pepys; reprinted in *BB* I, 22). The text of this ballad appears also in *Wits Cabinet*, c. 1700, and words and music are on an engraved single sheet bearing the second of the broadside titles (Harvard, BM H.1601 [39], dated 1705?). Under this title the words and music are to be found in all editions of *Pills*, 1719–1720, III, 41. Nothing is known of the history of the "Dutch

Womans Jigg," though it may well have been an independent tune before "The Whim" became associated with the "Bartholomew Fair" ballad.

The music of "Bartholomew Fair" was popular enough to be used in eight ballad operas; among them are Walker's *The Quaker's Opera,* 1728, Chetwood's *The Lover's Opera,* 1729, Coffey's *The Boarding-School,* 1733, and Henry Carey's *The Honest Yorkshire-Man,* 1735. Chappell noted the peculiar metrical organization of the tune: each musical phrase is three measures, as often happens in jigs and hornpipes.

Basse's Career,

or Hunter's Career

In *The Compleat Angler,* part I, chapter V, Piscator says: "I'll promise you I'll sing a song that was lately made, at my request, by Mr. William Basse; one that hath made the choice songs of the 'Hunter in his career,' and of 'Tom of Bedlam,' and many others of note . . ." Basse is thought to have died about 1653, the year in which Izaak Walton's book was first published. The earliest and fullest copy of his "Hunter" song is a broadside of about 1625, "Maister Basse his Careere, Or The new Hunting of the Hare," beginning "Long ere the Morne expects the re- turne," and sung "To a new Court tune" (Pepys; reprinted in *PB* II, 38). On the same sheet and to the tune "Basse his Careere," is "The Faulconers Hunting" in the same measure, beginning "Early in the morne, when the night's ouerworne" (*PB* II, 41).

Basse's song in abbreviated form and with many textual variants is found in Bodleian MS Rawl. Poet. 246, c. 1648–1660, in *Sportive Wit,* 1656, *Wit and Drollery,* 1682, *A Collection of Old Ballads,* 1723–1725, III, 196, in Sir Nicholas Harris Nicolas's edition of *The Complete Angler,* 1836, II, 420–421, and in R. W. Bond's *The Poetical Works of William Basse,* 1893, p. 129.[1]

---

[1] In *PB* Professor Rollins lists the variants in Bond's text, which is derived from *Wit and Drollery.* Chappell (*PMOT* I, 256) reprinted the text from *A Collection of Old Ballads,* not from "a vaguely specified manuscript," as Professor Rollins states; the manuscript references in Chappell's article are to the music and are reasonably specific. In *Wit and Drollery* the poem is followed by "The Hunt," beginning "Clear is the air,

A number of broadsides were sung to the tune, all of them in the distinctive stanza pattern of Basse's original. Perhaps the earliest is "Mount Taraghs Triumph. 5. Iuly. 1626," to the tune of "the Careere," beginning "King Charles be thou blest, with peace and with rest" (London Society of Antiquaries, No. 271, a Dublin imprint). "Wit's never good till 'tis bought" was licensed in 1634 to Thomas Lambert, and the one known copy of the ballad was printed for him. It begins "Once musing alone,/upon things many a one," to the tune of "Basses Carreere" (Roxburghe; reprinted in *RB* III, 63). Another citing the tune title in this form is "Huberts Ghost," beginning "What Serpent is this/That at me doth hiss" (Rawlinson, Pepys, Bagford; reprinted in *BB* I, 160).

"The Hasty Bride-Groom," beginning "Come from the Temple away to the Bed," to the tune "Bass His Carrier: Or, Bow Bells" (Manchester, Pepys, Rawlinson, Douce, Lord Crawford, Morgan, Roxburghe; reprinted in *RB* VII, 458), first appeared in *Mercurius Fumigosus,* May 16–23, 1655, and was licensed for separate publication the next year. Its popularity may be gauged by the fact that it was kept in print by successive syndicates of ballad publishers up to the end of the seventeenth century and was included in both the 1714 and 1719–1720 editions of *Pills.* In *Wits Cabinet,* c. 1700, it is followed by "The Lady's Loving Reply" in the same metrical pattern. "News from Frost-Fair, upon the River of Thames," beginning "Not many years ago/There fell a mighty Snow" (Harvard), derives its tune title "Come from the Temple to the Bed" from the opening line of "The Hasty Bride-Groom" and can be sung to "Basse's Career," as can "The Greenland Voyage; or, the Whale-Fisher's Delight," beginning "Why stay we at home, now the Season is come," to the tune "Hey to the Temple" (*Collection of Old Ballads* III, 172).

Lute arrangements of the tune, called "Hunters Cariere," can be found in Sir Robert Gordon of Straloch's MS Lute Book, 1627–1629, extracts from which, in tablature, were made by George F. Graham in 1847 (Natl. Lib. of Scotland, Adv. MS 5.2.18, pp. 16–17); another early Scotch set (for mandore) is in the Skene MS, printed in Dauney's *Ancient Scotish Melodies,* 1838, p. 235. The Bedford Cittern MS, fol. 18, preserves a mid-seventeenth-century version, and "humbers carrere" in Christ Church MS 437, fol. 8ᵛ (Fig. 25) is a virginal arrangement from the same period. The tune is used in *Pills* VI, 197, for "The Hunt," an interesting piece of sustained *double entendre* which quickly turns from its innocent opening "Some in the Town go betimes to the Downs,/ To pursue the fearful Hare" to the real subject: "But all my delight is a

and the morning is fair"; the opening and closing stanzas would fit the tune, but in the middle section the author has written stanzas of various lengths which are not adapted to singing.

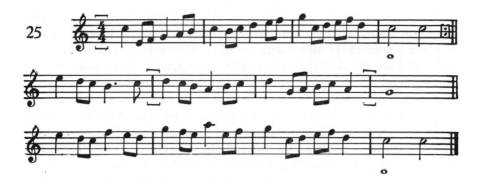

25

Cunney in the Night,/When she turns up her silver Hair." D'Urfey wrote a song "to a pretty Tune; She turns up her Silver hair" in honor of the Worthy Society of Archers, 1711 (*Pills,* 1719–1720, I, 150), which also fits the tune.

The Beggar Boy

The music is found in the first eight editions of *The Dancing Master,* 1651–1690 (1651, p. 5=Fig. 26); the treble-violin version of the tune requires division of several notes to fit the words sung to it.

26

Original is unbarred.

The tune may get its name from "The Begger-Boy of the North: Whose lin[e]age and calling to th' world is proclaim'd, Which is to be sung to a Tune so nam'd," beginning "From ancient pedigree by due descent" (Roxburghe; reprinted in *RB* III, 323). This ballad was printed for Francis Grove, whose apprenticeship was completed in 1623, and if it is the source of the tune name, it must have been issued by 1630. In 1631 Robert Guy's "The witty Westerne Lasse," beginning "Sweet Lucina, lend me thy ayde," to the tune of "The begger boy," was entered in the Stationers' Register (Pepys, Roxburghe; reprinted in *RB* III, 47). From Guy's ballad comes another name for the tune, "Lusina," which was cited on a broadside of 1632: "A most pleasant Dialogue: Or A merry greeting betweene two louers," by Charles Records, beginning "Good morrow, fair Nansie, whither so fast" (Pepys; reprinted in *PB* II, 225). It was named again in a ballad by S[amuel?] S[mithson?] called "The Parliament Routed . . . To the Tune of, Lucina: Or, Merrily and cherrily," 1653, beginning "Cheer up kind Countrey-men be not dismaid" (variant issues in Harvard, BM Thomason; reprinted in Wright's *Political Ballads*, p. 126, Wilkins's *Political Ballads*, I, 105, Mackay's *Cavalier Songs*, p. 102, and *RB* VIII, xlvii*, cxlv*).

Other ballads sung to "The Begger-boy" include Martin Parker's "Tryall brings truth to light," beginning "The world hath allurements and flattering shows" (Roxburghe; reprinted in *RB* III, 285), and "The Worlds Sweet-heart," beginning "Sweet Mistris Money I here will declare" (Roxburghe; reprinted in *RB* III, 81); both broadsides were issued by Thomas Lambert in 1634.

A-Begging We Will Go

This tune takes its name from the refrain of a stage song found in a late seventeenth-century broadside which went through many editions, both black-letter and roman. It is "The Beggars Chorus In the Jovial Crew," beginning "There was a jovial Beggar,/he had a wooden Leg," "To an excellent New Tune" (Bagford; reprinted in *BB* I, 216; found also in Lord Crawford, Wood 417, Roxburghe [2 editions], Douce [2 editions], Harvard, Madden). The song was evidently used in Richard Brome's *Jovial Crew, or The Merry Beggars* (produced 1641), but since it does not appear in the printed play before the 1684 edition, it may have been introduced only in a revival. This latter view is strengthened by the fact that the song (without music) in *Wit and Mirth*, 3d ed., 1684, has the title "A Song in the last revived Play called, The Jovial Crew, or the Bonny-Beggars"; moreover, a rash of songs capitalizing on the refrain formula suddenly appeared in the mid-eighties, showing that the stage song or the broadside—perhaps both—had suddenly caught the public fancy.[1]

Music to the song appeared first in *Choice Ayres and Songs,* Fifth Book, 1684, p. 26 (Fig. 27). It is also found on a broadside of that same year,

"The Swearers Chorus to the First Presbyterian Plot," beginning "There was a Monstrous Doctor" (Bodleian Ashmole G.16 [111 and 137], Clark). The publisher was Nathaniel Thompson, who included the song in *A Choice Collection of 120 Loyal Songs,* 1684, and in the expanded edition with music, 1685. The latter collection contains several other political songs to the tune, as well as the original playhouse song; see pp. 35, 37, 264.

"There was a jovial beggar" is found with its air in all editions of *Pills,* 1719–1720, III, 265; in the same work "I am a jolly toper, I am a raged Soph" (VI, 200) also contains the music. The continued popularity of the tune in the eighteenth century may be seen from the engraved single-sheet songs with the music; e.g., "The Basket Women The Words by Mr. A. Bradley," beginning "To th' Gin shop let us go,/where we may take our fill" (BM H.1601 [465], Huntington, c. 1720) and "The Stag Chace. by a West Country Gentleman," beginning "I am a jolly huntsman" (BM G.309 [38], Harvard; reprinted in Watts's *Musical Miscellany,* 1729–1731, VI, 145, and *Muses Delight,* 1754). Even more impressive is its appearance in no less than eighteen ballad operas, from Walker's *The Quaker's Opera,* 1728, to Brooke's *Jack the Gyant Queller,* 1749.

The tune is known under several names, deriving from some part of the original playhouse text: "Jovial Beggar(s)," "There was a jovial Beggar," "A Beggar I will be," "The Beggar with the Wooden Leg," "A Beggar of all Trades is the best," "The Sturdy Beggar." It is called "The

[1] "Colonel John Okei's [or Okie's] Lamentation, or a Rumper Cashiered," beginning "Of a Famous Brewer my purpose is to tell" (Harvard, Wood 416, BM Luttrell, BM Thomason) has the tune title "And a Begging we will go" and is dated 1660; but the stanza pattern does not fit this tune. The ballad can, however, be sung to "Which nobody can deny."

Jovial Crew" in Walsh's *New Country Dancing-Master,* c. 1728, III, 146.

A great many seventeenth- and eighteenth-century ballads were sung to the tune, all of them dating from 1684 or after. These include "Content's a Treasure," beginning "We are Jovial Topers" (Roxburghe; reprinted in *RB* V, 162; the black-letter edition published by J. Blare is later than Ebsworth's date, "c. 1681"). "The Merry Beggars of Lincolns-Inn-Fields," beginning "Three Beggars met together" (Pepys IV, 252); "Jolly Jack of all Trades, Or, The Cries of London City," beginning "I am a Jack of all Trades" (Pepys IV, 263, Douce I, 104); and the very similar "Jovial Tom of all Trades, or, The Various Cries of London City," beginning "My name is Tom of all Trades" (Harvard), were all licensed by Richard Pocock, which dates the editions 1685–1688. Professor Rollins reprinted four political broadsides of 1689 calling for the tune (*PB* IV, 87, 116, 120; V, 76), but he did not reprint an amatory ballad of 1692, "Age renewed by wedlock," beginning "Come all ye Ancient Women" (Pepys V, 159). "The Gipsies Song," 1684, beginning "I'd rather be the Gipsies Lord and Soveraign" (Clark), has no tune direction, but its refrain "And a Gipsie I will be . . ." follows the pattern found in ballads sung to "A-Begging."

Other songs to the tune will be found in such miscellanies as *Political Merriment,* 1714–1715, *A Pill to Purge State-Melancholy,* 1715, and *A Collection of State Songs,* 2d ed., 1716. M. O. Percival, *Walpole Ballads,* 1916, p. 86, reprinted one political broadside to the tune and noted the existence of several other contemporary specimens.

The Black Almain

"The Black Almain" was used as the tune of three and perhaps four sixteenth-century ballads. The earliest of these, licensed in 1570–1571, is Steven Peell's "A proper new balade expressyng the fames, Concerning a warning to al London dames," beginning "You London dames, whose passyng fames" (Huntington; reprinted in Collier's *Old Ballads,* 1840, p. 53, and in Collmann, No. 71). "A pleasant Poesie, or sweete Nosegay . . . gathered in . . . the Bible," 1572, was written by John Symon and begins "A stock of flowers, bedewed with showers" (BM Huth; reprinted in *A Collection of Seventy-Nine Black-Letter Ballads,* p. 5). *A Handefull of Pleasant Delites,* 1584, ed. Rollins, p. 39, contains still another to the tune: "A proper Sonet, Intituled, Maid, wil you marrie," beginning "Maid, wil you marie? I pray sir tarie." A broadside of 1570, whose tune is named "Blacke Almaine upon Scissillia," is in the same stanza pattern as Peell's ballad and may well be intended for the same tune. It is "A new Ballade, intituled, Agaynst Rebellious and false rumours," beginning "What rumores now are raised of late,/Within this English lande" (BM Huth; reprinted in *A Collection of Seventy-Nine*, p. 239).

A contemporary set of the tune, called "Ein schöner Englischer Dantz," has been preserved in the keyboard *Tabulatur* of the elder Bernhard Schmid published in Strassburg, 1577 (see Wilhelm Merian, *Der Tanz in den deutschen Tabulaturbüchern*, 1927, p. 103). As "The Black Almaine" the tune is found in a late seventeenth-century manuscript formerly in the collection of the Sacred Harmonic Society, now Royal College of Music MS 1119, fol. 24 (Fig. 28).[1] The unusual stanza pattern

28

combines a ballad-meter quatrain, a trimeter couplet, a tetrameter couplet, and three or four irregular tetrameters. The music, comprising four four-measure phrases plus a two-bar coda, will fit the elastic stanza if the first strain is repeated. The two pieces with twelve-line stanzas—the Peell broadside and that sung to "Blacke Almaine upon Scissillia"—require as well a repetition of the coda.[2]

[1] See *Catalogue of the Library of the Sacred Harmonic Society*, 1862, No. 1601. I am indebted to Professor John Ward for calling my attention to both musical settings. He has meantime published the seventeenth-century tune in "Music for *A Handefull of Pleasant Delites*," *JAMS*, X (1957), 163.

[2] Mr. Ward's disposition of the lines is different, for he does not repeat the first strain and he omits a line from the *Handefull* stanza.

Blue Cap

Music to this tune is found in all editions of *The Dancing Master*, 1651–c. 1728 (1651, p. 2=Fig. 29), in *A Musicall Banquet*, 1651, in *Mu-*

Original is a minor third higher and unbarred.

sicks Recreation On the Lyra Viol, 1652, and in *A Booke of New Lessons for the Cithern & Gittern*, 1652, in the mid-century Bedford Cittern MS, fol. 1, and in John Gamble's MS Commonplace Book, 1659, Nos. 51 and 74. An arrangement for virginals in New York Public Library MS Drexel 5612, p. 181, may be earlier than these; and a version in the Skene MS (*Ancient Scotish Melodies*, ed. Dauney, 1838, p. 234) is almost certainly later.

"Blew Cap for me . . . To a curious new Scottish tune called Blew-cap" was licensed to Thomas Lambert March 22, 1634, and the Roxburghe copy of the ballad (reprinted in *RB* I, 75) is a Lambert issue of about this date. The title and tune name are drawn from the burden "Gif ever I have a man,/Blew-cap for me," and the ballad begins "Come hither, the merri'st of all the nine." The Gamble MS, No. 51, contains a seven-stanza version of the broadside with air and bass, and a text without music or tune direction is preserved in *An Antidote against Melancholy*, 1661.[1]

Lambert entered another ballad to the tune in May, 1634: "Robin and Kate," by Martin Parker, beginning "Farre in the North Countrey (as I haue heard tell)" (Roxburghe; reprinted in *RB* II, 414). Still another

---

[1] The ballad makes explicit the identification of the blue cap or bonnet with Scotsmen. An allusion to another ballad on the subject is found in *Vox Borealis*, 1641, sig.

Parker ballad to the tune was licensed in 1634: "The good Fellowes best Beloved," beginning "Among the nine Muses, if any there be" (Roxburghe; reprinted in *RB* III, 249). Others using the tune include: "The Subjects Thankfulnesse," 1640, beginning "Long time hath sweet England injoy'd her peace" (BM Huth); a song on events of 1640–1641, beginning "Let Scots now return at Lesleys demand" (*Rump*, 1662, and *Loyal Songs*, 1731); and a topical parody on the original ballad, set to the "Blue Cap" music and beginning "Come hither y[o]u merriest of all ye land" (Gamble's MS, No. 74). The words of the latter song appeared without tune direction as "The Gallants of the Times. Supposed to be made by Mr. William Murrey of His Majesties Bed-chamber" in Sir John Mennes and Dr. James Smith's *Wit Restor'd*, 1658, pp. 16–17.

Blush Not Redder
Than the Morning

This tune title takes its origin from the first line of a song "To Bellamira" in Nathaniel Lee's *Caesar Borgia*, 1680, IV, i. The verses, without music, were reprinted in *Wit and Drollery*, 1682, p. 308, and in *Female Poems on Several Occasions*, 2d ed., 1682, p. 124; they appear with music by Thomas Farmer in *Choice Ayres and Songs*, Third Book, 1681, p. 10 (Fig. 30). A very similar version of the music is found in Fitzwilliam Museum MS 30.G.20, p. 6 (c. 1680). The setting in *Pills*, 1719–1720, VI, 195, is by an unknown hand.

The stage song was expanded into a broadside, "The Virgins Happiness: or, Love in Triumph . . . To a New play-house Tune, Sung at the Dukes Play-house: Or, Blush not Redder than the Morning" (Douce II, 237). One other broadside was set to the tune: "Loves tyrannick conquest," beginning "Cupid, leave thy Tyranizing;/Thou art still new pains devising" (Bagford, Roxburghe; reprinted in *RB* VI, 290). Corrupt music

B2: "There was a poore man . . . who to get a little money, made a Song of all the Capps in the Kingdome, and at every verse end concludes thus,

> Of all the Capps that ever I see,
> Either great or small, Blew Cappe for me."

This ballad maker's Scottish sympathies were not appreciated once the Bishops' Wars had broken out, and he "was clapt up in the Clinke."

30

on the Bagford and Roxburghe sheets is improper printing of "Great York has been debarred of late," q.v. That tune does not fit the stanza form of "Blush not."

Bobbing Joe, or Bobbing Joan

This tune is found in every edition of *The Dancing Master* (1651, p. 7 = Fig. 31); in *A Booke of New Lessons for the Cithern & Gittern,* 1652;

31

Original is unbarred.

in *Musick's Delight on the Cithren,* 1666; in Walsh's *Compleat Country Dancing-Master,* 1718; and in Gay's *Polly,* 1729. It is named in four other ballad operas, including Fielding's *The Author's Farce,* 1730, Odingsells' *Bays's Opera,* 1730, Worsdale's *A Cure for a Scold,* 1735, and *The Mad House,* 1737. The Lincolnshire version of "Shepherd's Daughter" (a fragment of Child No. 110, "The Knight and Shepherd's Daughter") has a traditional tune markedly similar to "Bobbing Joan," as is pointed out in a note by Cecil J. Sharp, *JFSS,* III (1908), 222–223.

Although we possess only a late seventeenth-century edition of it, the

broadside giving rise to this tune seems to be "Bobbin Io: Or; The Long-
ing Lass Satisfied at last," beginning "These was a Maid liv'd in the
North,/which had of late a sore mischance," to the tune of "The Bobbin
Jo" (Rawlinson 106); its refrain is

> The bobbin jo, the bobbin jo,
> And canst thou dance the bobbin jo.

Despite the reference to dancing, the ballad makes it obvious that "bobbin jo" is equivalent to the "green gown," a euphemism for the sexual
act. Among the ballads and songs sung to the tune are the following:
"My Dog and I," beginning "You that are of the merry Throng," to the
tune of "My Dog and I; or, Bobbing Jone" (Pepys IV, 229, and Rawlinson 108, both black-letter editions; Roxburghe, Chetham, Douce, and
Harvard, eighteenth-century Newcastle editions; it is not reprinted in
RB—see VIII, 188). A song in Patrick Cary's *Trivial Poems*, 1820 (MS
dated 1651) to the tune of "Bobbing Joane" begins "I nere yett saw a
lovely creature/(Were she a widdow, mayd, or wife)." "New Bob-in-Jo"
is mentioned as a tune in *Mercurius Democritus, or a True and Perfect
Nocturnall*, No. 38, December 22–29, 1652 (BM Thomason). This tune
may be indicated for an eighteenth-century broadside: "In and Out and
Turn About: A New C[our]t-Dance," beginning "Ye People at Home/
Who H[a]n[ove]r hate," to the tune of "John Bob'd in, and John Bob'd
Out; Or, Bob in Joan; Or, The Miller of Mansfield" (BM 1871.e.9 [204]),
although the stanza is not quite long enough to fit the music. An American broadside of 1814, "Patriotic Diggers," beginning "Johnny Bull, beware,/Keep at proper distance," has the tune direction "Great way off
at sea, a Negro Song, or Bob and Joe" (Harvard photostats of two editions from an unknown source). This ballad "from the pen of a celebrated Poet," recounting the throwing up of a breastwork on Brooklyn
Heights during the War of 1812, will fit the "Bobbing Joan" tune somewhat awkwardly, provided both strains are repeated. One edition of the
ballad bears the tune title "Love and Whiskey," about which I have
no information.

   "The Rakes of Stony Batter," an eighteenth-century slip song (Roxburghe III, 386), does not fit the tune, despite the reference in the refrain:

> Hey for Bobbin Joan,
> Hey for Stony Batter,
> Keep your Wife at Home,
> Or I will have at her.

The Bonny Christ Church Bells

Some years before he became Dean of Christ Church, Oxford, Henry Aldrich (1647–1710) composed the very popular three-part catch that begins "Oh! the bonny Christ Church bells!/One, two, three, four, five, six." It was first published in John Playford's *The Musical Companion,* 1673, Supplement, p. 1 (Fig. 32); it was the opening selection in *Catch*

that *Catch Can,* 1685; it also appeared in *The Second Book of the Pleasant Musical Companion* in editions from 1686 to 1707, and in its successor *The Pleasant Musical Companion,* the last edition of which was issued c. 1740. The tune was included in *The Dancing Master,* commencing with the supplement to the 6th ed., 1679, in *Musicks Recreation on the Viol, Lyra-way,* 1682, and in Thomas Greeting's *The Pleasant Companion . . . for the Flagelet,* 1683.

Despite the complex stanza form and the general unsuitability of the musical movement for ballads, the tune was used for several broadsides, including one published in 1683 by Nathaniel Thompson: "Russel's Farewel," beginning "Oh, the mighty Innocence/Of Russel, Bedford's Son," to the tune of "Oh, the merry Christ-Church Bells!" (Harvard, with the music; the words appear in Thompson's *120 Loyal Songs*, 1684, and both words and music are in *180 Loyal Songs*, 1685, whence Ebsworth apparently took them for republication in *RB* V, 324). Another is "Innocent Love in Triumph," beginning "See how the charming Celia lies," to the tune of "The Oxford Bells" (Pepys III, 77, Lord Crawford 1041, BM C.22.f.6 [51], Harvard). The first of the six broadside stanzas appears in modified form, beginning "See how fair and fine she lies," in *180 Loyal Songs*, p. 140 and in *Pills*, 1719–1720, V, 252.

Another broadside, preserved in several eighteenth-century editions but perhaps older, is "The Cries of London," beginning "Hark! how the cries in every street/Make lanes and allies ring," to the tune of "The Merry Christ-Church Bells" (Douce, Chetham, Harvard, Roxburghe; reprinted in *RB* VII, 57).

Wit and Mirth, An Antidote against Melancholy, 3d ed., 1682, contains the original song and three other catches, including a political one, "Oh the Presbyterian Whiggs," and a version of "See how Charming Celia lyes." A third, "Hark, the merry Tinker's crew," had appeared in *The Musical Companion*, 1673, on the same page with the original catch; the two are likewise found together in *Wit and Drollery*, 1682. Another song to the tune, beginning "Oh, the Plot Discoverers," in *120 Loyal Songs* and *180 Loyal Songs*, may have had its origin in an undiscovered broadside. Henry Bold supplemented the original text with a Latin translation in his *Latine Songs, with their English*, 1685, p. 122.

The tune, usually called "Christ-Church Bells," was used in Gay's *Polly*, 1729, Johnson's *The Village Opera*, 1729, Phillips's *The Chambermaid*, 1730, and three other ballad operas.

Bonny Dundee

This is the "proper tune" of the broadside ballad, "Bonny Dundee: or Jockey's Deliverance, being his Valiant Escape from Dundee And the Parson's Daughter, whom he had Mow'd," beginning "Where got'st thou the Haver-mill Bonack," [1] to the tune of "Bonny Dundee" (Pepys V, 262, Lord Crawford 1334, both sheets published by Charles Bates, c. 1690 or shortly thereafter; a later Sarah Bates issue is in Madden II, 436). Eighteenth-century editions commonly are titled "Jockeys Escape from bonny

---

[1] Havermeal bannock: an oatcake.

Dundee . . . To it's own proper Tune" (Douce, Roxburghe; reprinted in *RB* VIII, 453), but a late copy in the Chapin Library of Williams College has the older "Bonny Dundee" title. The song is said to have been "written about Monmouth, by Tom D'Urfey" (Crawford *Catalogue*). Ebsworth (*RB* VIII, 455) concedes that it may "possibly" have been written by D'Urfey in 1684 but resists associating the poem with Monmouth. Evidence is not conclusive on either point. T. F. Henderson, *Scottish Vernacular Literature*, 3d ed., 1910, pp. 376–377, doubts that the ballad is wholly D'Urfey's on the ground that he did not elsewhere equal the "Dundee" refrain.

The ballad text was reprinted in *Compleat Academy of Complements*, 1705, and in *A Collection of Old Ballads*, 1723–1725, I, 275; both words and music are preserved in *Pills* V, 17. The first appearance of the tune is on page 9 of a "New additional Sheet," c. 1688, a second supplement to the seventh edition of *The Dancing Master*, 1686 (Fig. 33). It is also

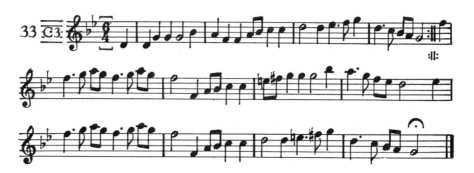

found in the body of the eighth and later editions of that work, as well as in Walsh's *Compleat Country Dancing-Master*, 1718. The tune was used in Gay's *The Beggar's Opera*, 1728, in Mitchell's *The Highland Fair*, 1731, and in Coffey's *The Boarding-School*, 1733; and it is cited in four other ballad operas, sometimes under the title "The Charge is prepar'd," from the first line of Gay's *Beggar's Opera* song to the tune.

An early eighteenth-century broadside to be sung to "Bonny Dundee" is "Queen Elizabeth's Day: or, The Down-fall of the Devil, Pope, and Pretender," beginning "Let us sing to the Mem'ry of glorious Queen Bess" (Roxburghe; reprinted in *RB* IV, 334). The original is about 1711; it was reprinted in *Political Merriment*, 1714, and in *A Pill to Purge State-Melancholy*, 1715.

Although "Bonny Dundee" was a London broadside, it was one of the English songs taken up by the Scotch as peculiarly their own. "Those with the blew Bonnets," noted a contemporary work, *"split their Wems in hollowing out—Bonny Dundee, Valiant Jocky, Sawny was a Dawdy*

Lad, and *'twas within a Furlong of* Edinborough *Town"* (Sir Thomas Burnet and George Duckett, *A Second Tale of a Tub: or, The History of Robert Powel, the Puppet-Show-Man,* 1715, p. 179). None of these songs was made in Scotland.[2] An example of currency north of the border is "Adew Dundee," a recognizable variant of the tune without words, preserved in Part V of the Skene MS (late seventeenth century?), whence it was printed in *Ancient Scotish Melodies,* ed. Dauney, 1838, p. 225. It is thus possible that we have here an example of a Scotch air which owed its English popularity (and later Scotch vogue) to its use by such effective versifiers as D'Urfey. The dating of the Skene MS is important but remains uncertain, despite statements placing it in the first quarter of the seventeenth century (cf. *Grove's Dictionary of Music and Musicians,* 5th ed., 1954, VII, 677).

The Bonny Grey-Eyed Morn

This tune takes its title from the opening line of "A New Scotch Song in the (*Fond Husband*) Sung by Mrs *Willis.* Sett to Musick by Mr. [Jeremiah] *Clarke.* 1696," a Library of Congress single sheet (Fig. 34). No edition of D'Urfey's *A Fond Husband* contains the song, and it is doubtful that he wrote its words; moreover, the sudden popularity of the tune at the end of the century suggests that it was not added to the old play of 1677 until the mid-nineties. Another edition of the playhouse song appeared as an engraved single sheet, the BM copy of which is conjecturally dated 1698; a further edition of about 1730 testifies to its continued popularity. The song is found, with music, in all editions of *Pills,* and its inclusion in the third volume of the 1719–1720 edition is a further argument against D'Urfey's authorship, since he gathered his own songs into the first two volumes.

In 1697 the two-stanza stage song was expanded to a five-stanza broadside: "An Excellent New Scotch Song, Called, The Bonny Grey-Eyed Morn; or, Jockey Roused with Love. To a Pleasant New Scotch Tune," beginning "The bonny Grey-ey'd morn began to peep" (Pepys, Lord Crawford, Roxburghe; reprinted in *RB* VII, 302). Music in the variant Pepys and Lord Crawford copies is meaningless; in the Roxburghe copy

---

[2] "Valiant Jockey," q.v., and " 'Twas within a furlong" (see "The Scotch Haymakers") were written by D'Urfey. On the "Sawny" song, compare "Sawney is a bonny lad," the work of Peter Motteux and Henry Purcell (*Pills* III, 225).

34

the title begins "An excellent new Play-House Song . . ." and the sheet contains no music. It is worth noting that the Scotch quality of the piece derives chiefly from the use of the proper name "Jockey"; neither text nor music has any real Scotch accent. But Scotch songs were becoming fashionable in the theater, and not unnaturally the titles began to advertise even such incidental Scotch quality as is here.

Clarke's tune is found also in *Youth's Delight on the Flagelet,* 11th ed., 1697, in *The Dancing Master,* Second Part, 2d ed., 1698, and in Walsh's *Compleat Country Dancing-Master,* 1718. A harpsichord setting entitled "The bonny grey eyd" is in BM MS Add. 22099, fol. 7 (c. 1704–1707). The air had a considerable vogue in ballad opera, its music appearing in editions of Gay's *The Beggar's Opera,* 1728, Ramsay's *The Gentle Shepherd,* 1730 (music in 1786 ed.), *The Prisoner's Opera,* 1730 (Air 11, untitled), and Theophilus Cibber's *Patie and Peggy,* 1730. In six other ballad operas the tune is cited, either under its usual title or as " 'Tis Woman that seduces," from the opening line of the *Beggar's Opera* song.

Among numerous broadsides sung to the tune are the following which have not been reprinted: "Susan's Courtship: or, Sweet William Woo'd by the Farmer's Daughter of Devonshire," beginning "Sweet William, prithee tell me, wilt thou wed" (Pepys III, 24), and "Coy Moggy: or, The Scotch Lass's Lamentation," beginning "Gid faith Ise was a blith and bonny Lass" (Pepys V, 265, c. 1697–1699). A characteristic use of the tune for an eighteenth-century song is found in "An Epithalamium," beginning "Let Joy alone take place and Musick sound," in Walsh's *British Musical Miscellany,* 1734–1736, II, 45.

Bonny (or Pretty) Kate
of Edinburgh

"Pretty Kate of Edenborough; being A New Scotch Song Sung to the King at Windsor," beginning "Just when the young and blooming spring," is a broadside version of a song written by Thomas D'Urfey (Pepys IV, 35, Wood 417 [113], with inaccurate but recognizable musical texts, the latter copy bearing the MS date 1682; Lord Crawford, Roxburghe, with meaningless music; reprinted in *RB* VII, 304). D'Urfey published his song with its music in *Several New Songs*, 1684, p. 1 (Fig. 35), and in *Pills*, 1719–1720, II, 30. In *180 Loyal Songs*, 1685, there is a

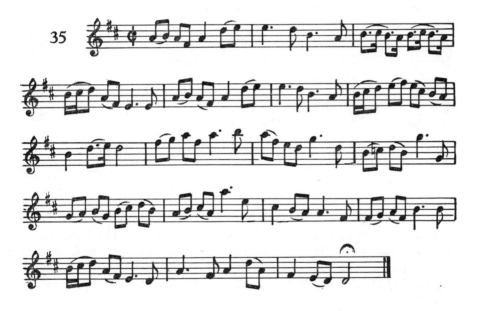

35

political parody without music: "A Loyal Scotch Song. To the Tune of, Bony Kate of Edingborough," beginning "Just as the Mist of Errour fled." Although Ebsworth reprinted its three stanzas in *RB* V, 597, there is no evidence that these verses appeared on contemporary broadsides.

"Nancy's Ghost," a song by Dr. Thomas Blacklock beginning "Where waving pines salute the skies," in Johnson's *Scots Musical Museum*, 1787–1803, II, 205, uses the tune of "Bonie Kate of Edinburgh." Earlier in the century the air appeared in the first book of William McGibbon's *Scots Tunes,* 1742, p. 3. The tune would seem to be Scotch only by adoption, through the curious circumstance that its original words, made in London, had a Scotch flavor.

Bonny Katherine Ogie

The earliest appearance of this tune is in the Additional Sheet, c. 1687, No. 8, appended to the seventh edition of *The Dancing Master* (Fig. 36).

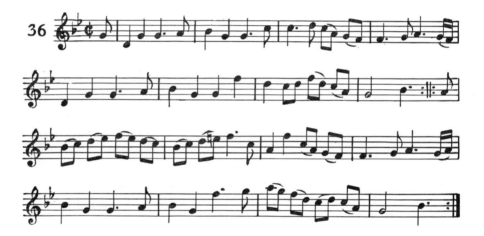

It is called "Lady Catherine Ogle, a new Dance," but no dancing instructions accompany it, and it is not in succeeding editions. The same title is used for one setting in *Apollo's Banquet,* 5th ed., 1687, and another version in the same volume is called "A Scotch Tune." Under the name "Katharine Ogie" two settings are preserved in Dr. John Leyden's MS Lyra Viol Book (after 1690).

D'Urfey wrote "A New Scotch Song" to the tune, beginning "Walking down the Highland Town,/There I saw Lasses many," which appears in *Pills,* 1719–1720, II, 200. The 24-line song calls its heroine "Catherine Logy"; it contains almost no dialect. Another version of D'Urfey's song is "Bonny Kathern Oggy as it was sung by Mr. [John] Abell at his Consort in Stationers Hall [1716]," beginning "As I went forth to view the Spring,/upon a morning early" (Harvard, Huntington, BM H.1601 [48], the latter copy catalogued as "1705?"). A number of other eighteenth-century versions of the song, usually called "Katharine Ogie," begin "As walking forth to view the Plain,/upon a Morning early" (Ramsay's *Tea-Table Miscellany*, 1723, Thomson's *Orpheus Caledonius*, 1725, Watts's *Musical Miscellany*, II, 1729, *The Hive*, 1732, Alexander Smith's *The Musical Miscellany*, 1786). "Bonny Kathern Oggy for the Harpescord" is a single-sheet song of c. 1740 beginning "As I went forth to view the Spring" (Harvard, BM G.316.d [37]). *Katharine Ogie's Garland*, c. 1765, contains "The handsome Maid; or, a Song in Praise of Katharine Ogie," beginning "As I went forth to view the Plain," together with "The Answer to Katharine Ogie."

The same music is used for a single-sheet song "Bonny Kathern Loggy" (Harvard, BM G.306 [27], Huntington; reprinted in *The Merry Musician*, I, 1716, and *Pills*, 1714, V, 170, 1719–1720, VI, 274). In heavy Scotch dialect, it begins "As I came down the hey Land Town,/and there was lasses many." The first stanza follows D'Urfey's text, but thereafter the song blackens the heroine, for "four and twenty Highland Lads,/Were following Kathern Loggy" and taking their pleasure of her; the song ends "And had I kend shaw had been a Whore,/I had ne'r Lov'd Kathern Loggy."

Other songs to the tune include "The Clans Lamentation, Against Mar and their own Folly," beginning "As I did Travel in the North" (Roxburghe; reprinted in *RB* VI, 622; the broadside contains no imprint, but the ballad narrates events of 1715); "The New Way of Catherin Ogie, by G [line torn away]," beginning "Why does thy sparkling Eyes so kill" (National Library of Scotland Ry III.a.10 [28], an eighteenth-century broadside without imprint); and "Victory and Beauty, A New Song By Mr. Ramondon, Senior," beginning "I Sing not of Affairs of State," to "the good old Tune of Catharine Ogie," without music (BM 1871.e.9 [183]). *The Vocal Miscellany*, 2d ed., 1734, pp. 57, 264, and *A Complete Collection of . . . English and Scotch Songs*, 1735–1736, III, 140, I, 157, reprint not only the original song on Katherine Ogie, but another to the tune, beginning "As I went forth to view the Spring,/Which Flora had adorned," every stanza of which ends "Omnia vincit Amor." Neither of these contains music.

The tune was used for ten ballad operas, among them the following in which the air has been reprinted: Walker, *The Quaker's Opera*, 1728, Gay, *Polly*, 1729, Chetwood, *The Lover's Opera* (music in 3d ed., 1730), Theophilus Cibber, *Patie and Peggy*, 1730, and Mitchell, *The Highland Fair*, 1731.

Bonny Lad, Prithee
Lay Thy Pipe Down

This tune title is derived from the first line of a song written by Thomas D'Urfey for Act III of his play *The Marriage-Hater Match'd*, 1692. With a tune by Thomas Tollet, it appears in *The Banquet of Musick*, Sixth Book, 1692, p. 8 (Fig. 37). The same music, for treble

violin, is in *Apollo's Banquet*, 7th ed., Third Part, 1693. Words and music are in all editions of *Pills*, 1719–1720, III, 230.

D'Urfey's song was expanded into a broadside of the 1690s, with meaningless music on the sheet: "Unconstant Peggy: or, Scotch Jemmy's sorrowful Lamentation for the Loss of his Love," beginning "Bonny Lad, prithee lay thy Pipe down," "To an Excellent New Scotch Tune" (Pepys V, 297). The sequel to this ballad is "Peggys Kind Answer; or Languishing Jemmy Crown'd with Comfort," beginning "Prithee Bonny Lad let thy Pipe play," to the tune of "Bonny Lad, prithee lay thy Pipe down" (Pepys V, 244, also with meaningless music).

The tune is used in one ballad opera: Coffey's *The Beggar's Wedding*, 1729.

Bonny Lass, Gin Thou Wert Mine

This is a song in Otway's *The Souldiers Fortune,* 1681, Act IV. With music by Thomas Farmer it appears in *Choice Ayres and Songs,* Third Book, 1681, p. 17 (Fig. 38), and in every edition of *Pills,* 1719–1720, III,

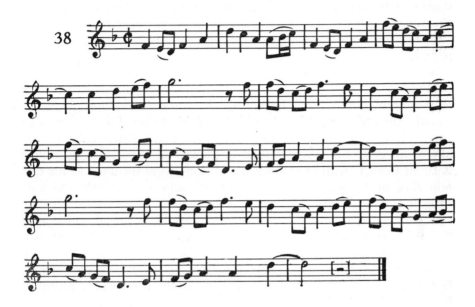

257. In expanded broadside form it is "The Longing Virgins Choice: or, The Scotch Lasses Delight," beginning "Bonny Las, gin thou art mine,/ and with twenty thousand pound about thee," "To a Modish new Scot[c]h Tune, Sung at the Dukes Playhouse" (Lord Crawford 183, Harvard, BM C.22.f.6 [142]).

Bonny Nell

This tune takes its name from a lost ballad alluded to in Thomas Robinson's *The Anatomy of the English Nunnery at Lisbon in Portugall,* 1622, p. 13: ". . . at sundry times playing upon their instruments for their fathers recreation, they sing him ribaldrous Songs and jigs, as that of *Bonny Nell,* and such other obscene and scurrilous Ballads, as would make a chaste eare to glow at the hearing of them . . ."[1]

C. J. Sisson, in his *Lost Plays of Shakespeare's Age,* 1936, p. 201, quotes a song found among papers relating to a Nottingham trial of 1617, which is "Better to be song, then to be redd to the tune of Bonny Nell," and which begins "My muse arise and truth then tell." The tune is also named on a contemporary broadside: "A battell of Birds Most strangely fought in Ireland, upon the eight day of September last, 1621 . . . To the tune of Shores wife. Or to the tune of Bonny Nell," beginning "Marke well, Gods wonderous workes, and see" (Pepys, reprinted in *PG,* p. 150).[2]

A curiosity set to the tune is "A graue Poem, as it was p[rese]nted by deuines and other of yᵉ Un: of Cambridge rather to be sunge then read, to yᵉ tune of Bonny Nell," beginning "It is not now a fortnight since/ Lutetia intertaind yᵉ Prince" (BM MS Add. 22603, fol. 43ᵛ; another version is in Bodleian MS Ashmole 36–37, fol. 258).[3] This English version of a Latin entertainment presented to James I in 1615, made by Bishop Richard Corbet "with some liberall additions," was included in his *Certain Elegant Poems,* 1647, p. 58, and was reprinted in John Nichols, *Progresses,* 1828, III, 66.

A more popular piece which has left its traces in ballad and song is "The deceased [*or* diseased] Maiden-Louer. . . . To an excellent new tune, Or to be sung to the tune of Bonny Nell," beginning "As I went forth one summer's day,/To view the meadows fresh and gay" (Pepys, Douce, Lord Crawford, Wood E.25, Rawlinson, Roxburghe; reprinted in *RB* I, 260). On the same sheet in some copies is a continuation entitled "The Faithless Lover . . . To the same Tune," beginning "When I had seen this Virgins end." Four stanzas drawn from the first part of the broadside appear, with music by Robert Johnson, in *Select Musicall Ayres, and Dialogues,* 1652, p. 3 (Fig. 39), *Select Ayres and Dialogues,*

---

[1] In Middleton, Rowley, and Massinger, *The Old Law,* c. 1618, IV, i, Gnothoes refers to Helen of Troy in the following terms: "As long as shee tarried with her Husband, shee was *Ellen,* but after she came to *Troy* shee was *Nel* of *Troy,* or Bonny *Nell* whether you will or no." This allusion may attest to the currency of the ballad, but it is idle to press the point.

The song in Lodge's *Rosalynde* containing the line "She simpred smooth like bonny bell" was altered to read "She simpered much like bonny *Nell*" in *Westminster Drollery,* I, 1671; but the allusion here is undoubtedly influenced in part by the popularity of Nell Gwyn.

[2] The tune of "Shore's Wife," cited also in broadsides reprinted in *SB,* p. 106, and *A Collection of Old Ballads,* 1723–1725, III, 43, has not survived.

[3] In the BM manuscript "A graue Poem" is followed by "A Reply on yᵉ former So[ng]," without tune direction but not in the "Bonny Nell" stanza.

39

1659, and in all editions of *Pills*. Johnson's air is not "Bonny Nell" but a new tune composed for the ballad stanzas.

The original tune has not survived. The "Bonny Nell" in *Apollo's Banquet*, 1670, No. 28, is a contemporary dance tune unsuited to the six-line octosyllabic stanza pattern uniformly associated with the ballad tune.

Bonny Sweet Robin, or My Robin
Is to the Greenwood Gone

This tune is preserved under several names in printed and manuscript music of the late sixteenth and early seventeenth centuries. It is called "Bonny sweet Robin" in Antony Holborne, *The Cittharn Schoole*, 1597, in Byrd's arrangement for virginals, New York Public Library MS Drexel 5612, p. 192 (reprinted in William Byrd, *Forty-five Pieces for Keyboard Instruments*, ed. Stephen Tuttle, 1939, p. 139), and in Giles Farnaby's set in *The Fitzwilliam Virginal Book*, II, 77. The latter collection contains another arrangement, by John Munday, entitled "Robin," I, 66. In Thomas Robinson, *The Schoole of Musicke*, 1603, the piece is named "Robin is to the greenwood gone."

Other titles include "My Robin is to the," BM MS Add. 17786, fol. 15; "Bonni well Robin van Doct^r. Jan Bull" in a 1628 virginal arrangement, BM MS Add. 23623, fol. 13^v (Fig. 40); "Jolly Robbin," BM MS

Original contains varied repeat of each strain.

Add. 31392, fol. 25; and "Sweet Robyne," BM MS Egerton 2046, fols. 22^v, 35. The Euing Lute MS contains both an untitled treatment of the tune, fol. 31, and a set by "Mr Ascue" called "Robin hoode," fol. 46^v; William Ballet's MS Lute Book, pp. 27, 113, includes one version under the name "Bonnie sweet Robin" and another called "Robinhood is to the greenwood gone." [1] Three lute arrangements and one for lyra viol entitled "Robin" are among the Cambridge University musical manuscripts (Dd.2.11, fols. 53, 66; Dd.9,33, fol. 29^v, by Dowland; Nn.6.36, fol. 19^v). Another lute arrangement entitled "Robin is to the Greenwood gone" (Dd.3.18, fol. 11) resembles one with the same title in Folger MS 1610.1, fol. 16^v. A ricercare treatment of the tune for four strings and keyboard appeared in Thomas Simpson, *Taffel Consort*, 1621 (reprinted in *Jacobean Consort Music*, ed. Thurston Dart and William Coates, 1955, p. 195). A viola da gamba MS of c. 1660 in the Henry Watson Music Lirary, Manchester, includes an arrangement of "Roben is to the greensewoode gon" by Richard Sumarte.

A lost ballad, "A Dolefull adewe to the last Erle of Darby. to the tune of Bonny sweete Robin," was licensed to John Danter, April 26, 1594 (Rollins, *Anal. Index*, No. 617). Another to the tune may be an Elizabethan production, although the earliest extant edition was issued by

[1] This latter title led Chappell (*PMOT* I, 233) to conjecture that the tune had served for a Robin Hood ballad now lost—a belief strengthened by the title of the Ascue set in the Euing MS.

Henry Gosson, who flourished c. 1603–1640: "A Courtly New Ballad of the Princely Wooing of the Fair Maid of London, by King Edward," beginning "Fair Angel of England, thy beauty most bright" (Pepys, Euing, Lord Crawford, Bagford, Rawlinson, Douce, Roxburghe; reprinted in *RB* I, 181).[2] The first line of this ballad became the tune title for a number of broadsides noted below.

Further evidence of the currency of the tune is suggested by dramatic references. In *Two Noble Kinsmen*, IV, i, "Bonny Robin" is named as a song the jailer's daughter knows, and in *Hamlet*, IV, v, Ophelia sings "For bonny sweet Robin is all my joy," which may be the closing line of a stanza from the original song.

"Bonny sweet Robin" is also used for religious purposes, being cited for singing "An other Carrell, for the same day" in *Good and True, Fresh and New, Christmas Carols*, 1642, as well as one "For Twelfth-day" in *New Carolls*, 1661. "The delicate wooing between 2 Royal lovers," beginning "I Salute thee sweet love with the ti[t]le of grace," names the tune "Robin Hood is to the Greenwood gone" in *The Royal Garland of Love and Delight*, 1681, and "My Robin is to the Greenwood gone" in the version contained in *The Garland of Delight*, 1681.

We have already seen that "Fair Angel of England" as a tune title derives from the opening line of a ballad sung to "Bonny Sweet Robin." The two tune names can thus be considered equivalent, or alternate, titles of the same air, and there is no evidence that there was ever an independent tune called "Fair Angel of England." This relationship between tune and tune names becomes further complicated, as we shall see, but it is essentially a repetition of the pattern we have just discussed.

Two broadsides cite both tune names: "Englands Monthly Predictions for this present yeare 1649," beginning "Fair England, the Garden of Europe was call'd," to "Faire Angell of England. Or, Bonny sweet Robin" (Manchester; reprinted, with facsimile, in *CP*, p. 215); and "Good Admonitions, or Wholesome Counsel," by I. P., beginning "Good people I wish you/a while to attend," to the tune of "Bonny sweet Robin, Or, Fair Angel of England" (Douce I, 89, a broadside of c. 1675).

To "Fair Angel of England" was sung "The Poor Man's comfort," beginning "My heart is oppressed with sorrow, dear Wife" (Pepys IV, 92, Rawlinson 39). And "The Poor Man's Comfort" becomes the tune title for "The poor Mans Councillor, Or, The marryed mans Guide," be-

---

[2] The ballad was reprinted in such characteristic seventeenth-century miscellanies as Richard Johnson's *Golden Garland of Princely Pleasures*, 3d ed., 1620, sig. D8ᵛ, and his *Crown Garland of Golden Roses*, 1659, ed. Chappell, 1845, p. 34. In both collections the original ballad is followed by "The fair maid of London's answer to King Edward's wanton love," a continuation (sung to the same tune) found in columns 3 and 4 of the original broadside in the Roxburghe, Lord Crawford, and some other copies.

ginning "Come friend if thy leisure permit thee to stay" (Lord Crawford, Pepys, Harvard, Roxburghe; reprinted in *RB* VIII, 103). "The poor mans Counsellour" in turn is one of the tune titles (along with "My Life and my Death") cited for "The bad Husbands Reformation, Or, The Ale-Wives daily Deceit," beginning "I was a bad Husband, that had a good Trade" (Lord Crawford, Harvard, BM C.22.f.6; reprinted in *RB* VIII, 796), and for "The Wonderful Praise of a Good Husband," beginning "Dear Daughter, i'de have thee to take special care" (Pepys, Lord Crawford, Roxburghe; reprinted in *RB* VII, 147). These two latter ballads, licensed by Richard Pocock, date from 1685–1688. "My Life and my Death" is an independent tune, q.v.

Another ballad to the tune of "Fair Angel of England" takes us off in another direction. "Loves fierce desire, and hopes of Recovery" by L[aurence] P[rice] begins "Now the Tyrant hath stolen/my dearest away" (Pepys, Lord Crawford, BM C.22.f.6, Harvard, Douce, Euing, Roxburghe; reprinted in *RB* VI, 67). "A Looking-Glass for a Covetous Miser," by T[homas?] J[ordan?], beginning "Come listen kind neighbours with heart and good will," has the tune direction "The Fair Angel of England, or the Tyrant" (Pepys II, 19, Lord Crawford 259, BM C.22.f.6 [7], Harvard), and is exceptional in its long stanza of eight anapestic tetrameters. The usual pattern is four or six such lines or their equivalent, which will fit our original tune (the last eight bars being repeated for a six-line stanza).

"The Tyrant" or "Now the Tyrant hath stolen" becomes a popular tune title with its own offshoots. One of the most important is "Love and Honour: Or, The Lovers Farewel to Calista," beginning "Farewel my Calista, my joy and my grief," to the tune of "Now the Tyrant hath stolen" (Lord Crawford, Douce, Roxburghe, two editions each; Harvard; reprinted in *RB* VI, 40). This is an expanded version of a song, perhaps by Dryden, appearing first without music in several miscellanies of 1672: *Covent Garden Drolery, Westminster Drollery, Windsor Drollery,* and *New Court-Songs,* beginning "Farewell fair Armeda my joy and my grief." With music by Robert Smith it is in *Choice Songs and Ayres,* First Book, 1673.[3] The song was inspired by the death of Captain Francis Digby in a naval engagement of 1672, and "Digby's Farewell," q.v.,

[3] In *Apollo's Banquet,* 5th ed., 1687, the Smith tune is entitled "The Earl of Sandwich's Farewel." This title serves for a different air in *Musicks Recreation on the Viol, Lyra-way,* 1682, and that music, called "Captain Digby's Farewell," immediately follows "The Earl of Sandwich's Farewell" in *Apollo's Banquet.* Confusion is deepened by the fact that a ballad on the death of Captain Digby, "The Sorrowful Ladies Complaint," beginning "One morning I walk'd by my self on the shoar" (Harvard, Pepys, Lord Crawford, Roxburghe; reprinted in *RB* IV, 398) is to the tune of "The Earl of Sandwich Farewel." A three-stanza song in *Westminster Drollery,* 1672, II, 1, to be sung to "my Lord Sandwiches Farewell," is entitled "Mr. Digbyes Farewell"; beginning "Oh pitty Arminda those Passions I bear," it returns us to the "fair Armeda" of the original 1672 song on Captain Digby.

became an extremely popular broadside tune. Among its earliest uses are those in which it is associated with tune names derived from the "Love and Honour" broadside. Thus "The Faithful Shepherdess," beginning "Amintas was walking one evening alone," is to the tune of "Farewel fair Armeda; or, Captain Digby's Farewel" (Douce I, 75). "The Lovers final Farewel. To his Faithless false Mistress," beginning "I lov'd thee wel once, but il'e love thee no more," is to "Love and honour or Digby's farwell" (Rawlinson 147). From the first line of "Love and Honour" comes the tune title "Farewel my Calista" named in "Love and Gallantry," a ballad beginning "Farewel my Clarinda my life and my soul" (Roxburghe; reprinted in *RB* VI, 438).

Still another ballad sung to "Now the Tyrant hath stolen" generates a fresh tune title: "The two Jeering Lovers . . . Dick Down-right of the Country, and . . . Nancy of the Citie," by L[aurence] P[rice] (BM C.20.f.14; reprinted in *CP*, p. 415) is the likely origin of the tune title "Dick and Nan" which is named on two broadsides: "The Couragious Plow-man," beginning "There was a brave Citizen/walkt forth of late" (Harvard, Douce, Lord Crawford, Rawlinson, Roxburghe; reprinted in *RB* III, 613), and "Cupid's Power," beginning "To cure melancholly,/ I travers'd the fields" (Lord Crawford; reprinted in *RB* VIII, cxxxiv*).

Yet another tune title was generated from a proverbial phrase "Laugh and lie down," and its use in a ballad may be connected with one of the "Tyrant" broadsides. "The Shepherds Delight," beginning "What an innocent loving life/Shepherds do lead," is to the tune "Now the Tyrant has stolen my dearest away" (Rawlinson 48, Pepys III, 55). The ballad is an expansion of a song beginning "Thus all our Life long we are frolick and gay" in Shadwell's *The Royal Shepherdess*, 1669, Act III, reprinted in *Westminster Drollery*, 1671, and, with music by John Banister, in Playford's *Choice Songs and Ayres*, First Book, 1673, and in all editions of *Pills*. The ballad refrain is:

> With our shepherdesses
> we laugh and lie down
> And to each pretty damosel
> we give a green gown.

This may be the source of "Laugh and Lye down," the tune title of "The Young mans Rambles, Or The Batchellors shifts," beginning "I Courted a Maiden/was handsoma [sic] and fair" (Rawlinson; reprinted in *RB* VIII, 858), and "The Constant Maidens Resolution," beginning "I am a young Damsel/that's plunged in Woe" (Douce I, 32); both ballads are in a twelve-line stanza equivalent to six lines of anapestic tetrameter, the commonest "Tyrant" stanza form.[4]

4 A less likely source of the tune name is the ballad entitled "Laugh and lie Down: or, A Dialogue between a young Gentleman and his Sweetheart," beginning "As I was

It is uncertain whether all these ballads, and many more to "Fair Angel of England" and "Tyrant" not cited, were in fact sung to the original "Bonny Sweet Robin" tune. In the absence of tunes bearing these alternate names, we can only conjecture whether the popularity of new ballads kept the old tune in vogue under new names. We do have a setting of "Though the Tyrant hath ravish'd my Dearest away" by John Playford in *Catch that Catch Can,* 1667, but it shows only that the original words were familiar enough to inspire a parody which Playford could make into a fresh part-song. The variation in length of stanzas associated with "Tyrant" ballads suggests that other tunes unknown to us were being used.

Bow Bells

John Playford admired "Bow Bells" enough to use it in a number of his music instruction books. It is first found in lyra-viol tablature in his

Original lyra-viol set is a fifth lower.

A Musicall Banquet, 1651, Part I, No. 12 (Fig. 41). His *A Booke of New Lessons for the Cithern & Gittern,* 1652, includes versions for both cittern

a walking one evening most clear," to the tune "As I was a walking one Sun shining day" (Pepys; reprinted in *RB* VIII, 859). The stanza pattern of four anapestic tetrameters offers no rhythmic difficulties, though the quatrain is less common than either the six- or eight-line stanza in the "Tyrant" ballads. Nothing is known of the tune title here named.

and gittern, the former purged of some incorrect note values when it reappeared in *Musick's Delight on the Cithren,* 1666, No. 32. A keyboard setting is in *Musicks Hand-maid,* 1678.

The tune direction "Bass His Carrier: Or, Bow Bells" is given for singing "The Hasty Bride-Groom," a ballad of 1655 beginning "Come from the Temple away to the Bed" (Manchester, Pepys, Rawlinson, Douce, Lord Crawford, Morgan, Roxburghe; reprinted in *RB* VII, 458). A version of this text in *Pills,* 1719–1720, VI, 198, has the music of "Basse's Career," q.v., which fits it admirably. But "Bow Bells," with a strain of duple and one of triple rhythm, is not adapted to the regular alternations of anapestic tetrameter and trimeter in the ballad. Although some allowance may be made for the indistinct melodic line often found with instrumental arrangements, it seems doubtful that the tune preserved is the one to which the ballad might have been sung.

Bread of God

This tune (Fig. 42) is printed on two editions of a broadside published by Alexander Banks in 1682: "The Loyal Scot; An Excellent New Song. To an Excellent New Scotch Tune," beginning "Bread of Geud! I think the Nation's mad" (Harvard, BM C.38.i.25 [15], Bodleian Ashmole G.16 [156], Chetham 4 and 292). Copies without the music (Huntington, Yale) are piracies, according to a statement made in April, 1682, by Na-

thaniel Thompson (see *PB* V, 240). The text was reprinted in *120 Loyal Songs,* 1684, and appears with its music in *180 Loyal Songs,* 1685. Under the title "Bred a gad" the tune is found in Humphry Salter, *The Genteel Companion . . . for the Recorder,* 1683. A treble-violin arrangement appears as "A Scotch Tune" in *Apollo's Banquet,* 5th ed., 1687, and as "Bread of Gad" in the 6th ed., 1690; both editions contain "The Second Part of Bread of God," which has a rhythmic pattern almost identical with that of the original melody.

It is not remarkable that no further broadsides were set to this tune; what is noteworthy is that such an unmelodious air should have had the little vogue it enjoyed. The explanation may lie in the attraction of the political verses accompanying this artificially Scotchified melody.

The Bride's Good-Morrow

The ballad whose title gives this tune its name begins "The night is passed, & ioyfull day appeareth" and is sung "To a Pleasant New Tune" (Roxburghe; reprinted in *RB* I, 62). Although the only entry of the ballad in the Stationers' Register is dated 1624 and the single surviving copy is of about the same time, it is evidently a reissue of a sixteenth-century original, for "The Bride's Good-Morrow" was named as a tune before the end of that century.

Music of "The Bride's go[o]d-morrowe" is preserved in the Shirburn MS, fol. 187ᵛ (reproduced in *SB,* p. 186), for singing "A pleasant ditty, which doth pleasantly display the ioyfull walkes in the month of Maye," beginning "Rise vp, my darling;/Abroad let vs be walking" (Fig. 43).

Original is unbarred.

The broadside from which this was copied does not seem to have survived. Moreover, the tune, which would require six repetitions for each stanza, is very likely incomplete.

A familiar narrative to the tune is "A most pleasant Ballad of patient Grissell," beginning "A Noble Marques as he did ride on hunting" (BM Huth; reprinted in *A Collection of Seventy-Nine Black-Letter Ballads,* 1867, and *RB* II, 269). The unique Huth text, which has been dated c. 1600, is the oldest broadside edition extant, although Deloney's version of the story may have circulated in this form before being gathered into his *Garland of Good Will* (apparently licensed in 1593; earliest surviving edition 1631, reprinted in *Works,* ed. Mann, p. 346). The title varies in later broadside editions, one common form being "A most excellent and vertuous Ballad of the Patient Grissell" (Roxburghe, Douce, Euing, Lord Crawford, Pepys, Bagford, Harvard, Morgan). The ballad appears in the Percy Folio MS (ed. Hales and Furnivall, III, 423–430) but not in the *Reliques.* The Percy Collection at Harvard contains an eighteenth-century edition of the ballad, published by Dicey, which, along with its inclusion in *A Collection of Old Ballads,* 1723–1725, I, 252, attests to its currency over more than a century.

Bright Was the Morning

D'Urfey's poem, beginning "Bright was the morning," appeared originally in his *New Collection of Songs and Poems,* 1683. In the same year it was reprinted with music by Thomas Shadwell in *The Newest Collection of the Choicest Songs,* p. 60 (Fig. 44). The same music is in Humphry

Measures 4–8 rebarred upon expansion of cadences.

Salter's *Genteel Companion . . . for the Recorder,* 1683. Words and music are in all editions of *Pills,* 1719–1720, I, 260, in Bodleian MS Mus.

Sch. G.640 (37), and in BM MS Add. 19759, fol. 20 (the latter reprinted in facsimile in C. L. Day, *The Songs of Thomas D'Urfey,* p. 87). Another setting of D'Urfey's poem, by William Turner, is in *The Theater of Musick,* First Book, 1685. Both musical texts are rather self-conscious pieces in characteristic pastoral rhythm, though Turner's is the more highly ornamented.

The words to D'Urfey's song are found in such miscellanies as *Wits Cabinet,* c. 1700, and *The Hive,* 3d ed., 1727, II, 257. In expanded form it had appeared as a broadside, with meaningless music printed on the sheet: "The Loyal Lovers Farewel," to the tune "Bright was the morning" (Harvard, Lord Crawford 195, a black-letter edition of the 1680s). Apparently no other broadsides were sung to the tune.

The Broom, the Bonny Broom,
or The Broom of Cowdenknows

The music of "Broome, Broome, The bonny bonny Broome" is in the first fourteen editions of *The Dancing Master,* 1651–1709 (1651, p. 74 = Fig. 45). A three-part song, beginning "Ho, the Broome, the Bonny,

Original is a fourth higher and unbarred.

bonny Broome," is in BM MS Add. 11608, fol. 55, 1656–1659. The tune is called "The Bonny Broom" in *Musick's Delight on the Cithren,* 1666. Eighteenth-century versions of the melody abound: it is in William Thomson's *Orpheus Caledonius,* 1725, No. 10, Watts's *Musical Miscellany,* 1729–1731, I, 76, *The Merry Musician,* c. 1729 (Harvard), p. 43, Johnson's *Scots Musical Museum,* 1787–1803, I, 70, and Ritson's *Scotish Songs,* 1794, I, 118, and on a number of single sheets from c. 1735 to 1785.

Johann Christian Bach composed a full instrumental score for the song, c. 1784, and Haydn harmonized it for George Thomson's *A Select Collection of Original Scottish Airs*, 1802, III, 28. The tune was used in eight ballad operas, including Gay's *The Beggar's Opera*, 1728, Mitchell's *The Highland Fair*, 1731, and Potter's *The Decoy*, 1733, whose printed editions contain the music.

Perhaps the earliest ballad that can be associated with the tune is "The New Broome," beginning "Poore Coridon did sometime sit" (Pepys, reprinted in *RB* VIII, 586). It is without tune direction, but the stanza pattern is similar to that of other ballads known to be to the tune (eight lines of ballad meter plus a refrain of four). The refrain is:

> The bonny Broome, the well favour'd Broom,
>   the Broome bloomes faire on hill,
> What ail'd my Love to lightly mee,
>   and I working her will?

Although the Pepys edition probably dates from the second quarter of the seventeenth century, the language of the ballad suggests a considerably earlier date of composition.[1]

In existence by 1632, when it was entered in the Stationers' Register, is "The lovely Northern Lasse, Who in the Ditty here complaining, shewes What harme she got milking her Daddies Ewes." It begins "Through Liddersdale as lately I went" and is to be sung "To a pleasant Scotch tune, called, The broom of Cowdon knowes" (Euing, Rawlinson, Douce, Roxburghe; reprinted in *RB* I, 588, and in Child, Appendix to No. 217). The tune name evidently derives from the refrain of the ballad:

> With O, the broome, the bonny broom
>   the broome of Cowdon knoes,
> Faine would I be in the North Countrey,
>   to milke my daddies Ewes.

Chappell (*PMOT* II, 459–460), anxious to minimize the Scotch element in early balladry, is probably correct here in insisting that the tune is called Scotch because of the subject matter of the ballad. All the

---

[1] The second line of the ballad refrain is probably related only thematically to the "Broom on hill" whose "foote" or burden Moros sings in Wager's *The Longer Thou Livest*, 1569:

> Brome, Brome on hill,
> The gentle Brome on hill hill:
> Brome, Brome on Hive hill,
> The gentle Brome on Hive hill,
> The brome standes on Hive hill a.

It is not possible to identify "Brome," one of the songs the jailer's daughter can sing in *The Two Noble Kinsmen*, IV, i.

evidence points to the British origin of the tune, for it appears exclusively in English publications until after the first quarter of the eighteenth century. A traditional ballad popular in Scotland is called "The Broom of Cowdenknows" in some nineteenth-century texts (Child No. 217). Its relation to the broadside is uncertain. Aside from the central motif of the lass got with child while milking her father's ewes, the story lines are independent. Child believes that the broadside poet may have known only the refrain of the Scotch ballad and "built his very slight tale on that." But only a few traditional texts (notably those recovered by Scott and Peter Buchan) contain a "Cowdenknows" refrain, and the possible influence of print upon tradition cannot be wholly dismissed.[2]

Another early black-letter ballad to the tune is "The Complaint of a Sinner. To the tune of the bonny broome," beginning "Christ is my loue he loued me/when I was wretch forlorne" (Pepys; reprinted in *RB* VIII, 585), and with a refrain echoing that of "The New Broome":

> The bonny Broome, the well favour'd Broom
> the broome bloomes faire on hill:
> Him have I lost that loved me best,
> my love against his will.

The first line of this ballad becomes the tune title for "The Dream of Judas' Mother Fulfilled," beginning "Who that antique story reads,/ and ancient tales of old," to the tune of "Christ is my love" (Roxburghe; reprinted in *RB* VIII, 583). This is an early eighteenth-century roman-letter copy without imprint, but Ebsworth conjectured that it must have originated at least a century before. It is in the usual octave stanza with no refrain.

Other seventeenth-century ballads to the tune include the following: "Iohn Hadlands advice: Or a warning for all young men . . . to forsake lewd company Cards, Dice, and Queanes. To the tune of the bonny, bonny Broome," by R[ichard] C[limsell], beginning "To all men now I'll plainly shew" (Roxburghe; reprinted in *RB* III, 268); "The Bonny Bryer," by M[artin] P[arker], beginning "One morning early by the breake of day,/walking to Totnam-Court," to the tune of "the Bonny Broome" (Roxburghe; reprinted in *RB* VII, 165), with the refrain:

> Sing O the Bryer, the bony bony Bryer,
> the Bryer that is so sweet:

[2] Gavin Greig's *Last Leaves of Traditional Ballads and Ballad Airs*, 1925, pp. 151–152, contains an Aberdeenshire text which opens with lines similar to the broadside refrain. The tunes are not clear analogues of the seventeenth-century "Bonny Broom," but a note calls attention to a tune in W. Christie's *Traditional Ballad Airs*, 1876–1881, I, 126, which is close enough to the broadside tune and Greig's 1 b-c to be a link between print and tradition.

> Would I had stayd in Lancashire,
> to milke my mothers Neate.

"Slippery Will, or The old Bachelors complaint," beginning "Long have I liv'd a bachelors life" (Euing, Roxburghe; reprinted in *RB* II, 503); both copies of this ballad were printed by E. B., who may be Edward Blackmore (fl. 1618–1633); and, lastly, "The forlorn Lovers Lament," beginning "Sir, do not think these lines have flow'd/from youthful hearts or hands" (Roxburghe; reprinted in *RB* VI, 586).

The Scotch version of "The lovely Northern Lasse," popular throughout the eighteenth century, is called "The Broom of Cowdenknows" in Allan Ramsay's *Tea-Table Miscellany*, 1723, p. 25 (9th ed., 1733, I, 14), where the verses are identified as "new Words by different Hands." Its sentimentalized account of the maid's fall—without the happy ending of the broadside—begins "How blyth ilk Morn was I to see," and the refrain is as follows:

> O the Broom, the bonny, bonny Broom,
> The Broom of Cowdenknows;
> I wish I were with my dear Swain,
> With his Pipe and my Ews.

Alexander Stuart included the familiar air in his *Musick for Allan Ramsay's Collection of Scots Songs*, c. 1725, p. 26. The *Tea-Table* text is in *A Collection of Old Ballads*, 1723–1725, III, 236, in *The Wreath*, 1753, *The Bonny Boatman's Garland*, c. 1765, a Newcastle imprint, and, with the tune, in most of the eighteenth-century songbooks cited in the opening paragraph of this discussion.

A political ballad of the Jacobite uprising is "An excellent new Song Entituled, the New way of the Broom of Cowden Knows," beginning "Hard Fate that I should banisht be/And Rebell called with Scorn" (National Library of Scotland, Ry III.a.10 [7]), without tune direction but with a stanza form that fits the "Broom" music.

Thomas A. Arne wrote new music for "The Bonny Broom," an abbreviated version of the *Tea-Table* text. It is in *Gentleman's Magazine*, XXII (Oct., 1752), 471, *The Muses Delight*, 1754, p. 82, and *Clio and Euterpe*, 1759–1762, II, 26.

Robert Crawford's "Broom of Cowdenknows," beginning "When summer comes, the swains on Tweed," is a lyrical adaptation of motifs in the earlier Scotch verses. The song appeared in Johnson's *Scots Musical Museum* I, 71, and in Ritson's *Scotish Songs* II, 245, as addenda to the *Tea-Table* text. Single-sheet editions of c. 1780 with different music are in BM H.1994.d (61), BM G.313 (187), and Huntington.

Buff Coat

This tune is in the fourth and all subsequent editions of *The Dancing Master,* 1670–c. 1728 (1670, p. 149=Fig. 46). Initially it is a modal air in common time, but from the seventh edition it is in 6/4 and major.[1]

46

It is also in Walsh's *Compleat Country Dancing-Master,* 1718. In Thompson's *Compleat Collection of 200 Favourite Country Dances,* c. 1760–1780, the tune appears as "Miss Peachey's Delight" (I, 59) and as "The Retreat" (II, 77). As "Buff Coat" or "Buff Coat has no Fellows," it was popular in ballad operas, appearing in at least a dozen, from Gay's *Polly,* 1729, to *The Country Coquet,* 1755.[2]

The tune title "Buff Coat hath no Fellow" probably comes from the refrain of a ballad not now extant. The buff coat was a conspicuous piece of military uniform during the early seventeenth century, and allusions in popular song probably stem from that period. A soldiers' song in Fletcher and Massinger's *The Knight of Malta* (performed c. 1618) contains the refrain

---

[1] Chappell (*PMOT* I, 343) states that in later editions of *The Dancing Master* "Buff Coat" and "Excuse Me" appear as alternate names for the same tune. In point of fact, "Excuse Me," first introduced in the seventh edition, is an independent tune not interchangeable with "Buff Coat." It can be traced back to a setting in Thomas Robinson's *New Citharen Lessons,* 1609, but no broadsides seem to have been sung to the tune.

[2] *Polly* includes both "Buff Coat" and "Excuse Me," with music for each. The two tunes are named in Chetwood's *The Lover's Opera,* 1729, but only "Buff Coat" is retained in the 1730 edition which contains music. In Chetwood's *The Generous Free-Mason,* 1731, and Fielding's *The Intriguing Chambermaid,* 1734, the title "Excuse Me" is given to the music of "Buff Coat"; and since Chappell reprints a strain of the air from the former source, he may have thus been led to equate the tune names.

Each toss his can, until his throat be mellow
Drink, laugh, and sing; the soldier has no fellow

but no direct connection between the end of the refrain and our tune title can be argued, especially since the rhythmic pattern of the theater song is incompatible with that of "Buff Coat." Chappell is impressed by the three half-notes at the beginning of the tune, which imply strongly accented monosyllables, and he rephrases the playhouse refrain to read "Drink, laugh, sing, boys . . . " in order to make words and music fit—a dangerous overinterpretation of the evidence.

Broadsides to "Buff Coat" include one printed c. 1660–1665: "The merry Hoastess" by T[homas] R[obins], beginning "Come all that loves good company" (Roxburghe; reprinted in *RB* III, 307); and one dating from 1686–1688: "The Coy Maids Repentance; or, The Old Maids Wish," beginning "When I was young and handsome too" (Pepys III, 150). In both broadsides the opening line requires the long notes to be divided, but not so extensively as in the jigging rhythm of the *Generous Free-Mason* version of the tune. The song in *Polly,* beginning "Why that languish!" illustrates the metrical pattern necessary for the older version of the air.

Buggering Oates, Prepare Thy Neck

This tune title is from the first line of "The Kings-Bench Salutation," beginning "Come Buggering Oates, prepare thy Neck," which is found

47

with the music in *180 Loyal Songs,* 1685, p. 367 (Fig. 47). The notoriety of Titus Oates, or the quality of the tune itself, was sufficient to couple the air to three broadsides, all of which are probably products of the 1680s. One is "You'l never get her up, Or, Love in a Tree," beginning "A Week ago as I did walk/When it was almost twilight" (Lord Crawford 1254, Harvard, BM C.22.f.6 [225]). Another, which fits its first tune "The Doubting Virgin" somewhat better than its second, "Buggering Oats prepare thy Neck," is "The Lovers Prophesie," beginning "Would you know when I will marry/To a pretty comely Lass" (Lord Crawford; reprinted in *RB* VII, 299). A third is "Portsmouths Lamentation; Or, A Dialogue between Two Amorous Ladies, E[llen, i.e., Nell] G[wyn] and D[uchess of] P[ortsmouth]," beginning "I Prithee, Portsmouth, tell me plain,/without dissimulation," to the tune of "Tom the Taylor, or, Titus Oats" (Bagford; reprinted in *BB* II, 606). On "Tom the Taylor" see "Daniel Cooper."

Bugle Bow

"Bugle Boe" is one of several tunes named for singing the respective sections of "Frauncis new Jigge," written by George Attowell and licensed for publication in 1595 (Pepys; reprinted in *PG*, p. 2; a contemporary MS copy is printed in *SB*, p. 245). Of about the same date is a lute setting of the simple tune with variations in Cambridge University MS Dd.2.11, fol. 82, entitled "Buggle Bowe" (Fig. 48).

Apparently unrelated to the Elizabethan tune is the late seventeenth-century broadside "The Bugle-Bow: or, A Merry Match of Shooting," beginning "Upon a time it chanced so," to the tune of "My husband is a carpenter or, The Oyl of Care" (Pepys III, 118, Lord Crawford 1231, BM C.22.f.6 [90]).[1] An eighteenth-century slip song "Bougel a Boy," beginning "My Name it is Bougel a Boy./As you may plainly see" (BM

[1] I have no information on either tune named for singing this ballad.

1871.e.9 [27]) is without tune direction and is rhythmically incompatible with the old "Bugle Bow" air.

Burton Hall, or London's Loyalty

"A New Ballad, Of Londons Loyalty" to the tune of "Burton Hall," beginning "Rowze up Great Monarch of this potent Land" (BM C.38.i.25 [12], BM 1872.a.1 [122ᵛ], Bodleian Vet.A.3.c.29 [3], Chetham 3, Harvard) is a broadside dated 1681 which furnishes the several alternative names given to the tune. Another edition of the same date begins "Rowze up Great Genius of this Potent Land" (Wood 417 [60]); it appeared with music as one of D'Urfey's *Several New Songs,* 1684, p. 19 (Fig. 49),[1] and in the next year words and music were included in *180 Loyal Songs* together with four other songs to the tune. The D'Urfey authorship is further attested by its inclusion in the 1719–1720 edition of *Pills* among those songs which D'Urfey claimed for his own (II, 132).

The music of "Burton Hall" seems to have been printed first in 1683. In that year it is found as "London's Loyalty" in Thomas Greeting's *Pleasant Companion . . . for the Flagelet* and Humphry Salter's *Genteel Companion . . . for the Recorder;* and as "Burton Hall, or London's Loyalty" on two dated broadsides, "Ryot upon Ryot: or, A Chant upon the Arresting the Loyal L. Mayor & Sheriffs," beginning "Rowze up Great Monarch/In the Royal Cause" (Bodleian Ashmole G.16 [51], Harvard, Huntington, Yale, Clark; reprinted in *180 Loyal Songs*); and "Coll. Sidney's Lamentation . . . Condemn'd for High-Treason," beginning "Now, now too weak, alas! I find our Cause" (Clark, reprinted in *180 Loyal Songs* without music but with tune title "What Name"—which may be a printer's query). In an undated broadside of c. 1683 with music, the tune is called "Rowze up Great Monarch": "The Couragious Loyalists, or a Health to the Royal Family," beginning "Drown'd Melancholly/in a Glass of Wine" (Lord Crawford, BM C.39.k.6; reprinted in *180 Loyal Songs* and *OPB,* p. 100). The tune was apparently not included in *The*

1 Ebsworth, who reprinted D'Urfey's 1684 text (*RB* V, 245), erroneously dated the ballad 1683, doubtless because of a reference in stanza 5 to a £300 fine, which he equated with a levy of 500 marks against Sir Thomas Player in June, 1683. The context suggests rather that Madame Cresswell, with whom Player was intimate, was liable for the payment of a £300 bond, to which no precise date can be assigned. Other topical allusions in the ballad are to affairs of 1679–1681.

49 [3]

* G in original.   ** E in original.   *
** B♭ in original.

Dancing Master until the fifteenth edition, 1713; there and in Walsh's *Compleat Country Dancing-Master,* 1718, it is called "London's Loyalty."

Other political broadsides to the tune include one of 1682, "London's Joy and Loyalty on . . . the Duke of York's Return out of Scotland," beginning "Rouze up ye Tories," to the tune of "London's Loyalty" (Bodleian Ashmole G.15 [65]), and one of 1683, "No Protestant Plot, Or, The Whigs Loyalty: with the Doctor's New Discovery," beginning "Hells restless Factious Agents still Plot on," to the tune of "Burton House, Or, Londons Loyalty" (Bodleian Ashmole G.16 [103], Harvard, Clark). Both of these are included in *180 Loyal Songs.* Appearing early in the reign of James II is "Seasonable Advice to Doctor Oates," beginning "Oh Doctor! now repent, since at the last/For thy gross crimes thou art in prison cast" (Chetham 1043). The tune is cited as "London's Loyalty," but the sheet contains badly printed music of "Hey, boys, up go we" to which the ballad could not in any case be sung.

Busy Fame

The song giving rise to this tune title first appeared without music in [Joan Philips's] *Female Poems*, 1679. With music by Thomas Farmer, and with the protagonists' names changed from Phylena and Celadon to Velinda and Coridon, the two-stanza pastoral poem is found in *Choice Ayres and Songs*, Fifth Book, 1684, p. 19 (Fig. 50), and in the 1714 and

50

1719–1720 editions of *Pills*. A broadside text of c. 1680 expands the poem and changes the heroine's name once more: "Coridon and Parthenia," beginning "When busie Fame o're all the Plain,/Parthenia's Praises rung," to the tune of "When busie Fame" (Euing, Lord Crawford, Harvard, two editions each; Douce, Yale, Roxburghe; reprinted in *RB* III, 568). During the next several decades the tune was frequently cited for ballad singing, often as an alternative to other familiar melodies fitting the double ballad-meter stanza, such as "Jenny gin," "Hey, boys, up go we," "Young Phaon," and "The fair one let me in." The Lord Crawford *Catalogue* lists ten broadsides to "Busy Fame," and more than a dozen to the tune are reprinted in the *Roxburghe Ballads*. By the time of the ballad operas, however, the tune had so fallen out of favor that it is not cited in the hundred or more printed librettos.

Although only a few broadsides using the tune can be noted here, the following deserve mention: "Loyalty unfeigned, Or, The true Protestants Admonition," beginning "Hold fast thy Sword & Scepter Charles/sad Times may else come on," to the tune of "Busie Fame, Young Pheon, or,

The Fathers Exhortation" (Lord Crawford, Douce, Harvard, Roxburghe; reprinted in *RB* IV, 640). This appeared in the early 1680s, when Protestants were still confident, if wary; reprinted in *180 Loyal Songs,* 1685, it was brought up to date by the substitution of "James" for the earlier monarch's name.[1] "Loves Boundless Power," c. 1681, beginning "Hail to the Mirtle Shade," is directed to be sung to "When Busie Fame" (BM C.22.f.6, Douce, Lord Crawford, Harvard, Pepys; reprinted in *RB* V, 422), though that tune fits the ballad rather poorly. This broadside was expanded from a stage song in Nathaniel Lee's *Theodosius,* 1680, III, ii, with its own music which in time became a well-known ballad tune. One can only surmise that at the launching of "Loves Boundless Power" the tune of "Busy Fame" enjoyed the greater popularity and so was cited to the exclusion of the theater air.

Several ballads calling for "Busy Fame" have apparently not been reprinted: "Falle[n] Man's cruelty," beginning "When Cupid's fierce and powerful Dart," to be sung to "Jenny Gin, Busie Fame, or, The fair one let me in" (Pepys III, 385); "The Dispairing Maiden Reviv'd By the Return of her Dearest Love," beginning "As I walkt forth to take the air,/one morning in the Spring," to the tune of "The fair one let me in; Or Busie Fame; Or, Jenny Gin" (Pepys III, 181, Douce I, 54ᵛ); "The Tormented Lovers Admonition," beginning "Cassandra's Beauty Charm'd mine eye," to the tune of "Busie Fame" (Douce II, 218); "The Charming Eccho," beginning "As I was walking all alone,/one Evening fair and clear," to the tune of "Oh love whose unconfined Wings; Or, Busie Fame: Or, Young Pheon" (Douce I, 47ᵛ; another edition, Pepys III, 187, omits "Busie Fame" from the list of tune titles); "The Brave Boys of Bristol," beginning "Brave Bristol Boys, where e're you be," to the tune of "Hey Boys up go we; Jenny Gin; Busie Fame; Or, Russels Farewel" (Douce I, 19); "The Amorous Petitioner," beginning "As I did lately walk abroad," to the tune of "Cloris full of harmless thought, Young Phaon, Busie Fame, or the Lanthorn Horns grow dimn" (Pepys III, 109).[2]

[1] A competing version of the ballad, "Popery Unvail'd" (Douce II, 174ᵛ), has a similar opening, "Hold fast thy Sword and Scepter Charles/sad times are coming on," but only "Young Pheon" is cited as tune; despite similar subject matter, there are no verbal parallels with "Loyalty unfeigned" after the first few lines.

[2] I have found no information on the fourth tune title.

Callino Casturame

Commentators on this tune name agree that it is an English rendering of an Irish phrase, the first element of which has come into modern usage as *colleen*. Beyond that the suggestions are numerous but conflicting. W. H. Grattan Flood says the words are *Cailín óg a stiuire me* ("My dear little girl");[1] H. E. Rollins offers *Cailín óg a stór* ("Young girl, O treasure");[2] Gerard Murphy gives *Cailín ó chois tSiúire mé* ("I am a girl from beside the [river] Suir");[3] and J. Maclean suggests *Chailin Og, an Stiuir Thu Mi* ("Young maid, will you guide me").[4]

"Callin o custure me" was entered in the Stationers' Register, March 10, 1582 (Rollins, *Anal. Index,* No. 259); and this ballad, or an imitation of it, is in *A Handefull of Pleasant Delites,* 1584 (ed. Rollins, 1924, p. 38), as "A Sonet of a Louer in the praise of his lady. To Calen o Custure me: sung at euerie lines end." With the interpolation of the Irish refrain as directed, the tune must be sung three times over to accommodate each six-line octosyllabic stanza. Shakespeare uses the Irish words in *Henry V,* IV, iv, 4, where they are Pistol's gibberish reply to the French soldier's words which he has not understood. An epigram in *The Scourge of Folly* (lic. 1610) by John Davies of Hereford (*Works,* ed. Grosart, 1878, II, 16) alludes to the refrain, perhaps in the form associated with the *Handefull* poem:

> No word proceeds from his most fluent tong,
> But it is like the burden of the song
>   Call'd Callino, come from a forraine Land,
>   Which English people do not vnderstand.

The tune is in William Ballet's MS Lute Book of the late sixteenth century. As theme and variations for virginals by William Byrd, it is found in *The Fitzwilliam Virginal Book* and BM MS Add. 30485, fol. 96ᵛ (in *Collected Works,* ed. Fellowes, 1937–1950, XX, 5). The music manuscripts in the Cambridge University Library contain one setting of

[1] *A History of Irish Music,* 3d ed., 1913, p. 170. Flood summarized his argument in a letter to *The Irish Statesman,* June 25, 1927, pp. 376f.

[2] *Handefull,* ed. 1924, p. 99. In a further note on the tune name in *J. Q. Adams Memorial Studies,* 1947, p. 472, Rollins called attention to an earlier discussion by James Lecky in the New Shakspere Society *Transactions,* 1887–1890, pp. 140–142, which contains several additional interpretations, including that adopted by Rollins.

[3] See *Grove's Dictionary of Music and Musicians,* 5th ed., 1954, III, 289.

[4] London *Times Literary Supplement,* May 9, 1958, p. 255.

"Callinoe" for lute (Dd.3.18, fol. 3) and two in cittern tablature, the first of which (Fig. 51) is by [Thomas] Robinson (Dd.4.23, fols. 19, 23ᵛ). A four-part song in J. Playford's *Catch that Catch Can*, 1667, beginning

"Callino Callino Calino Castore me" and entitled "An Irish Tune," is in duple rhythm, and the music bears no relation to the familiar version of the tune.

At least one seventeenth-century ballad was sung to the tune of "Culino" or "Calino": "A Pleasant Song made by a Souldier," beginning "In summer time when Phoebus raise [i.e., rays]" (Pepys, Wood 401, Roxburghe; reprinted in *RB* VI, 284). Each eight-line stanza requires the air to be sung twice.

Calm Was the Evening

This tune takes its name from the opening line of a song which seems to have appeared first in *A New Academy of Complements*, 1669, p. 179. It is twice printed in *Merry Drollery Complete*, 1670, pp. 220, 292, and is found in several later poetical miscellanies. Its fame followed its introduction in Dryden's *An Evening's Love, or the Mock-Astrologer*, 1671, Act IV, where it begins "Calm was the Even, and cleer was the Skie." A musical setting for voice and bass by Alphonso Marsh is in

52 — C 3 —

Basses throughout imply flatted E.

Choice Songs and Ayres, 1673, p. 9 (Fig. 52); the three-stanza poem with Marsh's air is in the Keith MS Book, p. 58, and in all editions of *Pills,* 1719–1720, III, 160.

The song, with its conspicuous *ha ha* refrain, was expanded into an eleven-stanza broadside in which the pastoral figures Amyntor and Sylvia are renamed: "Amintas and Claudia; Or, The Merry Shepherdess" (Harvard, Lord Crawford, Euing, Douce, Bagford; reprinted in *BB* II, 499). The tune, here named "Calm was the Evening, and Clear was the Skie," serves also for a sequel, "The Amorous Shepherd, and coy Shepherdess, Or, An answer to Amintas and Claudia," beginning "Clear was the morning, and azure the Skie" (Douce I, 9).[1]

[1] C. L. Day, in *The Songs of John Dryden,* 1932, prints a facsimile of Marsh's setting, p. 27, and notes further reprints, imitations, and parodies of the original song, pp. 149–150. Day does not list the two miscellany appearances of the song which antedate Dryden's play, and which may cast some doubt on his authorship of the verses.

Cam'st Thou Not from Newcastle?

The tune "Newcastle" appears in the first eight editions of *The Dancing Master,* 1651–1690 (1651, p. 77=Fig. 53). With a few slight wrench-

53

Original is unbarred.

ings of accent, it fits a sixteen-line fragment in the Percy Folio MS (ed. Hales and Furnivall, I, 253), beginning "Came you not from Newcastle?/ Came yee not there away." The two stanzas include the following refrain:

> Why shold not I loue my loue?
>   why shold not my loue loue me?
> why shold not I loue my loue,
>   gallant hound sedelee?

In Fielding's *The Genuine Grub-Street Opera,* 1731, "Why should not I love Robin" is to be sung to "Why shou'd not I love my love," but no music is printed; a variant edition of the same year, *The Grub-Street Opera,* directs the song to be sung to "Mad Moll."

Miss Evelyn K. Wells, in her notes on tunes of the 1651 *Dancing Master* in *JEFDSS* III (1936–1939), 268, proposes a relationship between the "Newcastle" air and a ballad of c. 1625, "The contented Couckould, Or a pleasant new Songe of a New-Castle man . . ." (Pepys; reprinted in *PB* II, 24). Since no tune is named on the sheet, one can only speculate whether the Newcastle tune and text were ever intended to go together; on metrical grounds the linking is possible but fairly rough. Verbal echoes of "Walsingham" are discussed under the tune of that name.

In *The Famous Historie of Fryer Bacon,* a chapbook of 1627, "Cam'st thou not from New-Castle" is named as a "Northren tune" to which Miles, accompanying himself on pipe and tabor, sings a song beginning "To couple is a custome,/all things thereto agree" (ed. 1629, sig. C1ᵛ). The trimeter quatrains are so lyrical that it is difficult to accept the forcings necessary in putting them to the dance tune. In all likelihood the surviving tune is not the one which must have had some currency in Elizabethan days and in the early part of the seventeenth century.

Can Life Be a Blessing?

Originally a song in Dryden's *Troilus and Cressida,* 1679, III, ii, "Can life be a Blessing, or worth the possessing?" is in *Choice Ayres and Songs,* Third Book, 1681, p. 3, with music by Thomas Farmer (Fig. 54), and,

with the same music in another key, in Fitzwilliam Museum MS 30.G.20, c. 1680, p. 4. The Dryden song was expanded into a ten-stanza broadside version, "Loves Power and Greatness," beginning "Can Life be a Blessing,/That's worth our possessing?" (Pepys III, 133, Lord Crawford 201),

"To a New Play-house Tune," presumably Farmer's. A political ballad of c. 1680 must have followed "Loves Power and Greatness" into print; it is "Unfeigned Friendship, or, The Loyalists Cordial Advice," beginning "How happy's the State where no discords are breeding," to "a new Playhouse Tune, called, How happy's the State, or, Can Life be a Blessing" (Harvard, BM C.22.f.6, Lord Crawford, Pepys; reprinted in *PB* III, 82). If "How Happy's the State" is a separate tune, it has not survived.

John Eccles wrote incidental music for a revival of Dryden's play, c. 1695, and it was presumably about this time that he composed a fresh setting for "Can life be a blessing" (in his *Collection of Songs*, c. 1704, p. 137). So far as is known, this air had no connection with broadside history.

Canst Thou Not Weave Bone-Lace?

This tune derives its title from the opening line of "Another Scotch Song, by way of Dialogue, Set to a very pretty Northern Tune," which appeared in Thomas D'Urfey's *A Compleat Collection*, 1687, p. 15. D'Urfey's song, which may be an adaptation of an earlier text, was expanded into a broadside of about the same date: "Chastities Conquest, Or, No Trusting before Marriage," beginning "Canst thou not weave Bonelace,/yea by Lady that I can," to the tune of "Canst thou not weave Bone-lace" (Lord Crawford, Douce, Harvard, Euing, Pepys, Roxburghe; reprinted in *RB* III, 497).

No contemporary copy of the music has been found, but it appears as a spirited dance tune in one ballad opera, George Lillo's *Silvia*, 1731, Air 51 (Fig. 55). Lillo echoes the ballad in his second line:

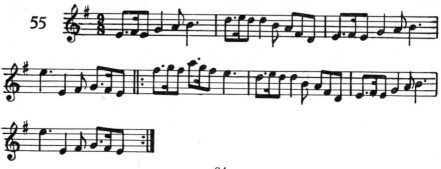

Thou canst do Housewife's Work!
Yea, by'r Lady, that I can.

Chappell (*RB* III, 496) equates the tune with "A Trip to Marrowbone," found in the twelfth and succeeding editions of *The Dancing Master* and used by D'Urfey for his song "Maiden fresh as a rose" (in *Merry Musician*, 1716, I, 189, and *Pills*, 1719–1720, I, 56–57). The two tunes are similar in their basic rhythm and in their final cadence, but they differ melodically. "A Trip to Marrowbone" contains a second strain not paralleled in "Canst thou not weave Bone-lace."

The Carman's Whistle

This tune, arranged by William Byrd as a set of variations for the virginals, is in his *My Ladye Nevells Booke*, *The Fitzwilliam Virginal Book*, BM MS Add. 30485, fol. 65, BM Add. 30486, fol. 19 (Fig. 56), and

Will Forster's MS Virginal Book, p. 130 (see *Collected Works*, ed. Fellowes, 1937–1950, XX, 7). A keyboard transcript, c. 1700, attributed to Byrd in BM MS Add. 31403, fol. 25ᵛ, is entitled "The Carter's Whissell." Early seventeenth-century lute tablatures are in BM Egerton MS 2046, fol. 32ᵛ, and Cambridge University MS Dd.5.78.3, fol. 48ᵛ. The staff notation setting in David Lumsden's *An Anthology of English Lute Music*, 1954, No. 26, is a composite.

The presence of "The Carmans Whistle" in *My Ladye Nevells Booke* establishes the vogue of the tune before 1591. A ballad with this title must have circulated contemporaneously, for in 1592 Henry Chettle, in a letter prefixed to Anthony Munday's translation of *Gerileon of England* (Part 2, sig. A4), condemned it by name: "I maruell who the diuell is his Printer [who] . . . would bee so impudent to print such odious and lasciuious ribauldrie, as Watkins Ale, The Carmans Whistle, and sundrie such other."[1]

The musical ability of carters was legendary, as Chappell (*PMOT* I, 138) showed through quotations from Elizabethan and Jacobean plays. Most of the allusions are general, in the spirit of Falstaff's characterization of Justice Shallow: "'A came ever in the rearward of the fashion, and sung those tunes to the over-scutch'd huswives that he heard the carmen whistle, and sware they were his Fancies or his Good-nights" (*2 Henry IV*, III, ii, 342–345). Here the whistling of carmen is signified, but not without the possibility of a pun on the tune name.

The following may be the original ballad to the tune, though it is extant only in editions of the late seventeenth century: "The Courteous Carman, And the Amorous Maid. or, The Carmans Whistle," beginning "As I abroad was walking/by the breaking of the day," to the tune of "The Carman's Whistle; or, Lord Willoughby's March" (Lord Crawford 86 and 87, Douce I, 32ᵛ and 38, Harvard, BM C.22.f.6 [104]; an emasculated partial text is reprinted in Chappell, *PMOT* I, 139–140). One of the Douce copies contains the following MS addition: "Tune I wish I was a fair maid as I am a Bonnie Then I would have a whitser &c." On this tune I have no information. "Lord Willoughby," which fits the ballad, is an independent Elizabethan tune, q.v.

Closely paraphrasing "The Courteous Carman," using its first tune, and sharing with it the *double entendre* of phallic symbolism, is "The Combers Whistle or, The Sport of the Spring," beginning "All in a pleasant morning,/in the merry month of May," licensed by Sir Roger L'Estrange, and so not later than 1685 (Rawlinson, Wood E.25, Lord Crawford, Roxburghe; reprinted in *RB* III, 564).[2] Another to the tune is "All is ours and our Husbands, Or the Country Hostesses Vindication," beginning "Come all you Tribes of Hostises," to the tune of "Carmans

[1] The letter is signed "T. N." but in the preface to *Kind-Harts Dreame*, 1592, Chettle absolved Thomas Nashe of any responsibility, blamed the printer, and acknowledged the authorship of the strictures quoted. In the body of *Kind-Harts Dreame* Chettle renewed his attack on this and other objectionable ballads.

[2] A variant form of this text, called "A Pleasant New Sounge called the carmans Whistle," is in Bodleian MS Rawlinson Poet. 185, fol. 21, a commonplace book dated c. 1590; this earlier version is to the tune of "O Neighbor Roberte," another name for "Lord Willoughby."

Whistle, Or High Boys up go we" (Lord Crawford, Harvard, Roxburghe; reprinted in *RB* III, 380).

Cavalilly Man

This tune is in *The Dancing Master,* commencing with the fourth edition, 1670, p. 140 (Fig. 57); it is without key signature and in common time through the eighth edition and thereafter is in F and in 6/4 time. Music is also found in *180 Loyal Songs,* 1685, pp. 200, 254; on a broadside "Love and Loyalty" (Fig. 58) properly sung to "Tender hearts of

London City" (Douce, Lord Crawford, Pepys, Roxburghe; text reprinted in *RB* VII, 497); and in *Pills,* 1719–1720, II, 118, IV, 12, 317. In Walsh's *Compleat Country Dancing-Master,* 1718, the tune is called "Cavalier." The music is used in but one ballad opera: Johnson's *The Village Opera,* 1729.

The original ballad giving rise to the tune name was published by Francis Grove and is probably to be dated about 1640. It is: "The North-country Maid's resolution & love to her Sweetheart . . . To a pleasant new Northern Tune," beginning "As from Newcastle I did pass" (Euing 257). In it a Scottish lass, loyal to her "Cavalier blade," repeats the words, "I'll follow my Cavalilly man," reinforcing them with the refrain:

O my dainty Cavalilly man,
　My finnikin Cavalilly man,
For Gods Cause and the Protestants,
　I prithee le me gang with thee man.

It may be questioned whether this ballad was sung to the tune we know, for each stanza of eight lines, with the four-line refrain, would require that our eight-measure tune be sung three times over; but this is by no means an unheard-of practice.

What is certain, however, is that the tune enjoyed a great vogue during the political struggles of the 1680s. The usual stanza form, analogous to that of "Which nobody can deny," is three lines of anapestic tetrameter plus a one-line refrain. A typical broadside sung to the tune is "A Litany from Geneva; in Answer to that from St. Omer's," 1682, beginning "From the Tap in the guts of the Honourable Stump" (Wood 417, Bodleian Ashmole G.16, BM 1872.a.1; reprinted in *180 Loyal Songs,* 1685, and *RB* V, 196; some editions have no tune direction). The refrain "Libera nos, Domine" links this ballad with a large class, including "A Letany for St. Omers" alluded to above, in which political or religious factions are represented as complaining of contemporary ills from which they would like to be freed. Litany stanzas usually end with the Latin phrase or its English equivalent, "For ever good Lord deliver us." Although not always designed for singing, the litanies nonetheless often call for such tunes as "Cavalilly Man" or "The Queen's Old Courtier" or "When Jockey first the wars began," and most of them can be sung to one of these tunes.

In 1684 Thomas D'Urfey composed "A New Littany, design'd for this Lent, and to be Sung in all the Conventicles, in and about London, for the Instruction of the Whiggs," beginning "From Counsels of Six, where Treason prevails," to the tune of "The Cavalilly Man" (Bodleian Ashmole G.16, BM 1872.a.1, Harvard, Clark; reprinted in *180 Loyal Songs* and in *RB* V, 343). Another Tory piece from the same year is "Song of the Light of the three Nations turn'd into Darkness. Or Otes made Free man of Whitington's Colledge, for Perjury, andalum Magnatum, and something like Treason," beginning "Come all our Caballers & Parliament Votes" (Bodleian Ashmole G.16 [66], Clark; reprinted in *120 Loyal Songs* and *180 Loyal Songs*). "Oates Well Thresh't," beginning "Our Oates last Week not worth a Groat," is a broadside of 1681 to the tune "Which no Body can deny" (Harvard, Wood 417 [184], Bodleian Firth b.20 [86]). In *180 Loyal Songs* it is reprinted with the tune direction of the broadside but with music of "Cavalilly Man." This political songster of 1685 contains several other "Cavalilly" pieces probably derived from broadsides which have not survived.

Other ballads include "A New Song Lately come from Ireland," beginning "There was an Irish Army brave," to the tune of "Cavaleiro-man," licensed by J. F[raser], who succeeded Richard Pocock upon the accession of William and Mary (Harvard). The five-line stanza, in which the fifth line repeats the fourth, can be sung to the tune with a repetition of the two closing bars. Another is "The Conditional Recantation or A Dialogue between the Oracle of St. Patrick and the late King," beginning "If both the Indies were my own" (BM MS Harl. 7319, p. 659). A pair of related ballads to the tune revert from politics to romance: "The Well-shap'd West-Country Lass," beginning "Hi-ho, my heart it is light" (Pepys III, 281, Lord Crawford 509), actually an ironic portrait of physical un-pleasantness; and restoring the perspective on the ideal lover, "Roger, The West-Country Lad . . . his . . . Sweet-heart Described, in Answer to the Well-shap'd Country Lass," beginning "Hie-hoe, pray what shall I doe?" (Pepys V, 218, Lord Crawford 510, both with meaningless music).

Celia, That I Once Was Blest

This tune by Henry Purcell takes its name from a song originally set to it in Dryden's *Amphitryon*, 1690, Act III. It was printed in *The Songs in Amphitryon, with the Musick,* 1690, p. 1 (Fig. 59), in a contemporary

59

single-sheet edition (BM C.180.a [17]), and in all editions of *Pills,* 1719–1720, IV, 257. A treble-violin arrangement of the tune appeared in *Apollo's Banquet,* Second Book, 1691.

· 89 ·

The stage song was expanded from three to ten stanzas in the broadside version: "Coy Celia's Cruelty . . . sung . . . in . . . Amphitryon. To an excellent new playhouse tune" (Lord Crawford 208, Pepys V, 301, both with meaningless music). And half a dozen other broadsides were written to the tune: "Constant Cloris," beginning "Cloris in a Mirtle Grove" (BM C.39.k.6, with meaningless music; reprinted in *OPB*, p. 59); "The Mistaken Bride: or, The faithful Friend," beginning "In fair London late did dwell" (Lord Crawford, Euing, Harvard, Roxburghe; reprinted in *RB* VIII, 133); "The False-hearted Lover," beginning "Loyal Lovers far and near" (Pepys; reprinted in *PB* VII, 150), with its answer, "The Young-Mans Lamentation," beginning "Is my sweetest Creature Dead" (Pepys; reprinted in *PB* VII, 154); "The Lovers Lamentation: or, a New Mock-Song On the Cruelty of Coy Lucinda," beginning "Pitty here a Loyal swain" (Pepys III, 85); and "The Forsaken Nimphs Complaint," beginning "Strephon vow'd and swore to be" (Pepys V, 300, with meaningless music).

The tune is cited as Air 12 in the original edition of Chetwood's *The Lover's Opera*, 1729, but is not named in the third edition, 1730, which contains music. Words of the original stage song continued to be popular during the eighteenth century, appearing in such poetical miscellanies as *The Compleat Academy of Complements*, 1705, and volume one of *The Hive*, 3d ed., 1726.[1]

Charles of Sweden, or First of August

In the second volume of *The Dancing Master*, 3d ed., 1718, p. 337 (Fig. 60), and in Walsh's *Compleat Country Dancing-Master*, Second Book, 1719, this tune is entitled "Frisky Jenny, Or: The tenth of June," the second of these names deriving from the birthday of James, the Pretender. In the third volume of *The Dancing Master*, c. 1728, it is called "The constant Lover." [1] By the time of the ballad operas, the tune had acquired two new names: (1) "First of August" or "Glorious first of August," in allusion to the accession date of George I in 1714, becomes the tune title in Coffey's *The Beggar's Wedding*, 1729, *Chuck*, 1729, and *The*

---

[1] For a more detailed listing of reprints, see *The Songs of John Dryden*, ed. C. L. Day, 1932, pp. 169–170.

[1] An entirely different tune is that entitled "The constant Lover" in *The Dancing Master*, 1714, 1718, 1728, II, 181.

Sharpers, 1740; (2) "Charles of Sweden," used in Coffey's *The Devil to Pay,* 1731, Drury's *The Rival Milliners,* 1737, and *The Sailor's Opera,* 1745. The same tune, untitled, is Air 22 in Johnson's *The Village Opera,* 1729. In BM MS Add. 29371, fol. 55ᵛ, which may be of the mid-eighteenth century, a violin arrangement of the tune is called "Tenth of June, or King of Sweedland."

Several ballads were directed to be sung to the tune under its various names. An Irish broadside of 1727 capitalized doubly on the tune title and its relation to the calendar: "A New Song . . . on . . . Procession of . . . Society of Scriblers . . . Tuesday the first of August, 1727," beginning "Good People all I pray draw near,/This Glorious first of August" (BM 839.m.23 [164]). In another to the same tune, the beginning of the title may be cropped: "Made on the . . . Glory of the Twenty Four Corporations of . . . Dublin," beginning "All you that fain would Jolly be" (BM 839.m.23 [17]).

The original poem on the death of Charles XII seems to be "The Soldiers Remembrancer: or Valient Charles of Sweeden," beginning "Glorious Hero are you dead"; every stanza ends "Great glorious Charles of Sweeden," and though no tune direction is given, this song has the same stanza as others sung to the tune (Madden III, 713, a late eighteenth-century broadside edition; found also in *The Unconstant Moggy's Garland,* Newcastle, 1765?). The taking of Portobello in 1739 was occasion for a ballad to the tune of "Glorious Charles of Sweden": "English Courage Display'd, or Brave News from Admiral Vernon," beginning "Come Loyal Britains all Rejoyce with joyful acclamations" (Madden slip songs I, No. 531, reprinted in C. H. Firth's *Naval Songs and Ballads,* 1908, p. 177). On the same sheet is a reworking of the Portobello ballad to fit an event of 1741: "English Courage Display'd: on Admiral Vernon's Taking of Carthagena," beginning "Brave loyal Britons all rejoice,/With joyful acclamation," to the tune of "Glorious Charles of Sweden" (reprinted in M. O. Percival, *Walpole Ballads,* 1916, p. 166). To the same tune is "Whittington reviv'd, or the City in Triumph: On Alderman Parson's being Chose twice Lord-Mayor of . . . London," beginning "Great Alderman Parsons now is Chose" (BM 1876.f.1 [120]), celebrating an event of 1740. "A New Song, on the sharp and B[l]oody Battle . . . the 16th Instant, between the English . . . and the French," beginning "Brave Britons let your Voices Ring,/with joyfull acclamation" (BM 1876.f.1 [128]), is on the battle of Dettingen in 1743, the last occasion on which a British king has commanded in person. Also to the tune is "A copy of Verses made on the Public Fire-Works, in Honour of Peace . . . 27th of April 1749, in St. James's Park," beginning "Come free Brittons lets all rejoice,/upon this Solemn occasion" (BM C.116.i.4 [116]).

Among the single-sheet songs using this music (but without giving it a name) may be mentioned "A Jigg Danc'd in the Schoole of Venus: or the 3-Penny Hops Burlesq'd by Mr. John Vernham," beginning "Oh how I Doat upon that Lass" (Harvard, BM H.1601 [346], dated 1715?).

In Coffey's ballad opera *The Devil to Pay*, the song to this tune begins "Come, jolly Bacchus, God of Wine," whence another name for the tune.

Charon Make Haste

This tune flourished during the reign of James II and for a year or so afterward. Almost all the ballads to the tune were licensed by Richard Pocock, whose term extended from late in 1685 until early 1689 (cf. Rollins, *PB* III, 210, IV, 226); those not licensed by Pocock may be dated within the early months of William and Mary's reign. The tune title derives from the opening line of "The Dispairing Lovers Address to Charon," beginning "Charon make haste, and ferry me over" (Pepys, Lord Crawford, Douce, BM C.22.f.6; reprinted in *RB* VI, 24; the title is sometimes "A Call to Charon . . .").

Music to the tune (Fig. 61) is found on a Pepys broadside, "A New Song, called, The Duke of Grafton's Welcome Home . . . from his Forreign Travels," beginning "All Loyal Subjects resolve to be merry" (Pepys V, 31; text reprinted in *PB* III, 295). The music is corrupt in spots but is well above par for broadsides. Debased notation is printed with "True Lovers Extremity; or, The Maidens miserable Moan," beginning "I having an hour of time and leisure" (Euing, Harvard, BM C.39.k.6; reprinted in *OPB*, p. 140). A tune called "Caron make hast" is in *Youth's Delight on the Flagelet*, 9th ed., c. 1690, but it appears to be either a crude attempt at an accompanying part or an independent air.

61

* F on sheet.

Other broadsides to the tune include: "The Dying Damsels Doleful Destiny," beginning "Among the Violets, fair Lillies and Roses" (Douce I, 66, with the additional tune direction in MS: "True Love it is a Tormenting pain"; reprinted in *Seventeenth Century Lyrics*, ed. N. Ault, 2d ed., 1950, p. 482); "Charon's Kindness, or the Languishing Lass releas'd from her sorrowful destiny," beginning "As I was ranging the Forest of Fancy" (Douce I, 41ᵛ); "A Third Touch of the Times," beginning "Brave English Boys now rejoyce and be merry" (Pepys, dated 1688; reprinted in *PB* III, 329); "The Languishing Swain," beginning "Down by the side of a fair Christial Fountain" (Harvard, Lord Crawford, Roxburghe; reprinted in *RB* VI, 29); [1] "The Young Man and Maids Recreation or, The Spring Birds Notes," beginning "My Dearest lets walk through the Meaddows this weather" (Douce II, 265ᵛ); "Cupids Kindness to Constant Coridon," beginning "Silvia the Fair by the side of a River" (Douce I, 48, Lord Crawford 1057, Harvard, BM C.22.f.6 [38]); "A New

[1] Since the tune "Languishing Swain" is associated with ballads in octosyllabic quatrains, its name is probably not derived from this ballad, which is in the dactylic tetrameter octaves characteristic of "Charon" ballads. More likely candidates are two broadsides discussed under the tune "He that loves best must suffer most." "Charon" and "Languishing Swain" are not comfortably interchangeable, despite the remarks of Rollins (*PB* V, 319) and Lord Crawford (*Catalogue*, p. 597).

Song, called The Lover's Tragedy: or Parents Cruelty," beginning "A Virgin fam'd for her Vertue and Beauty" (Euing 186, Lord Crawford 1236, Harvard, BM C.22.f.6 [13]; reprinted in John Ashton, *A Century of Ballads*, 1887, p. 161); "The True Pattern of Loyalty," beginning "William and Susan they happily meeting" (Harvard, BM C.22.f.6, Lord Crawford; reprinted in *RB* VII, 502).

Three "Charon" ballads express the Protestants' joy after 1688: "Great Brittains Joys compleated, Or, Londons Triumph in the Proclaiming of the Prince and Princess of Orange King and Queen of England, on the 13th. of this Instant February," beginning "Protestants now we have cause to be chearful" (Pepys; reprinted in *PB* IV, 150); "The Kingdoms Cares Endu'd with Comfort, By The Coronation . . . the 11th. of this Instant April, 1689," beginning "Let all true protestants now in this Nation" (Pepys; reprinted in *PB* IV, 246); and "The Protestant's satisfaction in a Prosperous Reign," beginning "You that would have this a prosperous Nation" (reprinted in *RB* VII, 712, from an unidentified copy published by J. Blare in 1689).

The following pair of "Charon" ballads is related, as the titles show: "The Damosels Tragedy: Or, True Love in Distress," beginning "You Loyal Lovers attend to my Ditty" (Lord Crawford 1406, Harvard, BM C.22.f.6 [108]); and "The Young-Mans Complaint, Or, An Answer To The Damosels Tragedy," beginning "Now for the loss of my amorous Jewel" (Douce, Lord Crawford, Harvard, Roxburghe; reprinted in *BB* II, 938).[2]

A trifling curiosity attaches to "The Faithful Squire: or, The Fortunate Farmer's Daughter," beginning "There was I'll tell you a wealthy young Squire" (Lord Crawford, Harvard, Bagford; reprinted in *BB* I, 454), for it has been conjectured that the ballad may have been the germ of Richardson's *Pamela*. The verse prefixed to the ballad summarizes the idea of the novel, to be sure, but in a very general way:

> Had she consented to his will,
>   when he rid first that way,
> She might have been unmarried still,
>   though now a Lady Gay.

Such a miscellany as *Pills* is full of songs of the same tenor for which the same argument could be made, and in the absence of some specific acknowledgment by Richardson, it seems dangerous to attribute to this "Charon" ballad anything beyond the interest of a mere parallel.

[2] Ebsworth erroneously thought that the ballad to which this was the answer was "The True Lovers Lamentable Overthrow; Or, The Damosels Last Farewell" (*BB* I, 154). This latter ballad, to the tune of "Cruel Bloody Fate," has a stanza pattern distinctly different from that of the "Charon" ballads.

This dance tune appears in Paris Conservatoire MS Rés. 1185, No. 108, a mid-seventeenth-century virginal set (Fig. 62), in Elizabeth Rogers's MS Virginal Book (BM MS Add. 10337, fol. 21, before 1656), and in *A Booke*

62

* Varied repeat in MS.

of New Lessons, 1652, arranged for both cittern and gittern. In *The Dancing Master,* 1651–1690, it is entitled "Chestnut (or Doves Figary)." [1]

A ballad registered in 1656 calls for the tune: "The Batchelor's Choice, or, A Young-man's Resolution

> To have his Love and Sweet-heart Nancy,
> Whom he most heartily doth fancy,"

beginning "Fye upon this paultry Cupid,/he hath shot me with his shaft," to the tune of "Chess-nut, Or, Cat after kinde" (Rawlinson 45). The burden,

> But I fancy Lovely Nancy,
> and she alone enjoyes my heart,

is apparently an echo of "I could fancy pretty Nancy," used as a tune title by C[harles] R[ecords] in a ballad of the 1630s, "Friendly Counsaile" (*RB* I, 65); but the six-line iambic stanza contrasts with the eight-line trochaic pattern of our "Chestnut" ballad, and the two cannot well be associated.

[1] "Doves Figary" may be explained by a passage in Deloney's *Thomas of Reading* (*Works,* ed. Mann, pp. 217–218) which relates how a song made on the hospitable Tom Dove of Exeter eventually became a dance. Deloney quotes a stanza which can with little difficulty be fitted to the *Dancing Master* tune. See *JEFDSS,* IV (1942), 124.

One of Patrick Cary's *Trivial Poems* (ed. W. Scott, 1820; the MS is dated 1651) is to the tune of "But I fancy Louely Nancy" and begins "Surely now I'me out of danger,/And noe more need feare my heart." It has the trochaic movement of "The Batchelor's Choice" but antedates the registry of that broadside by five years. Since we do not know whether the broadside had been issued earlier, we cannot be sure where Cary got his tune title.[2]

"Cat after kinde" recalls the proverbial phrase, but I have no data on the tune.

Chevy Chase

Although "Chevy Chase" is named as the tune for some three dozen ballads before 1700, the only seventeenth-century musical setting I have found is an untitled air and bass, coupled with the opening stanza of the "Chevy Chase" ballad, in Edinburgh University Library MS Dc.1.69, fol. 113 (reversed), c. 1650–1675 (Fig. 63). The music is printed eight times in the 1719–1720 *Pills,* once with the ballad text (IV, 289); and the same tune (Fig. 64) is once specifically identified as "Chivy-Chase" (IV, 1). Music and tune name are again associated in several ballad operas, including Gay's *The Beggar's Opera,* 1728, Kelly's *The Plot,* 1735, and Fabian's *Trick for Trick,* 1735. The identity of the tune would therefore seem to be beyond question.

But the ballad itself, of which there are many seventeenth-century editions,[1] is to the tune of "Flying Fame," and there are at least two other ballads reprinted in *Pills* with "Chevy Chase" music whose broadside

---

[2] "The Redeemed Captive" (*BB* II, 549, *OPB,* p. 199) is a Restoration broadside with first line as in Cary's poem; thereafter, however, the two texts are independent, and the ballad is to the tune "When Aurelia first was [courted]," q.v.

[1] Perhaps the oldest edition is "A memorable song vpon the vnhappy hunting in Cheuy Chase . . ." (Pepys I, 92), printed for Henry Gosson, who flourished 1601–1640; another edition with the same title and of about the same date (Manchester II, 7) was printed for Edward Wright, fl. 1615–1648; an edition of c. 1658–1664 was printed for Coles, Vere, and Gilbertson (Euing 212, Wood 402 [30]). None of these copies is noticed in *STC* or Wing. Later editions during the seventeenth century include those printed for Coles, Vere, and Wright, c. 1663–1674 (Roxburghe III, 66, Douce I, 27^v) and for Coles, Vere, Wright, Clark, Thackeray, and Passinger, c. 1678–1680 (Harvard), the latter entitled "An unhappy memorable song on the hunting in Chevy Chace . . ." The ballad is in the Percy Folio MS (ed. Hales and Furnivall, II, 7), reprinted in the *Reliques,* in *RB* VI, 740, and in Child No. 162 B.

editions name "Flying Fame."[2] The question then is whether the music preserved as "Chevy Chase" was originally known as "Flying Fame" or whether there are two independent tunes. The ballad from which "Flying Fame" or "When flying fame" takes its name is lost;[3] moreover, no music with those titles has survived. We can be sure, however, that "Flying Fame" was known as a tune when the broadside texts of "Chevy Chase" began to be issued. And whereas "Chevy Chase" continued to be

[2] These are "The Shepherd and the King," beginning "An elder time there was of yore" (Wood 401, Pepys, Euing, Lord Crawford, Harvard, Douce, Roxburghe; reprinted in *RB* III, 211), licensed in 1578, but no surviving copy earlier than c. 1625; found in *Pills* V, 289. And Deloney's "A mournefull Dittie on the death of faire Rosamond," beginning "When as King Henrie rul'd this land," which first appeared in the 1607 edition of his *Strange Histories* (many broadside copies with varying titles; reprinted in *RB* VI, 673, in Mann's *Deloney*, p. 297); found in *Pills*, 1714 ed. only, V, 154.

[3] The phrase "flying fame" occurs in two poems in *A Gorgeous Gallery of Gallant Inventions*, 1578, ed. Rollins, p. 61: "If that the flying fame therof, to others eares attayne," and p. 120: "That dare I not? for feare of flying fame." The currency of the phrase tells us nothing specific about the lost ballad, but from other evidence we can be reasonably sure that it was a product of the Elizabethan muse.

named as a tune for new ballads throughout the eighteenth century, "Flying Fame" is found only on reissues of old ballads. We may conclude either that the older tune virtually died with the seventeenth century or that the great popularity of the "Chevy Chase" ballad produced a new name for the tune which gradually displaced the old name. The latter hypothesis seems the more probable, but it must be kept in mind that we do not have the evidence for a positive conclusion.

Among the early ballads to the tune of "Flying Fame," the following may be noticed: Deloney's "The Noble Acts of Arthur of the round Table," beginning "When Arthur first in court began," was included in his *Garland of Good Will*, 1631 (*Works*, ed. Mann, p. 323), but it was licensed in 1603 as a broadside and must have circulated even earlier, for in *2 Henry IV*, 1598, II, iv, Falstaff sings the opening lines. A broadside edition published by W[illiam] I[aggard], c. 1615, is at Harvard. Later texts, chiefly of the last quarter of the seventeenth century, are represented by the reprint in *RB* VI, 722. A five-stanza burlesque of the ballad, with identical beginning, is in *Sportive Wit*, 1656; another is in *Windsor Drollery*, 1672; and an imitation beginning "When James in Scotland first began," to the tune of "When Arthur first in Court began," is in *Choyce Drollery*, 1656.

Also to the tune is Deloney's story of Alphonso and Ganselo, called "Of the faithfull friendship that lasted betweene two faithfull friends," beginning "In stately Rome sometimes did dwell" (*Garland of Good Will*, in *Works*, ed. Mann, p. 338; Percy Folio MS, ed. Hales and Furnivall, III, 507; Roxburghe, reprinted in *RB* III, 205). And in *SB*, p. 204, is preserved "A newe Ballad . . . fall of Christ's Church pinnacle in Norwitch . . . Aprill 1601," beginning "If euer words did moue a wight." Other well-known ballads to the tune are: "A worthy example of a vertuous wife, who fed her father with her owne milk," licensed in 1596 and found in many editions (*RB* VIII, 4); "The Wanton wife of Bath" (*RB* VII, 213); a ballad on the battle of Agincourt, variously titled, and beginning "A Counsell graue our King did hold" (*PB* I, 12; the version in *Pills* V, 49, has a musical text which begins as in "The Children in the Wood," but after two bars becomes "Chevy Chase"); and "A Lamentable Song of . . . King Leir, and his Three Daughters" (*Golden Garland of Princely Pleasures*, 1620; reprinted in *RB* VI, 714, from an eighteenth-century copy without tune direction).

Deloney's ballad on Fair Rosamond (see note 2 above) gave another name to the tune of "Flying Fame." Early editions of "The Lady Isabellas Tragedy" are to the tune of "Fair Rosamond, Or, Chivy Chase" (Douce I, 111, Wood E.25 [54]; later editions are to "The Ladies Fall"; see "In peascod time" for a discussion).[4] Several eighteenth-century ballads also call for "Fair Rosamond," including "The Glorious Warriour:

or, A Ballad in Praise of General Stanhope," 1710 (BM C.20.f.2 [234], Lord Crawford 1277); "A New Ballad. To the Tune of Fair Rosamond," beginning "When as Qu--- A--- of great Renown," on Abigail Hill, Lady Masham, the Queen's favorite (BM 162.m.70 [11], Harvard; reprinted in *Political Merriment,* 1714); and such obvious imitations as "A New Song" on Robert Harley, first Earl of Oxford, beginning "When as Queen Robin rul'd this Land,/Both Knave and Queen was he" (BM 112.f.44 [35]; reprinted in *Political Merriment,* 1714, and *A Pill to Purge State-Melancholy,* 1715, all without tune direction; the table of contents of the latter directs the song "to all Tunes").

The ballad of "Chevy Chase" is itself a broadside reworking of an earlier version preserved in Bodleian MS Ashmole 48, fol. 15^v (mid-sixteenth century), popularly titled "The Hunting of the Cheviot." [5] It may well have circulated in print as well as orally, but no printed copies have survived. "Chevy Chase" was licensed in 1624 and again in 1675, both entries very likely representing transfers of ownership. We have seen (note 1, above) that one issue before 1640 has survived. It may be significant that "Chevy Chase" is not named as a tune on any ballads before 1624, and that it is found on only a handful before the middle of the century. One of the earliest of these is "The World's Wonder" (Euing 401), printed for Francis Grove, who was active during the years 1623–1661. John Taylor's *A Three-fold Discourse,* 1642, concludes with a ballad on a fire at Oxford, "Zeale over-heated," to be sung to "Chivey Chace" (a contemporary copy is in Bodleian MS Ashmole 36–37, fol. 160). The Thomason Tracts in the British Museum contain two broadsides written to the tune during the same decade: "Strange and true Newes of an Ocean of Flies dropping out of a Cloud," 1647, by T. W., and "A Loyal Song of the Royal Feast, kept by the Prisoners in the Tower, in August 1648," by Sir Francis Wortley, both reprinted in Wright's *Political Ballads,* 1841.[6]

---

4 An ambiguous tune direction is "Chevy Chase, or the Lady Izabell's Tragedy," found in "The Patient Wife Betrayed, or the Lady Elizabeth's Tragedy," beginning "Of Turkey lately I did read" (Euing 289). But since this ballad was issued by J. Clark, probably before he joined a syndicate c. 1674, it is fairly likely that the second tune direction here can be referred to the earlier form of "The Lady Isabellas Tragedy," both editions of which were published by c. 1675. In that case the tune name "Lady Izabell's Tragedy" comes to stand for "Flying Fame" or "Chevy Chase."

5 Child No. 162 A. In his article "Concerning Bodleian MS. Ashmole 48," *MLN,* XXXIV (June, 1919), 350, Professor Rollins convincingly refutes the notion held by some ballad scholars that Richard Sheale was the author of the manuscript.

6 Wortley's concluding stanza contains the direction for singing:

> This if you will rhime dogrel call
> (That you please you may name it)
> One of the loyal traytors here

In "The Royal Patient Traveller," a ballad by Henry Jones on Charles II's escape from Worcester, written in 1660, the tune is named as "Chivy Chase, Or, God prosper long our Noble King" (Wood 401; reprinted in *RB* VII, 639, and in A. M. Broadley's *The Royal Miracle*, 1912, p. 93). A manuscript ballad beginning "Come all you Youths that yet are Free," one copy of which gives the author as Rochester and the date as 1682, has the tune direction "Chevy-chace or when as King Henry rul'd y^s Land" (BM MS Harl. 6913, p. 275, MS Harl. 7319, p. 170), the latter tune name deriving from Deloney's "Fair Rosamond." "The Spanish Virgin," beginning "All tender hearts that ake to hear," is to "Chievy Chase; Or, Aim not too high" (BM C.22.f.6, Lord Crawford, Pepys; reprinted in *PB* III, 197). Neither tune will fit the six-line stanza made up of a ballad-meter quatrain plus a couplet of octosyllabics. Likewise "The Life and Death of Sir Hugh of the Grime," whose broadside copies name no tune (*RB* VI, 595), is reprinted in *Pills*, VI, 289, with the tune direction "Chevy Chase," inappropriate to the four roughly octosyllabic lines of the stanza. On the other hand, "The Unfortunate Forrester, or, Fair Elener's Tragedy," beginning "Amongst the Forresters of old,/ one Thomas of great fame," names "Chevy Chase" for which it is metrically suited (*RB* VI, 645); whereas the commoner version in longer lines, entitled "A Tragical Ballad on the Unfortunate Love of Lord Thomas and Fair Eleanor," beginning "Lord Thomas he was a bold Forester" (*RB* VI, 647), is either to its own tune "Lord Thomas," which has survived only in tradition, or is without tune direction.

An interesting feature of eighteenth-century "Chevy Chase" popularity is the rash of ballads employing the opening formula of the original. For instance, "A Happy Memorable Ballad," on the battle of Audenarde, July, 1708, begins

> God prosper long our Gracious Queen,
>   Our lives and Safeties all,
> A woful Fight of late there did
>   Near Audenarde befal.

(*BB* I, 393; *Pills* VI, 4, with the music). Another, beginning "God prosper long our noble King,/His Turks and Germans all," describes an altercation between George I and the Prince of Wales at the christening of the latter's son Frederick in 1717 (Douce IV, 20^v, BM C.116.i.4 [20]). Many other ballads with comparable echoes can be found on broadsides and

> Did for a Ballad frame it;
> Old Chevy Chase was in his mind,
>   If any sute it better,
> All these concerned in the Song
>   Will kindly thank the setter.

in such topical songbooks as *Political Merriment* and *A Pill to Purge State-Melancholy*.

The tune continued in vogue for new ballads of all kinds, of which two examples must suffice. One is "The Discovery: or, The Squire turn'd Ferret," an eight-page production which reached three editions in 1727. It begins "Most true it is, I dare to say,/E'er since the Days of Eve," and the tune direction is "High Boys! up go we; Chevy Chase; Or what you please" (BM C.116.i.4 [30], BM 1850.c.10 [60]). The other is "The Hunter Hunted; or, Entertainment upon Entertainments," 1728, beginning "Come all you Sportsmen far and near,/And all that follow Feasting," to "an Old Tune—God prosper long, &c." (BM 1875.d.6 [32]). Probably more ballads were sung to "Chevy Chase" in the eighteenth century than in the seventeenth. It was by all odds the tune most frequently used with the ballad-meter quatrain. And yet it is not graceful or memorable, nor is it rhythmically distinctive. But if it does not accord with latter-day taste, it yet has a firm, rugged quality of an earlier age when its double tonality was not a mark of peculiarity.

Chi Passa

"Chi passa per questa strada" is a song by Filippo Azzaiuolo first printed in his *Il primo libro de Villotte alla Padoana,* 1557. It was widely popular on the Continent during the second half of the sixteenth century,[1] and a number of English settings of the celebrated tune have been preserved, most of them too full of embellishment to reveal the original air. It appears twice among the gittern and cittern pieces at the end of the Mulliner Book (see *The Mulliner Book: A Commentary,* by Denis Stevens, 1952, Appendix, Nos. 3 and 7).[2]

Other manuscripts containing the tune include the William Ballet Lute Book, pp. 86–87, the Thomas Dallis Lute Book, p. 3, and the Marsh Lute Book, p. 360. In the Lord Middleton Lute MS (called also the Francis Willoughby Lute Book), the tune appears no less than five times in arrangements for lute (fols. 83ᵛ, 84ᵛ, 85) and cittern (fols. 87ᵛ, 90).

[1] A large number of instrumental arrangements are cited in *The Dublin Virginal Manuscript,* ed. John Ward, 1954, p. 54. Azzaiuolo's song has been reprinted by Oscar Chilesotti, "Jacomo Gorzanis, Liutista del Cinquecento," *Rivista Musicale Italiana,* XXI (1914), 90–91; the melody alone is in Ward, p. 55, with the first stanza of the *Handefull* ballad cited below. Chilesotti notes that when Duke William V of Bavaria married in 1568, Orlando di Lasso sang "Chi passa" to his own lute accompaniment.

[2] Stevens renders the title of No. 7 as "[Cin]quepasse."

Keyboard arrangements include an untitled piece at the end of the Dallis MS (reprinted in *Dublin Virginal Manuscript,* No. 30); and William Byrd's "Qui passe: for my Ladye Nevel" in *My Lady Nevells Booke,* ed. Hilda Andrews, 1926, no. 2, found as "Kapasse" in Will Forster's MS Virginal Book, No. 9 (in Byrd's *Collected Works,* ed. Fellowes, 1937–1950, XVIII, 69). Seventeenth-century settings are in Cambridge University MS Dd.3.18, fol. 7ᵛ (lute) and MS Dd.4.23, fol. 31 (cittern). In addition to the many Continental examples cited by Ward, mention may be made of the version of c. 1600 called "Gailliarde Chi passa per questa strada" in *Het Luitboek van Thysius,* No. 131 (Fig. 65).

65

At least two Elizabethan ballads call for the tune. William Elderton's "A proper newe Ballad sheweing that philosophers learnynges are full of good warnynges," licensed in 1568–1569, beginning "Philosophers learnings are ful of good warnings,/In memorye yet left to scoole vs," is to the tune of "my Lorde Marques Galyarde, or the firste traces of Que passa" (BM Huth; reprinted in *A Collection of Seventy-Nine Black-Letter Ballads,* 1867, p. 138). "A Sonet of two faithfull Louers, exhorting one another to be constant," beginning "The famous Prince of Macedon,/whose wars increst his worthy name," is to "Kypascie"; it was probably published as a broadside before being gathered into *A Handefull of Pleasant Delites,* 1584 (ed. Rollins, p. 53). Although the ballads differ markedly in stanza pattern, the tune is flexible enough to accommodate either. In each the first strain is sung twice; the *Handefull* ballad then moves to the second strain, whereas the Elderton text, as the tune direction indicates, continues to repeat the first phrase with its embellishment.

The Children in the Wood,
or Now Ponder Well

The old ballad of two children abandoned to die in the wood was licensed in 1595, and the Stationers' Register entry reproduces the common form of the title as it appears in seventeenth-century editions: "The Norfolk gent his will and Testament and howe he Commytted the keepinge of his Children to his owne brother whoe delte moste wickedly with them and howe God plagued him for it" (Rollins, *Anal. Index,* No. 1962; a reissue was licensed in 1675—No. 1963). The ballad, which begins "Now ponder well you parents deare," is in the Pepys, Bagford, Lord Crawford, Douce, Euing, Harvard, Manchester, Wood, and Roxburghe collections, reprinted in *A Collection of Old Ballads,* 1723–1725, I, 222, in Percy's *Reliques,* and in *RB* II, 216. Broadside issues continued to appear in the eighteenth and nineteenth centuries, along with chapbook and slip-song texts. Ten New England editions suggest the American popularity.[1] Addison's admiration for the ballad (*Spectator,* No. 85) is too well known to require quotation. The pretty detail of a robin's covering the children's bodies with leaves is echoed, or at least paralleled, in the mad Cornelia's song, "Call for the robin redbreast and the wren" (Webster, *The White Devil,* V, iv), and in "I am no Robbin-red-breast to bring strawes/To cover such a coarse" (Dekker, *The Wonder of a Kingdom,* III, i). The robin motif is central in "Babes in the Woods," beginning "Oh don't you remember (*or* My dear, do you know), a long time ago," a brief derivative of "The Children in the Wood" probably dating from the early nineteenth century.[2]

[1] See Worthington C. Ford, *Broadside Ballads . . . Printed in Massachusetts, 1639–1800,* 1922, Nos. 3014–3022a. G. Malcolm Laws, *American Balladry from British Broadsides,* 1957, Q 34, lists late British texts, together with a few American traditional survivals clearly founded on broadsides.

[2] For references to traditional survivals of "Babes in the Woods," see Margaret Dean-Smith, *A Guide to English Folk Song Collections,* 1954, p. 51, and *The Frank C. Brown Collection of North Carolina Folklore,* 1952–1964, II, 388.

Most seventeenth-century broadside copies contain the tune direction "Rogero," q.v., and it is possible that this air is intended for a ballad of 1663 by C. H., "The Divils cruelty to Mankind," beginning "Good Christian People lend an Eare," which is directed to be sung "To the Tune of The Two Children in the Wood" (Wood 401; reprinted in *PA*, p. 122).

The air most commonly associated with our ballad is usually called "Now ponder well," from the opening line of "The Norfolk Gentleman." It was called for in nineteen ballad operas, including the following in which the music is printed: Gay's *The Beggar's Opera*, 1728, Act I, Air 12 (Fig. 66), Chetwood's *The Generous Free-Mason*, 1731, *The*

66

Jovial Crew, 1731, Coffey's *The Devil to Pay*, 1732, and Fielding's *An Old Man taught Wisdom*, 1735. The tune is called "The Children in the Wood" in Mottley and Cooke's *Penelope*, 1728, where it is used for a parody of "Chevy Chase." This air can be traced to an untitled *alla breve* form in *Pills*, 1719–1720, V, 1, where it is coupled with a reprint of Sir John Birkenhead's ballad "The Four-Legg'd Elder." [3] A variant tune combining features of "Now ponder well" and "Chevy Chase" is used in *Pills* V, 49, for "The most Famous Ballad Of King Henry the 5th; his Victory over the French at Agencourt," which is usually directed to be sung to "Flying Fame" (*PB* I, 8).

The music of "Now ponder well" appears on engraved single-sheet editions of "A new song of old similies. to ye tune of Chevy Chace or ye Children in the Wood by Dean Swift" (Harvard). The poem, which is more probably by John Gay, begins "My passion is as mustard strong,/ I sit all sober sad." Another Harvard edition with music lists only the first tune title; and still a third version (BM G.310 [91]) is without tune

[3] It appeared in the 1707 and 1712 editions of volume III, and may have been in the first edition of that volume, 1702, of which no copies are known. Broadside editions of the ballad direct it to be sung to "The Lady's fall" (Lord Crawford 23; another edition, "Printed in . . . 1647. And Reprinted 1677," Lord Crawford 24, Bagford III, 57, and Harvard, is to "The Lady's Fall, or Gather your Rose-buds; and Fourty other Tunes"; the text reprinted in *The Rump*, 1660, p. 1, names the same pair "and 50 other Tunes"). For further discussion of text and tune, see "In peascod time."

title but contains the same music.[4] In Watts's *Musical Miscellany*, 1729–1731, IV, 81, *The Merry Musician*, c. 1731, III, 153, and *The Convivial Songster*, c. 1782, p. 46, the music to this song is "Now ponder well," though untitled; and in such poetical anthologies as *A Complete Collection of . . . English and Scotch Songs*, 1735–1736, II, 124, and *The Merry Companion*, 2d ed., 1742, p. 315, the tune direction is "Children in the Wood." Ritson reprints the piece in his *English Songs*, 1783, and the "Now ponder well" music in volume III bears the title "Babes in the wood."

According to Chappell, the tune of "Now ponder well" can be found on "Chevy Chase" broadsides. I have encountered no examples, but there is indirect evidence to link text and tune in the eighteenth century. A late eighteenth-century song sheet, containing "Now ponder well" music and beginning "John Bull we know/Did long ago/Do many noble things," has the title: "The Metamorphosis of John Bull and his M[ini]st[e]rs or the Manoeuvres of the Grand Fleet. To the Warlike Tune of Three Children Sliding on the Ice" (Harvard, BM G.309 [86], California). This tune title derives from a seventeenth-century ballad entitled "The lamentation of a bad Market" (*PB* III, 58), which the broadside copy directs to be sung to "The Ladies Fall," but the text in *Pills* IV, 1, is to "Chivy-Chase," with the music. Earlier texts, without tune indications, are found in *The Loves of Hero and Leander*, 1651, and *Merry Drollery*, 1661. These relationships permit us to infer that in the eighteenth century "Three Children Sliding on the Ice" was sung to "Now ponder well"; it may also be sung satisfactorily to "The Ladies Fall" or "Chivy-Chase." The three tunes, while interchangeable, may more plausibly reflect preferences shifting from one generation to another.

Chloris, Full of Harmless Thoughts

The ballad giving rise to this tune title was sung to at least three airs. The original broadside (deriving from a miscellany poem by the Earl of Rochester in *The Last and Best Edition of New Songs*, 1677, beginning "While Chloe . . .") is "Corydon and Cloris Or, The Wanton Sheepherdess" [sic], to the tune of "Amorett and Phillis," q.v., and be-

[4] The BM *Catalogue of Printed Music* II, 182, erroneously identifies the tune as "Rogero."

gins "As Cloris full of harmless Thought/Beneath the Willows lay" (Douce, with additional tune direction in MS: "or Hye boys up go we"; Roxburghe, reprinted in *RB* VI, 134). The music of "Amoret and Phyllis" by Staggins is entitled "when Clori full of" in *Youth's Delight on the Flagelet*, 9th ed., c. 1690, suggesting that the association of ballad and tune had generated a new tune title. Rochester's poem was set by James Hart in John Banister and Thomas Low's *New Ayres and Dialogues*, 1678, p. 14 (Fig. 67), and in John Playford's *Choice Ayres & Songs*,

67

Second Book, 1679, beginning "While Chloe . . ." And a third tune, anonymous, is on a single-sheet edition of the song, c. 1700, beginning "As Cloris . . ." (BM H.1601 [13], Huntington). This latter combination of tune and text, entitled "The Lucky Minute," appeared in *The Merry Musician*, c. 1729, II, 73, and in Watts's *Musical Miscellany*, 1729–1731, I, 146, and continued in vogue as late as *The Convivial Songster*, c. 1782, p. 89. The anonymous tune is found in three ballad operas: Coffey's *The Beggar's Wedding*, 1729, Johnson's *The Village Opera*, 1729, and its condensation by Phillips, *The Chamber-maid*, 1730; it is cited in *The Country-Wedding*, 1749, without the music. In the absence of evidence to establish the currency of the anonymous tune before 1700, it must be supposed that the Staggins or Hart music was used with ballads, which are all black-letter editions of the late seventeenth century.

The tune is called "Ah Cloris . . ." in "The Dying Shepherdess," which begins "Alas my youthful Coridon" (Pepys III, 380). Other ballads cite several alternate tunes: "The Amorous Petitioner," beginning "As I did lately walk abroad," to the tune of "Cloris full of harmless thought, Young Phaon, Busie Fame, or the Lanthorn Horns grow dimm" (Pepys

III, 109); "Celinda's last Gasp: or Her Farewel to False Coridon," beginning "Attend true Lovers and give ear," to the tune of "Young Phoeon, Busie Fame: Or, Cloris full of Harmless thoughts" (Lord Crawford, Harvard, Roxburghe; reprinted in *RB* III, 488); and "Loyal Constancy; Or, The Seamans Love-Letter," beginning "Till from Leghorn I do return," to the tune of "Cloris full of harmless thoughts; Jenny Gin. The fair one let me in" (Lord Crawford, Pepys, Harvard, Bodleian Don.b.13, Roxburghe; reprinted in *RB* VII, 542).[1] With the exception of "the Lanthorn Horns grow dimn," on which I have no data, the tunes cited in these ballads are all well known and are actually interchangeable, since they all accommodate an eight-line ballad-meter stanza.

Chloris, Since Thou Art Fled Away

This tune title takes its origin from an early seventeenth-century pastoral song by Sir Robert Aytoun (*Poems,* ed. Charles Roger, 1844, pp. 62–63) which appeared anonymously in 1656 in *Sportive Wit* and *Choyce Drollery.* The former contains five stanzas and an "Answer" of equal length; the latter contains six stanzas but no Answer. Bodleian MS Ashmole 38, p. 238, contains both an English and a Latin version of five stanzas each, in a seventeenth-century hand. Henry Lawes set the poem in his *Ayres, and Dialogues,* Third Book, 1658, p. 10 (Fig. 68), where the poem is credited to Dr. Henry Hughes. Other printed versions of words and music are in *Musick's Delight on the Cithren,* 1666, and in all editions of *Pills,* 1719–1720, III, 154. A good musical text, closely following Lawes, is preserved in John Gamble's MS Commonplace Book, 1659, No. 194; the version in Edinburgh University Library MS Dc.1.69, p. 162, c. 1650–1675, preserves the melodic contours but not without serious distortion of note values.

No expanded broadside version of Aytoun's verses seems to have survived. But the first line became a tune title for a very popular ballad, "The New Courtier," beginning "Upon the Change where Merchants meet" (Wood E.25, Pepys, Lord Crawford, Douce, Rawlinson, Euing, Harvard, Roxburghe; reprinted in *RB* VII, 266). This ballad must have been in circulation during the 1660s, for it was reprinted in *The New Academy of Complements,* 1669, 1671, whence Ritson secured his ver-

1 The latter ballad is accompanied by an answer on the same sheet: "Vertue the Reward of Constancy," beginning "My dear to thee I'le surely be," "To the same Tune."

sion for *Ancient Songs,* 1790. The stanza pattern is distinctive, comprising three iambic tetrameter couplets plus a three-syllable burden which is "Well-a-day" in Aytoun's poem and "Have at all" in "The New Courtier."

This latter tag is presumably the origin of the tune title used for a song in one of Thomas Jordan's annual pageants, *London Triumphant,* 1672, beginning "Oh! who would fix his Eyes upon/These fading Joyes under the Sun?" to the tune of "Have at all," and with a burden "Touch and go." "Have at all" is named also as the tune for a ballad which in Wood's copy bears the MS date of 1678: "The Popes Great Year of Iubilee," beginning "Let me extol (these fickle times,)/The Church of Rome in ballad rimes" (Wood 416, Rawlinson, Roxburghe; reprinted in *RB* IV, 118). Here the stanza pattern is the customary six octosyllabics plus "Come all away, come all away," a burden which cannot be accommodated to Lawes's tune. A similar difficulty occurs in "Devol's Last Farewel," beginning "You bold undaunted Souls attend" (Euing, Bagford; reprinted in *BB* I, 14), where a double "Well-a-day" refrain lies outside the six-line stanza; the tune name, "Upon the Change," seems to be drawn from the opening line of "The New Courtier," cited above.

The Clean Contrary Way

This tune is preserved in a lyra-viol setting of the mid-seventeenth century in Cambridge University MS Dd.6.48, fol. 17ᵛ (Fig. 69). The

69

Original an octave lower and unbarred.

only piece I have found which seems to have been written for the music is "A New Presbyterian Ballad To the old Tune of, The clean contrary way," 1681, beginning "[Ala]ce poor Whiggs, our Senat's gone" (Roxburghe; reprinted in *RB* V, 61; roman-letter issues of the same year are in Bodleian Ashmole G.16 [98], Huntington, Harvard). The eight-line ballad-meter stanza with its burden "The clean contrary way" is paralleled in several ballads with the same burden but designated to be sung to "Hey, boys, up go we," q.v.

"The clean contrary way" is also named as an alternative tune to "Whoop! do me no harm" in a ballad with a different stanza pattern. The discussion of the latter tune contains references to other ballads intended for a setting—not known to us—of "The clean contrary way" which would be metrically interchangeable with "Whoop! do me no harm."

A still different metrical scheme is used in "Halfe a dozen of good Wives. All for a penny," a ballad licensed in 1634, beginning "If any standers by/that leads a single life" (Roxburghe; reprinted in *RB* I, 451).

This tune is distinctly related to "Gilderoy," q.v., and to such traditional airs as "Dives and Lazarus" and "Come all ye faithful Christians."

[The Clear Cavalier]

"On Loyalty in the Cavaliers" appeared in *Westminster Drollery*, 1672, II, 48, and as "The Cavaliers Song" is preserved in *Wit and Mirth*, 1682, and (with the music) in all editions of *Pills*, 1719–1720, III, 128. Eighteenth-century versions, with slightly variant texts, may be found in the suspect *Posthumous Works* of Samuel Butler, 1715–1717, in *Loyal Songs*, 1731, and *The Aviary*, c. 1750.

A ballad version of the poem, somewhat altered to fit the circumstances of William III's reign, appeared about 1690. Entitled "The Old Cavalier," it begins "He that is a clear/Cavalier/will not repine" (Lord Crawford, Harvard, BM C.39.k.6, Pepys; reprinted in *OPB*, p. 53, and *PB* V, 305). The ballad sheets direct "To an Excellent New Tune" and

contain music, which is actually Akeroyde's setting of "Sabina in the dead of night," and by no means adapted to the complex stanza pattern of the ballad. Music as found in *Pills* is less correctly printed than that in Colley Cibber's ballad opera, *Love in a Riddle,* 1729, Act I, Air 2, with words beginning "He that wears a Heart/Void of Art" (Fig. 70).[1]

In Shadwell's *Epsom-Wells,* 1673, V, i, Bisket wants those present to sing *"Hey for Cavaliers, ho for Cavaliers, Dub, a dub, dub, have at old Belzebub, Oliver stinks for fear,"* echoing the *Westminster Drollery* text. And in the opening chapter of Scott's *Peveril of the Peak,* Sir Geoffrey Peveril greets the Restoration with an "elegant effusion of loyal enthusiasm" consisting of several lines from the ballad.

The Cloak

This tune is named, in a ballad of c. 1688, "The Voice of Fame: Or, The Taylor's Glory," beginning "Of all the Professions that ever were nam'd" (Pepys; reprinted in *PB* III, 312). The broadside is without music, but Thomas Jordan's pageant of 1680, *London's Glory,* p. 12, contains his song from which the ballad derives, together with an anonymous tune (Fig. 71). It may or may not be "The Cloak," but the music fits the ten-line stanza form of poem and ballad.[1] A further possibility, however, is that the tune title "The Cloak" derives from "The Ballad of the Cloak: Or, The Cloaks Knavery," which is sung to the tune of "From Hunger and Cold, or Packington's Pound," qq.v. This familiar broadside is in stanzas of eight anapestic tetrameters or the equivalent, whereas the Jordan stanza is two lines longer; but a number of "Packington's Pound" ballads also are in this longer stanza form, requiring a repetition of the final four bars of the music.[2] Such a treatment would

---

[1] Chappell (*PMOT* II, 448) cites earlier occurrences of the tune in John Banister's MS Division Violin, in a MS "once the property of Charles Morgan, of Magdalen College" dated 1682, and in *Apollo's Banquet.* The tune is not in editions of the latter which I have seen; the manuscripts have eluded me.

---

[1] Both versions contain seven stanzas. In Jordan's poem, written during the reign of Charles II, the final stanza begins "Nine Kings of the brave Merchant-Taylers are free," which the ballad alters to "Ten . . . ," thus dating the broadside within the reign of James II.

[2] No ballads in swollen ten-line stanzas call for "From Hunger and Cold," perhaps because the final phrase of the tune, repeating the phrase preceding it, does not lend itself to further echo. This tune has therefore been left out of account in the speculation over "The Cloak."

71 G3

allow the Jordan poem or the ballad to be sung to "Packington's Pound," in which case "The Cloak" could be considered but another name for "Packington's Pound" music. It is not unusual for ballads to be sung to either a popular or a contemporary composed tune.

Cock Up Thy Beaver

One of D'Urfey's popular successes was "The Horse-Race; a Song made and sung to the King at Newmarket," beginning "To Horse, brave Boys of Newmarket, to Horse," and "Set to an excellent Scotch Tune, called, Cock up thy Beaver."[1] It was first published, with its music (Fig. 72), in D'Urfey's *Choice New Songs*, 1684, p. 3 (facsimile in C. L. Day, *The Songs of Thomas D'Urfey*, 1933, pp. 60–62). It appears in all editions of *Pills*, and was issued as a single-sheet song, c. 1720. The

[1] The tune evidently takes its name from the closing line of a refrain, "Hey, brave Johnie lad, cock up your beaver," associated with a song touched up by Burns in Johnson's *Scots Musical Museum* IV, 319, where it appears with the melody D'Urfey used. The text itself must be much older, but I have not traced it beyond Herd's *Scottish Songs*, 1776.

tune, usually called "Johnny, cock thy Beaver," is in *The Division Violin*, 1685, *The Dancing Master,* 7th ed., 1686, in Walsh's *Compleat Country Dancing-Master,* 1718, and Thompson's *Compleat Collection of 200 Favourite Country Dances,* II, c. 1764. In *Youth's Delight on the Flagelet,* 9th ed., c. 1690, it is called "The Horse Race," and in Johnson's *The Village Opera,* 1729, the title is "To Horse, to Newmarket." The one other ballad opera using the tune is Mitchell's *The Highland Fair,* 1731, in which it is called "Johny, Lad, cock up your Beaver." As an untitled air it appears in Kane O'Hara's comic opera *Midas,* 1764.

"The Call to the Races At New-Market" was a broadside expansion of D'Urfey's song, published 1685–1688 when Richard Pocock was licenser, and directed to be sung to the tune "To Horse brave Boys," which is clearly another name for "Cock up thy Beaver" (Lord Crawford

1192, BM C.22.f.6 [91], a black-letter edition; a roman-letter issue of c. 1700 is in the Bagford collection, reprinted in *BB* I, 80).

The tune of "Hooly and Fairly" in Johnson's *Scots Musical Museum* II, 199, bears some resemblance to "Cock up thy Beaver," but the kinship is exaggerated in the comments of James C. Dick, *Notes on Scottish Song by Robert Burns*, 1908, p. 98. The tune had appeared earlier in William McGibbon's *Scots Tunes*, Fourth Book, c. 1770.

Come, Boys, Fill Us a Bumper

"A Drinking Catch" beginning "Come Boys fill up a Bumper" appears, with the music, in Matthew Taubman's *An Heroick Poem . . . with Some choice Songs*, 1682, p. 8 (Fig. 73). The words alone had been

73

Original incorrectly barred 6/4, without time signature.

published in *A Choice Compendium*, 1681, and Henry Bold added a Latin version of the two-stanza text in his *Latine Songs, with their English*, 1685. The music, whose harmonic pattern does not permit it to be a catch, is in *Musicks Recreation on the Viol, Lyra-way*, 1682, in Thomas Greeting's *The Pleasant Companion . . . for the Flagelet*, 1683, and in *Apollo's Banquet*, 5th ed., 1687.

A ballad version of the poem probably dates from the early 1680s. It is "The Courtiers Health; Or The merry Boyes of the Times," beginning "Come boyes fill us a Bumper,/we'l make the Nation Roare," to "a new Tune, Come Boyes fill us a Bumper, Or, My Lodging is on the Cold ground" (Lord Crawford, Harvard, Roxburghe [three copies]; reprinted in *RB* III, 631, and again at V, 90). At least two other ballads were written to the tune: "Islington Wells a Song Of all the Virtues of those old Waters," dated 1684 and beginning "London Lasses make ready,/Repair for Islington" (BM C.20.f.2 [167]); and one from early 1689, "The Royal Health," beginning "Come Boys cast away sorrow" (Pepys; reprinted in *PB* IV, 177). Musical notation on the latter broadside comprises eight bars of "Lilliburlero" plus several bars of garbled musical characters. "Lilliburlero," of course, does not fit this ballad; the tune title named on the broadside is "Come, Boys, Fill up a Bumper," and to this the ballad can be sung.

Come Hither, My Own Sweet Duck, or Hey, Ho, My Honey

These two tune titles appear to derive from the first line and refrain of a song, "The insatiate Lover," which was printed in *Merry Drollery*, 1661, II, 106, though it must have been known before the Restoration. It begins "Come hither my own sweet duck/And sit upon my knee" and has as its refrain:

> With hey ho my honey,
> My heart shall never rue,
> For I have been spending money
> And amongst the jovial Crew.

No tune direction is cited for the song.[1]

Late in 1659 appeared "A proper new Ballad on the Old Parliament. Or, the second part of Knave out of Doores," beginning "Good morrow my Neighbours all, What news is this I heard tell?" and citing as its tune title the lines that form the refrain of an unidentified ballad (here an imitative refrain text that varies with each stanza):

> Hei ho my honey, my heart shall never rue,
> Four and twenty [now] for your mony, and yet a
> hard pennyworth too.

[1] Reprinted by J. W. Ebsworth in his *Choyce Drollery*, 1876. A parody of this song, beginning "Mine own sweet honey bird," also in *Merry Drollery*, is among those "reserved" for a supplement which Ebsworth separated from the body of his reprint.

(Wood 416, with MS date Oct. 1659; Harvard, with MS date November 10, 1659; BM Thomason, with MS date November 11, 1659; BM Luttrell, Bagford, Lord Crawford; reprinted in *The Rump*, 1660, in *Loyal Songs*, 1731, in Wright, *Political Ballads*, 1841, and in Mackay, *Cavalier Songs*, 1863).

A ballad with MS date of September, 1660, is "Englands Object," a piece on Hugh Peters, "Sower of Sedition" (Wood 401; reprinted in *CP*, p. 486). Its tune title is "Come hither my own sweet Duck" and its refrain (varies) is:

> Then hey ho, Hugh Peters
>   cannot you find a Text,
> To please your fellow Brethren,
>   they are so highly vext.

This ballad establishes an association of the "Come hither" and the "Hey ho my honey" motifs prior to the issuance of *Merry Drollery*. Another ballad of approximately the same date is "The Valiant Seaman's Congratulation to . . . King Charls the second," beginning "Great Charles, your English Seamen," to the tune of "Let us drink and sing, and merrily troul the bowl. Or, The stormy winds do blow. Or, Hey Ho, my Hony" (Euing 368).[2]

Other ballads to "Hey ho my honey" are: "A Lecture for all Sects and Schismaticks to read," by I. P., beginning "What ayles the Anabaptists" and with an occasional refrain which begins "With hey ho base Quakers . . ." (Wood 401 [164]); "The West-Country Cheat upon Cheat, or No Jest like a true Jest," beginning "Brave West-Country blades come listen" (Pepys IV, 247, Wood E.25 [130]); and "A Caveat for Young Men. Or, The Bad Husband turn'd Thrifty," by John Wade, beginning "All you young Ranting Blades" (Pepys, Euing, Lord Crawford, Harvard. Roxburghe; reprinted in *RB* III, 518).

Among the sizable number of ballads to the tune of "Come hither my own sweet duck" are the following: "The Bad-Husbands Folly; or, Poverty made known," beginning "To all good fellows now" (BM C.22.f.6, Pepys, Roxburghe; reprinted in *RB* VI, 493); "Wit never ought, till it be bought; & then it is stark nought," beginning "Of all spendthrifts in this Land," to the tune of "The Bad Husband's Folly, or, Come hither my own sweet duck" (Pepys IV, 260); "The Yorkshire Maids Fairing," by T[homas] R[obins], beginning "As I abroad did walk" (Pepys III, 384); "The Royall Subjects Warning-Piece to all Traytors," also by Robins, beginning "Old England now rejoyce" (Euing 310); "Iockeys complaint for want of his Ienny," beginning "I have an awd

---

[2] I have not found the first tune; on the second, see "When the stormy winds do blow."

woman wed,/doth nothing but scold and rail" (Rawlinson 133), with stanzas often ending:

> Would my awd wife were dead,
> and Jenny were here again.

From the last line of this refrain is derived another name for the tune, as used in the ballad "What is that to you? Or, The Northern Lad, his Discription of a Northern Lasse," beginning "I heard a Northern Lad," to the tune of "Jenny were here again" (Rawlinson 102). This ballad, issued c. 1670, is an expanded version of a song beginning "Poor Jenny and I we toiled" in *The New Academy of Complements*, 1669, *A Jovial Garland*, c. 1670, and *Pills*, 1719–1720, V, 146.[3]

One further ballad to the tune "Come hither my own sweet duck" is "The Loyal Maids good Counsel to all her Fellow-Maids," beginning "Young Maidens I pray you be carefull" (BM C.22.f.6 [145], Harvard, Yale, Lord Crawford 1453, Douce I, 128ᵛ). These copies of the ballad were licensed by Richard Pocock and hence can be dated 1685–1688.

The tune "Hey ho my honey" appears in *The Dancing Master*, in the seventh (1686) and subsequent editions; it had been included earlier among the violin tunes at the end of the third edition, c. 1662, No. 32 (Fig. 74), and 1665, No. 16, as "A New Dance or Maheney" and was incorporated into *Apollo's Banquet*, 1670, under the title "Hey ho, my Love and my Honey." In the second volume of *The Dancing Master*, 3d ed., 1718, the tune is called "A poor Shepherd in Love." In Walsh's *Compleat Country Dancing-Master*, 1718, it is called "Hey ho, my Honey," but in the Second Book, 1719, it is "A poor Shepherd in Love." This new tune name evidently originated with a song "The Distress'd Shepherd," beginning "I am a poor Shepherd undone," the words fitted to "Hey ho my honey" music in *Pills*, 1714, V, 185, 1719–1720, VI, 284, and in *The Merry Musician*, 1716, I, 269. This song had a considerable vogue in the eighteenth century, in anthologies as well as on single sheets with the music. Under its new tune title "I am a poor Shepherd undone," the old "Hey ho my honey" air is used in Gay's *The Beggar's Opera* and is named in three other ballad operas printed without music: *The Wanton Jesuit*, 1731; *The Fox Uncas'd*, 1733; and *The Sturdy Beggars*, 1733.

[3] Stanzas 2–6 of the broadside correspond roughly to the song text. "What's that to you," beginning "My Jeany and I have toil'd," is a touched-up version of the song which Allan Ramsay prepared for his *Tea-Table Miscellany*, 1733, II, 170. (To it he assigned the tune "The glancing of her Apron," for which see "In January last.") The song continued in vogue through the later eighteenth century, appearing in *London Magazine*, July, 1774, as "sung by Mr. Vernon at Vauxhall," and in *Convivial Songster*, c. 1782. None of the eighteenth-century settings, including that in *Pills*, bear any relation to the "Hey ho my honey" music.

The usual stanza form for ballads and songs cited here is eight trimeters (6–8 syllables each) plus a refrain of four; this fits the "Hey ho my honey" music. An occasional ballad with the equivalent of twelve lines plus the refrain can be sung to the music with a repetition of the last strain. Some ballads are in an eight-line stanza without a refrain; they can be sung to the music only with the omission of the final strain. Music in *Pills* V, 146, for "Poor Jenny and I we toiled," bears no relation to that of "Hey ho my honey," but it fits the eight-line stanza form admirably.

Come Live With Me

and Be My Love

According to an allusion in C. T.'s *Laugh and lie downe: or, The worldes Folly*, 1605 (reprinted in *The Works of Cyril Tourneur*, ed. Allardyce Nicoll, 1930, p. 284), Marlowe's famous lyric was sung to the tune

"adew my Deere." If the air has survived, it is not known by that name.[1]
A tune entitled "Come live with me, and be my love" has, however, been
preserved among the lyra-viol lessons at the end of William Corkine's
Second Book of Ayres, 1612, sig. G2ᵛ (Fig. 75). Another version of this

75

Original an octave lower.

air, "lately discovered in a MS. as old as Shakespeare's time," was contributed by Sir John Hawkins to the Johnson-Steevens *Shakespeare,* 2d
ed., 1778, I, 298 (Fig. 76). The Hawkins tune, whose source has not been
discovered, was reprinted in Ritson's *English Songs,* 1783 (1813, III, 151)
and (inaccurately) in Chappell's *NEA,* No. 180; the air in *PMOT* I, 215,
does not quite reproduce either version. The music is suitable for singing tetrameter quatrains. Some of the ballads noted below which are
in six-line stanzas require a repetition of the second strain, or they may
be intended for a tune not now extant.

Marlowe's pastoral poem was printed in Shakespeare's *The Passionate
Pilgrim,* 1599, and *England's Helicon,* 1600; two years later a stanza of
it was sung in *The Merry Wives of Windsor,* III, i. Its continued vogue
can be judged from numerous reprints of the poem, frequent allusions
to it, and perhaps most significant, the many parodies written by poets
as diverse as Donne and C. Day Lewis.[2]

---

[1] A poem of the mid-sixteenth century, with refrain "Adew my dere adew," is in
BM MS Harl. 2252, fol. 140, printed in Ritson's *Ancient Songs.* The meter does
not accord with that of "Come live with me"; moreover, no tune accompanies the
poem.

[2] For further information on the poem and some of its imitations, see R. S.
Forsythe, "*The Passionate Shepherd;* and English Poetry," *PMLA,* XL (1925), 692–
742; Sir Nicholas Harris Nicolas's notes in his edition of Walton's *The Complete
Angler,* 1836, I, 118ff.; and *England's Helicon,* ed. H. E. Rollins, 1935, II, 186ff.

76

Original a fourth higher.

Marlowe's poem and a reply which Izaak Walton attributed to Raleigh are both contained on a broadside entitled "A most excellent Ditty of the Louers promises to his beloued," with first line and tune title "Liue with me and be my Loue" (Roxburghe; reprinted in *RB* II, 3). In this version lines 3–4 of each stanza are repeated to make a six-line pattern. Another ballad with a six-line stanza and the same tune title is "A most sorrowfull Song . . . of Banister, who betraied the Duke of Buckingham," beginning "If euer wight had cause to rue" (Pepys; reprinted in *PB* II, 134; the ballad was first issued in 1600, but Rollins dates the Pepys copy c. 1630). One of the most popular ballads to the tune "Live with me" is "The woful Lamentation of Mistris Jane Shore," beginning "If Rosamond that was so fair," with a stanza of four lines plus a burden of two (Pepys, Manchester, Wood 401, Euing [two editions], Bagford [two editions], Douce, Morgan, Harvard [several late editions], Roxburghe [three editions]; reprinted in *A Collection of Old Ballads*, 1723–1725, I, 148, in *A Complete Collection of . . . English and Scotch Songs*, 1735–1736, IV, 80, in Percy's *Reliques,* and in *RB* I, 483).

The ballad on Jane Shore was influential enough to produce new names for the tune. It is called "Shore's wife" in "The lamentation of Henrye Adlington," beginning "Oh gratious god, looke downe vpon/the wicked deeds that I haue done" (*SB,* p. 106), and in "The Life and death of the great Duke of Buckingham," beginning "A tale of grief I must unfold" (Richard Johnson, *Crown Garland of Golden Roses,* 1612, ed. Chappell, 1842; eighteenth-century broadside versions are in Harvard [Percy Coll. II, 52], Chetham 3048, and Madden II, 505; reprinted in *A Collection of Old Ballads* III, 43). The tune is called

"Shore's wiue's Lamentation" in "A warning for all Souldiers . . . lamentation of William Wrench . . . executed [for desertion] . . . 1600," beginning "With hart opprest with griefe and care" (*SB,* p. 200). "Jane Shore" is the tune name given in "The Age and Life of Man," by B. Fancy, beginning "As I was wandring all alone" (Pepys II, 32, Euing 11, Douce I, 3); and it is written in as an alternate tune to "Banstead Downs" on both copies of "The Sea-Martyrs; Or, The Seamen's sad Lamentation for their Faithful Service, Bad Pay, and Cruel Usage," beginning "Good People, do but lend an Ear" (Harvard, Pepys; reprinted in *PB* VI, 10). The instability of stanza pattern is seen in the fact that the five ballads cited here are written in units of six, four, four, ten, and six lines respectively. The ten-line stanza can be accounted for and perhaps adjusted to the music, for it is in eight lines plus a two-line burden; if the tune be sung twice for the stanza proper and the second strain repeated yet again for the burden, our known melody will serve.[3]

Other ballads to the tune of "Come live with me" include Deloney's "The Imprisonment of Queene Elenor, wife to King Henrie the second," beginning "Thrice woe is me vnhappy Queene" (*Strange Histories,* 1602; *Works,* ed. Mann, pp. 397ff.), in a six-line stanza, with unmelodious and unbarred music which fits the words; and two ballads on unrequited love, either of which may be intended by Thackeray's listing "Hugh Hill and Sarah": "The dying teares of a trewe Lover forsaken, made upon his deathbed," beginning "Those gentle harts which trew loue craue" (*SB,* p. 120; later broadside copies in Pepys, Euing, Harvard, Manchester, Lord Crawford, Douce, Roxburghe; reprinted in *RB* IV, 420); and its sequel, "The repentant Songe of Sara Hill unto the maydes of W[o]rcester," beginning "Come, louely lasses, listen well" (*SB,* p. 212; *RB* IV, 422). Incongruously, the surname of both lovers is Hill. The tune title in Shirburn copies is "Liue with me and be my loue," whereas in later editions it is "Come live with me."

Among the parodies on Marlowe's poem, "The Wooing Rogue," beginning "Come live with me and be my Whore" (*Westminster Drollery,* 1671, I, 16), deserves notice because its seven-line stanza cannot be sung to the tune. The tune direction given is "My Freedom is all my Joy," which is equivalent to "I am a poor and harmless maid" (q.v.), a tune fitting this unusual stanza pattern.

[3] "The Ballad of Jane Shore" appears in only the 1714 edition of *Pills* V, 213; the eight-bar tune, which seems old, is marked for a repetition of bars 5–8, to fit a six-line stanza. It may well be the tune intended for all the ballads cited in the paragraph above.

[Come, Love, Let's Walk

Into the Spring]

Henry Youll's *Canzonets to Three Voices,* 1608, contains an anonymous poem of three stanzas beginning "Come, love, let's walk into the Spring," set to Youll's music (reprinted in *English Madrigal School,* ed. E. H. Fellowes, XXVIII, 5–20). A five-stanza text without tune direction or music is preserved in Harvard MS Eng. 628, p. 322 (first half of the seventeenth century). A 26–stanza expansion of the original poem was issued as a broadside of c. 1620: "The Lover's Delight: or, A pleasant Pastorall Sonnet. To a new Court Tune" (Roxburghe; reprinted in *RB,* I, 611).

Almost certainly the ballad was sung, not to Youll's madrigal set, but rather to a song tune associated with the original verses throughout the century. This simple anonymous tune is found, for example, with a four-stanza text in a part-book of the Scotsman Thomas Wode, now preserved in Dublin, Trinity College MS F.5.13, p. 66 (Fig. 77). Forbes's *Cantus,*

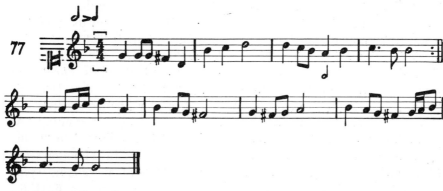

77

Original is unbarred.

Songs and Fancies, 1662, contains a version of the poem in three stanzas (five in the 1666 and 1682 editions), and, to the same tune, a spiritual parody beginning "Come, Lord, let's walk on Sion Hill" and a setting of "The thoughts of men do daily change." Further evidence of the Scotch popularity of this music is reflected by its presence in the Skene MS (Dauney, *Ancient Scottish Melodies,* 1838, No. 62), in Dr. John Leyden's MS Lyra Viol Book, and, with one stanza of text, in Louis de France's music book (known also as the Keith MS Book), c. 1680. For a composite musical score printed with the Forbes 1682 verses, and for references to other textual and musical sources, see *Music of Scotland, 1500–1700*, ed. Kenneth Elliott and Helena M. Shire (*Musica Britannica, XV*, 1957, No. 64). The tune seems to have been used for no other broadsides.

Come, Open the Door, Sweet Betty

A ballad licensed by Richard Pocock and so dating from the reign of James II is "John's Earnest Request: Or, Betty's compassionate Love extended to him in a time of Distress," beginning "Come open the Door sweet Betty,/for 'tis a cold Winters night," sung "To a Pleasant new Tune much in request" (Lord Crawford, Euing, Harvard, Pepys, Roxburghe; reprinted in *RB* VI, 202). There seems to have been no contemporary reprinting of this ballad or immediate re-use of its tune. But it was well enough known to be drawn upon in four ballad operas. The music is printed in Ryan's *The Cobler's Opera*, 1729, Air 30 (Fig. 78), Hippisley's *Flora*, 1729, Gay's *Achilles*, 1733, and Phillips's *The Livery Rake*, 1733. In the latter the tune is called "Fly, fly from the Place, fair Flora," from the first line of the song in Hippisley's ballad opera.[1]

A Scotch song, "Blink over the Burn, Sweet Betty," beginning "As gentle Turtle Doves,/By Cooing shew Desire," is not related to "Come open the Door, Sweet Betty." Words and music are in Thomson's *Orpheus Caledonius*, 1725, No. 15, in Watts's *Musical Miscellany*, 1729–1731, III, 65, and Walsh's *British Musical Miscellany*, 1734–1736, II, 66. Stanzas 3–5 are in Ramsay's *Tea-Table Miscellany*, 1723, p. 53, and in Johnson's *Scots Musical Museum*, 1787–1803, I, 52. But Burns, in his note on this Scotch song, recalls two stanzas of "old words," the first of which is clearly related to the English broadside:

[1] "Tom a Nokes Jigg" in *Apollo's Banquet*, 1670, No. 66, begins like the ballad-opera tune, but as Chappell has observed (*PMOT* II, 505), the jig has an underlying 9/4 rhythm while "Come, open the door" is in 6/4. Aside from a similarity in the opening bars, the two tunes are distinct.

78

Original is a fifth higher.

> Blink over the burn sweet Betty,
>> It is a cauld winter night;
> It rains, it hails, it thunders,
>> The moon she gies nae light:
> It's a' for the sake o' sweet Betty,
>> That ever I tint my way;
> Sweet, let me lie beyond thee
>> Until it be break o' day.
>
> O, Betty will bake my bread,
>> And Betty will brew my ale
> And Betty will be my love,
>> When I come over the dale:
> Blink over the burn, sweet Betty,
>> Blink over the burn to me,
> And while I hae life dear lassie,
>> My ain sweet Betty thou's be.[2]

Shakespeare's reference in *King Lear,* III, vi, to "Come o'er the bourn, Bessy, to me" alludes to a ballad of 1558 by William Birch, "A Songe betwene the Quenes maiestie and Englande" (London Society of Antiquaries, reprinted in *The Common Muse,* ed. V. de Sola Pinto and A. E. Rodway, 1957, p. 37). It bears no metrical relation to the later ballad or to the Scotch song.

[2] *Notes on Scottish Song by Robert Burns,* ed. James C. Dick, 1908, p. 18. G. F. Graham, in his *Songs of Scotland,* 1848–1850, III, 148, uses the old words recalled by Burns, altering a few details, and, to suit modern taste, changing "lie beyond" to "sit beside" in line 7. Graham's tune is the *Scots Musical Museum* air as arranged by T. M. Mudie.

Come, Shepherds, Deck
Your Heads

"The Shepheards Lamentation. To the tune of the plaine-dealing Woman," beginning "Come Shepheards, deck your heads," is a ballad published about 1615 (Pepys; reprinted in *PB* I, 85). The tune title is derived from the closing line of most stanzas in the first part of the ballad, but no music of "The Plain-Dealing Woman" has been found under that name. A seventeenth-century air (Fig. 79) with lute accompaniment is coupled with the first four ballad stanzas in MS 1019, fol. 2ᵛ, of St. Michael's College Library, Tenbury; the text varies in detail from that of Bodleian MS Ashmole 38, p. 127, and from others noted by Rollins in *PB* I, 83. Another tune, called "Com Shaepherders deck jour heds," is in Dirck P. Pers's Dutch songbook *Bellerophon,* beginning with the edition of 1633, p. 120 (Fig. 80). A different air under the same title—perhaps an inner part, not an independent melody—is found in J. J. Starter's *Friesche Lust-Hof,* 1621, p. 73 (Fig. 81), and in A. Valerius's *Neder-Landtsche Gedenck-Clanck,* 1626. Only this latter tune makes allowance for the repeated syllables in line 7 of many stanzas in the Pepys text.

"Come, Shepherds, deck your heads" is referred to in Walton's *Compleat Angler* as one of the ballads which Maudlin, the Milkwoman's

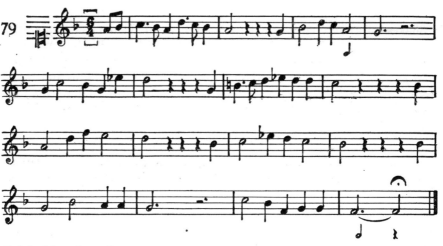

79

Original is unbarred.

80

Original is unbarred.

81

Original is unbarred.

daughter, can sing. None of the three tunes she might have used seems to have served for other ballads.

Come, Sweet Lass, or Greenwich Park

This tune, called "Greenwich Park," appeared first in *The Second Part of the Dancing Master,* 2d ed., 1698, p. 33 (Fig. 82),[1] and in the eleventh

1·*The Second Part of the Dancing Master,* 1st ed., 1696, is to be distinguished from the second *volume* of the work; there were only two editions of the second part, whereas there were four of volume II: the first undated, c. 1713, the others 1714, 1718, 1728.

82

and subsequent editions of the primary volume. The music is also found
under this title in Walsh's *Compleat Country Dancing-Master*, 1718. A
harpsichord setting by Jeremiah Clarke appears in BM MS Add. 22099,
fol. 6ᵛ, c. 1704–1707. Music is also found on a single-sheet song, Chetham
1381: "A Scotch Song Sung by Mrs. Cross at the Theatre Royal," beginning "Come sweet Lass, this bonny Weather, lets together." [2] As "Come
Sweet Lass" it is an air in Gay's *The Beggar's Opera*, 1728, and in *The
Fox Uncas'd*, 1733.

As the Chetham copy indicates, "Come Sweet Lass" began as a dramatic
song. Two broadside editions, probably from the 1690s, are in the Pepys
collection: "An Excellent New Scotch Song, Cald, Jockey's Complaint for
His Beloved Moggy . . . Lately Sung in a New Play at the Royal Theatre" (Pepys V, 263, with meaningless music and without tune direction);
and "Slighted Jockey: Or, Coy Moggy's Unspeakable Cruelty. Being An
excellent Scot[c]h Song much in Request. To a Pleasant new Tune"
(Pepys V, 274, reprinted in *A Collection of Old Ballads*, 1723–1725, I,
278). The former is in seven stanzas, three of which are "Moggy's Kind
Answer," and all but the two opening stanzas are in pseudo-Scotch dialect; the latter is in eight stanzas, plus an "Answer" of two stanzas, with
only slight suggestion of dialect.[3] Other versions of the text are usually
shorter: "Jockey's Love to Moggy" in *Wits Cabinet*, c. 1700, is in four
stanzas; the version in *Compleat Academy of Complements*, 1705, is the

2 The music is attributed to "Mr. Clarke." The engraved sheet is undated, but
Mrs. Cross was singing in London theaters in the 1690s. See Day-Murrie, Index IV.

3 Chappell (*PMOT* II, 600–601) reprinted this version, but without the "Answer."
He also eliminated the three occurrences of "I'se" to suppress the Scotch element
entirely and removed the sensuality from "Kiss and enjoy her still" by changing the
second verb to "delight." Ordinarily he used inverted commas to indicate textual
change, but they are wanting here.

same length, but stanzas three and four are in dialect and have no relation to those in *Wits Cabinet*. The version in *Pills*, 1719–1720, III, 217, includes only the first two stanzas—common to all the texts—with the music.

One other broadside was sung to the tune of "Come Sweet Lass." It is "Perjur'd Billy," beginning "In the West/A weeping Lover" (Pepys V, 275, a roman-letter edition published near 1700).

Cook Lorrel

This tune appears, under the name of "An Old Man is a Bed full of Bones," in all editions of *The Dancing Master* (1651, p. 76=Fig. 83).[1]

Original is unbarred.

As "Cook Lawrel" the music is found in *180 Loyal Songs*, 1685, p. 103, set to "A new Song made by a Person of Quality, and Sung before His Majesty at Winchester," beginning "A Tory came late through Westminster-Hall." With music (Fig. 84), this ballad had already appeared in

---

[1] This tune title is referred to in William Rowley's *Match at Midnight*, 1622, I, i; and a snatch, "An old man with a bed full of bones," is sung in James Shirley's *Constant Maid*, 1638, II, ii. There is a reference to "An old man's a bagge full of bones" in *The Partiall Law*, c. 1615–1630, II, iv. No extant ballads were sung to the

broadside form in 1683 (Harvard, three copies, BM 806.k.16, Yale, Clark; the text is reprinted in *RB* V, 335, apparently from *180 Loyal Songs*). The tune appears in all editions of *Pills*, and in the 1719–1720 edition it is printed three times: II, 98, IV, 101, IV, 110.

The sardonic song of Cook Lorrel's banquet for the Devil was written by Ben Jonson for his masque *The Gypsies Metamorphos'd*, 1621.[2] In expanded form it was popular on broadsides: "A Strange Banquet: Or, The Devil's Entertainment by Cook Laurel At The Peak in Derby-Shire," beginning "Cook Laurel would have the Devil his Guest" (Lord Crawford, Harvard, Euing, Rawlinson, Pepys, Roxburghe, BM C.20.f.2; reprinted in *RB* VII, 219). Manuscript versions are in Bodleian MS Rawlinson Poet. 160, fol. 175, Gamble MS, 1659, No. 92, and the Percy Folio. It was reprinted in *Merry Drollery*, 1661, *An Antidote against Melancholy*, 1661, *Merry Drollery Complete*, 1670, *New Academy of Complements*, 1671, *Wit and Mirth*, 1682, and, with the music, in all editions of *Pills*.

A large number of broadsides were sung to "Cook Lorrel," and only a partial listing can be given. Emphasis will be upon those ballads that give rise to other titles for the tune. An obvious parody on Jonson's poem is that by M[artin] P[arker], c. 1637, "A Bill of Fare: For, A Saturday nights Supper, A Sunday morning Breakfast, and A Munday Dinner," beginning "Ile tell you a Jest, which you'l hardly belaeue," to the tune of "Cooke Laurell, or Michaelmas Terme"[3] (Roxburghe; reprinted in *RB* I, 70). The generally unpleasant exploitation of mankind's foibles in Jonson's poem was heavily drawn upon in a number of pieces against the Rump Parliament. Most of them were issued as broadsides and afterward reprinted in *Ratts Rhimed to Death*, 1660, or *The Rump*, 1660, another ed. 1662, reprinted 1874. Characteristic titles are "A Proper New Ballad of the Devill's Arse a Peak, or Satan's Beastly place. Or, in plain tearms, of the Posteriors and Fag-end of a Long-Parliament"; "A New

tune under this name, unless we except one in a hand of c. 1700 in BM MS Harl. 6913, p. 59, which fits the music with difficulty. It begins "In a famous Street near Whetstones Park/Where there's commonly Fiddlers as soon as 'tis dark."

[2] Cook (*or* Cock) Lorrel was already famous as a rogue, and Cock Lorrel's boat, the subject of a tract printed by Wynkyn de Worde, c. 1510 (ed. E. F. Rimbault, Percy Society, 1843), was a ship of fools. S[amuel] R[owlands?], in his *Martin Mark-all*, 1610, speaks of him as "the most notorious knaue that euer liued. By trade he was a Tinker, often carrying a panne and a hammer for a shew: but when he came to a good booty, he would cast his profession in a ditch, and play the padder."

[3] "Michaelmas Terme" is a tune name derived from the title of a ballad licensed in 1633 (Rollins, *Anal. Index*, No. 1758) and sung to the tune of "The Rambling Clerk" (*BB* I, 401). Both Parker's ballad and "Michaelmas Term" are in eight-line stanzas, and the tunes may therefore be considered interchangeable. Music for "The Rambling Clerk" apparently has not survived.

Kickshaw for the queasie Stomack of Sathan and all those that fight under his Banner"; "The Rump Roughly but Righteously handled." [4]

Other ballads include "A pair of Prodigals Returned . . . a Conference between an Englishman and a Scot, concerning the Restauration of Charles II," beginning "Tush Jocchee, we have no more Kings to Betray" (BM Luttrell II, 157, BM Thomason 669.f.25 [52], both dated 1660); "The Dutch-Miller, and New Invented Wind-Miller . . . who undertakes to Grind all sorts of Women," beginning "I am a brave Miller but newly come o're" (Wood E.25 [53]). "I Father the Child that's none of my own," beginning "If every Woman was serv'd in her kind," is to the tune of "Cook Laurel: Or, Give me the Lass" (Lord Crawford, Douce, Harvard, Roxburghe; reprinted in *RB* VIII, 440; with music of "Cook Lorrel," in all editions of *Pills*). The second tune title is from the opening line of "The Country Miss new come in Fashion" (*RB* IV, 402) which is sung to "The Mock Tune to the French Rant," an air which apparently has not survived. "The Country Miss" itself became a tune title, appearing as an alternate to "Cook Lorrel" in "The Plow-mans Prophesie: Or, The Country-mans Calculation," beginning "Come listen all you that to mirth are inclin'd" (Pepys IV, 297, Rawlinson 120, Wood E.25 [81]). The same two airs are indicated by a still different combination of tune names in "The Merry Wives of Wapping," beginning "A knot of Women in Wapping do meet," to the tune of "The Country Miss: Or, The Plowmans Prophesie" (Wood E.25 [126]).

Another name for the tune "Cook Lorrel" is generated from the burden of "The Plow-mans Prophesie," which is "Then covetousness out of England will run." This phrase became the tune title for several ballads, having in common the idea that when the impossible happens, covetousness, or Popery, or some other comparable evil will vanish. These include "The Quakers Prophesie," beginning "Come all my kind Neighbours and listen awhile" (Lord Crawford, BM 1876.f.1; reprinted in *RB* VI, 6); "The Countryman's Prophecy," beginning "All you that strange Prophecies love for to hear" (Pepys; reprinted in *PB* IV, 68); "Good News for England, Or, The Worst is past," beginning "Come listen to me and I will declare," to the tune of "the Woody Querristers, or Covetuousness [sic] out of England shall run" (Pepys IV, 296, *temp.* Charles II); and "A New Ballad, called, The Protestants Prophesie," beginning "Come hearken to me whilst the truth I do write" (Wood E.25 [117], with MS date "Jan or Feb 1688"; Bagford; reprinted in *BB* I, 439). The title of this last ballad became the tune title used in "Wavering Nat and kind Susan," beginning "Come all you brave Sawyers and listen a while," to

[4] For full bibliographical details on songs in *The Rump*, see H. F. Brooks, "Rump Songs: an Index with Notes," *Oxford Bibliographical Society Proceedings & Papers*, V (1936–1939), 283–304.

the tune of "The Protestants Prophesie" (Roxburghe; reprinted in *RB* VIII, 471). The burden of "The Protestants Prophesie" is "Then Popery out of this land will be gone," and apparently it was upon the model of this ballad that "The Prophesie" was written. It has no tune direction, but its burden is "And Popery out of this Nation shall run"; it begins "When the K[ing] leaves of[f] S[al]ly, and holds to the Queen," and like the other prophecies just noticed, describes the Utopia that must exist before the present state of affairs can be reversed. It is found in *The Muses Farewel to Popery and Slavery,* Supplement, 1689.[5]

"The Painters Pastime: or, A Woman Defin'd after a New Fashion," beginning "Assist me Appolo [sic], and help my conceit," to the tune of "Cook Laurel, or, Sing Tidne Too" (Douce II, 173) is a ballad of the last quarter of the seventeenth century which fits the tune (I have no data on the second tune title). Chappell (*PMOT* I, 161) is inclined to equate "Cook Lorrel" with a sixteenth-century tune name, "The Painter," on the strength of the ballad title above; but the metrical patterns are entirely dissimilar.[6]

"Cook Lorrel" is sometimes cited for ballads whose meter ill fits the tune. Such are "A New Letany," beginning "From Jesuitical Polls, who proudly expose" (*A Third Collection of . . . Poems . . . against Popery,* 1689), and "A Short Letany," beginning "From an old Inquisition, and new Declaration" (*Fourth and Last Collection of Poems against Popery,* 1689; reprinted in *RB* IV, 297); the three long lines plus a burden "For ever good Lord (*or* Heaven) deliver me" comprise the usual litany form, but it is not easily adapted to the "Cook Lorrel" tune. Another, "The Ingenious Braggadocia," beginning "I Have a Mare her Colour is White,/ Sweet if thou love me tell me now" (Pepys, Lord Crawford, Harvard, Roxburghe; reprinted in *RB* VIII, 600), has a stanza of four lines which fit the tune without difficulty; but the burden, especially in its first two lines, seems to call for different musical movement:

[5] "The French Prophet. Or, A New Touch of the Times," beginning "I am an old Prophet, and newly come over," has no tune direction and is in an irregular eight-line stanza pattern. Ebsworth (*RB* VIII, 239) feels that it is related to the "Covetousness" ballads referred to above, but the similarity is chiefly in theme.

[6] "The Painter," for which no music has survived, probably took its name from "ye paynter in his pryntyshod," a ballad licensed in 1565–1566, followed shortly by moralizations and other related pieces, none of which are extant (Rollins, *Anal. Index,* Nos. 530, 2032–2035). A ballad entitled "The Louer compareth some subtile Suters to the Hunter," to the tune of "the Painter," is preserved in *A Handefull of Pleasant Delites,* 1584 (ed. Rollins, p. 33). Also to the tune is a song beginning "Stand backe, ye slepinge iackes at home" in John Pickering's *Horestes,* 1567 (*Quellen und Forschungen,* LXXX [1898], 517), and "A new song of an hostisse and her guests" in Richard Johnson's *Crown Garland of Golden Roses,* 1612 (ed. Chappell, 1842, p. 72). The stanza pattern of the three poems is syllabically 8.4.8.4.8.8.8.8, for which the "Cook Lorrel" tune will not serve.

With hey my Nanny, with ho my Nanny,
with hey my Nanny, my Nanny, Nanny;
The more I do look, the more I love thee,
thou art kinder then ever thou used to be.[7]

Could Man His Wish Obtain

A single stanza with this beginning is found in *A New Collection Of the Choicest Songs*, 1682. With music by James Paisible, a two-stanza

85

Original is an octave lower.

version appears in *Choice Ayres and Songs,* Fourth Book, 1683, and in all editions of *Pills*. Paisible's tune, entitled "Could Man his wish obtain," is in *Musicks Recreation on the Viol, Lyra-way,* 1682, p. 64 (Fig. 85), in

[7] Ebsworth (*RB* VIII, 600) is surely wrong in stating that "The true tune must have been an adaptation of 'Come hither, my own sweet Duck!'" Stanza pattern and rhythm are so disparate as to make any such musical affinity unlikely.

Thomas Greeting's *The Pleasant Companion . . . for the Flagelet,* 1683, Humphry Salter's *The Genteel Companion . . . for the Recorder,* 1683, *Apollo's Banquet,* 5th ed., 1687, and in Fitzwilliam Museum, Cambridge, MS 30.G.20, p. 55.

The song, lengthened into a broadside of six fourteen-line stanzas, is called "The Mournful Shepherd: Or Torment of Loving, and not being Lov'd again . . . Play'd and Sung at the King's Play-House . . . To a Pleasant New Tune, called Could Man his Wish Obtain" (Lord Crawford, Douce, Euing, Harvard, Pepys, Roxburghe; reprinted in *RB* VI, 62). No other broadsides seem to have been sung to Paisible's graceful but rather ornate music.

The Country Lass

Martin Parker's ballad, "The Countrey Lasse," beginning "Although I am a countrey lasse,/A lofty mind I beare-a" (Pepys, Roxburghe; reprinted in *RB* I, 165), was to be sung to "a dainty new note" or "The Mother beguiles the Daughter" (in the Roxburghe copy it is "The mother beguild daughter").[1] Laurence Price wrote "Good Ale for my money," beginning "Be merry, my friends, and list awhile," to the tune of "The Countrey Lasse" (Roxburghe; reprinted in *RB* I, 412), probably soon after the issuance of Parker's ballad. A cittern set of "Countrey Lasse" in *A Booke of New Lessons,* 1652, No. 15 (Fig. 86), may have no relation to these texts; it will, however, suit the stanza pattern once initial notes are added to first and last phrases to accommodate the iambic meter. I have elsewhere discussed these ballads (see "Stingo") in relation to the music of "Cold and Raw," to which a song echoing Parker's ballad is printed in *Pills,* 1719–1720, IV, 152. With differences in detail, the *Pills* text was adopted by Allan Ramsay, who included it in the second volume of his *Tea-Table Miscellany,* 1729, "To its ain Tune," but without music.

The air commonly associated with "What tho' I am a Country Lass"

---

[1] The ballad from which this tune title probably originated is lost, but "The father beguild his son" was entered in the Stationers' Register in June, 1629, and "The sonne beguils the Father" in July, 1630 (Rollins, *Anal. Index,* Nos. 872, 2480). A date of around 1630 can therefore be postulated for Parker's ballad. Chappell (*PMOT* I, 356) equated this tune title with "I have but a mark a year," but later (II, 780) presented evidence which in effect nullified the relationship he had earlier described. It is safest to say that we do not possess music to "The Mother beguiles the Daughter."

in the eighteenth century is found on engraved single sheets, as for example "The Country Lass: or the Lofty Shepherdess" (BM G.313 [81], dated 1725?; Harvard). With the same title it is in *The Merry Musician,* c. 1731, III, 9 (Fig. 87). The tune is used in seven ballad operas, includ-

* G in original.

ing Coffey's *The Devil to Pay,* 1731, and Potter's *The Decoy,* 1733, whose editions contain music. An imitation using the same tune is "The London Lass," beginning "What tho I am a London Dame/And lofty looks I bear a," in Walsh's *British Musical Miscellany,* 1734–1736, I, 94. "The Discontented Virgin," beginning "What tho' I am a Courtly Lass,/And handsome too as may be," is a parody appearing on a quarto broadside of 1727 without music or tune direction (BM 1871.e.9 [190]). Ramsay's *Tea-Table* text was included in William Thomson's *Orpheus Caledonius,* 2d ed., 1733, II, No. 38, and in Johnson's *Scots Musical Museum,* 1787–

1803, IV, 356, but the tunes, which differ from each other, are distinct from the familiar eighteenth-century air.[2]

Chappell declared (PMOT II, 646) that Henry Carey's "Sally in Our Alley," originally sung to Carey's own music, has, since about 1760, been coupled with the slightly older tune of "The Country Lass." [3] I find no such early record of the shift, but George Thomson's *Select Collection of Original Scottish Airs*, 1818, V, 230, contains Carey's words with the music of "The Country Lass," as harmonized by Beethoven.

The Court Lady

A tune called "Confesse" and "Confesse his Tune" in the first edition of *The Dancing Master*, 1651, p. 19 (Fig. 88), and "Confess, or the Court Lady" in the second through tenth editions, is very likely named for an early seventeenth-century dancing master "Mr. Confesse." [1] Whether its alternate title is to be associated with ballads calling for the tune of "The Court Lady" is dubious, for the second half of the tune demands octosyllabics instead of the alternating tetrameters and trimeters of ballad meter. It is more probable that some other tune is intended, for the citations noted below are separated from the dance tune by half a century or more, and the tune name is commonplace enough to be reinvented.

To "The Court Lady" is sung "The Unfortunate Concubine: Or, Rosamond's Overthrow. Occasion'd by her Brother's unadvisedly praising her Beauty to Two Young Knights of Salisbury, as they rid on the Road," beginning "Sweet youthful charming Ladies fair" (Harvard Percy

[2] The *Museum* tune served also for singing "Geordie" (IV, 357), a version of the traditional ballad (Child No. 209) which exists in a number of Scotch analogues. A loosely related English broadside, "The Life and Death of George of Oxford" (*RB* VII, 70, and Child No. 209, Appendix), calls for the tune "Poor Georgy," which has apparently not survived, unless in oral tradition. Almost all the American "Geordie" texts derive from the "George of Oxford" broadside. See the discussion in Tristram P. Coffin, *The British Traditional Ballad in North America*, rev. ed., 1963, pp. 124ff.

[3] R. G. Noyes, "The Contemporary Reception of 'Sally in Our Alley,'" *Harvard Studies and Notes in Philology and Literature*, XVIII (1935), 165–175, discusses the vogue of Carey's song. He observes that a basic similarity between the cadences of "The Country Lass" and Carey's tune led to confusion of the two; the older air is free from the florid ornamentation of Carey's tune and was thus easier to sing. While Noyes's explanation cannot be urged as a general principle of popular selection, it is very likely correct here.

[1] See Margaret Dean-Smith's annotations in her facsimile edition of *The English Dancing Master*, 1957, p. 19.

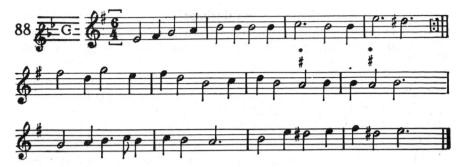

88

Original is a minor third higher and unbarred.
* Note is sharped in later editions.

collection, Douce, Roxburghe [without tune direction]; reprinted in *RB* VI, 676). Three different eighteenth-century editions are represented by these copies, though the subject matter is much older. The version reprinted in *A Collection of Old Ballads*, 1723–1725, I, 1, is probably derived from a contemporary Dicey print.

An untitled version of Deloney's ballad on the death of Rosamond, beginning "When as King Henry rul'd this land," has the tune title "Court Lady" in *A Complete Collection of . . . English and Scotch Songs*, 1735–1736, III, 143, though it is usually sung to "Flying Fame." In the same volume of this musicless collection, "Queen Eleanor's Confession," which on broadsides is directed "To a pleasant new Tune," is to "Court Lady." [2]

Courtiers, Courtiers,

Think It No Harm

"Courtiers, courtiers" evidently originated as a theatrical song. Although Day-Murrie list its source as Richard Brome's *The Jovial Crew*, 1652, it is not in that edition or the one of 1684. It may, however, have

[2] Chappell (*PMOT* I, 174) printed a traditional tune for "Queen Eleanor's Confession" which is substantially that published in William Motherwell's *Minstrelsy, Ancient and Modern*, 1827 (reprinted in John Goss, *Ballads of Britain*, 1937, p. 68) and in E. F. Rimbault's *Musical Illustrations of Percy's Reliques*, 1850. The air has no relation to "Court Lady."

been interpolated into performances during the 1680s, when it suddenly achieved popularity. The broadside version was called "The Beggars Delight, As it was Sung at the Theatre-Royal," and an edition with music is dated 1684 (Bodleian Ashmole G.15 [167], Clark); another, without music, is dated 1685 (Douce I, 18). Other seventeenth-century editions are in Pepys IV, 253, Harvard Dyson Perrins 49, Lord Crawford 293, Douce I, 16ᵛ, BM C.22.f.6 (85).

The broadside text is followed in every edition of *Pills*, 1719–1720, IV, 142, where the tune is somewhat corrupted by echoes of "Cold and Raw" in the first few measures. A single-sheet version of the ballad, "The Beggar's Dear Joy, Set for yᵉ German Flute," beginning "Courtiers, Courtiers think it no Scorn," is in the British Museum (G.316.h [21], dated 1730?) and in the Julian Marshall collection, Harvard (Fig. 89).

The tune appears as "The King of Poland" in *The Dancing Master*, 7th ed., 1686, and in *Apollo's Banquet*, 5th ed., 1687. It is called "Courtiers, Courtiers think it no harm" in Gay's *The Beggar's Opera*, 1728, and in an anonymous ballad opera, *The Judgment of Paris*, 1731.

The Cramp

William Elderton named "The Crampe" as the tune for "A newe ballad, entytuled, Lenton stuff,/for a lyttell munny ye maye have inowghe" beginning "Lenton stuff ys cum to the town" (Bodleian MS

Ashmole 48 [60]; reprinted in Thomas Wright, *Songs and Ballads . . .
Chiefly of the Reign of Philip and Mary*, 1860). The ballad was licensed
to William Pekering in 1569–1570, but Rollins believes that it must
first have appeared about 1562–1563; the Ashmole version he believes
was copied from the broadside now lost to us.[1]

The only extant tune that might be identified with "The Crampe" is
the air sung by the medius voice in "A Round of three Country dances
in one," Ravenscroft's *Pammelia*, 1609, No. 74 (Fig. 90). The words here

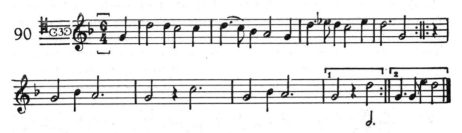

Original is an octave lower and unbarred.

are "The crampe is in my purse full sore," but it should be noted that
the second half of the tune, well adapted to the "Hey hoe the Crampe a"
refrain, does not fit the latter part of Elderton's complex seven-line
stanza. Moreover, the adaptation of a tune to the harmonic requirements
of a round does not guarantee a reliable musical text, as may be seen
by comparing the version of "Robin Hood, Robin Hood, said Little
John" in this round with other examples of the music. Elderton's ballad
was evidently intended to be sung to some other tune than the one we
possess.

Another Lenten piece sung to "The crampe," also licensed in 1569–
1570, is "A ballad from the countrie sent to showe how we should fast
this lent," by Thomas Preston. It begins "Prepare yourselves to fast this
lent" and is printed in *SB*, p. 347, from Bodleian MS Rawlinson Poet.
185, fol. 7ᵛ, where the copy is dated 1589. The seven-line stanza agrees
metrically with Elderton's, offering another bit of evidence that the surviving tune has little relation to the ballads here cited.

1 Hyder E. Rollins, "Concerning Bodleian MS. Ashmole 48," *MLN*, XXXIV (1919),
340–351.

The Cremona Fiddle

"A Ballad, Upon a Gentleman's sitting upon the Lady W[eymouth]'s Cremona Fiddle," dated 1720 and beginning "Ye Lads and ye Lasses that live at Longleat," is directed to be sung to "King John and the Abbot of Canterbury," a tune more commonly known as "Derry down" (Harvard Percy collection). Engraved single-sheet versions of c. 1730, usually titled "A Song made upon a Gentleman's sitting upon a Cremona Fiddle" (BM H.1601 [550], Harvard) or "The Long-leat Ballad" (Harvard), contain variant versions of "Derry down" music with its characteristic refrain. But "The Cremona Fiddle" in Watts's *Musical Miscellany,* 1729–1731, II, 162 (Fig. 91), *British Melody, or the Musical Maga-*

91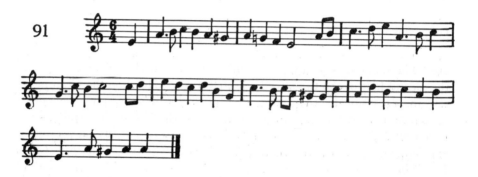

zine, 1739, No. 3, and *The Convivial Songster,* c. 1782, p. 40, has its own tune and naturally omits the "Derry down" refrain tags. The words are reprinted in *The Hive,* 3d ed., 1727, II, 262, without tune direction. The text in *A Complete Collection of . . . English and Scotch Songs,* 1735–1736, III, 113, is to the tune of "Cremona Fiddle," an ambiguous direction in the absence of music. Attribution of this humorous song to Jonathan Swift is now discounted; it does not appear in Harold Williams's edition of Swift's poems.

Crimson Velvet

This tune title takes its origin from a description of the princess's dress in "An excellent Ballad of a Prince of England's Courtship to the King of France's Daughter, and how the Prince was disasterously slain; and how the aforesaid Princess was afterwards married to a Forrester," beginning "In the Days of Old/when fair France did flourish," to the tune of "Crimson Velvet" (Lord Crawford, Wood 401, Wood 402, Wood 276b, Douce, Morgan, Pepys, Bagford, Euing, Roxburghe [two editions]; reprinted in Thomas Deloney's *Garland of Good Will*, 1631 [*Works*, ed. Mann, p. 333], in *A Collection of Old Ballads*, 1723–1725, I, 181, and in Percy's *Reliques*, and *RB* I, 309). An earlier copy than any of the extant printed editions is in the Shirburn MS, c. 1585–1616 (*SB*, p. 192).

"In the dayes of old," from the opening line of the ballad just cited, is the tune title for "Rochell her yeelding to the . . . French King, on the 28. of October 1628. after a long siege," by Martin Parker, beginning "You that true Christians be/assist me with your sorrow" (Pepys; reprinted in *PG*, p. 293).

A considerably older ballad, to the tune of "Crimson Velvet," is "The lamentable complaint of Queen Mary for the unkind departure of King Philip, in whose absence she fell sick, and died," beginning "Mary doth complain;/Ladies, be you moved" (Richard Johnson, *Crown Garland of Golden Roses*, 1659, ed. Chappell, 1845). Despite its seventeenth-century publication, this may have been written soon after Mary's death in 1558. The capture of Calais by the Spaniards in 1596 is the subject of a topical ballad to the tune of "Crimson veluet," soon copied into the Shirburn MS (printed in *RB* VIII, xx***, and *SB*, p. 241): "Callis, his wofull Lamentation for her haplesse spoyle," beginning "If euer wofull tale/moved man to pittye."

"Constance of Cleueland . . . and her disloyall Knight," beginning "It was a youthfull Knight/lou'd a gallant Lady," to the tune of "Crimson Velvet" (Pepys [two editions], Lord Crawford, Roxburghe; reprinted in *RB* VI, 572), was licensed in 1603 and again in 1624 (Rollins, *Anal. Index*, Nos. 824, 1266). The first lines of this ballad provide the name under which the tune (Fig. 92) is found in J. J. Starter's *Friesche Lust-Hof*, 1621, p. 40: "Twas a youthful knight, w[hi]ch loved a galjant Lady." The same music in Forbes's *Cantus*, 1662, No. 57 (Fig. 93), is coupled with verses from *England's Helicon*, 1600, beginning "Shepherd, saw thou not my fair lovely Phylis." The air in the Straloch MS, 1627–1629, and in the Skene MS (Dauney, p. 248) also takes its title from

92

Original is unbarred.

93

Original is unbarred.

these verses. The tune appears in D. P. Pers's *Bellerophon*, 1633, pp. 167–168, but without indication of its English associations.

In the British Museum copy of W. S[latyer]'s *Psalmes, or Songs of Sion*, 1642, "Crimson Velvet" has been written in as the tune to which Psalm 43 may be sung. It begins "Judge my cause, O Lord,/And give sentence for me."

The popularity of this tune is remarkable in view of the fact that it calls for a complex stanza, usually written in twenty lines. But the tune itself, despite its rather monotonous repetitions, has a moving solemnity appropriate to most of the songs written for it.

The Crossed Couple,
or Tantara Rara Tantivy

The ballad giving this tune one of its names is "The crost Couple, Or A good Misfortune," beginning "Ille tell you a tale no stranger than true," to "a new Northern Tune, much in fashion," but without the music itself (Euing, Roxburghe; reprinted in *RB* III, 648). To the tune of "The Crost Couple" is a ballad of early 1660, "King Charles his Glory, And Rebels Shame," beginning "Charles the first was a Noble King" (BM Luttrell; reprinted in *RB* VII, 661). Other editions, probably issued shortly after the regicide executions of October, 1660, have the title "The Traytors Downfall, or a brief Relation of the Downfall of that Phanatic crew who traiterously Murthered the late Kings Majesty of blessed Memory" (Euing, Manchester; reprinted in *RB* VIII, liii*). The Manchester copy has substituted a new opening stanza, beginning "Come hither to me and I will declare." The Euing stanza is a composite, following the original text in its opening lines. In both Euing and Manchester versions, the tune title is given as "Fa la la," from the refrain in lines 2, 4, and 8, the full form of which is "with a fa la la la lalero."

Another to the tune of "The Crost Couple" is "News from Hide-Park," beginning "One evening a little before it was dark" (Pepys, Douce, Euing, Lord Crawford, Wood E.25, BM Luttrell, Harvard [Percy collection II, 69, an eighteenth-century imprint], Roxburghe; reprinted in *RB* VI, 496). This ballad, with music, appears in all editions of *Pills*, 1719–1720, IV, 138 (Fig. 94).

An internal refrain (variable) of "sing tan tara tara tantivee" disap-

94

Original is a fourth higher.

pears as the ballad gets under way, but it is conspicuous enough to have become another name for the tune. Thus we have "Tan tarra rara, tan tivee" cited as the tune for two ballads featuring Nell Gwyn and the Duchess of Portsmouth: "A Pleasant Dialogue betwixt two Wanton Ladies of Pleasure," beginning "Brave Gallants now listen and I will you tell" (BM Luttrell, Bagford; reprinted in *BB* II, 599); and "The Duchess of Portsmouths Farewel," beginning "I Prithee dear Portsmouth now tell me thy mind" (BM Luttrell; reprinted in *RB* IV, 283). In both, the threefold burden is "With a fa la la la fa la la." The same stanzaic structure is found in a Manchester (I, 28) ballad whose first part is missing, but whose second part, to the tune of "Fa la la," begins "O come my own Deere lets dally a while" and constitutes an independent ballad of a lovers' tryst interrupted when a Peeping Tom falls out of a tree into their midst. Another with similar stanza form is "The Jacobite tossed in a Blanket," beginning "I pray Mr. Jacobite tell me why," to the tune of "Fa la: Or, Tan tara Tantroy [i.e., Tantivy]" (Lord Crawford, Pepys; reprinted in *PB* VI, 198).[1] "Tom Tell Truth," beginning "I killed a man and he was dead," to the tune of "Tanta ra ra ra, Tantivee" (Harvard, Lord Crawford, Roxburghe; reprinted in *RB* VIII, 425), also has a "fa la la la la la" refrain.

Two other ballads with the same metrical pattern dispense with a nonsense refrain in favor of more meaningful phrases: "The Merry Milk-Maid['s] . . . longing desire after matrimony," beginning "As I through a Meadow one morning did pass," to the tune of "Tan-Tivee" (Pepys IV, 13, dated 1691, Lord Crawford 100, Harvard) confines its refrain to "It is a fine thing to be marry'd" at the close of each stanza. In "The Good-Fellows Counsel: Or, The Bad Husbands Recantation," beginning "I had no more wit, but was trod under feet," to the tune of "Tan Tivye" (Wood E.25, Harvard, Rawlinson, Lord Crawford, Roxburghe; reprinted in *RB* VI, 499), the tripartite burden is usually "and all was for want of money" or "when I have no want of money."[2] Still another, "The Peni-

---

[1] Rollins, following Chappell and Ebsworth, equated the tune of "Fa la," used for eight-line stanzas, with "Sir Eglamore" or "The Friar in the Well," tunes found only with seven-line stanzas. Each pattern calls for the refrain in the second, fourth, and final lines of the stanza, and this common feature doubtless led to the assumption that the stanza patterns were identical. Chappell (*PMOT* I, 276), failing to note the tune title, also erroneously assigned "The Jacobite tossed in a Blanket" to the tune of "Sir Eglamore." His quoting of the refrains is below his usual standard of accuracy.

[2] This burden has a tenuous verbal connection with the tune titles "Never a Penny of Money" and "Without ever a penny of Money," which are named on two Restoration broadsides: "Stand too't Whetston-Park Ladies," beginning "I am a brave Lass, and I Travel'd about" (BM C.22.f.6 [77], Douce II, 188v, Lord Crawford 537, Harvard); and "The Scotchmans Lamentation for the loss of his Pack," beginning

tent Gallant," beginning "There was, I must tell you, a Jocular Spark," to the tune "Hide Park" (Pepys IV, 138), closes each stanza with "the thirteen poor Cuckolds of Branford" or a variation of the phrase.

All these ballads may be sung to the *Pills* tune accompanying the verses of "News from Hide-Park." A different tune called "Hide Park" appears in the first three editions of *The Dancing Master,* 1651–1665; it will fit none of these ballads, but it can be used with Richard Climsell's "The praise of London . . . To the tune of the second part of Hide Parke" (Pepys; reprinted in *PB* II, 220). Neither tune will fit the following ballad, which requires a "Cupid's Courtesy" musical form: "A New Ditty: Of a Lover, tost hither and th[i]ther, That cannot speake his mind when they are together," to the tune of "Hide Park" (Roxburghe; reprinted in *RB* II, 235). "The defence of Hide Parke . . . To a curious new Court tune" (Manchester, Pepys; reprinted in *PB* II, 146) is in a uniquely complex stanza pattern unsuited to either tune. Chappell evidently cited the ballad merely because it was another on the subject of Hyde Park.

Cuckolds All A-Row

The closing line of the nursery rhyme "Mistress Mary, quite contrary" is usually known as "And pretty maids all in a row," but it once read "And cuckolds all arow." It is not clear whether the dance- and ballad-tune name was influenced by the nursery rhyme, or the converse.[1] The

"There was a brisk Scotchman as I do understand" (Pepys III, 340). In both the burden is "with a fa la la la la lero" (variously printed) in lines 2, 4, and 8 of each stanza. These ballads could be, and perhaps were, sung to the "Crossed Couple" tune, for the refrain pattern is identical to that of "The Traytors Downfall," an earlier edition of which, "King Charles his Glory," was sung to "The Crossed Couple," as almost certainly were the later editions.

Another ballad with the same refrain pattern calls for the tune "Oliver was of Huntington"; it is Abraham Miles's account of the posthumous hanging of Cromwell, Ireton, and Bradshaw on Jan. 30, 1661, entitled "The Last Farewel of three bould Traytors," and begins "Who did not hear of Olivers Nose" (Harvard). Although the tune title is a prosy commonplace, a similar phrasing, "This Oliver was of Huntington," opens a stanza of "King Charles his Glory," published the preceding year. Again, we can but point to the possibility that the later ballad was sung to "The Crossed Couple," the tune of the earlier.

[1] See Iona and Peter Opie, *The Oxford Dictionary of Nursery Rhymes,* 1951, No. 342, where two citations from the last quarter of the eighteenth century are noted. Evidence is lacking for the date of the rhyme in its older form.

Original is unbarred.

tune of this name is found in every edition of *The Dancing Master* (1651, p. 67 = Fig. 95), in *A Booke of New Lessons for the Cithern & Gittern*, 1652, in *Musicks Recreation on the Viol, Lyra-way*, 1682, and in Walsh's *Compleat Country Dancing-Master*, 1718. It was also well known during the first half of the seventeenth century.

The lost ballad "Cuckolds all a row" was registered in June, 1637; it is presumably the song with this title, beginning "Not long agoe as all along [*or* alone] I lay upon my bed," which is found in *Wit and Drollery*, 1661, p. 85, reprinted in *Pills*, 1719–1720, IV, 77 (there with the music of "London is a fine town"). No tune is named, but the refrain is "Cuckolds all arow." A ballad to the tune by Humphrey Crouch, published c. 1640, implies a familiarity with the song in its parodying of details. It is "A pleasant new song that plainely doth show, that al are Beggers . . . ," beginning "Come cease your songs of Cuckolds row," with stanzas ending "Beggers all a row" (Manchester; reprinted in *CP*, p. 114). Another to the tune before 1640 is "The Cruell Shrow: or, The Patient Mans Woe," by Arthur Halliarg, beginning "Come bachelors and married men" (Roxburghe; reprinted in *RB* I, 94).

A song written by Francis Quarles about 1641, beginning "Know then my Brethren, Heaven is cleare," contains the burden "Hey then up go wee," which gave rise to a very popular tune title of the 1680s, "Hey, boys, up go we," q.v. Quarles's song, printed first in an anonymous tract, *The Distractions of our Times*, 1642, was reprinted in his eclogue, *The Shepheards Oracle*, 1644, with no tune direction. It was reprinted in *Rump*, 1662, and *Loyal Songs*, 1731, with the tune direction "Cuckolds all a-row." A broadside version of 1681 is noted under "Hey boys." Unrelated to either of these tunes is the stately air found in a setting of Quarles's verses for solo voice (Bodleian MS Don.c.57, p. 52), probably from the third quarter of the seventeenth century.

A ballad of 1660, with burden "Cuckolds all-a-Row," has the tune title "Is there no more Cuckolds but I," which may be internally inspired; in contemporary reprintings, the tune name is given as "Cuckolds all-a-Row." The ballad, beginning "You cowd-hearted [or coward-hearted] Citizens," has the broadside title: "Roome for Cuckolds: or my Lord Lamberts Entrance into Sodome and Gomorrah" (Harvard, BM Luttrell II, 182, BM C.20.f.2 [284] and [315], BM Thomason, dated 1 Feb 1659/60, Wood 416 [27]). In *The Rump,* 1660, it is called "The She-Citizens Delight," and in *Ratts Rhimed to Death,* 1660, it is called "London's true Character."

In his diary Pepys wrote that at a New Year's Eve ball, Dec. 31, 1662, Charles II called for "Cuckolds all awry" as the first of the country dances and led the company in "the old dance of England." And the tune is mentioned in "London is a Fine Town" (*Pills,* 1719–1720, IV, 41):

> Then they go to *Greenwitch* all in the City Barge,
> And there they have a Noble Treat all at the City Charge;
> And when they come to *Cuckold's-Point,* they make a Gallant Show,
> Their Wives bid the Musick play *Cuckolds-all-a-row.*

The natural association of the phrase "Cuckolds all a Row" with marital infidelity was probably responsible for its use as a burden in a ballad periodically reissued during the eighteenth century and since. A typical form, "A General Summons . . . To assemble at Horn Fair October 18," begins

> You horned fumbling cuckolds
>   In city, court or town,
> You're summon'd here and must appear,
>   Your fine to render down . . .

and the stanzas end "Cuckolds all of a row" (BM 1876.f.1 [152], without tune direction).

Cupid's Courtesy

"Cupids Courtesie: or, The young Gallant foild at his own Weapon. . . . To a pleasant Northern Tune," by J. P., was licensed in 1664 to John Conyers. Although no edition with his imprint has survived, copies issued by Francis Coles are contemporary, antedating Coles's death in 1680 (Douce I, 46, Euing 39). The ballad, which begins "Through the cool shady Woods,/as I was ranging," was frequently reprinted for a century or more. Copies of later editions are in Pepys, Douce, Lord Crawford, Harvard, and Roxburghe collections (*RB* III, 530, is a reprint from a late seventeenth-century issue without author's initials).[1] The text was reprinted also in *A Jovial Garland*, c. 1670, sig. F8, and with music in *Pills*, 1719–1720, VI, 43 (Fig. 96).[2]

A sequel to the ballad is "Cupids Tryumph . . . Being an Answer to Cupids Courtesie. . . . The tune is Saraban, used in Dancing-Schools. Or, Cupid Courtesie," beginning "A Gallant Lady Gay,/as she was walking" (Rawlinson; reprinted in *RB* IV, 13).[3] Another, which seems to echo the opening formulas of the original ballad, is "Cupids Cure: or, An Answer to Cupids Cruelty," beginning "All in a shady Grove,/ as I was musing," to the tune of "Cupids Curtesie" (Douce I, 47). I have not found a "Cupids Cruelty" broadside to which this might be an answer.

"The Virgin's Complaint Against Young Mens Unkindness," beginning "I am so deep in love,/I cannot hide it," to the tune of "Cupid's Courtesie" (Lord Crawford 566, Douce II, 235, Harvard), gives us two

[1] J. P. Collier, in *A Book of Roxburghe Ballads*, 1847, p. 80, reprinted the text later used in *RB*. His reference to "a manuscript copy of it dated 1595" cannot be taken seriously.

[2] The music is also found in *Pills* IV, 165, with "A Ballad on New Bethlem," beginning "This is a Structure fair,/Royally raised." The poem had originally appeared in *Wit and Mirth*, 1682, p. 256, as "On New-Bedlam," without tune direction.

[3] The exact saraband tune cannot be confidently identified, although the tune of "The Saraband" in *The Dancing Master*, 1651–1686, will fit the ballad if repeats are omitted.

new names for the tune.[4] In the sequel, entitled "The Young Mans Vindication against The Virgins Complaint," and beginning "Sweet Virgin, hath disdain/mov'd you to passion," the tune direction is "the Virgins Complaint; or, Cupids Courtesie" (Douce, with the additional tune name in MS "So Deep in Love," Rawlinson, Pepys, Roxburghe; reprinted in *RB* VI, 255). "The Bashful Virgin: or, The Secret Lover," beginning "O what a pain it is/to be a Lover," is to the tune of "I am so deep in Love: or, Little Boy" (Douce, Pepys, Lord Crawford, Harvard, Roxburghe; reprinted in *RB* III, 430). The second tune name is derived from the original "Cupids Courtesie" ballad, where the god of love is frequently called "Little boy."

The opening line of the original ballad is levied on for another name of the tune in "The Valiant Seamans happy return to his Love, after a long seven Years absence," beginning "When Sol did cast no light,/being darken'd over," which is to be sung to "I am so deep in love: Or, Through the cool shady Woods" (Wood E.25, Douce; reprinted in *RB* VII, 518; an eighteenth-century issue is in the Percy collection, Harvard).[5] Another version of the story, which breaks off before the sailor can identify himself, is "The Pensive Maid," beginning "When Soll will cast no light,/all darkned over." Here the order of tune names is reversed: "Through the cool [or cold] shady Woods, Or, Deep in Love" (Pepys, BM 11621.l.2, Lord Crawford, Wood E.25, Bagford, Harvard, Roxburghe; reprinted in *RB* VII, 516). An eighteenth-century copy of "The Pensive Maid" (Harvard) gives the first tune name only.

"When Soll will cast no light" is still another name for the tune, found in "Love and Loyalty," beginning "When Soll with golden Rayes" (Pepys III, 123), and in "The Shoomakers delight. Or. A New Dialogue betwixt a West Country Shoooemaker & his Love," beginning "On Midsummer day as I/abroad was walking" (Lord Crawford, Harvard, Roxburghe; reprinted in *RB* VII, 33, and *OPB*, p. 201). John Wade's "A Serious Discourse between two Lovers," beginning "My pretty little Rogue/do but come hither," is to the tune "When Sol will cast no Light, Or, Deep in Love" (Pepys, BM C.22.f.6, Lord Crawford, Wood E.25, Harvard; reprinted in *RB* VII, 254, and *OPB*, p. 194). And Wade's ballad is the source of the tune name "My pritty little Rogue," found along with "When Sol will cast no light" in "The West Country

[4] The ballad was licensed in 1678 as "The maiden's complaint against young mens unkindnesse," and a copy with that title is in Pepys III, 220. In later issues the title begins "The Kind Virgin's Complaint . . ." (Douce, Roxburghe; reprinted in *RB* VI, 253).

[5] An earlier version signed Cuthbert Birket is "A pleasant new Song between a Seaman, and his Love." It begins "When Sol could cast no light,/But darked over," uses the same stanza pattern, and calls for a tune "Robin the Devil," on which I have no information (Roxburghe; reprinted in *RB* III, 127).

Wooing," beginning "My Joy and only Dear" (Lord Crawford, Euing, Harvard, Roxburghe; reprinted in *RB* VII, 252).

A pair of related ballads, both issued before 1680 and sung to "I am so deep in love, Or, Cupids Courtesie," may lead us to another popular tune name, "Ring of Gold." The ballads are "The Seamen and Souldiers last Farewel," beginning "Farewel my dearest Dear,/now I must leave thee" (Pepys IV, 216, Euing 328); and "The Maidens Lamentation. Or, An Answer to the Seamen and Souldiers last farewel," beginning "Alas my dearest joy,/why wilt thou leave me?" (Wood E.25 [139]). The second of these contains the lines "Take here this Ring of Gold,/dear love and accept it" (stanza 11), from which the "Ring of Gold" tune may derive. This latter tune name appears on "An Answer to the Covetous-Minded Parents," a ballad with meaningless music (Pepys; reprinted in *RB* VIII, lxxiv*) answering "The Covetous-minded Parents," for which the tune named is "Farwell my dearest Dear" (Pepys V, 294, with meaningless music; another edition, without music, in Euing, Lord Crawford, Harvard, Roxburghe; reprinted in *RB* III, 616, VIII, lxxiii*). It would appear that "Farwell my dearest Dear" is derived from the opening of "The Seamen and Souldiers last Farewel" and "Ring of Gold" from that ballad's sequel, and thus that both tunes might be the equivalent of "Cupid's Courtesy."

Such a theory, however, is clouded by the existence of another ballad, "The Unconstant Maiden, Or, The Forsaken Young-Man. . . . To a pleasant New tune." It begins "Farewell my Dearest Dear,/now I must leave thee," and its second stanza has the lines "Here is a Ring of Gold,/my Dear accept it" (Pepys; reprinted in *RB* VIII, lxxvi*; an edition of c. 1700 is in Madden III, 779). Music in both copies is meaningless, but the ballad is in the "Cupid's Courtesy" stanza (eight lines alternating six and five syllables). Although the Pepys copy cannot have been issued before 1682, we have no assurance that it was the original edition. It is, therefore, impossible to know whether "Farewell my Dearest Dear" and "Ring of Gold" are mere echoes in "The Unconstant Maiden" or whether they actually originate in this ballad. Consequently we cannot say whether these two tune names are to be identified with the unnamed "pleasant New tune" or with "Cupid's Courtesy." They are interchangeable with the latter; beyond that we cannot go.[6]

One further ballad sung to our tune should be noted. It is "The Sweet Salutation on Primrose Hill," beginning "In the pleasant month of May," to the tune "Though Father Angry be: Or, Deep in Love" (Pepys; reprinted in *RB* VIII, lxxxvi*). The second tune name is distinctly an afterthought here. For the ballad is written in an eight-line stanza of

[6] For a list of ballads sung to "Ring of Gold" or its offshoots, see *RB* VIII, lxxix***.

full trimeters, whereas "Deep in Love" (i.e., "Cupid's Courtesy") calls for alternate lines of five syllables with feminine rhymes; the tune can be used, but the effect is frequently awkward. I have not found the first tune.[7]

Two ballad operas introduce the tune of "Cupid's Courtesy," but no music is printed with either. In Chetwood's *The Lover's Opera*, 1729, it is called "When Sol did cast no light" (omitted from the 3d ed., 1730, which contains music). In the anonymous *Vanelia*, 1732, it is called "I am so sick of Love, I cannot hide it."

Cupid's Trepan

This tune takes its primary title from a Restoration ballad, "Cupid's Trappan: or, Up the Green Forrest: Or, The Scorner Scorn'd: or, Willow turn'd into Carnation. Described in the Ranting Resolution of a Forsaken Maid. To a pleasant new Tune, now all in Fashion" (Lord Crawford, Euing, Douce, Rawlinson, BM C.22.f.6, Pepys; reprinted in *RB* VII, 359). It begins "Once did I love a bonny bonny Bird," from which comes another name for the tune; its second stanza begins "Up the green Forrest, and down the green Forrest," whence yet another tune name.

A sequel to the original ballad is "The Batchellors Fore-Cast, or Cupid Unblest, being an Answer to Cupids Trappan, or Up the Green Forrest," beginning "Once did I love and a very pretty Girl," to the tune of "Cupids Trappan" (Euing; reprinted in *RB* VII, 361). Another answer is "A young Man put to his Shifts: Or, The Ranting young mans Resolution," beginning "Of late did I hear a young damsel complain" (Lord Crawford, Harvard, Douce, BM C.22.f.6, Pepys, Roxburghe; reprinted in *RB* VII, 179).

In a pair of related ballads the war between the sexes reaches the farm: "The Plowmans Art in Woeing," beginning "I am a young man that do

---

[7] "The merry Maid of Middlesex," a ballad licensed in 1656, has a stanza of eight trimeters plus a refrain of four; it begins "Let Father angry be,/Let Mother brawl and chide" (*RB* VIII, clxxiii*). The same twelve-line unit is found in "The Maidens Choice," to the tune of "let Father angrey be" (BM C.20.f.14 [15]). The refrain of "The merry Maid" might be the source of the tune name "Though Father Angry be," despite the association of the latter with an eight-line stanza. "The merry Maid" is sung to "The Maid that lost her way," a tune which I have not discovered. On metrical grounds Ebsworth is wrong (*RB* VIII, lxxxviii*) in tracing it to "A pleasant new Song, if you'le heare it you may,/Of a North-Country-Lasse that had lost her way," a ballad in a 6.6.8.6 quatrain.

follow the Plow" (Lord Crawford, Harvard, Roxburghe; reprinted in *RB* VI, 526, and *OPB*, p. 216), is countered by "The Milkmaids Resolution," beginning "Of late I did hear a young man domineer" (Lord Crawford, Harvard, Roxburghe; reprinted in *RB* VI, 529).

Other seventeenth-century ballads used the tune under other names, whose origins have been discussed: "The Patient Husband and the Scoulding Wife," beginning "All you gallants in City or Town," is sung to "Bonny bonny bird" (Roxburghe; reprinted in *RB* VII, 182); "A New Song Made in the Praise of the West of England," beginning "Unto West-Country men/These few lines I do pen," is to "The Protestant Prince; or, Vp the green Forrest" (Pepys; reprinted in *PB* IV, 80). In the latter ballad, the first tune title is another name for "The Prince of Orange's Delight," q.v.

The tune continued to be popular in the eighteenth century, stimulated principally by a new song issued on single sheets about 1700: "The Maid's Twitcher. Sung by Mr. Pack at the Theatre in Lincolns Inn Fields," beginning "A damsell I'm told of delicate mould" (BM H.1601 [12]). As "The Twitcher" it was reissued about 1710 (BM G.306 [14], Harvard). A version of the tune under the former title is in BM MS Add. 38189, fol. 25 (c. 1695–1725), arranged as an air for violin. It is cited in no less than fifteen ballad operas, as either "The Twitcher" or "A damsel I'm told," and the music is found in Mottley and Cooke's *Penelope*, 1728, Air 12 (Fig. 97), Coffey's *The Beggar's Wedding*, 1729, Ralph's *The Fash-*

ionable Lady, 1730, Coffey's *The Female Parson*, 1730, and his *The Devil to Pay*, 1731. The tune is cited in *The Sailor's Opera*, 1745, as "He that has the best Wife," from the first line of the "Twitcher" song in *The Devil to Pay*, and the music is called "I have left the World, as the World found me" in Hippisley's *Flora*, 1729.

Still another single-sheet song using the "Cupid's Trepan" music is "Song in The Fair [1751]. Sung by Mr. Beard," beginning "In story we're told/How our monarchs of old" (BM G.309 [7]; Harvard, Julian Marshall collection, with "Cupid's Trepan" and "Brave Boys" added in MS at the top of the sheet). This version of the music repeats the last six bars as a chorus.

Henry Carey wrote the words and music of "The Huntsman's Rouze," beginning "The Hounds are all out and the Morning does peep" (BM G.315 [157]); the poem follows the "Cupid's Trepan" stanza pattern, even to the tag "my brave Boy" in line four of each stanza, which may be the reason Chappell associated the song with the eighteenth-century vogue of "Cupid's Trepan." [1]

The *Journal of the Folk Song Society*, II (1905), 82–83, prints the words and music of a song beginning "I once had a boy and a bonny boy too," as sung in Westmoreland and Norfolk. Lucy Broadwood's note points out that the texts are versions of "Cupid's Trepan," but this and other traditional survivals of the old ballad are sung to different music.

The Damask Rose,

or Omnia Vincit Amor

Martin Parker's ballad "Loues Solace," licensed in 1632, begins "The Damaske Rose nor Lilly faire"; it is sung "to a new court tune called the Damaske Rose" (Roxburghe; reprinted in *RB* I, 623) and has the refrain "So sweet is the lass that loves me." No music is extant for "Damaske Rose," but an eighteenth-century edition of Parker's ballad (Harvard 25243.29* [20]), exploiting his refrain line, is entitled "Sweet is the Lass that Loves me. A young Mans Resolution to prove constant to his sweet heart." It bears the tune title "Omnia vincit Amor," under which name a crabbedly written air appears in the Skene MS and is transcribed with justifiable emendation of time values in Dauney's *Ancient Scotish Melodies,* 1838, p. 238 (Fig. 98). Although the tune calls for trochaic

---

[1] Carey's fourth line rhythm is distinctly different from that of "Cupid's Trepan," for his air trips along steadily to form a ten-measure musical sentence, whereas the older tune comes to a strong stand at "brave boys." Since songster versions of Carey's poem reduce the refrain tag to its form in "Cupid's Trepan," it is natural to assume, as Chappell did, that this tune rather than Carey's was to be used. Songsters I have seen do not, however, make this association.

98

Dauney's transcript is a fourth higher. First ending has been supplied in measure 8, and tablature is followed in measure 23, restoring a note omitted by Dauney.

meter, it is fairly well adapted to Parker's stanza of eight lines alternating eight and seven syllables.[1]

A ballad in the same stanza form, whose only known edition probably dates from the last quarter of the seventeenth century, is "The Resolved Lover, or, So Sweet is the Lass that loves me," beginning "Oh that I were with my true Love," to the tune of "The Lilly and the Rose, or, So sweet is the Lass that loves me" (Rawlinson 118). The first tune title may be in loose allusion to Parker's opening line; the second echoes title and refrain of both ballads and presumably is another name for the original tune, not the name of another tune. If this is so, the handful of ballads sung

[1] A broadside of c. 1670, in the same stanza form, entitled "Omnia Vincit Amor," beginning "As I went forth to view the Spring,/which Flora had adorned" (BM 1871.e.9 [48]), is without tune direction. Each stanza ends with the title phrase. Other editions of this ballad, with the title "The Last Lamentation, of the Languishing Squire," have the tune direction "Billy and Molly: Or, Jockey's Jealousie" (RB VI, 228). No music exists for the former; for the latter, see under "Jockey's Jealousy." Still another edition of the ballad, "Omnia Vincit Amor; Or, The Disconsolate Swain's Lamentation," has the tune title "The Battle of Almanza" (Douce III, 71ᵛ, an eighteenth-century Newcastle copy). Of this tune, I know only that it could not have received its name before 1707, the date of the battle. Allan Ramsay reprinted the ballad, with changes, as "Omnia vincent amor" in his *Tea-Table Miscellany*, 1733 ed., I, 106.

to "Sweet is the lass that loves me" are related to "Damaske Rose" or its successor.

These include: "The true Lovers Admonition," beginning "You pretty little young men all,/come listen to my Ditty" (Harvard, Lord Crawford, Roxburghe; reprinted in *RB* VI, 219); "The Map of Mock-begger Hall," beginning "I reade, in ancient times of yore," to the tune of "It is not your Northerne Nanny; or, Sweet is the Lasse that Loves me" (Roxburghe [two editions, one before 1642]; reprinted in *RB* II, 132, VI, 762); [2] "To her brown Beard. For i'le warrant the Girl he'l Love the," beginning "You pretty Ladies all/That merrily are disposed," to the tune of "Sweet is the Lass, or my maidenhead will not o're load me" (Lord Crawford 1418, Harvard, Douce II, 217, BM C.22.f.6 [218]).[3]

Unrelated to "Damaske Rose" is the tune title "Like to the Damaske Rose," cited in a ballad beginning "Like to a Dove-cote never haunted." [4] The comparison of unmarried and married women is made in a series of long complex stanzas, requiring "the second strain to be sung twice over," in a rhythm totally at variance with that of the eight-line stanza in the ballads just discussed.

The Dame of Honor

"The Dame of Honnour or Hospitallity. Sung by Mrs. Willis in the Opera call'd the Kingdom of the Birds," beginning "Since now the Worlds turn'd upside down," was written by Thomas D'Urfey for his

[2] The second Roxburghe copy, a variant edition issued by the publisher of the first, is entitled "Mock-Beggers Hall" and begins "In ancient times when as plain dealing/Was most of all in fashion." On the first tune title, see "Northern Nancy." A late seventeenth-century ballad, "The Ruined Lovers," is directed to be sung to the tune of "Mock-Beggers Hall stands empty" (*RB* VII, 411); this tune title, drawn from the refrain line of the "Mock-begger Hall" ballad, is evidently another name for one of the two tunes named on the earlier ballad.

[3] The second tune title is apparently derived from a ballad in the same meter, but without tune direction, called "The faithfull woings of two Country Lovers," whose refrain in alternate stanzas is "my Maiden-head will not load me" (*RB* VI, 250; Ebsworth's title, "A Pleasant Song of The Faithful . . ." is not derived from the Roxburghe exemplar, whose heading is almost completely shorn. Other copies I have seen give the title as I quote it).

[4] The unique copy in the Roxburghe collection has been shorn of its title, but the word "or" remains, showing that what Chappell gives as the title (*RB* II, 12) is actually the subtitle: "Prettie Comparisons wittily grounded,/Which by scornful Maidens may best be expounded."

opera *Wonders in the Sun, or, The Kingdom of the Birds,* 1706, I, ii. The music has been attributed to G. B. Draghi on very doubtful evidence.[1] A single-sheet edition of the song with the music (Fig. 99) was probably

published while the opera held the stage (BM H.1601 [388], dated 1706?; Harvard, Julian Marshall collection). It was immediately reprinted, with the title as on the song sheet, in *Pills,* 1706, IV, 146 (1719–1720, I, 212). With or without music, the song was printed in many poetical miscellanies of the eighteenth century, and its popularity may be gauged from the parodies and imitations it inspired.

One of the earliest broadsides using the tune is "The Dutchess of C[leveland]'s Memorial," beginning "What tho' my Name is toss'd about,/For quarreling with Beau F[eildi]ng" (BM 1872.a.1 [158]), which recounts the unhappy marriage of Barbara Villiers to Major General Robert Feilding. In 1706 the General was sentenced to Newgate for maltreating his wife, and the ballad writers were ready with "General Fielding's Answer to the Dutchess of C—'s Memorial," beginning "If I was by misfortune sent,/To Newgate in a huff Sirs," also to the tune of "The Dame of Honour" (BM 1872.a.1 [158ᵛ]).

A Scotch imitation of D'Urfey's song, without tune direction but with the burden "When I was a Dame of Honour" and in the appropriate stanza form, contains the notation "printed Feb. 1707." It is "The Knights of the Horn Orders Address to the Fruit Maids of Edinburgh," beginning "The Nations Sins are many fold,/And Scotland has no name" (National Library of Scotland Ry III.a.10 [19]). A political squib on Abigail

---

[1] Sir John Hawkins, *History of Music,* 1776, IV, 427, confused Draghi with Lully, one of whose pieces was introduced into D'Urfey's opera; see *Grove's Dictionary of Music and Musicians,* 5th ed., 1954, II, 761.

Masham and her influence over Queen Anne is "A ballad to the Tune of the Dame of Honour," beginning "All things are chang'd in Court and Town," in *A Pill to Purge State-Melancholy*, 1715; a longer version in *Political Merriment*, Part III, 1715, is called "Mass - - - m display'd."

In the second volume of *The Dancing Master*, 2d ed., 1714, and succeeding editions, the tune is called "Queen Bess's Dame of Honour," and in Walsh's second volume of *The Compleat Country-Dancing Master*, 1719, it is called "Dame of Honour." It was used for sixteen ballad operas under the following titles: "Since all the world's turn'd upside down," in Gay's *Polly*, 1729; "Since all the World" in *The Court Medley*, 1733; "In good Queen Bess's Golden Days" in Breval's *The Rape of Helen*, 1737. It is called "Dame of Honour" or "When I was a Dame of Honour" in others, including the following that reprint the music: Ralph's *The Fashionable Lady*, 1730; Coffey's *The Devil to Pay*, 1731; *The Jovial Crew*, 1731; Lillo's *Silvia*, 1731; Fielding's *The Lottery*, 1732; Potter's *The Decoy*, 1733; and Langford's *The Lover his own Rival*, 1736.

Pills contains two other songs to the music: "Perkin in a Cole-Sack: Or, the Collier's Buxome Wife of St. James's," which begins "Come all that are disposed a while,/And listen to my Story" and has all the marks of a street ballad (VI, 254); and "The Man of Honour: Or, the Unconstant World turn'd upside down," beginning "How is the World transform'd of late," and with burden, "When I was a Man of Honour" (VI, 257).

Damon and Pythias

Virtually the only Elizabethan broadside containing music is "A Newe Ballade of a Louer Extollinge his Ladye," by M. Osb[orne?], dated 1568, and beginning "Alas, my harte doth boyle,/and burne with in my breste" (BM Huth; reprinted in *A Collection of Seventy-Nine Black-Letter Ballads*, 1867, p. 24). The unbarred music on the sheet, called "Damon and Pithias," contains occasional errors in notes and rests which make it difficult to join words and music. The tune (Fig. 100) requires a key signature of one flat, and on two occasions a flatted seventh is appropriate; the time value of several notes remains conjectural.[1] Despite the unsatis-

---

[1] For a facsimile of the broadside and a transcription of the tune in modern notation, see John Ward, "Music for *A Handefull of Pleasant Delites*," *JAMS*, X (1957), 167–169. Ward does not bar the tune, nor does he resolve the mensural anomalies, but he suggests the inflection of B and E as indicated in Fig. 100. He properly compares the "recitation-like" setting with other near-contemporary oddities, including the airs in BM MS Add. 38599 (the Shanne commonplace book) and those in

factory printing of the air, it remains valuable to us as a contemporary record of a musical style prevalent in the 1560s, yet quite unlike the usual Elizabethan ballad tune.

"Damon & Pithias" is named for singing "The lamentation of a woman being wrongfully defamed," a ballad beginning "You Ladies falsly deemd,/of anie fault or crime," which is preserved in *A Handefull of Pleasant Delites*, 1584 (ed. Rollins, p. 56). From its association with the tune, Professor Rollins argued that this ballad could have been included in the lost 1566 edition of the *Handefull*. The tune was also named for singing "Can my poore harte be still" in John Phillip's play, *Pacient . . . Grissill*, lic. 1566, sig. C4, and for a song introduced in Edmund Elviden's *Historie of Pesistratus and Catanea*, c. 1570, sig. C1.

The tune may get its name from Richard Edwards's *Damon and Pithias*, which was apparently performed in 1564–1565; the earliest extant edition was "Newly Imprinted" in 1571. In the play, a song beginning "Awake ye wofull Wightes,/That longe haue wept in wo" [2] has the stanza pattern of the 1568 broadside, a comparable refrain form, and two lines which are, except for the word *wo* (*loue* in the broadside), identical in the two texts:

> My wo no tongue can tell,
> ne Pen can well descrie: . . .

Deloney's *Strange Histories*, 1602, calling them "mavericks of the ballad-tune literature" and suggesting that such a tune as "Damon and Pithias" may be "a remnant of popular style hitherto unnoted." The group needs study, particularly in its possible relationship to plainsong. For a typical Shanne tune, see "O man in desperation."

[2] A contemporary transcript of the song is in BM MS Cotton Vespasian A.xxv, fol. 135 (olim 144), reprinted by K. Böddeker, *Jahrbuch für roman. und engl. Sprache,* N. F. II (1875), 210. The hypermetrical refrain line, "Damon my frende ys judged to dye," will not fit the tune.

The evidence suggests that the broadside author built his verses on the model of Edwards's dramatic song and took his tune name (and presumably the tune) from the play. A puzzling entry of 1565–1566 in the Stationers' Register, "a ballett intituled tow lamentable songes Pithias and Damon," may indicate that two songs from the play were issued in broadside form. An entry of 1562–1563 is more troublesome, for if "the lover extollynge hys Ladyes" (Rollins, *Anal. Index*, No. 1586) refers to an earlier edition of the Osb[orne?] broadside, it must have antedated the play, and the direction of influence would be reversed, a process more difficult to explain. It is clear, however, that for a brief period early in Elizabeth's reign, the tune "Damon and Pithias" enjoyed a modest popularity.

The Danger Is Over

A four-stanza broadside, "The Charming Bride, and Jovial Bridegroom," beginning "The Danger is over, is over, is over, the danger is over" (BM 11621.l.2 [11], Morgan 38), takes its tune name from the opening line. Music on the sheet is meaningless. The broadside is an expansion of a two-stanza song in Southerne's *The Fatal Marriage*, 1694, III, ii, with musical setting by Henry Purcell. It was published in *Gentleman's Journal*, March, 1694 (Fig. 101), and a single-sheet copy of words and

music is among those in a British Museum made-up collection known as *Joyful Cuckoldom*. The original verses, without the considerable repetition necessary in singing, are included in *Pills*, 1719–1720, III, 295, with Purcell's music. Apparently no other broadsides were sung to the tune.

Daniel Cooper

This tune is known under a variety of names: "Daniel Cooper," "Tom the Tailor," "A Job for a Journeyman Shoemaker," "Oxfordshire Damosel," and "My child must have a father." That these are alternate names for the same tune is shown by the genealogical relationships among the members of this complex family. The music is found in *The Dancing Master,* beginning with the 9th ed., 1695, p. 169 (Fig. 102), in Walsh's *Com-*

pleat Country Dancing-Master, 1718, and in *Pills,* 1719–1720, V, 88. The commonness of the stanza form (eight lines alternating eight and seven syllables) accounts for the large number of alternate tunes cited along with members of the "Daniel Cooper" family.

A ballad known as "Daniel Cooper; Or, The High-land Laddy" was issued by P. Brooksby in 1683, with corrupt music. It begins "There's ne'r a Lad in our town,/that's worth an ounce of Powder"; the second stanza begins "Daniel Cooper and his Man"; and the musical directions are "To a Scotch Tune, called, Wally on't, Or, We'l welcome you to Yarrow. Up go we, Or, Jenny Gin" (BM C.22.f.6 [42], Douce I, 51). I have no data on the two Scotch tunes named, though the first suggests "Waly, Waly" printed in W. Thomson's *Orpheus Caledonius*, 1725, to which the stanzas could be sung. The third is "Hey, boys, up go we," and both it and the familiar "Jenny Gin" fit the stanza. No direct connection can be traced between the ballad of Daniel Cooper and the tune of that name.

Among the ballads sung to the tune of "Daniel Cooper" the following may be mentioned: "The Crafty Barber of Debtford," beginning "Come and hear my pleasant Song" (Lord Crawford 229, Harvard, Douce I, 48ᵛ; music printed on the broadside comprises the opening and closing measures of "Hey, boys, up go we," crudely engraved with pitches only approximate); "A New Song called Love in a Tub," beginning "A Female Quaker in Cheap-side,/She lov'd a presbyterian," a roman-letter ballad of c. 1683 printed for Absalon Chamberlain (BM 1876.f.1 [24], Lord Crawford 391); "Whose there Agen," beginning "Good People all I pray give ear" (Pepys IV, 127); "Sport upon Sport: or, The Man in the S[hift?]," dated 1685, beginning "A Lusty Lad there was of late" (Pepys III, 208); "Tobia's Advice, Or, A Remedy for a ranting Young-Man," by Tobias Bowne, beginning "On May morning as I walkt forth,/I to myself was musing" (Harvard, Lord Crawford, Pepys, Roxburghe; reprinted in RB VII, 151). An anti-Jacobite ballad of c. 1715, to the tune "Daniell Cooper and his Man," is "The Pretender," beginning "Wee have too Kinges; the one is true,/The other a Pretender" (Huntington).

A new name for the tune comes from the chief character in "Poor Tom the Taylor His Lamentation," beginning "Tom the Taylor near the Strand,/he met a pretty Creature," to the tune of "Daniel Cooper" (Pepys, Lord Crawford, Roxburghe; reprinted in RB VII, 472). To the tune of "Tom the Taylor" is "The Wanton Maids of Lambeth," beginning "I am a Maid both Brisk and Bold" (Pepys IV, 172). "Jolly Ralph the Joyner, or Kind Kate the Cookmaid," beginning "Brisk Ralph of late he came to Kate," is to the tune of "Daniel Cooper, or, Tom the Taylor" (Pepys III, 176). The same pair of tune names are cited for "A Nosegay of Pleasure growing in Venus's Garden," 1685, beginning "A bony Lad came to the Court,/His Name was Donald Cowper" (Clark; reprinted in *180 Loyal Songs*, and with the music in *Pills* V, 88). "Portsmouths Lamentation. Or, A Dialogue between Two Amorous Ladies, E. G. and

D. P. [i.e., Nell Gwyn and the Duchess of Portsmouth]," beginning "I Prithee, Portsmouth, tell me plain,/without dissimulation," is to "Tom the Taylor, or, Titus Oats" (Bagford; reprinted in *BB* II, 606). For the second tune title see "Buggering Oates, prepare thy neck."[1]

Another ballad to the tune "Tom the Taylor" is "A Jobb for a Iourneyman-Shoomaker," whose title becomes another name for the "Daniel Cooper" tune. It begins "A Seamans Wife, a buxome Dame" (Pepys IV, 180). It is followed by "The Seamans Safe Return, or, an answer to the Job for a Journeyman-Shoomaker," beginning "At length the seaman he came home," to the tune of "Tom the Taylor near the Strand" (Pepys IV, 181).[2] "Bouncing Bess of Brumley, or, The Bob-Tail'd-Bob," beginning "A Kentish Maid to London came,/on Monday morning early," is to the tune of "Tom the Taylor, Or, The Journey-man Shoomaker" (Douce I, 15^v; licensed by Sir Roger L'Estrange, and so no later than 1685). "Poor Anthony's Complaint . . . against his miseries of marriage," beginning "Was ever Man so vext with a wife," is also to the tune of "Tom the Taylor, the Journey-man Shoomaker, or Billy and Molly" (Pepys IV, 121, Euing 275).

"Billy and Molly," an independent tune which has not survived, is a familiar alternate for "Journeyman Shoemaker." Sung to these two tunes are: "The Victorious Wife: or, The Hen-peckt Husband," beginning "Good people stay and hark a while" (Pepys IV, 134); "The Witty Chamber-Maid; or, Dick the Weaver strangely Cheated," beginning "There was a lass in London town,/she was both fair and witty" (Pepys III, 143); and "An Invitation to Lubberland," beginning "There is a ship we understand,/now riding in the river" (Lord Crawford, Roxburghe; reprinted in *RB* VII, 564).

Of the several other ballads sung to "A Job for a Journeyman Shoemaker," it must suffice to mention the following, which have not been reprinted: "The Jolly Coach-Man; Or, The Buxome Taylors Wifes Late folly," beginning "A Taylors wife exceeding fair,/a Coach-man often courted" (Lord Crawford 1107, BM C.22.f.6 [54], both copies dated 1685); and "The Seamans Deceit," beginning "You Maids that live in London town," to the tune of "The Journey-man Shoo-maker" (Pepys IV, 220).

"The London Lasses Folly, or, The Maiden Beguil'd" has a variable refrain from which "My child must have a father" emerges as yet another name for the tune. It begins "Not long ago it chanced so,/abroad as I was walking," to the tune of "The Journey-man Shooe-maker" (Pepys;

---

[1] See "Crossed Couple" for two other dialogues between Nell Gwyn and the Duchess of Portsmouth.

[2] A second sequel, referred to in *RB* VII, 135, is sung to "Touch of the Times," a frequently cited tune which has not survived.

reprinted in *RB* III, 351).[3] To the tune of "My child must have a Father" are the following: "The Huntington-shire Plowman; or, The Plowmans Complaint," beginning "Young Men and Maids I pray attend/unto a plowmans Ditty" (Pepys, BM C.22.f.6, Lord Crawford, Douce, Roxburghe; reprinted in *RB* VII, 31; the Douce copy has an additional tune direction in MS, "Cold and Raw," which would fit the ballad); "The Valiant Dairy-Maid; or, Three Taylors well Fitted," beginning "There were three Taylors, Taylors three," to the tune of "My child must have a Father; Or, Billy and Molly" (Pepys IV, 283); and "The Unfortunate Damsel," beginning "In Debtford liv'd a Bonny Lass," to the tune of "My Child must have a Father. Or, She got money by 't" (Pepys; reprinted in *PB* III, 274). "She got money by 't" is an independent tune, q.v.

One further tune title emerges from this complex; it originates in "The Oxfordshire Damosel, Or, The London Merchant's Choice," beginning "There was as fine a London Blade,/as ever trod on Leather," to the tune of "The Jobb for a Journeyman-Shoomaker" (Pepys, Lord Crawford, Roxburghe; reprinted in *RB* VII, 134). To "Oxford-shire Damosel" is sung "Doctor Experience's excellent Advice to the Virgins," beginning "You Maidens all that would be wise" (Pepys III, 100).

All these ballads that can be dated seem to have been issued during the 1680s. But there are indications that the tune continued to be popular for another century. "Daniel Cooper" is cited in one ballad opera, without music: George Farquhar's *The Stage-Coach*, 1730. And it is used as the tune for "The Briton's Wish," in George A. Stevens's *Songs, Comic and Satyrical*, 1772.

Daphne

"A pleasant new Ballad of Daphne: To a new tune," beginning "When Daphne from faire Phoebus did flie," appears in an early seventeenth-century broadside (Euing, Roxburghe; reprinted in *RB* II, 530). A paraphrase of line six of the broadside in Rowley, Dekker, and Ford's *The Witch of Edmonton*, performed 1621, III, i ("Tarry and kiss me; sweet Nymph stay") may help to fix the date of the ballad. Moreover, two stanzas, with empty musical staves, are found in Giles Earle's songbook

---

[3] A sequel is "The Answer to The London Lasses Folly: or, The New-found Father Discover'd at the Camp," beginning "You Maidens wild, that were beguil'd," to the tune of "The Journey-man Shooe-maker" (Lord Crawford, Pepys, Douce, Harvard, Roxburghe; reprinted in *RB* III, 353).

(BM MS Add. 24665, fol. 67ᵛ, c. 1615–1626, ed. Peter Warlock, 1932, p. 86). The ballad was reprinted in such chapbooks as T. D.'s *Royal Garland of Love and Delight*, 1674, *The Garland of Delight*, 1681, and *Cupid's Garland set round about with Guilded Roses*, n.d. (the two latter in Pepys's collection of Penny Merriments).

An arrangement of "Daphne" by Giles Farnaby is in *The Fitzwilliam Virginal Book*, II, 12, and a somewhat later virginal set is preserved in Paris Conservatoire MS Rés. 1186, fol. 55ᵛ. The melody is used for a five-part instrumental "Daphne," an early seventeenth-century piece in

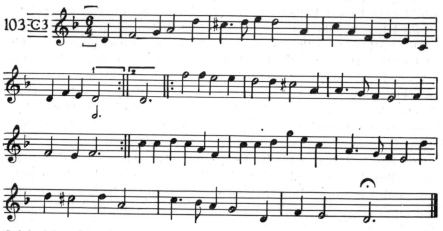

Original is unbarred.

BM MS Add. 17786, fol. 7 (Fig. 103). In the first eight editions of *The Dancing Master*, 1651–1690, the tune appears as "Daphne, or The Shepherdess." A religious parody beginning "When Father Adam first did flee" is coupled with the tune in Forbes's *Cantus*, 1662. A viola da gamba setting of "Daphne" by Richard Sumarte, c. 1660, is preserved in a manuscript in the Henry Watson music collection, Manchester Free Reference Library.

J. J. Starter's *Friesche Lust-Hof*, 1621, prints the tune as "When Daphne did from Phoebus fly," and in Adriaen Valerius's *Neder-Landtsche Gedenck-Clanck*, 1626, it is called "Engelsche Daphne." [1] In Jacob van Eyk's *Der Fluyten Lust-Hof*, 1654, there are three settings of the tune, called "Doen Daphne." F. van Duyse, in *Het Oude Neder-landsche Lied*, 1903–1908, II, 1667ff., reprints the *Friesche Lust-Hof* music (from the 1627 edition, overlooking its presence in the edition of 1621) and cites a large number of appearances of the tune direction in various forms to indicate its long popularity in the Netherlands.

[1] "Prins Daphne" in the latter work is a different tune.

Dargason

A florid arrangement of this tune for lute, probably done near the close of the sixteenth century, is in Cambridge University MS Dd.2.11, fol. 8. The skeleton tune can be seen amid the ornamentation, but it could scarcely be constructed from this source alone. Fortunately the tune is also found in *The Dancing Master* (1651, p. 71=Fig. 104).[1] The

104

Original is unbarred.

treatment of the final cadence in the fourth to eighth editions differs from that of the early editions, but both forms end on the chord of the dominant, making of this an "endless" tune. Chappell (*PMOT* I, 65) combined the later and the earlier states into a double strain to accommodate the eight-line stanza found in two of the three ballads sung to "Dargason." Another version of the tune is in Ravenscroft's *Pammelia*, 1609, No. 30, where three old melodies are arranged to be sung simultaneously. The cadence has been altered to conform to the harmonic demands of the other tunes. The air appears with the words:

> Oft haue I ridden vpon my gray nag,
>   and with his cut tayle he plaid the wag,
>   and down he fell vpon his cragge,
>   fa la re la, la ri dan dino.

Strong traces of "Dargason" remain in the familiar "Irish Washerwoman" and in the American play-party song, "Skip to my Lou." [2]

The tune was current in the sixteenth century, for "A mery Ballet of the Hathorne tre," beginning "It was a maide of my countre," is "To be

1 In the first edition the music is called "Sedanny, or Dargason"; some later editions have "Dargason, or the Sedany." The tune of "Dargason or Sedany" in *A Booke of New Lessons for the Cithern & Gittern*, 1652, follows that of the 1651 *English Dancing Master*.

2 For a note on further traditional currency of the tune, see Margaret Dean-Smith's edition of *Playford's English Dancing Master, 1651*, 1957, p. 60.

songe after Donkin Dargeson" (BM MS Cotton Vespasian A.xxv, fol. 154ᵛ, olim 163ᵛ; reprinted in Ritson, *Ancient Songs*, 1790, Evans's *Old Ballads*, 1810, in Peele's *Works*, ed. Dyce, and in K. Böddeker, *Jahrbuch für roman. und engl. Sprache*, N. F. II [1875], 360–362).[3] The four-line stanza fits the tune.

Allusions to "Dargason" in John Day's *Isle of Gulls*, 1606, and Jonsons' *Tale of a Tub*, 1640, treat it as a place-name, not as a dance or ballad tune. But two seventeenth-century ballads were sung to the tune. One of them is "Londons alacritie . . . to keepe out all the desperate Cavaliers, and blood thirsty Papists," dated 1643 and beginning "By hearesay our foes they are coming to towne,/And threaten to kill us & beat our workes downe," to the tune of "Michaelmas Terme, or Dargeson" (BM 1870.d.1 [8]). For a note on the first tune title, see "Cook Lorrel." The octave stanza of anapestic tetrameter can be sung to "Dargason" by repeating the strain and dividing all quarter notes into eighths—a common enough practice, but seldom necessary on such a scale as is here required.

Another ballad to the tune is "The Shrop-shire Wakes. or, Hey for Christmass. Being the Delightful Sports of most Countries," beginning "Come Robin, Ralph, and little Harry,/and merry Thomas at our Green" (Rawlinson 144, Douce II, 207). Our two copies of this ballad were published by P. Brooksby, who flourished in the latter decades of the century, but the ballad may have been written earlier. Its stanza pattern of four lines with a refrain of four calls for a double strain of "Dargason"; the refrain of tetrameter lines fits the music, but the stanzas themselves are irregular and require some division of notes as in "Londons alacritie."

Dear Catholic Brother

This tune gets its name from "The Catholick Brother," which begins "Dear Catholick Brother, are you come from the Wars." Written near the end of the War of the Spanish Succession, this song was issued on single sheets, perhaps as early as 1710 (BM H.1601 [134], Harvard Julian Marshall Coll.=Fig. 105). It was included in the 1714 and 1719–1720 edi-

---

[3] Böddeker interprets the name appended, probably in a seventeenth-century hand, as "G. Poete." It seems rather to be "G. Peele," but this attribution carries no authority: Peele would have been in his teens in the 1570s, by which time most of this MS had been compiled.

105

tions of *Pills* (V, 177; VI, 277), and in *The Merry Musician,* 1716. The usual stanza format is an anapestic tetrameter quatrain, plus a burden "With a fa, la, la," which is sometimes omitted.

A number of political ballads were written to this tune in the early years of the reign of George I. "Poor Teague: Or the Faithful Irishman's Joy, for the Duke of Ormond's Happy deliverance," beginning "Ab, ab bue, by my shoul I was quite almost mad/when I heard cozen Ormond was grown very sad," describes a threat to the life of James Butler, Second Duke of Ormonde, c. 1715 (BM 1876.f.1 [72]). "A Song," beginning "Of Quarrels, and Changes, and Changelings I sing," is a Jacobite piece of c. 1715 naming the tune "Dear Catholick Brother, or, The Irish Dear-Joy" (Clark). The second tune title is probably inspired by a phrase in the opening stanza of the original "Catholick Brother" ballad. *A Collection of State Songs,* 1716, prints two pieces to the tune: "The High-Church Expedition" and "On the Pretender's Expedition to Scotland." Two more appear in *Mughouse Diversion,* 1717, 5th ed., 1719: "The Somersetshire Man's Account of the Roebuck Mughouse," and "The Irish Bulls, on the King's Publick Entry." "A Dialogue between Morgan, Sawney, and Teague, on the 19th of October, 1714" is in *A Collection of Old Ballads,* 1723–1725, II, 224. Later uses of the tune include a song "By Mr. Fielding" in Watts's *Musical Miscellany,* 1729–1731, VI, 170, with the music: "A Dialogue between a Beau's Head and his Heels, taken from their Mouths as they were spoke at St. James's Coffee-House." And a verse pamphlet of 1740, "Michaelmas Term, or the Battle of the Loggerheads," names the tune for singing (Harvard; an issue of c. 1750 is in BM 11630.b.5 [9]).

The tune is cited in four ballad operas, including Walker's *The Quaker's Opera,* 1728, Johnson's *The Village Opera,* 1729, and Phillips's

· 167 ·

one-act condensation, *The Chamber-maid,* 1730, Ralph's *The Fashionable Lady,* 1730, and Peterson's *The Raree Show,* 1739. Music is printed with all save the last of these.

Dear Pickaninny

In the Third Part of his *Don Quixote,* 1696, Act IV, Thomas D'Urfey introduced a duet "Intended to be Sung by 2 Poppets one representing A Captain tother a Town Miss." *New Songs* from the play appeared in the same year, and although the gathering of engraved sheets was not uniform throughout the edition, some copies contain this song, beginning "Dear Pinkaninny/if half a Guinny/to Love will win ye," and including the tune which is identified only as a minuet (Fig. 106). The song was

reprinted with music in *Pills,* 1719–1720, I, 282, and without music in *A Complete Collection of . . . English and Scotch Songs,* 1735–1736, III, 96. Meantime the stage song, expanded to eight stanzas, was issued as a broadside entitled "The Captains Courtship to a Town Miss" (Pepys V, 214, with meaningless music). No other broadside seems to have used the tune, but it was called for in two ballad operas of 1731—Coffey's *The Devil to Pay* and Lillo's *Silvia.*

Death and the Lady

In the second recitative of "A New Year's Ode," Henry Carey introduced a tune not his own and noted the fact: "The Melody stolen from an Old Ballad called Death and the Lady" (*The Musical Century*, 1737–1740, I, 53). The ballad may be older than the earliest extant copy, a roman-letter edition printed for J. Deacon, who flourished at the close of the seventeenth century. Later editions are common, and the ballad continued to be popular with the Seven Dials printers of the nineteenth century. It is usually titled "The Great Messenger of Mortality; Or, a Dialogue betwixt Death and a beautiful Lady," and begins "Fair Lady, lay your costly Robes aside" (Wood 417, Douce, Lord Crawford, BM 1871.e.9 [111], Yale, Madden, Roxburghe; reprinted in *RB* VII, ix). Most editions have no tune direction, but the Roxburghe copy and one or two others list the tune as "Farewel my Heart's Delight." This title echoes the opening line of "The two faithful Lovers" (*BB* II, 471), a ballad sung to "Franklin is fled away," q.v.; but the "Franklin" music does not fit the "Messenger" verses, which are in the decasyllabic quatrains characteristic of "Fortune my foe." Indeed, there is a suggestion of a link with "Fortune" in the fact that a Byrd setting of the latter in the Clement Matchett MS Virginal Book, 1612, bears an added title "Farwell delighte." But the tune Carey appropriated is wholly independent of "Fortune."

Carey may have had his attention called to "Death and the Lady" by the presence of the tune in two ballad operas: Ryan's *The Cobler's Opera*, 1729, Air 6 (Fig. 107), and Ralph's *The Fashionable Lady*, 1730.

In any case, it is remarkable that this old tune should have been printed three times in less than a decade after having been in popular circulation for a considerable period. The music itself is of another age.

"Fair Lady, lay your costly Robes aside" is given as the tune to which a late eighteenth-century broadside is to be sung. It is titled "A true and

Tragical Song, concerning Captain John Bolton . . . Trial . . . 27th of March, 1775 . . . strangled himself in the Cell" and begins "Good Christian people all, both old and young" (Roxburghe; reprinted in Ritson's *Yorkshire Garland,* 1788, Halliwell-Phillipps's *Yorkshire Anthology,* 1851, and *RB* VIII, 724). There may be other eighteenth-century uses of the tune which I have not seen.

Chappell (*PMOT* I, 167) advances the interesting thesis that some ballads directed to be sung to "Aim not too high" (a tune name deriving from the first line of a "Fortune my foe" ballad) could not easily be sung to the tune of "Fortune" because of the initial trochaic foot the music demands. He believes that ballads with a strong iambic beginning, as in "Fair Lady, lay your costly Robes aside," were sung either to the tune we know as "Death and the Lady" or to an altered version of "Fortune" which would accommodate this different rhythmic pattern. Chappell's idea is somewhat weakened by the fact that most "Aim not" ballads will fit one tune as well as the other; in other words, there is not the sizable body of ballads he implies which would be difficult to sing to "Fortune" as we know it. And both tunes have a dirgelike quality which makes it possible to wrench the metrical accents without severe dislocation.

The Delights of the Bottle

This was originally a two-stanza solo of Bacchus in Shadwell's *Psyche,* 1675, Act V, with music by Matthew Locke. The vocal music of the opera was published in that year, and this song, beginning "The delights of the Bottle & the charms of good Wine," includes a four-part chorus, repeating the last two lines of each stanza (Fig. 108). Words and music were reprinted in *Choice Ayres, Songs & Dialogues,* Book I, 1676, and in *The Second Book of the Pleasant Musical Companion,* 2d ed., 1686. Shadwell's words may be found in *Wit and Mirth,* 3d ed., 1682, and *RB* VIII, clxvi*; a seventeenth-century MS version is in Arthur Clifford's *Tixall Poetry,* 1813.

The stage song was lengthened to twelve stanzas and published as a broadside, with an apology in the headpiece:

> Some Lines were drawn by a more skilful hand,
> And which they were you'l quickly understand,
> Excuse me therefore if I do you wrong,
> I did but make a Ballad of a Song.

The title is "The Delights of the Bottle: Or, The Town-Gallants Declaration for Women and Wine . . . To a most Admirable New Tune, every where much in request" (Lord Crawford, Harvard, Douce, Rawlinson, Euing, Wood E.25, Roxburghe; reprinted in *RB* IV, 44). The Wood copy's MS note "made about 1650" is clearly in error.

A number of ballads were written to this tune during the reign of Charles II. Richard Burton, a bookseller who flourished into the 1670s, published "The Prodigal Son Converted, Or The Young-man return'd from his Rambles," beginning "The delights & the pleasures/of a man without care" (Douce, Roxburghe; reprinted in *RB* IV, 49). The following ballads to the tune were licensed by Roger L'Estrange and so are no later than 1685: "The Rich and Flourishing Cuckold well Satisfied," beginning "The delights of a Cuckold that doth not repine" (Wood E.25, Rawlinson; reprinted in *RB* VIII, clxiv*); "Poor Robin's Prophesie, or, The merry Conceited Fortune-teller," beginning "All you that delight for to hear a new song" (Pepys, Rawlinson, Harvard, Douce, BM C.22.f.6, Lord Crawford; reprinted in *RB* VIII, lxxviii*); and "Old Christmass Returnd . . . a Looking-glass for rich Misers," beginning "All you that to Feasting and mirth are inclin'd" (Pepys; reprinted in *PB* III, 53). "The Wine-Cooper's Delight," beginning "The Delights of the Bottle are turn'd out of doors,/By factious fanatical Sons of damn'd Whores," is a ballad of 1681, some editions of which contain music (Harvard, BM

82.1.8, Wood 417, Wood 276a, Roxburghe; reprinted in *RB* IV, 53). Words and music are also in *180 Loyal Songs,* 1685.

D'Urfey wrote a song to the tune beginning "Farewell my Lov'd Science, my former delight" for his *Sir Barnaby Whigg,* 1681, III, ii, reprinted in his *New Collection of Songs and Poems,* 1683. Another song of D'Urfey's, "Away with the Causes of Riches and Cares," originally used in his *Madam Fickle,* 1677, I, i, has its own tune by Matthew Locke in *Catch that Catch Can,* 1685, and *The Second Book of the Pleasant Musical Companion,* 1686; a broadside version, "The Young Gallants Tutor," is to the tune of "The Delights of the Bottle" (Pepys IV, 246, Douce II, 259).

"News from the West; Or, . . . what lately happened in that part of the World," beginning "Come listen all you who to mirth are inclin'd," is "To a New Tune, Or The Delights of the Bottle, Or, Would you know how we Drink" (Bodleian Ashmole G.15 [163], licensed by Richard Pocock, 1685–1688); the broadside contains unidentified music which may be the "New Tune" itself. The last tune name may be an imprecise reference to the Purcell music for "Would you know how we meet o're our jolly full Bowls," q.v. "The Birds' Harmony," beginning "As I was walking in the shade/Which Summer's heat with leaves had made," is to be sung to "The delights of the Bottle" (Pepys, Douce; reprinted in *RB* VI, 782); but instead of six anapestic tetrameter lines, its stanza pattern is a mixture of four- and five-foot iambics which do not fit the tune.

"The Fathers good Counsel to his Lascivious Son . . . against Wenching," beginning "Come Son, you are young, yet I oft have been told," is to "The delights of the bottle" (Roxburghe; reprinted in *RB* VIII, 578); the imprint has been cropped, but it probably dates from c. 1680–1690. Only eighteenth-century Bow Church Yard imprints remain of "Simple Simon's Misfortunes, and his Wife Margery's Cruelty," beginning "Come listen a while and here I will relate" (Harvard Percy collection, Roxburghe; reprinted in *RB* VIII, 428).

Derry Down

This tune, one of the most popular in the eighteenth century, was called "Derry Down," "The Abbot of Canterbury," "The King and the Lord Abbot," "King John and the Abbot of Canterbury," and "A Cobler there was." Its stanza form is distinctive, comprising an anapestic

tetrameter quatrain plus a burden "Derry down, down, hey derry down."
A great many broadsides without tune direction were probably designed
for this tune, if we may judge from the presence of the characteristic
refrain or some adaptation of it.

A version of "Kinge John and Bishoppe," without refrain or tune indication, is in the Percy Folio MS (ed. Hales and Furnivall, I, 508; reprinted in Child, No. 45 A).[1] The ballad giving rise to the tune, though
it may have been written as early as the Percy text, is known to us only
from broadside editions of the late seventeenth century and after. It is
"A New Ballad of King John and the Abbot of Canterbury," beginning
"I'le tell you a Story, a Story anon,/Of a noble Prince, & his Name was
King John," to the tune of "the King and the Lord Abbot" (Euing, Lord
Crawford, Pepys, Bagford, Harvard, Douce, Roxburghe; reprinted in *RB*
VI, 747, and Child No. 45 B). Black-letter copies, licensed by Roger
L'Estrange, are no later than 1685, and the ballad was in Thackeray's list
of c. 1689. *Pills* contains a reprint of the broadside along with the
earliest appearance of the tune (1700, II, 28; 1719–1720, IV, 28=Fig. 109).

Many versions of the music may be found on single-sheet songs and
in poetical miscellanies of the eighteenth century. The tune as in *Pills*
appears with "A Song made upon a Gentleman's sitting upon a Cremona
Fiddle," beginning "Ye Lads & ye Lasses y^t live at Longleat" (Harvard,

[1] As Child's notes make clear, folktale analogues of this riddling ballad are widespread. Walter Anderson's *Kaiser und Abt*, Folklore Fellows Communications No. 42,
1923, is an impressive study of more than five hundred versions of the story. Anglo-
American tradition is usually represented by the ballad form, of which there are at least
two seventeenth-century versions metrically and musically distinct from our "Derry
down" ballad. They are: "The King and the Bishop," beginning "In Popish time when
Bishops proud," to the tune of "Chievy-Chase" (Pepys, Douce, Roxburghe; reprinted
in *RB* VI, 751), and "The Old Abbot and King Olfrey," beginning "In old times past
there was a King we read," to the tune of "The Shaking of the Sheets" (Pepys, Douce;
reprinted in *RB* VI, 753).

110

Original is in A minor; time signature mistakenly given as 6/8 on song sheet.
* Misengraved a whole tone too low in original.

BM H.1601 [550], dated 1730?). Another edition, engraved by Cross and so perhaps earlier, bears the title "The Long-leat Ballad. Occasion'd by a Gentleman's Sitting upon a Cremona Violin" (Harvard) and has a distinctive cadence (Fig. 110).[2] Three other single-sheet songs contain identical music, notably more syncopated than the *Pills* version. They are: "The Norfolk Freeholders, Set for yͤ German Flute" (Fig. 111), a

111

ballad of c. 1733 opposing Walpole's tax plans, beginning "You Norfolk Freeholders whose generous Hearts" (BM G.316.f [147]); "The Country Wedding; or, The Plough Yoak'd to yͤ Cupbord," beginning "All you that e'er tasted of Swatful Hall Beer" (Harvard); and "The Snipe. [A] ballad to yͤ tune of yͤ Abbot of Canterbury," by the Rev. Phanuel Bacon, beginning "I'll tell ye a story, a story yᵗ'ˢ true" (Harvard, BM G.309 [1], dated 1750?). The tune as arranged by Richard Leveridge for

[2] A broadside version of 1720, without music, has the tune direction "King John and the Abbot of Canterbury" and is entitled "A Ballad, Upon a Gentleman's sitting upon the Lady W[eymouth]'s Cremona Fiddle" (Harvard Percy collection). This ballad is sung also to its own tune; see s.v. "Cremona Fiddle."

"The Cobler's End,"[3] beginning "A Cobler there was, and he liv'd in a Stall" (Watts, *Musical Miscellany*, 1729–1731, II, 170), and for "The Snipe" (*ibid.*, VI, 136), differs in no important respect from the *Pills* version. But the music on a single-sheet edition of Matthew Prior's "The Thief & Cordelier," beginning "Who has ever been at Paris, must needs know the Greve" (Harvard, BM G.313 [83], dated 1725?) has a considerably different movement in three-quarter time and ends with a major cadence (Fig. 112).

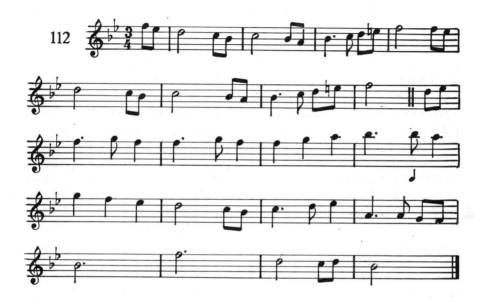

112

Under the name "Abbot of Canterbury" or "A Cobler there was," the tune is one of the most popular used in ballad operas, being called for in no less than twenty-six productions. It was not in the original version of Gay's *The Beggar's Opera* but was added as an unnumbered air to the fourth state of the first edition, and it appeared as Air 56 in the second edition. Music is printed for the tune in other ballad operas, as follows: Mottley and Cooke, *Penelope*, 1728, Coffey, *The Beggar's Wedding*, 1729, Johnson, *The Village Opera*, 1729, Ralph, *The Fashionable Lady*, 1730, Coffey, *The Devil to Pay*, 1731, Coffey, *The Boarding-School*, 1733, Langford, *The Lover his own Rival*, 1736. The tune is referred to in *Court and Country*, 1743, as "Who's e'er been at Paris," from the opening line

[3] This ballad, which appeared in many contemporary collections, gave rise to the name Henry Carey applied to the tune when, using it for a song in his *Musical Century*, 1737–1740, I, 53, he speaks of the melody as "stolen from an Old Ballad called Death and the Cobler."

· 175 ·

of Prior's ballad; and the last of the operas using the tune is Brooke's *Jack the Gyant Queller,* 1749.

Some indication of the most popular songs set to the tune may be gained from the opening stanza of "The Battle of the Colliers," an eighteenth-century broadside to the tune of "King John, and the Abbot of Canterbury" (BM C.116.i.4 [23]):

> I tell not, as whilom did merry Mat. Prior,
> A Tale of a Hangman, a Thief, and a Fryar;
> Nor will I the King, and the Abbot repeat,
> Or the Fiddle's Mischance that befel at Long-Leat.

The three ballads here referred to have already been noticed. At least a hundred other ballads and songs to the tune (or written in the stanza form with a "Derry down" refrain) could be cited from eighteenth-century literature. Almost every verse anthology from *Political Merriment,* 1714, to *British Lyre,* 1793, contains pieces to the tune, and single broadsides covering a wide range of topics—amatory, political, religious—find the distinctive tripping stanza appropriate for humorous or satiric effects. It was as popular in Ireland as in England (see the broadsides gathered in BM 1890.e.5 and BM 839.m.23). The threat of a Napoleonic invasion in 1803–1804 led to a sheaf of English ballads sung to this tune (uncatalogued Harvard broadsides, Accession No. 44W-2001). One can only conclude that a good tune has almost unlimited uses. Recognizable variants of the air, changed in contour but preserving the eighteenth-century movement, occur with half a dozen texts of "King John and the Bishop" recovered during the twentieth century in England and America (see B. H. Bronson, *The Traditional Tunes of the Child Ballads,* 1959– , I, 357–361). Other "Derry down" variants have recently been found associated with "The Little Brown Bulls" and "Red Iron Ore" (Franz Rickaby, *Ballads and Songs of the Shanty-Boy,* 1926, pp. 65, 161) and "Blue Mountain Lake" (Helen H. Flanders *et al., New Green Mountain Songster,* 1939, p. 176. A variant is recorded by Frank Warner, *American Folk Songs and Ballads,* Elektra LP-3, 1952).[4]

---

[4] For further references, see G. Malcolm Laws, *Native American Balladry,* 1950, C 16, D 9, C 20.

[The Devil Assist
the Plotting Whigs]

"The Whigs Lamentable Condition, or the Royalists Resolution. To a pleasant new Tune," beginning "The Deel assist the Plotting Whigs," is found with music in *180 Loyal Songs,* 1685, p. 210. With small modifications the same tune (Fig. 113) is printed on a broadside

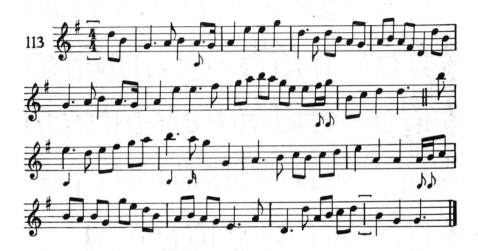

which may be dated c. 1683: "The Bloody Siege of Vienna," beginning "The Gods are now in Council sat" (Harvard, Clark).

Chappell (*PMOT* II, 609n.) incorrectly associates this tune with one by Purcell commonly called "Peggie, I must love thee," q.v. Aside from sharing a common pseudo-Scots character, the tunes are completely unalike.

De'il Take the War

"A Scotch Song in the last New Play, Sung by Mrs. Cross," beginning "De'el take the Warr that hurri'd Willy from me," was issued by Henry Playford and Samuel Scott in 1696 (Chetham 2058),[1] the year in which D'Urfey's unpublished play, *A Wife for Any Man,* was performed. Charles Powell's florid and rather uninteresting tune appeared on the single sheet (Fig. 114). A broadside issue of 1696 with meaningless music is entitled

"An Excellent New Scotch Song, Being lately Sung in . . . A Wife for any Man" (Pepys V, 259). Within the next few years several other editions were issued with music (Harvard, California, Huntington, BM G.304 [49], BM H.1601 [128]). Words and music are in all editions of *Pills,* 1719–1720, I, 294. The tune is also to be found in *The Dancing Master,* Second Part, 2d ed., 1698, and in Walsh's *Compleat Country Dancing-Master,* 1718. D'Urfey's verses alone are in *Compleat Academy of Complements,* 1705. A late eighteenth-century song-sheet version, titled simply "De'el Tak the War" (Huntington), testifies to the long vogue of the piece.

[1] Since the sheet is designated "Numb. 1," it is probably the first in a series of "Scotch" songs which Playford and Scott announced early in 1696. See Day-Murrie, Book No. 160, for information on the second, third, and fourth songs in the series. "Numb. 1" has not been previously identified.

The tune is cited in six ballad operas, including the following which print the music: Coffey's *The Beggar's Wedding,* 1729, Ryan's *The Cobbler's Opera,* 1729, Chetwood's *The Lover's Opera,* 1729 (music in 3d ed., 1730), and Potter's *The Decoy,* 1733. Watts's *Musical Miscellany,* 1729–1731, V, 118, reprints the song and air from *The Beggar's Wedding,* beginning "Behold, I fly on Wings of soft Desire."

The Devil's Progress

One of the ballads reprinted in *Rump,* 1662, and in *A Collection of Loyal Songs Written against the Rump Parliament,* 1731, is "The Sence of the House, or the Reason why . . . The Remnant . . . of Parliament cannot consent to Peace, or an Accommodation. To the Tune of, The New-England Psalm, Huggle Duggle, ho ho ho the Devil he laught aloud." It begins:

> Come come beloved Londoners, fy fy you shame us all,
>> Your rising up for Peace, will make the close Committee fall;
> I wonder you dare ask for that, which they must needs deny,
>> There's 30. swears they'll have no Peace, and bid me tell you why.

A broadside copy among the Thomason Tracts in the BM is dated March 10, 1642/43; other copies are in Bodleian A.3.18.Art and Ashmole H.23 (69), and a manuscript version is in Ashmole H.23 (63).

I know of no ballad entitled "New England Psalm," but *Pills,* 1719–

1720, III, 82, prints what may formerly have been a ballad with that title. Here, however, it is called "The Devil's Progress on Earth, or Huggle Duggle, &c." and begins "Friar Bacon walks again,/And Doctor Forster too." The *Pills* refrain "Huggle Duggle Ha! ha! ha!/The Devil laugh'd aloud," establishes a kinship with the older broadside and suggests that "The Devil's Progress" must have been known before 1642. The *Pills* music (Fig. 115) opens with a phrase reminiscent of Dr. Aldrich's "The bonny Christ Church bells," q.v.

Diana's a Nymph

This tune takes its origin from "Diana's Darling, Or The Modish Courtier," whose first line is "Diana's a Nymph so chast and so fair." [1] This ballad, whose stanza is six anapestic tetrameter lines, is sung to "Diana's a Nymph" (Lord Crawford, Pepys, Harvard, BM C.22.f.6, Roxburghe; reprinted in *RB* IV, 58). William Turner wrote a musical setting to the words for *Choice Ayres & Songs,* Second Book, 1679, p. 48 (Fig. 116). "Diana's a Nymph" is the tune cited for "Tyrannick Love," beginning "I Languish all night, and I sigh all the day" (Roxburghe; reprinted in *RB* IV, 63), a broadside with an eight-line stanza requiring a repetition of the final eight bars of music. An independent musical setting of a poem beginning "I languish all night and sigh all the day" is in *Choice Songs and Ayres,* First Book, 1673; but the verse has a different movement (lines 2, 4, and 8 are trimeters) and cannot be considered to have any relationship to the broadside except for the coincidence of first lines. [2] The opening line of "Tyrannick Love" is also imitated

[1] "Diana's Darling" is to be distinguished from the ballad on Diana and Actæon beginning "Diana and her darlings dear" (*RB* II, 520), one edition of which (Manchester I, 29) is to the tune of "Rogero." This is in ballad quatrains. Still different music, unpreserved, is presupposed in the tune direction "Diana," for singing the octosyllabic quatrains of "The Lamentable Song of the Lord Wigmoore" (Richard Johnson, *Crown Garland of Golden Roses,* 1612, ed. Chappell, 1842, p. 14).

[2] The song was introduced into Edward Ravenscroft's *The Citizen turn'd Gentleman,* 1672, I, i, and the text is found in several contemporary drolleries. See Ebsworth's discussion in *RB* IV, 61–62. Assuming a relationship between stage song and broadside, Ebsworth dated "Tyrannick Love" about 1672–1673; the argument fails from incompatibility. Our only evidence for dating the broadside concerns the one edition known, which was published for Coles, Vere, Wright, Clark, Thackeray, and Passinger, a partnership active 1678–1680.

116 ＝C3＝

in a song found in *The Newest Collection of the Choicest Songs,* 1683, sig. K2. Its stanza would fit "Diana's a Nymph" but no tune is named for singing, and the text diverges from broadside wording after the first line.

Digby's Farewell

Captain Francis Digby lost his life in an encounter of his warship *Henry* with Dutch vessels in Southwold Bay, May 28, 1672. But in 1671 a poem, "Captain Digby's Farewell," beginning "I'le go to my love, where he lies in the Deep," appeared in *The New Academy of Complements,* and, without reference to Digby in the title, in *Oxford Drollery* and *Windsor Drollery.* With music by Robert Smith, it appears in *Choice Songs and Ayres,* First Book, 1673, p. 14 (Fig. 117), without title; in the second edition, 1675, it is titled "Captain Digby's Farewell." The stanza of this song is four anapestic tetrameters plus the refrain:

Ah! Ah! Ah! my Love's dead!
There was not a Bell,
But a Triton's shell
to Ring, to Ring out his Knell.

Another poem, "Mr. Digbyes Farewell, To the Tune of my Lord Sandwiches Farewell," beginning "Oh pitty Arminda those Passions I bear," is in what Ebsworth calls "the extremely scarce 'second impression'" of *Westminster Drollery,* Part Two, 1672. Its stanza pattern is six

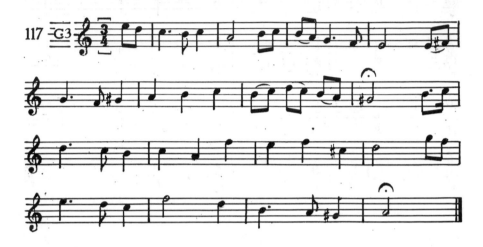

lines plus a refrain of two lines to be repeated, all of anapestic tetrameters. But a ballad to the tune of "The Earl of Sandwich Farewel" called "The Sorrowful Ladies Complaint," beginning "One morning I walk'd by my self on the shoar" (Harvard, Pepys, Lord Crawford, Roxburghe; reprinted in *RB* IV, 398), is an expansion of the 1671 poem, retaining its stanza form including the refrain:

Of ah! ah! ah! my Love's dead
There is not a Bell
But a Triton's shell
To ring, to ring, to ring my Love's knell.

Another tune by Robert Smith, different from that for "I'le go to my love," is called "The Earle of Sandwich Farewell" in Thomas Greeting's *The Pleasant Companion . . . for the Flagelet,* 2d ed., 1673, and in *Apollo's Banquet,* 5th ed., 1687. The same music is in *Choice Songs and Ayres,* First Book, 1673, p. 10 (Fig. 118), with the song (perhaps by Dryden) beginning "Farewell fair Armida my Joy and my Grief." The same tune is called "Farewell fair Armida" in *Musicks Recreation on the Viol, Lyra-way,* 1682, and "Farewel, my Calista" in Johnson's *The*

Village Opera, 1729.[1] This music, unlike that for "I'le go to my love," fits the stanza pattern (eight anapestic tetrameters) of ballads assigned to "Digby's Farewell."

Still another tune remains to be considered. It is called "Digbys Farwell" in *Musicks Hand-maid,* 1678, No. 75 (Fig. 119); "Captain Digby's Farewel, or, Carman's Whistle" in *Apollo's Banquet,* 6th ed., 1690; and—to compound the confusion—"The Earl of Sandwich's Farewell" in *Musicks Recreation on the Viol, Lyra-way,* 1682. This tune will also fit the stanza pattern of "Digby's Farewell" ballads.

[1] A broadside version, beginning "Farewel my Calista, my joy and my grief," has the title "Love and Honour: Or, The Lovers Farewel to Calista: Being sent from Sea in the late Engagement against the Dutch, to his Mistress, under the Name of Calista." Though it would fit the music of "Digby's Farewell," it contains the tune direction "Now the Tyrant hath stolen" (see "Bonny sweet Robin"). The ballad is reprinted in *RB* VI, 40. The poem on which the broadside is based appeared originally in *New Court-Songs, and Poems, Covent Garden Drolery, Westminster Drolery,* and *Windsor Drolery,* 2d ed., all of 1672.

"Armida," or "Calista" as she became in the ballad, is thought to have been Frances Stewart, Duchess of Richmond. G. Thorn-Drury, in his edition of *Covent Garden Drolery,* 1928, pp. 126–129, doubts the attribution, though the *DNB* supports it. Thorn-Drury argues too against Dryden's authorship of the poem; for a contrary view, see *The Songs of John Dryden,* ed. C. L. Day, 1932, pp. 152–155.

119

*Double bar in original is at end of measure 4.

The problem facing us is, first, the relationship between the 1671 poem, written before Digby's death, and the verses which memorialize him from 1672 onward. It is singular that "I'le go to my love, where he lies in the Deep" could have been written about a Digby who was absent on naval duty but still alive. Yet only on that premise can we explain the existence of the song, coupled with Digby's name, a year before his death. A second problem is to establish the relationship between the "Digby's Farewell" and "Earl of Sandwich's Farewell" tunes. The poem in *Westminster Drollery* indicates that "The Earl of Sandwich's Farewell" was known as a tune before 1672; and associating that tune with a poem called "Mr. Digbyes Farewell" suggests that "Digby's Farewell" as a tune derives from "The Earl of Sandwich's Farewell." But we have three tunes under consideration: one by Robert Smith called "Captain Digby's Farewell"; another by Smith called "The Earle of Sandwich Farewell"; and an anonymous tune which goes by both names. We can eliminate the first of these because it does not fit the "Digby" ballad stanza.

But the fact remains that one tune name has not given way to another; rather, the two tunes and two tune names exist side by side (note that *Musicks Recreation* and the fifth and sixth editions of *Apollo's Banquet* print both tunes). The two tunes might be said to be interchangeable, in that both can be used with the eight-line "Digby" stanza; but they are not musically identical. The one ballad to be sung to "The Earl of Sandwich Farewel" can be sung with Robert Smith's tune to "Farewell fair Armida" if the last two phrases of the music are repeated. And all the ballads directed to "Digby's Farewell" can be sung to the anonymous tune. It may or may not be significant that, although an astonishing number of "Digby" ballads list an alternate tune, in none have I observed "The Earl of Sandwich's Farewell" cited as an alternate tune.

"Digby's Farewell" enjoyed undoubted popularity as a ballad tune during the last decade or so of Charles II's reign. It was used with: "Great B[r]ittains Ioy, and Good News for the Netherlands . . . Peace Concluded . . . 9th of February . . . [1674]," beginning "Come all Loyal Subjects I pray you draw near" (Wood E.25 [101]); "News from the Coast of Spain," on the sea battle at Cadiz, February, 1674, beginning "Come all you brave Sea-men of Courage so free" (Wood E.25 [100], Rawlinson 82); "The bad Husband's Information of ill Husbandry," beginning "You bonny boon blades that are company keepers," to the tune of "Digby's Farewel: Or The Jovial Crew" (Lord Crawford 1385, Pepys II, 89, Harvard, Rawlinson 135; the latter copy is dated 1676 and the tune title is "The Jovial Crew");[2] "The Musical Shepherdess, or, Dorinda's Lamentation for the loss of Amintas," by W[alter] P[ope], beginning "Adieu to the Pleasures and follies of Love," to the tune of "Amintas farewel: or, Digby's Farewell" (Lord Crawford, Pepys, Douce, Wood E.25, BM C.22.f.6, Roxburghe; reprinted in RB IV, 462). This last-named broadside was an expansion of a three-stanza song in Shadwell's Tempest, 1674; it was not printed in the play, but the words appeared in The Several Songs Now in Mode, 1675, and with music by James Hart, in Choice Ayres, Songs, & Dialogues, 2d ed., 1675, and in all editions of Pills, 1719–1720, III, 178. "Amintas farewel" seems to be an internally inspired tune title, probably a name for Hart's tune. "Good News in Bad Times; or, Absaloms Return to David's Bosome," a political ballad of 1683, beginning "Adieu to the hopes of the Whigs of the State," is to the tune "Adieu to the pleasures and Follies of Love" (Harvard, Clark, Roxburghe; reprinted in RB V, 399), a name derived from the first line of "The Musical Shepherdess," mentioned above.

The tune was popular for execution ballads: "The Plotter Executed . . . Edward Coleman . . . [Dec. 3, 1678]," beginning "Forbear your vile Ploting, all you that design," to the tune of "Captain Digby, or, Packington's Pound" (Roxburghe; reprinted in RB IV, 125); "Treason Rewarded at Tiburn . . . Ireland and Grove . . . Executed . . . the 24th of January [1679]," beginning "Let all Loyal Subjects look well to their Hits" (Wood E. 25; reprinted in RB IV, 136); "Sir Thomas Armstrong's Farewell," supposedly written before his execution June 20, 1684, beginning "Farewel Worldly Pleasures and fading delight," to the tune of "Digbys Farewel: or, Packingtons Pound" (Roxburghe; reprinted in RB V, 483).

2 "The Jovial Crew" is the title of a ballad beginning "Come let's to the Tavern there's nothing so sweet," to the tune of "Let the Bay-liffs be hang'd, and the Serjeants accurst, or, Digby's Farewell" (Rawlinson 141). I have no data on the first tune title cited, but it is again coupled with "Digby's Farewel" in "A farewel to Hackney Iades. Or, Be Kind to One and no more," beginning "Let Mally, and Jenny, and Peggy sit still" (Rawlinson 90).

Among other ballads to the tune, the following do not appear to have been republished: "The Royal Health," beginning "You Peers of this Nation, pray never Rebel" (Clark, with MS date 27 March 1684); "The Winchester Health: Or, An Excellent New Pleasant Song of his Majesty," dated 1684, beginning "Here's a Health to Great Charles, our Soveraign King" (Chetham 1047); "The Constant Couple, Or, The Glory of True Love," beginning "Of late I did walk in a pleasant fair day," to the tune of "Bonny Currant: or, Digbys farewel, or Packington's Pound" (Douce I, 31, Pepys III, 163); [3] "The Maltster caught in a Trap Or, The Witty Ale-Wife," beginning "I pray you draw near and attend now a while," to the tune of "What should a young woman do with an old man: Or, Digby's Farewel" (Lord Crawford 606, BM C.22.f.6 [149], Harvard); [4] "The Kind Lovers . . . Amandus and Coriana," beginning "Hark, hark, in yon Grove the fair nymph she does sing," to the tune of "Hark, hark, in yon Grove, or Digbyes Farwell" (Pepys III, 228); [5] "The City Caper: Or, The Whetstones-Park Privateer," beginning "The Jenny a small Pickaroon in the Park" (Lord Crawford 724, Rawlinson 129, Douce I, 26, BM C.22.f.6 [92], Harvard); "The Couragious Cook-maid," beginning "Of late in the North a fine frolique did pass," to the tune of "The City Caper, Or: Digby" (Lord Crawford 961, BM C.22.f.6 [101]).

"Love Crownd with Victory," beginning "My Dear canst thou love me, I pray tell me true," has the tune direction "Ile crown thee my dearest &c. Digby's Farwel, Or Packintons Pound" (Harvard, BM C.22.f.6 [56], Lord Crawford 831, Douce I, 123). The first tune title is from the refrain of the broadside. "The merry Pastime of the Spri[ng]," by L[awrence] W[hite], begins "All young men and maidens,/come listen a while" (Rawlinson 115); its sixteen-line stanza, the equivalent of eight anapestic tetrameters, will fit "Captain Digby," to which it is to be sung. "The Lovers final Farewel. To his Faithless false Mistress," beginning "I lov'd thee wel once, but il'e love thee no more," is sung to "Love and honour or Digby's farwell" (Rawlinson 147). The first tune

---

[3] "Bonny Currant" is probably a dance tune, but I have not found the particular coranto that may be intended.

[4] The first tune title is associated with "Digby's Farewell" in several other ballads, including "The Politick Maids Device," beginning "All Maidens come hither and hearken a while" (Lord Crawford 41, Pepys III, 166), and its sequel, "The Young-Man's Answer to the Politick Maids Device," beginning "For certain and sure, this Girl will go mad" (Pepys III, 167). The same tunes, plus "Packington's Pound," are cited for "An Amorous Dialogue between John and his Mistris" (RB III, 395).

[5] The first tune title, internally inspired, may imply an independent tune, as is often the case with stage songs. Although this broadside may have originated in the theater, there is no record of such a song with music.

title, equivalent to "The Tyrant," is from the broadside "Love and Honour" cited in note 1 above.

"A We[st]minster Wedding: Or, A Whore-Master Buried Alive" begins "A Curse on blind Cupid his name I do hate" (Rawlinson 142). "The Gossips Meeting, or, The merry Market-Women of Taunton," beginning "Come all my kind neighbours, & hear me a while," is to "The Parliament of Women: Or, Digby's Farewell" (Wood E.25 [120], Rawlinson 112); the first tune title may be suggested by the subject of the ballad.

Diogenes Surly and Proud, or The Tippling Philosophers

Ned Ward, author of *The London Spy,* wrote "Wine and Wisdom: or, The Tipling Philosophers, a lyric poem," 1710,[1] beginning "Diogenes surly and proud, who snarl'd at the Macedon Youth." It was popular in many forms through the eighteenth century, thanks to Richard Leveridge's assistance in writing a tune for it and singing the ballad publicly. Thus a contemporary song-sheet issue with music (Fig. 120) bears the title "The Tippling Philosophers. Set and Sung by Mr. Leveridge at the Theatre in Lincoln's Inn Fields" (BM Gren. 559 [17], Huntington, Harvard, Yale). Other editions of the song sheet with London and Dublin imprints attest its continued popularity. It was printed on broadsides without music (Douce II, 271ᵛ, BM 1872.a.1 [165ᵛ]) and was included in such songbooks as Watts's *Musical Miscellany,* 1729–1731, I, 154, *The Convivial Songster,* c. 1782, p. 138, and Ritson's *English Songs,* 1783, II, 34. Leveridge's tune, called "The Tipling Philosophers," is in *The Dancing Master,* c. 1728, III, 49, and in an arrangement for harpsichord or spinet in *The Ladys Banquet,* Fifth Book, c. 1735, p. 27. Commonly called "Diogenes surly and proud," the air was introduced into seven ballad operas, of which the following include the music in printed editions: Coffey's *The Beggar's Wedding,* Chetwood's *The Lover's Opera* (music in 3d ed., 1730), and Johnson's *The Village Opera,* all dating from 1729.

Ballads sung to the tune include "The High German Doctor," 1720, beginning "Praestigius Legerdemain, with strange Artificial Slights," to

[1] H. W. Troyer, in *Ned Ward of Grubstreet,* 1946, lists the original issue as 1708.

120

the tune of "Diogenes surly and proud" (BM 1850.c.10 [54], Harvard), and a song "When Honesty first was in vogue," to the tune of "The Tippling Philosophers," in William Goodall's *The True Englishman's Miscellany*, 1740, p. 104. Another ballad of Ned Ward's, which appears on a Dublin song sheet of 1720 with Leveridge's tune, is "A South-Sea Ballad, or, Merry Remarks upon Exchange-Alley Bubbles," beginning "In London stands a famous Pile" (Harvard). Other editions without music name the tune "The Grand Elixir; or, The Philosopher's Stone discover'd" (National Lib. of Scotland Ry III.c.36 [132], Harvard, BM 1876.f.1 [88, 89]; reprinted without specification of source in *RB* VIII, 258). Leveridge's music, ideal for the anapestic rhythms of Ward's original song, does not fit the iambics here. I have not found the tune of "The Grand Elixir"; but another edition with music, entitled "The Prophetick Ballad, with merry Remarks . . . ," prints the tune of "London is a fine town," to which the piece can be sung (BM H.1601 [252]).

A composer known only as Mr. Yoslington wrote a fresh air for "The Second Part of The Tipling Philosophers," a single-sheet song of about 1715, beginning "Wise Solon who carefully gave good laws" (BM H.1601 [513], Harvard). The text is sometimes printed on broadsides along with the first part. But Yoslington's tune seems not to have been used for any other songs.

The Doubting Virgin

This tune title is derived from a ballad by Thomas Bowne, "The Doubting Virgin, And The Constant Youngman," c. 1680, beginning "Oh my dearest do not slight me" (Lord Crawford, Harvard, Pepys, Douce, Roxburghe; reprinted in *RB* IV, 344). This ballad is to be sung to "The Repriev'd Captive," a tune now unknown; the Douce copy contains an added tune direction, written in, "O that I had been marryed." [1] A related ballad is "The Doubting Virgins Satisfaction," beginning "Dearest know I do not slight thee," to the tune of "The Repriev'd Captive; Or, The doubting Virgin" (Douce, Roxburghe; reprinted in *RB* IV, 347). Following these, a large number of ballads, several of them by Bowne, were directed to "The Doubting Virgin," all of them in an eight-line stanza alternating eight and seven syllables and characterized by a strong trochaic meter.

The only music that can be associated with "The Doubting Virgin" is found in a ballad opera, *Momus turn'd Fabulist*, 1729, Air 10 (Fig. 121),

121

under the name "Woman's Work is never done." This title is derived from a ballad "Womens Work is never done," beginning "Oh that I had never been married," of which only a mid-eighteenth-century slip-song version is extant (Lord Crawford 939). It is directed to be sung to "the Doubting Virgin," and one may therefore presume that the music from the ballad opera belongs to this tune title. The Douce MS notation is evidently in allusion to the first line of "Womens Work is never done." [2]

---

[1] In the Douce collection this manuscript addition or a variant, "O that I had never married," is found on almost every broadside directed to be sung to "The Doubting Virgin."

[2] An earlier ballad entitled "A Womans Work is never done" begins "As I was wandring on the way" and has the tune direction "A Womans work is never done, Or,

The music is perfectly adapted to the trochaic meter of the ballads, for both musical and poetic phrases begin on the accent throughout.

Among the ballads to the tune are several which are related through their refrains. "Shall I? shall I? No, No," beginning "Pretty Betty now come to me,/thou hast set my Heart on fire," has the refrain:

> Come let's dally, shall I? shall I?
> but she answered No no no.

(Lord Crawford, Douce, Roxburghe; reprinted in *RB* VI, 157). "Kind William, Or, Constant Betty," beginning "Constant Betty that sweet creature," has a very similar refrain:

> Let's not dally, shall I, shall I,
> But she answered, no, no, no.

(Lord Crawford, BM C.22.f.6, Douce, Harvard, Pepys; reprinted in *RB* VII, 201). Its sequel, without a refrain, is "The Hasty Wedding; or, William's Patience Rewarded. With the consent of Pretty Nancy," beginning "Sitting with my Dearest Dear,/by a Little purling Spring," to the tune of "The Man of Fashion, or, The Doubting Virgin" (Euing, Lord Crawford, Douce, Roxburghe; reprinted in *RB* VII, 203). The first tune title here cited is usually "Will [*or* Would] you be a man of fashion" and is often found as an alternate to "The Doubting Virgin," as in the following ballad, whose subtitle relates it to the ballads just noticed. "The Dumb Lady, Or, No, no, not I I'le Answer," beginning "Underneath a little Mountain," is to the tune of "the Doubtful Virgin, or the new Borey, or Will you be a Man of Fashion," and has the refrain "Still she answered no not I" (Pepys, Douce, Harvard, Lord Crawford, Roxburghe; reprinted in *RB* IV, 352).

Among the numerous ballads sung to "The Doubting Virgin," the following do not appear to have been reprinted: "William's Seven-Years

The Beds making" (Roxburghe; reprinted in *RB* III, 302). This ballad was entered in the Stationers' Register, June 1, 1629, as a part of the estate of Margaret Trundle, who followed her late husband's profession of ballad printing from June, 1627, to June, 1629. The Roxburghe copy is a reprint which probably dates from the early years of the reign of Charles II. Its stanza form is eight lines in couplets, unlike the typical rhyme scheme ababcdcd found in "Doubting Virgin" ballads; more important, the ballad contains occasional pentameters, to which the music is not adapted.

One other ballad was sung to "Womens Work is never done": "The Unhappy Voyage . . . [of] the Royal Anne . . . split to Pieces . . . on the Lizzard the 10th of November, 1721" (*RB* VIII, 260). It is in the "Doubting Virgin" stanza form, though the scansion is often irregular.

"Women's work will never be done" in Leyden's Lyra Viol MS (after 1690) is a different tune which had some eighteenth-century currency in Scotland as "The black Eagle" (*Scots Musical Museum*, III, 237). See *Notes on Scottish Song by Robert Burns*, ed. James C. Dick, 1908, pp. 101–102.

Love Compleated," beginning "Late abroad as I was walking,/by a Little Shady Grove" (Douce II, 252); "The Windsor Frolick: or, A Hue and Cry after a couple of Maiden-Heads," beginning "Two brisk Country Girls did agree,/to go unto Windsor-Fair," to the tune of "Oh so Ungrateful a Creature; Or, The Doubting Virgin" (Douce II, 251ᵛ); [3] "Real Reality, or; The Souldiers Loyalty," beginning "Tho' at present I must leave thee" (Pepys IV, 43); "The Seamans Constancy," beginning "Dearest dear we must be parted" (Pepys IV, 190).

A ballad of 1688, "Monmouth Routed," beginning "Now the fatal Fight is over," has the tune direction "The Souldiers Departure" (Lord Crawford, Pepys; reprinted in *RB* V, 674), which is derived from "The Souldiers Departure From his Love," beginning "Now my love has Crost the Ocean," to the tune of "The Doubting Virgin" (Bagford; reprinted in BB I, 355). The first line of "Monmouth Routed" in turn becomes the tune name in "The Bloody Fight of Flanders," beginning "Here is News from famous Flanders," to the tune of "Now the fatal Fight is over" (Pepys; reprinted in *PB* VI, 229), and "A New Coppy of Verses Of General Schomberg's Happy Success . . . in Ireland," beginning "Now Duke Schomberg he is Landed," to the tune of "Now the Fight is Over" (Pepys; reprinted in *PB* V, 18).

The ballad called "The Souldiers Departure From his Love" was licensed by Richard Pocock (1685–1688), and a number of other ballads employ this name for the tune of "Doubting Virgin." They include "The Mariners Misfortune, or, The Unfortunate Voyage of two Constant Lovers," beginning "A Seaman lov'd a Maiden pretty" (Bagford; reprinted in *BB* I, 250); another edition is entitled "The She-Mariners Misfortune," and is to "Doubting Virgin" (Pepys IV, 187). Several ballads on military campaigns of the period also use "The Souldiers Departure": "Monmouth Worsted in the West," beginning "Now we see the fight is over" (Wood E.25, Pepys; reprinted in *RB* V, 669); "Monmouth's Saying In the West of England," beginning "Now our bloody Fight is over" (Pepys; reprinted in *RB* V, 678); "The Protestant Seaman's Resolution To Fight for King William," beginning "Come brave noble hearted Sea-men" (BM C.22.f.6, Lord Crawford, Harvard, Pepys; reprinted in *PB* IV, 214); and "The Valiant Souldier's Misfortune: or . . . the Duke of Schomberg's last Farewell," beginning "Let all noble stout Commanders" (Pepys, Bagford; reprinted in *BB* I, 350).[4] "The Hasty Damosel," beginning "Mother, pray when shall I marry,/and receive a womans due,"

[3] "Oh so Ungrateful a Creature" is an independent tune, though no satisfactory music has been preserved. See "Joy to the Bridegroom."

[4] Another tune title, for which no music has been found, is added in "Dunkirk's Lamentation . . . set to the Tune of, The French Dancing-Master: or, The Soldiers Departure" (*PB* VII, 186).

has the tune direction "The Seamans Departure, or, Doubting Virgin" (Pepys IV, 178, Harvard, Douce I, 94ᵛ). The first tune title is either a transfer from "The Souldiers Departure" or (less likely) is derived from the content of such a sailor's ballad of farewell as "The Seamans Constancy," noted above.

One other ballad of the 1680s deserves mention: "The Bashfull-Maidens No, no, no, turn'd to I, I, I . . . To a New Tune much in Fashion, Or, the Soldier's Departure," beginning "When the Kine had given a Pail full" (Pepys III, 183). It is a slight expansion of a poem by D'Urfey, published in his *Choice New Songs*, 1684, p. 16, the music of which is the "New Tune" referred to in the broadside. The ballad was reprinted with music in *180 Loyal Songs*, 1685, p. 252, and in all editions of *Pills*, 1719–1720, II, 26. The "New Tune," named from the first line, is found in seven ballad operas, including *Momus turn'd Fabulist,* where "Woman's Work is never done" also appears. Thus there can be no doubt that the two tunes were independent. Moreover, though D'Urfey's refrain pattern is basically the "Shall I? Shall I?" form, he has individualized it by adding a ninth line, further repeating "no" or "I," for which the music supplies a two-bar coda. The ballad can be sung to "Doubting Virgin" by the elimination of the extra line.

Down in a Bottom, or The Parliament Sat as Snug as a Cat

A Cavalier ballad of c. 1654 in Bodleian MS Rawlinson Poet. 152, fol. 9, begins "The Parliament sat as snug as a Cat"; the music (Fig. 122) is included, with the direction "To the tune of Downe in a bottome &c.," but there is no other heading. Ballads associated with this tune are in six-line stanzas or the equivalent, syllabically pairs of 5.5.8 or 6.6.9. The music calls for the repetition of the last line of each stanza, but in none of the texts is such a repetition indicated.

"Down in a bottom" is named as the tune for "A City Ballade," beginning "Since the Realm has lost its head," in *The Rump,* 1660, *Rump,* 1662, reprinted in *Loyal Songs,* 1731. "Last Parliament sat as snugg as a Cat" is the tune for "Rump Rampant . . . set out by Sir T. A. Perfumer to his late Highnesse," beginning "In the name of the fiend, what the Rump up again" (Harvard, BM Luttrell, Wood 416 [25], dated January,

122

Original is unbarred.

1659[/60]; reprinted in *The Rump,* 1660, *Ratts Rhimed to Death,* 1660, *Rump,* 1662, and *Loyal Songs,* 1731). Another contemporary broadside, "The History of the Second Death of the Rump," beginning "Come buy my fine Ditty/Of News from the City," is to "The Parliament sate as snugg as a Cat" (Harvard, Wood 416, BM Thomason, dated March 7, 1659/60; reprinted in *The Rump, Rump,* and *Loyal Songs*).

Several other ballads in these collections have no tune titles but are in the same distinctive meter: "The Rump Dockt," beginning "Till it be understood/What is under Monck's Hood" (Harvard, BM Thomason, BM Luttrell, BM MS Harl. 2127, fol. 14, Bodleian Firth b.20 [12]; reprinted in *Ratts Rhimed to Death, The Rump, Rump, Loyal Songs*). "The Rebells Reign," probably written in 1654, begins "Now we are met in a knot, let's take t'other pot"; it has no tune direction, but stanza 14 reproduces the opening lines of the manuscript ballad:

> The Parliament sate as snug as a Cat,
>   And were playing for mine and yours:
> Sweep-stakes was their Game, till Oliver came,
>   And turn'd it to Knave out of doors.

It appeared in *Merry Drollery,* 1661, *Merry Drollery Complete,* 1670, *Rump,* and *Loyal Songs.* One contemporary broadside not reprinted in these collections, but written in the same meter, is "The Noble Souldiers Advice to his Comrades: or, The Red-coats Resolution," dated 1661, beginning "When honest Red-Coats,/Leave cutting of throats" (BM Luttrell II, 207).

D'Urfey recalled the old words as he launched into a contemporary lampoon, "The Church Jockey, a Comick Satyr. The Words made to a pretty Play-house Tune":

> The Parliament sate
> As snug as a Cat;

> In Old loyal Brome you may read,
> And ours in their House,
> Were as close as a Mouse,
> Legislating the Nation with Speed.

This poem appears only in the 1719–1720 edition of *Pills* (II, 66), and unhappily D'Urfey does not print a tune. The allusion may be to Henry Brome, one of the printers of *The Rump*, in the 1662 edition of which appears "The Rebells Reign," quoted above. Or perhaps the gifted Alexander Brome wrote this or some other poem containing the phrase which D'Urfey echoes.

The Downright Squire

A lute arrangement of "Downeright Squyre" dating from c. 1600 is preserved in Cambridge University MS Dd.2.11, fol. 70 (Fig. 123); another set of the same tune appears without title in the Marsh Lute Book,

Transcription omits varied repeat of each strain.

c. 1590, p. 40. Still a third variant is a lute tablature in Folger MS 448.16, fol. 18ᵛ, dating from the early years of Elizabeth's reign; though called "The upright esquiere," it is nonetheless a variant of our tune.[1]

Of the four ballads sung to the tune, the earliest is that found in an untitled manuscript version beginning "Ons dyd I aspyre to loves desyre/ And wot yow not whye," in Bodleian MS Ashmole 48 (reprinted in *Songs and Ballads . . . Chiefly of the Reign of Philip and Mary,* ed. Thomas Wright, 1860, p. 191). Professor Rollins has shown that the manuscript

[1] John Ward, "Music for *A Handefull of Pleasant Delites,*" *JAMS,* X (1957), 155–156, gives a transcript of the Folger tablature with the first stanza of "L. Gibsons Tantara."

was compiled before the end of 1565,[2] and the fact that the tune was known by that date lends strength to the supposition that two ballads calling for the tune in *A Handefull of Pleasant Delites*, 1584, may have appeared in the lost edition licensed for publication in 1566. They are "L. Gibsons Tantara, wherin Danea welcommeth home her Lord Diophon fro[m] the war," beginning "You Lordings, cast off your weedes of wo," and "A new Sonet of Pyramus and Thisbie," beginning "You Dames (I say) that climbe the mount" (*Handefull*, ed. Rollins, pp. 7, 35). Still another to the tune is T. Rider's "A merie newe Ballad intituled, the Pinnyng of the Basket," a broadside of c. 1590 beginning "Twas my hap of late to heare/A pretie ieste" (BM Huth; reprinted in *A Collection of Seventy-Nine Black-Letter Ballads*, 1867, p. 105).

The Dragon of Wantley

"A True Relation of the Dreadful Combate between More of More-Hall and the Dragon of Wantley," beginning "Old Stories tell how Hercules," appeared in 1685, with music (Fig. 124) on the broadside

(Pepys V, 391, BM 1872.a.1 [129*], Clark, with MS date 28 Nov. 1684).
In later editions, without music, the title usually begins "An Excellent Ballad of that most Dreadful Combate . . ." (Douce, BM

[2] "Concerning Bodleian MS. Ashmole 48," *MLN*, XXXIV (1919), 340–351.

1871.e.9, Roxburghe; a bowdlerized reprint is in *RB* VIII, 417). The ballad appears with music in all editions of *Pills*, 1719–1720, III, 10, also in *The Convivial Songster*, c. 1782, and in Ritson's *English Songs*, 1783; it was reprinted without music in *A Collection of Old Ballads*, 1723–1725, I, 38, and in Percy's *Reliques*. Another song to the tune, beginning "I heard much talk of Oxford Town," is found in *The Convivial Songster*.

Because of verbal irregularities, neither the broadside music nor that in *Pills* fits every stanza equally well. Aside from a few differences in pitch and harmony, the two versions differ chiefly in division of some quarter notes into eights. Some stanzas therefore can be sung better to one version of the tune, some to the other.

Drive the Cold Winter Away

This tune name is derived from "A pleasant Countrey new Ditty: Merrily shewing how To driue the cold Winter away," where the title phrase is the concluding line of each stanza. The ballad begins "All hayle to the dayes/That merite more praise," and the tune is given as "When Phoebus did rest" (Pepys, Roxburghe; reprinted in *RB* I, 84). Now a song beginning "When Phoebus addres'd [*or* had drest] his course to the West" in *Wit and Drollery*, 1656, and *Merry Drollery*, 1661, has the refrain "O do not, do not kill me yet,/For I am not prepared to dye." [1] And in the *Boertigheden* section of J. J. Starter's *Friesche Lust-Hof*, 1621, sig. C4^v (Fig. 125), is music entitled "O doe not, doe not kil me yet for I am not &c," which may be considered the tune of "When Phoebus did rest." A somewhat different tune, called "Drive the cold winter away," is in all editions of *The Dancing Master*, 1651–c. 1728 (1651, p. 39=Fig. 126), in *Musick's Delight on the Cithren*, 1666, and in Walsh's *Compleat Country Dancing-Master*, 1718. An untitled virginal set of the mid-seventeenth century is preserved in Paris Conservatoire MS Rés. 1186, fol. 54, and the melody is coupled with an abbreviated form of "All hail to the days" in *Pills*, 1719–1720, IV, 241.[2]

Broadside copies of "All hail to the days" were printed for Henry

---

[1] A copy in the Percy Folio MS (ed. Hales and Furnivall, IV, 7) is probably no later than 1640; the poem itself is considerably earlier.

[2] The same music is inappropriately printed on a broadside containing a Latin version of "The Catholick Ballad," properly sung to the tune of "Eighty-eight," for which see "Jog on."

125

Original is unbarred.

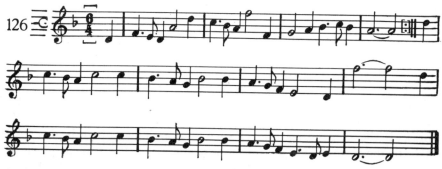

126

Original is unbarred.

Gosson, who flourished c. 1603–1640. A suggestion that the ballad may be even older is seen in a Scotch song with the same movement and with a comparable occasional refrain:

> The wind blawis cauld, furius & bauld,
>   This lang and mony day:
> But Christis mercy, we man all die,
>   Or keip the cauld wind away.

It is found in the 1567 edition of *A Compendious Book of Godly and Spiritual Songs* (ed. A. F. Mitchell, Scottish Text Society, 1897).[3]

The following ballads to the tune of "To drive the cold winter away" date from the reign of Charles I: "The father hath beguil'd the sonne," by Martin Parker, beginning "I Often haue knowne,/And experience hath showne" (Pepys; reprinted in *PG*, p. 309); "A Health to all Good-Fellowes," beginning "Be merry, my hearts, and call for your quarts"

[3] Mitchell (p. 288) doubts that the spiritual song is a parody of the secular ballad; if it is, "it has retained nothing . . . save the tune and the catch-words."

(Roxburghe; reprinted in *RB* I, 447); G. B.'s "A New Song, called Jacke Dove's Resolution," beginning "To all my good Friends these presents I send" (Roxburghe; reprinted in *RB* I, 475); a ballad by N. P. with title cropped, beginning "Come, come my brave gold/Which I love to behold" (Roxburghe; reprinted in *RB* I, 129); W[illiam?] B[lunden?]'s "Hang Pinching, Or, The good Fellowes Observation, Mongst a Ioviall Crew, Of them that hate Flinching, But is always true blew," beginning "All you which lay clame/to a good fellowe's name" (Roxburghe; reprinted in *RB* III, 255);[4] and possibly the incomplete ballad, "Oh faine would I marry," beginning "Oh faine would I wive" (Manchester II, 47).

One of the political songs in *The Rump,* 1660, "The Second Part of Saint George for England," beginning "Now the Rump is confounded," had earlier appeared on broadsides, some copies of which bear the MS date March, 1659/60 (BM Thomason, BM Luttrell, Wood 416, Bagford; reprinted in Wright's *Political Ballads,* Mackay's *Cavalier Songs,* and *RB* VIII, xiii*). Still another song to the tune is the unlovely portrait entitled "Sir Grigory Cow T - - - on his Mistress, Madam Dowzabell," beginning "I now will not fail,/To tell you a Tale" (*Mock Songs,* 1675).

A ballad of 1664 to the tune "All Hail to the dayes" is entitled "I warrant thee Boy, Shee's Right" (Lord Crawford 250), from which is derived one of the tune titles cited in "Hey ho, for a Husband," beginning "You maidens that are fair and young," to the tune of "Ile warrant thee boy she's right, Or, a little o' th tone with 'tother" (Pepys IV, 9).[5] On the second tune title, see "Stingo."

The Duke of Monmouth's Jig

This tune is found in Thomas Greeting's *The Pleasant Companion . . . for the Flagelet,* 1680, No. 70 (Fig. 127), but the ballads sung to it date from the previous decade. One of them, licensed by Sir Roger L'Estrange on February 8, 1676/7, is "Love and Honesty: Or, The

---

[4] Chappell (*PMOT* I, 194) suggests that the tune title "True Blue" may derive from the burden of this ballad; but the movement of pieces sung to that lost tune is incompatible with that of "Drive the cold winter away" ballads, and on metrical grounds the relationship must be denied.

[5] "Hey ho, for a Husband" was registered by Francis Grove in 1657, but the Pepys copy is a later edition. A reworking of the ballad, with music by Samuel Akeroyde, is in *Pills,* 1719–1720, IV, 56, beginning "There was a Maid the other Day."

Modish Courtier," beginning "A Curse on the zealous and ignorant crew" (Rawlinson, Roxburghe; reprinted in *RB* VI, 56); it is the expansion of a playhouse song found in *The Wits Academy,* 1677.

Another to the tune is "The Batchelors Ballad," beginning "No more silly Cupid,/will I pine and complain" (Douce, Rawlinson; reprinted in *RB* VII, 334), expanded from a song entitled "Ungrateful after Enjoyment" in *The Last and Best Edition of New Songs,* 1677. A sequel is "The Maids answer to the Batchelors Ballad," beginning "Who's here so ingenious/mis[s]pending his time," to the tune of "No more silly Cupid: Or, The Duke of Monmouth's Jig" (Harvard, Lord Crawford, Rawlinson, Douce, Roxburghe; reprinted in *RB* VII, 336). The first tune title, of course, echoes the opening line of "The Batchelors Ballad."

"The Politick Girle," beginning "My dearest Katy, prethee be but constant now," is a song directed to be sung to "The Duke of Monmouths Jigge" in *Westminster Drollery,* 1672, II, 106; but the eight-line stanza cannot be fitted to the tune in Greeting's collection.

Duke Upon Duke

"Duke upon Duke, An Excellent New Play-house Ballad," beginning "To Lordings Proud I tune my Song," is an oft-reprinted piece in 37 quatrains thought to have been written by Swift or Gay or Pope upon a quarrel by Nicholas (afterward Baron) Lechmere and Sir John Guise.

128

Perhaps the earliest edition is the 1720 six-page folio text issued by A. Moor, "Set to Musick by Mr. Holdecombe" (Fig. 128), a copy of which is Bodleian Pamph. 357 (11).[1] A number of broadside and pamphlet copies are extant, with and without music (BM, Harvard, Huntington, Chetham 1883). At least one of the British Museum copies (1876.f.1 [94]) contains the MS tune direction "Cheavey Chace," and one edition (Harvard, BM C.116.i.4 [52]) contains a corrupt version of that tune.

An edition without music is titled "An Excellent Old Ballad, called Pride will have a Fall, As set forth in the . . . History of the deadly Strife between the Dukes of Guise and Lancastere . . . in the Reign of Richard Coeur de Lion" (Douce IV, 39, BM 1871.f.3 [25]).

"An Answer to Duke upon Duke &c.," beginning "Thou Pope, Oh Popery burning Hot," also set to Henry Holcombe's music, is in the British Museum (1876.f.1 [81]); versions with corrupt "Chevy Chase" music are BM C.116.i.4 (54) and Morgan 17.

A violin arrangement of Holcombe's tune in BM MS Add. 38189, fol. 6, is entitled "Duke upon Duke."

Dulcina

The ballad of Dulcina and her shepherd Coridon was in circulation before 1615, for on May 22 of that year it was transferred from one printer to another (Rollins, *Anal. Index,* No. 650) as "Dulcina, to the

---

[1] The ballad was reprinted in *The Hive,* 3d ed., 1726, I, 109, as "Duke upon Duke. Written in the Year 1719." One of the Harvard copies bears the MS notation "Aug. 1720." The *DNB* dates the ballad c. 1725. Norman Ault, *New Light on Pope,* 1949, pp. 186ff., considers the case strong for attributing the authorship to Pope.

tune of fforgoe me nowe come to me sone." Two extant ballads might qualify as the one alluded to in the Stationers' Register entry; both use the "Forego me now" refrain, though the tune title in each is "Dulcina." It may be that the tune we now know as "Dulcina" was earlier called "Forego me now, come to me soon," but it is also possible that the refrain line became simply another name for the "Dulcina" tune. One of the ballads is "An excellent newe dyttye, wherein fayre Dulcina complayneth for the absence of her dearest Coridon, but at length is comforted by his presence," beginning "The golden god Hyperion/by Thetis is saluted," which was copied from a broadside into the Shirburn MS (printed in *SB*, p. 64, and in *RB* VIII, clv*). The second, and more familiar, ballad is "An Excellent Ditty, called the Shepherds wooing Dulcina," beginning "As at noon Dulcina rested," and formerly attributed to Raleigh. Broadside copies date from after the Restoration (Pepys, Harvard, Manchester, Lord Crawford, Douce, Roxburghe; reprinted in *RB* VI, 166); but the ballad was entered in the Stationers' Register March 13, 1656 (*Anal. Index*, No. 2419). Perhaps the earliest copy is a fifteen-stanza version with music, dated 1615, in Giles Earle's songbook, BM MS Add. 24665, fol. 35ᵛ (Fig. 129).

129

Original is unbarred.

A contemporary keyboard setting of the tune is called "Daunce" in *The Fitzwilliam Virginal Book* II, 268. Eight stanzas of the Earle text are to be found in the Percy Folio MS (ed. Hales and Furnivall, IV, 32, 49), and six stanzas in Harvard MS Eng. 628, p. 323—both transcripts of the first half of the seventeenth century. A twelve-stanza version is in

Westminster Drollery, 1672, II, 59, reprinted in *Pills,* 1719–1720, VI, 206, with a later tune (Fig. 130).

A number of ballads to "Dulcina" date from the first half of the seventeenth century. "Two pleasant Ditties, one of the Birth, the other of the Passion of Christ," beginning "Ivry [i.e., Jewry] came to Ieru-salem," has been preserved in several editions, one of which was printed by the assignees of Thomas Symcocke, c. 1628 (Roxburghe; reprinted in *RB* II, 549; other editions are in Pepys, Euing, Bagford, Rawlinson, Manchester). That the original edition was issued even earlier is seen from a transcript of both parts preserved in the Shirburn MS, c. 1585–1616 (*SB,* pp. 59ff.). Harvard MS Eng. 628, p. 308, contains four stanzas, without tune direction. "A Pleasant New Song betwixt a Saylor and his Love," beginning "What doth ayl my love so sadly" (Euing, Pepys, Rawlinson, Bagford, Roxburghe; reprinted in *RB* II, 470), was, in its earliest edition, printed for John Grismond, who flourished 1618–1638.[1]

Martin Parker wrote at least three ballads to the tune: "A Prouerbe old, yet nere forgot, Tis good to strike while the Irons hott," beginning "All you Young-men who would Marry" (Pepys; reprinted in *PG,* p. 229, dated 1625?); "A Penny-worth of good Counsell," beginning "Of late it was my chance to Walke" (Roxburghe; reprinted in *RB* II, 295); "The desperate Damsells Tragedy. Or The faithlesse young man," beginning "In the gallant month of Iune" (Lord Crawford, Roxburghe; reprinted in *RB* I, 265).

[1] The burden of this ballad is the source of the tune title "Kisse and bid me welcome home" associated with "A new Carroll of the birth of . . . Jesus Christ" (*New Carrolls,* 1661, sig. A3; two stanzas reprinted in *RB* VII, 792); presumably "Kisse . . ." becomes another name for the tune "Dulcina."

One additional ballad remains to be mentioned, to indicate that the tune continued to be popular after the Restoration under the full title, "As at Noon Dulcina rested." This is "The True-Lovers Good-morrow," beginning "In the month of February,/the green leaves begin to spring" (Lord Crawford 687, Pepys III, 64, BM C.22.f.6 [187], Rawlinson 125, Douce II, 219ᵛ, 228, Harvard). On one of the Douce copies is the added MS tune title "Oh that I had never marryed." The ballad is named in Thackeray's list of c. 1689, signifying that it was then in print.

The tune is sometimes called "Robin Goodfellow" from a ballad first printed by Henry Gosson (fl. 1603–1640): "The mad-merry prankes of Robbin Good-fellow," beginning "From Obrion in Fairy Land/the King of Ghosts and shadowes there," to the tune of "Dulcina" (Euing, Bagford, Pepys, Roxburghe; reprinted in *RB* II, 81). Among ballads sung to the tune under its later name are: "The Downfall of Dancing; or the over-throw of three Fidlers and three Bagg-Pipe-Players," beginning "Three Pipers, and three Fidlers too" (Douce I, 62ᵛ, Pepys III, 188); "A New Song," beginning "Though S[haftesbury] is cleared by/The Cunning Ignoramus Sway," dated 1682 (Harvard, Huntington; the publisher's name is given as "C. Tebroc," i.e., Charles Corbet); "The Bare-faced Tories: A New Song," beginning "What a Pox care we for Law," dated 1682 (Bodleian Ashmole G.16 [55]).

Since the "Robin Goodfellow" ballad stanzas end "ho ho ho," Ebs-worth (*BB* I, 148) conjectured that the tune "Yo, ho, ho" in "Beauties Warningpiece or, Advice to the Fair" derives from (or is a mistake for) the "Robin Goodfellow" burden. But this ballad has a six-line stanza, whereas all the ballads associated with "Dulcina" have an eight-line stanza or its equivalent, and neither older nor later tune can be cut off at the three-quarter point. Ebsworth added the bracketed tune title "Ho, ho, ho! or Robin Goodfellow" in printing "Robin Good-Fellow: the King of Pharies" (*RB* VIII, cxi*) from an Oriel College, Oxford, MS of c. 1656. No ballad seems actually to have used "Ho, ho, ho" as a tune title; Ebsworth made the addition gratuitously.

Surviving from the first half of the seventeenth century are several edi-tions of "A delicate new Ditty, composed upon the Posie of a Ring, being; I fancie none but the alone," beginning "Thou that art so sweete a creature" (Manchester, Euing, Pepys, Roxburghe; reprinted in *RB* I, 244), to the tune of "Dulcina." Its refrain is "I fancy none but thee alone," from which is derived the tune title for a mutilated broadside of c. 1640, "[Th]e true hearted Lo[ver]," beginning "My loving friend I doe commend" (Harvard). The tune is called "I fancy none but thee" in "The Maids Song in praise of her Love," beginning "Were my Love a silly Shepherd," in Richard Climsell, *Cupid's Soliciter of Love,* 1680.

In the British Museum copy of William Slatyer's *Psalmes, or Songs of Sion,* 1642, a former owner has noted that "Dulcina" is a tune to which Psalms 15 and 16 could be sung. "As at noone Dulcina rested" is indicated as a tune for "A Caroll for Innocents day" in *Good and True, Fresh and New, Christmas Carols,* 1642, and "Dulcina" for "A Carrol for Christmas-day in the morning" in *New Christmas Carrols,* c. 1662.

Enfield Common

"Enfield Common," beginning "On Enfield Common I met a Woman," to "an Excellent New Tune," is a broadside without music in BM C.39.k.6, reprinted in *OPB,* p. 89. The text appeared in all editions of *Pills,* 1719–1720, IV, 224, with a tune by Purcell (Fig. 131), an entr'acte

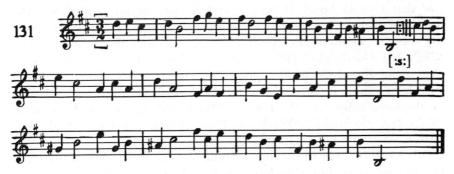

Original a minor third higher; time signature erroneously given as 3/4.

hornpipe composed for *Amphitryon,* 1690 (published in his *Collection of Ayres for the Theatre,* 1697, and reprinted in *Works,* XVI, 29–30). The tune does not seem to have been used for any other broadsides, but under the name of "Enfield Common" it is in *The Dancing Master,* eleventh edition *et seq.,* 1701–c. 1728, and in Walsh's *Compleat Country Dancing-Master,* 1718.

Essex' Last Good-night

This tune is found in Elizabeth Rogers's MS Virginal Book (BM MS Add. 10337, fol. 7, before 1656, Fig. 132) and in a Cambridge University

Library MS of about the middle of the seventeenth century (Dd.6.48, fol. 15, inaccurate lyra-viol tablature). The tune takes its name from "A lamentable new Ballad upon the Earle of Essex death," beginning "All yow that crye O hone! O hone!" and recounting sympathetically the details of Robert Devercux's career and his supposed last words upon the scaffold, February 25, 1601. Early copies give the tune as "The King's last Goodnight" (*SB*, p. 328; Manchester I, 37, facsimile in *A Century of Broadside Elegies*, ed. J. W. Draper, 1928, No. 1; Pepys I, 106); later copies, usually printed on the same sheet with another ballad on the same subject to the tune of "Welladay" (q.v.), list the tune as "Essex last goodnight" (Wood 401, Pepys, Euing, Lord Crawford, Bagford, Roxburghe; reprinted in *RB* I, 571).

Other ballads sung to the tune include one licensed to Thomas Pavier, October 23, 1607, but now lost: "A ballad of Gods Wrath shewed at Lyons in Fraunce vppon a College of Jesuytes in A stage play. to the tune of Essex good night" (Rollins, *Anal. Index*, No. 986). Also to the tune of "Essex good-night" is "A dolefull dittye of five . . . persons . . . drowned . . . crossing . . . the Thames . . . 15 of October last, 1616," beginning "What hart so hard, but will relent" (*SB*, p. 68). Another, "The Story of Ill May-Day in the Time of King Henry the Eighth," beginning "Peruse the stories of this land," is found in Richard Johnson's *Crown Garland of Golden Roses*, 1659 (ed. Chappell, 1845, p. 39), reprinted in J. P. Collier's *Broadside Black-Letter Ballads*, 1868, p. 96, as from a Gosson edition, c. 1603–1640, which I have been unable to trace; Collier's statement that the ballad is in Deloney's *Strange Histories*, 1607, is not correct.[1] *New Carrolls*, 1661, contains "Another for Christmas

---

[1] See *CP*, p. 33, for references to an imaginary ballad of 1647 to the tune.

day," beginning "All you that in this house be here," to the tune. A Scotch ballad in praise of James, Duke of Albany (afterward James II), is to the tune of "the Last Good-night," by which may be intended "Essex' Last Good-night." [2] It is "The Banishment of Poverty by his Royal Highness, J. D. A.," attributed to Francis Sempill,[3] beginning "Pox fa that pultron povertie/Wa worth the time that I him saw" (National Library of Scotland, Harvard; reprinted in Watson's *Choice Collection of . . . Scots Poems,* 1706, and *The Poems of the Sempills of Beltrees,* ed. James Paterson, 1849).[4]

In "The wofull death of Queene Jane, wife to King Henry the Eight: and how King Edward was cut out of his mother's belly," beginning "When as King Henry rul'd this land,/He had a queene I understand," the tune is called "The Lamentation for the Lord of Essex" (*Crown Garland of Golden Roses,* 1612, ed. Chappell, 1842). This may be another name for "Essex' Last Good-night," for the meter corresponds to the usual eight-line tetrameter stanza associated with the latter. A Dutch version of this tune title, "Lammetacie vande Graeve Essex," cited without music in B. J. Wellens, *T'Vermaeck der Jeught,* 1612, p. 96, is joined to words with a different rhythmic pattern. It may be equated with "Essex Lamentatie [or] Wat if a daye &c," in Camphuysen's *Stichtelyche Rymen,* 1647, the music of which is actually "What if a day, or a month, or a year." This Dutch songbook also contains "Galliarde Essex," which is the same as "Gaillarde du comte essex" in Nicolas Vallet's *Tablature de Luth, intitulé Le Secret des Muses,* 1618–1619, but is unrelated to "Essex' Last Good-night." [5] One other suggestive tune title, "the Ladies of Essex Lamentacon," is found with an untitled song beginning "Sighinge sore in woofull wise" in a jig, *Michael and Frances,* written in

[2] The octosyllabic meter fits the tune, and the closing line, "And gart him take his last goodnight," echoes "and lately took his last good-night" of the original Essex ballad.

[3] Wing D 30A, misreading the title, assigns the broadside to "J. D." and dates it 1695. The two Harvard copies and that in the Rosebery collection of the National Library of Scotland are without imprint, but a safer date, at least of composition, would be c. 1680.

[4] An eighteenth-century ballad may derive its tune name "Pultring Poverty" from the first line of the Sempill ballad. It is "The Good-man of Auchter Muchty; Or The Wife turned Good-man," beginning "In Auchtermuchty lived a Man" (Douce III, 36v, Lord Crawford 636, Chetham 254, Madden II, 367), and is in tetrameter quatrains; the Sempill ballad is printed variously in quatrains, eight-line stanzas, and without stanza division.

[5] "The Earl of Essex' Galliard," variously titled, is derived from John Dowland's "Can she excuse my wrongs," *First Booke of Songs or Ayres,* 1597, No. 5. Dowland's instrumental arrangements are preserved in his *Lachrimae . . . with diuers other Pauans, Galiards, and Almands,* 1604, in Robert Dowland's *Varietie of Lute Lessons,* 1610, and in several contemporary lute manuscripts, including the Euing Lute Book, fol. 24, and Cambridge University Dd.2.11, fols. 40v, 62v.

1601 and only recently discovered (C. J. Sisson, *Lost Plays of Shakespeare's Age,* 1936, p. 138). The stanza pattern, six lines in tetrameter couplets with a three-line refrain in irregular meter, is difficult to adjust to "Essex' Last Good-night."

The Evening Ramble

This tune was originally a jig in Purcell's *Fairy Queen,* 1692. Under the name of "Old Batchelor" it was incorporated into *The Dancing Master* in the 9th ed., 1695, p. 165 (Fig. 133); it is also in Walsh's *Compleat Country Dancing-Master,* 1718, and in *Pills* from 1706 (IV, 222) to 1720 (VI, 74). The same music is given in *Pills,* 1719–1720, V, 261, with "The Maiden Lottery," beginning "Young Ladies that live in the City," which had appeared as a broadside, c. 1695, without music, but with the tune direction "The Evening Ramble" (Pepys V, 420). I have not found a ballad called "The Evening Ramble" from which the tune title may derive; nor can we be absolutely certain that the broadside was calling for the Purcell tune, though the *Pills* conjunction of words and music is better evidence than none. There is no denying the great popularity of "The Evening Ramble" as a ballad tune during the last decade of the seventeenth century.

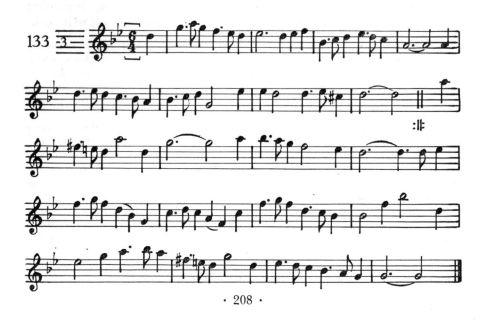

It is used for another lottery ballad, "The Fortunate Lasses of London . . . a brief Account . . . of the Late Maiden-Lottery," beginning "The Lottery now is compleated" (Pepys V, 431). Also sung to it were the following: "The Triumph of Namur [1695]," beginning "Come listen, you Protestant Subjects" (Harvard, Pepys; reprinted in *PB* VII, 97); "King William's Welcome Home . . . from Flanders," beginning "Great William's returned in Triumph" (Pepys; reprinted in *PB* VII, 105); "The Shooe-maker's Triumph . . . sung at a General Assembly of Shooe-makers, on the 25th of Octob. 1695," by Richard Rigby, "a Brother of the Craft," beginning "I Sing in the Praise of Shooe-makers" (Lord Crawford, BM C.39.k.6, Pepys; reprinted in *OPB*, p. 86, and in *PB* VII, 109); "The Royal Progress," beginning "King William returning from Flanders" (Pepys; reprinted in *PB* VII, 113); "The Plough-man's Praise," beginning "Dear Mother I reckon to marry" (Lord Crawford, Harvard; reprinted in *RB* VIII, 682); "The Royal Regulation . . . of the Coin of this Kingdom," beginning "You Merchants, rich Farmers and Grasiers" (Pepys; reprinted in *PB* VII, 172), concerning an act of January, 1696; and "Great Britain's Triumph . . . Peace . . . Sign'd the 10th of this Instant Sept. 1697," beginning "You Nobles, and Peers of the Kingdom" (Pepys; reprinted in *PB* VII, 267).

The tune is called "The Maiden-Lottery" in "The Cruel Lover: Or, The False-hearted Saylor," an account of the jilting of Mary Shalford, who "took grief to Heart and dyed the 2d Day of this Month [1695?]," beginning "You Lovers that have been False-hearted" (Pepys; reprinted in *PB* VII, 158).

Fain I Would If I Could

This air is found in the first three editions of *The Dancing Master* as "Faine I would if I could," or "Faine I Would" (1651, p. 46=Fig. 134). In editions from 1670 to 1690 it is called "Parthenia, or Fain I would." In Elizabeth Rogers's MS Virginal Book, BM MS Add. 10337, fol. 30 (before 1656), "The Kings Complaint" is a version of the tune, with interesting melodic differences (Fig. 135). "Fain I would" in *Musicks Recreation on the Viol, Lyra-way*, 1682, is a twelve-measure dance tune of undeniable charm, but it is unrelated to the other tune of that name and will not fit the ballads directed to be sung to the tune.

"A Coffin for King Charles: A Crowne for Cromwell: A Pit for the People," bearing a MS date of April 23, 1649, is sung to "Fain I would"

134

Original is a fourth higher and unbarred.

and begins "So, so the deed is done" (BM Thomason, Harvard [undated]; reprinted in Wright, *Political Ballads*, 1841, Wilkins, *Political Ballads*, 1860, Mackay, *Cavalier Songs*, 1863). Another ballad, to the tune of "Fain would I if I could, Or, O brave house," is "The Matchless Shepheard, Overmatcht by his Mistress," by Laurence Price, beginning "Fain would I, if I might/by any means obtain" (Rawlinson; reprinted in *CP*, p. 440). Price's ballad was written about 1656, though the broadside edition was doubtless printed after the Restoration. Its stanza pattern of eight iambic trimeters fits "Faine I would " better than does "A Coffin for King Charles," whose double ballad-meter stanza requires some division of notes for the tetrameter lines. Because the line "Fain would I if I could" appears several times in the Price ballad, it would be tempting to think that our tune title is internally inspired. But it is

135

clearly older than Price's text and probably belongs to a ballad now lost, unless it be considered such a commonplace phrase that one need not look for specific origins. I have no data on the other tune, "O brave house."

A tune called "Parthenia" but unrelated to the *Dancing Master* music is in Playford's *A Brief Introduction to the Skill of Musick*, 4th ed., 1664, his *Musick's Delight on the Cithren*, 1666, and *Musicks Recreation on the Viol, Lyra-way*, 1669, 1682, Thomas Greeting's *The Pleasant Companion . . . for the Flagelet*, 2d ed., 1673, No. 6 and No. 14, *Musicks Handmaid*, 1678, and *Apollo's Banquet*, 6th ed., 1690. This air appears among the violin tunes at the end of *The Dancing Master*, 1665, and, with the title of "The Jovial Beggars," in the eleventh and succeeding editions, 1701–c. 1728. In the original edition of *Apollo's Banquet*, 1670, it is called "The Duke of York's Delight." It is not interchangeable with "Fain I would," and no ballads were sung to it.

The Fair One Let Me In

This tune takes its name from a song by Thomas D'Urfey, with music by Thomas Farmer, which appeared in three collections in 1683: *Choice Ayres and Songs*, Fourth Book, p. 8 (Fig. 136); D'Urfey's *A New Collection of Songs and Poems*, and *The Newest Collection of the Choicest Songs*. In the D'Urfey volume the song is called "The Generous Lover, a New Song," and it begins "The night her blackest Sables wore." The first stanza closes "This angel let me in," but in other texts the reading

· 211 ·

is "The fair one let me in," whence the common form of the tune title. Farmer's music, entitled "On night her blackest Sables where," is in Salter's *Genteel Companion . . . for the Recorder,* 1683, and the song appears with the music in all editions of *Pills,* 1719–1720, I, 324.

The broadside version of D'Urfey's song was called "The Kind Lady Or, The Loves of Stella and Adonis. A new Court song much in request. To a new tune. Or, Hey boys up go we, the charming Nymph, or Jenny Gin" (Lord Crawford, Pepys, Roxburghe; reprinted in *RB* VI, 195). The "new tune" was evidently Farmer's music; the other tunes are often named as alternates to "The fair one let me in," for they are all adapted to an eight-line stanza in ballad meter.[1] During the last ten or fifteen years of the seventeenth century a large group of ballads were written to this tune, only a few of which can be noted here.

At least half a dozen are reprinted in *The Roxburghe Ballads,* and one is in *The Pepys Ballads.* The following do not appear to have been reprinted: "The Virgins Tragedy: Or, the Faithful Maiden, and the Faithless Young man," beginning "Young Gallants all and Ladies fair," to the tune of "Ginny Gin Or, fare one let me in" (Harvard, Lord Crawford 1446); "The Dispairing Maiden Reviv'd By the Return of her Dearest Love," beginning "As I walkt forth to take the air,/one morning in the Spring," to the tune of "The fair one let me in; Or Busie Fame; Or, Jenny Gin" (Pepys III, 181, Douce I, 54ᵛ); "Falle[n] Man's cruelty," beginning "When Cupid's fierce and powerful Dart," to the same three tunes, given in reverse order (Pepys III, 385); "The Kind Shepherd, and the Amorous Shepherdess," beginning "The smart of Love who can endure" (Douce I, 110ᵛ); "Love without blemish," beginning "Farwel, farwel my hearts delight" (Pepys III, 331, Douce I, 126); "The Subtle Damosels Advice," beginning "Give ear a while unto my Song," to the tune of "Jenny Gin, Or, The fair one let me in, Or, Young Pheon, Or, Busie Fame" (Lord Crawford 417, BM C.22.f.6 [182]); "Flora Happily Revived By Strephons Return," beginning "When Phoebus with her glittering Beams" (Pepys III, 193); "The Milk-Maids Morning Song," beginning "A Merry Milk-Maid on a time," to the tune of "Ginny Gin, Or, The fair one Let me in" (Pepys III, 198); "The Careless Drunkards," beginning "Come let us merry be, brave boys," to the tune of "The Fair one let me in: Or, Jenny Gin" (Pepys IV, 238); and "True love without deceit or, The Country Girles Happiness," beginning "We that are bonny Country girles," to the tune of "The Fair one let me in; or, Hey boys up go we" (Pepys III, 101).

A pair of ballads published by J. Deacon offer some curious paradoxes. "Strephon's Comforts: or, Phillis Reviv'd," beginning "Ranging the Plain

---

[1] "The charming Nymph" apparently has not survived.

one Summers night" (Wood 417 [112]), is a 1682 broadside version of a song that had appeared in Joan Philips's *Female Poems,* 1679. The sheet contains music of "Jenny gin" with the direction "To a Pleasant New Tune: or, The fair one let me in." The implication of these facts is that "The fair one let me in," though not published until 1683, was known in the preceding year. The "Pleasant New Tune" is not "Jenny gin," for copies of the song in *The Newest Collection of the Choicest Songs* and *Choice Ayres and Songs* have a still different tune, which is also used with the song in *Pills,* 1719–1720, III, 188. A second ballad likewise displays an inconsistency between tune direction and music printed. "Loves Extasie: or, Strephon and Cloas Corronation," beginning "As Strephon did unfold his Flocks," has the tune direction "Jenny Gin," but the music actually printed on the undated broadside is a rather indifferent copy of "The fair one let me in" (Wood 417 [153]).

Despite the clearly authenticated authorship of D'Urfey's song, it appears on a contemporary broadsheet entitled "Four of the choicest New Songs . . . Written by a person of Quality, named E. G." (BM 1876.f.1 [26]). And in Scotland it had a strange history, indeed. One is not surprised to see "She rose and let me in," beginning "At Night when all Souls were asleep," a refacimento of D'Urfey's poem, probably printed in Edinburgh in the eighteenth century (Harvard). Allan Ramsay included a softened version of D'Urfey's original, beginning "The night her silent sables wore," to the tune of "She raise and loot me in" (marked "Z," i.e., old song) in his *Tea-Table Miscellany,* 1733, II, 133, and this text appears in Thomson's *Orpheus Caledonius,* 1733, II, No. 14, where the music too has undergone considerable change in detail. The Scotchified song is also found in Alexander Smith's *The Musical Miscellany* (Perth, 1786) and in Johnson's *The Scots Musical Museum.* As Burns soundly remarked, Ramsay "took it into his head to clear it of some seeming indelicacies, and made it at once more chaste and more dull." [2] But the unreliable Stenhouse, whose notes in the *Museum* are often dedicated to claiming Scotch origin for everything sung in Scotland, declared that the original poem was the work of Francis Semple of Beltrees, about 1650. Whereupon an unscholarly editor reprinted Ramsay's text as being the mid-seventeenth-century production that Stenhouse groundlessly claimed.[3]

Although Chappell (*PMOT* II, 510) says the tune of "The fair one let

[2] *Notes on Scottish Song by Robert Burns,* ed. James C. Dick, 1908, pp. 20–21.

[3] *The Poems of the Sempills of Beltrees,* ed. James Paterson, 1849, p. 71. Paterson even claimed that "the original Scotch words" were in *Choice Ayres and Songs,* 1683, though there is probably not a Scotch word in the entire text. He made no mention of D'Urfey.

me in" was "introduced into many ballad-operas," I have failed to find it under any of the several titles by which it is ordinarily cited.

The Fairest Nymph the Valleys

Perhaps the earliest appearance of this tune is the lute version entitled "graysin maske" in BM MS Add. 38539, fol. 30, dating from c. 1613–1616.[1] Keyboard settings with this title are preserved in Christ Church MS 437, fol. 5, and in Priscilla Bunbury's MS Virginal Book, fol. 13ᵛ; Orlando Gibbons's arrangement, called "A Maske," is in BM MS Add.

137

Original is unbarred.

36661, fol. 60ᵛ (reprinted in *Complete Keyboard Works*, ed. M. H. Glyn, 1925, I, 14). All these sources date from the first half of the seventeenth century. The tune is called "The fairest Nymph those Valleis, or Mountaines ever bred" in J. J. Starter's *Friesche Lust-Hof*, 1625, p. 194 (Fig. 137), and in mid-century keyboard arrangements in Elizabeth Rogers's

---

[1] The name was applied to a number of tunes associated with annual festivals at Gray's Inn during Elizabeth's reign and after. The present tune is particularly to be distinguished from the "Gray's Inn Masque" more commonly known as "Mad Tom," q.v.

Virginal Book (BM MS Add. 10337, fol. 3) and Paris Conservatoire MS Rés. 1186, fols. 36ᵛ, 39. The flyleaf of the latter MS contains a reference to "Gregories Maske" beside the listing of "yᵉ fairest Nymphes." Another corruption of the original tune name is seen in Pers's Dutch songbook *Bellerophon,* 1656–1657, where the tune is called "Gravesande."

"The fairest Nymphs" takes its name from the first line of a song preserved with empty musical staves in Giles Earle's songbook, c. 1615–1626 (BM MS Add. 24665, fol. 76ᵛ, ed. Peter Warlock, 1932, p. 104). A broadside version without imprint is titled "The Obsequie of faire Phillida, With the Shepheards and Nymphs lamentation for her losse. To a new Court tune" (Euing, Roxburghe; reprinted in *RB* II, 345).

In the British Museum copy of Slatyer's *Psalmes, or Songs of Sion,* 1642, p. 22, a former possessor has noted that "The fairest Nymph the valleys" may be used for singing Psalm 84, "Lord how amiable/Thy Tabernacles be."

[*Farewell, Ungrateful Traitor*]

Captain Simon Pack contributed the musical setting of "Farewell ungratefull Traytor,/Farewell my perjur'd Swain" to Dryden's *The Spanish Fryar,* 1681, V, i. The three stanzas of Dryden's song were reprinted in *Wit and Drollery,* 1682, in John Shirley's *Complete Courtier,* 1683, and with Pack's music in *Pills,* 1719–1720, V, 334 (Fig. 138).[1]

138

---

[1] A contemporary manuscript version with Pack's air (BM MS Add. 19759, fol. 20ᵛ) is reprinted in facsimile in *The Songs of John Dryden,* ed. C. L. Day, 1932, p. 59. On eighteenth-century reprints and imitations, see Day's notes on the song (pp. 160–161).

* E♭ in original; emendation from *Pills*, 1707, IV, 122–123.

A broadside version of ten stanzas appeared as "Olimp[i]a's Unfortunate Love . . . To a pleasant new Play-House Tune" (Pepys, Roxburghe; reprinted in *RB* VI, 21).

Farinel's Ground

In the early 1680s, the violinist Michel Farinelli wrote some "divisions on a ground," a favorite form of variations in which the same sequence of bass notes is employed throughout. The common English name of the composition is misleading, however, for both the melodic line of the opening section and the ground bass itself had been in use for more than a century. The *folia* or *Les folies d'Espagne* was the name given to the ostinato bass, one of a handful of harmonic patterns upon which the Renaissance built so much of its music. Its origins seem to lie in a boisterous sixteenth-century dance of the Iberian peninsula; and, to make the definition of *folia* more difficult, the name was also applied to descant melodies erected upon the bass pattern. In all its ramifications the *folia* was a widely disseminated and popular musical phenomenon. John Ward, one of its most recent students, has noted that its music has been preserved in more than a thousand sources, not only in Spain and Portugal, but also in Italy and northern Europe.[1] Corelli's use of the basic structural pattern in his twelfth sonata, Op. 5, is well known. It has

---

[1] "The Folia," in the *Report of the Fifth Congress*, International Society for Musical Research, Utrecht, 1952. See also Andreas Moser, "Zur Genesis der Folies d'Espagne," *Archiv für Musikwissenschaft*, I (1918–1919), 358–371, and Otto Gombosi, "Zur Frühgeschichte der Folia," *Acta Musicologica*, VIII (1936), 119–129. An incomplete list of composers employing the theme may be found in Percy Scholes, *Oxford Companion to Music*, s.v. Folia, where the D'Urfey song of 1684 mentioned below is erroneously dated c. 1718.

attracted such other composers as Vivaldi, Domenico Scarlatti, Bach, Grétry, Cherubini, Liszt, and Rachmaninov.

"Mr. Fardinels ground" appeared first in Humphry Salter's *The Genteel Companion . . . for the Recorder,* 1683, pp. 40–41. Among the unnumbered pages of this volume, a somewhat altered version bears the name "The Kings health," derived from the title of Thomas D'Urfey's panegyric on Charles II, using the tune. Beginning "All joy to great Caesar, long Life, Love, and Pleasure," it appears in D'Urfey's *Several New Songs,* 1684, p. 13 (Fig. 139). We may surmise that the unnumbered

First strain only.

pages of Salter's recorder book were added after the publication of D'Urfey's song, for the melodic line of "The Kings health" is the same in both.[2]

In *The Division-Violin,* 1685, the tune is called "Faronells Division on a Ground." A late seventeenth-century English manuscript (Paris Conservatoire Rés. 1186 bis, Part I) contains a version based on the old ostinato bass, "The Spanish follye," and another setting called "Mr. ffaranella's Ground." In *Apollo's Banquet,* 5th ed., 1687, it is "The Tune of Farrinel's Ground, to the Song of (All Joy to Great Caesar)"; in another arrangement for violin, BM MS Add. 38189, fol. 8 (c. 1695–1725?), it is called simply "All joy to Great Caesar."

D'Urfey, accepting the challenge of the melodic variations, has ingeni-

2 The music, with Farinelli's *folia* bass, may be conveniently seen in the facsimile from *Several New Songs* reproduced in *The Songs of Thomas D'Urfey,* ed. C. L. Day, 1933, pp. 48–53. The music of the opening section is also in Hawkins's *History of Music,* 1776, V, Appendix, No. xxiv.

ously fitted words to all six sections of Farinelli's piece. Probably the earliest single-sheet edition, with words interlined throughout, bears D'Urfey's original title and the tune direction "Farrinel's Grounds"; a copy in the Clark Library contains a MS date 9 July 1684 (later variant issues are in Harvard and BM H.1601 [240]). The D'Urfey verses appear without music in *180 Loyal Songs*, 1685, and with all six musical strains in editions of *Pills* from 1706 (1719–1720, II, 152).

Broadsides sung to the tune include "The Loyal Health . . . His Majesties . . . Deliverance from the Late . . . Conspiracy, by the Fire at Newmarket. 1684," beginning "Ye Monarchy haters,/And Whigs of that Leven" (Bodleian Ashmole G.16 [31], Clark). This piece contains no tune direction but reprints the music of "Farinel's Ground." Another is "A New Song. on King William & Queen Mary. 1689," beginning "Let Crowns, Fame and Treasure/Love and Joy without measure," to the tune of "Joy to great Caesar," with music on the broadside (Harvard).[3] *A Pill to Purge State-Melancholy*, 1715, contains belatedly "The Royal Health," beginning "Here's a Health to Queen Anne, Sir," and modeled somewhat on D'Urfey's poem but without music. D'Urfey himself had written to the tune "A Royal Ode" on Queen Anne's coronation (BM G.304 [139], California); reprinted in the 1706 and later editions of *Pills* (1719–1720, II, 157).

In Gay's *The Beggar's Opera*, 1728, and *Chuck*, 1729, the tune is cited as "Joy to great Caesar"; in Aston's *The Restauration of King Charles II*, 1732, it is called "The First Strain of Joy to Great Caesar." In Mottley and Cooke's *Penelope*, 1728, the tune title is "The Medley," evidently from a single-sheet song of the same title, c. 1710, which begins "State and Ambition, all Joy to great Caesar" and combines snatches from many popular songs in stanzas sung to "Farinel's Ground" (BM H.1601 [407], Huntington).

The Fit's Come on Me Now

This proverbial phrase, indicating desire (often sexual), is echoed in several Renaissance plays (cf. Dekker's *If It Be Not Good*, II, ii, Ford's *The Lady's Trial*, III, i, and his *'Tis Pity She's a Whore*, II, i). In

---

[3] Rollins, *Anal. Index*, No. 1905, is an entry of this ballad in the Stationers' Register: "A new song to the tune of Joy to Great Caesar," licensed Sept. 8, 1689, to Dorman Newman, who may have been the printer. The ballad was issued by E. Hawkins.

Fletcher's *Wit Without Money*, c. 1614, V, i, Vallentine sings a stanza of what must have been a familiar song:

> The fits upon me now, the fits upon me now,
> Come quickely, gentle Lady, the fits upon me now,
> The world shall know they are fooles,
> And so shalt thou doe too;
> Let the Cobbler meddle with his tooles;
> The fits upon me now.

No contemporary air is known for the stage song, but a tune to which it could be sung is found in *The Dancing Master*, 7th ed., 1686, p. 205, as "The Fit's come on me now" (Fig. 140). Through the eleventh edition,

1701, it appears unchanged, but in the latter the same tune is printed a second time, with a few differences in detail and with the title "Bishop of Chester's Jigg." [1] In twelfth and later editions the tune bears both names and with the double title is in Walsh's *Compleat Country Dancing-Master*, 1718.

A ballad of 1655 written to the tune is called "The Young-Mans Tryal: Or, Betty's Denial," beginning "Oh Fie upon Cupids skill" (Wood E.25 [49]). The broadside record is then blank until the nineteenth century, when Pitts of Seven Dials issued a slip song called "The Fit Comes On Me Now" (BM C.116.i.1 [211]). Its subject matter is familiar, but in its new garb it cannot be sung to the old jig tune, and the sheet contains no singing direction. It begins:

> It was on a Easter Monday, in the spring time of the year,
> A mother and her daughter, as you shall quickly hear,
> Jane said as they were walking, I'll tell you what I'll do,
> I must and will get married the fit comes on me now.

[1] Under this title the variant form of the tune had first appeared in *The Dancing Master*, Second Part, 1696.

Chappell (*PMOT* I, 176) records the last line of the stanza as being familiar to one of his friends through traditional singing. Something similar has remained in tradition to the present day. For American survivals, see: "I Must and I Will Get Married" in Sharp-Karpeles, *English Folk Songs from the Southern Appalachians*, 1932, II, 159; "Rolly Trudum" and notes thereon in Vance Randolph, *Ozark Folksongs*, 1946–1950, III, 77. The old phrase is variously preserved as "I'm in the notion now," "the fidget's on me now," and "the fit is on me now."

The Flatteries of Fate

Although several ballads were sung to this tune, much of its history is shrouded in shadow. Apparently the tune name derives from the opening of a song in *Westminster Drollery*, Part I, 1671, "All the flatteries of Fate, and the glories of State." [1] It is cited as the tune for "The unequal Marriage: or The Old Bridegroom, and young Bride," beginning "Young Ladies be wary/Who yet are to marry" (Rawlinson 91); for "Fidelia's Lamentation, Or, A Lady bewailing her Unfortunate Love," beginning "You Ladies draw near/whilst I speak of my Dear" (Douce I, 78); and for "The new made Gentlewoman Or, The dishonest Lady," beginning "Come Gallants and lis[t]en unto me a while" (Lord Crawford, Roxburghe; reprinted in *RB* VIII, 562). This latter broadside, a production of the 1670s by L[awrence] W[hite], links to the original tune title several ballads sung to the tune of "The New made Gentlewoman." Among these is "The Longing Maid," beginning "As I walk't in the Forest/one Evening of late," an amatory broadside of Harry and Doll, a printed copy of which dates from 1674–1679 (Rawlinson 113). It is an expansion of a three-stanza poem appearing in *Westminster Drollery*, 1672, II, 87, without tune direction or music, and partially reprinted in Playford's *Choice Songs and Ayres*, 1673, p. 44, with music by Robert Smith (Fig. 141). The *Drollery* text and the Smith music are in all editions of *Pills*, 1719–1720, III, 168. [2]

[1] The same song appears in *Tixall Poetry*, ed. Arthur Clifford, 1813, p. 112, from a late seventeenth-century MS commonplace book.

[2] The pages of the 1672 *Westminster Drollery* contain also "A mock to the Song of Harry gave Doll, and to that Tune," beginning "As I walk't in the woods one Evening of late." But this song had appeared in Act II of Shadwell's *The Miser* (produced in January, 1672), and it contains no references to Harry or Doll. It seems likely, indeed, that this was the original and "The Longing Maid" the "mock."

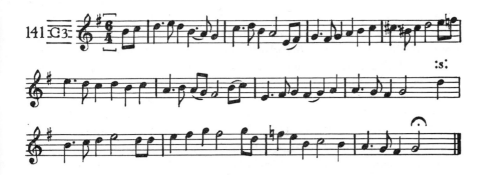

Other ballads to the tune of "The new made Gentlewoman" are: "The Subtile Damosel: Or, Good Counsel for Maids" by J. Wade, beginning "I once had a Servant,/as other Maids have" (Lord Crawford, Harvard; reprinted in *RB* VIII, 565; both ballad collections have copies of another edition listing the tune as "The foolish Husband," about which I have no information); and "The Damosels hard shift for a Husband," beginning "I am a young Damosel/both beautious and fair," to the tune of "Oh how I sigh; Or, The Tyrant, Or, The New made Gentlewoman, Or, Jenny" (Rawlinson 131).[3]

"The Flatteries of Fate" is linked with an alternate tune "Jenny, Jenny" in two ballads: "A Tryal of True Love: Or, The Loyal Damosels Resolution," beginning "You Loyal young Damosells/whose Lovers are bent" (Roxburghe; reprinted in *RB* VI, 293), and "The Volunteers kind Answer, to The Loyal Damosels Resolution," beginning "My Fairest and Rarest,/I Joy for to hear" (Pepys III, 307). The tune of "Jenny, Jenny," cited for several other ballads, has not survived.[4] Nor has "Mall Cooper is grown so gallant and gay," which appears along with "The Flatteries of Fate" in the tune direction of "The Trappaner Trappand or, A cunning Gossip caught in a trap," beginning "You Female Trappanners/ I pray you draw near" (Wood E.25 [51], Douce II, 221).

Robert Smith's music, in a different key and with slight alterations, is set to "The Town Gallant," beginning "Let us drink and be merry, dance, joke and rejoice," in *Choice Ayres, Songs, & Dialogues*, I, 1676, 95. This song was written by Thomas Jordan for his municipal pageant,

[3] The first tune title is from the opening line of a ballad sung to "Riding to Rumford," a tune not extant; on "The Tyrant" see "Bonny Sweet Robin"; the others are discussed in the present article.

[4] Ebsworth (*RB* VI, 292), in seeking to trace the derivation of the tune title "Jenny, Jenny," ignores metrical considerations when he associates it with a ballad of the same title (*RB* VII, 350); for the latter has a stanza of eight lines in ballad meter, whereas broadsides naming "Jenny, Jenny" as the tune are in stanzas of four or six anapestic tetrameters or their equivalent.

The Triumphs of London, 1675, where it was called "The Epicure. Sung by one in the habit of a Town Gallant." As "The Careless Gallant" it appeared in a number of broadside versions without specific tune direction (*BB* II, 722, *RB* III, 484). The song is in all editions of *Pills*, 1719–1720, III, 175, with music and text as in the Playford 1676 songbook.[5] The words alone are found in *Wit and Mirth*, 3d ed., 1682, and in Ramsay's *Tea-Table Miscellany*, 1740, IV, 424. The refrain line, ". . . a hundred years hence," is used also in a broadside of 1697 with a similar stanza pattern: "The True English Prophet: Or, Englands Happiness A Hundred Years Hence. To a New Play-House Tune," beginning "Come chear up your Hearts, Boys, & all hands to Work" (Lord Crawford 237, BM 1872.a.1 [156ᵛ]).

Flying from Olinda

This broadside tune derives its name from the first line of an untitled song, beginning "Fly from Olinda, young and fair,/fly from her soft engaging Air," in *The Theater of Music*, First Book, 1685, p. 38 (Fig. 142). There the composer is identified as Robert King, who wrote a different air for "Olinda's Answer," beginning "Ah, poor Olinda, never boast"; it too appears in the *Theater*, but was probably first used in Nahum Tate's farce, *A Duke and No Duke*, 1685. Each song is found with its respective tune in *A Collection of Twenty Four Songs*, 1685. The original Olinda song is in all editions of *Pills*, 1719–1720, IV, 305. The answer appears, without music, in a garland licensed by Pocock

---

[5] Jordan's poem was set also by Johann W. Franck in *Remedium Melancholiae*, 1690, p. 16, and by George Vanbrughe in *Mirth and Harmony*, c. 1713. Vanbrughe's tune appears on eighteenth-century single-sheet editions in which the song is entitled "The Good Fellow" (BM G.316.e [75], Harvard), but Smith's music is used for the song in *The Convivial Songster*, c. 1782, and in Ritson's *Select Collection of English Songs*, 1783.

(1685–1688), *The True Lover's New Academy*, where it is entitled "The Virgins Complaint," and the tune is called "Flee from Olinda." Presumably the earlier King air is meant, though either will fit the six-line stanza.

Apparently the only broadside sung to the tune "Flying from Olinda" is "A New Song, Of Father Petre, and the Devil," 1689, beginning "Pluto Arise: Great Master come" (Pepys; reprinted in *PB* V, 36). Two of its three-line stanzas are required for each repetition of the 24-bar air.

Fond Boy

The popularity of this tune may be gauged from the fact that more than two dozen ballads were sung to it. Its vogue was chiefly in the 1690s, and at least eight broadside texts contain musical notation—all meaningless save one in which the first fifteen bars, though wretched, are not garbled beyond recognition. This musical text appears on the broadside from whose opening line the tune title is derived: "An Excellent New Song, Of The Two Happy Lovers," beginning "Fond Boy what dost thou mean, thus my Heart to surprize" (Lord Crawford 394, Pepys V, 184).

The link to an adequate musical text is a broadside of 1694, "An Excellent new Playhouse Song, Call'd, The Faithful Lovers, Or, The Young Man's Earnest Request To His Mistress . . . ," beginning "Such commands ore my fate has your love or your hate"; the tune named is "Fond Boy," but the printed music is meaningless (Lord Crawford 1095, Pepys

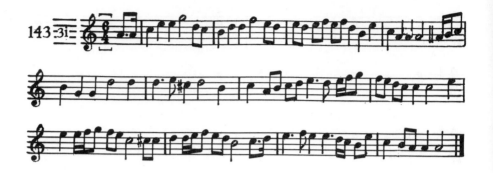

143 :31:

V, 206). This broadside derives from a song in *Thesaurus Musicus,* First Book, 1693, p. 12, whose air is credited to Thomas Tollet (Fig. 143); it is reprinted in *Pills,* 1719–1720, VI, 113. With these two good musical texts in hand, it becomes possible to recognize the gropings toward accuracy in the notation of the "Two Happy Lovers" broadside.

At least eight ballads give the singer a choice between the tunes of "Fond Boy" and Purcell's "If love's a sweet passion," drawn from his *Fairy Queen,* 1692, Act III. Examples are: "The Shooemaker Outwitted," beginning "Good people I pray now attend to my moan" (Pepys III, 271); "The Noble Funeral Of . . . the Duke of Grafton . . . Slain at the Siege of Cork," beginning "As two men was walking down by the sea side" (BM 1876.f.1 [30], Morgan 76); and "The Dorset-shire Damosel," beginning "In Dorset-shire lived a young Miller by Trade" (Harvard, Pepys, Lord Crawford, Roxburghe; reprinted in *RB* IV, 339). A broadside "The Indifferent Lover, or The Roving Batchelor," expanding a song in Dryden's *Amphitryon,* Act IV, beginning "For Iris I sigh," is to be sung to the playhouse tune by Purcell or to "Fond Boy" (Pepys V, 197, Lord Crawford 395, BM C.39.k.6 [48]; reprinted in *OPB,* p. 123).[1] Other ballads sung to "Fond Boy" have been reprinted from the Pepys, Bagford, and Roxburghe collections, but a large number, developing amorous or frolicsome subjects, have not been reprinted. Alone among ballad operas, Johnson's *The Village Opera,* 1729, uses the tune, calling it "Such Command o'er my Fate" from the opening line of Tollet's *Thesaurus* song.

[1] The broadside contains meaningless music. A single-sheet version, with Purcell's music, is in BM C.180.a, a made-up collection known as *Joyful Cuckoldom* (Day-Murrie, Book No. 133); the same words and music appear in all editions of *Pills,* 1719–1720, IV, 246.

Fortune My Foe

The stately strains of "Fortune my foe" are among the most familiar in ballad music, so frequently has this tune been coupled with solemn or lugubrious accounts of murders, natural disasters, warnings to the impious, deathbed confessions, and the like. The tune evidently takes its name from "A sweet Sonnet, wherein the Lover exclaimeth against Fortune for the loss of his Ladies favour, almost past hope to get again, and in the end receives a comfortable answer, and attains his desire, as may here appear." The ballad begins:

> Fortune my foe, why dost thou frown on me
> And will thy favour never better be?
> Wilt thou I say, forever breed my pain,
> And wilt thou not restore my joys again?

Surviving black-letter editions of this broadside (Pepys, Roxburghe, Lord Crawford, Bagford; reprinted in *BB* II, 961) are probably later than 1660, but there is ample evidence that it was in existence before 1590. In 1565–1566, John Cherlewood was granted a license to print a ballad "of one complaynynge of ye mutabilite of fortune"; this may or may not be "Fortune my foe." But on Feb. 28, 1589, a license was issued to Richard Jones for a ballad "of the life and deathe of Dr. Ffaustus the great Cunngerer," which has survived, and which is to the tune of "Fortune my foe." [1]

Several other sixteenth-century broadsides testify to the immediate vogue of "Fortune my foe": "A mournfull Dittie on the death of certaine Judges and Justices of the Peace . . . after the Assises holden at Lincolne last past," dated 1590 and beginning "Recounting griefes and dolors long tyme done," to the tune of "Fortune" (BM Huth; reprinted in *A Collection of Seventy-Nine Black-Letter Ballads,* 1867, p. 197); a lost ballad licensed in July, 1592, "The Lamentacion of John Parker whoe for consentinge to the murder of John Bruen was hanged in Smithfeild the 28 of June 2 yeres after the fact was committed to the tune of fortune"; and in all likelihood three ballads relating to the execution in March,

[1] "The Judgment of God shewed upon Jhon Faustus, Doctor of Divinitye," beginning "All Christian men, give eare a whyle to me." The earliest version, probably copied from a broadside of the 1590s, is found in *SB,* p. 72; late seventeenth-century copies are common (Wood 401, Euing, Harvard, Bagford, Pepys, Lord Crawford, Douce, BM C.22.f.6, Roxburghe; reprinted in *RB* VI, 703).

1590, of Mrs. Eulalia Page, her paramour, and two accomplices for the murder of her husband.[2]

After 1600, ballads to the tune of "Fortune" became so numerous that only a few of the more interesting may be mentioned. "Titus Andronicus Complaint," beginning "You noble minds and famous martial wights," has survived in a number of early and late seventeenth-century editions (*SB*, p. 227, and Percy's *Reliques* represent earlier, *RB* II, 544, later copies). A song beginning "Come ffrauncis Come make hast and goe with me," to the tune of "ffortune," appears in the recently discovered jig *Michael and Frances,* written in 1601 (C. J. Sisson, *Lost Plays of Shakespeare's Age,* 1936, p. 137). "The Araignement of Iohn Flodder and his wife . . . for burning the Towne of Windham . . . 1615," "Anne Wallens Lamentation, For the Murthering of her husband . . . 1616," and "The lamentable Burning of the Citty of Corke . . . by Lightning . . . 1622," all reprinted in *PG*, illustrate characteristic subjects associated with the tune throughout the century, whether applied to contemporary crime and disaster or to such famous murders as those of Arden of Feversham (*RB* VIII, 49) or the young Edward V and his brother (Richard Johnson, *Golden Garland of Princely Pleasures,* 3d ed., 1620, sig. E3).

The tune of "Fortune" is found in a number of late sixteenth- and early seventeenth-century manuscripts. Florid variations without a clear melodic line are in William Ballet's MS Lute Book, c. 1600, p. 14; another setting, at p. 111, presents the air in recognizable form.[3] Settings of uncertain date but within this period are among the manuscripts in the Cambridge University Library: Dd.2.11, fol. 56, "Complaint J:D,"

[2] See *RB* I, 555, 559, 561, from an edition of c. 1640 without imprint. The three pieces, which were printed on the same sheet, can be found in a number of late seventeenth-century editions (Lord Crawford 1227, 1228, Bagford II, 42, Pepys II, 170, Euing 192, Harvard, Douce I, 113v) and some eighteenth-century copies (Lord Crawford 1229, Roxburghe III, 742, 744, Douce III, 61, 62). J. P. Collier reprinted the ballads in his *Broadside Black-Letter Ballads,* 1868, pp. 63ff., from a copy in his own possession said to be dated 1591 and signed T. D. Without seriously questioning Collier's attribution, F. O. Mann reprinted two of the three in his edition of Deloney, pp. 482, 504. It is curious that Collier's copy did not turn up in Lord Crawford's collection, the repository of all the ballads that Collier passed to his son-in-law Frederick Ouvry; nor is a sixteenth-century edition listed in the *STC*. The earliest extant printed edition is that in the Pepys collection I, 126–127, dated 1609; the text in *SB* is from a manuscript copy of the broadside dated 1601. Since no surviving copy of the ballads contains Deloney's initials, it may be suspected that Collier "cooked" the pedigree.

[3] Although this manuscript is preserved in the Library of Trinity College, Dublin, it is of English origin. W. H. Grattan Flood, *A History of Irish Music,* 3d ed., 1913, p. 172, refers to "Fortune" as "an exquisite sixteenth-century Irish melody" but without making a case for its Irish origin. He does, however, contribute evidence on the vogue of the tune when he notes that in February, 1649/50, "Irish pipers attached to Lord Inchiquin's army drew off from Naas to the march of 'Fortune my Foe.'"

and Dd.4.22, fol. 11ᵛ (arrangements by John Dowland), Dd.9.33, fols. 50ᵛ, 89, all for lute; Dd.14.24, fol. 21ᵛ, "Complaint att Fortune," in cittern tablature; and Nn.6.36, fol. 15, in lyra-viol tablature. Another Dowland version is in Euing Lute MS, fol. 27. Anonymous keyboard settings are in Christ Church MS 431, fol. 20, and in Paris Conservatoire MS Rés. 1186, fol. 24 (Fig. 144). The version in Thomas Tomkins, *Keyboard*

144

Music, ed. S. Tuttle, *Musica Britannica*, V, 1955, 128, derives from Paris Conservatoire MS Rés. 1122, p. 174. A treatment by Byrd is preserved in *The Fitzwilliam Virginal Book* I, 254, in Will Forster's MS Virginal Book, 1624, and, with added title "Farwell delighte," in the Clement Matchett MS Virginal Book, 1612 (ed. Thurston Dart, 1957, p. 11; the piece is printed also in W. Byrd, *Collected Works*, ed. E. H. Fellowes, 1937–1950, XX, 11). A viola da gamba setting of the later seventeenth century by Richard Sumarte is in a manuscript in the Henry Watson music collection of the Manchester Free Reference Library.

The earliest printed version of the tune I have seen is a lute setting by I. D[owland?] in Barley's *New Booke of Tabliture*, 1596; it is also in William Corkine's *Ayres, to Sing and Play to the Lute and Basse Violl*,

1610, with variations for lyra viol. On the Continent the tune was popular: Jan P. Sweelinck (*Werken,* ed. M. Seiffert, 2d ed., I, 1943, No. 65) and Samuel Scheidt (*Tabulatura Nova,* 1624, ed. Seiffert, 1892, p. 126) wrote keyboard variations on the theme during the first quarter of the seventeenth century. Valentin Haussmann used the tune in his *Venus-garten,* 1602, No. 3, a work which I have not seen. In at least a dozen Dutch songbooks of the seventeenth century the tune is referred to, usually as "Enghelsche Fortuyne" or "Fortuyn Anglois" or some variation of these formulas, and the music is often printed. The earliest such reference I have noted is in *Den Nieuwen Verbeterden Lust-hof,* 3d ed., 1607, where the tune title is listed three times. Music is found in Nicolas Vallet, *Le second Livre de Tablature de Luth,* 1616; Adriaen Valerius, *Neder-Landtsche Gedenck-Clanck,* 1626; and D. R. Camphuysen, *Stichte-liche Rymen,* 1647, where the Eighth Psalm is set to the untitled tune.

The association of the tune with the Faustus story gave rise to several ballads which use "Doctor Faustus" as a tune name: "Witchcraft discovered and punished," beginning "Now listen to my Song good People all," to the tune of "Doctor Faustus: or, Fortune my Foe" (*RB* VI, 706); "Youths Warning-peice," dated 1636 and beginning "What mournefull ditty, or lamenting verse," to the tune of "Doctor Faustus" (*RB* III, 1); and a satire on Nathaniel Lee included by Dr. Robert Wild in his *Iter Boreale,* 1671, but probably circulated earlier in broadside form as "The Recantation Of a Penitent Proteus Or the Changling, As It was Acted . . . 1663," beginning "Attend good people, lay by scoffs and scorns," to the tune of "Doctor Faustus" (Harvard, Yale, London Society of Antiquaries, BM C.20.f.2 [54], BM 1871.f.3 [37], BM 1872.a.1 [14], Wood 416 [99]; all copies are in roman letter, without imprint).

References to the tune abound in Jacobean drama. In *The Maydes Metamorphosis,* 1600, II, ii, Joculo sings the first stanza of the original ballad; Venturewell begins it in Beaumont's *The Knight of the Burning Pestle,* V, iii; in Brome's *The Antipodes,* III, v, Joyless whistles the tune. John Fletcher's *The Wild-Goose Chase,* III, i, contains a song parodying "Fortune my foe" and doubtless sung to that tune:

> My Savoy Lord, why dost thou frown on me?
> And will that favour never sweeter be?
> Wilt thou I say, for ever play the fool?
> De-Gard, be wise, and Savoy go to school! . . .

Less elaborate references appear in Beaumont and Fletcher, *The Custom of the Country,* I, i; Shirley, *The Grateful Servant,* V, i; Jonson, *The Case is Altered,* IV, viii, and *The Gypsies Metamorphos'd,* 1640, p. 75; and also in the closing scene of Act III in Tomkis, *Lingua.* In Rowley's

The Noble Soldier, III, i, the Poet presumably has the "Fortune" tune in mind when he says:

> The king! shoo'd I be bitter 'gainst the King,
> I shall have scurvy ballads made of me,
> Sung to the Hanging Tune.

In later drama "Fortune" is not forgotten. John Tatham's comedy, *The Rump, or The Mirror of the Late Times*, 1660, V, i, mentions the tune for dancing; Thomas Rawlins's *Tom Essence*, 1677, II, ii, contains a reference; and in Aphra Behn's *The Roundheads*, 1682, V, v, fiddlers play "Fortune my Foe" while Hewson the cobbler dances as the play ends.

The first line of another ballad to the tune of "Fortune my foe" is the source of one of the most popular alternate names for the tune. It is "An excellent Song, wherein thou shalt finde Great consolation for a troubled minde," and begins "Aime not too high in things above thy reach" (Manchester, Rawlinson, Pepys, Roxburghe; reprinted in *RB* I, 326). Both "Fortune" and "Aim not too high" are named on a few ballads, as for example "A Looking Glass for Traytors . . . Edward Coleman . . . Executed . . . December [1678]," beginning "Let all bold Traytors here come take a view" (Wood E.25; reprinted in *RB* IV, 130). Other combinations occur: "The Bedfordshire Prophesie," beginning "Good People all I pray you to attend," is to the tune of "Bernard's Vision, or, Aim not too high" (*PB* V, 108); [4] "The Disturbed Ghost," beginning "Good Christian people all pray lend an ear," is to the tune of "Aim not two [sic] High, or Kings Tryal" (Douce; reprinted in *PA*, p. 174); [5] "Englands Tribute of Tears . . . Duke of Grafton [mortally wounded] 9th of October, 1690," beginning "Unwelcome Tydings over-spreads the Land," is to the tune of "The Watch for a Wise Man's Observation; Or, Aim not too high" (*RB* VII, 740). [6]

A number of dull moralizing ballads with a variety of tune titles all stem from "Aim not too high," the tune named for the first in the series: "The Godly Mans Instructions," beginning "Good People all, I pray

[4] The first tune title is derived from "Saint Bernard's Vision," to the tune of "Fortune, my Foe" (*RB* II, 491); some copies (Pepys II, 4–5, Euing 316–318, Lord Crawford 96) are directed to be sung to "Flying Fame," a tune suitable for ballad meter but not for the iambic pentameter quatrains of "Fortune" ballads.

[5] "Kings Tryal" emerges as a tune name from "The True Manner of the Kings Tryal at Westminster Hall . . . ," to the tune of "Aim not too high" (Euing 357; reprinted from later editions in *RB* VII, 622). This ballad on Charles I's trial, based upon two of the most reliable contemporary pamphlet sources, was phenomenally popular after the Restoration and was still a stock item when Thackeray published his list, c. 1689.

[6] "A Watch for a Wise Man's Observation," beginning "One God there is, of Wisdom, Glory, Might," is a devotional poem in the "Fortune" stanza, but without tune direction (BM Thomason 669.f.15 [9], dated 1650, BM Luttrell II, 231, dated 1677, BM 82.l.8 [61], dated 1698).

hear what I read" (Lord Crawford 442; reprinted in *RB* VII, 830, VIII, clxxxii*). "A Letter for a Christian Family," beginning "Both young and old, both rich and poor give ear," is to the tune of "The Godly Mans Instruction," the ballad just cited (*RB* VII, 811). "The Letter for a Christian Family" is in turn given as the tune of "A Lesson for all true Christians," an acrostic ballad by J. C., beginning "All you whose minds be high & heavenly bent" (*RB* VII, 814). And "A Lesson for all True Christians" is the tune title listed for several ballads, including the following: "A godly song for all penitent Sinners," beginning "Good people all, I'le tell you here in short" (Pepys II, 50); "The Troubles of these Times," beginning "Poor England now is full of care and grief" (*RB* VII, 692); and an acrostic ballad entitled "The Youths Guide," beginning "Prepare good People to give ear with speed," whose stanza capitals spell out "Paul Burgis," followed by the alphabet from A through O (Lord Crawford 1014, BM C.22.f.6 [216]).[7]

The earliest surviving edition of "The Young-Mans A. B. C.," dated 1684, an acrostic ballad beginning "Accept dear Love/these shadows of my grief," is to the tune "Aim not too high" (Euing 407); the copy in the Bagford collection is to "The Virgins A, B, C," while the Roxburghe and Morgan copies give the tune as "The Young-mans A. B. C." (*RB* II, 655). Several editions of the feminine counterpart of this broadside, "The Virgins A. B. C.," beginning "All youthfull Virgins to this Song give eare," list its tune as "The Young-mans A. B. C." (*RB* II, 651). This mixture of tune titles arose chiefly because both ballads were popular for half a century or more. Chappell (*RB* II, 650) noted that later copies recast the first line into a hendecasyllable ("All you faithful virgins . . ."), requiring a division of the initial note of the tune. But since the rest of the ballad is in regular pentameters, there seems virtue in Chappell's suggestion that some other tune may have superseded the original air. I have not encountered another under any of the tune names cited in previous paragraphs. What is singular, indeed, is the unusual melodic and rhythmic persistence of "Fortune." Persistent also is the title "Fortune" in connection with the air. I have found no copy of the tune which bears the label "Aim not too high," or any of the other alternate names by which the tune was signified on ballad sheets.

"The Midnight Messenger . . . a dialogue between death and a rich man," sung to "Aim not too high" (Douce III, 64, a late roman-letter copy without imprint) contains a few lines beginning with such strong iambics ("Amounting," "Extorted," "The time") that to Chappell

[7] A second tune listed for "The Youths Guide" is "My bleeding Heart," a lost air used with tetrameters and hence unsuitable for this broadside.

(*PMOT* I, 167) "Fortune" did not seem a suitable tune. Accordingly, he theorized that some ballads naming "Aim not too high" as their tune were sung to another air, perhaps "Death and the Lady." The choice of this melody rests, so far as one can see, on the dubious ground of similarity of subject matter, plus the fact that the tune's twelve bars accommodate an iambic pentameter quatrain.

Chappell's argument, though interesting, breaks down at a number of points. For example, each of the four musical phrases of the "Fortune" tune begins with two accented notes; technically, neither an iambic nor a trochaic foot is as appropriate as a spondee here, but all three types of feet are found among the broadsides, with iambs as common in old ballads sung to "Fortune" as in those sung to "Aim not." I have been unable to discover a significant metrical difference between ballads bearing the two tune names, though there is great variation in versifiers' awareness of the tune contours. Chappell adds another hypothesis, as if even he were not satisfied with equating "Aim not too high" and "Death and the Lady": it is that *Fortune, being altered by the singer to the accent of those ballads, and sung in a major key, gradually acquired a different shape.* This suggestion has the merit of keeping "Fortune" and at the same time gratuitously destroying its distinctive metrical shape. But there is no musical evidence to support the hypothesis. Many tunes do exist in both major and minor modes, but I have not seen "Fortune" so altered, nor am I persuaded that change of mode has any bearing on the changes of rhythmic pattern suggested. In summary, we have no evidence for more than one melody, various as the tune names may be; and there is but one basic verse pattern, subjected to no more than ordinary warping at the hands of careless and unskilled "poets."

Forty-Nine

"Poor Robbin turn'd Seeker; or The Seekers Ballad," a sectarian production dating from about 1674 and beginning "Oh where am I now?/which way shall I go?" was to the tune "49" with music printed on the Harvard broadside (Fig. 145). Summing up the dilemma of an unorganized group of religious dissenters, Robbin's monologue weighs the claims of Protestant, Presbyter, Anabaptist, Independent, Socinian, Quaker, and Papist. He finds none of them wholly to his liking and concludes, "A true Seeker still,/For my self will I be."

The tune probably was named with reference to the year of Charles I's execution. I have encountered it nowhere else.

Franklin Is Fled Away

This tune takes its origin from the eighth line of "A mournful Caral: Or, An Elegy, Lamenting the Tragical ends of . . . Frankin [sic] and Cordelius . . . ," beginning "Frankin my loyal friend, O hone, o hone" (Douce, Bagford, Pepys, Roxburghe; reprinted in *RB* VII, 418). It was licensed to William Gilbertson in 1656, and the Douce copy was issued by him; other copies date from the early 1680s. In all texts the name is given as "Frankin" except in the tune title, where it is properly spelled. Five stanzas of the ballad have been copied into John Gamble's MS Commonplace Book, 1659, No. 273; the musical staves are empty. An ornamented version of the tune, called "Franklin," is in *Musicks Recreation on the Viol, Lyra-way,* 1669; in unembellished form it appears in *Apollo's Banquet,* 1670, No. 67, as "Francklyn" (Fig. 146). In *180 Loyal Songs,* 1685, it appears as "O hone," and in *Pills,* 1719–1720, V, 129, as "O Hone, O Hone." In the

146 G3.

Original a fifth higher.

ballad opera *The Jovial Crew*, 1731, it is called "You gallant Ladies all."

What may have been an answer to "A mournful Caral" is "The two faithful Lovers," beginning "Farewel my hearts delight,/Lady adieu," to the tune of "Franklin is fled away" (Pepys, BM C.22.f.6, Lord Crawford, Euing, Douce, Bagford; reprinted in *BB* II, 471). This ballad was also licensed to Gilbertson in 1656, but extant copies are a generation later.[1]

"Franklin" is the tune name given for "The Queens Lamentation . . . upon the Death of . . . Prince Henry Duke of Glocester . . . 1660," beginning "Sweet Heavens have been pleas'd" (Euing 290), but the tune is called "O hone, O hone" in a ballad on the death of Princess Elizabeth, daughter of Charles I: "The Lamenting Ladies Last Farewel . . . 1650," beginning "Mournful Melpomany,/assist my quill" (Pepys, Manchester, Douce, Lord Crawford, Euing, Wood 402, Harvard, BM C.22.f.6, BM 1876.f.1, Roxburghe; reprinted in *RB* VII, 631; the Wood copy is signed ES). The tune is also named "O Hone, O Hone" in "Whig upon Whig: or, A Pleasant Dismal Ballad," dated 1683 and beginning "Beloved hearken all,/O Hone, O Hone" (Harvard, Clark; reprinted in *180 Loyal Songs* and *RB* V, 317); and in "Teagve and Monsievr's Lamentation . . . at Limerick [1690]," beginning "Poor Teague, what shall we do?/O Hone, O Hone" (Pepys; reprinted in *PB* V, 206). Two ballads without tune direction contain the "O hone" refrain and are in the distinctive "Franklin" stanza form: "The Downfall of Chancery. or, The Lawyers Lamentation," beginning "Farewell Lords Commissioners,/Your Hon'r lies a bleeding" (BM 82.l.8 [22], BM Luttrell II, 66, the latter containing the MS date 1684); and "The Whigs Lamentable Lamentation,"

[1] The first line of this ballad, "Farewel my Heart's Delight," is listed as the tune for "The Great Messenger of Mortality; Or, a Dialogue betwixt Death and a beautiful Lady," beginning "Fair Lady, lay your costly Robes aside" (Roxburghe, an eighteenth-century Newcastle edition; reprinted in *RB* VII, ix; other copies are likewise late and are usually without tune direction). The iambic pentameter quatrains of this ballad require constant wrenching to adapt them to the music of "Franklin." For a discussion of more plausible tunes, see "Death and the Lady" and note that "Farewll Delighte" is the name given to one keyboard setting of "Fortune my foe," q.v.

beginning "What have the Whigs to say?/O hone! O hone!" (*RB* V, 534; reprinted without source—apparently from *180 Loyal Songs*).

"The distressed Damosels downfall," c. 1675, beginning "You pritty Maidens all/I pray draw near," to the tune of "Frankling is dead and gone, O hone o hone" (Rawlinson 80, Douce I, 59ᵛ), exists in at least two other forms beginning "You pretty Maidens all I pray give ear," but with considerable variation in title and text. One is "An Excellent New Song, Call'd The Injur'd Lady . . . To a pleasant new tune much in request at Court" (Pepys V, 292, dated 1691); the other is "An Excellent New Song, called, The Ruined Virgin . . . To an Excellent New Play-house Tune" (BM C.39.k.6; reprinted in *OPB*, p. 118). An eighteenth-century version has the title "The Broken Contract, Or, The Betray'd Virgin's Complaint" and is without tune direction (Roxburghe; reprinted in *RB* VIII, 807). "You Pritty Maidens all" is the tune title for "The Childrens Cryes Against Their Barbarous Cruel Father [1696]," beginning "Children both far and near, hear the sad fate" (Harvard, Pepys; reprinted in *PB* VII, 226); metrically this ballad is also in the "Franklin" pattern.

Yet another name for the tune is found in "The two Unfortunate Lovers," beginning "In Flintshire liv'd, we hear, a 'Squire young," to the tune "The Ruined Virgin, or Franklin is Fled Away" (Pepys III, 363). "The Ruined Virgin," evidently derived from a title cited in the preceding paragraph, is also used as the tune title in the following: "Love in Despair," beginning "You Loyal Lovers all help me to moan" (Pepys V, 313); "The Banish'd Duke," beginning "Pity a noble Peer, fam'd for renown" (Pepys; reprinted in *PB* VII, 122); and "The Dorsetshire Tragedy," beginning "A Damsel with a Knight lived of late" (Pepys; reprinted in *PB* VII, 133).[2]

In contrast to the doleful lamentations usually associated with the tune, there is a parody ridiculing the excessive grief of a lady whose dog Daphne "Was by a careless Maid . . . In the Night over-laid" and smothered. The song, beginning "Oh! let no Eyes be dry,/Oh Hone, Oh Hone," appeared with the music in *Pills*, 1719–1720, V, 129, and in *The Convivial Songster*, c. 1782.

[2] Rollins (*PB* VII, 121) considers the tune "The Ruined Virgin" to be "evidently interchangeable" with "Welladay." But the latter tune fits an eight-line stanza pattern of 6.6.6.5s, whereas "The Ruined Virgin" is used for a syllabic pattern which is 6.4.6.4.6.6.6.4 or its equivalent; the movement of the two patterns is strikingly different. Rollins does not note the relationship between "The Ruined Virgin" and "Franklin." "The Ruined Virgin" appears as a tune title on two ballads in octosyllabic quatrains (*PB* VII, 282, 285); these could not be sung to either "Franklin" or "Welladay." Either "The Ruined Virgin" was the name of two different tunes or its association with tetrameter quatrains was careless.

"Ohone," as a common Scotch and Irish word of lamentation, is found in some refrains and tune titles that are not to be identified with "Franklin." "The Ladye's replye to the answere made to her lamentation," to the tune "Oh Hone" (*SB*, p. 146), has a stanza of six octosyllabics plus a two-line Gaelic refrain. "A Broadside for the Dutch, With a Bounce, a bounce, bounce," to the tune "O hone, O hone: Or, The Great Boobie" (BM Luttrell III, 82) fits the tune of "Sellenger's Round," with which "The Great Boobie" is identified, but its anapestic meter is ill-suited to "Franklin"; and such a poem as "The Irish footmans, O hone" in *Westminster Drollery*, 1672, II, 52, is simply a lament with no tune direction and no relation to "Franklin."

The Freemason's Song

A Dublin broadside of 1729–1730, entitled "A View of the Irish Bar" and beginning "There's M[arla]y the neat,/Who in primitive State," has no music but contains the tune direction "The Free-Mason Tune, Come let us prepare, &c." (BM 839.m.23 [172]). The tune title is derived from "The Enter'd 'Prentices Song. By our late Brother Mr. Matthew Birkhead, deceas'd," beginning "Come let us prepare,/We Brothers that are" (Rev. James Anderson, *The Constitutions of the Free-Masons*, 1723, pp. 84, 90). Anderson includes the music, which he identifies as "Compos'd by its Author, Mr. Birkhead." It may be doubted that Birkhead was the composer, for in all substantial respects the tune (Fig. 147) had appeared as early as 1714 coupled with verses which D'Urfey wrote, probably in 1702: "On the Queen's Progress to the Bath," beginning "Dear Jack if you mean,/To be cur'd of the Spleen" (*Pills*, 1714, V, 61; 1719–1720, II, 230).[1] Once the tune was associated with Masonic words, it became known as "Come let us prepare" or "The Freemason's Song [*or* Tune *or* Health]," and it was widely popular throughout the eighteenth century. Single-sheet editions of the song appeared (Harvard, Huntington, BM H. 1601 [87], G. 307 [12]); it was reprinted in such collections as Watts's *Musical Miscellany*, 1729–1731,

[1] In *The Merry Musician*, 1716, I, 1, where the same words and music appear, the direction reads "to a comical Tune, in a Masque, call'd, Hob's Wedding." Another D'Urfey song, without music but in the same stanza pattern, is directed to be sung "to a Comical Tune, call'd Hobb's Wedding" (*Pills*, 1719–1720, I, 197). The tune called "Hobb's Wedding: A Kissing-Dance in the Country Wake" (*Dancing Master*, Second Part, 1696, p. 16) does not fit the meter of D'Urfey's song.

147

III, 72, *British Melody, or The Musical Magazine,* 1739, Allan Ramsay's *Tea-Table Miscellany,* 1740, IV, 362, without music, and *The Free Masons Songs,* c. 1760. In two collections the song, printed without music, is directed to be sung to "Ye Commons and Peers," a well-known tune composed by Richard Leveridge (*A Complete Collection of . . . English and Scotch Songs,* 1735–1736, and *The Merry Companion,* 2d ed., 1742).

Other poems are directed to be sung to "Come let us prepare"— presumably the old tune ascribed to Birkhead; examples are "Cupid turn'd Tinker," beginning "Fair Venus, they say," in *The Hive,* 4th ed., c. 1733, III, 92;[2] songs 205 and 206, by George Alexander Stevens, in *Muses Delight,* 1754; and "A Song," beginning "Here's a health to the King," in *The True Loyalist,* a Jacobite collection of 1779.

The tune itself, called "Free Mason's Health," was reprinted in *The Dancing Master,* c. 1728, III, 125, and in Walsh's *New Country Dancing-Master,* c. 1728, III, 22. As "Come let us prepare" or "Free-Masons Song [or Tune]" it was used in at least nine ballad operas; the music was reprinted in editions of Coffey, *The Beggar's Wedding,* 1729; Johnson, *The Village Opera,* 1729; Phillips, *The Chamber-maid,* 1730; Coffey, *The Devil to Pay,* 1731; Fielding, *The Lottery,* 1732; and Langford, *The Lover his own Rival,* 1736.

[2] In the first edition (1725, III, 83) the song appears without tune direction.

The French Levalto

The *volte* or *volta* was a lively dance in triple time, deriving its name from the turn which was a conspicuous feature. The *lavolta* of Provence is one of the oldest French dances and is an ultimate ancestor of the waltz. It was popular in the courts of Elizabeth and James I, and we are told that it was banished from the court of Louis XIII because it was thought unseemly for the man to lift the woman into the air.[1] A Shakespeare reference to the dance is suggestive:

> They bid us to the English dancing-schools,
> And teach lavoltas high and swift corantos.[2]

A tune called "The French Lavolta" (spelled also *Lauata, Levalto, Lavalto*) is used with the popular "A pleasant new Ballad of the Miller of Mansfeild in Sherwood; and of King Henry the seconde," beginning "Henry, our royall Kinge, would go on hunting," the earliest version of which is among the *Shirburn Ballads*. There are editions in most of the great collections: Wood 401, Harvard, Pepys, Bagford, Lord Crawford, Douce, Morgan, Percy Folio MS, Roxburghe; reprinted in *RB* I, 539. The *Shirburn Ballads* also contains the sequel, to the same tune: "A merry Ballad of the miller and king Henry the second; shewing howe he came to the Court . . . ," beginning "When as our noble king came home from Notingham" (reprinted also in *RB* I, 543).

Versions of the tune are in *Het Luitboek van Thysius*, No. 383, as "Volte de France"; in Paris Conservatoire MS Rés. 1186, fol. 85^v, as "ye reuolto" (Fig. 148); and in Cambridge University MS Dd.3.18, fol. 8, as "Y^e French Volta."[3] None of the three sets is well adapted to the

<hr/>

[1] Curt Sachs, *World History of the Dance*, 1937, p. 374, describing the turns and leaps, speaks of the "impetuous energy, meridional *gaillardise*, and self-confident vigor" which the dance introduced into the ballroom. The famous painting of Queen Elizabeth dancing the volta with Robert Dudley, Earl of Leicester, is conveniently reproduced in Mabel Dolmetsch, *Dances of England and France*, 1949, p. 128; the dance is described on pp. 129–132.

[2] *Henry V*, III, v, 32–33. He alludes to "the high lavolt" in *Troilus and Cressida*, IV, iv, 88.

[3] Reprinted in Wooldridge, *OEPM* I, 232–233. Another setting, most closely resembling that of the Paris MS, was reproduced in E. F. Rimbault's *Musical Illustrations of Percy's Reliques*, 1850, p. 109, and with different harmonization in Chappell, *PMOT* I, 169. Its source is said to be a manuscript of virginal music once owned by T. Birch, Esq., of Repton, Derbyshire. In his 1850 volume Rimbault claimed ownership of the MS, but its present whereabouts is unknown.

Wooldridge, I, 233, reprints the Rimbault air and notes that "the version in Sir John Hawkins' transcripts, where it is called *The Revolto*, is practically the same as

six-line stanza of the ballad, although the opening strain is suitable for the first four lines. The Dutch version contains three sections, providing far more thematic material than could be utilized, and the Paris MS in its second section is rhythmically unsuitable. Apparently no recorded version of the tune was set down with the ballad in mind.

It should be added that two eighteenth-century broadsides citing a tune "The King and the Miller" cannot have been sung to "The French Levalto": "Argyle's Advice to Sir R[ober]t W[al]p[ol]e," beginning "In days of Yore, when Statesmen wore,/Clean Hands and honest Faces" (Roxburghe; reprinted in *RB* VIII, 286), is in four-line stanzas; "The Harlot Un-mask'd," beginning "How happy a State does the Damsel possess?" (BM C.116.i.4 [22]) has stanzas of nine anapestic tetrameters.

The Friar and the Nun

Two tunes bear the name of "The Friar and the Nun," but the more recent one, usually associated with the poem beginning "A lovely lass to a friar came," is treated under the latter rubric, q.v. The old tune, found in all editions of *The Dancing Master*, from 1651 to c. 1728 (1651,

this." The tune closely resembles that of the Paris MS, and inasmuch as most of the contents of that MS, including "yᵉ reuolto," were copied into the New York Public Library MS Drexel 5609, it is possible that this latter MS of the eighteenth century is the elusive collection of Hawkins's virginal transcripts.

p. 84=Fig. 149), and in *Musick's Delight on the Cithren*, 1666, appears several times in *Pills* and was used in four ballad operas.

149

Original is unbarred.

I have not found a ballad of a friar and a nun, but in Erasmus' *Apophthegmes*, tr. Nicholas Udall, 1542, fol. 245, there is a reference to the contemporary practice of singing "songes of the Frere and the Nunne, with other sembleable merie iestes, at weddynges, and other feastynges." If "A lovely lass to a friar came" is a secularized treatment of the story, it contains no remnants of the lines from "The Friar and the Nun" quoted in Chettle's *Kind-Harts Dreame*, 1592:

> He whipt her with a foxes taile, Barnes minor,
> And he whipt her with a foxes taile, Barnes maior.

The context makes it clear that the sons of old Barnes took delight in ballads Chettle considered indecent.

Among the broadsides sung to this tune, at least two date from the seventeenth century: "The Wiltshire Wedding," beginning "All in a misty morning,/cloudy was the weather," sung "To an excellent North-Country Tune" (Lord Crawford, Pepys, Harvard, all black-letter editions; Douce, BM C.20.c.30 [15], Roxburghe; reprinted in *RB* VII, 205). The broadsides are without music, but the *Pills* version (1719–1720, IV, 148) contains the tune; moreover, the same music, entitled "All in a misty morning," appears in Gay's *The Beggar's Opera*, 1728, *The Jovial Crew*, 1731, and in Carey's *The Honest Yorkshire-Man*, 1736 ed.[1]

---

[1] In the 1735 edition the tune was titled "A Beggar got a Beadle." Carey's song to the tune, called "The Old One outwitted," was published in a single-sheet edition while his ballad opera was in vogue (BM G.316.f [15]).

A political ballad of 1681 against Shaftesbury and Stephen College is to the tune of "The Fryar and the Nun": "Have You any Work for a Cooper?" beginning "The Cooper, and the Joyner, are Two famous Trades" (Wood 276a [554], Harvard, Huntington, Yale, Clark, BM Luttrell II, 95, Library of Congress [1689 ed.]). Black-letter copies of "The Pope's Pedigree," beginning "A Begger got a Beadle,/a Beadle got a Yeomen," are to the tune "London is a brave Town" (RB IV, 101); but engraved editions dating from about 1705 contain the music of "The Friar and the Nun," though the tune is called "the London Prentice" (Harvard, Huntington, BM H.1601 [50]); with the same music it appears in all editions of *Pills,* 1719–1720, III, 63. Imbedded in the poem, which had appeared in *Wit and Drollery* as early as 1656, there is a stanza related obliquely (and probably only incidentally) to the tune title:

> Thus as it was feigned,
>   The Pedigree did run:
> The Pope he got a Fryer,
>   The Fryer he got a Nun:
> The Nun by chance did stumble,
>   And on her back she sunk,
> The Fryer fell a top of her,
>   And so they got a Monk.

The "Friar and the Nun" music is used for a song, "Strawberry," found in *Pills* (1714, V, 276; 1719–1720, VI, 348) and in *The Merry Musician,* 1716. In John Kelly's ballad opera, *The Plot,* 1735, the music bears the title "The merry Songster." A late eighteenth-century song sheet, "Sir John Barleycorn," beginning "There was four Men Came out of the North" (Harvard) also reprints the tune.

The Friar in the Well

This tune appears in the first eight editions of *The Dancing Master,* 1651–1690, as "The Maid peept out at the window, or the Frier in the Well." It derives its second title from the theme of a broadside "The Fryer well fitted; or, A pretty Jest that once befell; How a Maid put a Fryer to cool in the Well. To a Merry Tune," beginning "As I lay musing all alone,/fa, la, la, la, la" (Rawlinson, Douce, Wood E.25, Harvard, Lord Crawford, Bagford, Pepys, Roxburghe; reprinted in RB

VII, 222).[1] The poem also appeared in *Wit and Mirth,* 3d ed., 1682, and in *Pills,* 1719–1720, III, 325. Although the broadside copies date from the last third of the seventeenth century, the subject (and probably the ballad itself) is alluded to in John Skelton's *Colyn Cloute,* c. 1522:

> But when the freare fell in the well,
> He coud not syng himselfe therout
> But by the helpe of Christyan Clout.   (ll. 879ff.)

Munday and Chettle's *Downfall of Robert, Earl of Huntington,* 1601, IV, ii, also refers to a friar's falling into a well as the subject of a merry jest. It seems probable that the first tune title, "The Maid peept out at the window," was a line in some earlier version of the ballad not extant.

F. J. Child, who reprinted "The Fryer well fitted" as No. 276 A in *The English and Scottish Popular Ballads,* included as 276 B a traditional Scottish version recorded several times in the early nineteenth century. Its stanza form, though retaining a nonsense refrain, is so changed that the old tune could not have served.

An eighteenth-century broadside, "The Merchant's Son, and the Beggar-Wench of Hull," beginning "You Gallants all I pray draw near," and without tune direction (*RB* VII, 379), has a stanza of four octosyllabic lines plus a *fa la* refrain. Ebsworth associates it with the tune of "The Friar in the Well," but it might equally well be sung to "Sir Eglamore"; in either case the refrain line would have to be sung after the first, second, and fourth line of each stanza. As many broadside versions of various Robin Hood ballads attest, printers were often lax in indicating refrain patterns.[2]

In early editions of *The Dancing Master* the tune is printed with one flat in the signature (1651, p. 42=Fig. 150). Later editions containing the air in the same position on the staff are without key signature (1670, p. 72=Fig. 151). The former version is in Aeolian mode; the latter is in G major, with the added oddity that the final strain, twice printed, contains no sharped F in the first statement but, when repeated, sharps every F. These musical texts offer a good illustration of the gradual but steady abandonment of modality during the seventeenth century, a

---

[1] A copy which substantially follows the broadside text is reprinted in *The Common Muse,* ed. V. de Sola Pinto and A. E. Rodway, 1957, p. 296, from an unspecified and undated MS of the Duke of Portland in Nottingham University Library.

[2] "The Shepher'ds Lamentation For His Phillis," beginning "As I lay musing all alone," has a tune name drawn from its first line (Lord Crawford, BM C.39.k.6; reprinted in *OPB,* p. 77). The broadside seems to owe nothing to "The Fryer well fitted," whose first line is identical, but whose stanza pattern and refrain organization differ from that of the pastoral piece.

Original is unbarred.

phenomenon undoubtedly complicated by the relatively careless printing of popular music. Only in tablature notation can one be sure of the actual intention with reference to modes.

The Frog Galliard

In John Dowland's *First Booke of Songes or Ayres,* 1597, No. 6, this tune appears with the familiar words, "Now O now I needs must part" (Fig. 152). Two years later, in Thomas Morley's *First Booke of Consort*

Lessons, an arrangement for flute and five stringed instruments is called "The Frog Galliard." Lute settings of c. 1600 with the same title are in Folger MS 1610.1, fol. 12ᵛ, and in Cambridge University Library MSS Add. 3056, fol. 42ᵛ, and Dd.2.11, fol. 93 (Dd.2.11, fol. 40ᵛ is untitled). Other contemporary versions include "Frayge Gallarde" in *Het Luitboek van Thysius,* No. 366, and an untitled set of variations in the Euing Lute MS, fol. 26ᵛ. It is called "The Frogge" in the Clement Matchett MS Virginal Book, 1612 (ed. Thurston Dart, 1957, p. 14), and in Thomas Robinson's *New Citharen Lessons,* 1609. Adriaen Valerius's *Neder-Landtsche Gedenck-Clanck,* 1626, reprints it as "Nou, nou," and in D. R. Camphuysen's *Stichtelycke Rymen,* 1647, it is given as "Forgs [sic] Gaillarde." The tune is in the Skene MS, and Dauney says it "may be presumed" to be related to "The Frog cam to the Myl dur," whence "A Frog he would a wooing go." He seems to realize that his conjectures find no support in the music to which he alludes; moreover, he seems not to have known of Dowland's authorship of the tune (*Ancient Scotish Melodies,* 1838, pp. 242, 289).

Two broadsides were sung to the tune: "The True Lovers Knot Untyed," a ballad on the imprisonment of the unfortunate Arabella Stuart in 1611, beginning "As I from [*or* to *or* through] Ireland did pass,/I saw a ship at anchor lye," to the tune of "Frog's Galliard" (Wood E.25, Manchester, Euing, Lord Crawford, Harvard, Pepys, Bagford, Douce, BM C.22.f.6 [188], Roxburghe; reprinted in *RB* VII, 601); and "The Shepheards Delight," beginning "On yonder hill there springs a flower" (Euing, Roxburghe; reprinted in *RB* II, 528). The broadsides are in iambic meter, as opposed to the strong trochees of Dowland's "Now O now," for which the music is suited. The tune can easily be adapted to the broadside rhythm, but I have seen no versions in which an anticipatory note was provided at the beginning of each musical phrase.

From Hunger and Cold

This tune is distinct from "Packington's Pound," though the two are interchangeable and are listed together as alternate tunes for a few ballads. It is later in origin than "Packington" and is superseded, as we shall see, by the more popular tune. "From hunger and cold" takes its name from the beginning of a song in Richard Brome's *A Jovial Crew,* 1652, Act I. The play was acted in 1641, and the song appears to have been first printed in *The Academy of Complements,* 1650. Under the title "The Jovial Beggar," both words and music are found in *Select Ayres and Dialogues,* 1659, and *The Musical Companion,* 1673, the latter of which attributes the music to J. G.[1] As "A Catch of the Beggars" it appears without music in *Merry Drollery,* 1661, and *Merry Drollery Complete,* 1670.

The most popular broadside associated with the tune is "The Ballad of the Cloak: Or, The Cloaks Knavery," beginning "Come buy my new Ballet, I have't in my Wallet." Editions of around 1680 bear the tune direction "From Hunger and Cold, or Packington's Pound" and contain the music of the former, Fig. 153 (Bagford III, 8, Lord Crawford 235, BM Luttrell II, 43, Bodleian Ashmole G.16 [129b], Morgan 92, Harvard [four copies], Wood 417 [4] with MS date June, 1679). An earlier copy,

[1] Perhaps John Goodgroome, who contributed other songs to both collections, or the prolific John Gamble.

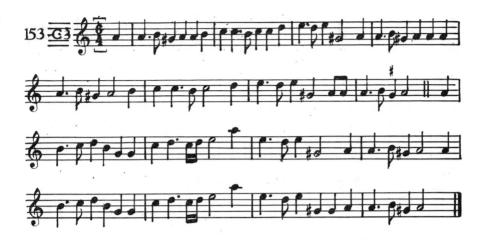

153

without music or tune direction, is entitled "The Tyrannical Usurpation of the Independent Cloak over the Episcopal Gown" (BM 1871.e.9 [8]). It is dated 1663, and the authors are given as "A. C. and P. C."; the initials may have been intended as a part of the poem's symbolism, unrelated to any personal identification. The general topicality of the ballad was preserved into the 1680s by continued alterations of the text. One version refers to the Popish Plot, another to James as the rightful successor to his brother Charles II. The words were reprinted in *Wit and Mirth,* 3d ed., 1682. Other broadside editions include BM 1876.f.1 (8), BM 1871.f.3 (26) dated 1732, and two in the National Library of Scotland: LC.Fol.76, p. 39, temp. Charles II; and Ry III.a.10 (121), an engraved edition bearing the MS date May, 1718 (or 1710), and containing the music. A copy in the Roxburghe collection (reprinted in *RB* IV, 605) has no tune direction but contains the music of "Packington's Pound." This same coupling of words and music appears in all editions of *Pills,* 1719–1720, III, 1.

At least two other ballads were sung to "From hunger and cold." They include "The Joviall Crew: or, Beggars-Bush," beginning "A Beggar, a Beggar,/a Beggar I'le bee" (Lord Crawford, Euing, Harvard, Bagford; reprinted in *BB* I, 195),[2] and "The High-way Hector," beginning "I am a brave Padder,/You ne're knew a Madder," to the tune of "Hunger and Cold, or Packingtons pound" (Harvard, Lord Crawford 538, BM C.22.f.6 [124]; two stanzas are reprinted in *RB* VIII, 846).

---

2 The words had appeared in *Windsor Drollery,* 1671. They are in all editions of *Pills,* 1719–1720, III, 99, with music by John Church. As "The Beggar" or "The Beggars Song" it was popular in the mid-eighteenth century. *The Muses Delight,* 1754, reprints it with a syncopated version of Church's tune, substantially as it is found on engraved song sheets of c. 1750 (Harvard, BM I.530 [18]).

The Gaberlunzie Man

"The Gaberlunzie-Man," beginning "The Pauky auld Carle came o'er the Lee," seems to have been first printed with its music in William Thomson's *Orpheus Caledonius*, 1725. The version in *The Merry Musician*, c. 1731, III, 29 (Fig. 154), supplements the title: "The Words and

Tune compos'd by King James V. of Scotland, on occasion of an Adventure of his in Disguise after a Country Girl." Percy, who reprinted it in the *Reliques*, noted only that "tradition informs us" of the ballad's connection with James V, whereas Ritson accepted the king as "the reputed author" (*Scotish Songs*, 1794, I, xxxv, 163). James C. Dick demolished the quaint attribution (*Notes on Scottish Song by Robert Burns*,

1908, pp. 68, 118–119). Allan Ramsay included the poem without comment in the 1733 edition of the *Tea-Table Miscellany*. E. F. Rimbault reprinted the *Orpheus* music in his *Musical Illustrations of Percy's Reliques*, 1850, observing that the tune is "evidently ancient, although no old copy of it has been preserved."

A broadside text, without tune direction or imprint, is "An Excellen Balladt [sic] Intituled The Gaberlunzie-Man," beginning "The silly poor Man came o'er the Lee" (Lord Crawford 1055). Crawford's conjectural date, 1680–1690, may be sound. In any case, this ballad is earlier than "The new Way of the Gaberlunzy Man . . . To it's own proper Tune," beginning "Once in a Morning sweet and fair,/As I went out to take the Air," a broadside without imprint or music (BM 1876.f.1 [34], dated 1690?; another issue, Lord Crawford 976, dated c. 1720).

"Gaberlunzie," as the context of both ballads makes clear, is a Scotch word for wandering beggar. There is ample tradition for ballads of kings' adventures in such disguise, but "The Gaberlunzie Man" is unconventional in concluding without the usual disclosure of identity.

Gather Your Rosebuds

Herrick's famous poem, "To the Virgins, to make much of Time," appears in BM MS Add. 31432, fol. 33ᵛ, with music in William Lawes's autograph. Contemporary with this is a version in Edinburgh University Library MS Dc.1.69, p. 89 (Fig. 155).[1] Words and music appear, without

attribution, in *A Booke of New Lessons for the Cithern & Gittern*, 1652, and in *Musicks Recreation on the Lyra Viol*, 1652; Lawes is credited

[1] John P. Cutts's inventory of this manuscript in *Musica Disciplina*, XIII (1959), 169–194, lists several other manuscript versions of Lawes's setting. For additional appearances of the poem see *The Poetical Works of Robert Herrick*, ed. L. C. Martin, 1956, p. 473.

with the music in *Select Musicall Ayres, and Dialogues,* 1652. The song is to be found also in Playford's *Introduction to the Skill of Musick,* 1655, John Gamble's MS Commonplace Book, 1659, No. 141 (the familiar tune in 6/4 instead of common time), *Musick's Delight on the Cithren,* 1666, *Catch that Catch Can: or the Musical Companion,* 1667, and in many other seventeenth-century collections. It was introduced into one ballad opera, *The Jew Decoy'd,* 1733.

A broadside by Sir John Birkenhead cited Lawes's music for singing: "The Four-Legg'd Elder," beginning "All Christians and Lay-Elders too," to the tune of "The Lady's Fall, or Gather your Rose-buds; and Fourty other Tunes" (Harvard, Lord Crawford 24, Bagford III, 57). It was originally directed to "The Lady's fall" only (Harvard, Lord Crawford 23, BM Thomason), but the later edition, "Printed in the year 1647. And Reprinted 1677," contains the fuller tune direction, itself an alteration of the rubric (". . . and 50 other Tunes") appearing with the poem in *The Rump,* 1660. A related Birkenhead ballad in *The Rump* is "The Four-Legg'd Quaker. To the Tune of the Four-Legg'd Elder," beginning "All that have two or but one ear." In *Ratts Rhimed to Death,* 1660, this poem is directed to be sung "To the Tune of the Dog and Elder's Maid; Or, The Lady's Fall," and these tunes are also named on the contemporary broadside edition in Wood 416 (70). "The Four-Legg'd Elder" is reprinted in *Pills,* 1719–1720, V, 1, with music which is an imperfect form of "Children in the Wood." Neither this tune nor "Gather your Rosebuds" is well adapted to the ballad-meter stanza of "The Four-Legg'd Elder," which contains eight lines plus a four-line refrain. On the tune of "The Lady's fall," see "In peascod time."

The Gelding of the Devil

"The Gelding of the Devil" was entered as a broadside in the Stationers' Register in 1656, and in the same year a version was printed in *Sportive Wit.* As the title suggests, the matter of the ballad is indelicate: the devil, admiring a fine gelding belonging to a baker of Mansfield, requests a similar operation, and then in a delirium of pain resolves to repay the baker in kind a week later. But the baker's wife dresses in her husband's clothes and the devil is merrily thwarted in a scene inspiring lines of Chaucerian wit. The poem was often reprinted, appearing in *An Antidote against Melancholy,* 1661, *Merry Drollery,* 1661, *Merry Drollery*

Complete, 1670, *Wit and Drollery,* 1682, *Wit and Mirth,* 3d ed., 1682, in all editions of *Pills,* 1719–1720, III, 147, and in other seventeenth- and eighteenth-century collections. Henry Bold's *Latine Songs, with their English,* 1685, preserves the stanza form in Bold's translation.

The oldest surviving broadside version dates from the 1670s; it begins "A Pretty jest I will you tell,"[1] and the tune direction is: "The Gelding of the Devil: Or, the Card Players" (Pepys, Bagford, Douce, Roxburghe; reprinted in *RB* VIII, cii***). Ebsworth could scarcely bring himself to include the ballad in *RB.* He pointedly deferred it, and when he finally did print it, with large excisions and substitutions, he inserted another sheet with duplicate pagination:

> For use where deem'd needful, with edges gumm'd down,
> To shut out the "Baker of fam'd Mansfield town."

A ballad bearing the manuscript date "1660. Nov. 29" and sung to "the guelding of the Divel" is "Hugh Peters last Will and Testament: or, The Haltering of the Divell," beginning "A Joyful story I will you tell/

Original key is B♭.

Of the haltering of the Divel of hell." It relates the hanging of Hugh Peters, a clergyman implicated for his part in the execution of Charles I (BM Thomason 669.f.26 [32]; reprinted in Thomas Wright, *Political Ballads,* 1841).

The tune is found with the original ballad text in *Pills* (Fig. 156). A

[1] Other versions begin "A story strange . . . ," "A Merry Jest . . . ," and "Now listen a while and . . ." On the international diffusion of the story, see Stith Thompson, *The Types of the Folk Tale,* 1961, No. 1133.

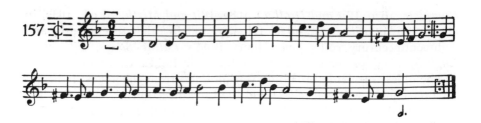

treble-violin version entitled "Gelding of the Devil" is in *The Dancing Master,* 3d–8th eds., 1665–1690; though it is not well adapted to singing, it may be made to fit the ballad and is undeniably an older tune (Fig. 157).

An entirely different piece is a sow-gelder's song in *The Beggar's Bush,* III, i, mentioned in the 1647 folio edition of Beaumont and Fletcher's plays, but not printed in the play until the second folio, 1679. It had meantime appeared in *Wit Restor'd,* 1658, and in *Merry Drollery,* 1661. It was included in *Pills,* 1719–1720, V, 330, with music by Thomas Wroth. An earlier, and perhaps the original, setting, is found with the words in John Gamble's MS Commonplace Book, 1659, No. 67. The song begins "I met with the devil in the shape of a ram" and describes the vain efforts of the devil to escape the sow-gelder by transforming himself into one animal after another, or by disguising himself as a woman or a priest. The stanza pattern is unlike that of "The gelding of the Devil," and music of the two is not interchangeable.

Gerard's Mistress

This tune derives its title from the subject matter of "The Love-sick-Maid: Or, Cordelia's lamentation for the absence of her Gerhard. To a pleasant new Tune," beginning "Be gone/Thou fatall fiery Feaver, now be gone" (Manchester, Pepys, Bagford, Euing, Douce, Lord Crawford, Harvard, Roxburghe; reprinted in *RB* VI, 563). Although the ballad was licensed in 1656, an edition printed by John Hammond must have been in circulation during 1641–1651, the decade in which he flourished. Moreover, the tune was printed in *A Musicall Banquet,* 1651, and the next year in *Musicks Recreation on the Lyra Viol* and *A Booke of New Lessons for the Cithern & Gittern;* the latter contains two arrangements, one of

158

them titled "Gerards Mistresse" (Fig. 158), the other "Colonel Gerrards Mistresse." [1] Words and music of the ballad are preserved in the contemporary Trinity College, Dublin, MS F.5.13, p. 104. A lyra-viol set of the tune is in Cambridge University MS Dd.6.48, fol. 18ᵛ. Virginal arrangements include "Gerrards Tune" by Thomas Heardson in New York Public Library MS Drexel 5611, p. 50, and an anonymous setting in *Musicks Hand-maid*, 1678.

"The Weeping Widdow," to the tune of "Gerhard," in which Charles I's queen gives advice to her children, may have been written in 1649, soon after the execution (Manchester; reprinted in *CP*, p. 238). Another Charles I ballad to the tune is "The Kings last Speech at his time of Execution," beginning "I Come/My blessed Saviour, now behold I come" (Pepys, a late seventeenth-century copy; reprinted in *RB* VII, 625); it too was probably written at the time of the event.

Other ballads to the tune include "The pensive Prisoner's Lamentation . . . taken out of the Cronacle of Edward the second," beginning "You Gods,/And Goddesses that rules in Hellicon" (Manchester II, 5), and "An Excellent Sonnet of the Unfortunate Loves of Hero & Leander," beginning "How fares/my fair Leander? O vouchsafe to speak" (Pepys, Douce, Euing, Roxburghe; reprinted in *RB* VI, 560). Since some editions of the latter are signed H[umphrey] Crouch, it is not unlikely that the ballad was written during the years of the Commonwealth. Ebsworth has noted that Crouch's imperfect knowledge of the classical story led him to reverse the roles of Hero and Leander.[2] Also to the tune is "The Rump Ululant . . . being, The Recantation of the . . . Rump," beginning "Farewell/False Honours, and usurped Power Farewell," which

[1] In *A Musicall Banquet* it is called "Colonel Gerards Tune." No contemporary Colonel Gerard—and there were several—can be confidently associated with the ballad or its tune.

[2] For further information on Humphrey Crouch, see *CP*, pp. 144–145.

appeared not only in broadside form (BM Thomason 669.f.23 [57], Wood 416 [45], both with MS date Feb. 1659/60, Harvard), but also in *Ratts Rhimed to Death*, 1660, *The Rump*, 1660, and *Loyal Songs*, 1731. "The Maids Complaint," beginning "Adieu thou cold companion of my bed, adieu," is a song to the tune in William Hicks's *Oxford Drollery*, 1671, p. 92.

Henry Bold, in his *Poems, Lyrique, Macaronique, Heroique*, 1664, p. 105, reprinted the first part of the original "Gerhard" broadside, interpolating his own parody after each stanza.

The extraordinary feature of "Gerard's Mistress" is that its complex tune, made up of two five-measure phrases, should have lent itself to a number of broadsides in which the versification requires an unusual 18-line stanza or its metrical equivalent. Although the poetry itself is not sophisticated, the total impulse is certainly the antithesis of popular. It is conceivable that one man, perhaps Crouch, wrote all the broadside texts fitted to this tune. Ebsworth's conjecture that the original ballad may have been the expansion of a stage song is worth noting, but he did not have the information to date it earlier than about 1660, whereas we have seen that its origin was a decade before, when theatrical activity was relatively slight.

Gilderoy

Gilderoy, or Gilroy, was an alias of Patrik M'Gregour, a notorious outlaw belonging to the proscribed clan whose later history furnished Scott with rich materials for his *Rob Roy*. Gilderoy was executed in Edinburgh with others of his gang, July 29, 1636,[1] and he became enough of a folk hero for legend to connect his name with exploits against Cardinal Richelieu and Cromwell. It was inevitable that the marauder and blackmailer should be glorified in memory, romanticized into a type of Robin Hood, and celebrated in a ballad. Although probably written much earlier, a broadside published in the 1690s develops the theme as viewed by his beloved (thought by some to be one Meg Cunningham). It is "The Scotch Lover's Lamentation: or, Gilderoy's Last Farewell . . . To an excellent new Tune, much in request," beginning "Gilderoy was a bonny

[1] For an account of the trial, see John Spalding, *Memorialls of the Tr[o]ubles in Scotland and in England, A.D. 1624–A.D. 1645* (Spalding Club, 1850), I, 437–446. In other accounts the date of Gilderoy's execution has been given as 1638 and 1658, but the authority of the trial proceedings would seem conclusive.

boy" (Pepys, Lord Crawford, Bagford; reprinted in *A Collection of Old Ballads*, 1723–1725, I, 271, in *BB* I, 105, and in *OPB*, p. 183). A different version, having only one stanza in common with the broadside and beginning "Was ever grief so great as mine," was included in *Westminster Drollery*, 1671, I, 112. A variant broadside text of c. 1700 "To its own Proper Tune" is "Gilderoy," beginning "My Love he was as brave a Man" (Lord Crawford 838). That the original ballad was a good deal earlier seems to be substantiated by the existence of a broadside "Two Strings to a Bow; or, The cunning Archer . . . To an excellent Scotish Tune, call'd Gilderoy," beginning "Give ear you lads and lasses all" (Roxburghe; reprinted in *RB* VIII, 542); it was issued by the stationer Charles Tyus, who is known to have flourished for a few years before and after 1660.[2]

Editions of *Pills* from 1707 to 1719–1720 (V, 39) contain "Gilderoys last Farewel," derived from the broadside text. The music is badly garbled, however, and the earliest satisfactory tune is "Gilder Roy" in Alexander Stuart's *Musick for Allan Ramsay's Collection of Scots Songs*, c. 1725, p. 94 (Fig. 159). A closely related variant of the tune appears in

the second volume of William Thomson's *Orpheus Caledonius*, 1733, with a somewhat different text of the ballad. Percy's version, from which "indecent luxuriances" had been pruned, seems to have been the work of the "Hardyknute" improver, Lady Elizabeth Wardlaw; it is followed by Pinkerton, Herd, and Ritson.[3]

[2] See H. R. Plomer, *Dictionary of Booksellers . . . 1641 to 1667*, 1907.
[3] The table of contents of Johnson's *Scots Musical Museum*, vol. I, associates the name of Sir Alexander Halket (brother of Lady Elizabeth Wardlaw) with "Gilderoy," although the ballad is not reprinted with the tune. Ritson (*Scotish Songs*, 1794, II,

Sir Charles Sedley's song in Act III of *The Mulberry Garden*, 1668, beginning "Ah Cloris! that I now could sit," found its way into Allan Ramsay's *Tea-Table Miscellany*, 1723, p. 89, where it is directed to be sung to "Gilder Roy." [4] Text and tune are in Alexander Smith's *Musical Miscellany*, Perth, 1786, p. 196, and in the *Scots Musical Museum*, I, 66. The *Orpheus Caledonius* melody, in a more florid form as found in William McGibbon's *Scots Tunes*, Book III [1755], and in the *Museum*, was arranged by Pleyel for vocal duet in George Thomson's *Original Scottish Airs*, 1801–1805, I, 20. Both the ballad and Sedley's song are printed with the music.

Because the original broadside was published in London, Maidment considered the air to be English; but we cannot be sure of the original form of the tune. A rhythmically distorted variant used in the ballad opera *The Jovial Crew*, 1731, will not easily fit the meter of the ballad. What is certain is that "Gilderoy" had a long vogue in Scotch tradition and was reprinted in many eighteenth- and nineteenth-century collections of Scotch songs. But that it may never have been wholly Scotch property is suggested by its evident kinship with tunes of the traditional carol "Come all ye faithful Christians" and the murder ballad "Maria Martin" collected in England early in the twentieth century.[5] Moreover, there is a remarkable resemblance between "Gilderoy" and the tune commonly used for the traditional "Dives and Lazarus" and "We are poor frozen-out Gardeners." [6] Finally, the seventeenth-century English air, "The Clean Contrary Way," q.v., seems harmonically to be the ancestor of this entire tune cluster.

24) accepts Halket as the author of the ballad on the *Museum's* authority. More recent opinion has vacillated between brother and sister; see James Maidment, *Scotish Ballads and Songs*, 1868, II, 220ff.

[4] John Banister's original setting of the stage song seems not to have been preserved. Because of Ramsay's tune direction, there has been speculation that "Gilder Roy" might be Banister's air. The prior currency of the ballad would, however, weaken the supposition, and it is difficult to believe that Pepys, when he heard Mrs. Knipp rehearse Sedley's song with its "slight, silly, short ayre" (*Diary*, May 7, 1668), was listening to the tune we know as "Gilderoy."

[5] *JFSS*, II (1905), 115–123. In addition to four traditional tunes of the carol and the ballad (three of each being closely related to the "Gilderoy" tune), Lucy Broadwood reproduces and discusses other parallels from Ireland and Scotland. For further traditional variants of "Gilderoy" text and tune, see *JFSS*, II (1906), 239–242.

[6] See *The Oxford Book of Carols*, No. 60 (second tune), and Chappell, *PMOT* II, 747–748.

The Glories of Our Birth

and State

James Shirley's play, *The Contention of Ajax and Ulysses*, 1659, closes with a solemn song in three stanzas beginning "The glories of our blood and state." The song "was afterwards sung in parts, the Musick excellently composed by Mr. Ed[ward] Coleman," according to the original edition. Coleman's music, with Shirley's words, beginning "The Glories of our Birth and State," appears in *Catch that Catch Can: or the Musical Companion*, 1667, p. 146 (Fig. 160), as a composition for two and (chorus) three voices. Words and music were also reprinted in *Select Ayres and Dialogues*, Second Book, 1669, *The Musical Companion*, 1673, Banister and Low's *New Ayres and Dialogues*, 1678, and *Synopsis of Vocal Musick*, 1680.

The stage song was the basis for a ten-stanza broadside published in the late 1670s, "The Vanity of Vain Glory," beginning "The gloryes of our birth and state" (Roxburghe; reprinted in *RB* V, 578). I have found no other broadside using the tune.

The Glory of the West

This tune is in *The Dancing Master,* first seven editions, 1651–1686, tenth and after, 1698ff. (1651, p. 94=Fig. 161), *A Musicall Banquet,*

Original is unbarred.

1651, *Musicks Recreation on the Lyra Viol,* 1652, 1669, *A Booke of New Lessons for the Cithern & Gittern,* 1652, *Musick's Delight on the Cithren,* 1666, *Musicks Hand-maid,* 1678; and in Walsh's *Compleat Country Dancing-Master,* 1718.

Two ballads were sung to the tune: "The Fame, Wit, and glory of the West," beginning "A Faire and comly creature" (Manchester; reprinted in *CP,* p. 257); and an imitation by Charles Hammond, "The credit of Yorkshire, or the Glory of the North . . . To the tune of the right Glory of the West," beginning "Of late I heard a dity" (Manchester; reprinted in *CP,* p. 266). Rollins dates both pieces about 1649; dates are printed on each, but these unique copies are both mutilated.

The extant musical texts are all instrumental arrangements, and though the general rhythmic pattern fits the complex ballad stanza, the tripping syllables require a division of many notes. A further awkwardness is that the tunes fall short of the length necessary to fit the ballads, and only by the repetition of the final two-measure phrase can the tune be adapted to the verse pattern.

Two other ballads bear the title "The Glory of the West": one a celebration of General Monk's approach to London early in 1660 (Wood 416 [39] and other copies; reprinted in *The Rump*), without tune direction but in the rhythmic pattern of "Which nobody can deny"; the other a political ballad of 1685 to the tune of "Winchester Wedding" (Lord Crawford 659, Wood 417 [144]). These of course bear no relationship to the mid-century tune "The Glory of the West."

Go from My Window

"Go from my Window" is named as the tune for singing the fourth section of "Frauncis new Iigge," c. 1595 (Pepys; reprinted in *PG*, p. 1, and in C. R. Baskervill, *The Elizabethan Jig*, 1929, pp. 450–464; a MS version entitled "Mr. Attowel's Jigge" is reproduced in *SB*, pp. 245–254). A ballad called "Goe from the windowe goe" was licensed March 4, 1588, but it is lost unless parts of it are echoed in Merrythought's song in Beaumont's *The Knight of the Burning Pestle*, III, v:

> Go from my window, love, go;
> Go from my window, my dear.
> The wind and the rain
> Will drive you back again;
> You cannot be lodged here.

After a bit of dialogue Merrythought sings another stanza:

> Begone, begone, my juggy, my puggy,
> Begone, my love, my dear.
> The weather is warm,
> 'T will do thee no harm;
> Thou canst not be lodged here.

That the original ballad was considerably older than 1588 is suggested by the religious parody in *A Compendious Book of Godly and Spiritual Songs*, 1567 (ed. A. F. Mitchell, 1897, pp. 132–133):

· 257 ·

Quho is at my windo, quho, quho?
Go from my windo, go, go.
Quha callis thair, sa lyke ane stranger,
  Go from my windo, go.

Lord I am heir, ane wratcheit mortall,
That for thy mercy dois cry and call,
Unto thé my Lord Celestiall,
  Sé quho is at my windo, quho.

The first of Merrythought's stanzas is paraphrased in Fletcher's *Monsieur Thomas,* III, iii, and his *The Woman's Prize,* I, iii, in Otway's *The Soldier's Fortune,* V, i, and Middleton's *Blurt Master Constable,* IV, i. The second song at the end of Thomas Heywood's *The Rape of Lucrece,* beginning "Arise, arise, my Iuggie my Puggie," elaborates Merrythought's other stanza. It was reprinted in *Wit and Drollery,* 1661, and with music of "Tomorrow is St. Valentine's Day" in *Pills,* 1719–1720, IV, 43.

The tune of "Go from my Window" enjoyed wide popularity. It is in William Barley's *A New Booke of Tabliture,* 1596, as theme and variations for the orpharion "made by I[ohn] D[owland?]," in Antony Holborne's *The Cittharn Schoole,* 1597, in Thomas Morley's *First Booke of Consort Lessons,* 1599 (a six-part setting by Richard Alison), and in Thomas Robinson's *The Schoole of Musicke,* 1603, arranged for lute. *The Fitzwilliam Virginal Book* contains two virtually identical sets of keyboard variations, one ascribed to Thomas Morley, the other to John Munday. Other virginal pieces on the tune are in New York Public Library MS Drexel 5612, p. 31 (Dr. John Bull); Paris Conservatoire MSS Rés. 1122, p. 153 (a fragment, in Thomas Tomkins, *Keyboard Music,* ed. S. Tuttle, *Musica Britannica,* V, 1955, 153), Rés. 1186, fol. 119, Rés. 1186 bis, Part II, p. 46; Will Forster's MS Virginal Book, fol. 163ᵛ (in William Byrd, *Forty-five Pieces for Keyboard Instruments,* ed. S. Tuttle, 1939, p. 113); and in Cosyn MS, p. 157 (in *Twenty-five Pieces from Benjamin Cosyn's Book,* ed. Fuller-Maitland and Barclay Squire, 1923, p. 14).

Late sixteenth-century versions for lute are in Folger MS 1610.1, fol. 17 (Fig. 162), and in Cambridge University MSS Dd.2.11, fol. 3, Dd.3.18, fol. 34ᵛ, and Dd.5.78.3, fol. 39ᵛ (Dowland), fol. 40ᵛ. Cambridge MS Dd.4.23, fol. 5ᵛ, is in cittern tablature, as is Richard Alison's set in the Mills College Cittern MS, No. 33. Other lute arrangements include: BM MS Egerton 2046, fol. 29ᵛ (Dowland); BM MS Add. 31392, fol. 26ᵛ (Francis Pilkington); and Euing Lute MS, fol. 17ᵛ (Dowland), fol. 48ᵛ. A song "Come gentle heardman sitt with me" (found in Francis Davison's *Poetical Rhapsody,* 1602) is set to "Go from my Window" with lute accompaniment in BM MS Add. 15117, fol. 10ᵛ, after 1614. As "The

162

* Followed in the original by four variations.

New Exchange" or "Durham Stable" the tune appears in *The Dancing Master*, 1651–1686, cast not in the usual 4/4 time, but in more fluid 6/4; the Aeolian mode of 1651 disappears after the early editions.

In addition, the tune is named in several seventeenth-century Dutch songbooks without music: *Den Bloem-Hof Van de Nederlantsche Ieught*, 1608, pp. 22, 25, the latter naming the tune "Gophromowinde Milort"; B. J. Wellens, *T'Vermaeck der Jeught*, 1612, p. 95; and *Cupido's Lusthof*, c. 1613, p. 22.

Chappell (*PMOT* I, 142) printed a stanza of the old song recovered from oral circulation, with a tune whose opening and closing cadence reminded him of Ophelia's song, "How should I your true love know." Within the twentieth century further traditional traces have appeared: "One night as I lay on my bed," a ballad collected in Dorsetshire, has a refrain:

> So it's open the window, my love, do
> So, begone from my window, my love, do
> So open the window, my love, do.

And a Scottish version has a tune clearly related to Chappell's nineteenth-century traditional version.[1]

[1] *JFSS*, III (1907), 78, 80. See also *JEFDSS*, III (1936–1939), 161–164.

The Gods of Love

This tune takes its name from the opening line of a ballad by William Elderton. Apparently no printed copy has survived, but a good text is preserved in an Elizabethan manuscript now in the possession of the American collector, James M. Osborn, who printed it in the London *Times*, November 17, 1958. It begins:

> The God of love that sits above,
> And knows me, and knows me,
> How sorrowful I do serve: . . .

The lost broadside was licensed as "the godes of Love &c" in 1567–1568 (Rollins, *Anal. Index*, No. 987). But its first publication must have been earlier, for in 1562–1563 "the answere to the iiijth ballett made to the godes of loue" was entered (*Anal. Index*, No. 83), as was William Birch's "The complaint of a sinner . . . After W. E. moralized" (*Ballads and Broadsides*, ed. H. L. Collmann, 1912, No. 7), beginning:

> The God of loue, that sits aboue,
> Doth know vs, Doth know vs,
> How sinfull that we bee: . . .

Another extant moralization, "The ioy of Virginitie," beginning "I Iudge and finde, how God doth minde,/to furnish, to furnish," is to be sung to "The Gods of loue" (*A Handefull of Pleasant Delites*, 1584, ed. Rollins, p. 42). It too may date from the 1560s and may have been included in the first state of the *Handful*, licensed in 1566.

Elderton's opening phrase is echoed in *The Rare Triumphs of Love and Fortune*, 1589, Act IV. In *Much Ado about Nothing*, V, ii, Benedick sings a snatch of the ballad. Shakespeare's fourth line is, as Mr. Osborn has noted, perhaps a deliberate conflation of Elderton's sixth line, "Some pity when I deserve," and his third.

> The god of love,
> That sits above,
> And knows me, and knows me,
> How pitiful I deserve . . .

In Thomas Heywood's *Fair Maid of the Exchange*, 1607, sig. E, Frank sings "Ye gods of Loue that sits aboue," but the meter of his song is incongruent with Elderton's.

A cittern arrangement of "The goddes of love" appears in fol. 88ᵛ of the Francis Willoughby Lute Book (called also Lord Middleton's Lute MS). The tune is among the untitled keyboard pieces of c. 1570 at the end of Thomas Dallis's MS Lute Book, printed in *The Dublin Virginal Manuscript,* ed. John Ward, 1954, p. 25. Professor Ward has shown that the popular Elizabethan dance tune "Turkeylony," found in William Ballet's MS Lute Book, p. 91, is but another version of "The Gods of love." The tune has been considerably reworked in Susanne van Soldt's virginal manuscript of 1599 (BM MS Add. 29485, fol. 17), where it is called "Pavan dan vers [d'Anvers?]." [1] None of the several instrumental settings is free enough from embellishment to be well adapted for singing, but the Ballet version is the most nearly satisfactory (Fig. 163). With a repetition of its first and third strains (as called for in the Willoughby

163

---

[1] Ward, pp. 52–53, prints both the Ballet and the van Soldt settings in modern notation. In a subsequent study of "Music for *A Handefull of Pleasant Delites*," *JAMS,* X (1957), 164–165, Ward prints a transcript of the Willoughby setting. He calls attention to several Continental appearances of the tune under various names, the earliest of which is "Gentil madonna" in Antonio Rotta's *Intabolatura de Lauto,* First Book, 1546.

* Bass note is C in tablature (fifth instead of sixth string stopped).
** Bass notes are G in tablature (fourth instead of fifth string stopped).

set) it will fit the quatorzains of the broadsides with which "The Gods of love" is associated. It is observable that the echoing phrases which mark the distinctive stanza form are not paralleled by equally distinctive melodic contour.

Gramercy Penny

To the tune of "Gramercy penny" Martin Parker wrote "A Fayre Portion for a Fayre Mayd . . . Who liues at London for a Marke a yeare," licensed May 1, 1633, and beginning "Now all my friends are dead and gone" (Roxburghe; reprinted in *RB* I, 365). The eight-line stanza concludes with the burden:

> Though I have but a mark a year,
> And that my mother gave me.

It is reprinted in *Sportive Wit*, 1656, and a brief but cynical modernization is in *Pills*, 1719–1720, IV, 116, with music (Fig. 164). We cannot know whether this tune is that named on Parker's ballad, but it will serve in want of one with unmistakable antecedents.[1]

[1] Chappell (*PMOT* I, 356) assumed that the tune was named from "But god a mercy penny," the burden of "There's nothing to be had without money . . . To a new

164

* E in original.

In the same meter, and to the tune of "Though I have but a marke a yeare," is "The Praise of Nothing," beginning "The praise of wisedome some doe write" (Euing, Roxburghe; reprinted in *RB* II, 340). This ballad, for which there is no Stationers' Register entry, presumably derives its tune name from Parker's ballad.

Gray's Inn Masque, or Mad Tom

To the tune of "Grayes Inne Mask" two ballads are directed to be sung. They are "A New Mad Tom of Bedlam," beginning "Forth from my sad and darksome Cell," and, usually printed on the same sheet, "The Man in the Moon drinks Claret, As it was lately sung at the Curtain Holywel, to the same tune," beginning "Bacchus the Father of drunken Nowls" (Euing, Pepys, Bagford, Lord Crawford, Harvard, Roxburghe; reprinted in *RB* II, 259, 256). Allusion to the Curtain suggests that

Northerne tune, Or the Mother beguil'd the Daughter" (*RB* II, 565). This ballad was registered July 8, 1633, two months after Parker's was licensed, but we cannot be sure that either was being printed for the first time. Chappell later (II, 780) derived the tune name from a ballad of c. 1628, "Oh Gramercy Penny . . . To the tune of, Its better late thriue then neuer," by Laurence Price (*PB* II, 100). But Price's ballad is in a nine-line stanza not interchangeable with that of Parker. Other ballads were written to be sung to each of the tunes named in this note, but no music has been found for either.

the "Claret" ballad was written during the first quarter of the seventeenth century, before the theater fell into disuse. The Euing broadside, earliest of the printed editions, can be dated c. 1658–1664; the others were published during the next forty years. The first ballad of the pair is preserved in BM MS Harl. 7332, fol. 42, in an early seventeenth-century hand said to be that of "Fearegod Barbon, of Daventry, in the county of Northampton." [1] From the same period comes a variant text, "Darkesome Cell," in the Percy Folio MS (ed. Hales and Furnivall, III, 123). As "Tom of Bedlam" the song appears, without music, in *Le Prince d'Amour*, 1660, p. 169, in *Wit and Mirth*, 3d ed., 1682, p. 56, and in all editions of *Pills*, 1719–1720, III, 43. It continued to be popular in eighteenth-century miscellanies, from *The Hive*, 1732, IV, 181, to Ritson's *English Songs*, 1783, II, 146—to cite but two among many appearances.

A number of tunes are named "Gray's Inn Masque," from their connection with the celebrated entertainments periodically given by the inns of court, including Gray's Inn, during the reigns of Elizabeth and James I, and combining music, dancing, and allegorical pageantry. John Coperario (born Cooper), the celebrated English lutenist and composer, is credited with the music used for Francis Beaumont's *The Masque of the Inner Temple and Grayes Inne*, performed at Whitehall on February 20, 1613.[2] One of his instrumental pieces for the masque is "Cuperaree or Graysin," preserved in BM MS Add. 10444, fol. 28^v. This MS (dated after 1635) contains many other tunes from masques, including "Graysin Anticke Masque," fol. 41^v, and three others entitled "Grayes Inne Masque," fols. 44, 53^v, leading Chappell (*PMOT* I, 330) to suggest that all of them may have been written for the 1613 performance, presumably by Coperario. The tune in which we are presently interested is that on fol. 44, which we can establish as the one meant for ballad singing because a variant in lute tablature, dating from c. 1613–1616, has the title "Mad Tom of Bedlam" added in a later hand (BM MS Add. 38539, fol. 29 = Fig. 165). The tune is also in the first ten editions of *The Dancing Master*, the title "Graies Inne Maske" being expanded to "Grayes-Inn Mask, or (Mad Tom)" with the fourth edition. The virginal arrangement in Drexel MS 5612, p. 59 (New York Public Library), is entitled "The man in the moone" and therefore dates from after the appearance of the two ballads. A contemporary untitled virginal set is preserved in Christ Church MS 437, fol. 7.

In *Choice Songs and Ayres*, 1673, p. 66, "Tom of Bedlam," with a vari-

[1] Related to Praise-God Barbon or Barebone(s), the London leather seller and M. P., in whose dubious honor the parliament of 1653 was named?

[2] See *Grove's Dictionary of Music and Musicians*, 5th ed., 1954, II, 427. The attribution seems first to have been made by E. F. Rimbault, *Notes and Queries*, Ser. I, I (1850), 265.

165

* First ending and repeat sign supplied by editor.
** Second ending supplied.

ant first line, "Forth from the dark and dismal Cell," is arranged for bass voice. It is reprinted in later editions of that work as well as in *Catch that Catch Can: or, The Second Part of the Pleasant Musical Companion,* 1685, No. 71 (in the 1686 and 1687 editions, called *The Second Book of the Pleasant Musical Companion,* the song is Part II, No. 25). Song-sheet editions of c. 1710, with the voice part in the treble clef, are titled "Old Tom of Bedlam" (BM H.1601 [149], Huntington, Harvard). The tune was introduced into Mottley and Cooke's *Penelope,* 1728, and Odingsells' *Bays's Opera,* 1730, with music in printed copies of the former.

Although the tune antedates Purcell's birth by almost half a century, his name became associated with it through the inclusion of the "Mad Tom" ballad in *Mr. Henr[y] Purcell's Favourite Songs,* c. 1725, whence

Ritson and others picked up the attribution. A passage in Walton's *The Compleat Angler* identifies William Basse as the author of "The Hunter in his career" (see "Basse's Career") and of "Tom of Bedlam," but because several songs with this latter title were written during Basse's lifetime—he died in 1653—we cannot be sure that he was the author of "Forth from my sad and darksome cell." [3] Sir John Hawkins credited Basse with the verses and named Henry Lawes as the composer of the setting in *Choice Songs and Ayres,* without benefit of documentary evidence.[4]

The Great Booby

No wholly satisfactory music for "The Great Booby" seems to have survived. Nor does the tune exhibit an independent life, for the ballads which cite it name an alternate air in each instance. A five-stanza poem beginning "My friends if you will understand" is found in a seventeenth-century hand in Bodleian MS Rawlinson Poet. 152, fol. 208, together with "The tune of a great Boobye," an eight-measure air which will accommodate only half the double ballad-meter stanza (Fig. 166). Its three final minims seem especially designed for the words "great Boobee," with which each stanza ends. An expanded broadside text, entitled "The Great Boobee," is directed to be sung to "a pleasant New Tune; Or, Sallengers Round" (Pepys, Euing, Douce, Roxburghe; reprinted in *RB* VII, 273). The ballad was licensed in 1656 but surviving copies probably date from the next decade. The "New Tune" was evidently that of the Rawlinson MS; "Sellenger's Round," q.v., sometimes called "The beginning of the world," is a tune whose *a b a* form occupies 24 measures, whereas only the first two strains are needed for singing this ballad. Since the second strain ends on the dominant, the effect is circular, but the fit is admirable.[1]

Another ballad calling for either the old or the new tune is "The Merry

[3] I have discussed some of these other songs, s.v. "Tom of Bedlam." A convenient collection of texts and some musical settings is *Loving Mad Tom: Bedlamite Verses of the XVI and XVII Centuries,* ed. Jack Lindsay, 1927.

[4] See Sir Harris Nicolas's edition of *The Complete Angler,* 1836, I, 124n. R. W. Bond, though accepting the uncertainty of Basse's authorship, nevertheless reprinted "Forth from the dark and dismal Cell" in his edition of *The Poetical Works of William Basse,* 1893, p. 135.

[1] Eight bars of music unsuited to the verse are printed with the full text in *Pills,* 1719–1720, V, 94.

166

Original is unbarred.

Wooing of Robin & Joan the West-Country Lovers," beginning "O Mother chave been a Batchellor," sung to "The beginning of the World, or Sellingers Round, or Great Boobe" (Pepys, Roxburghe; reprinted in *RB* VII, 308). The version printed in *Wit Restor'd,* 1658, names only the first of these tune titles; the text in *Wit and Drollery,* 1682, is without tune direction.

The tune is called for in a third ballad, "A Broadside for the Dutch, With a Bounce, a bounce, bounce," beginning " 'Twas lately we met with the vapouring Dutch," to the tune of "O hone, O hone: Or, The Great Boobie" (BM Luttrell III, 82, dated 1672). "O hone" is another name for "Franklin is fled away," q.v., a tune which fits these verses with some difficulty. The Rawlinson "great Boobye" music can be used, with some division of notes to accommodate the anapestic meter.

Great York Has Been Debarred of Late

A ballad of about 1680, having as both tune name and first line "Great York has been debar'd of late," is entitled "The Loyal Tories Delight, Or, A Pill for Fanaticks" (Roxburghe; reprinted in *RB* IV, 636). The ballad sheet contains two lines of music fitting the distinctive five-line stanza form (Fig. 167).

The tune apparently was not used for other ballads, but I have found the music printed on four other broadsides, none of which can be sung to the tune. Moreover, the tune is usually garbled by the reversal of the two musical lines. On the following ballads, then, the presence of a musical score is only a printer's stratagem to give an up-to-date look to

167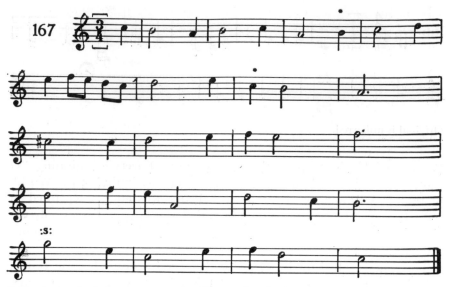

* Conjectural pitches; stems are headless on broadside sheet.

his broadside. Three of the four name an appropriate tune for singing the respective verses (but it is not, of course, related to "Great York"): "Loves tyrannick conquest," to the tune "Blush no redder than the morning" (Pepys V, 233, Roxburghe II, 280); "The Statesmans Downfal," to the tune "Hold fast thy Sword and Scepter Charles, or, Russels farewel" (Harvard); "England's Joy in the merry month of May," to the tune "Ah! how pleasant 'tis to Love" (Pepys V, 37); "The Whiggs Lamentation, For the Tap of Sedition," dated 1683, without tune direction (Wood 417 [118], Harvard).

Greensleeves

One of the most popular of broadside tunes, "Greensleeves" is also one of the few still current in the twentieth century. Ralph Vaughan Williams's orchestral "Fantasie" on this air, drawn from his opera *Sir John in Love,* 1929, has reached a large public. Several American hymnals couple the tune with a nineteenth-century carol text beginning "What Child is this." Richard Dyer-Bennet and others have recorded shortened forms of the original "Greensleeves" ballad. And, most interesting of all, modal sets of the tune have been preserved traditionally in association with the morris dance. Cecil J. Sharp and H. C. MacIlwaine noted three local variants of the tune used with "Bacca Pipes Jig," in which the dance centers around crossed churchwarden pipes, and they recorded also a "Wyresdale Greensleeves Dance" (*Morris Dance Tunes,* 1907–1913, Sets IV and X; rev. ed., Sets IV, V, VI and X; instructions for dancing are found in the same authors' *The Morris Book,* 1907–1913). Through the centuries the tune has persisted in several forms under a variety of names, but its distinctive harmonic pattern may help to explain why its identity has been so well preserved.

The earliest reference to "Greensleeves" in the Stationers' Register is dated September 3, 1580, when Richard Jones was licensed to print "A newe northen Dittye of ye Ladye Greene Sleves." No broadside print of this ballad exists, but it was included in *A Handefull of Pleasant Delites,* which Jones issued in 1584 (ed. Rollins, p. 19). It begins "Alas my loue, ye do me wrong,/to cast me off discurteously," and the refrain is:

> Greensleeues was all my ioy,
> Greensleeues was my delight:
> Greensleeues was my heart of gold,
> And who but Ladie Greensleeues.

On September 3, 1580, a license was also issued to Edward White to print "ye Ladie Greene Sleves answere to Donkyn hir frende," a rather puzzling suddenness unless we assume that a forehanded ballad maker had anticipated public demand by writing both pieces before either was published. The original ballad must have immediately caught the public fancy, for on September 15 Henry Carr was licensed to print a "Greene Sleves moralised," and three days later White registered "Greene Sleves and Countenaunce in Countenaunce is Greene Sleves." In December Jones entered another, "A merry newe Northen songe of Greenesleves begynninge the boniest lasse in all the land," and the next February still another, "A Reprehension againste Greene Sleves by William Elderton." Before a twelvemonth had passed, White swelled the number with "Greene Sleves is worne awaie, Yellowe Sleves Comme to decaie, Blacke Sleves I holde in despite, But White Sleves is my delighte," registered in August, 1581. Unhappily all these have vanished, but another by Elderton, licensed May 30, 1581, has survived in a contemporary issue. It is "A new Ballad . . . Treason . . . against the young King of Scots [prevented by] one Andrewe Browne . . . the Kings Chamberlaine," beginning "Jesus God what a griefe is this," to the tune of "Milfield, or els . . . Greensleeues" (London Society of Antiquaries [Lemon, *Catalogue,* No. 71]; reprinted in Percy's *Reliques;* an imperfect version is in Percy Folio MS, ed. Hales and Furnivall, II, 266; cf. Child No. 180). And "The Lord of Lorne and the false Steward," licensed on October 6, 1580, is to be sung to "Greensleeves" or "Greensleeves and Pudding-pies" in seventeenth-century issues, the earliest that have survived (Wood 401, Euing, Pepys, Harvard, Morgan, Douce, Chetham, Madden, Lord Crawford, Roxburghe; reprinted in *RB* II, 56, and as Child No. 271).[1]

At least one other sixteenth-century ballad was sung to the tune: "A warning to all false Traitors by example of 14 . . . executed . . . August, 1588," beginning "You Traitors all that doo deuise" (Lord Crawford; reprinted in *Broadside Black-Letter Ballads,* ed. J. P. Collier, 1868). Another to the tune, "A most excellent Godly new Ballad . . . abuses of this wicked world" (Manchester; reprinted in *PA,* p. 3), has survived only in an early seventeenth-century edition, but it was originally licensed in 1586 (Rollins, *Anal. Index,* Nos. 7, 1021) and may have been sung to the tune then.

Since many ballads in this period are without tune designation, it is tempting to assign tunes wherever possible; thus Chappell noted that Elderton's "A new Yorkshyre Song, Intituled: Yorke, Yorke, for my monie," beginning "As I came thorow the North Countrey" (Roxburghe; reprinted in *RB* I, 4), might, because of its twelve-line stanza, be intended for singing to "Triumph and Joy." Chappell suggested further that the lost "Triumph and Joy" might prove to be identical with "Greensleeves." [2]

Shakespeare alludes twice to the tune in *The Merry Wives of Windsor.* Mrs. Ford, contrasting Falstaff's disposition and his words, says that

[1] Chappell (*PMOT* I, 228) suggests that the ballad and hence the tune may be older, quoting the Satyra Prima of Edward Guilpin's *Skialetheia, or a Shadowe of Truth,* 1598:

> Yet, like th'olde Ballad of the Lord of Lorne,
> Whose last line in King Harries dayes was born . . .

But though the ballad were familiar in the time of Henry VIII, we may not conclude that the tune "Greensleeves" is of equal antiquity, for we cannot be sure that "The Lord of Lorn" was originally sung to the tune. What we do know is that editions of the second half of the seventeenth century call for the tune. An earlier version in the Percy Folio MS is without tune direction.

[2] He conjectured that "Triumph and Joy" originated in "The Tryvmphe Shewed before the Queene and the Ffrenche Embassadors," entered in the Stationers' Register July 1, 1581. But this lost work seems, from the fee paid, to have been a book rather than a ballad. At least seven ballads to the tune of "Triumph and Joy" are extant, in stanzas of four, eight, or twelve tetrameter lines. They could be sung to "Greensleeves," with the necessary contraction or expansion of the tune, but the twelve-line stanza would require a most monotonous repetition of the second strain, itself containing a conspicuous repetition. Moreover, the oldest of these, "A new Ditty, shewing the Wonderful Miracles of our Lord," beginning "When Jesus Christ was 12 years Old," was licensed in 1578, two years before the first "Greensleeves" ballad. "Triumph and Joy" would appear, therefore, to be an independent tune. For texts, see *CP,* p. 78; *PG,* p. 185; *RB* II, 379, VI, 393, VII, 791, VIII, xv***; *SB,* pp. 103, 322.

168

Original is a fifth lower.

"they do no more adhere and keep place together than the Hundredth Psalm to the tune of 'Green Sleeves'" (II, i); and later Falstaff, embracing Mrs. Ford, says, "Let the sky rain potatoes; let it thunder to the tune of Green Sleeves, hail kissing-comfits and snow eringoes; let there come a tempest of provocation, I will shelter me here" (V, v). There are further references to the tune in Fletcher's *The Loyal Subject,* III, ii, and Shirley's *The Imposture,* V, i. Dr. John Rainoldes's *Overthrow of Stage Plays,* 1599, p. 90, describes the Bishop of Ely, "who, to saue his honour and wealth, became a greene-sleeues, going in womans raiment lesse way then twenty miles, from *Douer* castle to the Sea side." *Green-sleeves* was by now a metaphor for a handsomely dressed woman, or more usually a courtesan; Barnabe Rich, *Roome for a Gentleman,* 1609, sig. C1, speaks of women whose "impudent boldnes of behauiour . . . were more fitting for my Lady Greene-sleeues, then decent for those women, that are of any good sort or reputation."

During the late sixteenth-century period of popularity, the tune was recorded in William Ballet's MS Lute Book, p. 104 (Fig. 168); in Folger MS 1610.1, fol. 5, treble and ground in tablature for two lutes; in BM MS Add. 31392, fol. 29, a lute arrangement by "maister Cuttinge"; and in the Cambridge University Library MSS Dd.3.18, fol. 8ᵛ (lute) and Dd.4.23, fol. 25 (cittern).[3] The tune is preserved in a Continental manuscript of c. 1600, *Het Luitboek van Thysius,* No. 70. An early seventeenth-

[3] The first and last of these settings are transcribed in Germaine Bontoux, *La Chanson en Angleterre au temps d'Élizabeth,* 1936, pp. 101–102 (facsimile of the Ballet tablature, Plate IV). The Folger version is transcribed by John Ward, "Music for *A Handefull of Pleasant Delites," JAMS,* X (1957), 157. Ward properly notes that the

169

Original is unbarred and a fourth lower.

170

century medley for four voices by William Cobbold includes the tune of "Greensleeves" (Fig. 169) and some lines from the original ballad (BM MS Add. 18936, fol. 58). Other contemporary arrangements include the virginal set in Paris Conservatoire MS Rés. 1186, fol. 101, and one for cittern in *A Booke of New Lessons for the Cithern & Gittern*, 1652.

Folger ground is the well-known ostinato pattern, the *romanesca*, which underlies most of the Renaissance settings of "Greensleeves," requiring one statement for the stanza and a second for the refrain. Where the *romanesca* begins on the tonic, the closely related *passamezzo antico* begins a third below; otherwise they are alike. Several arrangements, including Ballet's and the Cambridge cittern setting, follow the *passamezzo antico* in the first strain and are slightly at variance from both formulas in the second. For the notation of these ground basses, see Gustave Reese, *Music in the Renaissance*, 1954, p. 524, Ex. 121.

The tune does not appear in *The Dancing Master* until the seventh edition, 1686, p. 186 (Fig. 170), where it is called "Green-Sleeves and Pudding-Pies"; in the seventeenth edition, 1721, it is called "Green Sleeves and Yellow Lace." [4] Under the former title it is found in Walsh's *Compleat Country Dancing-Master,* 1718. In volume two of *The Dancing Master,* 3d ed., 1718, and of Walsh's *Compleat Country Dancing-Master,* 1719, it appears, considerably altered, as "Buckingham House." The earlier form of the *Dancing Master* tune is used in *Pills,* 1719–1720, I, 257, II, 164, and (with slight modification) IV, 259.

In *Good and True, Fresh and New, Christmas Carols,* 1642, the tune was named for singing "A Caroll for New-yeares day" (partially reprinted in *The Oxford Book of Carols,* 1928, No. 28). "Another for Christmas-day at Night" was set to "Greensleeves" in *New Christmas Carrols,* c. 1686.

Allan Ramsay's "Ye watchful Guardians of the Fair," written to the tune, appears in his *Tea-Table Miscellany,* 1723, p. 77 (reprinted in David Herd's *Ancient and Modern Scots Songs,* 1769, and in his collections of 1776 and 1791). A keyboard arrangement of the air is in Alexander Stuart's *Musick for Allan Ramsay's Collection of Scots Songs,* c. 1725, p. 82. Ramsay's verses, with music, found a place in James Johnson's *Scots Musical Museum,* 1787–1803, IV, 402.

"Greensleeves" was one of the tunes used in Gay's *The Beggar's Opera,* 1728, Act III, Air 26, and it was named in three ballad operas printed without music: Thomson's *The Disappointed Gallant,* 1738, *Court and Country,* 1743, and Brooke's *Jack the Gyant Queller,* 1749. The short form of the tune was much more popular with ballad-opera authors, as we shall see.

In more recent times, to cite but two examples, "Greensleeves" appeared in very rudimentary form as a fiddle tune in a manuscript book of 1838 (reprinted in Frank Kidson and Mary Neal, *English Folk-Song and Dance,* 1915, p. 28); about 1852 a Limerick piper played a florid major-mode variant of the air which P. W. Joyce transcribed and included in his *Old Irish Folk Music and Songs,* 1909, No. 142. These, coupled with the morris-dance survivals already noted, suggest that "Greensleeves" has been dependent on both oral and written avenues of transmission, that it has appealed to a wide variety of publics, and that it has kept its identity despite the disfigurements of decay and embellishment.

In 1656 James Smith's poem "The Blacksmith" was published in *Wit and Drollery.* [5] It begins "Of all the Trades that ever I see,/There's none

[4] For a possible source of both tune titles see *Songs from David Herd's Manuscripts,* ed. Hans Hecht, 1904, p. 177.

[5] Often reprinted, e.g., in *Wit Restor'd,* 1658, *An Antidote against Melancholy,* 1661, *Merry Drollery,* 1661, *Merry Drollery Complete,* 1670, and *Pills,* all editions.

to the Black-smith compared may be," and its three-line stanza is capped with the catchy refrain "Which no body can deny." [6] Although the song is here without tune direction, "Greensleeves" was named on a broadside version almost immediately issued under the verse title, "A merry new Ballad, both pleasant and sweete, In praise of the Black-smith, which is very meete" (Roxburghe; reprinted along with the version from *Antidote against Melancholy*, 1661, in *RB* II, 127).[7] A somewhat later broadside version, called "The bonny Black-smiths delight," bears the tune direction "Nobody can deny" (Pepys IV, 264, Rawlinson 191).[8]

The tune, which was vastly popular for a century or more, consists of the first strain of "Greensleeves," sometimes lengthened from eight to ten measures to accommodate a repetition of the refrain line.[9] Its most popular name was "Which nobody can deny," but several other tune titles were generated by ballads set to the air. Moreover, a large number of songs and ballads without tune direction are cast in the "Blacksmith" mold, some with the "Which nobody" refrain, others with an internally inspired stanza tag of the same metrical pattern. Some of these poems may not be intended for singing, but it is inevitable that most of them should suggest the tune to any reader familiar with its vogue. Only a small fraction of these can be noticed here.

[6] Two other miscellanies of 1656 contain poems with the "Which no body can deny" refrain, and priority among the three volumes is uncertain (see *Choyce Drollery*, ed. J. W. Ebsworth, 1876, p. 33; and *Parnassus Biceps*, ed. G. Thorn-Drury, 1927, p. 159). The refrain is also in a poem on "Admiral Dean's Funeral," describing an event of June 24, 1653. Although the earliest known text is in *Merry Drollery*, 1661, it is possible that a broadside print was circulated immediately after the event. Whichever of these pieces may have first introduced the refrain, it is clear that "The Blacksmith" was the most influential, generating parodies and imitations; during the rest of the century "Which nobody can deny" and "The Blacksmith" displaced "Greensleeves" as names by which the tune was known.

[7] "Greensleeves" is also named as the tune in a version of the ballad preserved in Bodleian MS Ashmole 36–37, fol. 195. The text in "The Innovation of Penelope and Ulysses," a mock-poem by J. S. in *Wit Restor'd*, 1658, is fuller than those in broadsides and miscellanies, and Anthony Wood's statement that Smith was probably the author of the ballad (*Athenae Oxoniensis*) cannot be lightly dismissed. A ballad entry in the Stationers' Register, March 21, 1635 (Rollins, *Anal. Index*, No. 204) cannot be confirmed as relating to the broadside under discussion.

[8] The title of this ballad is probably the source of the tune name "The bonny Blacksmith" cited in "A View of the Popish-Plot," beginning "Come listen a while both Young and Old" (Pepys; reprinted in *PB* IV, 194).

[9] In "Oates Well Thresh't," beginning "Our Oates, last Week not worth a Groat," the tune direction is explicit: "Which no Body can deny. The Burden must be Twice Repeated" (BM Luttrell III, 125, Wood 417 [184], Harvard, Yale, Huntington, Union Theol. Sem.). "The Jesuits Character," beginning "The Jesuits they are a sort of Men," has a comprehensive tune title: "To the Black-Smiths Tune, Which no body can deny" (Bodleian Ashmole G.16, Harvard, Yale, BM Luttrell; reprinted in *RB* IV, 140).

Another song on the blacksmith, beginning "Of all the Sciences under [or beneath] the sunne," was apparently inspired by Smith's verses; it is found, with music, in John Gamble's MS Commonplace Book, 1659, No. 121 (printed, without music or tune direction, in *Merry Drollery*, 1661, *Merry Drollery Complete*, 1670). In part a parody, in part a political squib on Cromwell, is "The Brewer. A Ballad made in the year 1657" (actually 1658 or 1659) to the tune of "The Blacksmith," beginning "There's many a Clinching verse is made/In honor of the Blacksmiths trade,/But more of the Brewer may be said" (*Antidote against Melancholy*, 1661, *Merry Drollery*, 1661, *Rump*, 1662, *Pills*, all editions; a broadside version of c. 1670, "The Praise of Brewers," is in Rawlinson 187, Wood E.25 [63]). Another Cromwellian parody, "The Brewer," begins "Of all the trades that ever I see/There's none to the Brewer compared may be" (*Wit and Drollery*, 1661; reprinted in *RB* VIII, c*); an expanded text, entitled "The Protecting Brewer," c. 1657, begins "A Brewer may be a Burgess grave" (*Merry Drollery*, 1661, *Rump*, 1662, *Loyal Songs*, 1731, Wilkins, *Political Ballads*, 1860).

Ratts Rhimed to Death and *The Rump*, published in 1660 almost entirely from broadside sources, are filled with crude Royalist attacks on the Rump Parliament; many of them were directed to be sung to "Which nobody can deny" or "The Blacksmith." [10] Another class of ballads for which the tune might be used is represented by "The City of Londons New Letany," beginning "From Rumps that do Rule against Custom and Lawes," to the tune of "The Black-Smith" (BM C.20.f.2 [24], BM 82.l.8 [3]; reprinted in *The Rump*, 1660). Its refrain is "Good Jove deliver us all"; a great many other mock litanies with the burden "Libera nos Domine" are in the same stanza pattern but lack tune directions. Tune names when found include also "Cavalilly Man," "When Jockey First the Wars Began," and "An Old Soldier [or Courtier] of the Queen's." The second of these tunes is not known; the others, qq.v., are musically interchangeable with "The Blacksmith." [11]

"Old England turn'd New," beginning "You talk of New England, I truly believe," sung to the tune of "The Blacksmith," appears in *Pills*, 1719–1720, III, 120 (music at III, 20). When it had begun to appear in miscellanies (*Merry Drollery* and *Wit and Drollery*, 1661, *Wit and*

---

[10] *Rump*, an enlarged edition of *The Rump* issued in 1662 and reprinted 1874, contains twenty-one pieces in the "Blacksmith" stanza. Many of these are to be found also in *A Collection of Loyal Songs Written against the Rump Parliament*, 2 vols., 1731. For a detailed listing of broadside copies and reprints, see H. F. Brooks, "Rump Songs: An Index with Notes," *Oxford Bibliographical Society Proceedings & Papers*, V (1936–1939), 283–304.

[11] The general absence of tune directions suggests that many litanies were conceived as verse satires, not as poems for singing.

Mirth, 1682; also in Bodleian MS Ashmole 36–37, fol. 114), no tune was named; but this was the usual practice. The *Pills* reprint with its identi-fied air leads us, through the refrain "And is not Old England grown New," to another name for the tune. A related broadside, with the same refrain and some stanzas in common, is "A Description of Old England," beginning "Was ever the like in any age known," sung "To a pleasant new tune, Or, is not old England grown new" (copies of c. 1675 in Rawlinson 103, Wood E.25 [72], Lord Crawford 1244, Harvard). Thomas Lanfiere's "The Citty Prophisier," beginning "All you Honest Men in Country and town," is sung to "Oh is not Old England grown New" (Rawlinson 101); and "Englands Present State," beginning "Poor Eng-land the world at thee doth admire," is sung to "Old England's now grown New" (Pepys; reprinted in *PB* III, 162).

Another subsidiary tune name is "Lulla by baby," which takes its origin from the refrain of a ballad of 1688, "A New Song of Lulla By, or Father Peter's Policy Discovered," beginning "In Rome there is a most fearful rout," to the tune of "Green Sleeves, or, my Mistriss is to Bulling Gone" (Wood E.25 [110], Harvard).[12] "Lulla by baby" is the tune named for "Epithalamium . . . 1689," beginning "Pray rub up your ears, and I'll tell you a thing" (Lord Crawford, Pepys; reprinted in *PB* IV, 206), and for "The French Cryer Newly arriv'd in England," be-ginning "If any in Town or Country can" (Pepys IV, 321). "In Rome there is a most fearful rout," from the first line of the "Father Peter" ballad, is the name given to the tune of "The Frightened People of Clarkenwel . . . 1689," beginning "In Clerkenwell-Church there was a Rout" (Pepys IV, 343).[13]

Other tune names are more difficult to associate positively with the short form of the "Greensleeves" air. "Vanity of Vanities," a popular broadside of 1660 (BM Thomason, BM Luttrell, Wood 416; reprinted in *Ratts, Rump,* &c.), is "To the Tune of Jews Corant" but has the "Which nobody" stanza form and refrain. If "Jews Corant" is an inde-pendent tune, it does not seem to have survived.[14] The case is similar with "Tumble down Dick," named as the tune of "A Whigg Ballad, or, a Summons To a fresh Association," c. 1682 (BM 1871.f.3 [6], Bodleian Ashmole G.16 [198], Huntington, Harvard, Yale). But "A Display Of

[12] A briefer edition, entitled "Father Peter's Policy Discovered" and without tune direction, is Lord Crawford 674, BM C.20.f.2 (320), Harvard; see *PB* IV, 205, for a note on other broadside copies and contemporary reprints. The tune of "my Mistriss is to Bulling [i.e., Boulogne] Gone" is not known.

[13] In Lillo's ballad opera *Silvia,* 1731, Air 28, the music of "Which nobody" is called "At Rome there is a terrible Rout."

[14] "The Jews Corant" in *Apollo's Banquet,* 1670, No. 175, is much too long and elaborate to be used for singing the broadside.

the Headpiece and Codpiece Valour of . . . Colonel Robert Jermy," whose tune is "A Turd, or the Black-Smith" (Bagford I, 73, Harvard; reprinted in *Ratts* and *Rump*), contains a number of lines which suggest that the first tune title is not the name of an independent ballad or melody, but an integral part of the vilification directed against Jermy. "The Lancashire Sham-Plot," beginning "Projecting and Plotting for the Publick Good," has the "Which nobody" refrain and the tune name "A. Smith" (Harvard); the reference is to Aaron Smith, an unsavory anti-Jacobite whose "sham-plot" was exposed in 1694.

In the 1680s at least two broadsides in short stanza form reverted to "Greensleeves and Pudding Pies" for their tune title (in 1686 this title had been used for the full form of the tune in *The Dancing Master*). "The 2d Part of Perkin's Sucking bottle," beginning "The Ladies, I hear take it in great Scorn," is clearly a sequel to the "Father Peter" ballad cited above, for its refrain is "In my Lulla by Baby by by" (BM MS Harl. 7319, p. 605). Another with the same tune title is "Will ye buy any Woylfleet Oisters," beginning "All you that will any Oysters buy" (BM 1871.f.3 [4]).

Broadsides of the eighteenth century reveal the continued popularity of the tune through the frequent appearance of the "Which nobody" refrain. In about half the specimens I have collected from broadsides and miscellanies, the tune is named, usually "Which nobody can deny" and only occasionally "The Blacksmith" or "Greensleeves." [15] Examples abound in such collections of political satire as the following: *Poems on Affairs of State*, eds. 1697–1716; *A Collection of Poems for and against Dr. Sacheverell*, 1710–1711; *Political Merriment*, 1714–1715; *Tory Pills to Purge Whig Melancholy*, 1715; *A Pill to Purge State Melancholy*, eds. 1715–1718; *A Collection of State Songs*, 1716; and *Mughouse Diversion*, eds. 1717–1719. Broadside versions of many miscellany pieces are extant, chiefly in the British Museum.

The earliest musical example I have encountered of the short tune is an eight-bar version in the Gamble MS, 1659, No. 121 (Fig. 171). Of about the same date is the "Blacksmith" in the Bedford Cittern MS, fol. 43A. In *The Second Book of the Pleasant Musical Companion*, 1686, Part II, No. 23, "The Blacksmith" set to "A Song made on the Power of Women" is in ten bars to accommodate a repetition of the refrain line (Fig. 172). The same music is also printed in *Pills*, 1719–1720, III, 20; IV, 15; V, 5, 92, 270; VI, 223; in this collection some sixteen songs are set to

---

[15] When "Greensleeves" is named, the full tune is usually intended. A peculiar hybrid is "An Excellent New Song, call'd Mat's Peace," 1711 (BM 1876.f.1 [59]; reprinted in *Political Merriment*, 1714, Part 2, p. 61), in which the nine-line stanza requires not only the full form of the tune, but also the repetition of the two final bars, as is often found with the short "Which nobody" music.

it. "Which nobody can deny" is called for in at least eleven ballad operas (as compared with four for "Greensleeves"), and the music, somewhat altered melodically but in the common ten-bar form, is printed in Mottley and Cooke's *Penelope,* 1728, *The Jovial Crew,* 1731, Air 42 (Fig. 173), Lillo's *Sylvia,* 1731 (called "At Rome there is a terrible Rout"), and Coffey's *The Merry Cobler,* 1735.

Grenadiers' March

The earliest appearance of this tune I have found is in *A Collection of the Newest and Choicest Songs*, 1683, p. 4, where it is set to a single-stanza, 19-line song, beginning "Hail the Mighty Monarch, Valiant Pole," which requires a repetition of each strain in turn (Fig. 174). Words

174

and music were reprinted in *A Collection of Twenty Four Songs* and *180 Loyal Songs*, both of 1685; the latter volume contains another song in the same complex stanza, beginning "Hail! thou Mighty Monarch Valiant James," and the tune is named from the first line of the original song (the two reprinted in *RB* V, 384, 545).

The tune of "Grenadiers March" is also found in Humphry Salter's *Genteel Companion . . . for the Recorder*, 1683, among the unnumbered pages added probably in 1684; in *The Dancing Master*, 1686 and later eds.; and in Walsh's *Compleat Country Dancing-Master*, 1718.

"The Granadees March" in *Musicks Recreation on the Viol, Lyra-Way*, 1682, is perhaps a descant version, which in a few spots is harmonically incompatible with the air under discussion. The 1682 tune does, how-ever, make the better fit with "A New Song," c. 1685, in eight-line stanzas beginning "Come my Lads let's March away" (BM 807.g.5 [47]).

The tune is not to be confused with the popular march "British Grenadiers." Nor is it related to "The Granadeers new March," a tune named along with "Hark the thundring Cannons roar" for singing a ballad of 1685: "The Granadiers Loyal Health To the King and Royal Family," beginning "Dub a dub, a dub, stand your ground" (Morgan 15).

Music on the broadside is corrupt; the complex 16-line stanza pattern will not permit the ballad to be sung to "Grenadiers' March" or to "Hark the thundering cannons." A sequel, to the tune of "The Granadeers Loyal Health," is "The Couragious Seamens Loyal Health. Or, an Answer to Dub, a dub, a dub, &c.," beginning "Shall the Granadeer-Boys Proclaim/Their Loyalty to the Royal Train" (BM C.22.f.6, Lord Crawford; reprinted in *RB* VII, 528, 822). Still another "Granadiers Loyal Health" is in six-line octosyllabics and names the tune "Joy to the Bridegroom," q.v.

Grim King of the Ghosts

An anonymous two-stanza song "The Frantick Lover," beginning "Grim King of the Ghosts make hast," appeared without music or tune direction in *A New Collection of the Choicest Songs*, 1682, sig. B4ᵛ. A broadside expansion of the song, licensed by Richard Pocock (1685–1688), has the title "The Lunatick Lover: Or, The Young Man's Call to Grim King of the Ghosts for Cure. To an Excellent New Tune" (Pepys, Bagford, Lord Crawford, Douce, Roxburghe; reprinted in Percy's *Reliques*, Ritson's *English Songs*, and *RB* VI, 222). The Bagford copy names "Hail to the Myrtle Shades" as the tune, and that Purcell air of 1680 must have vied with the new "proper" tune for popularity, inasmuch as it is several times named as an alternate on "Grim King" broadsides.

The initial popularity of the tune was intense but brief, most of the broadsides sung to "Grim King of the Ghosts" having been issued by 1691. Among these are "A New Mournful Ballad, Called The Duke of Allbemarle's Farewell" (Pepys; reprinted in *PB* III, 308), "The Whipster of Woodstreet" (Pepys; reprinted in *PB* VI, 31), and two of less doleful content: "The Pensive Lover, or, The Damosels Crosses Crown'd with Comfort," beginning "O pitty a harmless Maid" (BM C.22.f.6 [160], Lord Crawford 923, Douce II, 176ᵛ, Harvard), and "The Father's wholsome Admonition," beginning "My Son if you reckon to Wed" (Lord Crawford, Pepys, Harvard, Roxburghe; reprinted in *RB* VI, 216).

That the musical charm of "Grim King of the Ghosts" outweighed the mournfulness of its name is evident from its use in a spate of broadsides welcoming the successors of James II. These pieces include: "Great Britains Earnest Desires For The Princess Marys Happy Arrival," beginning "Sweet Princess the Nations delight" (Pepys; reprinted in *PB* IV, 135); "The Subjects Satisfaction . . . Proclaiming of King William and Queen Mary," beginning "King William is come to the Throne" (Lord Crawford, Wood E.25, Pepys, Roxburghe; reprinted in *RB* VII, 720);[1] "The Protestants Joy; or An Excellent New Song on the Glorious Coronation . . . ," beginning "Let Protestants freely allow" (Bagford; reprinted in *BB* II, 612); "Englands Extasie . . . for the Happy Coronation . . . ," beginning "Hark how the Huzza's go round" (Pepys; reprinted in *PB* IV, 231); "An Excellent New Song on the Happy Coronation . . . ," beginning "King William and Mary is crown'd" (reprinted in *RB* VII, 719, source not identified); "The Loyal Subjects Free Choice . . . in the Calling of a New Parliament," beginning "Let all Royal Glory and State" (Pepys; reprinted in *PB* V, 81).

Despite the obvious popularity of the tune, or perhaps because of it, no immediately contemporary music seems to have survived. The earliest version I have found is on a single-sheet song of about 1710 (Fig. 175),

set to Nicholas Rowe's poem "Collin's Complaint," which begins "Despairing beside a clear stream" (BM H.1601 [135], Huntington, Harvard, several eds.). Words and music were reprinted in *Pills*, 1714 and 1719–1720, in *The Merry Musician*, 1716, and in Ritson's *English Songs*, 1783. The tune was used in at least ten ballad operas, and the music is found

[1] Both "Grim King" and "Hail to the Myrtle Shades" are cited as tunes to which this and the following ballad may be sung.

in editions of Gay's *The Beggar's Opera*, 1728, and Coffey's *The Devil to Pay*, 1731. Besides "Grim King of the Ghosts," other tune names derive from the title or first line of Rowe's poem, or from Gay's words, "Can Love be controlled." "Colin's Complaint" inspired parodies and imitations, most of them to the original tune.[2] These include: "Rosalind's Complaint. By Mr. Baker," beginning "On the Bank of a River so deep" (*Merry Musician*, c. 1729, II, 65; Watts's *Musical Miscellany*, 1729–1731, I, 126; without the music, in *A Complete Collection of . . . English and Scotch Songs*, 1735–1736, IV, 117); "Melinda's Complaint," beginning "By the side of a glimmering Fire" (single-sheet song, c. 1730, BM G.316.d [53], Harvard; reprinted in Walsh's *British Musical Miscellany*, 1734–1736, I, 62–63, and, without the music, in *Complete Collection*, III, 68); "The Scullion's Complaint," beginning "By the side of a great kitchen fire" (words only in *Complete Collection*, I, 82, Ramsay's *Tea-Table Miscellany*, 1740, IV, 329, *The Merry Companion*, 2d ed., 1742, p. 331). This last song replaces the elegant pathos of Rowe with a calculatedly inverted formula which develops its emotion around a youth's longing for a pudding. A generation later G. A. Stevens, in his *Songs, Comic and Satyrical*, 1772, p. 46, renewed this attack on the sentimental with his equally contrived parody, beginning "By the side of a green stagnate pool,/Brick-dust Nan she sat scratching her head."

"The Modest Question," by one Mr. Berkeley, beginning "Can love be controul'd by advice," is indebted to Gay for its first line but is thereafter independent; the music by D. Russell bears no relation to "Grim King of the Ghosts" (*Gentleman's Magazine*, XII [1742], 599; single-sheet editions, BM G.316.d [66], G.307 [32], G.305 [252]).

The Gunfleet

Common-time versions of this tune are found in *Apollo's Banquet*, 5th ed., 1687, and *The Dancing Master*, 17th ed., 1721. Exemplars in 6/4 time, more nearly suitable for singing, are in the sixth edition of *Apollo's Banquet*, 1690, No. 23 (Fig. 176), and in BM MS Add. 29371, fol. 57ᵛ, mid-eighteenth century. All four are violin sets.

---

2 Two that were not are "A short reply to Collins Complaint," beginning "Ah Collin! why shou'd'st thou despair" (BM H.1601 [40], Harvard, Huntington) and "The Answer to Collins Complaint. The Tune by Mr. Hendell," beginning "Ye Winds to whom Collin complains" (Harvard, BM G.314 [2], Huntington). Both are engraved single sheets; the Handel air is from the second version of his *Rinaldo*.

176

The name, referring to Gunfleet Sands off the Essex coast, may have come from a lost ballad on naval action against the Dutch in 1666. It is, in any event, older than the musical examples suggest, for William Hicks's *Oxford Drollery*, 1671, 1679, p. 25, names "The Gun-fleet" for singing "The Scornful Lass," beginning "A Gallant once did wooe a Lass." This was shortly followed by a song to the tune in *Westminster Drollery*, 1672, II, 110: "The two vertuous Sisters," beginning "My Cozen Moll's an arrant Whore/And so is her sister Kate." Another drollery piece to the tune is "The Suddain Wedding," beginning "I'me in Love says Noll./Indeed says Doll," in *Mock Songs*, 1675, p. 86, reprinted as "The Hasty Wedding" in Hicks's *Grammatical Drollery*, 1682, p. 39; a broadside edition of 1685–1688 entitled "Short and Sweet, or . . . Wooing of Oliver and Dorothy" (Pepys III, 65) adds a stanza not in the original song.

Guy of Warwick

"A pleasante songe of the valiant actes of Guy of War wicke. to the tune of, Was ever man soe tost in love" was entered in the Stationers' Register, Jan. 5, 1592, and re-entered in 1624 and 1675. No contemporary copy seems to have survived. Seventeenth-century editions, entitled "A Pleasant Song of the Valiant Deeds of Chivalry . . . Sir Guy of Warwick, Who for the Love of Fair Phillis became a Hermet . . . ," begin "Was ever Knight for Lady's sake/so tost in love, as I Sir Guy?" and the tune is "Was ever Man" (Lord Crawford, Wood 401, 402, Douce, Chetham, Morgan, Pepys, Harvard, Bagford, Roxburghe; reprinted in *RB* VI, 734; Percy's *Reliques* reprints the broadside, not the fragment found in the Folio MS). No tune of "Was ever Man" is extant; the tune title seems to derive from the first line of a lost ballad, and perhaps its opening furnished the model for the beginning of "Guy of Warwick." An air called "Sir Guy" appearing in the ballad opera *Robin Hood*, 1730, fits the stanza of eight octosyllabics, but we know nothing of its history (Fig. 177).

177

* Broadside does not require this repetition.

References to the legendary exploits of Sir Guy abound in Renaissance literature, doubtless recalling as often the figure of metrical romance as the ballad hero. Thus, the author of *The Arte of English Poesie,* 1589 (ed. Willcock and Walker, 1936, pp. 83–84), appears to have the former in mind when he speaks of "blind harpers or such like tauerne minstrels . . . their matters . . . for the most part stories of old time, as . . . Sir Topas, . . . Beuis of Southampton, Guy of Warwicke, Adam Bell, and Clymme of the Clough & such . . . made purposely for recreation of the co[m]mon people at Christmasse dinners & brideales, and in tauernes & alehouses and such other places of base resort." The references in Udall's *Ralph Roister Doister,* I, ii, and *Henry VIII,* V, iv, are general, but in *The London Chanticleers,* Scene III, the "Guy of Warwick" ballad is offered for sale by Ditty, and in Fletcher's *Little French Lawyer,* II, iii, and Beaumont's *The Knight of the Burning Pestle,* II, viii, the first line of the ballad is paraphrased.

One other broadside is sung to the tune, but since it is in a stanza of decasyllabic lines it does not correspond with the metrical pattern of the "Guy of Warwick" ballad, nor does it fit the tune we possess: "The Worldings Farewell," beginning "O Wretched man that lovest earthly things," to the tune of "Guy of Warwick: Or Troy Town" (Pepys II,

15).[1] This ballad has the solemn march of "Fortune my foe"; if that tune were not in fact intended, we probably have here a reference to a "Guy of Warwick" melody which has not survived, one which could not have been related to our ballad of that name.

Hail to the Myrtle Shades

Henry Purcell composed the music for "Hail to the Myrtle shade," sung after the third act in Nathaniel Lee's *Theodosius,* 1680 (Fig. 178). The tune is also found in *Choice Ayres and Songs,* Third Book, 1681,

Musicks Recreation on the Viol, Lyra-Way, 1682, Humphry Salter's *Genteel Companion . . . for the Recorder,* 1683, *180 Loyal Songs,* 1685, *Pills,* 1719–1720, III, 184, and on at least three broadsides.

"Loves Boundless Power" is the playhouse song expanded to fill a

[1] The tune of "Troy Town" is likewise unsuited to this ballad, being designed for a stanza of six octosyllabic lines. See the discussion of "Queen Dido."

broadside and directed to be sung to an already familiar tune, "When Busy Fame" (Pepys III, 194, Douce I, 127, 132ᵛ, Lord Crawford 475, BM C.22.f.6 [58], Harvard). But Purcell's music soon made its own way, for both political and nonpolitical subjects. In 1681 the first of a series of broadsides on Titus Oates called for the tune and echoed the first line of the stage piece: "A Song upon Titus," beginning "All Hail to the Chief of the Post" (Harvard, Yale). In the next year appeared "Titus Tell-Troth: or, The Plot-Founder Confounded," beginning "Hail to the Knight of the Post" (with the music, BM C.38.i.25 [6], Wood 417 [85], Harvard, Yale, Huntington; reprinted in *180 Loyal Songs*), and "Thompson Tell-lyes, or An Answer to Titus Tell-troth," beginning "Hail to the Devil and Pope" (Harvard, Yale). "The Hue-and-Song after Patience [Ward]," beginning "All hail [*or* Hail] to London['s] fair Town," appeared in 1683 (Natl. Lib. of Scotland, Wood 276a, Harvard, Huntington, Clark; reprinted in *180 Loyal Songs* and *RB* V, 279). Two broadsides of 1684 also reprint the music: "Oates Thrash'd in the Compter, And Sack'd-up in Newgate," beginning "Hail to the Prince of the Plot" (Harvard; reprinted in *180 Loyal Songs*), and "Pluto, the Prince of Darkness, his Entertainment of Coll. Algernoon Sidney," beginning "Room for great Algernoon" (Harvard, Clark; reprinted in *180 Loyal Songs* and *RB* V, 432).

"The Lunatick Lover," a broadside of James II's reign, was sung to both "Grim King of the Ghosts" and "Hail to the Myrtle Shades," as were two ballads on the accession of William and Mary, noticed under the former tune title.

A handful of nonpolitical ballads used Purcell's popular tune. They include: "The Loves of Damon and Sappho," beginning "Come turn thy Rosie face" (Lord Crawford, Harvard, Roxburghe; reprinted in *RB* VI, 153); "The Despairing Shepherds Advice to Rash Lovers," beginning "In a Grove where fair Nymphs dwell" (Pepys III, 361); "The faithfull Shepherd," beginning "Come my dear hearts delight" (Pepys III, 224); "The Country Lovers . . . Roger and Margaret," beginning "Remember the standing Corn" (BM C.22.f.6 [99], Lord Crawford 1028, Yale, Harvard); "The Mariner's Delight, or, The Seaman's Seaven Wives," beginning "My Dearest I must to the Sea" (Lord Crawford, Harvard, Roxburghe; reprinted in *RB* VII, 490); "The School of Venus," beginning "How long shall I sigh and mourn" (BM C.22.f.6 [172], Lord Crawford 530, Douce II, 188, Pepys III, 221, Harvard). The tune is also called for in a song beginning "Colonus and Bacchus did meet" in George Meriton's *The Praise of Yorkshire Ale,* 1685.

An engraved song sheet of the 1740s, "Hail to the Myrtle Shade, Sung by Master Budd at the new Wells" (BM H.1994.b [29], *Thesaurus*

Musicus, 1743?, fol. 32ᵛ) replaces Purcell's music with a contemporary setting by an unknown composer.

Hark the Thundering Cannons Roar

The lifting of the siege of Vienna in September, 1683, by forces under the leadership of John Sobieski, King of Poland, was the occasion of a ballad written by Thomas D'Urfey, with music by Christopher Fishburn. It exists in two broadside forms: "An Excellent New Song on the late Victories over the Turks," beginning "Hark! the thundring Canons roar" (Bodleian Ashmole G.16 [135ᵛ], with music; reprinted in D'Urfey's *Several New Songs*, 1684, *180 Loyal Songs*, 1685, *Pills*, 1719–1720, I, 300); and "A Carrouse To The Emperour, the Royal Pole, And the . . . Duke of Lorrain," beginning "Hark I hear the Cannons roar" (BM C.22.f.6, Pepys, Lord Crawford, Harvard, Roxburghe; reprinted in *RB* V, 366). The music is also found in Humphry Salter's *The Genteel Companion . . . for the Recorder,* 1683. In the same year Fishburn's tune was printed on another broadside, "The Whigs Drown'd in an Honest Tory-Health," beginning "Wealth breeds Care, Love, Hope & Fear" (Bodleian Ashmole G.16 [136]). This political drinking piece, for which the tune may originally have been written, is in *A Collection of the Newest and Choicest Songs*, 1683, followed by "Hark the thundring canons," which is directed to be sung to the tune of "Wealth breeds Care"; Fishburn is not named. The music is, however, credited to him in the reprint of "Wealth breeds Care" in *Choice Ayres and Songs*, Fifth Book, 1684, and in *Pills* V, 184, though it is anonymous in *180 Loyal Songs*. The tune was printed on several other political broadsides of the next few years, as noted below. *The Dancing Master* introduced the air as "Vienna" in the seventh edition, 1686, but apparently no broadsides called for the tune under that name.

Since more than three dozen ballads were sung to the tune, only a fraction of them may be cited here. Those containing music are as follows: "The Whig-Intelligencer," 1684, beginning "Hark! the fatal day has come" (BM 1871.e.9, Bodleian Ashmole G.16, Harvard [Fig. 179], Yale; reprinted in *180 Loyal Songs* and *RB* V, 80); "A Dialogue between Bowman the Tory, and Prance the Runagado," 1684, beginning "Come murthering Miles, where's your Sedan" (Bodleian Ashmole G.16 [74], Harvard, Clark, Huntington, Yale; reprinted in *180 Loyal Songs*); and

179

* E♭ in original.

"On the Most High and Mighty Monarch King James the II. His Exaltation on the Throne of England," 1685, beginning "Hark! the Bells and Steeples Ring" (Harvard; reprinted in *180 Loyal Songs*, and *RB* V, 520).[1]

Where music is not found, the tune is known as "Hark (*or* Hark how) the thundering cannons roar," "Hark I hear the cannons roar," "The thundering cannons roar," or "The cannons roar." "The Reward of Loyalty," cited as an alternative tune to the original stage music[2] for "Beauties Triumph," beginning "A pox upon this needless Scorn" (Harvard, BM C.22.f.6 [33], Lord Crawford 1007) derives its name from the title of a 1685 ballad beginning "Loyalty's a Noble thing," to the tune of "Hark the Thundering Cannons Rore" (Lord Crawford 787, Bodleian Ashmole G.16 [167], Library of Congress, Huntington).

A dozen ballads, most of them concerning the accession of William and Mary or other events of 1689, are reprinted in *The Pepys Ballads;* a number of others are in *The Roxburghe Ballads*, especially among the historical pieces which Ebsworth gathered in volume five. The following seem not to have been reprinted: "The Kings-Bench Cabal," 1684, be-

[1] "Englands Royal Reno[wn] . . . Coronation of . . . James the Second," beginning "Noble hearted English boys," to the tune of "The Cannons rore," exists in a black-letter edition without music (Bagford; reprinted in *BB* II, 593) and a roman-letter version which, despite the tune title, contains the music of "King James's Jig" (Wood 417 [143]). The latter tune, though possible, is not nearly so satisfactory as "Hark" for the words of this ballad.

[2] Introduced into Aphra Behn's *The Second Part of The Rover*, 1681, IV, i; the original verses with music by Capt. Simon Pack are found in *Choice Ayres and Songs*, Fourth Book, 1683, p. 24.

ginning "Eternal Whigs that still depends" (BM C.20.f.2 [168]); "A Song upon the Randizvous on Hounsley-Heath," 1685, beginning "Our Comet or the Blazing-Star" (Bodleian Ashmole G.15 [187], Harvard, Lord Crawford 991); "A Trick for Tyburn . . . a Song of the Prisoners of Newgate, at the Gaol-Delivery," 1685, beginning "Trumpets sound and Steeples Ring" (Bodleian Ashmole G.16 [170], Harvard); "Captain Gordon's Welcome Home . . . taking the French Privateers, and a Rich Prize," beginning "Now Brave Captain Gordon's come" (Natl. Lib. of Scotland Ry III.a.10 [22]). The less common nonpolitical ballad to the tune is represented by "The true Lovers Conquest," beginning "Fair Nymph! those sparkling eyes of thine" (Pepys III, 214) and "The Cheater Cheated," beginning "Kind Gentlemen let me request" (Pepys IV, 279).

The broadside vogue of Fishburn's tune was of scarcely a decade's duration. But its continued appearance in *The Dancing Master* and its use in several ballad operas helped to keep the air alive over a total span of more than half a century. It is found (with music) in Johnson's *The Village Opera*, 1729, and in Phillips's condensation called *The Chamber-maid*, 1730, in *The Whim: or The Miser's Retreat*, 1734, and (without music) in Aston's *The Fool's Opera*, c. 1730.

Harvest Home

Henry Purcell's song beginning "Your hay it is mowed and your corn is reaped" was written for a scene in Act V of Dryden's *King Arthur*, 1691, in which Comus and three peasants sing and dance before Arthur and Emmeline.[1] The tune gets its name from the refrain, "Harvest home, harvest home, and merrily roar out our harvest home"; it is also called "We've cheated the parson," from the beginning of the second stanza.

The song, with music (Fig. 180), was issued almost immediately on a small engraved sheet as "A New Song in the Dramatick Opera. Written by Mr. Dryden" (BM G.304 [188]; substantially the same words and music are in *Pills*, 1719–1720, V, 141). "We've cheated the Parson" appears as a tune for the treble violin in *Apollo's Banquet*, Second Book, 1691, on an added leaf in the BM copy, "A New Addition . . . ," No. 6. "The Hay it is mow'd" is an arrangement for harpsichord (c. 1704–1707) in BM MS Add. 22099, fol. 10.

1 See *Works*, Purcell Society Edition, XXVI, 157.

180 <u>31</u>:

An expanded broadside version without music is called "New Play-House-Song; of the Husbandman's Delight: suiting the Humours of a Country Life," 1691 (Pepys V, 410). Another edition, with some textual variation, is called "The Country Farmer's Vain-glory; in a New Song of Harvest Home," beginning "Our Oats they are how'd, and our Barley's reap'd" (Lord Crawford, Euing, Roxburghe; reprinted in *RB* III, 610); the second part of the ballad, which is "An Answer" critical of the farmer for cheating the parson of his tithe, names "Harvest Home" as the tune.

In *The Dancing Master*, c. 1728, III, 60, "Boys and Girls come out to Play, The New way" consists of four bars of the nursery song, called "Boys and Girls to Play" (from *The Dancing Master*, II, 3d ed., 1718), combined with the refrain of "Harvest Home." In this form the tune was used in fifteen ballad operas, usually titled "We've [*or* We, *or* I] cheated the parson." In Odingsells' *Bays's Opera*, 1730, it is "Boys and Girls come out to Play," and in Peterson's *Raree Show*, 1739, it is called "The State of old Virgins," from the first line of the song sung to the tune in Chetwood's *Lover's Opera*, 1729. Music is printed in Chetwood's 3d ed., 1730, in Gay's *Polly* and *Achilles*, in *The Jovial Crew*, 1731, Fielding's *The Mock Doctor*, 2d ed., 1732, and his *An Old Man taught Wisdom*, 1735, and Coffey's *The Merry Cobler*, 1735.

Another "Harvest Home," beginning "Come Roger and Nell, come Simkin and Bell," was composed by T. A. Arne for his *Harlequin Sorcerer* (see *London Magazine*, XXI [1752], 521). It is probably Arne's tune which was intended for a broadside of about 1756 on the hiring of Hessian mercenaries, "England's Alarum Bell" (BM 1876.f.1 [157^v]).

Have at Thy Coat, Old Woman

A tune of this title is in every edition of *The Dancing Master*, 1651–
c. 1728 (1651, p. 38=Fig. 181), in *Musick's Delight on the Cithren*, 1666,

181

Original is unbarred; F♯ in key signature is not found in first edition.

and in Walsh's *Compleat Country Dancing-Master*, 1718. The tune name
may derive from "A merry new Song of a rich Widdowes wooing, That
married a young man to her owne vndooing" (Pepys; reprinted in *PB* I,
258), the refrain of which is:

> Haue at thy coat old woman,
> Haue at thy coat old woman,
> Heere and there, and euery where,
> Haue at thy coat old woman.

This ballad of about 1625 is to be sung to "Stand thy ground old Harry,"
a tune which apparently has not survived. It may be mere coincidence
that the *Dancing Master* tune, sung twice over, will fit the ballad; for
"Have at thy coat, old woman" is a proverbial phrase which could have
attached itself to a tune without regard to this or any other broadside
ballad. For this reason I do not positively equate the two tune names or
argue any sequential relationship between the ballad refrain and the
later tune.

"Stand thy ground, old Harry" served for singing at least two other
early seventeenth-century ballads: "A knotte of good fellows," beginning
"Come hither, mine host, come hither" (*SB*, p. 91), and "A very pleasant
new Ditty," beginning "Come Hostesse fill the pot" (Pepys; reprinted in
PB I, 252). I have found but a single reference to "Have at thy coat, old
woman" as a tune title. To it is sung a ballad in the form of a verse
epistle titled "From Sʳ Roger Martin to D[uke of] Monmouth" and beginning "Twas a foolish fancy Jemmy." It is found in BM MS Harl. 6914,
p. 54 (the unspecified "early Manuscript" from which Ebsworth printed

the text in *RB* V, 215). The piece, evidently written c. 1682, appeared in *180 Loyal Songs*, 1685, minus title, tune direction, and music; moreover, the seven-line stanza does not fit the tune as we know it. At best, the relationship of song to tune is tantalizing.

Chappell (*PMOT* I, 365–366) reprinted a song beginning "My name is honest Harry," from *Westminster Drollery*, 1671, feeling that since it fit the music it might have some relationship with "Stand thy ground, old Harry." For further references, see the note in the appendix to Ebsworth's edition of the drollery, 1875, p. xxiv.

Chappell (*RB* III, 575) also associated with "Have at thy coat" several ballads sung to "Your humble servant, madam," q.v. But in the second half of each stanza the meter does not fit the tune.

We are thus left with a series of conjectures, but without documentary support for assigning the tune to any extant broadsides.

The Haymakers

This tune is found in the second volume of both *The Dancing Master*, 3d ed., 1718, p. 226 (Fig. 182), and Walsh's *Compleat Country Dancing-*

182

Master, 1719. With some division of notes to accommodate vocal requirements, it will fit "The Love-sick Maid quickly Revived," beginning "As I was walking forth of late,/within the Meadows gay," to the tune of

"What shall I do, shall I dye for love, &c. Or, the Hay-makers" (Lord Crawford, Roxburghe; reprinted in *RB* VI, 238).[1]

A broadside of the same stanzaic pattern is directed to be sung to "The Hay-makers march," which may or may not be the same air: "Loves Fancy, Or, The Young-mans Dream," beginning "She lay naked in her Bed/and I my self lay by" (Wood E.25 [88], a late seventeenth-century edition; found also in *Wit and Drollery*, 1656, and *Merry Drollery Complete*, 1691, sometimes with an answer beginning "She lay up to the navel bare"). For another tune which may be associated with this ballad and several offshoots, see "She lay all naked in her bed."

One of the songs in Adam Thomson's ballad opera, *The Disappointed Gallant*, 1738, is to be sung to "Hay Makers," but the rhythm of the song is unsuitable for either the *Dancing Master* "Haymakers" or "The Scotch Haymakers." Unhappily Thomson's printed text does not include music, so that we cannot know what air was intended.

He That Loves Best Must Suffer Most

This tune title takes its name from the final line of a three-stanza song, with music by Robert King, appearing in *Choice Ayres and Songs*, Fifth Book, 1684, p. 7 (Fig. 183). It was reprinted with the tune in all editions of *Pills*, 1719–1720, IV, 251. The last years of the seventeenth century saw two independent broadside expansions of the original song: a black-letter edition in eight stanzas "To an Excellent New Tune" with the title "The Languishing Swain made Happy: Or, The Kind Return of his Clorinda" (Pepys III, 247); and a roman-letter sheet with meaningless music and twelve stanzas of text, "An Excellent New Song, call'd, The Languishing Swain" (BM C.39.k.6; reprinted in *RB* VII, 832, and *OPB*, p. 157). The broadsides begin "Happy's the Man that's free from Love," whereas the original song began "Happy the Time when . . ."

"He that loves best must suffer most" is named as the tune for singing "Unconstant Damon: or, Clorinda's Languishing Lamentation," begin-

[1] The first tune derives its name from the burden of a ballad current c. 1600–1615: "The lovlye Lamentation of a Lawyer's daughter for lacke of a husband" (*SB*, p. 302). This piece, beginning "Now drawes on the fruitfull tyme," has the tune direction "An Oyster Pye, or Robinson's Galliard." The first tune has not come to light; the ballad does not fit either of the galliards in Thomas Robinson's *Schoole of Musicke*. A later seventeenth-century ballad with the same refrain is "Virginity grown Troublesome" (*RB* VI, 246), sung to "a pleasant New West-Country Tune" not now identifiable.

ning "Some mournful Muse attend my Quill" (Lord Crawford, BM
C.39.k.6; reprinted in *OPB*, p. 161). This ballad also contains meaningless music.

An unadorned anonymous tune "He that loves best" in *Youth's Delight
on the Flagelet,* 9th ed., c. 1690, n. p. (Fig. 184), will fit the octosyllabics
of these ballads and stands as close to the texts as does King's air. The
former is in sixteen bars, the latter in twenty-four, accommodating four-
and six-line stanzas respectively. In the original song the unit is a quatrain
plus a repetition of the third and fourth lines. "Unconstant Damon" is
likewise in a six-line stanza, made up of a quatrain plus two refrain lines.
Of the two broadsides expanding the original song, "The Languishing
Swain made Happy" repeats each pair of lines successively to make an
eight-line stanza, whereas the roman-letter "Languishing Swain" is in
octosyllabic quatrains. The flageolet tune fits this latter ballad, whereas
the King air is apter for the six-line stanza; with repetitions, either will
serve for an eight-line unit.

Since the two broadside amplifications of the *Choice Ayres* song do not
give us a tune name, we can state only that those ballads *could* be sung
to either of our tunes, not that they were. For this reason there can be
only a tenuous association between these airs and some twenty broadsides which cite the tune name "Languishing Swain." The octosyllabic
quatrain is the dominant stanza form in this group of ballads, and the

184

Original is a fifth higher.
* Ambiguous time values in tablature.

flageolet tune requires no modification to fit these pieces. Because of gaps in our evidence, the linkages suggested in the following paragraphs have but a speculative relationship to the available music.

A group of ballads having the closest affinity to the parent stem includes "Constancy Lamented," beginning "Alas! my dearest Dear is gone," with a double bond formed by its two tune titles, the first of which harks back to the opening line of the *Choice Ayres* song: "All happy times, &c., Or, Languishing Swain" (Pepys; reprinted in *PB* IV, 38). Several other ballads are sung to "All happy times," including four which have been reprinted (*PB* III, 232, VI, 249, 333, 337), two which apparently have not been reprinted,[1] and one with the tune direction "All happy times when free from love" which seems to confirm the link with the original song ("Love Overthrown," reprinted in *PB* VII, 137).[2]

A dozen ballads in octosyllabic quatrains naming as tune only "The Languishing Swain" offer no complication and may be summarily dealt with. They include "The Unfortunate Lady" (*PB* V, 320), "An Answer to . . . The Unfortunate Lady" (*PB* V, 323, and *OPB*, p. 72), "The Ladies Lamentation" (*PB* VI, 207), "The Perjured Sayler," 1693 (*PB* VII, 36), "The Bristol Tragedy" (*PB* VII, 143), "The Unjust Uncle" (*OPB*,

[1] They are "The Beautiful Barkeshire Damsel," beginning "There was a Damsel young and fair" (Pepys V, 239), and "The second part oth Barkshire Damsel," 1697, "To the same Tune," beginning "The Gallant Esquire nam'd before" (Pepys IV, 27).

[2] This ballad on the fears of being transported to America has circulated orally into our own era. For a rather bland text plus notes on traditional recoveries, especially in the United States, see *Frank C. Brown Collection of North Carolina Folklore*, 1952–1964, II, 253ff.

p. 120), "The Kentish Maiden" (*RB* VIII, 550), and "The Maiden's New Wish" (Pepys III, 88). Others, which seem not to have been reprinted, are: "The Woman's Victory," beginning "Young marry'd Women, pray attend" (BM C.22.f.6 [207], Lord Crawford 1454, Harvard); "The Northampton-shire Knight's Daughter," beginning "Near to a fountain all alone" (Pepys V, 176); "An Answer to The Northampton-shire Knight's Daughter," beginning "The Lady of Northampton-shire" (Pepys V, 177); and "The Hampshire Miller," beginning "A Miller liv'd near Overton" (Pepys III, 12).

Another group of ballads introduces the tune title "I loved you dearly," which may refer to an independent melody not discovered or may be another name for "Languishing Swain." The initial piece in the series is "An excellent New Song, Call'd, Nellys Constancy, or, Her Unkind Lover," beginning "I lov'd you dearly, I lov'd you well," to be sung "To a pleasant New Tune: or, Languishing Swain" (Pepys; reprinted in *RB* VI, 791; another issue, BM 1876.f.1 [33], is simply "To an Excellent New Tune"). This ballad, metrically irregular in its opening quatrains, settles into the octosyllabic pattern characteristic of the entire complex. The ambiguity of the tune direction is that, if taken literally, the "pleasant New Tune" originating with this ballad becomes "I loved you dearly" from the opening line; but the formula had become so stereotyped as to be often meaningless and is not a genuine indication of an alternative musical air. The ambiguity continues in the tune direction "I Lov'd you dearly, &c., Or, Languishing Swain" of the sequel, "The Sea-Man's Answer. To His Unkind Lover," beginning "Fair Maid you say you lov'd me well" (BM C.39.k.6; reprinted in *RB* VI, 792, and *OPB*, p. 94). The same pair of tune names appears in "The Sea-man's Complaint for His Unkind Mistress of Wapping," beginning "When I went early in the Spring" (Pepys V, 368; "Languishing Swain" is omitted from the tune direction in other issues: Lord Crawford, BM C.22.f.6; reprinted in *RB* VIII, 433). An answer names only "I lov'd you dearly" as the tune (*RB* VIII, 434, *OPB*, p. 75). The tune is called "I love you dearly" in "The barbarous and bloody Son, Who Shot his . . . Father-in-Law," 1696 (Pepys; reprinted in *PB* VII, 231); it has the full form "I love thee dearly, I love thee well" in "The Sussex Tragedy," beginning "Young Men and Maidens, pray draw near" (Pepys V, 314).

The same kind of ambiguity gathers around "The Jealous Lover," first found as the title of a ballad beginning "Farewel my love, farewel my dear," to be sung "To a new Tune, much in request" (Pepys V, 367).[3] In two ballads "The Jealous Lover" is coupled with "The Languishing

---

[3] This ballad is evidently the origin of the tune title "Fare well my Love," found with "The Ship-Carpenter's Love to the Merchants Daughter" (*RB* VIII, 146).

Swain" in the tune direction: they are "The Leicester-shire Tragedy" (*OPB*, p. 28) and "Crafty Kate of Cholchester" (Lord Crawford 1432, a late seventeenth-century exemplar; a reprint of an eighteenth-century Newcastle issue with tune direction "The Languishing Lover" is in *RB* VIII, 430).[4]

Finally, a small group of ballads display a metrically distinctive 4½ line stanza, the swelling caused by repetition of half the fourth line (e.g., "In wronging me, in wronging me/thou wrong'st thy own"). This series begins with "An Excellent New song, Called, The False-hearted young Man, or, The Injured Maiden," beginning "Why should not I complain on thee,"[5] to be sung "To a pleasant new Tune: or, The Languishing Swain" (Pepys; reprinted in *RB* VIII, x*). The first of these tune directions may indicate a new air (later known as "The False hearted Young Man"?), and the ballads that follow exhibit evidence to strengthen the guess. A sequel to the ballad just named is "The Distracted Young-Mans Answer To The Injured Maiden," sung "To the same Tune: or, The Languishing Swain" (*RB* VIII, 414, and *OPB*, p. 80; a variant issue is in Pepys V, 288). In "The Faithful Marriner" (*RB* VI, 793, and *OPB*, p. 147), the tune direction is "The False-hearted Young Man: or, The Languishing Swain," but only the former tune name is cited for singing "The Forlorn Lover," beginning "O yes, O yes, O yes, I cry" (Pepys V, 211).[6] If "The False-hearted Young Man" was an independent tune—not known to us today—it must have taken melodic account of the fourth-line repetition formula in this group of ballads. If the verbal repetition is suppressed, "The Languishing Swain" becomes a workable alternative tune.

[4] Ballads directed to be sung simply to "Jealous Lover" include "The Punish'd Atheist" (*PB* III, 184), "The Westminster Wonder" (*PB* VII, 76), "The Traveler's Repentance" (*PB* VII, 101), "The Chearful Husband" (*RB* III, 515), and three that have apparently not been reprinted: "The Deceitful Merchant," beginning "A Waterman near Gravel-lane" (Pepys V, 249); "Shameless Joan," beginning "You that in merriment delight/Pray listen well to what I write" (Pepys V, 423); and "The Mournful Maid of Berkshire," beginning "Attend you Friends and Parents dear" (Lord Crawford 153).

[5] "Why should not I complain on thee" is named as the tune of "An Excellent New Song, Called, The Politick Lovers," beginning "In London City late did dwell," with the same hypermetrical stanza form (Pepys V, 397).

[6] "The Forlorn Lover" may have been inspired by a much briefer D'Urfey song in *Pills*, 1719–1720, II, 262, which has the same opening line and a number of other verbal details found in the broadside. The song is without music and its stanza is a plain octosyllabic quatrain.

A Health to Betty

This tune is in every edition of *The Dancing Master* (1651, p. 21 = Fig. 185), in *Musick's Delight on the Cithren,* 1666, and in Walsh's *Compleat*

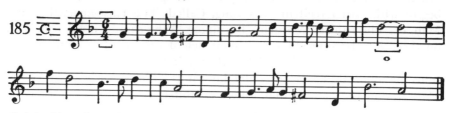

185

Original is unbarred.

Country Dancing-Master, 1718. A lute set of c. 1650 is in Trinity College, Cambridge, MS O.16.2, p. 136, and a lyra-viol tablature version dated 1692 is preserved in a transcript of part of the Blaikie MS, No. 38, in the Dundee Free Library. D'Urfey appropriated the dance tune for one of his songs (*Pills,* 1719–1720, II, 110), and it is used for a drinking song beginning "O let us Swim in Blood of Grapes" in William Thomson's *Orpheus Caledonius,* 1725, No. 25. "A health to Betty" is one of the airs in Gay's *Polly,* 1729, *Love and Revenge,* c. 1729, and Mitchell's *The High-land Fair,* 1731. In the latter ballad opera, the tune is called "My Moth-er's ay glowrin o'er me," from the first line of a song in Ramsay's *Tea-Table Miscellany,* 1723, p. 123 (the tune of "A health to Betty," un-named, is provided for it in Alexander Stuart's *Musick for Allan Ram-say's Collection of Scots Songs,* c. 1725, p. 124). Words and music were printed in Ritson's *Scotish Songs,* 1794, I, 28, and, as arranged by Haydn, in George Thomson's *Original Scotish Songs,* 1793–1818, IV, 194.

Despite this evidence of post-1650 vogue of the tune, it was associated chiefly with early seventeenth-century broadsides. These include Martin Parker's "Fourepence halfepenney Farthing: Or, A Woman will haue the Oddes" (licensed 1629), beginning "One morning bright, (for my de-light)," to the tune of "Bessy Bell, or a health to Betty" (Pepys; reprinted in *PG,* p. 323); [1] and "The paire of Northerne Turtles," c. 1635, begin-

---

[1] "Bess a Bell she doth excel" is cited in Burton's *Anatomy of Melancholy* (ed. Floyd Dell and Paul Jordan-Smith, 1927, p. 760) as a typical song of rustics. It apparently has no connection with "O Bessy Bell and Mary Gray," an eighteenth-century Scotch song. A tablature version of "Besse Bell" (BM MS Egerton 2046, fol. 51ᵛ), c. 1664–1678, seems to be in part a melody, in part an accompaniment, but it is metrically suitable

ning "Farewell, farewell, my dearest dear," sung "To a new Northerne Tune, or, A health to Betty" (Roxburghe; reprinted in *RB* II, 312; the second part only is in Pepys I, 372).[2] A broadside of 1689 to the tune of "Good Health to Betty: Or, Queen Marys Lamentation" is in the same meter: "The Boast of Great Britain," beginning "We had a Roman Queen of late" (Pepys; reprinted in *PB* V, 57).[3] All three ballads are written in an eight-line stanza or its equivalent, which requires a repetition of the tune. But a song entitled "Advice or, an Heroic Epistle to Mr. Fra. Villers," to the tune of "A Health to Betty" (BM MS Harl. 7319, p. 278) is in a short stanza form that fits the tune exactly. It begins:

> Leave off your Ogling Francis
> And mind your Sister Nancy's
> She's quite undone
> If once King John
> Shou'd get between her Haunches.

Another version, dated 1682, with the tune title "heres A health to Betty," is in BM MS Harl. 6914, p. 58, source of the text printed in *RB* V, 220.

Heart of Oak

"Heart of Oak," now part of the basic repertoire of British national song, first appeared in David Garrick's pantomime, *Harlequin's Invasion*, which opened on the last day of 1759. In its original intent it was a topical song, for its opening lines

> Come, cheer up, my lads, 'tis to glory we steer,
> To add something more to this wonderful year, . . .

refer to a series of British triumphs in Africa, Europe, and North America, climaxed by the capture of Quebec, which made 1759 a significant

for Martin Parker's ballad. It should be clear that "Bessy Bell" is an independent tune, not an alternate name for "A health to Betty."

2 From the closing lines of each stanza it appears that the "New northerne Tune" cited in this ballad may be "Lie lulling beyond thee," q.v.

3 "Queen Mary's Lamentation" is probably related, through "King James's Lamentation," to "Billy and Molly," for which no tune has survived. Professor Rollins's note equating "Billy and Molly" with the tune "I am a Maid, and a very good Maid" (*PB* IV, 167) ignores metrical considerations; the former is used with eight-line stanzas, alternating eight and seven syllables, whereas the latter calls for four eleven-syllable lines.

year of victory. The celebration of British pride is characterized by the refrain: "Heart of oak are our ships, heart of oak are our men. . . ," and with music by William Boyce, the song became instantly popular.[1] In the manner of the time, it was issued as a single sheet with music (Fig. 186), of which a number of contemporary editions survive (BM G.307 [74],

186

Chorus

BM G.316 [75], &c.). Among the other immediate reprints may be mentioned those in *The Royal Magazine*, II (1760), 153, *The Universal Magazine*, XXVI (1760), 152, and *Clio and Euterpe*, 1759–1762, III, 66.

Perhaps the next most famous use of the "Heart of Oak" tune is in "The Liberty Song" by John Dickinson, the Pennsylvania political writer and statesman. A broadside edition with music was published in Boston in September, 1768 (W. C. Ford, *Broadsides . . . Printed in Massachusetts, 1639–1800*, 1922, No. 1434), and was widely copied in newspapers and almanacs. It begins "Come join hand in hand, brave Americans all," and its refrain shows the clear imitation of Garrick's original song, turned to the immediate issue of the colonies' relation with Britannia:

> In freedom we're born, and in freedom we'll live;
> Our purses are ready,
> Steady, Friends, steady,
> Not as *slaves*, but as *freemen* our money we'll give.

In England at least two other songs to the tune were issued with music: "Keppel's Triumph," beginning "Bear a hand jolly Tars for bold Keppel appear" (BM G.306 [197], about 1779); and "The Hardy Tars of Old

---

[1] The common corruption "Hearts of oak . . ." changes the sense of the first clause, as the substitution "Jolly tars are our men" sentimentalizes the second.

England," beginning "Come cheer up my Lads, let us haste to the Main" (BM G.307 [85], about 1780). A conventional broadside of the 1790s, without music, is "King, Liberty, Laws," beginning "Ye true-hearted Britons, so brave and so free" (BM 1871.f.16, unnumbered folio), a ballad which reviles France and her "engine Tom Paine."

James Boswell, in *An Account of Corsica*, 1768, pp. 318–319, tells how, after he had played "Gilderoy" and some other Scots airs "indifferently" on his German flute, his Corsican friends asked him for an English song, and he sang them "Heart of Oak." He provoked "quite a joyous riot" among them when he translated the words into Italian.

Heart's Ease

Two entirely different tunes named "Heart's ease" have been preserved. A stately 26-bar air in lute tablature is among the Cambridge University MSS (Dd.2.11, fol. 44, probably late sixteenth century; transcribed in *OEPM* I, 97–98, and in E. W. Naylor, *Shakespeare Music*, 1912, p. xi, facsimile, p. x). A five-part setting of this tune, called "The Honie Suckle," is in Antony Holborne's *Pavans, Galliards* . . . , 1599. A strongly rhythmic dance tune is in *The Dancing Master*, editions of 1651–1690 (1651, p. 54 = Fig. 187).

Original is unbarred.

It is clear that "Heart's ease" was known by the beginning of Elizabeth's reign, for in the interlude *Misogonus*, II, ii, attributed to Laurence Johnson, c. 1560–1577, Cacurgus appoints the parts for a four-voice song

· 301 ·

to the tune, beginning "Cast care away with sport and play/Pastime is all our pleasure." In *Romeo and Juliet,* IV, v, Peter asks the musicians to play the air, punning on the title.

Two ballads found in the Shirburn MS, and so dating from near the beginning of the seventeenth century, call for the tune. One of them, to "Hart's ease," is "A pleasant new Ballad, shewing how Loue doth bereaue a man of health, witt, and memorye," beginning "Wit, whither wilt thow? woe is mee!" (*SB,* p. 268); [1] the other, naming the tune as "Wit whither will thow," is "The description and qualitye of an vnconstant Lover," beginning "What greater griefe then losse of loue" (*SB,* p. 281).

Both the *Misogonus* song and the two ballads fit the *Dancing Master* tune better than the lute air, although the ballads require some stretching. The early stage song was clearly written with a tune in mind, and from what we know of the age of many tunes in the *Dancing Master,* it is not farfetched to surmise that this version was intended.

The Hemp-Dresser,

or The London Gentlewoman

"The London Gentlewoman Or the Hemp-Dresser" is in all editions of *The Dancing Master* (1651, p. 58 = Fig. 188); in some editions the tune

188

Original is unbarred.

is entitled "The Hemp-dresser, or The London Maid." As "Hemp Dresser(s)" it is in Walsh's *Compleat Country Dancing-Master,* 1718, and

---

[1] The quotation of the opening words in *As You Like It,* IV, i, is evidence that the ballad (though not necessarily the Shirburn transcript) was written before 1600.

Rutherford's *Compleat Collection of 200 . . . Country Dances,* c. 1756. The tune derives its titles from an old poem which might have gone unpublished but for Henry Bold's including it, alongside his translation, in *Latine Songs, with their English,* 1685. The first two of its four stanzas are:

> There was a London Gentlewoman
> That lov'd a Countrey man, a;
> And she did desire his company
> A little now and than, a.
> > Fa, la, &c.

> This man he was a Hemp-dresser,
> And dressing was his Trade, a;
> And he doth kiss the Mistress, Sir,
> And now and then the Maid, a.
> > Fa, la, &c.

A broadside of 1679, attributed to Charles Blount, "The Sale of Esau's Birth-right: Or, The New Buckingham Ballad," beginning "A Wondrous Tale I will relate," is to the tune of "The London Gentlewoman, or Little Peggey Ramsey" (Lord Crawford, BM C.20.f.2, Wood 417, Bodleian Ashmole G.16, Harvard, Huntington, Bagford; reprinted in *BB* II, 764).[1] Thomas D'Urfey wrote "The Winchester Christening," a sequel to his "Winchester Wedding," to "the tune of a pretty Country Dance, called, The Hemp-dresser." It appeared in his *Third Collection of New Songs,* 1685, p. 7 (Fig. 189), in *Two New Songs,* 1685, in every edition of *Pills,* in *The Convivial Songster,* c. 1782, and in *The Winchester Garland,* a late eighteenth-century Newcastle print. All but the last contain the music.[2]

D'Urfey's first line, "The sun had loos'd his weary team," became the name of the tune in many ballad operas, including Gay's *The Beggar's Opera* (with music); *The Wanton Jesuit,* 1731; *The Court Legacy,* 1733; Drury's *The Mad Captain,* 1733; *The Sturdy Beggars,* 1733; Drury's *The Rival Milliners,* 1737; and *Court and Country,* 1743. In Mottley and Cooke's *Penelope,* 1728 (with music), and *Love and Revenge,* c. 1729, the tune is called "Joan stoop'd down," probably from the first line of an undiscovered song.

Robert Burns used the tune for his song, "The Deil's awa wi' the

---

[1] For the second tune, see "Peg a Ramsey."

[2] A variant text of D'Urfey's ballad, somewhat sentimentalized in the closing stanzas, was issued as a broadside to the tune of "Cold and Raw": "Roger's Delight: or, The West-Country Christning," beginning "When Sol had left his weary Teams" (Pepys, BM C.22.f.6, black-letter editions printed before 1700; Roxburghe, a later issue, reprinted in *RB* VII, 210). Both texts of the ballad may be found in *A Complete Collection of . . . English and Scotch Songs,* 1735–1736, I, 124, III, 136.

189 C3.

Original is a fifth higher.

Exciseman," beginning "The deil cam fiddlin thro' the town" (Johnson's *Scots Musical Museum* IV, 412). Chappell (*PMOT* I, 312) noted that the tune was still commonly heard in the middle of the nineteenth century.[3]

The eight-bar tune fits the quatrains associated with it; when a "fa la" refrain is added, the stanza is sung to the first strain with its repetition, and the second strain is reserved for the refrain. D'Urfey's poem in octave stanzas requires repetition of both musical strains. It will be observed that the *Dancing Master* version of the tune is in Mixolydian mode.

Hey, Boys, Up Go We

About 1641, when an intense pamphlet warfare broke out between the high-church party and the Puritans (the latter group symbolized by persons whose initials formed the word "Smectymnuus" and with whom John Milton worked closely), Francis Quarles wrote a political song whose chief distinction was the concluding line of each stanza, "and Hey then up go wee." Quarles introduced it into an eclogue, assigning it to Anarchus. It pictures the systematic overthrow of institutions, an up-

---

[3] Margaret Dean-Smith's notes to the tune in her edition of *The English Dancing Master*, 1957, p. 50, include references to its traditional survival in Wales ("Flaunting Two" in Edward Jones's *Relicks of the Welsh Bards*, 1784) and the Isle of Man ("A Pair of white gloves" in *JFSS*, VII [1922–1926], 173–174; cf. 309). Miss Dean-Smith perpetuates a mistake of Chappell's in implying that the tune of "The Hemp-Dresser" is to be found in John Playford's *Choice Ayres, Songs and Dialogues*, 1675. Chappell had actually stated that D'Urfey's song was to be found in *Choice Ayres and Songs*, Third Book, 1681, but there is no record of the song before 1685; indeed, the song to which "The Westminster Christening" is the sequel was not published until 1684.

heaval which the Puritans could be presumed to favor but which would seem anarchistic to a person of Quarles's stripe. The song, entitled "The Tryumph of the Round-heads, or yᵉ reioycing of the Smects" in a contemporary manuscript (Bodleian MS Ashmole 36–37, fol. 81),[1] originally had no tune assigned, but in *Rump*, 1662, it is directed to be sung to "Cuckolds all a-row," and its immediate history is to be associated with that tune, q.v. But a broadside version of 1681, "A Proper New Brummigham Ballad," beginning "Know now my Brethren Heaven is clear," expands Quarles's text to twelve stanzas and names the tune as "Hey then up go we" (Bodleian Vet.A.3c.29 [6], Harvard, Yale, Huntington).

In 1682 Thomas D'Urfey reworked Quarles's song for his play *The Royalist*, Act IV, composing a new opening stanza but levying substantially on Quarles in the rest of the song. He did not change the refrain, nor is a tune named in the play. But the stage song, expanded and made even more topical in broadside form, was the basis of an immediate vogue in which the altered refrain, "Then Hey Boys up go we," played a great part. It appeared with music (Fig. 190) as "The Whig's Exalta-

tion; A Pleasant New Song of 82. To an Old Tune of 41," beginning "Now Now the Tories all shall stoop" (BM C.38.i.25 [5], BM Luttrell II, 236, Bodleian Ashmole G.16 [160], Harvard, Huntington, Yale). Another edition was published in the same year, without music (Bodleian Ashmole G.16 [56]); still another contemporary edition without music bears the title "The Whig Rampant: or, Exaltation. Being a Pleasant New Song of 82. To a New Tune of, Hey Boys up go We" (Lord Crawford, Euing,

---

[1] Chappell (*PMOT* II, 425) misread the last word of the title "Saints," thus losing some of the central associations of the song.

Roxburghe; reprinted in *RB* IV, 264). It seems doubtful that the tune was new in 1682, although I have been unable to discover an earlier instance of it; it is clear, however, that the new name became firmly attached to it, and for half a century political songs used both the tune and the infectious refrain line. D'Urfey's own song was duly printed in his *New Collection of Songs and Poems*, 1683; it was reprinted in *Wit and Mirth*, 3d ed., 1682, in *180 Loyal Songs*, 1685, and in *Pills*, 1719–1720, II, 286, with music in the two latter.

Music is also found in *The Dancing Master*, Supplement to the 6th ed., 1679, printed c. 1682, and in all editions thereafter, originally in common time but in 6/4 beginning with the 9th ed., 1695. It is also in Thomas Greeting's *Pleasant Companion . . . for the Flagelet*, 1683, Humphry Salter's *Genteel Companion . . . for the Recorder*, 1683, in *180 Loyal Songs*, 1685, pp. 6, 221, 257, and in Walsh's *Compleat Country Dancing-Master*, 1718. The tune was used in at least five ballad operas, including the following which were printed with music: Odell's *The Patron*, 1729; *The Prisoner's Opera*, 1730; Coffey's *The Devil to Pay*, 1731; and Lillo's *Silvia*, 1731.

The following broadsides, both issued in 1682, print the music and identify it as "the Tune of 41, or Hey Boys up go we": "Great York and Albany: or, the Loyal Welcom to His Royal Highness on His Return from Scotland," beginning "Now now the Zealots all must droop" (Harvard; another edition, without the first tune title, Bodleian Ashmole G.15 [64], Harvard, Huntington; reprinted with music in Matthew Taubman's *An Heroick Poem*, 1682); and "An Excellent New Hymne to the Mobile, exhorting them to Loyalty The Clean Contrary Way," 1682, beginning "Let us advance the Good Old Cause, Fear not Tantivitiers" (BM 1871.e.9 [70], Harvard; a variant issue with music but without tune direction, Bodleian Ashmole G.16, Wood 417, Huntington; reprinted in *120 Loyal Songs*, 1684, and *RB* V, 60). This last is an adaptation of Alexander Brome's song of 1643, "The Saints Encouragement" (*Songs and Other Poems*, 1661; reprinted in *Rump*, 1662, as "Collonel Vennes Encouragement to his Souldiers"), beginning "Fight on brave Souldiers for the cause,/Fear not the Caveleers," with a burden "The clean contrary way" preserved in the later broadside.

"The clean [or clear] contrary way" is the burden of at least two other broadsides sung to "Hey boys": "Animadversions on the Lady Marquess," c. 1682, beginning "The Lady Marquess and her gang" (Roxburghe; reprinted in *RB* V, 67); and "A New Ballad from Whigg-Land," 1682, beginning "Brave Monmouth's out of Favour now" (Bodleian Ashmole G.16 [159], Natl. Lib. of Scotland, Chetham, Huntington, Harvard). "The clean contrary way" was an independent tune, q.v., and the phrase never became an alternate name for the "Hey boys" tune.

The case is different with "41" or "the tune of 41," for we have found it in conjunction with the music of "Hey boys." Among the ballads without music which cite the tune under this name are: "The Jacobites Lamentation and Confession," 1696, beginning "Old Sandcroft he began the Dance" (BM 1871.e.9 [100]); and "The Tories Confession, Or, A merry song in Answer to The Whigs Exaltation: To the same Tune of Forty One," 1682, beginning "A Pox on Whigs we'l now grow wise" (Lord Crawford, Bodleian Ashmole G.16 [two issues], Chetham, Huntington, Harvard; reprinted in *Rome Rhym'd to Death,* 1683, and *RB* IV, 268).[2]

All told, more than fifty broadsides were written to the tune under one or another of its names, and most of these pieces were on political subjects. Aside from the large number reprinted in *RB* and a few in *PB* and *PG,* the following seem not to have been reprinted: "The Whigg and Tory's Friendly Dialogue," 1682, beginning "Now now yon [i.e., you] Tories pray give o're" (Huntington); "A Looking-glass for a Tory; or the Bogg-Trotter's Glory," 1682, beginning "The Devil and we have done brave things" (BM 807.f.36 [20], Bodleian Ashmole G.16 [54], Harvard); "The Whigs Elevation," 1683, beginning "Now, now brave Monmouth's come again" (Clark); "The Explanation," beginning "Our Priests in holy Pilgrimage" (Wood 417 [164] with MS date 1688, BM C.20.f.2 [317], Library of Congress, Harvard; found also in *A Collection of the Newest . . . Songs . . . against Popery,* 1689, in *The Muses Farewel to Popery and Slavery,* 1689, and *Poems on Affairs of State,* 2d ed., 1716, III); "The Jacobites Exultation Upon their conceiv'd hopes of the Present Plot," beginning "Now, now the Stubborn Whigs may Rot" (Lord Crawford 892, Harvard, without tune direction but with burden "High Boys up go we"); and "Mall in her Majesty," beginning "The Tories wish for James again/The Papists for his Spouse" (BM MS Harl. 7319, p. 672; no tune direction, but the poem ends "then Hey Boys up go we").

The following are among the nonpolitical ballads to the tune which apparently have not been reprinted: "The Country Lass for me," beginning "Come Lovers all, both great and small" (BM C.22.f.6 [98], Lord Crawford 265, Harvard); "A Dialogue between a Baker and his Wife," beginning "Where have you been, you drunken Dog" (Pepys IV, 147); "Love in a Mist," beginning "A Thumping lusty Country Lad" (BM C.22.f.6 [57], Lord Crawford 1182, Douce I, 125, Harvard); "Money money, my Hearts," beginning "Good Folks look to your Purses" (Pepys IV, 319); and two by Thomas Bowne: "Tom and Rogers Contract," beginning "As Tom met Roger upon the Road" (Pepys IV, 18, Douce II,

[2] Another "Answer" with similar first line but different contents is "The Popish Tories Confession: Or, An Answer to the Whiggs Exaltation . . . to the Tune of, Hey Boys up go We" (Douce II, 182).

214); and "The West-Country Maids advice," beginning "Fair Maids draw near to me a while" (BM C.22.f.6 [224], Lord Crawford 372, Douce II, 250ᵛ, Harvard). Because of its common meter, a ballad fitting "Hey Boys" could also be sung to many other tunes; witness but two such from among a large number: "Great News from a Parliament of Women . . . in Rosemary Lane," 1684, beginning "Through London streets as I did pass," to the tune of "Hey-Boys up go We: Or Genny Gynn" (BM 1876.f.1 [27]); and "The Brave Boys of Bristol," beginning "Brave Bristol Boys, where e're you be," to the tune of "Hey Boys up go we; Jenny Gin; Busie Fame; Or, Russels Farewel" (Douce I, 19).

A few curiosities deserve note. A ballad entitled "The Knight of the Wooden Ruffs Exaltation," beginning "Come stand to thy Tackle Nat," designed to be "Sung to a delicate Tory Tune, by the Manks Lady his Wife," contains the "Hey boys" refrain in its closing stanzas. It was printed at the end of a tract (*Trincalo Sainted,* 1682) which celebrated Nathaniel Thompson's punishment in the pillory on July 5 of that year. Thompson, who published most of the 1682 Tory broadsides we have noted, is referred to as "the Jesuits Implement, and Printer General," and his wife from the Isle of Man is rather unnecessarily drawn into this bit of political jockeying.

"The Discovery: or, The Squire turnd Ferret," beginning "Most true it is, I dare to say," is to the tune of "High Boys! up go we; Chevy Chase; Or what you please" (BM C.116.i.4 [30], an eight-page pamphlet, 2d ed., 1727). The four-line stanza form fits "Chevy Chase" but "Hey boys" requires two stanzas for each repetition of the tune. Another eighteenth-century piece has the "Hey boys" burden and an ambiguous historical description of tune or song: "The Tories Triumph . . . Being a New Song to a merry Old Tune, made in the Year 1641. reviv'd in 1683. and lately performed at the Bell-Tavern in W———r [Windsor?]," 1711, beginning "Now, now the Whigs shall all go down" (Lord Crawford 894; reprinted in *Political Merriment,* 1714, and *A Pill to Purge State-Melancholy,* 1715).

"Monmouth and Bucleugh's Welcom from the North," 1682, beginning "When stout young Jemmy went abroad," has the tune title "York and Albany's Welcome to England" (Harvard, Yale, Huntington), which in turn was the title of an earlier ballad "To a New Play-House Tune, much in request," with the distinctive "Hey boys" beginning made familiar by D'Urfey: "Now, now the Duke is safe return'd" (BM C.38.i.25 [11]).

A single-sheet song of about 1712, "We have been Banter'd & Bubbl'd & Cheated & Banter'd & Bubbl'd," beginning "Your melancholly's all a folly,/The Peace I'm sure is sign'd," contains the first eight bars of "Hey boys" and ten bars of new music to accommodate the nine-line stanza (BM G.314 [34], Harvard; reprinted in *Pills,* 1719–1720, VI, 334).

The Highlanders' March

This air is found in both supplements to the third edition of *The Dancing Master*, c. 1662, No. 46 (Fig. 191), 1665, No. 22, and in *Musick's*

Delight on the Cithren, 1666. Contemporary virginal sets include those of John Stone and Robert Wintersall in Christ Church Mus. MS 1175, fols. 12ᵛ, 13ᵛ, and the anonymous lessons in New York Public Library MS Drexel 5612, p. 50, and *Musicks Hand-maid*, 1678.

Two broadsides call for the tune: "The Ladies Lamentation. For the losse of her Land-lord," 1651, beginning "All in a fair morning for sweet recreation" (BM C.20.f.14; reprinted in *CP*, p. 315), and "A Loyal Subjects Admonition, or a true Song of Brittains Civil Wars," beginning "Great controversie hath been in England" (Euing 160). The latter ballad cites as an alternative tune "General Moncks right march that was sounded before him from Scotland to London," which apparently has not survived.[1]

---

[1] A tune known variously as "Monk's March," "The Lord Monck's March" and "General Monk's March" is found in *The Dancing Master*, 3d ed. supplements; *Musicks Hand-maid*, 1678; *Musicks Recreation on the Viol, Lyra-way*, 1682; volume two of *The Dancing Master*, 3d ed., 1718, and of Walsh's *Compleat Country Dancing-Master*, 1719. It does not fit the Euing ballad, nor is it adapted to other ballads citing such tune titles as "Monk's March," "My Lord Monks March to London," "General Monks March," "General Monk hath advanc'd himself since he came from the Tower," "Monk hath confounded," "General Monk sail'd through the Gun-Fleet," "General Monk was a nobleman." These tune titles, associated with ballads written in a variety of rhythmic and stanzaic patterns, have nothing in common save their reference to the first Duke of Albemarle.

The Hobbyhorse

The hobbyhorse has had a long and honorable history as one of the accessories of the morris dance, and remnants of traditional ceremonies associated with it and their music survive in England today. During the Restoration, when frowns of the Puritans had lost some of their force, "The Hobby Horse Dance" as a tune found its way into *Musick's Delight on the Cithren,* 1666, Greeting's *Pleasant Companion . . . for the Flagelet,* 2d ed., 1673, *Musicks Recreation on the Viol, Lyra-way,* 1682, and *Apollo's Banquet,* 1670, and subsequent editions. A contemporary MS version for lyra viol is in Cambridge University MS Dd.6.48, fol. 35^v. If it did not appear in *The Dancing Master,* the reason is clear: its tune had not been adapted for the relatively fashionable long or round dances which Playford's series of volumes popularized.

It was used as a broadside tune as early as 1666, when Sir John Birkenhead wrote a ballad on a decisive naval battle against the Dutch on St. James's day of that year, in which Prince Rupert and the Duke of Albemarle (formerly General Monk) led the British sea power. It is "A New Ballad Of a famous German Prince and a renowned English Duke, who . . . fought with a Beast with Seven Heads, call'd Provinces," beginning "There happen'd of late a terrible Fray," to "a new French Tune, call'd Monsieur Ragou,[1] or, The Dancing Hobby-horses" (Lord Crawford 1115, Wood 416 [111], BM C.20.f.2 [68], Bagford I, 77, Harvard). The distinctive stanza pattern fits the music, notably in the burden at the end of the first and second strains, where "With a Thump Thump Thump &c" is sung to a rocking, thumping rhythm. That this was a conspicuous feature of the nautical ballad is borne out by a lampoon in the same meter, beginning "O Berkenhead how hast thou tyr'd thy Muse,/With a Burden that no body else could chuse/Of a Thump a Thump &c" (Bodleian MS Ashmole 36–37, fol. 262). Another broadside containing the "Thump" burden is "The Protestant-Flayl: An Excellent New Song," 1682, beginning "Listen a while, and I'l tell you a Tale," to the tune of "Lacy's Maggot; Or, The Hobby-Horse" (Lord Crawford, Huntington, containing the music of the latter tune [Fig. 192]; *180 Loyal Songs,* 1685, with the music of the former, unsuitable to the text; reprinted in *RB* V, 35). A Dublin ballad of 1725, to the tune of "Protestant Flail," has a "Thump" refrain and can be sung to "Hobbyhorse" music: "Whiteacre's Glory: Or, the Drubbing of Seignior Stapha. At

---

[1] "La Ragou," No. 82 of the French dances appended to *The Dancing Master,* 3d ed., 1665, is not the tune called for, its structure being unsuitable for singing the broadside.

Figg's Amphitheatre in London," beginning "All you that to true English Blood do belong" (BM 839.m.23 [60]).

To a somewhat different "tune of a Pretty Country Dance, call'd the Hobbyhorse," Thomas D'Urfey wrote a song beginning "Jolly Roger Twangdillo of Plowden Hill" (*The Second Collection of New Songs and Ballads*, 1699, p. 15 [Fig. 193]; *Pills*, all editions, 1719–1720, I, 19; *The Merry Musician*, 1716; volume two of *The Dancing Master*, 3d ed., 1718—in the latter called "Jolly Roger"). The rocking burden here is largely nonsense, but the same octave skips and insistent reiteration of the keynote are present here. This tune is used in five ballad operas, as "Jolly Roger Twangdillo" or "Jolly Roger": *The Jovial Crew*, 1731, and Phillips's *The Livery Rake*, 1733, with music; Odingsells' *Bays's Opera*, 1730, Drury's *The Mad Captain*, 1733, and Breval's *The Rape of Helen*, 1737, without music.

Hold Fast Thy Sword
and Scepter, Charles

This tune takes its origin from "Loyalty unfeigned, Or, The true Protestants Admonition," which begins "Hold fast thy Sword & Scepter Charles/sad Times may else come on" (Lord Crawford, Harvard, Rox-

burghe; reprinted in *RB* IV, 640).[1] The tune direction on the broadside is "Busie Fame, Young Pheon, or, The Fathers Exhortation"; of these the first two are familiar and the third is the title of a lost ballad licensed in 1675. "Loyalty unfeigned" was reprinted in *180 Loyal Songs,*

[1] For another possible source of the tune name, see a discussion of the ballad "Popery Unvail'd," s.v. "Young Phaon."

1685, p. 292, with the ruler's name changed to James, and with a tune (Fig. 194) which fits this and the following song in the volume. The latter, beginning "O Poland Monster of our Isle," had appeared in broadside form in 1682 as "A New Song upon the K[in]g of Poland and the Prince of the Land of Promise," to "a Theater Tune: Or, Hold fast thy Crown and Scepter, Charles" (Harvard, Huntington).

Still another broadside to the tune is "The Statesmans Downfal, Or, His Lamentation for being put in the Tower," beginning "What cursed fate hath thus of late" (Harvard). The tune direction is "Hold fast thy Sword and Scepter Charles, or, Russels farewel," and either tune would fit; but music contained on the sheet is a garbled version of "Great York has been debarred of late," a tune requiring a totally different stanza pattern.

How Blest Are Shepherds

"How blest are Shepherds, how happy their Lasses" was a song in the second act of Dryden's *King Arthur*, 1691, with music by Purcell. Two broadside versions were published, one, with imperfect musical text, entitled "The Shepherds Happiness: or, An Advice to Ladies" (Pepys V, 189, dated 1691); the other, undated and with meaningless music, titled "The Happy Shepheard: Or, The Young Gallants Courtship to his Coy Lady" (Lord Crawford 520, BM C.39.k.6 [25]; reprinted in *OPB*, p. 65). In both issues the text is expanded from two stanzas to seven. The original words and music are reprinted in all editions of *Pills*, 1719–1720, III, 290; the music alone is in *Apollo's Banquet*, Second Book, 1691 (in a supplementary section "A New Addition," No. 8=Fig. 195), and in Purcell's posthumous *A Collection of Ayres*, 1697.

One other broadside was sung to the tune: "The Young Mens Advice to Proud Ladies," 1692, beginning "Ladies of London I strange [sic] and admire" (Lord Crawford 744, with meaningless music). The tune was used in three ballad operas: *Chuck,* 1729, Johnson's *The Village Opera,* 1729 (with music), and Drury's *The Mad Captain,* 1733.

How Can I Be Merry or Glad

This tune is found in *Youth's Delight on the Flagelet,* 9th ed., c. 1690, 11th ed., 1697 (Fig. 196). Its name derives from the first line of

196

Original an octave higher.

"The Unconstant Shepherd," a ballad of about 1690 "To an Excellent New Tune," beginning "Oh, how can I be merry or glad" (Pepys, Lord Crawford, Douce, Madden, Euing; reprinted in *BB* II, 981). "An Answer to the Unconstant Shepherd," beginning "My Dear let nothing trouble thy Heart," is also "To an excellent New Tune" (Pepys, Bagford; reprinted in *BB* II, 508; Lord Crawford 832 contains the music).

The following ballad and its sequel name the tune as "O How can

I be merry or glad": "The Merchants Son of Exeter," beginning "Susan a Mercers Daughter dear" (Pepys III, 365); "An Answer to The Merchants Son of Exeter," beginning "Disloyal lovers listen now" (Pepys III, 366). The tune is "How can I be merry or glad" in "The Undutiful Daughter of Devonshire," beginning "Behold I am an aged Man" (Pepys III, 388, BM C.22.f.6 [195], Lord Crawford 175, Douce I, 58ᵛ, Harvard). It is "How can I be merry and glad" in "The Loyal Soldier of Flanders," beginning "Young Thomas he was a proper Lad" (Pepys, Euing, Lord Crawford, Harvard, Roxburghe; reprinted in *RB* VII, 750); and it is "Merry and Glad" in "The Pretended Country Squire," 1692, beginning "Come Listen, while I here unfold" (Pepys V, 393, Chetham 1035), and "The West-Country Lady," beginning "Young Lasses now of beauty bright" (Pepys IV, 14).

How Can the Tree

This tune takes its name from Lord Vaux's poem, "No pleasure without some paine," beginning "How can the tree but waste and wither away" (*Paradise of Dainty Devices,* 1576, ed. Rollins, 1927, No. 71). The tune is found with Vaux's text in William Barley's *A New Booke of Tabliture,* 1596, Part III, sig. C3ᵛ (Fig. 197); in BM MS Add. 24665, fol. 27ᵛ, c. 1615–1626 (printed in *Giles Earle His Booke,* ed. Peter Warlock, 1932, p. 37); and in the Leyden MS, fol. 14ᵛ, 1639 (Natl. Lib. of Scotland). Lute accompaniment to the song appears in Brogynton MS 27, p. 125

(c. 1595, Natl. Lib. of Wales), and consort parts are in Cambridge University MSS Dd.4.23, fol. 23 (cittern) and Dd.5.20, fol. 2 (bass viol). A version of the text without music is preserved in BM MS Harl. 6910, fol. 168ᵛ. Vaux's poem is echoed in the anonymous *Sir Clyomon and Sir Clamydes*, 1599, sig. D4ᵛ, where Neronis reads or recites verses beginning "How can that tree but withered be."

"How can the tree" is cited as a tune for singing a ballad "Of King Edward the second, being poysoned," beginning "The Kings curst keepers ayming at reward," in Thomas Deloney's *Strange Histories*, 1602 (*Works*, ed. Mann, pp. 405ff.).[1]

How Cruel Is Fortune Grown

An anonymous poem beginning "How cruel is Fortune grown,/to turn all my hopes to despair" in *The Wits Academy*, 1677, is found with music in *Choice Ayres and Songs*, Second Book, 1679, p. 9 (Fig. 198). A broadside version with expanded text is "Unconstant Phillis. Or, The Infortunate Shepherds Lamentation . . . To an excellent new play-

198

---

[1] Deloney's text is accompanied by unbarred music in recitative style, suitable for singing four of the six lines in each stanza; "How can the tree" is an alternate tune whose familiarity to the reader could be assumed.

house Tune: Or, Tell me no more you love" [1] (Wood E.25 [13], Rawlinson 121, Lord Crawford 525). The playhouse tune was evidently that printed in *Choice Ayres*. "How cruel is Fortune Grown" is named as the tune for singing a ballad of 1686, "The faithful Subjects new Song, of the Kings Royal Person," beginning "How patient is our King,/Against those that Rebell" (Library of Congress Broadside Portfolio 265, No. 4; the sheet, headed "The Royal Songs," contains two other encomiums upon James II).

How Happy's the Lover

A playhouse song beginning "How happy's the [*or that*] Lover who after long Years," with music composed by Bernard Berenclow, was included in *Comes Amoris*, Third Book, 1689, p. 1 (Fig. 199), and in *The*

199

---

[1] The second tune gets its name from the opening line of "Love al-a mode," which is "to an Excellent, and Familiar new Tune" whose identity I cannot establish (Pepys III, 102). "Tell me no more you love" is also the tune for singing "The Bridewel Whores resolution," beginning "The sorrows that I have known" (Rawlinson 98).

Banquet of Musick, Fourth Book, 1690. It was expanded to ten stanzas in a broadside entitled "The Happy Lovers: Or, The Damsel's Invitation to her Gallant to Prepare to be happy to Morrow" (Lord Crawford 527, with meaningless music). A half-stanza parody, beginning "How happy's that Husband who after few Years," is in *Pills,* 1719–1720, VI, 241, with the tune named but not reproduced.

How Lovely's a Woman

A song beginning "How lovely's a Woman before she's enjoy'd," with music by John Reading, appeared in *The Theater of Music,* Fourth Book, 1687. It was reissued on a small quarto engraved sheet under the title "A Song in commendation of Musick, Women and Wine," c. 1690 (BM C.180.a [40]). A broadside dated 1695 (Manchester I, 49) expands the verse from four to nine stanzas and includes a good musical text (Fig. 200); undated variant issues (in Pepys V, 220, and Lord Craw-

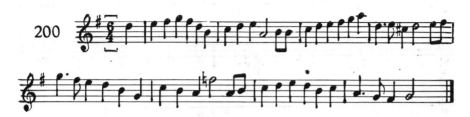

* E in original; D in *Theater* and *Pills*.

ford 534) contain meaningless music. *Pills,* 1719–1720, III, 205, reprints the original 1687 text and tune.

Another broadside to the tune is "An Excellent new Song, Called, The slighted Lover, or The Scornful Miss," beginning "O why am I allways perplexed in mind" (Pepys V, 355, Lord Crawford 941).

How Unhappy a Lover Am I

"Towzer Discover'd; or a New Ballade on an Old Dog That Writes Strange-Lee," 1683, an attack on Sir Roger L'Estrange, beginning "How unhappy a Mastiffe am I," is to the tune "Oh how unhappy a Lover am I" (Bodleian Ashmole G.16 [4], Harvard, Yale). The tune name links the broadside with the song which it parodies—a dialogue in Dryden's *Conquest of Granada,* Part II, 1672, IV, iii, beginning "How unhappy a lover am I." Words of the song were reprinted in 1671 in *The New*

Academy of Complements and *Westminster Drollery*,[1] in *Windsor Drollery*, 1672, and with music by Nicholas Staggins, in *Choice Songs and Ayres*, 1673, p. 38 (Fig. 201), and *Pills*, 1719–1720, III, 166.

How Unhappy Is Phyllis in Love,
or Let Oliver Now Be Forgotten

Thomas D'Urfey wrote "An Excellent New Ballad," 1681, beginning "Let Oliver now be forgotten," to the tune of "How Unhappy is Phillis in Love" (BM Luttrell, Bodleian Ashmole G.16, London Society of Antiquaries, Harvard, Huntington, Clark, Yale; 1682 ed., Lord Crawford

[1] In *Westminster Drollery* the song is directed to be sung to the tune "How severe is forgetful old age." A poem with that opening line appeared in *The New Academy of Complements*, 1671, in *Westminster Drollery*, and with music by Pelham Humphrey, in *Choice Songs and Ayres*, First Book, 1673. If an earlier tune for "How severe" existed, it apparently has not survived.

759). The verses were printed in D'Urfey's *New Collection of Songs and Poems,* 1683, as "Tony: A Ballad made occasionally by reading a late Speech made by a Noble Peer" (reprinted in *RB* V, 267). The ballad with music is in *180 Loyal Songs,* 1685, and the tune title is named as on the broadside. Words and music in *Pills,* 1719–1720, II, 283, bear the title "Old Tony, a song. The Tune, How happy is Phillis in Love." D'Urfey pictured Anthony Cooper, Earl of Shaftesbury, in an unattractive light as a vacillating statesman with traitorous heart; his ballad was calculated to make a strong appeal to those who sided with the king and James, Duke of York. D'Urfey's song gave new names to the tune—"Let Oliver now be forgotten" and "Tony" or "Old Tony"— though the original name (which I have been unable to trace to its source) was not entirely displaced.

Music of "Let Oliver now be forgotten" is found in Matthew Taubman's *An Heroick Poem,* 1682, p. 9 (Fig. 202), coupled with a song "Philander" beginning "A pox on the factious o' th' C[it]y," in *Musicks Recreation on the Viol, Lyra-way,* 1682, and in Humphry Salter's *Genteel Companion . . . for the Recorder,* 1683. And the following broadsides contain the music: "Tony's Lamentation: or, Potapski's City-Case," 1682, beginning "Alas! poor Unfortunate Tony" (Chetham 243, Harvard, Yale, Huntington); "The Conspiracy: or, The Discovery of the Fanatick Plot," 1683, beginning "Let Pickering now be forgotten" (Wood 276a, Harvard, Clark; reprinted in *180 Loyal Songs* and *RB* V, 311); "The Loyal Caution To all the Kings Friends" [1683?], beginning "Let Plotters never be forgotten" (Harvard, Yale).

The tune is cited in a number of political ballads without music: "The Ignoramus Ballad," 1681, beginning "Let Fourty eight now be remember'd" (BM 1871.e.9 [64], Harvard, Yale, Huntington); "An Excellent New Ballad, Of the Plotting Head," 1681, beginning "You Presbyters now Relent," to "How Unhappy is Phillis in Love, Or, Let Oliver now be forgot" (BM 1872.a.1 [74], Chetham 171, Huntington); "A New Ballad of the Protestant Joyner. Or of Colledges Lamentation since his Condemnation," beginning "The Protestant Joyner is carried," to the tune of "Tony, Or, How unhappy in love is Philander" (Harvard); "The Traytors Last Farewel . . . Sir Thomas Armstrong . . . Executed . . . 20th . . . June, 1684," beginning "Old Tony he led you to Ruin" (Harvard).

Among the nonpolitical ballads to the tune are "The Quarrelsome Lovers: Or, The successless Woeing," beginning "Of late I did hear of a Woeing," to the tune of "Old Tony, Or let Oliver now be forgotten" (BM C.22.f.6 [169], Harvard, Lord Crawford 960), and "[The?] Lovers Paradice, or, The Transported Lover," beginning "[?Let Nym]phs and kind Shepherds Caress it" (Douce I, 129ᵛ).

202 [G3]

* Note lacking in Taubman; supplied from *180 Loyal Songs,* p. 1.

The first strain of "How unhappy is Phyllis in love" is approximated in "An old woman clothed in grey," but the second part of this eighteenth-century tune is entirely different in harmony, phrasing, and total length, so that the two airs are not interchangeable. On the latter tune, see "Kind husband and imperious wife."

[How Vile Are the Sordid Intrigues]

Thomas D'Urfey wrote "How vile are the sordid intrigues of the town" for his play *The Marriage-Hater Match'd,* 1692, II, i, and introduced it also into *The Richmond Heiress,* II, ii, the following year. With music (Fig. 203) it appears in *Comes Amoris,* Fourth Book, 1693, p. 8 (facsimile in C. L. Day's *The Songs of Thomas D'Urfey,* p. 99),

203

and in an engraved song sheet entitled "The Disconsolate Ladys Complaint" (BM C.180.a [30], c. 1693), the music there attributed to Purcell.

A broadside entitled "The Discontented Lady" containing meaningless music expands the text to six stanzas (Lord Crawford, BM C.39.k.6; reprinted in *OPB*, p. 31).[1] A text of three stanzas without music is in *The Compleat Academy of Complements*, 1705.

The Hunt Is Up

Lute arrangements of this tune are in Folger MS 448.16, fol. 12, c. 1570 (Fig. 204) and *Het Luitboek van Thysius*, c. 1600, No. 77 (Fig. 205); early seventeenth-century versions are BM MS Egerton 2046, fol. 32, and Cambridge University MS Dd.3.18, fols. 4, 13ᵛ. Simpler settings for cittern are in Thomas Robinson's *New Citharen Lessons*, 1609, Cambridge University MSS Dd.4.23, fol. 4ᵛ, and Dd.14.24, fol. 11, and *Musick's Delight on the Cithren*, 1666. Still another tablature version is in

[1] Rollins (*Anal. Index*, No. 600) would associate a Stationers' Register entry "The discontented lady," 1656, with the Crawford-Osterley Park broadsides of the 1690s (Charles Bates, the printer, was apprentice until July 7, 1690); but D'Urfey's authorship is decisive.

204

Tablature contains no time signs above the notes; values given to the C–E♭ chord in measure 3 and B♭–D in measure 8 are arbitrary.

Musicks Recreation on the Viol, Lyraway, 1661. J. J. Starter's Dutch songbook *Friesche Lust-Hof*, 1621, contains an example of the tune, here called "O myn Engeleyn, ô myn Teubeleyn." [1] An untitled virginal set of the mid-seventeenth century, signed R. Cr[eigton], is preserved in Paris Conservatoire MS Rés. 1186, fol. 59ᵛ. A set of keyboard variations by Byrd on a different "Hunt's up" tune, in his *My Ladye Nevells Booke*, No. 8, appears in *The Fitzwilliam Virginal Book*, No. 276, as "Pescodd Time," though having no relation to the usual form of the latter tune. Another Byrd setting of "The Hunt's up" with a different order of variations and two new sections is in *Fitzwilliam*, No. 59. As is often the case with very popular tunes, most of these settings assume a prior familiarity with the air and seldom state it in an unembellished form.

A ballad "ye hunte ys up" licensed in 1565–1566 has not survived. Professor Rollins has pointed out (*Anal. Index*, No. 1175) that J. P. Collier's texts in his *Extracts*, I, 129–130, are spurious. A moralized version in *A Compendious Book of Godly and Spiritual Songs*, 1567, ed. A. F. Mitchell, 1897, pp. 174–175, may echo the original text in its opening lines:

> With huntis vp, with huntis vp,
>   It is now perfite day,
> Jesus, our King, is gaine in hunting,
>   Quha lykis to speid thay may.

[1] A variant of the tune was used in a Thuringian "Singspiel" in 1630. See Erk and Böhme, *Deutscher Liederhort*, III, 18. In the second half of the tune Continental sources depart from the English versions both melodically and harmonically.

205

The strong doctrinal bias of the Scottish text is evident from the fourth stanza:

> The hunter is Christ, that huntis in haist,
>> The hundis ar Peter and Paull,
> The Paip is the Fox, Rome is the Rox,
>> That rubbis vs on the gall.[2]

"A pleasant newe Ballad, of . . . her Maiestye . . . entring into the three and fortith [year of her reign, Nov. 17, 1600]," beginning "Ring out your bels!/what should yow doe els?," is to the tune "The Queene's hunt's vp" (*SB*, p. 179). The six-line stanza fits the music, with the three-line refrain requiring a repetition of the second strain. A song to the tune "The Queenes Majesties new Hunt is vp" in four-line stanzas is Anthony Munday's "Women are strongest: but Trueth overcommeth all things," beginning "It neither is the mightie King,/nor any men beside," in his *Banquet of Daintie Conceits,* 1588. The measure fits the "Hunt is up" music, but I have found no copy of the tune called by Munday's extended title.

"Soet Olivier," the name given to the tune in *Het Luitboek van Thysius,* is probably derived from a lost ballad registered in 1584 as "O swete Olyuer Leaue me not behind the." [3] In *As You Like It,* III, iii, Touchstone sings a couple of scraps that indicate the stanza form (exactly fitting "The Hunt is up" tune), if not the actual beginning of the ballad:

> O sweet Oliver,
> O brave Oliver,
> Leave me not behind thee; . . .
>> Wind away,
>> Begone, I say,
> I will not to wedding with thee.

---

[2] An English religious parody is found in BM MS Add. 15233, fol. 33 (mid-sixteenth century), attributed to John Thorne. J. O. Halliwell[-Phillipps] reprinted this text at the end of his edition of *The Moral Play of Wit and Science,* Shakespeare Society, 1848, pp. 65–68.

[3] In 1586 a moralized parody "O Sweete Olyver altered to ye scriptures" was entered. Rollins (*Anal. Index,* No. 1995) notes a number of references to the ballad.

Merry Drollery, 1661, I, 20, and several other miscellanies of the period print "A Catch" in a single stanza which would fit the tune:

> The Hunt is up,
> The Hunt is up,
> And now it is almost day,
> And he that's abed with another man's wife,
> It's time to get him away.[4]

Inasmuch as "hunt's up" was a generic term for an aubade, or, more specifically, a hunter's reveille, it is not surprising that there should be "Hunt's up" songs in other rhythmic patterns designed for melodies other than the tune that became popular. In 1537, for instance, information was brought against John Hogon for singing a seditious song beginning "the hunte is vp, the hunte is vp," whose structural pattern is too ample and too irregular to fit the tune.[5] Likewise, Thomas Deloney's ballad to the tune "The hunt is vp" does not fit; it is "A New Sonnet, conteining the Lamentation of Shores wife," beginning "Listen, faire Ladies,/Vnto my misery" (*Garland of Good Will,* 1631; in *Works,* ed. Mann, pp. 302ff.). "A Hunts vp" by the madrigal composer John Bennet is a good example of the formal tradition at work with the common elements of a hunting song. It has the same short metrical phrases and can actually be sung to the popular tune, with a repetition of several strains, but it had its own four-part composed music, which Thomas Ravenscroft printed in his *Briefe Discourse,* 1614. The first stanza is:

> The Birds they sing, the Deare they fling,
>   hey nony nony nony no,
> The Hounds they crye, the Hunters they flye,
>   hey tro li lo, tro lo li lo, hey tro lo li lo li li lo.
>
> [Cho.] The hunt is vp, the hunt is vp,
>   Sing merrily wee, the hunt is vp.

The author (Puttenham?) of *The Arte of English Poesie,* ed. Willcock and Walker, 1936, p. 17, notes that "one Gray" was held in good esteem by Henry VIII and later by the Duke of Somerset "for making certaine merry Ballades, whereof one chiefly was, *The Hunte is vp, the hunte is vp.*" *The Complaynt of Scotland,* 1549, lists "The hunt is up" as a tune

[4] Reprinted in Ritson's *Ancient Songs,* 1790, p. lvi. As a catch the song would require a different tune, in which each pair of measures (possibly each group of four bars) must agree harmonically.

[5] *Ballads from Manuscripts,* ed. F. J. Furnivall, 1868–1872, I, 310.

for dancing. In neither case can we be sure whether ballad or tune is that presently under discussion, although there is no strong reason to doubt the antiquity of the tune.

Hyde Park

As "Hide Parke" this tune is in the first three editions of *The Dancing Master* (1651, p. 91 = Fig. 206), but it is called "New hidd parke" in a

Original is unbarred and a major third higher.

seventeenth-century virginal arrangement in New York Public Library MS Drexel 5612, p. 183.[1] Though it was probably not so intended, Richard Climsell's ballad of 1632 to the tune of "the second part of Hide Parke" may be satisfactorily sung to it: "The praise of London: Or, A delicate new Ditty, which doth invite you to faire London City," beginning "All you that delight in Pastime and Pleasure" (Pepys; reprinted in *PB* II, 220).

"A Song, call'd Hide Park. The tune, Honor invites, you to delights, Come to the Court and be all made Knights," found in *Westminster Drollery*, 1671, begins "Come all you noble, you that are neat ones,/ Hide-Park is now both fresh and green" and can also be sung to the tune of "Hyde Park."[2] The tune named in the drollery is apparently derived from the two-line refrain of a song, without tune direction, entitled

[1] The Drexel MS contains another "Hidd Parke" in the same rhythmic pattern, except that its twelve bars are in two groups of six, instead of the usual four-measure units.

[2] Another version, beginning "Come all you nobles that are great ones," is in Bodleian MS Ashmole 421, fol. 177ᵛ.

"Verses upon the Order for making Knights of such persons who had £40 per annum in King James I Time," beginning "Come all you farmers out of the country" (BM MS Add. 5832, fol. 205; reprinted in Chappell, *PMOT* I, 327, and in Ebsworth's edition of *Choyce Drollery*, p. 295). The date is uncertain; the poem is in an eighteenth-century manuscript collection but is said to have been copied from the Crewe MS, on which I have no data. In the same meter is "The Honest Mans immaginary Dreames," c. 1648, beginning "You that desire for to be inriched," to the tune "Honour Invites" (Manchester; reprinted in *CP*, p. 225).

"The Penitent Gallant," beginning "There was, I must tell you, a Jocular Spark," is to the tune of "Hide Park" (Pepys IV, 138); it appears to have been sung, not to the *Dancing Master* tune, but to "The Crossed Couple," q.v.

I Am a Poor and Harmless Maid, or In My Freedom's All My Joy

One of John Playford's earliest musical instruction volumes, *A Booke of New Lessons for the Cithern & Gittern*, 1652, contains a cittern setting of a four-stanza poem beginning "I am a yong and harmlesse Maid/And some are pleas'd to call me faire," with a refrain "Yet in my freedome is my joy." The song was included in a later edition of this work, *Musick's Delight on the Cithren*, 1666. A version of the poem in Bodleian MS Ashmole 36–37, fol. 190ᵛ, may be older than either printed copy; it is without music and begins "I am a poore & harmeles Maid." With similar opening line a contemporary vocal setting of the tune (air and bass with one stanza of the poem) is preserved in Edinburgh University Library MS Dc.1.69, p. 131, c. 1650–1675 (Fig. 207).

An expansion of the text to nineteen stanzas appeared on a broadside titled "The Vertuous maids Resolution," registered in 1656. The tune is named "I am a poor and harmless maid," and two stanzas of narrative precede the soliloquizing lines of the original poem (Manchester, Pepys, Rawlinson, Roxburghe; reprinted in *RB* VII, 144).

An imitation of the original poem is "The Committe[e]-mans Complaynt," beginning "I am a poore Committee man/Some men are

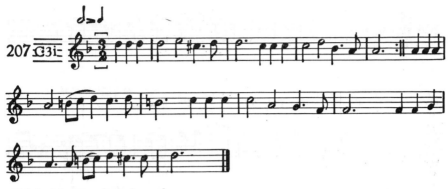

207 𝄵

Original is irregularly barred.

pleas'd to terme me knaue," with a burden "For in my Couzonage was my ioy" (BM MS Add. 22603, fol. 67, a mid-seventeenth-century commonplace booke).[1]

An early Restoration broadside to the tune is "The Royall Oak, or the wonderfull Travells . . . of . . . Charles the Second," by J. W[ade?], beginning "Come friends and unto me draw near," to the tune "In my freedom is all my Joy" (Euing; reprinted in *RB* VIII, lxv*). *Westminster Drollery,* 1671, contains two poems to the tune "My freedom [which] is all my joy": "The Wooing Rogue," a rather gamey parody beginning "Come live with me and be my Whore"; and "On a Gentleman," beginning "Poor Cloris wept, and from her eyes."

A distinct feature of this tune is that it calls for a seven-line stanza in which the sixth line is the burden, repeated in the seventh.

I Am Come to Lock All Fast

"An Excellent New Song, Call'd, Lock all Fast, or Secret Love," 1693, beginning "I am come to lock all fast" (Pepys V, 200), with the music (Fig. 208), is an expanded version of the stage song in Purcell's *The Fairy Queen,* 1692, Act II. The tune was added to *Apollo's Banquet,* 7th ed., 1693, Third Part, and the words were reprinted in such miscellanies as *Wits Cabinet,* c. 1700, *The Compleat Academy of Complements,* 1705, and *Pills,* 1719–1720, VI, 77 (one stanza with music).

[1] A broadside of 1647 among the Thomason Tracts in the British Museum is entitled "The Committee-mans Complaint, and the Scots Honest Vsage" but is unrelated to the MS poem.

208

No other broadside seems to have been sung to the tune. In Cibber's ballad opera, *Love in a Riddle*, 1729, the fourth air in Act III is Purcell's music, untitled.

I Am Confirm'd

This tune takes it name from the opening line of a poem by Suckling set to music by Henry Lawes in *Select Musicall Ayres and Dialogues*, 1652, Part I, p. 10 (Fig. 209). This song is found also in John Gamble's

209

MS Commonplace Book, 1659, No. 114, and in *Musick's Delight on the Cithren,* 1666.

The music was used for at least one broadside: "A New and True Ballad of the Poet's Complaint," c. 1675, beginning "Faith i'm a Dog if I can guess," to the tune of "I am Confirm'd" (BM C.22.f.6 [10], Lord Crawford 378, Douce II, 179, Harvard).

I Am the Duke of Norfolk

This tune appears as "Pauls Steeple" in the first ten editions of *The Dancing Master,* 1651–1698 (1651, p. 69=Fig. 210). In another Playford publication, *The Division-Violin,* 1685, there are two sets of variations on the tune, the first called "Duke of Norfolk or Pauls Steeple," the second reversing the order of the two names. Elizabeth Rogers's Virginal Book (BM MS Add. 10337, fol. 33), compiled before 1656, uses the tune as the basis of an untitled piece. It appears twice in John Gamble's MS Commonplace Book, 1659, No. 49, set to a political ballad beginning "God bless our noble King, was there ever such a thing"; and No. 70, beginning "The purelinges of the City both zealous men & witty." "Johne Andersonne My Jo" in the Skene MS (printed in Dauney, *Ancient Scotish Melodies,* 1838, p. 219) is clearly the same tune, even though the musical accent is shifted somewhat in the second strain.

While the original ballad on the Duke of Norfolk does not seem to have survived, an interesting traditional fragment fitting the tune has been preserved. A health sung at the Horkey, or harvest supper, is as follows:

To the Duke of Norfolk

I am the Duke of Norfolk,
Newly come to Suffolk,

210

Original is unbarred.

> Say, shall I be attended
> Or no, no, no?
> Good Duke, be not offended,
> And you shall be attended,
> You shall be attended
> Now, now, now.[1]

The earliest reference to the ballad I have found is in Fletcher's *Monsieur Thomas*, 1639, III, iii, where the Fiddler names it first among eight ballads he can sing. The earliest broadside calling for the tune is "A Lanthorne for Landlords," c. 1640, beginning "With sobbing grief my heart will break" (Pepys, Roxburghe; reprinted in *RB* I, 547). Another to the tune is a mock-heroic piece by John Taylor, the Water-Poet, "A dreadful Battle between a Taylor and a Louse," c. 1655, beginning "There was upon a time/A Taylor neat and fine" (BM C.20.f.14 [25], presumably the source of the reprint in *RB* VII, 479).[2] "God Speed the Plow, And Bless the Corn-Mow," beginning "My noble friends, give ear," is a dialogue between a servingman and a husbandman, the earliest

---

[1] *The Suffolk Garland,* Ipswich, 1818, p. 402. The compiler adds: "At the 'Harvest Supper,' one of the guests is crowned with an inverted *pillow,* and a jug of ale is presented to him by another of the company, kneeling, as represented in the vignette [reproduced at p. 337]. This custom has most probably some allusion to the homage formerly paid to the Lords of Norfolk, the possessors of immense domains in this county."

[2] A later edition of this broadside is entitled "The War-like Taylor" and begins "Once upon a time" (Lord Crawford 979, Pepys IV, 282, Harvard). A modernized reworking without tune direction is "A Bloody Battle between a Taylor and a Louse," beginning "A Taylor and a Louse,/Liv'd together in a House" (Roxburghe; reprinted in *RB* VII, 478).

edition dating from 1665 or earlier (Euing, Lord Crawford, Pepys, Rox-burghe; reprinted in *RB* VI, 523).[3]

A satirical ballad on Charles II, beginning "I am a senseless thing, with a Hey, with a Hey/Men call me a King, with a Ho," was written no later than 1680 to the tune of "I am the Duke of Norfolk." Though attributed to Rochester, it is not found in editions of his work, but it is included in such a miscellany as *Poems on Affairs of State*, 1704, III, 70. In 1681 the notorious Stephen College wrote "A Ra-Ree Show," beginning "Come hither, Topham, come, with a hey, with a hey,/Bring a Pipe and a Drum, with a ho," to the tune of "I am a Senceless Thing" (BM 1871.f.3 [5], Harvard, Huntington). The refrain tags, which include a closing line "With a hey, tronny, nony, nony, no," are common to both ballads and appear in at least three other contemporary poems having the same stanza structure. One of them, "A Satyrical Sonnet," 1678, on College, begins "Let the Commons hunt their Plots w[i]th a hey" (BM MS Harl. 7319, p. 68); another, "The Ballad," dated in MS 4 Feb. 1680/1, begins "Assist me some good spright with a hie, with a hie" (BM Lut-trell II, 10), and, like the preceding piece, is without tune direction; a third, entitled "Some nonsense," is to the tune of "the Magpyes" (on which I have no information) and begins "Old Wainscote is ith right with a hey with a hey" (BM MS Harl. 6913, p. 193; a modern transcript of a variant text is in Harvard MS Eng. 633, p. 150). Although the first two ballads cited in this paragraph are allied to "I am the Duke of Norfolk" and all five can be sung to that tune with slight adjustment of note values, the stanza pattern is much more closely akin to that asso-ciated with "Sound a Charge," q.v.

Other ballads to "I am the Duke of Norfolk" include: "The Maids new All-a-mode Pincushing," beginning "I am a maid of Flushing" (Pepys III, 178); and "The Lamentation of Seven Journey men Taylors," be-ginning "Attend and you shall hear" (Lord Crawford, Pepys, Douce, BM C.22.f.6, Harvard; partially reprinted in *RB* VII, 487). "The Tavern Query, or The Loyal Health" is a ballad upon the accession of Queen Anne, 1702, beginning "True English Boys be merry," to the tune of "Jolly Bacchus, or I am the Duke of Norfolk" (Pepys; reprinted in *PB* VII, 313). The first of these tune titles comes from "Bacchus's Health," an audience-participation song beginning "Here's a Health to Jolly

---

[3] A similar dialogue, beginning "Well met, my friend, upon the high-way, walking on" (*The Loyal Garland*, 1686, ed. J. O. Halliwell-Phillipps, 1850, p. 66), names no tune but can be sung to "I am the Duke of Norfolk." A nineteenth-century traditional sur-vival from Sussex is printed in J. H. Dixon's *Ancient Poems, Ballads, and Songs of the Peasantry of England*, 1846, p. 42. For references to reprints of this text and further discussion, see Margaret Dean-Smith, *A Guide to English Folk Song Collections*, 1954, s.v. "Husbandman and Serving-man."

Bacchus," which first appeared in *Apollo's Banquet*, Second Book, 1691, No. 75, with the music of "I am the Duke of Norfolk" and was reprinted with the music in all editions of *Pills* (1719–1720, III, 274). The tune was printed a second time in *Pills* (VI, 247) for a coarse song beginning "A Broad as I was walking, I spy'd two Maids a wrestling."

The tune is found in at least seven ballad operas, usually under the title "There was a bonny [or jolly] blade," as in *The Jovial Crew*, 1731; Phillips's *The Livery Rake*, 1733; Langford's *The Lover his own Rival*, 1736; all with music. In Ryan's *The Cobler's Opera*, 1729, it is called "My Wife she is dumb" in the text, but the tune is printed at the end under the old name, "I am ye Duke of Norfolk."

An eighteenth-century engraved song sheet uses the music for singing "The Lass with the Velvet A-se," beginning "There was a buxom Lass" (BM G.305 [26], c. 1710, BM H.1601 [459], c. 1720); new music is added for the chorus.

The same music in *Pills* serves for a song (1699, I, 293; 1719–1720, III, 276) beginning "There was a bonny Blade,/Had marry'd a Country Maid,/And safely conducted her home, home, home." An earlier version is a black-letter broadside of c. 1680, "The Dumb Maid: or, the Young Gallant Trappan'd," to the tune of "Dum, dum, dum: or, I would I were in my own Country" (Euing, Harvard, Lord Crawford, Roxburghe; reprinted in *RB* IV, 357).[4] The *Pills* text seems to be the source of later slip-song versions; Ebsworth printed one from his own nineteenth-century collection (*RB* IV, 356), and several American issues are extant (see G. Malcolm Laws, *American Balladry from British Broadsides*, 1957, Q 5), including one in *The Songster's Companion*, a Brattleboro, Vermont, publication of 1815. "The Dumb Wife" is frequently encountered in American tradition, the text strongly conditioned by modern stall copies. The old tune has, however, been displaced by a variety of airs (see the references to traditional texts and tunes in Laws).

A distant relative of "The Dumb Wife" is an eighteenth-century song beginning "There was a little Man, and he woo'd a little Maid,/And he said my little Maid will you wed?" The *Journal of the Printing-Office at Strawberry Hill*, ed. Paget Toynbee, 1923, p. 13, records that some copies of this ballad were struck off on May 31, 1764, and names the author as Sir Charles Sedley (great-grandson of the Restoration wit).[5] Facsimiles believed to be reprints of the original issue are conveniently reproduced in *A Bibliography of the Strawberry Hill Press*, ed. A. T. Hazen and J. P. Kirby, 1942, pp. 187–188. The copies are without music or tune direction. But a violin version of "I am the Duke of Norfolk,"

---

[4] The first tune title is internally inspired. "I would I were in my own country," q.v., is an independent tune, harmonically similar to "I am the Duke of Norfolk."

[5] Some catalogues erroneously credit the authorship of the ballad to Silvester Harding.

211

called "The little Man & Maid," appears in Thompson's *Compleat Collection of 200 Favourite Country Dances,* c. 1765–1775, II, 34. The same music is found with Sedley's verses in two Scotch songsters: Alexander Smith's *The Musical Miscellany,* 1786, p. 154, and David Sime's *Edinburgh Musical Miscellany,* 1792–1793, II, 266.[6]

English broadside editions with music include a Harvard exemplar of "The Little Man & Maid" (Fig. 211) and the second of "Two Favorite Madrigals for Three Voices" (BM G.808.g [22]). Sedley's poem in six stanzas (requiring a double repetition of the last syllable at middle and end of each stanza) concerns the simple courtship of a sentimental couple. Despite a few verbal echoes, it has no relationship to the narrative thread of "The Dumb Wife"; but a twelve-stanza amplification of Sedley, a Boston broadside of c. 1800 entitled "Matrimony" (Harvard; partially reprinted in *JAF,* LXII [1949], 425–426), shows the wife turning into a scold until sweet reason and motherhood dissolve the domestic friction. By contrast, the older poem was more forthright in depicting human nature: when the well-meaning husband has a physician loosen the tongue of his mute wife, she becomes a scold and there is no undoing the mischief.

6 Hazen and Kirby, p. 186, quote Mr. W. N. H. Harding on the initial Scotch popularity of the ballad and its appearance in *The Scots Nightingale,* 1778, and in the 1782 edition of *The Charmer.* For further information on currency, including its presence in *Mother Goose's Melody,* see Iona and Peter Opie, *Oxford Dictionary of Nursery Rhymes,* 1951, No. 326.

I Live Not Where I Love

The two earliest ballads related to this tune are:

1. The Constant Lover,
           Who his affection will not move,
           Though he live not where he love.

           To a Northerne tune called, Shall the absence of my Mistresse.

It was written by P[eter] L[owberry] and licensed in 1638 to Henry Gosson, whose edition is extant (Lord Crawford, Roxburghe; reprinted in *RB* I, 213). Its first stanza is as follows:

> You loyall Lovers that are distant
> from your Sweet-hearts many a mile,
> Pray come helpe me at this instant
> in mirth to spend away the while
> In singing sweetly, and compleately,
> in commendation of my love;
> Resolving ever to part never,
> though I live not where I love.

2. A Paire of Turtle Doves; Or, A dainty new Scotch Dialogue between a Yong-man and his Mistresse, both correspondent in affection, etc. To a pretty pleasant tune, called, The absence of my Mistresse, or I live not where I love.

This was written by Martin Parker and published by Thomas Lambert about 1640 (Roxburghe; reprinted in *RB* II, 317). Its first stanza is as follows:

> Must the absence of my mistresse,
> Gar me be thus discontent
> As thus to leave me in distresse
> And with language to lament?
> Nothing earthly shall divorce me
> From my deerest, but disdaine;
> Nor no fortune shall enforce me
> From my fairest to refraine.
> [Refr.] Oh! my deerest,
>   My heart neerest,
>   When shall I so happy bee
>   To embrace thee
>   And to place thee
>   Where thou nere maist part from me?

The dating of Parker's ballad is only approximate, and it is difficult on other evidence to assign priority here. Parker apparently derives his second tune title from the burden of Lowberry's ballad. But Lowberry's tune title appears to be a paraphrase of Parker's opening line. It is, of course, possible that both authors are alluding to a tune used in a lost ballad beginning "Shall the absence of my mistress"; and if this is the case Parker may be pointedly paraphrasing in his opening line. It is worth noting, too, that the stanza patterns are different. But the internal rhyme in the second half of Lowberry's stanza is paralleled in Parker's refrain, and one may assume that both ballads could be sung to the same tune if the first strain were repeated for lines 5–8 of Parker's stanza. While the dominant trochaic meter in the latter is not paralleled uniformly in Lowberry's verse, the differences could easily be accommodated through a division of an occasional musical note or a slight shift in time value.

Another ballad of about 1640 in Lowberry's stanza pattern is John Lookes's "The Ragman," beginning "There was a Ragman and a Mad man," to the tune of "Upon the highest Mountaines, or, The absence of my Mistresse" (Manchester, Roxburghe; reprinted in *RB* VII, 78, VIII, 777).[1]

"The absence of my mistress" is apparently not used again as a tune title, but "Though I live not where I love" appears on one other ballad that provides fresh links. It is T. R[obins]'s "The Valiant Trooper and pritty Peggy," beginning "Heard you not of a valiant Trooper" (Pepys IV, 40) with the burden

> But unconstant woman, true to no man,
> is gone and left me her bird alone.

This broadside, like the others to be cited, has an eight-line stanza with internal rhyme in lines 5 and 7; but the rather strict dissyllabic meter of the earlier pieces now gives way to a more fluid line, and, where there had been a maximum of eight syllables, we now find nine and ten in the verses of the first quatrain. With many musical texts such variation is of little consequence. Our only music which appears to be related to the ballads of around 1640, however, cannot easily be used with the Restoration broadsides. Forbes's *Cantus*, 1662, No. 45 (Fig. 212), beginning "With my Love, my life was nested," has the burden "Sith I live not where I love," and its music will fit the older ballads; but only with severe distortion can it be adapted to "The Valiant Trooper" and later broadsides.[2] Even this tune is advanced with diffidence, for the burden

---

[1] I have no data on the first tune title.

[2] Words and music are also preserved in Trinity College, Dublin, MS F.5.13, p. 37. In addition, Paris Conservatoire MS Rés. 1186, fols. 23, 57, contains two keyboard set-

212

Original is unbarred.

is too nearly a commonplace to support any positive relationship with ballads calling for the tune "I live not."

A reworking of "The Valiant Trooper," beginning "Did you not hear of a gallant Sailor," appears in *Pills,* 1719–1720, V, 80, with the refrain:

> Unconstant Woman proves true to no Man,
> She has gone and left me all alone.

Music printed with this text is clearly adapted to all but the three earliest broadsides, and although I have found no appearances of this tune before the 1707 edition of *Pills,* III, 156 (Fig. 213), there is every reason (because of the close similarity of the *Pills* poem to that of "The Valiant Trooper") to assume that the tune was in circulation a generation earlier than its record in print.

"A Voyage to Virginia: or, The Valliant Souldiers Farewel to his Love," beginning "My pretty Betty I now must leave thee,/the Drums doth summon me away," in some editions has the tune direction "She's gone and left me Bird alone," in others ". . . here alone" (Lord Crawford, Douce, Pepys, Roxburghe; reprinted in *RB* VII, 508, and in C. H. Firth's *An American Garland,* p. 46).[3] In "Cupids Delight," beginning "There was two Lovers that met together," the tune is "If the Door is locked where I have knocked; Or, The Valiant Trooper" (Roxburghe; reprinted in *RB* VII, 98).[4]

Two ballads of 1702 to the tune "Did you not hear of a Gallant Sailor" establish the existence of the reworked "Valiant Trooper" by that date. They are: "The Protestant Queen . . . Ann [proclaimed] 8th of March, 1702," beginning "I must confess that we all lamented,/the suddain Death of our Gracious King" (Lord Crawford, Pepys; reprinted in

tings of the mid-seventeenth century which take their titles from the opening line of the song.

[3] Firth believes that "A Voyage to Virginia" was originally written c. 1676, despite the date of 1685 on the Pepys copy, for Bacon's Rebellion was the only occasion requiring the dispatch of troops to America up to 1685.

[4] I have no data on the first tune title.

213

[Fine]   [D.C. al Fine]

214

Original is in key of F.

PB VII, 305); and "The Vigo Victory; or, The happy Success of the Duke of Ormond," beginning "Come listen now to the Nations glory" (BM 1871.f.3 [16]).

In *The Beggar's Opera* and *Achilles,* Gay calls the tune "Did you ever hear of a gallant sailor"; in Hippisley's *A Sequel to Flora,* 1732, Air 8 (Fig. 214), it is named "Inconstant Woman" from the burden of "Valiant Trooper."

Chappell (*PMOT* II, 452–453, 782) discusses the survival in tradition of the *Pills* song, "Unconstant Woman," sung in the nineteenth century to a different tune, which he prints. Here and there it has affinities with the *Cantus* tune of 1662, despite the obvious difference of movement and harmonic contour. Chappell also notes a survival, perhaps aided by print in the intervening generations, of Lowberry's "The Constant Lover" in much altered form. At the opening of the twentieth century, a song was collected in Sussex beginning "Farewell lads, and farewell lasses" which, though to a different tune, perpetuates some remnants of the old text, including the burden "I live not where I love" (*JFSS,* I [1904], 273).

I Loathe That I Did Love

Lord Vaux's poem "The aged louer renounceth loue," beginning "I loathe that I did love," was included in *Songs and Sonnets* (i.e., *Tottel's Miscellany*), 1557, and a broadside edition, now lost, was licensed in 1563–1564. Several MS commonplace books of the period contain the verses.[1] BM MS Add. 4900, fol. 62ᵛ, early seventeenth century (Fig. 215), is a

215

Original is unbarred.

setting with lute accompaniment, which seemed to Chappell the "regular composition of a musician," doubtless because of the repetitions required to swell the four-line stanza to a melody designed for six lines. In *Hamlet*, V, i, the gravedigger sings the first, third, and eighth stanzas of the ballad, distorted to suit his character.

A second tune for "I loathe that I did love" has been preserved. According to Chappell (*PMOT* I, 216) it was "written in characters of the times . . . on the margin of a copy of the Earl of Surrey's poems, in the possession of Sir W. W. Wynne." A dozen of these tunes, extracted from Wynne's volume, were reproduced in an edition of *Songs and Sonnets*, which G. F. Nott designed to augment his two-volume edition of *The Works of Surrey and Wyatt*, 1815–1816. This third volume was printed in 1809 but was never published.[2] Copies in the British Museum are with-

---

[1] Among them, Bodleian MS Ashmole 48, reprinted in Thomas Wright's *Songs and Ballads . . . Chiefly of the Reign of Philip and Mary*, Roxburghe Club, 1860, and BM MS Add. 38599, fol. 134ᵛ. See Professor Rollins's edition of *Tottel's Miscellany*, 1928–1929, II, 284.

[2] According to *CBEL* I, 403, the edition was destroyed by fire.

out music, but a copy preserved in the library of Arundel Castle contains the tunes, of which "I loathe that I did love" is No. 11, printed with five others on a leaf following p. 154 (Fig. 216). On a second leaf tipped in at

216

Original is unbarred.

the same spot, songs Nos. 10, 11, and 12 are harmonized by William Crotch.[3] Through the kindness of Professor Ruth Hughey, who has examined the Arundel Castle copy, I am able to give a transcript of the tune, which may date from the latter half of the sixteenth century.[4]

Some tune, at any rate, was used with the poem well before Shakespeare's time, for a song in the *Gorgeous Gallery of Gallant Inventions*, 1578 (ed. Rollins, p. 35), is "the Louer complayneth of his Ladies vnconstancy to the Tune of I lothe that I did loue," beginning "You graues of grisly ghosts/Your charge fro[m] coffins send."

I Love You More and More Each Day

This tune name is derived from the first line of a late seventeenth-century ballad, "The Constant Lover's Lamentation," with music on the sheet (Fig. 217) to fit the distinctive nine-line stanza (Pepys V, 299). The words alone are found in *Wits Cabinet*, c. 1700, and *The Compleat Academy of Complements*, 1705. Two other ballads sung to "I love you more and more each day" are printed with meaningless music: "The Witty Harlot; Or, The French King in the Powdering Tub," beginning "Great Lewis in a mighty heat" (Pepys; reprinted in *PB* V, 223), and "Oxford-

[3] Crotch apparently supplied Chappell with the music printed in *PMOT* I, 217, for Wooldridge's version of the text in *OEPM* I, 52, was "taken from a copy of the one printed by Dr. Nott, in the handwriting of Dr. Crotch," which was among Chappell's papers.

[4] E. F. Rimbault, in his *Musical Illustrations of Percy's Reliques*, 1850, p. 7, is inclined to attribute the airs to Surrey, but without evidence to support the suggestion.

217

* A in original.

shire Betty," beginning "Poor Tom the Tailor don't lament" (Pepys, BM C.39.k.6; reprinted in *RB* VII, 481, and *OPB*, p. 46).

A black-letter ballad "The Knight's Tragedy, or The Unfortunate Lovers last farewel," beginning "Forgive me if your looks (I thought)" (Pepys III, 379), has the same text as a roman-letter edition entitled "The Esquires Tragedy, or the Unfortunate Lovers last Farewel" (Pepys; reprinted in *RB* VIII, 637), both without music but with the tune direction "I love you more and more each day." From these sources the two opening stanzas of "The Despairing Lovers Complaint for Celias Unkindness" (Pepys V, 336, with meaningless music) are derived; the remaining four are new, and the stanzas are shortened by omitting the customary half-line repetition preceding the last line of each. Moreover, "The Despairing Lovers" is "To an Excellent New Tune," presumably the music by Robert King which had been printed with the first two stanzas in *The Banquet of Musick*, Second Book, 1688, p. 1 (Fig. 218).

At least five ballads name the tune "Forgive me if your looks I thought." These are: "Hells Nightwalker: Or, The Devil in Petticoats," beginning "Good people all I pray give ear" (Lord Crawford 441); "An Excellent New Copy of Verses . . . Thomas Cooke . . . Executed at Tyburn . . . 11th of August 1703," beginning "Unto my sad Complaint give ear" (Bagford; reprinted in *BB* I, 54); "The Barbarous Uncle," 1706, beginning "A Wealthy Squire in the North" (Lord Crawford 1252); "The Fatal

218

Virgin . . . Drowning herself In the River of Thames . . . 23d. of July, 1710," beginning "Good People listen and you'll find" (BM Huth 75); and "The Unfortunate Couple or The Unkind Father . . . Shot himself . . . L-d-g-te street," beginning "You Cruel Parents, most severe" (Harvard).

The original air "I love you more and more" remained in memory until beyond the middle of the eighteenth century, for "The Crafty Lover: Or, The Lawyer Outwitted," 1697, beginning "Of a Rich Counsellor I write" (Morgan 30), survives not only in *A Collection of Old Ballads,* 1723–1725, II, 234, but also in Aldermary and Bow Church Yard editions (Douce III, 14, Madden I, 182, Chetham 301, Harvard) which preserve the nine-line stanza and name the tune "I love thee more and more."

I Loved Thee Once,
I'll Love No More

This tune takes its name from the opening line of a poem, "To an Inconstant Mistress," composed by Sir Robert Aytoun about 1625 and found in *Le Prince d'Amour,* 1660. Henry Lawes wrote a sophisticated musical setting for it (*Select Ayres and Dialogues,* Second Book, 1669, p.

219

Original is unbarred.

30), but a simpler tune more suitable for ballad singing appeared in the second and third editions of *The Dancing Master,* 1652 and 1665 (1652, p. 51=Fig. 219).

It is probably to the earlier dance tune that the following ballad was sung: "The Passionate Louer," beginning "As I sate in a pleasant shade," to the tune of "I Lou'd thee once Ile loue no more" (Pepys; reprinted in *PB* II, 4).

I Never Saw a Face Till Now

This tune derives its name from the first line of a song written by Colonel (later Major General) Sackville for Southerne's play *The Disappointment,* 1684, I, i. With music by Simon Pack it was included in *A Collection of Twenty Four Songs,* sig. B1ᵛ (Fig. 220), in *180 Loyal Songs,* and in *The Theater of Music,* First Book, all 1685; it is found also in *Pills,* 1719–1720, IV, 303. The music alone appears in Humphry Salter's *Genteel Companion . . . for the Recorder,* 1683, among the unnumbered pages which were added at the end, in all likelihood a year or two after the original publication of this edition. The music is erroneously printed on some broadside copies of "State and Ambition" (Pepys V, 404), which has its own tune, and on "The Young Mans Joys Compleated" (Douce II, 263), which is to be sung to "O so ungrateful a Creature," an unrecorded air. Sackville's poem was included in *A New Garland,* c. 1685–1688, as "Love and Constancy."

"The Lovesick Shepherd Cured," beginning "Tell me, O Shepherd, why so sad," is to be sung to "We all to Conquering Beauty Bow, or, I

220

* Measure 5 appears twice in the original.
** Cadence note in measures 7, 14, 21, and 28 should extend through two measures.

never saw a Face till now" (Pepys V, 330, with meaningless music printed on the sheet). The first tune, q.v., is named from the beginning of a D'Urfey poem set to music by Dr. John Blow; despite the fact that D'Urfey's third line is "But I ne'er saw [or knew] a Face till now," the two tunes and their original words are entirely independent.

I Often for My Jenny Strove

This tune is named from the first line of a song published in *The Banquet of Musick*, Third Book, 1689, p. 23 (Fig. 221). The same air appears in *The Dancing Master*, 8th ed., 1690, *et seq.*, in *Apollo's Banquet*, 6th ed., 1690, and in Walsh's *Compleat Country Dancing-Master*,

1718; both words and music are in *Pills,* 1719–1720, III, 263. The original song was expanded into ten stanzas on a broadside, "The Constant Lovers," beginning "I often for my Joaney strove," on which the printed air is identified as a "New Northern Tune. I often for my Joaney, &c." (Pepys V, 253).

Among the many ballads sung to the tune, one is of special interest: "Cupid's Revenge," beginning "A King once Reign'd beyond the Seas,/ As we in ancient stories find" (Pepys, Harvard; eighteenth-century editions include Douce, Lord Crawford, Clark, Roxburghe; reprinted in *RB* VI, 661). This is a version of "King Cophetua and the Beggar Maid," a story several times referred to by Shakespeare (e.g., *Romeo and Juliet,* II, i; *2 Henry IV,* V, iii). An early ballad form appeared in Richard Johnson's *Crown Garland of Golden Roses,* 1612, sung, of course, to some older, unnamed tune. Percy prints a version of Johnson's text in his *Reliques.*

The following do not seem to have been reprinted: "The Disdainful Damosel," beginning "Now fifteen years are gone and past" (Pepys V, 209); "The Noble and Imprison'd Protestants . . . in the Castle of Dublin," beginning "What Protestant can now forbear" (Pepys IV, 63); "The Ploughman's Love and Loyalty," beginning "Sweet Joan my joy and hearts delight" (Pepys IV, 69); "The Surprized Lord & Lady," beginning "Of late we hear, in Devon-shire" (Pepys IV, 293); "The Ladies Looking-Glass; or, The Queen and the Cobler," beginning "A Queen beyond seas did command" (Pepys III, 95). The tune is called "I often with my Jemmy strove" in "Marage Forgotten, Or the Condiscending Shepherdess," 1689, beginning "As I was waliking [sic] over a Plain" (Pepys V, 231). Other ballads to the tune have been reprinted in *RB* or *PB;* the following was reprinted in *OPB,* p. 163: "The Contriving Lover," 1690, beginning "A Rich Old Miser of Renown" (Pepys, Lord Crawford, BM C.39.k.6).

The Jovial Crew, 1731, alone of the ballad operas, uses the tune and prints the music. Another late version of the air is found under the title "No charmes above her" in Dr. John Leyden's MS Lyra Viol Book, after 1690 (No. 73 in the G. F. Graham transcript). I have no information on the source of this tune name.

I Tell Thee, Dick

This tune is named from the opening line of a song written by Sir John Suckling upon the marriage of Roger Boyle, first Earl of Orrery, 1640. Conceived as a west-country rustic's humorous account of nuptials, the poem begins:

> I tell thee Dick where I have been,
> Where I the rarest things have seen;
>   Oh things without compare!
> Such sights again cannot be found
> In any place on English ground,
>   Be it at Wake, or Fair.

It was first published in Suckling's posthumous *Fragmenta Aurea,* 1646, and was reprinted in the following: *Wits Recreation Refined,* 1650; *Recreation for Ingenious Headpieces,* 1650; *Antidote against Melancholy,* 1661; *Merry Drollery,* 1661; *The New Academy of Complements,* 1671; *Wit and Drollery,* 1682; *Wit and Mirth,* 3d ed., 1682; *Pills,* all editions;

and also in such eighteenth-century miscellanies as *The Hive,* 3d ed., 1726, and *The Convivial Songster,* c. 1782. Ritson went back to the 1646 text in his *Ancient Songs,* 1790.

The music is found in *180 Loyal Songs,* 1685, pp. 244, 297; in *Pills,* 1719–1720, III, 132 (Fig. 222); and in the *Convivial Songster,* p. 10. Another tune (Fig. 223) is printed on a single-sheet edition of about 1720 entitled "A Comicall Parly between two Countrymen on sight of a Wedding" (BM H.1601 [218], Huntington, Harvard).

Although Suckling's poem does not appear to have been printed as a broadside, a number of ballads were written in imitation of it and were sung to the tune of "I [*or* I'll] tell thee, Dick." These include "The Cavaliers Complaint," 1661, beginning "Come Jack, let's drinke a pot of Ale" followed by "An Echo to the Cavaliers Complaint" on the same sheet (Chetham, Bagford, BM Thomason, BM Luttrell, Wood 416, Harvard; found also in *Merry Drollery* and *Antidote,* 1661, and in *New Academy of Complements,* 1671; reprinted in Wright, *Political Ballads,* 1841, p. 257). Another is "The Cavalier's Genius: Being a Proper New Ballad," c. 1663, beginning "Ch'ill tell thee Wat, ch'ave bin at Court," a clear imitation, despite the facetious tune title, " 'Ods bodikins chill work no more, and forty other good Tunes" (BM Luttrell II, 32, Wood 416 [78]). Two ballads of the 1680s to the tune are "The Plotting-Cards reviv'd, or the New Game of Forty One," c. 1681, beginning "Come, cut again, the Game's not done" (Huntington; reprinted in *180 Loyal Songs* and, incompletely, in *RB* V, 594); and "A New Ballad," on the restoration of Monmouth to Court after the Rye House Plot, beginning "Chil tell thee, Tom, the strangest story" (BM 1872.a.1, Bodleian Ashmole G.16, Wood 276a, Harvard, Clark; reprinted in *180 Loyal Songs* and *RB* V, 417).

Several comparable songs found their way into books rather than broadsheets. Of these the following name the tune: an unsigned song by Patrick Cary, c. 1651, beginning "And can you thincke that this translation/Will benefitt att all our nation" (*Trivial Poems,* ed. Walter Scott,

1820, p. 13); "A Christmas Song When the Rump was first dissolved," concerning events of 1653, beginning "This Christmas time, 'tis fit that we" (*The Rump*, 1660, *Rump*, 1662; reprinted in *Loyal Songs*, 1731, and Wilkins, *Political Ballads*, 1860, I, 117); "The Chequer Inn," 1675, beginning "I tell thee, Dick, where I have been,/Where I the Parliament have seen" (BM MS Harl. 7319, p. 33; printed, with an answer, in *Poems on Affairs of State*, 1704, III, 57). John Raymund's *Folly in Print, or a Book of Rhymes*, 1667, includes two pieces to the tune of "Sir John Sucklings Ballad." One is "A Ballad on a Friends wedding," beginning "Now Tom if Suckling were alive"; the other, which may be sung also to "I rode from England into France," is "Three merry Boyes of Kent," beginning "Of Mandeville, I do not tell."

A few pieces without tune direction are not only in the characteristic stanza form of "I tell thee, Dick" but imitate the opening lines of the original. These include "Upon Sir John Sucklings hundred horse," beginning "I tell thee Jacke thou'st give the kinge" (Bodleian MS Ashmole 36–37, fol. 53ᵛ, another copy, fol. 130; John Gamble's MS Commonplace Book, 1659, No. 104; printed in *Wit and Drollery*, 1656, p. 44, and *Le Prince d'Amour*, 1660). This lampoon on Suckling's raising a troop of horse at his own expense at the outbreak of civil war is followed in each copy by what purports to be Suckling's answer, beginning "I tell thee fellow [*or* fool] who e'er thou be." The Ashmole MS contains two copies of another poem beginning "I'le tell thee Dick where I have byne/ The rarest fights that I have seene" (fols. 51ᵛ, 292). *Merry Drollery Complete*, 1670, p. 317, has a poem "On the Printing of the Oxford Jests," beginning "I tell thee Kit, where I have been,/Where I the rarest Jests

have zeen"; and a very close imitation of Suckling's poem is "A Ballade on a Countrey Wedding," beginning "I Tell thee Jack as I zought out/ A stragling Lamb that stray'd about" (*Wit at a Venture*, 1674, p. 59). "A Song on a Wedding," beginning "Now that Loves Holiday is come" (William Hicks, *Grammatical Drollery*, 1682, p. 112), is similarly inspired.

Representative of a few broadsides which name the tune but do not imitate Suckling's poem are the following: "A New Ballad upon Dr. Oates His Retreat from White-Hall," 1681, beginning "Can'st tell me, Ceres, what curst fate" (Harvard, Yale, BM 806.k.16 [126]; reprinted in *180 Loyal Songs*, p. 248); and "The Countrymans Joy, At The Coronation Of King William & Queen Mary April the 11th 1689," beginning "Ods whirlikins! what mun Che do" (Pepys; reprinted in *PB* IV, 227).

A ballad on the battle of Audenarde, 1708, entitled "Jack Frenchman's Lamentation," beginning "Ye Commons and Peers," is directed to be sung to "I'll tell the[e] Dick, &c. Or, Who can but love a Seaman" (BM 1876.f.1 [40]); but the first tune does not fit the ballad. A song beginning "I'll tell thee, Dick, where I have lately been,/There's rare doings at Bath" (*Pills* VI, 282) has no relation to Suckling's ballad; it is usually titled "The Bath Teazers" and has its own music.

I Went from England into France

Music for this tune is found in John Gamble's MS Commonplace Book, 1659, No. 62 (Fig. 224), together with 21 stanzas of the poem whose opening line gives the tune its name. The verses are also found, without tune direction or music, in the second issue of Bishop Richard Corbet's *Certain Elegant Poems*, 1647, p. 80, and in his *Poems*, 1672, in *Musarum*

Deliciae, 1655, *Parnassus Biceps*, 1656, *Merry Drollery*, 1661, *Wit and Mirth*, 3d ed., 1682, in Bodleian MS Ashmole 36–37, fol. 44ᵛ, and in several other seventeenth-century manuscripts.[1]

I know of no broadside issue of "The Journey into France," but the tune was used for other broadsides. One was Sir John Denham's "Mr. Hampdens Speech against Peace at the close Committee," beginning "But will you now to Peace incline," to the tune "I went from England" (*Rump*, 1662, and *Loyal Songs*, 1731; earlier broadside copies, without tune title, are in BM Thomason, with the MS date 23 Mar 1642/3, in BM Luttrell and Bodleian Ashmole H.23; the piece was reprinted in Denham's *Poems and Translations*, 1668). The tune is called "I made a Voyage into France" in "An Exit to the Exit Tyrannus . . . Erasing that . . . Scandalous Motto . . . where King Charles the First Statue stood," beginning "After curs'd Traitors damned rage" (BM Thomason, Harvard, both copies bearing the MS date March 17, 1659/60; Wood 416, BM Luttrell, Bagford; reprinted in *RB* VII, 663).

"Three merry Boyes of Kent," beginning "Of Mandeville, I do not tell," is to the tune of "I rode from England into France, or Sir John Sucklings Ballad" (*Folly in Print*, 1667, p. 8). The second tune is "I tell thee, Dick," q.v.

I Would I Were in My Own Country

This tune appears as "Goddesses" in all editions of *The Dancing Master*, 1651–c. 1728 (1651, p. 52=Fig. 225), and in Walsh's *Compleat Country Dancing-Master*, 1718. An earlier keyboard setting by Giles Farnaby

[1] The poem has been attributed not only to Bishop Corbet but also to Suckling. G. Thorn-Drury, in his edition of *Parnassus Biceps*, 1927, p. 171, notes that in BM MS Egerton 923, fol. 77b, the poem is called "Goodwins Journey into ffraunce," and he follows Aubrey (*Brief Lives*, ed. A. Clark, 1898, I, 270) in proposing Thomas Goodwyn of Ludlow as the author. Thorn-Drury adds, "The whole tone of the piece seems to me quite out of keeping with anything Corbet is likely to have written, and I believe that the simple explanation of its ascription to him is that it has been confounded with a 'Iourney' he did write, the *Iter Boreale*." See Ebsworth's note in his edition of *Choyce Drollery*, 1876, p. 355, for references to MSS which assign the poem to Corbet and Suckling. V. de Sola Pinto and A. E. Rodway, who print the poem from the Taverham MS, c. 1600–1640, Nottingham University Library, in their collection *The Common Muse*, 1957, p. 133, make no reference to Corbet; moreover, their conjectured date of c. 1623 virtually removes Suckling from consideration, since he was born in 1609.

225

Original is unbarred.

in *The Fitzwilliam Virginal Book* is entitled "Quodling's Delight." [1] The form of the tune used in Gay's *Achilles*, 1733, as "Goddesses" is nearly identical with that which Chappell reproduced (*PMOT* II, 457) as from Sir John Hawkins's Transcripts of Music for the Virginals, where it was apparently called "I would I were in my own country."

The identity of the Hawkins Transcripts has not been established. The most likely candidate is New York Public Library MS Drexel 5609, an eighteenth-century compilation of keyboard pieces from many sources. This tune appears on p. 130 of the manuscript, evidently copied from the earlier Paris Conservatoire MS Rés. 1186, fol. 46 (Fig. 226). In neither manuscript, however, is the setting titled, and since it differs in detail from other musical texts, including the one Chappell printed, the case for the Drexel MS remains shaky. Furthermore, until it can be confirmed that this tune is somewhere called "I would I were in my own country," its association with ballads cited in the present discussion must be considered tenuous.

The ballad giving rise to the tune title is "The Northern Lasses lamentation, or The unhappy Maids Misfortune," beginning "A North Countrey Lass/up to London did pass," to the tune of "I would I were in my own Country" (Lord Crawford, Euing, Roxburghe; reprinted in *RB* VII, 168). This is a touching expression of homesickness, with a memorable refrain:

> O the Oak, the Ash, and the bonny Ivy Tree
> doth flourish at home in my own Country.

Nothing in the tenor of the ballad justifies Ebsworth in equating it with "The wanton Northerne lasse," licensed in 1640.

The same tune was probably used for "The Lancashire-Lovers: or, The merry Wooing of Thomas and Betty," beginning "My Betty thou knowst

---

[1] The tune does not fit the broadside "Loues up to the elbowes," which is directed to be sung to "Codlings" (*PB* II, 125). The Fitzwilliam collection also contains variations by Richard Farnaby on an air closely related to those cited; it is called "Fayne would I Wedd," from the concluding song in Thomas Campion's *Third and Fourth Booke of Ayres*, c. 1612, which begins "Faine would I wed a faire yong man."

I have courted thee long," to the tune of "Loves Tide: Or, At home would I be in my own Country" (Douce I, 134ᵛ; reprinted in *RB* VII, ix*).[2] The refrain here is strongly influenced by the earlier ballad:

> The Ash, and the Oak, and the Ivy-tree,
> Flourish bravely at home, in our own Country.

"The Dumb Maid: or, the Young Gallant Trappan'd," beginning "All you that pass along," is "To a new Tune, call'd, Dum, dum, dum: or, I would I were in my own Country" (Euing, Lord Crawford, Harvard, Roxburghe; reprinted in *RB* IV, 357). The first tune is another name for "I am the Duke of Norfolk," which is better suited to the four-line ballad stanza than is "I would I were in my own country." But the two tunes are closely related in both rhythmic and harmonic pattern.

I'll Go No More to the Old Exchange, or The New Royal Exchange

In *The Dancing Master*, 3d ed., 1665, p. 124 (Fig. 227), this tune appears as "The New Exchange"; the index lists it as "New New-Exchange"; in later editions it is called "The New Royal Exchange." [1]

[2] On "Love's tide" see "Wert thou more fairer."

[1] Another *Dancing Master* tune, which does not fit the necessary rhythmic pattern here, is called "The New Exchange" in the first edition, 1651; from the fourth edition,

227

Wit and Drollery, 1656, contains a song fitting the tune, though no tune direction is given: "On the Souldiers walking in the new Exchange to affront the Ladies," beginning "I'll go no more to the New Exchange,/ There is no room at all." In the same stanza pattern are a number of other poems inspired directly or indirectly by the poem of 1656, including another in *Wit and Drollery,* beginning "Wee'l go no more to Tunbridge wells,/The journey is too far." *Wit Restor'd,* 1658, contains "The Bursse of Reformation," beginning "We will go no more to the old Exchange,/ There's no good ware at all," and an answer beginning "We will go no more to the New Exchange,/Their credit's like to fall." *Merry Drollery,* 1661, contains "The New Exchange," a song licensed in 1658 which begins "I'll go no more to the Old Exchange,/There's no good ware at all," and continues in a nonpolitical vein, in contrast to the Royalist poems in *Wit Restor'd.*

A broadside to the tune "I'll go no more to the old Exchange" is "Loves Captivity and Liberty," beginning "Oft have I sworn I'll love no more" (Pepys IV, 5, Rawlinson 56). This is an expansion of a poem written by Henry Hughes, beginning "Oft have I swore," which Henry Lawes set to music in his *Ayres and Dialogues,* Third Book, 1658, p. 3. The tune title on the broadside clearly relates to the popular air and not to Lawes's music, for a refrain has been added to fill out the stanza to twelve lines, corresponding to the pattern in the other "Exchange" songs.

Another song to the tune of "I'll go no more to the New Exchange" is found in *Westminster Drollery,* 1672, II, 77, beginning "Never will I wed a girl that's coy."

1670, it is called "Durham Stable, or The New Exchange," in allusion to the fact that the Exchange, opened early in the seventeenth century, stood on grounds formerly occupied by the stables of Durham House.

I'll Never Love Thee More

This tune derives its name from the refrain of a song beginning "My dear and only love, take heed." Five stanzas of the text are found in *Wit and Drollery,* 1656, closely resembling the version in BM MS Harl. 2127, fols. 8, 5ᵛ (late seventeenth century). John Gamble's MS Commonplace Book, 1659, No. 274, contains a five-stanza text and the air with bass (Fig. 228). The tune, called "Never love thee more," is in *The Dancing*

Master, beginning with the 7th ed., 1686.[1] The words appear in *Pills,* 1719–1720, VI, 122, with a tune which appears to be a tenor part rather than a melodic line. The music printed for "William and Margaret. An old Scotch Ballad with the Original Scotch Tune" in Thomson's *Orpheus Caledonius,* 1725, No. 49, is actually a version of "I'll never love thee more." So is the tune called "Chevy Chase" in William McGibbon's *Collection of Scots Tunes,* 1742–1755, p. 108, and in a collection of airs for violin made by Samuel Wesley after 1774 (BM MS Add. 31763, fol. 18ᵛ); the same tune, printed with Montrose's "lines" in Johnson's *Scots Musical Museum* V, 464, is identified in Stenhouse's notes as "Chevy Chase." The broadside version is "Ile never Love thee more being a true Love Song between a young Man and a Maid," beginning "My dear and only

1 The tune was actually first printed in the 6th ed., 1679, Supplement, pp. 22–23. Page 22 is wanting in the only known (BM) copy, but the dance directions at the top of p. 23 agree perfectly with those accompanying the tune in the 1686 edition.

love take heed," to the tune of "O no, no, no, not yet" (Pepys III, 266, Rawlinson 190ᵛ).² Another broadside edition with the subtitle "Being the forsaken Lovers farewel to his fickle Mistress," is sung "To a rare Northern Tune, Or, Ile never love thee more," and begins "My dear and only joy, take heed" (Douce I, 101ᵛ).³ Both broadsides were printed in the neighborhood of 1675, but the ballad is more than half a century older, as we can see by the tune citations on other broadsides.

For example, "My deere and only Loue take heed" is the tune named in "The faythfull Louers resolution," printed for Philip Birch about 1620 (*PB* I, 169).⁴ "I'le neuer loue thee more" is named in "Tis not otherwise: Or: The praise of a married life," issued by George Blackwall about 1630 (*PG*, p. 356). Two ballads of about 1625 give the choice between "Oh no, no, no, not yet" and "I'll never love thee more": "Any thing for a quiet life" (*PB* II, 18), and "Good sir, you wrong your Britches" (*PB* I, 248).

Other ballads to "I'll never love thee more" include Thomas Jordan's "A Dialogue Betwixt Tom And Dick . . . March 28. 1660," beginning "Now would I give my life to see" (Lord Crawford, Bagford, BM C.20.f.2, BM Thomason, Bodleian Firth, Harvard, Roxburghe; ⁵ reprinted in *Ratts Rhimed to Death*, 1660, *Rump*, 1660, 1662, and *RB* VII, 672); "The Tragedy of Hero and Leander," beginning "Come mournful muse assist my quill" (Douce, Euing, Roxburghe; reprinted in *RB* VI, 558); ⁶ and "The Swimming Lady," beginning "The four and twentieth day of May" (Pepys, Douce, Morgan, Bagford; reprinted in *Pills* III, 96 [with different music] and in *BB* I, 142). To the tune of "I'le ever love the more" and in the same stanza pattern is "A Proper New Ballad, Being the Regrate of

² The tune name is from the burden of a second ballad on the sheet (without title, but beginning "A young man walking all alone/abroad to take the air"). In the versions of this piece found in the Percy Folio MS (ed. Hales and Furnivall, IV, 92) and in *Merry Drollery*, 1661, the refrain is "O nay, O nay not yet." A number of ballads, including several which originated in the first half of the seventeenth century, are sung to "O no, no, no not yet." I am inclined to consider this the name of an independent tune which has not survived, rather than a secondary name for "I'll never love thee more," with which it is sometimes coupled.

³ The first broadside is in eight stanzas, the second is in nine; the texts differ widely throughout, though they possess enough in common to be unmistakably related. The *Pills* text derives from the second broadside, but the other seventeenth-century versions cited are more closely akin to the first.

⁴ The first part of the ballad is reprinted in *Pills*, 1719–1720, IV, 59, with a new air by Samuel Akeroyde.

⁵ The Roxburghe copy has the title "A Pleasant Dialogue between the Country-Man and Citizen . . . March the 28, 1660."

⁶ "Hero and Leander, an Old Ballad" in W. Thomson's *Orpheus Caledonius*, 1733, II, No. 40, is a reworking of stanzas 2–5, 9–12 of the broadside; the music is a florid piece of contemporary composition.

a true Lover, for his Mistriss Unkindnesse," beginning "I wish I were those Gloves, dear heart" (Roxburghe; reprinted in *RB* VI, 584).

About 1643 James Graham, Marquis of Montrose, wrote a five-stanza poem to his mistress, beginning "My dear and only love, I pray," and incorporating the familiar refrain "I'll never love thee more." As we have already seen, the original ballad was well known some years before Montrose penned his lines. The poem is found in Watson's *Choice Collection of . . . Scots Poems,* Part III, 1711 (1869), p. 107, in Herd's *Scottish Songs,* 1776, I, 236, in *Poems of James Graham, Marquis of Montrose,* ed. J. L. Weir, 1938, p. 19, and on eighteenth-century broadsides; [7] in every case Montrose's poem is followed by a second part in thirteen stanzas, beginning "My dear and only love, take heed," which is in reality the original broadside. The 1733 edition of Allan Ramsay's *Tea-Table Miscellany* reprints Montrose's verses under the title "I'll never love thee more," I, 111, together with a song beginning "I toss and tumble thro' the night" to the tune of "Montrose's Lines," II, 152 (the latter reprinted in *A Complete Collection of . . . English and Scotch Songs,* 1735–1736, II, 81). The popularity of the song in Scotland is further suggested by the presence of the original tune, called "Montroses Lynes," in Dr. John Leyden's MS Lyra Viol Book, No. 59 (after 1690), and in the Blaikie Lyra Viol MS, No. 52, about 1745.[8]

Ianthe the Lovely

John Glanville's song, "The Happy Pair," beginning "Ianthe the Lovely, the Joy of her Swain," was first printed in *The Diverting Post,* 1705. It was soon thereafter issued as a broadside, "The Loyal Swain: or, The Happy Pair. Sung before Her Majesty . . . To a New Play-House Tune" (Bagford; reprinted in *BB* I, 110). This issue, with meaningless music, was published by Bridget Deacon, who succeeded her husband Jonah upon his death in 1704. A number of slip-sheet editions without music appeared during the eighteenth century (e.g., Roxburghe III, 502, 538, BM 1871.e.9 [125], BM 1876.f.1 [145]). Editions with music by John Barrett include "The Happy Pair. A Song Sung in York Buildings,"

---

7 "Montrose Lines: or, I'll never Love thee more," dated June 3, 1775 (BM 1876.f.1 [174]); another edition, "A Proper New Ballad," with tune direction "I'le never Love thee more" (Roxburghe; reprinted in *RB* VI, 581).

8 Both manuscripts exist only in transcripts; the former is in the National Library of Scotland, the latter in the Dundee Free Library.

229

c. 1710 (BM H.1601 [231]=Fig. 229), and another of c. 1715 (BM G.309 [71]). The tune, called "Ianthe," is found in *The Dancing Master*, 15th ed., 1713, and in Walsh's *Compleat Country Dancing-Master*, 1718. Words and music appeared in *Pills*, 1719–1720, V, 300, having been first included in the 1706 issue of volume IV.

Broadsides to the tune include "The Saylor's Complaint: or, the True Character of a Purser of a Ship," beginning "Of all the curst Plagues that e'er Fate did decree," to the tune of "Iantha" (Douce III, 85ᵛ, an early eighteenth-century issue published by William Onley, reprinted in *Naval Songs and Ballads*, ed. C. H. Firth, 1908, p. 233), and a ballad on Sir Robert Walpole's second marriage in 1738: "The Constant Lovers: or, the Pleasures of Matrimony," beginning "Lucinda the lovely,/The Joy of her Swain" (BM 1876.f.1 [110]). The latter, which does not name a tune, is in part a reworking of Glanville's original poem.

"A 'Squire's Choice," beginning "The World is a Bubble and full of Decoys," appears with Barrett's music in *Pills* VI, 38, and another song to the tune is at page 271 of the same volume: "Clarinda's Complaint," beginning "With sighing and wishing, and Green-sickness Diet." The tune was used in Gay's *The Beggar's Opera*, 1728, and in *Oxford Act*, 1733. And it appears in Johnson's *Scots Musical Museum* IV, 350, as the music for a song beginning "The tears I shed." Ebsworth (*BB* I, 112) reprinted a song to the tune from an undated pamphlet, *The Midship-Man's Garland*.

About 1750 Thomas A. Arne reset the poem, whose first line he gives as "Ianthe, the lovely, the joy of the plain" (BM G.316.c [8]). It was reprinted in the *London Magazine*, XXII (Jan. 1753), 37, and *Clio and Euterpe*, 1758–1762, I, 186. Another setting, by "Mr. Jackson of Exon.," is in *Vocal Music*, c. 1771, I, 175, and *Calliope*, 1788, p. 205. George A.

Stevens cites Arne's form of the first line as the tune name for his "Maria," beginning "One day, by appointment, Maria I met," in *Songs, Comic and Satyrical*, 1772, p. 151: presumably he intended that it be sung to Arne's rather than to Barrett's or Jackson's tune.

If Love's a Sweet Passion

Of all Henry Purcell's theater tunes, this was the most popular with the makers of broadsides. Introduced into the third act of *The Fairy Queen*, 1692, with words presumed to be by Elkanah Settle, the song was soon on the street in several forms, and within a short time some three dozen other ballads were capitalizing on the popularity of the tune.[1]

"If love's a sweet passion" was one of the ten included in Purcell's *Some Select Songs . . . in the Fairy Queen*, 1692, and an arrangement for strings appeared in his posthumous *Collection of Ayres*, 1697. The tune was added to *Apollo's Banquet* in the 7th ed., 1693. Meantime, the music had appeared on a broadside of 1692, "The Young Lovers Enquiry" (Pepys V, 173), which expanded the stage song from two to seven stanzas (Fig. 230).[2] And a correct score is to be found on two small engraved sheets probably dating from the early 1690s. One is "A Song in the New Opera call'd, The Fairy Queen," and the second is "A mock song to If love's a sweet passion," beginning "If wine be a cordial why does it torment."[3] Other engraved sheets of the original playhouse song appeared as late as 1740 (BM G.316.e [28], Harvard), and it is in all editions of *Pills* (1719–1720, III, 287). At least five ballads to the tune are on broadsides which contain meaningless music.

Ten ballads sung to "If love's a sweet passion" are reprinted in *PB*,[4]

[1] Some twenty-eight of these were collected by Pepys alone. See Roy Lamson, "Henry Purcell's Dramatic Songs and the English Broadside Ballad," *PMLA*, LIII (1938), 148ff. for a discussion of the variety of subjects upon which ballads were written to the tune. Both Lamson and Rollins (*PB* III, 223n.) list a number of eighteenth-century miscellanies reprinting the original song over a span of a century from its original appearance.

[2] Another contemporary edition, undated, contains meaningless music (Pepys V, 174). The seven-stanza text is found in later editions without music, which direct that it be sung "with its own proper Tune" (BM 1871.e.9 [34] and [49], Harvard).

[3] Nos. 13 and 12 respectively in BM C.180.a, a made-up collection of sheets known as *Joyful Cuckoldom*. "A mock song" was reprinted with the music in *Pills* VI, 82, and is sometimes found alongside the original song in eighteenth-century poetical miscellanies, e.g., *The Wreath*, 3d ed., 1753, Songs 4 and 5.

[4] Rollins, not taking account of the 1692 origin of "If love's a sweet passion," dates two ballads prematurely (*PB* III, 224 [1685?], V, 312 [1690?]). The historical basis of a

230

* E♭ in original.

and an almost equal number in *RB, BB,* and *OPB.* The following are among those apparently not reprinted: "The Wronged Lady," beginning "O Pity a Lover who lyes I declare" (Pepys V, 328, Lord Crawford 924), and "An Answer to The Wronged Lady," beginning "Was ever young Noble so tortur'd as I?" (Pepys V, 291); "The Unequal Match," beginning "I am a young woman, 'tis very well known" (Pepys III, 87); "Joan's Loving Letter," beginning "To thee, loving Roger, this letter I write" (Pepys III, 270); "The London Lottery," beginning "Attend to this Ditty, which fairly does treat" (Pepys V, 421, with meaningless music); "The Somersetshire Lady," beginning "I am a young wife that has cause to complain" (Pepys IV, 83); and "The Bucksome Lass of Westminster," beginning "You lusty young Batchelors pray now attend" (BM C.22.f.6 [89], Pepys III, 241, Lord Crawford 1409, Harvard).

The following are to be sung to either "Fond Boy" or "Love's a sweet Passion": "The Miserable Maulster," beginning "A Maulster that liv'd in the County of Kent" (Lord Crawford 799); "The Noble Funeral Of . . . the Duke of Grafton," beginning "As two men was walking down by the sea side" (BM 1876.f.1 [30], Morgan 76; partially reprinted in

third, "The Royal Dialogue," VI, 15, is an event of January, 1691, but the edition bearing this tune title could not have been published before the following year.

Sir A. W. Fitzroy, *Henry Duke of Grafton* [1921], p. 86);[5] "The West-Country Frolick," beginning "Pray did not you here of young frolicksome Kate?" (Douce III, 103ᵛ, Pepys V, 161, Lord Crawford 1008); and "The Shooemaker Out-witted," beginning "Good people I pray now attend to my moan" (Pepys III, 271). "The West-Country Wedding," beginning "Come all you old Bakers, attend and give ear," lists the full form of the tune title, "If Love's a sweet Passion," as well as "Fond Boy" (Pepys IV, 113). A ballad of 1696, "The Successful Commander . . . the Earl of Athlone, against the French at Givet," beginning "You true-hearted Protestants pray now attend," may be sung either to the Purcell tune or to the older "Let Caesar live long" (Pepys; reprinted in *PB* VII, 198).

The vogue of "If love's a sweet passion" was such that two songs were set to the tune in Abel Boyer's *The Compleat French-Master*, 1694: "L'Amour nous engâge pour nous rendre hûreux," No. 11, and "Helas! je Soûpire la Nuit & le jour," No. 12. The tune was also used in five ballad operas: Gay's *The Beggar's Opera*, 1728 (with the music), Odingsells' *Bays's Opera*, 1730, *Calista*, 1731 (the tune is called "When young at the Bar," from the opening line of Gay's song); *The Humours of the Court*, 1732; and *The Sturdy Beggars*, 1733. "When young at the Bar" is the name given to the tune of a song beginning "What ails thee, poor Shepherd, why looks thee so wan," in *A Collection of Loyal Songs*, 1750, p. 56.

In a Desert in Greenland

"A Dialogue betwixt Philander and Sylvia," beginning "In a Desert in Greenland,/where the Sun ne're casts an Eye," is a song by Thomas D'Urfey with music by William Aleworth which appeared in 1687 in *The Theater of Music*, Fourth Book, p. 10 (Fig. 231), and in *Comes Amoris*, First Book. The tune alone is in *Apollo's Banquet*, 5th ed., 1687, and the words were reprinted in D'Urfey's *New Poems*, 1690. Words and music are in all editions of *Pills* (1719–1720, II, 252).

A broadside version of c. 1690, expanding the text to seven stanzas is "The Suffering Lover . . . To an excellent new Tune" (Lord Crawford,

---

[5] If the funeral ballad was issued upon the death of the Duke of Grafton in October, 1690, it could not have been associated with the Purcell tune; our texts are evidently reissues.

BM C.39.k.6; reprinted in *OPB*, p. 134). Aleworth's tune was apparently not used for any other broadsides.

In Crete

"In Crete when Daedalus first began" is the opening line of an Elizabethan ballad which has been preserved in several manuscripts. A nine-stanza text of c. 1592 in Bodleian MS Rawlinson Poet. 112, fols. 18–17^v reversed, was published by Professor Rollins (*Review of English Studies,* III [1927], 336–337), who called attention to a four-stanza fragment in Bodleian MS Tanner 306, fol. 186. Special interest attaches to two stanzas in BM MS Harl. 7578, fol. 103; as Frank Sidgwick noted, the sheet originally contained religious verses, beginning "Christe ys rysynge," which have been "roughly deleted" and replaced by lines on Daedalus and Icarus.[1]

A moderately embellished lute tablature of "In Crete" is preserved in Folger MS 448.16, fols. 19ᵛ–20 (after 1571, according to Giles E. Dawson's dating of this part of the manuscript). The melodic line is more satisfactorily presented in an untitled version in William Ballet's MS Lute Book, p. 90 (Fig. 232); the last two bars, wanting in the Ballet tablature, are here supplied from the Folger set. A third arrangement for lute is "In creete when dadulus first began" in the Richard Mynshall MS Lute Book, 1599, fol. 8. An unbarred succession of notes in the Harleian

232

1 "Recovery of a Lost Ballad and Tune," *Gentleman's Magazine,* CCCI (1906), 179–181. The Harleian fragment was also printed by Rollins in his *Old English Ballads,* 1920, pp. 329–330.

text just discussed proves to be harmonically congruent with the lute settings, and is perhaps the alto of a four- or five-part vocal arrangement.[2]

Thomas Nashe, in his attack on Gabriel Harvey in *Have With You to Saffron-Walden*, 1596, named a number of ballads and singled out "In Creete when Dedalus" as a particular object of scorn. He charged that Harvey looked upon this ballad as "food from heauen, and more transporting and rauishing, than Platoes Discourse of the immortalitie of the soule was to Cato." Snatches from the ballad are sung in Beaumont's *The Knight of the Burning Pestle*, I, iv, and Fletcher's *Monsieur Thomas*, III, iii.

Thomas Deloney named "in Creete" as the tune for a ballad written before 1600, "How the Dukes daughter of Cornwall being married vnto King Locrine . . . was auenged," beginning "When Humber in his wrathfull rage" (*Garland of Good Will*, 1631, reprinted in *Works*, ed. Mann, p. 311; a version is also in the Percy Folio MS, ed. Hales and Furnivall, III, 437). Sir Edward Dyer's familiar poem, "My mind to me a kingdom is," was to be sung to the tune in its broadside versions (*SB*, p. 113, representing a MS text probably derived from a broadside issued

<hr />

[2] I am indebted to Prof. John Ward for calling this latter point to my attention. Dr. David Lumsden, in his unpublished Cambridge University dissertation, first identified the Ballet setting. Both scholars have recognized that one or more leaves are missing from the Ballet MS following the incomplete "In Crete" tablature; what next appears is the conclusion of John Johnson's version of "Rogero," and this title has been assigned to the composite of the two fragments in transcriptions printed by Germaine Bontoux, *La Chanson en Angleterre au temps d'Élizabeth*, 1936, pp. 84–86 (facsimile of lute tablature, pl. IV, opp. p. 102).

c. 1600; Pepys, an edition of c. 1624, reprinted in *PB* I, 229; later copies in Pepys II, 7, Douce II, 200ᵛ, 270ᵛ).[3]

In the oldest extant edition of "The Sinners Redemption," beginning "All you that are to mirth inclin'd," the tune direction is "The bleeding heart. Or, In Creet, &c." (Roxburghe; reprinted in *RB* II, 486).[4] Later editions, however, drop the second tune name, as if it had become too old-fashioned for a Restoration audience.[5] Three late seventeenth-century ballads called for the tune of "The Sinners Redemption," but it does not seem likely that "In Crete" was the melody intended.[6]

In January Last

This tune takes its name from the opening line of "A Scotch Song" which Thomas D'Urfey introduced into his play *A Fond Husband*, 1677:

> In January last on Munnonday at Morne,
> As along the Fields I past to view the Winter Corne,
> I leaked me behind, and saw come ore the Knough,
> Yen glenting in an Apron with a bonny brent brow.

In his dedicatory epistle D'Urfey says of the song that "a part of [it] was not mine; nor do I desire any Reputation from it." He evidently was not thinking of the tune, for he customarily worked with melodies not his own. Whatever his indebtedness may otherwise have been, he assumed enough of the credit that, when gathering his own songs into

[3] William Byrd set parts of Dyer's poem as No. 11 and No. 14 in his *Psalmes, Sonets, & Songs*, 1588. In BM MS Add. 15118, fol. 3ᵛ, of the first quarter of the seventeenth century, the poem is set to an unbarred air vaguely akin to the Harleian "In Crete" music. Unrelated musically is a three-part "My mind to me" of the same era in BM MS Egerton 2009, fol. 54ᵛ. Dyer's poem appears in all editions of *Pills* (1719–1720, IV, 88), with a fresh setting by Samuel Akeroyde.

[4] The only Stationers' Register entry of the ballad is dated 1656, and the Roxburghe copy may be of about that date, although it seems to be an older production.

[5] "My bleeding heart" is the opening of a ballad to the tune of "Sir Andrew Barton" (*RB* III, 23), and the ballad on Barton's life and death (*RB* I, 10, Child No. 167) is to the tune "Come follow my love," which has apparently not survived. Traditional tunes of "Andrew Barton" are modern.

[6] They are "The Sinners Care to Repent in due time" (*BB* I, 227), "A soluntary Song, for all stubborn Sinners" (Pepys II, 49, BM C.22.f.6 [18], Lord Crawford 456, Harvard), and "The Religious Man's Exhortation" (*RB* VII, 831).

the first two volumes of the 1719–1720 *Pills,* he included this among them, I, 306.

The song had meantime been introduced into Otway's *Friendship in Fashion,* 1678, Act III, and was printed with the music in *Choice Ayres & Songs,* Second Book, 1679, p. 46 (Fig. 233). Thomas Greeting added the

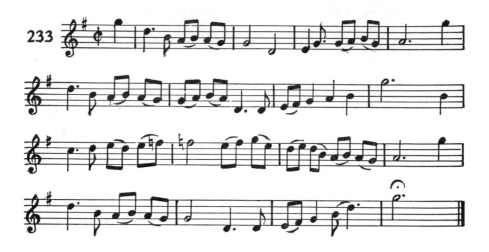

air to the 1680 edition of his *Pleasant Companion . . . for the Flagelet* as "A new Tune to a Northen Song." It appears in *Musicks Recreation on the Viol, Lyra-way,* 1682, as "Bonny Brow," from the last line of the opening stanza.[1] As "A Scotch Tune" the music is found in *Apollo's Banquet,* 5th ed., 1687. The six-stanza playhouse text, without music, was included in *Wit and Drollery,* 1682, and in D'Urfey's *Compleat Collection,* 1687.

An expanded broadside version of D'Urfey's song is called "The Scotch Wedding: or, A short and Pretty Way of Wooing . . . To a New Northern Tune" (Euing, Douce, Lord Crawford, Harvard, Roxburghe; reprinted in *RB* VIII, 458). This was followed by "The New married Scotch Couple: Or, The Second Part of the Scotch Wedding," beginning "As Jenny Crack and I/together ligg'd in Bed," and sung "To a New Northern Tune; Or, In January last" (Roxburghe; reprinted in *RB* VIII, 460). Both broadsides must have been issued shortly after the appearance of D'Urfey's play. Others to the tune include: "Northern Nanny," beginning "On Easter Monday last/when Ladds and Lasses

[1] Later settings with the same title are preserved in transcripts of the lost MS Lyra Viol books of Dr. John Leyden, No. 50, and Andrew Blaikie, No. 80. The latter collection contains another set entitled "In January Last," No. 94, as well as "Lady Binnys Lilt," No. 96, with a strikingly similar opening strain.

play" (Douce II, 163^v, issued no later than 1679); "Loves Quintessence. Or, The Frolick on Hackney Marsh," beginning "Down in a pleasant Valley" (Pepys III, 273); and a Monmouth ballad of c. 1681 based on a poem by Mrs. Aphra Behn, "Young Jemmy, Or, The Princely Shepherd," beginning "Young Jemmy was a Lad,/of Royal birth and Breeding," and sung "To a pleasant New Play-house Tune. Or, In Ianuary last, Or, The Gowlin" (Lord Crawford, Douce, Harvard, Roxburghe; reprinted in *RB* IV, 658).[2]

The six-stanza D'Urfey poem, "To its own Tune," is reprinted with minor changes in Allan Ramsay's *Tea-Table Miscellany*, 1733, II, 138. William Thomson followed Ramsay's text, entitling it "The Glancing of her Apron," and supplied a new tune for it in his *Orpheus Caledonius*, 1733, II, No. 42. Johnson's *Scots Musical Museum* V, 457, follows Thomson's title and tune but shortens the song text to three stanzas, beginning "In lovely August last, On Mononday at morn"; the original seventeenth-century tune is recognizable, though considerably modified. Ramsay also refined the old ballad "What is that to you" (see s.v. "Come hither, my own sweet Duck"), retaining the title and adding some Scotch embellishments, and assigned it to be sung to "The glancing of her Apron" (*Tea-Table Miscellany*, 1733, II, 170).

Alexander Campbell, in his *Albyn's Anthology*, 1816, I, 18–19, printed as a "Border Melody" a traditional version of the old "In January Last" air which he had received from a Miss M. Pringle of Jedburgh (I, 41), and coupled with it the words of "Jock o' Hazeldean," which Walter Scott had founded on the first stanza of Child No. 293 E.[3]

This tune is discussed by Stenhouse in his notes to the *Scots Musical Museum,* and by John Glen in *Early Scottish Melodies*, 1900, pp. 39–41. Stenhouse prints a tune "Willie and Annet" which is close to Campbell's "Jock of Hazeldean" and by inference is the original melody upon which the stage song was fashioned; the argument is not bolstered by dates or citation of tune source. Glen sees the origin of the tune in "Tantarra, or Lashleyes March," printed in *A Booke of New Lessons for the Cithern & Gittern,* 1652, but that piece is in 3/4 rather than common time and bears little resemblance to the stage tune.

---

[2] The playhouse tune is "Young Jemmy," q.v.; on "The Gowlin," see "London is a fine town."

[3] Chappell (*PMOT* II, 575) calls the "Border" attribution an error on Campbell's part; but the fact seems to be that whatever its origin, the old seventeenth-century tune was popular in Scotland and drifted naturally into traditional circulation.

This tune, called "Peascod Time" or "In Peascod Time," takes its name from a poem in *England's Helicon*, 1600, which begins:

> In Pescod time, when Hound to horne,
>   giues eare till Buck be kild:
> And little Lads with pipes of corne,
>   sate keeping beasts a field.

The music is preserved in the following: Antony Holborne's *The Cittharn Schoole*, 1597, sig. C1ᵛ; in the Mills College Cittern MS, c. 1600, No. 32;

234

Original is irregularly barred.

in New York Public Library MS Drexel 5612, p. 22 (Fig. 234), a virginal arrangement by Orlando Gibbons printed in his *Complete Keyboard Works,* ed. M. H. Glyn, 1925, II, 14; and in an untitled set of variations by William Byrd in Paris Conservatoire MS Rés. 1186, fol. 101ᵛ, copied into MS Drexel 5609, which is the source of the text in William Byrd's *Forty-five Pieces for Keyboard Instruments,* ed. S. Tuttle, 1939, p. 104. Byrd's setting of "Pescodd Time" in *The Fitzwilliam Virginal Book,* No. 276, is actually a version of his variations called "The Hunts Up" in the same collection, No. 59, and in his *My Ladye Nevells Booke,* No. 8; in these florid treatments neither melody is stated, though the harmonic basis common to both tunes may be faintly discerned beneath Byrd's free handling of chordal structure.

To this tune was sung "A lamentable ballad called The Ladye's fall," beginning "Marke well my heavy dolefull tale,/yow loyall lovers all," licensed in 1603. A contemporary copy is represented by the text in *SB*, p. 208; many editions survive from the second half of the seventeenth century (Euing, Pepys, Lord Crawford, Harvard, Roxburghe; reprinted in *RB* VI, 764) and later (Roxburghe III, 570, Douce III, 62ᵛ, Madden II, 477). It was reprinted in *A Collection of Old Ballads,* 1723–1725, in

Percy's *Reliques,* and in Ritson's *English Songs.*[1] Chappell (*PMOT* I, 196) has noted that early printed copies of "Chevy Chase" are to be sung to "In Peascod Time," but I have been unable to substantiate this claim.

Although no other ballads contain the tune direction "In Peascod Time," a great many are to be sung to "The Lady's Fall." [2] These include five manuscript pieces copied from early seventeenth-century broadsides (*SB,* pp. 25, 55, 76, 287, 293), and an equal number of Pepys broadsides, c. 1619–1630 (reprinted in *PG,* pp. 97, 110, 124, 288, 350), most of them dealing with crimes, monstrous births, or warnings of God's judgment. A very popular piece sung to the tune is "A Lamentable Ballad of the tragical end of a Gallant Lord, and a vertuous Lady," whose two children were murdered "by a Heathenish Blackamoor." A prose form of the story was licensed in 1569–1570, but no broadsides are earlier than the Restoration (Euing, Wood 401, Pepys, Lord Crawford, Douce, Bagford, Harvard, Morgan, Roxburghe; reprinted in *RB* II, 49). A calamitous ballad beginning "You dainty Dames so finely fram'd" tells how a woman "lying in Child-bed, was born away, and never heard of after"; licensed in 1603, it was reprinted until the nineteenth century under various titles. Perhaps the earliest is "A Warning for Maidens" (Roxburghe; reprinted in *RB* III, 194); other editions are called "A good Warning for all Maidens," "A Godly Warning for all Maidens," and, in some eighteenth-century copies, "Young Bateman's Ghost; Or, a Godly Warning . . . Tune Flying Fame" (Euing 128, Pepys I, 504, Wood 401 [106], Douce I, 87ᵛ, Lord Crawford 1386–1387; late copies, Bagford II, 43, Douce III, 110ᵛ, Roxburghe III, 766, Morgan, Harvard, Clark, Lord Crawford 1388–1389).

"The Bride's Burial," beginning "Come mourn, come mourn with me," to the tune of "The Lady's Fall" (*RB* I, 186) was licensed in 1603 and exists in numerous copies. From it comes the use of "The Brides Burial" as another name for the tune, cited in "A Looking-glasse for Young-men and Maids," c. 1655 (BM C.20.f.14; reprinted in *CP,* p. 367), and in "Two unfortunate Lovers," the tragedy of John True and Susan Mease (licensed in 1631; reprinted in *RB* II, 644). Both "Bateman" and "John True" appear as tune names, along with "The Fair Maid of Bristol," [3] in the broadside version of Child No. 243 ("James Harris [The

---

[1] Ritson presumed that "In Peascod Time" and "Children in the wood" were the same tune. They clearly belong to the same tune family, and harmonically as well as rhythmically they are closely related, but the points of difference entitle them to separate consideration.

[2] A memorandum book of John Locke's father, c. 1623–1655 (BM MS Add. 28273, fol. 102), contains directions for ringing "Ladies Fall" on five bells, by the numbers. The air is not the same as "In Peascod Time."

[3] A ballad entitled "The Fair Maid of Bristol" was licensed in 1623; it is conjectural whether this lost piece is represented by the late seventeenth-century broadside, "The

Daemon Lover]") entitled "A Warning for Married Women" (*RB* III, 200).[4] "Love's Overthrow," beginning "All you that know what tis to love," is also to the tune of "Bateman" (*RB* VII, 119). "The West-country Gentlemans last Will & Testament," beginning "A Gentleman that lately liv'd," is to the tune "I am James Harris call'd by name, or Ladies Fall" (Rawlinson 154), the first tune name an inexact echo of two lines in "A Warning for Married Women."

"The Lady Isabellas Tragedy, or the Step mothers cruelty," beginning "There was a Lord of worthy fame," names the tune as "Fair Rosamond, Or, Chivy Chase" on early editions (Wood E.25 [54], Douce I, 111) and as "The Ladies Fall" on a great many editions after about 1675 (*RB* VI, 651). The ballad is reprinted in *Pills*, 1719–1720, V, 53, with music (p. 49) which has affinities with "The children in the wood" in the opening bars but is otherwise a version of "Chevy Chase." Since the ballads "Fair Rosamond" and "Chevy Chase" were both sung to the tune of "Flying Fame," we have here one of many examples of confusion surrounding these several tune names. The broadsides of "Lady Isabella's Tragedy" suggest a shift from "Flying Fame" to "The Lady's Fall," but the *Pills* music leaves us on uncertain ground.

Fresh complexities are revealed in "The Four-Legg'd Elder Or, A horrible Relation of a Dog, and an Elders Maid," a ballad by Sir John Birkenhead written about 1647. Copies of what may be the original edition (Lord Crawford 23, BM Thomason, Harvard) are to the tune of "The Lady's fall." In *The Rump*, 1660, the tune is "The Lady's Fall, or Gather your Rose-buds, and 50 other Tunes"; in a broadside issue of 1677 this rubric becomes " . . . and Fourty other Tunes" (Harvard, Lord Crawford 24, Bagford III, 57); and in *Pills* V, 1, the ballad is reprinted with the music of "Children in the wood." Birkenhead also wrote "The Four-Legg'd Quaker," which in broadside form (Wood 416 [70]) and in *Ratts Rhimed to Death*, 1660, is "To the Tune of the Dog and Elder's Maid; Or, The Lady's Fall," but in *The Rump* of the same year is "To the Tune of the Four-Legg'd Elder." These would appear to be other names for "The Lady's Fall," as would "Help Lords and Commons," a phrase in the burden of both Birkenhead ballads cited as a tune name in "The Lawyers Plea, In the behalf of Young Tom of Lincoln," c. 1665, beginning "Lord help us all! what Story's this" (BM Luttrell II, 111).

One other ballad to the tune illustrates the ease with which the simple ballad-meter quatrain could become dissociated from its musical moor-

Fair and Loyal Maid of Bristow," sung to the tune of "Jenny ginn, Or, Busie Fame" (*RB* VI, 443).

[4] Some editions omit "Bateman" from the tune direction.

ings. "The lamentation of a bad Market, Or The Drownding of three Children on the Thames," beginning "Some Christian people all give ear," is sung to "The Ladies Fall" on broadsides (Lord Crawford, Harvard, BM C.22.f.6, Pepys; reprinted in *PB* III, 58), but in *Pills* IV, 1, it is reprinted with the music of "Chevy Chase." [5]

In Sad and Ashy Weeds

This tune takes its name from the opening line of a ballad of 1612, "The good Shepheards sorrow for the death of his beloued Sonne. To an excellent new tune" (Pepys; reprinted in *PB* I, 34). Professor Rollins believed that the broadside was probably the work of Richard Johnson, who included the text in his 1631 and 1659 editions of *A Crown Garland of Golden Roses*, along with another piece to the tune of "In sad and ashy weeds." [1] The library of the Duke of Norfolk contains a transcript of the first four stanzas in the hand of Anne, Countess of Arundel (1557–1630),[2] and it may be, as Professor Rollins suggests, that the poem was originally written earlier; the broadside adapts and enlarges the poem to apply to the King's loss of his son Henry, Prince of Wales, in November, 1612. For other manuscript and printed versions of the poem, see the full notes in *PB* I, 33. A further appearance of the song is in a commonplace book of c. 1625–1635, Harvard MS Eng. 686, p. 139, beginning "In pale and ashey weedes."

To this tune were also written "A Carrol for Innocents day," begin-

5 "Toney's Soliloquies," 1682, beginning "When the Plot I first invented, I was ravisht in Conceit," is to the tune of "Dagon's Fall. Or the Lamentation of a Bad Market" (BM C.38.i.25 [17], Harvard; reprinted in *180 Loyal Songs*, p. 285, without music and with only the second tune named). On the first tune, see "Ah cruel bloody fate"; the second seems to be derived from the title of the "Lady's Fall" ballad just cited.

1 "A Servant's Sorrow for the Loss of his Late Royal Mistress, Queen Ann, Who Died at Hampton Court [May 2, 1618]," *Crown Garland*, 1659 (ed. William Chappell, Percy Society, 1845, p. 1).

2 "Autograph Letters, 1585–1617," fol. 218ᵛ. For this reference I am indebted to Professor Ruth Hughey, who discovered the present whereabouts of the transcript. It was printed in Edmund Lodge's *Illustrations of British History*, 1838, III, 240–241. Lodge thought that the Countess of Arundel might have written "these pathetic effusions" upon the death of her husband, who had been a prisoner in the Tower for some years before his death in 1595. But Chappell (*PMOT* I, 201) believed that she merely wrote them from memory, altering some details to apply to her personal circumstances; that she could not have composed the verses is clear from her arrangement of the lines, which obscures some of the rhyme.

ning "Of Herod's bloody Reign/(with sad and grievous Soul I speak),"
New Christmas Carrols, c. 1662, sig. A8, and a broadside on the great
fire of 1666, "London mourning in Ashes," beginning "Of Fire, Fire,
Fire I sing" (Pepys; reprinted in *PB* III, 5), in which there is some dislocation of metrical pattern in the opening quatrain of each stanza.

"Who can blame my woe," from the burden of "The good Shepheards
sorrow," is cited, along with "I am a jovial Batchelor," [3] as the tune for
"The Distressed Pilgrim," beginning "I am a pilgrim poor and bare"
(Lord Crawford, Harvard, Roxburghe; reprinted in *RB* VIII, 93). The
British Museum copy of Slatyer's *Psalmes, or Songs of Sion,* 1642, contains a MS note stating that Psalm 137 could be sung to "In Sad & ashy,
or Who can blame my woe."

Music for "In sad and ashy weeds" is in Paris Conservatoire MS Rés.
1186, fol. 59ᵛ, a mid-seventeenth-century virginal set (Fig. 235). The

tune fits the original song, as well as the *Crown Garland* poem and the
psalm and carol verses; but the two late seventeenth-century broadsides require some shift in the tune to accommodate an opening quatrain in
8.6.8.6, as opposed to the earlier 6.8.6.8.

[3] This tune, which is used for half a dozen other ballads and is related ultimately
to the tune "Behold the man with a glass in his hand," does not appear to have survived.

In Summer Time

There must have been several tunes known by the name "In summer time," for the thirty-odd broadsides containing this tune direction fall into six distinct stanza patterns. Chief among these is the octosyllabic quatrain, followed by the stanza of eight octosyllabics, but no music has survived for either.[1] A badly printed tune in *Pills*, 1719–1720, V, 36 (Fig. 236), is set to words derived from a broadside by J. S., "The

young-mans Resolution to the Maidens Request," beginning "As I was walking under a Grove" (Pepys, Euing, Lord Crawford, Rawlinson, BM C.22.f.6, Roxburghe; reprinted in *RB* VII, 295). The tune title on the broadside is "In Summer time"; the eight-line stanza with alternating 8- and 9-syllable lines and the refrain "O then my love and I will marry" are retained in a sequel, "The maidens reply to the Young mans Resolution," beginning "Come prethee young man do not flout," to the tune of "the Young Mans Resolution" (Lord Crawford, Harvard, Roxburghe; reprinted in *RB* VII, 297). A late seventeenth-

[1] Other verse patterns, found in only a single ballad, include a six-line octosyllabic, an anapestic tetrameter quatrain, and an eight-line stanza whose syllabic makeup is 8x6y8x6y (the refrain lines x and y are respectively "down a down a down" and "hey down a down a down"). No music has survived for any of these.

century imitation of this last is "The Maidens Answer to the Young-Mans Request," beginning "A Damsel fair compleat and fine," to the tune "Then my love and I will marry" (Bagford; reprinted in *BB* II, 535). The tune titles relate both answers to the original ballad, and all three use a traditional formula of promising marriage when a number of impossible things shall have come to pass. Still another ballad in the same metrical pattern appears to be related to the foregoing through the tune title "My Love and I'll be married": it is John Wade's "Good Cou[n]sell for all Maids," beginning "You pretty Maidens listen well" (Douce I, 90, an edition of c. 1640–1665).

The *Pills* music for these ballads does not fit "In summer time" broadsides which have other stanza patterns. Our attempt to trace a tune compatible with the dominant form (four or eight tetrameter lines) continually runs aground. Alternative tune names found along with "In summer time" include: "Love's Tide"; "Fancies Phoenix"; "Flora Farewell" and its equivalent "My dearest dear and I must part"; "Suffolk Miracle" and "Bleeding heart," both deriving ultimately from "Come follow my love"; and "Joy to the Bridegroom." All these prove to be, not other names for "In summer time," but names of independent tunes, of which only "Love's Tide" (see "Wert thou more fairer") and "Joy to the Bridegroom" survive.

We may seek for origins in those ballads whose opening line begins "In summer time," but again the results are discouraging. At least eight broadsides begin with this commonplace phrase, and among them seven distinct stanza patterns are represented. One is in octosyllabic quatrains: "The Northampton-shire Lovers," beginning "In Summer-time when leaves are green/and Flora in her rich array" (*RB* VI, 274), to the tune of "True Love rewarded with Loyalty, or, Loves downfal"; both tune names are related ultimately to "Flora's Farewell," for which there is no music. Another has an eight-line octosyllabic stanza: "A Pleasant Song made by a Souldier," beginning "In summer time when Phoebus raise [i.e., rays]," to "Calino" (*RB* VI, 284). Since the music for "Calino" fits a four-line stanza, it might serve for the majority of "In summer time" broadsides. Both the "Calino" air and the earliest "In summer time" ballads are of the sixteenth century, however, and the conjunction of the two in a broadside of the mid-seventeenth century (apparently not issued earlier) does not satisfactorily account for the origin of our tune title.[2]

[2] The origin may lie in a Robin Hood ballad which is perhaps older than its 1631 licensing date. It is "The Noble Fisher-man: Or, Robin Hoods preferment," beginning "In Summer time when Leaves grow green,/when they doe grow both green and long" (Wood 402 [18], an issue printed for Francis Coles, one of the 1631 licensers; later editions are represented by the reprint in *RB* VIII, 486). The ballad is in quatrains.

Taken together, the various tunes that must have been sung as "In summer time" were in circulation for a century or more. Even limiting ourselves to the tune(s) suitable for an iambic tetrameter quatrain, we have a record of currency from about 1590 [3] to the end of the seventeenth century. But that popularity, as with hundreds of less frequently cited tune titles, has left no unmistakable musical trace.

[Iris on the Bank of Thames]

A song beginning "Iris on the Bank of Thames, with a sigh and weeping Eyes," with music by Thomas Tudway, appeared in *Choice Ayres and Songs,* Fourth Book, 1683, p. 62 (Fig. 237), and without music

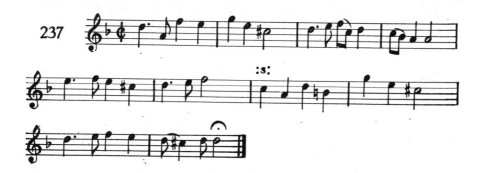

237

in *The Newest Collection of the Choicest Songs* in the same year. A broadside version of 1691 with meaningless music is in the Pepys collection, V, 198. No other broadsides appear to have used Tudway's tune, but a parody of the song, with music differing from Tudway's in detail, is "Iris' Caution," beginning "Iris, on a Bank of Thyme," in Watts's *Musical Miscellany,* 1729–1731, I, 150.

irregular but dominantly octosyllabic, and the tune direction is "In Summer time." But another ballad with identical first line and tune title has an entirely different metrical pattern; it is "A New Song to drive away cold Winter Between Robin Hood and the Jovial Tinker" (*RB* VIII, 527), with a double refrain, as cited in note 1, found in other Robin Hood ballads, but in no other ballads directed to be sung to "In summer time."

[3] This is a conjectural date for "A merry new Song how a Bruer meant to make a Cooper cuckold," *A Collection of Seventy-Nine Black-Letter Ballads,* 1867, p. 60.

This tune is found in *The Dancing Master,* 4th ed., 1670, p. 142 (Fig. 238), and in all subsequent editions. It is also in Walsh's *Compleat Country Dancing-Master,* 1718, and in all editions of *Pills.*

238

One of Thomas Jordan's civic pageants, *London Triumphant,* 1672, contained a song beginning "I Am a lusty lively Lad," [1] which was later issued in slightly longer form on broadsides, with the title, "The Prodigals Resolution, or My father was Born before me. To a Pleasant New Tune" (Pepys, BM C.22.f.6, Harvard, Lord Crawford, Roxburghe; reprinted in *RB* VI, 329). We cannot be sure of the tune originally used, but the song was reprinted in *Pills,* 1719–1720, III, 45, and in Ritson's *Ancient Songs,* 1790, p. 279, with the music of "Jamaica." The verses had meantime appeared in *Wit and Mirth,* 3d ed., 1682, without tune direction or music, and in John W. Franck's *Remedium Melancholiae,* 1690, set as an art song by Franck.

Also to the tune "Jamaica" is a song called "The Council," beginning "Two Toms and Nat,/In Council sat," in *The Muses Farewel to Popery*

[1] Although three stanzas were included in the 1722 edition of Sir Charles Sedley's *Works,* the attribution to him is considered doubtful by V. de Sola Pinto in his edition of *The Poetical and Dramatic Works,* 1928. Chappell suggests that the pageant verses may be indebted to an earlier song, a scrap of which has been preserved in "A Medly" in *Sportive Wit,* 1656, p. 30:

> Sing, Heigh—
> For a lusty lively lad,
> Heigh for a lad lacks kissing;
> Heigh for a lad that's seldom sad:
> But when he's dead . . .

and *Slavery*, 1689, Supplement, and in *Poems on Affairs of State*, 2d ed., 1697, I, Pt. 2, p. 140. Four other pieces are sung to the tune in *Pills:* "The Angler's Song" (III, 126), beginning "Of all the Recreations which/Attend on Humane Nature" (the broadside version is to be sung to "Amarillis," q.v., a tune not as well adapted to it as this); a ballad by Thomas Randolph, "Of the Downfal of one part of the Mitre-Tavern in Cambridge" (III, 136), beginning "Lament, lament you Scholars all" (found also in *Wit and Drollery*, 1656);[2] "The Jolly Trades-men" (VI, 91), beginning "Sometimes I am a Tapster new," with the music; and "The slow Men of London: Or, the Widow Brown" (VI, 93), beginning "There dwelt a Widow in this Town."

This last is in two parts and in other respects betrays broadside origin, though it cannot originally have been sung to this tune. It must have been in circulation before 1640, for it was about that year that Richard Climsell's ballad "The Ioviall Broome man" to the tune "Slow men of London" was issued (*RB* I, 499).[3] Moreover, the stanza form in the *Pills* text is eight lines plus a burden of four, which would require a repetition twice over of the first strain at beginning and end of each stanza.

The tune was used for several ballad operas. As "Jamaica" it is cited in *Love and Revenge*, c. 1729, and in Gay's *Polly*, 1729, with music; the same tune is found, untitled, in *The Prisoner's Opera*, 1730. In Drury's *The Mad Captain*, 1733, it is named "My Father was born before me." References to "Slow-Men of London" in *The Humours of the Court*, 1732, and to "There was three Lads" in Chetwood's *The Generous Free-Mason*, 1731, are to the 1729 tune referred to in note 3.

[2] No music appears with either ballad in *Pills*, but each is directed to be sung to the tune of "My Father was born before me," found earlier in the same volume. We cannot be sure that the direction indicates a tune name in general use, though its origin in the subtitle and pervasive refrain of "The Prodigals Resolution" is clear. It is sug-gestive that one ballad opera calls the tune "My Father was born before me."

[3] English interest in Jamaica seems to date from 1655, when the island was wrested from the control of Spain. It is doubtful that the tune, if it existed before that date, was then known as "Jamaica."

The possibility that a ballad "Slow Men of London" was current c. 1640 lends sup-port to a speculation of Chappell. He found, in Watts's *Musical Miscellany*, 1729–1731, II, 74, a four-quatrain song "Sung in the Play call'd Wit without Money," beginning "There was three Lads in our Town/Slow Men of London" (the song, with identical title and tune, is also found in *The Merry Musician*, c. 1729, p. 37, and the words alone are included in Ramsay's *Tea-Table Miscellany*, 1737, IV, 190, 1740, IV, 436); the verses are clearly related to the burden of the *Pills* "Slow Men," but the eight-bar tune is dif-ferent; the stanza form is identical with that of Climsell's ballad. Chappell supposed the song to have been introduced into Fletcher's play in an early eighteenth-century revival, as seems likely from the song title. His further suggestion that the ballad may have been used in seventeenth-century performances gains weight from the currency of "Slow men of London" implied by Climsell's tune direction.

Jenny, Come Tie My Cravat

A crabbed version of this tune was printed in an early edition of *Youth's Delight . . . on the Flagelet,* c. 1682.[1] More satisfactory is the music in *Apollo's Banquet,* 5th ed., 1687, Part I, No. 89 (Fig. 239). The tune is preserved on an "Additional Sheet," c. 1687, supplementing *The*

Dancing Master, 7th ed., 1686. It appeared also (this time with dancing directions) on a "New Additional Sheet," c. 1688, from whence it found its way into the eighth and succeeding editions. The tune is in Walsh's *Compleat Country Dancing-Master,* 1718, and Gay's *Polly,* 1729, and is named in two ballad operas without music.

The original broadside which gave the tune its name seems to be John Wade's "The Scotch Currant; Or, The Tying of Johnny's Cravant [sic]," beginning "As Johnny met Jenny on a Summers day/Johnny with Jenny began for to play," to the tune "Jenny, come tie my bonny

1 A reproduction of the tablature setting in F. W. Galpin's *Old English Instruments of Music,* 3d ed., 1932, Fig. 27, p. 146, is erroneously credited to a 1675 edition of Greeting's *Pleasant Companion . . . for the Flagelet.* The mistake is understandable, for the volume, now in the BM, has been supplied with a facsimile of the Greeting title page; but comparisons clearly reveal strong relationships with later editions of *Youth's Delight,* none with editions of Greeting, as Stanley Goodman has demonstrated in *Monthly Musical Record,* LXXXVI (Jan.–Feb., 1956), 20–26. An additional interest attaches to this copy of *Youth's Delight,* since it once belonged to Pepys. Oddly, Pepys recorded the purchase of Greeting's flageolet book, April 16, 1668, but his copy does not seem to have survived.

Cravant: or, Give me the Lass" (Douce; reprinted in *RB* VIII, 463).[2] The dance tune has the movement of a *courante,* as the ballad title suggests. Wade's piece was issued c. 1675 by the syndicate of Coles, Vere, Wright, and Clark. At about the same time another group of publishers, Thackeray, Passinger, and Whitwood, brought out a version whose contents were similar enough to constitute virtual piracy: "A New Scotch Jig: Or, The Bonny Cravat," beginning "As Johnny met Jenny a going to play," to the tune "Jenny come tie my" (BM C.22.f.6, Douce, Harvard, Pepys; reprinted in *RB* VIII, 466). The Thackeray partnership also issued "The Second Part of the new Scotch-Jigg: or, Jenny's Reply, To Johnny's Cravat," beginning "As Jenny sate under a Siccomore tree," to the same tune (Pepys, Lord Crawford, Douce, Euing, Harvard, Roxburghe; reprinted in *RB* VIII, 468).

Other ballads to the tune include: Thomas Lanfiere's "The Clothiers Delight . . . beating down their Work-mens wages," beginning "Of all sorts of callings that in England be," to the tune "Jenny come tye me &c. Packington's Pound, Or, Monk hath confounded" (Roxburghe; reprinted in *RB* VII, 7);[3] "A Good Wife is worth Gold," beginning "All Young men come hearken a while if you please" (Douce I, 91^v); and a ballad of 1681 on Shaftesbury, "A Dialogue between Mrs. Celier and the L. S[haftesbur]y," beginning "S[haftesbur]y, what's become of the Plot?" (Bodleian Ashmole G.16 [101], Harvard, Huntington), in stanzas of four lines which fit the music uncomfortably.

The usual eight-line stanza requires a repetition of each half of the tune. Three ballads using a six-line stanza can be accommodated with a repetition of the second strain only. They are: Robert Tippin[g]'s "The Rambling young Gallant," beginning "I am a brisk Gallant, all this I can tell" (Pepys III, 58); "The Bak'd Bully: or, Love in an Oven," beginning "[Y]ou Blades of the North,/to my Story give ear" (Douce I, 11); and "A Match at a Venture," beginning "As I in the Fields was walking along" (Roxburghe; reprinted in *RB* VII, 138).

Jenny Gin

This was one of the most popular broadside tunes of the late seventeenth century. It takes its name from a two-stanza Scotchified song, be-

---

[2] The second tune is named from the opening line of a ballad sung to "The Mock Tune to the French Rant" (*RB* IV, 401), on which I have no information.

[3] Music for "Monk hath confounded" has not survived.

ginning "Ah, Jenny, gen your Eyes do kill," in Aphra Behn's *The City Heiress*, 1682, III, i. It was quickly taken up by broadside makers, who not only expanded the song but also used the tune for some three dozen other pieces issued within the next decade or so. The double ballad-meter stanza is such a common form that it is not surprising to find "Jenny gin" cited as an alternative tune to "Hey, boys, up go we" or "Busy Fame" or "The fair one let me in"; what is unusual is that "Jenny gin" is very seldom named without alternates.

The earliest appearance of the tune is on a broadside of 1682, "Strephon's Comforts: or, Phillis Reviv'd . . . To a Pleasant New Tune [i.e., the music printed]: or, The fair one let me in," beginning "Ranging the Plain one Summers night" (Wood 417 [112]).[1] In the next year the air was included in Humphry Salter's *Genteel Companion . . . for the Recorder*. And the words and music of Mrs. Behn's song were reprinted in *The Newest Collection of the Choicest Songs*, 1683, in *Choice Ayres and Songs*, Fifth Book, 1684, and in all editions of *Pills*, 1719–1720, III, 262. A good version of the tune (Fig. 240), under the title "Ah Jenny! 'tis

240

your Eyn do kill," is found on a political broadside of 1683, "The Plot and Plotters Confounded," beginning "The Plot (God wot)/Is now broke out" (Clark; reprinted in *180 Loyal Songs*, 1685).

Mrs. Behn's song was expanded into two broadsides which are distinct after the first two stanzas. They are: "The Loves of Jockey and Jenny: or, The Scotch Wedding," to "a most pleasant new Tune"

[1] The song on which this broadside is based is coupled with new music in *Choice Ayres and Songs*, Fourth Book, 1683, *The Newest Collection of the Choicest Songs*, 1683, and *Pills*, 1719–1720, III, 188.

(Pepys, Euing, Lord Crawford, Harvard, Roxburghe; reprinted in *RB* VI, 178); and "Jockey's Lamentation turn'd into Joy: Or, Jenny yields at last . . . To a Pleasant new Play-house Tune" (Roxburghe; reprinted in *RB* VI, 181). Both ballads begin "Ah! Jenny Gin, your Eyn do kill," as though the printer conceived the Scotch word *gin* (if) to be a surname.

The following are among the ballads sung to "Jenny gin" or "Ah Jenny gin": "The Complaining Shepherdess Satisfied at last," beginning "One Summers night when all alone" (Pepys, Douce, Bagford; reprinted in *BB* II, 511); "The Love-sick Maid of Portsmouth," beginning "There is a lad in our Town" (Roxburghe; reprinted in *RB* VI, 186). To the tune "Ah Jenny" is "The Laundry-Maids Lamentation for the loss of her Seaman," beginning "Come mourn with me fair Nymphs, come mourn" (Pepys IV, 164). "Loves glorious Conquest," beginning "Adieu to grief and discontent" (Pepys III, 213), is to the tune "My love is on the brackish Sea," a name derived from the opening line of "The Seamans sorowful Bride," which is to the tune of "Ah! Jenny Gin" (Pepys, Harvard, Roxburghe; reprinted in *RB* VI, 444). The title of this last ballad may be the source of the tune name "Seamans mournful bride," cited along with "Hey boys up go we" and "The fair one let me in" for singing "The Good Fellows Frolick" (*RB* VI, 351).

The twenty-five or thirty ballads that name "Jenny gin" as an alternative tune contain the names of no less than thirteen other tunes that might be used, and as many as four are named on a single sheet. Typical of these is "The Subtle Damosels Advice," beginning "Give ear a while unto my Song," to "Jenny Gin, Or, The fair one let me in, Or, Young Pheon, Or, Busie Fame" (BM C.22.f.6 [182], Lord Crawford 417). Among others that do not seem to have been reprinted are: "Daniel Cooper; Or, The High-land Laddy," 1683, beginning "There's ne'r a Lad in our town," to "a Scotch Tune, called, Wally on't, Or, We'l welcome you to Yarrow. Up go we, Or, Jenny Gin" (BM C.22.f.6 [42], Douce I, 51, with corrupt musical score); "The Wounded Lover," beginning "Mythinks I feel fresh bleeding wounds," to the tune of "Some say there was a Papist plot; or, Jenny Gin" (Pepys III, 381); "The Brave Boys of Bristol," beginning "Brave Bristol Boys, where e're you be," to "Hey Boys up go we; Jenny Gin; Busie Fame; Or, Russels Farewel" (Douce I, 19).

"The New Blossom'd Marigold" is to the tune "Jenny Ginn, Or, as I walkt forth to take the air" (Pepys III, 210); the ballad, which begins "As I walkt forth to take the Air,/upon a Summers day," is, after the first line, unrelated to "The Dispairing Maiden Reviv'd By the Return of her Dearest Love," which begins "As I walkt forth to take the air,/ one morning in the Spring" and may be sung to "The fair one let me in; Or Busie Fame; Or, Jenny Gin" (Pepys III, 181, Douce I, 54ᵛ). It is impossible to say whether "As I walkt forth to take the air" was an independent tune.

Almost no political ballads were sung to "Jenny gin," perhaps because of the complex nature of the tune, which has all the earmarks of the trained composer. But there is no denying its popularity for songs of love and personal tragedy.

Jenny, My Blithest Maid

This tune is named from the opening line of a poem printed in *The Theater of Music*, First Book, 1685, *180 Loyal Songs*, 1685, p. 311 (Fig. 241), and all editions of *Pills*, 1719–1720, III, 252, with music by Samuel

Akeroyde. The tune alone is found in a supplement to Humphry Salter's *The Genteel Companion . . . for the Recorder*, 1683, and in *Apollo's Banquet*, 5th ed., 1687; in the former it is untitled; in the latter it is called "A New Scotch Tune."

The music also appears on a broadside of 1685–1688, "Jockies Happy Meeting with Fair Silvia in the Grove," beginning "Silvia, thou bright and charming Maid," to the tune of "Jenny my blithest Lass, &c. Or, Silvia thou brightest" (Pepys V, 267). The second tune title apparently derives from the opening of the ballad, but I have found no music with

this title. The broadside text in stanzas of eight tetrameters plus an irregular quatrain burden cannot be sung to the "Jenny" music on the
sheet.

Jenny's Cogwheel

"True Lovers Victory or the Northern couple agreed" is a broadside
of the early 1670s "To a rare Northern Tune or Jennys cog wheel"
(Wood E.25 [42], an issue printed for J. Clark; another issue, licensed
March 1, 1675, to the partnership of Coles, Vere, Wright, and Clark,
is in Lord Crawford, Harvard, Roxburghe; reprinted in *RB* VII, 176,
and *OPB*, p. 197). The ballad of twelve stanzas begins "A Boney blith
Lad/in the North Countrey," and its second stanza, commencing "Come
sit thee down by me/mine own sweet joy," opens a dialogue which is
the basis of a related ballad, "The Bonny Scottish Lovers . . . To a
pretty, yet common, Northern Tune," beginning "Sit thee down by
me, my own sweet joy" (Rawlinson 110; published by the partnership
named above). Both broadsides are expansions of a song printed in
Westminster Drollery, II, 1672.[1] A variant text appears with music in
Choice Ayres, Songs, & Dialogues, 1676, p. 76 (Fig. 242), and in all edi-

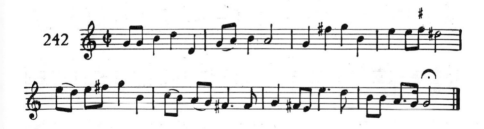

242

tions of *Pills,* 1719–1720, III, 256. In the absence of tune names we
cannot be sure whether the music in the two latter works is the "North-

[1] The first seven stanzas of "The Bonny Scottish Lovers" are roughly equivalent
to stanzas 2–9 of "True Lovers Victory"; stanzas 8–17 of the former are independent
of stanzas 10–12 of the latter. The problem of chronology is vexed by the fact that
"The Bonny Scottish Lovers" is the closer to the original drollery song, yet the
imprints would suggest that the other ballad was issued first. No problem of piracy
exists, for the same publishers controlled both broadside titles.

ern" tune or "Jenny's Cogwheel," nor can we know whether these two names stand for one tune or two when cited in "True Lovers Victory."

"Jenny's Cogwheel" seems to have been used for no other broadsides, although a possessor of the Douce I, 122ᵛ copy of "The loving Chamber-Maid" has written in "Sitt thee down by me" to supplement the ambiguous printed direction, "To a New Tune." The ballad (*RB* VII, 447, and *OPB*, p. 209) may, with some division of notes, be sung to the *Choice Ayres* and *Pills* tune. The same is true of two songs in William Hicks's *London Drollery*, 1673, which are to be sung "To the Scotch Tune Sit thee down by me": "On a Neat but Noble Cheese-feast lately in London," p. 21, and "The Welchmans Wooing his Mistris," p. 22.

Jenny's Delight

"The Amorous Gallant," beginning "How bonny and brisk, how pleasant and sweet," to the tune of "Jenny's delight" (BM C.22.f.6 [81], Lord Crawford 521, Rawlinson 88, Harvard), was issued c. 1673. It is an expanded version of a song in a miscellany *Methinks the Poor Town has been troubled too long*, 1673; in the same year, the original verses are found in *Choice Songs and Ayres*, p. 51, with music by Robert Smith (Fig. 243).

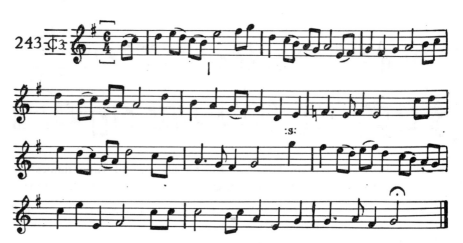

The tune name appears to have been inspired by Jenny's amorous role in the original poem. Apparently no other broadsides were sung to Smith's tune.

The Jewel in the Tower

A roman-letter ballad of 1712, with music for voice and flute (Fig. 244), is "On the Jewel in the Tower," beginning "If what the Tower of London holds,/Is valu'd for more than it's Power" (BM 1850.c.10 [20],

244

:S:

* Sharped in vocal air; uninflected in flute version on sheet.

Harvard). The words were reprinted in *A Pill to Purge State-Melancholy,* 1715. The tune is called "The Jewel in the Tower" in Johnson's *Village Opera,* 1729, and in the one-act condensation of the next year, Phillips's *The Chamber-maid.*

Jig a Jog-Goo

This tune, called "Jiggy Joggy," appears in lute tablature in the Cambridge University MS Dd.9.33, fol. 77, c. 1600 (Fig. 245). The Shirburn MS contains an amatory ballad of about the same date, "The second part of Jeamye," beginning "My hart is impure my body within," to the tune

245

Theme is followed by several variations in original.

of "Gigg-a-gogge, or Woddycocke" (*SB*, p. 189). An early Restoration ballad citing the tune is "A Job for a Ioyner or A good Workman well imploy'd," beginning "Come and attend young Virgins all," to the tune "Over the water, fain I would pass, or Jig a Jog-goo &c." (Wood E.25 [34]). Since the stanzas of this ballad end ". . . Jigg a Jog goo" and thus seem to have given the tune its name, it is likely that the piece originally dates from the very early years of the seventeenth century. Both ballads can be sung to the tune, but a condensed version of the second is in a different measure: "The Maid and the Joyner," beginning "There was a fair Maiden came out of Kent,"[1] *Wit and Drollery*, 1682, p. 112.

Joan to the Maypole

"The May-Day Country Mirth: or, The Young Lads and Lasses Innocent Recreation . . . To an excellent New Tune" begins "Joan to the Maypole away let's run" (Lord Crawford, Harvard, Roxburghe; reprinted in *RB* VII, 79; another edition, Douce II, 152, begins "Joan from the Maypole . . ." and contains meaningless music; a briefer copy in Pepys IV, 244, has the title "Rural Recreations"). The ballad is based on a short song in William Hicks's *Oxford Drollery*, 1671, and in *Windsor Drollery*, 1672;[1] the full broadside text is printed in all editions of *Pills*, 1719–1720, IV, 145, with music for which I can trace no title or earlier use (Fig. 246). "A Mock to Joan, to the May-pole away let us run, And to that tune," beginning "Tom to the Tavern away let us run," is in *Mock Songs*, 1675.

D'Urfey's song "The Disappointment," beginning "The Clock had struck faith I can't tell what," was first published in *Pills*, 1707, III, 25, with the tune of "Joan to the Maypole"; it was retained in succeeding editions, 1719–1720, I, 262, and was also issued as a single-sheet song with the same music (BM H.1601 [433], Huntington, Harvard). The tune is used in ballad operas, taking its names from D'Urfey's song: "The Clock had struck" in Ryan's *The Cobler's Opera*, 1729, and "The Clock

---

[1] The fourth stanza of the "Ioyner" ballad begins "There was a Maid came out of Kent." Neither text seems to be related to the song sung by Moros in Wager's *The Longer thou Livest*, 1569: "There was a Mayde come out of Kent, Deintie loue, deintie loue."

---

[1] E. F. Rimbault's *A Little Book of Songs and Ballads*, 1851, contains three stanzas from an unidentified "MS. volume of old Songs and Music," dated 1630; so the original song may go back to the time of Charles I. Rimbault printed no music with these verses.

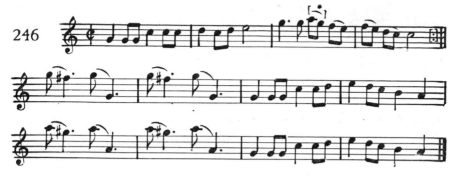

246

* F in 1719–1720 *Pills;* emendation from 1712, V, 145.

has struck I can't tell what" in Coffey's *The Female Parson,* 1730; in *The Wanton Countess* and *The Fox Uncas'd,* 1733, it is called "The Disappointment."

Joan's Ale Is New

The ballad "Jones ale is newe" was licensed in 1594, along with what seems like a moralizing counterpart, "the vnthriftes adiew to Jones ale is newe." The original ballad was re-entered in the Stationers' Register in 1656, to Thomas Vere, a copy of whose edition is found in Douce I, 105ᵛ. It was reissued during the second half of the century, and was part of William Thackeray's stock when he published his extensive list, c. 1689. The broadside text is followed in *Pills,* 1719–1720, V, 61, where it appears with the tune (Fig. 247).[1]

The broadside is titled "Joan's Ale is New; Or: A new merry Medley . . . To a pleasant New Northern Tune," and begins "There was a jovial Tinker/Which was a good Ale-drinker" (Pepys IV, 245, BM C.22.f.6 [52], Douce I, 99ᵛ, Lord Crawford 1130). The title echoes the refrain, which repeats the line three times in each stanza. No other ballads appear to have been sung to the melodious tune, but an anonymous play *The Partiall Law,* c. 1615–1630, II, iv, contains a reference to "Joane's ale's new" as a dance.

[1] "Under and over," q.v., has an opening strain clearly related to the first half of "Joan's ale is new"; thereafter the tunes diverge to fit stanza patterns which are not interchangeable.

247

Remnants of the old broadside have been recorded from tradition in this century. See, for instance, *JFSS,* II (1906), 234–236, "When John's sail was new" (Lancashire), and *ibid.,* VI (1918), 12–13, "When Joan's ale was new" (Surrey). The pioneer American collector John A. Lomax, in his *Adventures of a Ballad Hunter,* 1947, p. 240, noted that he had collected a piece known as "When Jones's ale was new" from a retired sailor.

Joan's Placket Is Torn

This tune must have derived its name from the refrain of a ballad now lost; it probably concluded in some such form as "The unfortunate Joan, her placket is torn,/'Tis rent and torn in twain." The tune first appeared in *180 Loyal Songs,* 1685, p. 143 (Fig. 248), but it had been in circulation for at least a generation before that.[1] The earliest broadside citing the

[1] George R. Gleig, in his *Family History of England,* 1836, II, 110–111, prints "the air which was played by the band at Fotheringay-castle, while Mary [Queen of Scots] was proceeding to her execution" in 1587. It is a military version of "Joan's Placket," in slow tempo. Chappell reprints it (*PMOT* II, 519) but does not share Gleig's confidence in "the tradition which connects it with this period in English history."

248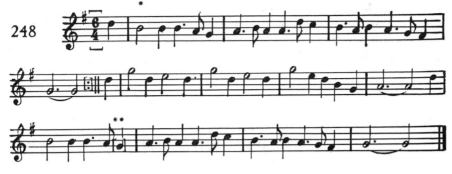

* C in original.
** Note missing.

tune is "Loves Carouse," by S[amuel?] S[mithson?], published about 1660, beginning "A Jovial crew of lively Lads" (BM Luttrell II, 133, printed for Francis Groves, who died in 1663; Luttrell's MS date "1674" can mean only date of acquisition). Pepys recorded in his *Diary* for June 22, 1667, that a trumpeter on board the *Royal Charles* sounded the tune of "Joan's placket is torn."

At least three political ballads of the strife-torn 1680s illustrate the catchiness of refrains adapted to topical purposes. "A New Song of the New Plot," begins "Have you not lately heard" (Bodleian Ashmole G.16 [101]; Harvard and Huntington copies are titled "A Song . . . Plot," the latter with MS date August 5, 1681; reprinted in *180 Loyal Songs*, as "The Plot Cram'd into Jones Placket," with music); it has a stanza of six lines and a refrain of equal length which reads in part:

> 'Tis rent and torn, and torn and rent,
>   and rent and torn in twain,
> For the Plot is rent and torn,
>   and will never be mended again.

Another political squib in *180 Loyal Songs* (reprinted in *RB* V, 623) is "The Plot Rent and Torn," beginning "Have you not heard of Knaves,/ that ne'er will be forgot"; and still another is "Romes Plots against the Present Government discovred [sic]," c. 1689, beginning "England must be Watchful now," to the tune "Jones Placket is Rent and Torn" (Pepys; reprinted in *PB* V, 65).

The tune appeared in *The Dancing Master,* 7th ed., 1686 (Additional Sheet), and in the tenth (1698) and following editions. It is found also in Walsh's *Compleat Country Dancing-Master,* 1718, and in Thompson's

Compleat Collection of 200 Favourite Country Dances, c. 1764, II, 91. It was called for in eight ballad operas, including the following which print the tune: Cibber's *Love in a Riddle,* 1729; [2] *Momus turn'd Fabulist,* 1729; Gay's *Achilles,* 1733; Potter's *The Decoy,* 1733; Kelly's *The Plot,* 1735.

Jockey's Gone to the Wood

Choice Ayres & Songs, Second Book, 1679, p. 12, contains a song beginning "Dear Jocky's gone to the Wood," with music by William Gregory (Fig. 249). The same tune is in *Musicks Recreation on the Viol, Lyra-*

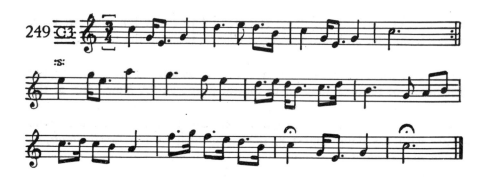

way, 1682, as "Jocky went to the wood," and in *Youth's Delight on the Flagelet,* 9th ed., c. 1690, as "The Wood Nimph or dear Jockey." The air is called "Jockies gaine to the Wood" in the Agnes Hume MS, dating from 1704. The words alone are reprinted in *Wit and Drollery,* 1682, p. 114.

The broadside expansion of the song is "The Scotch Wooing: Or, Jockey of the Lough, and Jenny of the Lee," to the tune of "Jockey's gone to the Wood" (Lord Crawford, Douce, Harvard, Roxburghe; reprinted in *RB* VII, 305). A sequel to the broadside, also in a nine-line stanza but with somewhat different metrical organization, is "A Maiden-Head Ill Bestowed; Or, A New Dialogue betwixt Kind Jenny of the Lough, And Unkind Jockey of the Lee," beginning "O Jockey thou art

[2] The proper tune name is not given; instead, the first lines of all the verses are listed as tune titles. Isaac Bickerstaffe took over both the tune and Cibber's words for a song in his *Love in a Village,* 1763, II, iii.

the Lad," to the tune "Would Jenny were here again" (Rawlinson; reprinted in bowdlerized fashion in *RB* VII, 348). I have no information on that tune.

Jockey's Jealousy

"Jockey's Jealousie . . . To an Excellent New Tune," beginning "I saw the lass whom dear I lov'd," with meaningless music, is a broadside of the 1680s (Pepys V, 261). The song of which this is an expansion appeared in *A Collection of the Choy[c]est and Newest Songs*, 1687, *Comes Amoris*, Second Book, 1688, p. 8 (Fig. 250), *The Banquet of Musick*, First

Book, 1688, and all editions of *Pills*, 1719–1720, III, 218; in each of these the verses are set to music composed by Moses Snow.

Another broadside employing the tune is "The Last Lamentation, Of the Languishing Squire," c. 1690, beginning "As I went forth to view The Spring,/which Flora had Adorned," to the tune of "Billy and Molly: Or, Jockey's Jealousie" (Lord Crawford, Pepys, Douce, Harvard, Roxburghe; reprinted in *RB* VI, 228). For other versions of this ballad, including a broadside edition of c. 1670 without tune direction, see "The Damask Rose," note 1.

Jog On, or Eighty-Eight

Early seventeenth-century versions of this tune appear as "Hansken" in *Het Luitboek van Thysius*, No. 25 (Fig. 251), and in a Richard Far-

naby arrangement in *The Fitzwilliam Virginal Book*, No. 297. It is called "Jog on" in the first ten editions of *The Dancing Master*, 1651–1698, perhaps from a song sung by Autolycus in *Winter's Tale*, IV, ii, to which the tune is nicely adapted:

> Jog on, jog on, the footpath way,
> and merrily hent the stile-a:
> A merry heart goes all the day,
> Your sad tires in a mile-a.[1]

The tune is named "Eighty-eight" from its association with "An old Song on the Spanish Armado in 88," beginning "Some yeares of late, in eighty eight/As I doe well remember," which is in Archie Armstrong's *Banquet of Jests*, 6th ed., 1640 (reprinted 1872, p. 87), in *The Academy of Complements*, 1670, in *Westminster Drollery*, 1671, I, 93, *Wit and Mirth*, 1682, and (with the title "Sir Francis Drake: Or, Eighty Eight") in *Pills*, 1719–1720, IV, 37. A slightly different version of the song, beginning "In eighty-eight, ere I was born,/As I can well remember," is in BM MS

---

[1] Autolycus sings only one stanza. The three-stanza song is in *An Antidote against Melancholy*, 1661, p. 73. Words and music are united in *Catch that Catch Can*, 1667, p. 85.

Harl. 791, fol. 59, and printed texts appear in *Choyce Drollery*, 1656, and *Merry Drollery*, 1661. In none of these versions is a tune title cited, but in *Pills* the music is "Jog on."

"The Catholick Ballad: Or An Invitation To Popery, Upon considerable Grounds and Reasons," by Dr. Walter Pope, is a popular broadside which appeared in 1674 in editions with and without music. It begins "Since Pop'ry of late is so much in debate," and is "To the Tune of 88" (Lord Crawford 1066, Wood 416 [126], Euing 24, BM 1871.e.9 [56], all with music; editions of this date without music include Harvard, Chetham 1103, Lord Crawford 1067; copies with music but with defective or cropped imprint include Bodleian C.6.2.Th [4], Chetham 30, and Roxburghe; reprinted in *RB* I, 89). Several copies bear later dates: 1675 (BM Luttrell III, 106), 1678 (BM 1872.a.1 [149], Euing 25), 1679 (Harvard), 1689 (Library of Congress). Music contained on these copies is deceptive, for with the first stanza interlined it appears to be carefully printed; the tune is grammatical, but it is rhythmically unrelated to the verse, and the final cadence on the seventh is improbable. It bears no relation to a tune printed with the ballad in *Pills* IV, 32, which follows the *Dancing Master* version of "Jog on" very closely, except for a division of some notes to accommodate anapestic meter (Fig. 252).

252

A still different tune, but one well suited to the metrics, is found on a broadside Latin translation dated 1675: "Canticum Catholicum, sive Invitatio ad Religionem Romanum," beginning "Ut Papisma reddatur jam nunc arguatur" (Huntington, Harvard; variant issues include Lord Crawford 1234 and BM Luttrell I, 169). The tune direction is "Latine reddita & Anglico-metris Pariter & Rythmis juste respondens 88," but the music is actually "Drive the cold winter away," q.v.

Dr. Pope apparently wrote the sequel entitled "Room for a Ballad, Or, A Ballad for Rome. . . . A Continuation of the Catholick Ballad," beginning "From Infallible Rome, once more I am come," to the tune of "The Powder-plot" (Lord Crawford, BM 1876.f.1, Wood 416; reprinted in *Rome Rhym'd to Death*, 1683, and *RB* IV, 105). Nothing is known of this tune title, but the meter of this ballad corresponds to that of "The

Catholick Ballad." From internal evidence it may be dated 1674. In the next year appeared "Reflections upon The Catholick Ballad," beginning "Since Drolling is grown, such a Trade in the Town" (BM Luttrell, Lord Crawford; reprinted in *RB* IV, 110). No tune direction is given, but the piece is metrically identical with "The Catholick Ballad."

The music of "Jog on" in *Pills* is used not only for the Armada song and "The Catholick Ballad" but also for "A Ballad called, The Jovial Bear-ward" (IV, 38), which originally appeared without tune direction in Ben Jonson's *Masque of Augures*, 1621. In the same volume of *Pills* the tune reappears (IV, 243) with Alexander Brome's "Ballad Upon the New Inn, with the famous Sign-Post, called the White Hart, at Skole in Norfolk," first printed in Brome's *Songs and Other Poems*, 1661. "Jogg on" is also named for singing a song beginning "There was a man two sons he had" in William Hicks's *Oxford Drollery*, 1671, p. 112.

John Anderson, My Jo

Bishop Percy alludes to this tune as one of those which the Reformation appropriated from the Latin service for profane use, but the earliest version of the tune I have found is "John Andersonne My Jo," an amateurishly notated tablature in the seventeenth-century Skene MS; Dauney has retained pitches and regularized time values in his transcription, *Ancient Scotish Melodies*, 1838, p. 219 (Fig. 253). Harmonically the tune

Original is a fourth higher and contains a 16-bar varied repeat.

is to be equated with "I am the Duke of Norfolk," although its melodic line has undergone independent development.

A broadside of the time of George I calling for the tune is "An Excellent new Ballad, Intituled the New way of the Turn Coat," beginning "I Loved no King in Fortie One" (BM 1871.e.9 [175]).[1] It may be intended for the Skene tune or, more probably, for the slightly different version found in Watts's *Musical Miscellany*, 1729–1731, VI, 202 (Fig. 254), in Gay's *Achilles*, 1733, in *The Convivial Songster*, c. 1782, p. 306,

and (with the familiar words by Burns) in Johnson's *Scots Musical Museum* III, 269, whence its appearance in many subsequent collections.

Percy's two-stanza Scottish text in the *Reliques* begins "John Anderson my jo, cum in as ze gae bye" and is a brief anecdote of cuckoldry in contrast to Burns's tender lyric of marital fidelity. Percy altered the five bairns to seven in later editions, on the highly questionable assumption that they symbolized Catholic sacraments.

The original "John Anderson, my jo, John," which Burns completely reshaped, is verbally unrelated to Percy's text. A sportive wife's immodest reproach of her husband's waning powers, it may be found in *Merry Muses of Caledonia*, c. 1800, ed. James Barke and Sydney Goodsir Smith, 1959, pp. 114–115.

1 Other editions contain the tune direction "London is a fine town," q.v.

John, Come Kiss Me Now

Perhaps the earliest version of this well-known air appears in an imperfect lute tablature of c. 1570, Folger MS 448.16, fol. 7. It is there entitled "The Antycke," and we may speculate whether its association with the verses of "John, come kiss me now" had not yet begun or was not then strong enough to have changed the tune name.

Under its familiar title it was a favorite subject for "divisions," or variations, throughout the seventeenth century. Keyboard sets include that of William Byrd in *The Fitzwilliam Virginal Book* I, 47 (Fig. 255), of

John Tomkins in BM MS Add. 29996, fol. 206ᵛ, and an anonymous arrangement of the unadorned air in Paris Conservatoire MS Rés. 1186, fol. 58. A set of lute variations is preserved in BM MS Add. 38539, fol. 11ᵛ (c. 1613–1616). Thomas Robinson's *New Citharen Lessons,* 1609, No. 27, entitled "Joan come kisse me now," may be the earliest printed form of the piece, but its emphasis is upon the chordal pattern rather than the melody. The tune with embellishments is found in the mid-century Bedford Cittern MS, fol. 10, in *A Booke of New Lessons for the Cithern & Gittern,* 1652, and in *Musick's Delight on the Cithren,* 1666. Playford's *Brief Introduction to the Skill of Music* contains "The Ground of John come Kiss" (1672, p. 97; in 1654, p. 32, and other early editions, the ground appears as an untitled lesson for viola da gamba); in the fourth edition, 1664, p. 110, *et seq.,* divisions on the air are among the pieces for treble violin. His *Apollo's Banquet,* 1670, includes the tune and a variation among the pages of treble-violin instruction preceding the pieces. His *The Division-Violin,* 1685, contains two sets of variations, No. 11 by David Mell, No. 12 by [Thomas?] Baltzar (Fig. 256).[1] Although not identified, a version of the tune is printed in *Pills,* 1719–1720, V, 58,

---

[1] The second strain as printed by Chappell (*PMOT* I, 148) appears in Baltzar's piece, but it may well be a variation itself, agreeing as it does harmonically with the original statement of the melody.

256

with a few stanzas of the coarse ballad "Stow the Friar." The air is suited to the verses, but no musical provision is made for the refrain. One ballad opera calls for the tune: Thomson's *The Disappointed Gallant*, 1738, printed without music.

The tune evidently takes its name from an old song whose opening stanza is preserved in the moralization found in *A Compendious Book of Godly and Spiritual Songs*, 1567 (ed. A. F. Mitchell, 1897, p. 158):

> Iohne, cum kis me now,
> Johne, cum kis me now,
> Johne, cum kis me by and by,
> And mak no moir adow.

The spiritual parody continues:

> The Lord, thy God, I am,
> That Johne dois thé call,
> Johne representit man
> Be grace celestiall; . . .

The same opening stanza is found, with the air and a variation (called "the running of it"), in Trinity College, Dublin, MS F.5.13, pp. 55–56, followed by "His answer to y[t] sam toone," in thirteen stanzas, beginning:

> Peace I'm angrie now now peace I'm angrie now
> Peace I'm angrie at the hert & knowe not q[t] to dowe.[2]

David Herd's *Scottish Songs*, 1776 (1869, II, 206), contains a fragmentary stanza plus the refrain lines of the original song, much as in Johnson's

[2] The portion of the MS containing "Airs and Sonnets" is in an early seventeenth-century hand. The words of the "answer" were printed by Andrew Lang in *Longman's Magazine*, XXVII (November, 1895), 107–108, and reprinted by Mitchell, p. 277.

Scots Musical Museum IV, 315, where a second strain is added to the familiar eight-bar tune. Anne Gilchrist, in her discussion of the tune (*JEFDSS*, III [1936–1939], 176–178) refers to an imitative song in James Hogg's *Jacobite Relics*, 1819, I, 144. Its concluding stanza begins "Great James, come kiss me now, now," and the tune also has a second strain.

I have found only one broadside ballad sung to the tune. It is "A dittie most excelent for euerie man to reade/that dothe intend for to amende & to repent with speede," to the tune of "a rich marchant man or John come kiss me now," beginning "Whoe loveth to live in peace: & marketh euerie change" (BM MS Add. 15225, fol. 56, c. 1616). This was a poem in *Tottel's Miscellany*, 1557 (ed. Rollins, 1928–1929, I, 196). A broadside version was entered in the Stationers' Register Sept. 4, 1564, but no printed copy survives; manuscript copies, without tune direction, include BM MS Sloane 1896, fol. 35ᵛ, c. 1576, and Bodleian MS Ashmole 48, fol. 37ᵛ, c. 1555–1565, the latter reprinted in Wright's *Songs and Ballads*, 1860, p. 57.

Since "John, come kiss me now" was an obvious favorite of John Playford, it is surprising that he did not include the tune in editions of *The Dancing Master*. Numerous allusions, however, point to its popularity as a dance tune throughout the seventeenth century (see Chappell, *PMOT* I, 147, II, 771).

John Dory

The ballad "John Dory" (Child No. 284) first appeared in print in Ravenscroft's *Deuteromelia*, 1609, where it is No. 1 of the Freemen's Songs for three voices. The same tune, shorn of embellishments and repetitions, is found with the ballad in *The Second Book of the Pleasant Musical Companion*, 1686, Part II, No. 22 (Fig. 257), and in *Pills*, eds. of 1699–1714, I, 25. The music is actually a three-part round or catch, and it may be suspected that Ravenscroft, who has clearly "worked up" the tune in other ways, has not provided us with very authentic notation.[1]

---

[1] The famous drinking song in William Stevenson's *Gammer Gurton's Needle*, "I can not eate but lytle meate," has been set as a four-part round to a common-time version of "John Dory," but on what authority remains a mystery. It is found in Ritson's *English Songs*, 1783, where without indication of origin it is said to have been "set, four parts in one, by Mr. Walker, before the year 1600." J. Stafford Smith, in his *Musica Antiqua*, 1812, credits the setting to Weelkes and gives *Deuteromelia* as his source, but only the three-part "John Dory" is in that work. Chappell (*PMOT* I,

257

The ballad begins:

> As it fell on a holy day,
>   and vpon an holy tide a,
> Iohn Dory bought him an ambling Nag,
>   to Paris for to ride a.

The account of John Dory's entering the service of King John II of France and of his being captured at sea by one Nicholl of Cornwall must have had wide currency during the seventeenth century, for frequent allusions treat it as a familiar or even a hackneyed subject.[2]

"John Dory" is openly parodied in a poem "Upon Sir John Sucklings most warlike preparations for the Scotish Warre," beginning:

> Sir John got him on an Ambling Nag,
>   To Scotland for to ride a,
> With a hundred horse more, all his own he swore
>   To guard him on every side a.

72) reprints the song without throwing further light on the source of the musical arrangement.

[2] Chappell (*PMOT* I, 67–68) has gathered a large number of references, which the following are intended to supplement. "Dr. Corbets Journey into France" in his *Certain Elegant Poems*, 1647, p. 81, refers to the ballad:

> But I to *Paris* rode along
> Much like *John Dory* in the song,
>   upon a Holy tide.

A song "On Gondibert" in *Merry Drollery*, 1661, I, 112, contains the following allusion:

> And all this stir to make a story,
> Not much superior to John Dory,
> Which thus in brief I lay before ye.

And "A Song made on the Power of Women" in *Pills*, 1719–1720, III, 27, begins:

> Will you give me leave, and I'll tell you a story, . . .
> It shall do more good than Ten of *John Dory*.

This was first printed in Sir John Mennes and Dr. James Smith's *Musarum Deliciae*, 1655, and was reprinted along with "John Dory" in the *Pleasant Musical Companion* and in *Pills;* Percy included it in his *Reliques*. It deals unflatteringly with events of 1639, and in *Vox Borealis*, 1641, are echoes which suggest that the ballad must have been in circulation at that time. After the singing of a seven-stanza song beginning "Sir John got on a bonny browne Beast/To Scotland for to ride a," Willie remarks that in his camp too there were songs sung of Suckling. "Mine is a sinister verse then yours, for it hath two foot more, and it is to be sung, To the Tune of *Iohn Dorie*, as followeth.

> "Sir John got on an ambling Nagge,
>   To Scotland for to goe,
> With a hundred Horse, without remorse,
>   To keep ye from the foe."

After four more lines he breaks off: "I had rather tell you the rest of it in plain Prose." [3]

For all its popularity, there is no record of "John Dory" or any of its parodies on extant broadsides. A ballad of c. 1675 contains an allusion in the tune name, but the verse is in the distinctive pattern associated with "The Spanish Pavan" and could not be sung to "John Dory" music. It is Thomas Robins's "Englands Gentle Admonition," beginning "Good People all I pray draw near," to the tune of "Poor Tom's Progress: Or, John Dory sould his ambling Nag for Kick-shaws" (Roxburghe; reprinted in *RB* IV, 477).

[3] A sale catalogue of the British bookseller Percy J. Dobell, No. 94, 1947, listed a copy of Suckling's *Fragmenta Aurea*, 3d ed., 1658, on a blank leaf of which was a poem in a contemporary hand, "A Song Sir John Suckling made of himselfe," beginning:

> As it fell on a Holyday
> All on a Holy day tide a
> Sir John bought him an ambling nag
>   To Scotland for to ride a.

This appears to be the *Musarum Deliciae* ballad, prefixed with the two opening lines of "John Dory." The attribution to Suckling is unfounded.

Johnny Armstrong

I have been able to find no satisfactory tune for "Johnny Armstrong" unless it be "Armstrong's Farewell" in James Oswald's *Caledonian Pocket Companion*, c. 1770, II, 75 (Fig. 258). It is an elaborate arrangement for German flute or violin, in three strains, the first of which, with its repetition, would accommodate the quatrains customarily associated with

the tune name. The second strain seems to be an addition designed to exploit the higher reaches of flute or fiddle, and the third is a quick 6/8 reprise of the first two. Only the first strain is well adapted to singing and may be much older than the two other parts. But because of the gap of almost 150 years between the ballads and the tune itself, it is not possible to propose the identification with much confidence.

The title "Armstrong's Farewell" is, however, at least reminiscent of the seventeenth-century broadside, "Iohn Arm-strongs last goodnight," by T. R., beginning "Is there never a man in all Scotland," and sung "To a pretty Northern Tune, called, Fare you well guilt Knock-hall" (Wood 401 [94]; published by F. Grove, to whom the ballad was licensed in 1658; many other copies, chiefly of late editions; reprinted in *RB* VI, 604; the Wood copy is Child No. 169 B). The tune name here is derived from a line in the ballad, in which Armstrong takes leave of his dwelling, fearful that he will never return from his appointment with the King in Edinburgh. Another version, "A Northern Ballet," begins "There dwelt a man in faire Westmerland," and is without tune direction (*Wit Restor'd*, 1658, *Wit and Drollery*, 1682; this is Child No. 169 A).[1] From the reference to the ballad of "Johnny Armstrong" in Walton's *The Compleat Angler*, 1653, Part I, Chap. IV, it may be inferred that the ballad was known either traditionally or from print some years before the editions known to us. The events of the ballad can be dated 1530.[2]

At least three broadsides of the latter part of the seventeenth century are sung to the tune of "Johnny Armstrong": "The Lovers Farewel to his Unconstant Mistris," beginning "All in a Morning clear and fair" (Douce II, 139); "The West-Country Damosel's Complaint," beginning "When will you Marry me William" (Lord Crawford, Euing, Douce, Roxburghe; reprinted in *RB* VI, 635); and "The married wives Complaint of her unkind Husband," beginning "Come all young Maids that are to Wed," to the tune of "jonny armstrong, or True love rewarded with Loyalty" (Wood E.25 [148], Douce II, 151ᵛ).[3]

There is apparently no relationship between the Johnny Armstrong of these ballads and the protagonist of "A pleasant new Ballad, shewing how Sir John Armstrong and Nathaniel Musgrave fell in love with the Lady

---

[1] The opening stanza of this version is the second stanza of the broadside, and the parallelism throughout is strong. But only the broadside contains a scene between Musgrave, the little footpage, and Armstrong's lady, to whom he brings news of Armstrong's death.

[2] A third version (Child No. 169 C) is found in Allan Ramsay's *The Ever Green*, 1724, II, 190, where it is described as having been taken down from an Armstrong descendant. Tunes associated with this text appear in Ritson's *Scotish Songs*, 1794, II, 7, and Johnson's *Scots Musical Museum*, 1787–1803, IV, 367.

[3] The second tune title is ultimately derived from "Flora's farewell," for which there is no music.

Dacres Daughter of the North . . . and how they wrought the Death of one hundred men . . . To a new Northern tune," beginning "As it fell out one Whitsunday" (Euing, Bagford, Lord Crawford, Roxburghe; reprinted in *RB* VII, 606).

Joy to the Bridegroom

This tune takes its name from the opening line of a poem written in 1681 upon the marriage of "Lady W——." It first appeared anonymously in *A Choice Compendium,* 1681, and is found also in *Wit and Drollery,* 1682, in D'Urfey's *A New Collection of Songs and Poems,* 1683, and *The Complete Courtier,* 1683.[1] The song, with music, is in all editions of *Pills,* 1719–1720, I, 323. An expanded broadside version, to the tune of "Joy to the Bridegroom," is "The Joys of Vertuous Love," beginning "Joy to the Bridegroom, fill the Sky" (Pepys IV, 93, Lord Crawford 729, BM C.22.f.6 [131]).

The music is contained on several broadsides, the earliest of which is "Loyalty Triumphant, On the Confirmation of . . . Sheriffs . . . Sung . . . September 30, 1682," beginning "Fill up the Bowl, and set it round" (Huntington, Harvard [Fig. 259]; reprinted with the music in *180 Loyal*

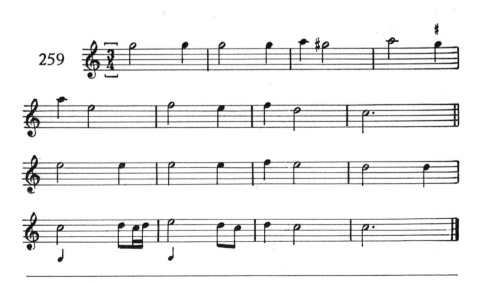

259

---

[1] See *PB* III, 251, for a listing of later reprints.

Songs, 1685, p. 156, whence the text in *RB* V, 271). Another with music is from January, 1683: "A New years Guift to the Templers . . . Sir Edmond Saunders, Chosen Lord Chief-Justice," beginning "Old Tony's fled, from Justice gone" (Bodleian Ashmole G.15 [111], Huntington, Harvard; reprinted in *180 Loyal Songs,* p. 158). Another ballad of 1683 containing the music is "The Granadiers Loyal Health," beginning "Old England's Glory now begins" (Harvard, Yale). The tune alone is in Humphry Salter's *The Genteel Companion . . . for the Recorder,* 1683, and, under the title "Minuet," in *Apollo's Banquet,* 5th ed., 1687. In some broadsides, the six-line verse pattern calls for a repetition of the first musical strain; in others the second is to be repeated.

The tune is named on several other broadsides containing no music: "The Mirror of Mercy," beginning "Heard you not of the Headborough," to "Joy to the Bridegroom: Or, In Summer time" (Pepys; reprinted in *PB* III, 252); and a ballad on the coronation of William and Mary, 1689, "Englands Holiday," beginning "Come all Loyal Subjects of every sort," to the tune of "Let Caeser live long, Now now the Fights done, The Plow-mans Health, Joy to the Bridegroom Or, My Life and my Death" (Pepys; reprinted in *PB* IV, 264).[2]

A broadside of 1685–1688, "The Young Mans Joys Compleated," beginning "Now to my true Lover Betty," is directed to be sung to "O so ungrateful a Creature" (BM C.22.f.6 [213], Lord Crawford 910, Harvard). Music on the sheet is "Joy to the Bridegroom," which fits the dactylic octaves with difficulty; nor can the ballad be comfortably sung to "I never saw a face till now," music for which appears on a variant issue of "The Young Mans Joys" (Douce II, 263). The tune of "O so ungrateful a Creature" seems not to have survived, although more than a half dozen ballads from the later 1680s were directed to be sung to it.

Joy to the Person of My Love

This tune is named from the opening line of a song found in the Leyden MS of 1639, fol. 2ᵛ, National Library of Scotland (Fig. 260), and in Forbes's *Cantus,* 1662, No. 34. A mandore arrangement of the tune is in the Skene MS (printed in *Ancient Scotish Melodies,* ed. Dauney,

2 Of these five tunes, all except "Joy to the Bridegroom" are usually associated with stanzas of six anapestic tetrameters, the pattern in "Englands Holiday" as well. The ballad can be sung to "Joy to the Bridegroom" by division of most of the long notes. No music is known for "The Plow-mans Health."

p. 241). The song was published c. 1625 as a broadside entitled "A Lover forsaken of his best beloved. To an excellent new Court tune" (Roxburghe; reprinted in *RB* II, 65); another contemporary issue, with slightly varying title, is represented by Euing 188. A later roman-letter edition is "Joy to the Person of my Love . . . To be Sung with its own proper Tune" (BM 1871.e.9 [50]).

260

Original is unbarred except for phrase ends.

"The True hearted Lover Deceived, by an Unconstant Woman," beginning "One Morning in green April's Month," is to the tune of "Joy to the Person of my Love" (BM 1871.e.9 [18], c. 1665), but the double ballad-meter stanza does not fit music designed for a complex fourteen-line form.

Kind Husband and Imperious Wife

In *A Collection of Old Ballads*, 1723–1725, II, 230, is found a nine-stanza text of "The Worcestershire Wedding, or, Joy after Sorrow," beginning "An old Woman cloathed in gray" and directed to be sung to "Kind Husband and Imperious Wife." Since this collection is largely a reprint of broadsides, it may be presumed that an edition of this ballad was in circulation during the latter part of the seventeenth century, but I have found no copy. Single-sheet editions of four stanzas with music have been preserved from the early years of the eighteenth century: "The old Woman cloathed in Grey," c. 1705 (Harvard, BM H.1601 [25]=Fig.

261), and "A Song" (Harvard, BM G.306 [71]). The tune, called "Unconstant Roger" in allusion to the matter of the ballad, appeared about 1728 in *The Dancing Master*, III, 77, and Walsh's *New Country Dancing-Master*, III, 86. Most familiar is its use as the opening air in Gay's *The Beggar's Opera*, there called "An old Woman cloathed in Gray."

"The Kind husband but imperious wife" is the title of an anonymous song without tune direction found in *Westminster Drollery*, 1671, *Wit*

and *Drollery*, 1682, and William Hicks's *Grammatical Drollery*, 1682.[1] The movement of the poem is only moderately well adapted to the eighteenth-century tunes we possess, and it may be doubted that the drollery poem has any vital relationship to the ballad. The first strain of the tune is reminiscent of "How unhappy is Phyllis in love," q.v.

King James's Jig, or The Country Farmer

This was an extremely popular broadside tune of the 1680s, used for some three dozen ballads under one of its several names or their offshoots. The music appears twice in *180 Loyal Songs*, 1685, pp. 322, 358, as "King

---

[1] In his reprint edition of *Westminster Drollery*, Appendix, p. xxiii, J. W. Ebsworth suggests that Hicks may be the author of the song, but his evidence is inconclusive.

Jame's Jig" (Fig. 262). A badly printed version of the tune is on a coronation broadside of 1685, "Englands Royal Renown," beginning "Noble Hearted English Boys" (Wood 417 [143]), although the tune direction is "[Hark] the [thundering] Cannons Roar," to which the verses are better adapted. The tune is called "Painted Chamber" in *The Dancing Master*, 7th ed. (New Additional Sheet, c. 1688), and in subsequent editions; in the seventeenth edition, 1721, it is titled "The Country Farmer's Daugh-

262

ter: or, The Painted Chamber." It is "Painted Chamber" in *Apollo's Banquet*, 5th ed., 1687, and in Walsh's *Compleat Country Dancing-Master*, 1718; it is "Country Farmer" in the ballad opera *Momus turn'd Fabulist*, 1729, Rutherford's *Compleat Collection of 200 . . . Country Dances*, c. 1756, and Thompson's *Compleat Collection of 200 Favourite Country Dances*, c. 1758. It is untitled in *Youth's Delight on the Flagelet*, 9th ed., c. 1690.

The commonest tune name found on broadsides is derived from the title "The Countrey Farmer; or, The Buxome Virgin." This ballad begins "There was a brisk Lass both Bonny and Brown" and is to the tune of "New-Market, or King James's Jigg" (Pepys, Douce, Lord Crawford, Harvard, Roxburghe; reprinted in *RB* III, 363).[1] "The Answer to the Buxome Virgin. Or, The Farmer well-fitted," beginning "The Country Farmer is now undone," names the tune "The Countrey-Farmer, or, The Buxome Virgin" (Pepys, Douce, Lord Crawford, Harvard, Roxburghe; reprinted in *RB* III, 366).[2] From these two related ballads come several

[1] The tune "Newmarket," found in *The Dancing Master*, beginning with the 5th ed., 1675, is in common time and does not fit the meter of this ballad.

[2] One other ballad cites the tune as "The Country-Farmer; or, The Buxom Virgin": "The Innocent Shepherd and the Crafty Wife," beginning "A Silly poor Shepherd was folding his Sheep" (Pepys III, 209, BM C.22.f.6 [129], Lord Crawford 1056, Harvard).

tune titles, the most important of which, "The Country Farmer," we shall reserve for separate discussion. The first line of the original ballad, "There was a brisk lass," becomes the tune name in "The Coy Cook-Maid," beginning "Joan scrub'd up her Rooms" (Pepys, Lord Crawford, Euing, Douce, Roxburghe; reprinted in *RB* III, 627); in "The Difficult French-Man's Unsuccessful Adventures," beginning "My Pockets begar, were lin'd very well" (Pepys III, 136, Douce I, 61ᵛ); and in "A New Ballad of an Amorous Gentleman," beginning "I went to the Fair to pick out a wife" (Pepys IV, 96, Douce I, 8). "The Countrey Farmer's now undone," from the opening line of "The Answer to the Buxome Virgin," becomes the tune title for "The Irish-mens prayers to St. Patrick," beginning "O Broder Teague, and Teague my Roon" (Pepys; reprinted in *PB* V, 25), though the original sheet contains a few bars of "Lilliburlero" interspersed with pied musical type, and that tune would fit the ballad equally well. A continuation of the original ballad is "The new Married Couple or, A Friendly Debate between the Countrey Farmer and his Buxome Wife . . . a second Song to the Tune of, The Countrey Farmer," beginning "Dear Gill I ne'r thought until last night" (Douce; reprinted in *RB* IV, 17).

"King James's Jigg" is cited as the tune for a few ballads, including: "Monmouth Routed and taken Prisoner," beginning "Five thousand Pound for James the Scot" (Pepys; reprinted in *RB* V, 663); "The Western-Triumph . . . of . . . James the II," beginning "Come listen awhile to the Lines which I bring" (Pepys; reprinted in *PB* III, 292); "Couragious Jockey," beginning "Young Jockey was jolly blithe and gay" (Pepys IV, 38); and "The Extravagant Youth, or, An Emblem of Prodigality," beginning "Come listen a while and I will relate" (Pepys, Lord Crawford, Harvard, Roxburghe; reprinted in *RB* IV, 443). In the two latter "The Country Farmer" is added as an alternative name for the tune.

On a number of broadsides "The Country Farmer" is named as an alternative for other distinct tunes. Thus it is cited along with "The New-Market Jigg" [3] in "The True-Lovers Glory," beginning "You Lovers most Loyal, where-e're you be" (Pepys III, 205). It is an alternate to "Why are my Eyes still flow. . .ing" in "The Cuckold's Lamentation of a Bad Wife," beginning "Young Batchelours all, come hear this new Song" (Douce, Lord Crawford, Roxburghe; reprinted in *RB* III, 635). It is cited along with "Packington's Pound" and "Digby's Farewell" in "A Full Description of these Times," beginning "Now let all true Protestants

---

[3] This tune is probably the same as "New-Market," cited on the broadside of "The Countrey Farmer; or, The Buxome Virgin." The identification is not positive, but it seems likely that the reference is to D'Urfey's song beginning "To horse, brave Boys of Newmarket, to Horse," sung to music otherwise known as "Cock up thy Beaver," q.v.

ever Rejoyce" (Wood E.25, BM 1871.f.3, Pepys; reprinted in *PB* IV, 46). It is an alternative to "The Devonshire Frolick" in "The Welch Wedding," beginning "Now sweet Shinny wilt thou be wed" (Pepys IV, 109, Douce II, 244, Lord Crawford 903, BM C.22.f.6 [203]), and to "The Devonshire Damosels" in "A Warning and good Counsel to the Weavers," beginning "You Gentlemen all come listen a while" (Pepys; reprinted in *PB* IV, 30). The two tune names here derive from "Maids a-washing," for which see "Where's my Shepherd?" In "The Loving Mistress, and The Wanton Clerk," beginning "A Lawyer in our Town did dwell" (Pepys III, 164), the tunes named are "A fig for France" (lost), "The Country Farmer," and "Where's my shepherd." Another lost tune is "A Touch of the Times," named along with "The Country Farmer" in "Advice to Batchelors," beginning "Both Robert and Richard, nay, William and Ned" (Douce, Lord Crawford, Harvard, Roxburghe; reprinted in *RB* III, 373).

"The Country Farmer" is named alone on a large number of ballads, including the following which do not seem to have been reprinted: "A Groats-worth of Mirth for a Penny," beginning "Come Gallants and welcome, partake of my cheer" (Pepys III, 207); "The Country Clowns Delight" by M. H., beginning "There was a young-man both handsome & rare" (Pepys III, 261); "The Country Damosels Lamentation For her Love" by Gabriel Owens, beginning "There was a young Damsel both bonny and brave" (Pepys III, 341); and "Evan's Gamesome Frollick," beginning "Come listen a while, and I here will unfold" (Douce I, 69). A pair of complementary ballads are further related by the use of the title of the first as the tune name for the second: "The Sorrowful Damsels Lamentation For Want of a Husband," beginning "I am a poor maiden lives in great distress," is to the tune of "The Country Farmer" (Douce II, 209, Lord Crawford 552, BM C.22.f.6 [180], Harvard); [4] "The Bachelour's Guide, and the married Man's Comfort," beginning "All Batchelors now, come hearken to me," is to "The Sorrowful Damsels Lamentation for want of a Husband" (Lord Crawford 21, BM C.22.f.6 [84], Harvard).

A piece by Sir Edward Morgan printed with the tune of "King James's Jig" in *180 Loyal Songs*, p. 322,[5] begins "If Sorrow the Tyrant Invade thy Breast." It appears in two broadside editions, one called "The Dis-

[4] A virtual paraphrase of "The Sorrowful Damsels Lamentation" is "The Maidens Moan . . . for want of a Husband," beginning "I am a poor Maiden in woful distress," to the tune of "A Touch of the Times. Or, The Country Farmer" (Pepys III, 267). The Pepys text is the more regular of the two, but it is difficult to assign priority; moreover, since both ballads were issued by Brooksby, the question of piracy is not raised.

[5] No tune name is given with the music, but on p. 358 the identical music is called "King James's Jig."

truction of Care" (Pepys V, 97), the other, licensed Nov. 1, 1687, called "A New Song made by a Person of Quality, in praise of the Mug" (Chetham 1887); both contain music as found in the *Pills* reprint of the song, V, 82. The tune is not "King James's Jig," but is harmonically related to it. Still another version is in *RB* V, 172, entitled "The Gallant's Worthy Commendation of the Mug. 1682," no source given.

King Solomon

The ballad giving rise to this tune name is William Elderton's earliest known production, "The panges of Loue and louers f[i]ttes," 1559, beginning "Was not good Kyng Salamon/Rauished in sondry wyse" (Huntington; reprinted in Collmann, No. 39). The piece was licensed in 1558–1559, and again in 1560 and 1624. It is without tune direction, but the stanza pattern is distinctive, for lines six and eight depart from the octosyllabic measure to produce a refrain, the respective lines here being "Lady lady" and "My deare lady." [1]

In 1561–1562 a license for printing was given to "a new ballett after the tune of kynge Salomon." This is probably R. M.'s "A newe Ballade," beginning "O Dere Lady Elysabeth, which art our right and vert[u]ous Quene" (BM Huth, London Society of Antiquaries [Lemon *Catalogue*, No. 48]; reprinted in *Harleian Miscellany*, 1813, X, 262, and in *A Collection of Seventy-Nine Black-Letter Ballads*, 1867, p. 30). This is also without tune direction, but the four-line stanza is the "King Solomon" pattern printed in compressed form, with refrains "Lady Lady" and "most dere Lady." A third contemporary ballad in this stanza pattern names the tune as "Kynge Salomon"—George Mell's "A proper New Balad of the Bryber Gehesie," beginning "Was not the bryber Gehesie/Rewarded iustly of the Lord" (BM Huth; reprinted in *Collection of Seventy-Nine*, p. 42). This was entered by Thomas Colwell, 1566–1567, who printed the extant copy. The refrain lines vary throughout but retain the usual four-syllable pattern.

Still another to the tune is "The Ballad of constant Susanna," beginning "There dwelt a man in Babylon" (Pepys, Roxburghe; reprinted in *RB* I, 190). The Pepys copy was printed for Henry Gosson and the Roxburghe copy for John Wright, both booksellers being among the six reg-

---

[1] On the great contemporary popularity of the ballad, see Hyder E. Rollins, "William Elderton," *SP*, XVII (1920), 201.

istering the ballad in 1624. It had earlier been entered in 1562–1563 and 1592, and the re-entry in 1675 is represented by later issues of the ballad (Pepys I, 496–497, Douce I, 30, Bagford II, 6).[2] This ballad too is without tune direction, but the identity is established by the "Lady, lady . . . of this Lady" refrain pattern. A fragment of another imitation of Elderton's ballad is preserved in *A Handefull of Pleasant Delites*, 1584, ed. Rollins, p. 29, with the refrain tags of the original. It seems probable that it was in the lost 1566 edition of the miscellany; it is fragmentary here because a leaf has been lost from the unique copy of the 1584 edition of the *Handefull*.

The "King Solomon" ballad form was imitated in two interludes of 1567, *The Trial of Treasure*, sig. E1, and Pickering's *Horestes*, sig. C2ᵛ, both of which introduce songs patterned on the "lady, lady" refrain formula. Marston's *Antonio and Mellida*, 1602, Act III, and Armin's *Two Maids of Moreclacke*, 1609, sig. C3ᵛ, echo the opening line of "The pangs of love." And in *Twelfth Night*, II, iii, Sir Toby sings a snatch from the Susanna ballad: "There dwelt a man in Babylon, lady, lady." The 1567 edition of *A Compendious Book of Godly and Spiritual Songs* (ed. A. F. Mitchell, 1897, p. 213) contains a moralized parody on Elderton, entitled "Ane Dissuasioun from Vaine Lust," whose stanza form indicates that it could be sung to the tune. It begins:

> Was not Salomon, the King,
> To miserie be wemen brocht?
> Quhilk wisdome out of frame did bring,
> Till he maist wickitly had wrought.
> A thousand wemen he did keip,
>   Allace, allace!
> Quhilk drownit him in Sin sa deip,
>   As come to pas.

The Bannatyne Manuscript, 1568 (ed. W. Tod Ritchie, 1928–1934, III, 254), exhibits further evidence of the widespread interest in Elderton's ballad through the Scottish version it contains, beginning "Was not gud king salamon/reuisit in sindry wyiss." Still later is the reference to "a dittie that I haue made to the tune of, Lady, Lady, my faire Lady" in C. T.'s *Laugh and lie downe*, 1605 (reprinted in *The Works of Cyril Tourneur*, ed. Allardyce Nicoll, 1930, p. 290).

The tune "Was not goode kinge Salamon" is found among some cittern and gittern pieces in BM MS Add. 30513, fol. 123, c. 1545–1585.

---

2 Other copies of the Susanna ballad include a Symcocke issue of c. 1628, Manchester II, 50; later editions are BM Huth 72, c. 1663–1674, and Lord Crawford 1138, c. 1690. A Welsh traditional survival, with a tune whose first strain is reminiscent of the original English air, is noted in *JEFDSS*, III (1936–1939), 170–171.

263

The manuscript, consisting largely of keyboard music, was made by Thomas Mulliner, master of the choir of St. Paul's (published as *The Mulliner Book,* 1951, ed. Denis Stevens; the cittern set is reprinted in the appendix to Stevens's *The Mulliner Book: A Commentary,* 1952). A somewhat better rendering of the tune is found among some keyboard pieces of c. 1570 at the end of Thomas Dallis's MS Lute Book (Trinity College, Dublin, MS D.3.30), reproduced in *The Dublin Virginal Manuscript,* ed. John Ward, 1954, No. 13 (Fig. 263). In several Continental collections the tune appears as the almain "Guerre guerre gay." [3]

King William's March,
or Hark, Hark, and Yonder

This tune derives its two names from a ballad celebrating the battle of the Boyne, July 1, 1690; it is called "King William's March" and begins

[3] In his commentary on the tune, Ward reprints the set in Sebastian Vreedman's *Carminum . . . Liber Secundus,* 1569, fol. 6, and notes the appearance of the tune in Pierre Phalèse's *Hortulus Cytharae,* 1570, and in Adriaen Valerius's *Neder-Landtsche Gedenck-Clanck,* 1626. Ward also sets the first stanza of "Was not good King Solomon" to the Dublin version of the tune.

264

"Hark! Hark! and yonder/Hear the Martial Thunder" (Lord Crawford, Pepys; reprinted in *PB* V, 200). The singing direction is "To a Pleasant New Trumpet Tune, call'd, King William's March." The Pepys copy, V, 55, contains an accurate musical score (Fig. 264); the Crawford sheet is a variant issue with meaningless music.

Music is also found in *Apollo's Banquet,* 6th ed., 1690, where it is called "An English March" and is attributed to Samuel Akeroyde.

The tune is named "Hark, hark, and yonder" in another broadside containing the music: "A Dialogue between My L. Hump, & his Valet dChambre," beginning "Jack, Tom, where are you" (Pepys V, 430); and in "England's Joy . . . King William safely Arrived from Flanders," 1691, beginning "The Jacobites do wonder," without music (Pepys; reprinted in *PB* VI, 148). "K. William's March in Flanders," the tune named in "Jockey and Willy, The Scotch Rivals" beginning "Ise love my dear Moggy, said Jockey, so fair" (Lord Crawford 607, with meaningless music), may identify another tune instead of being another name for "King William's March."

This was a very common tune in Restoration days. Two arrangements in lyra-viol tablature are in Cambridge University MS Dd.6.48, fols. 1ᵛ, 8ᵛ (mid-seventeenth century). It is found in John Playford's *A Brief Introduction to the Skill of Musick,* 4th ed., 1664; among the "Select New Tunes and Jiggs for the Treble-Violin" at the end of *The Dancing Master,* 3d ed., 1665, No. 32 (Fig. 265); in *Musick's Delight on the*

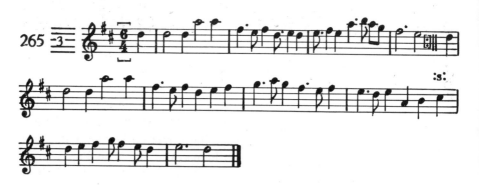

Cithren, 1666; in *Musicks Recreation on the Viol, Lyra-way,* 1669, in *Apollo's Banquet,* 1670; in Thomas Greeting's *The Pleasant Companion . . . for the Flagelet,* 2d ed., 1673; and it is set as a virginal lesson in *Musicks Hand-maid,* 1678. But the tune may be of earlier origin, for in D'Urfey's *The Fool Turn'd Critick,* 1678, IV, ii, "The King's Delight" is named as one of the tunes which "are incomparable to some of these we have now." Moreover, the earliest broadside to the tune probably dates from before 1640; it is "The Batchelors Delight," beginning "The world's a Blister sweld with care," to "the Kings delight, or, The young mans advice to his fellow Batchelors" (Lord Crawford, Harvard, Roxburghe; reprinted in *RB* III, 423).[1]

[1] The *STC* quotes the Roxburghe colophon as "G. F[airbeard, bef. 1622]," but on both Roxburghe and Lord Crawford copies, it is actually "F. G[rove] on Snow-hil." Grove was active from about 1623 until near his death in 1663. The second tune title is probably internally inspired and thus becomes another name for the tune. This conjecture is borne out by the existence of a ballad to the tune of "The Young Mans Advice," entitled "The Benefit of Marriage," beginning "A Man that had a pretty young Wife" (Euing 18, briefly quoted in *RB* VIII, 660, without source; the publisher is E[lizabeth] Andrews, a bookseller to whom Philip Brooksby was apprenticed in 1662). The stanza form is as in "The Batchelors Delight," with the addi-

A broadside written about the time of the Restoration is "A Turn-Coat of the Times," beginning "As I was walking through/Hide-Park as I us'd to do," to the tune "The King's Delight, Or, True Love is a Gift for a Queen" (Pepys, Douce, Lord Crawford, Euing, Harvard, Roxburghe; reprinted in *RB* IV, 517).[2] "The Turn-Coat of the Times" then becomes a tune name in several ballads, including "The Knight and the Beggar-Wench," beginning "I Met with a jovial Beggar,/And into the Fields I led her," to the tune of "The King's Delight, or Turn-Coat" (Pepys, Bagford, Euing, Rawlinson, Lord Crawford, Harvard, Roxburghe; reprinted in *RB* VII, 376). From this latter ballad come two other names for the tune: "The Knight and beggar-wench" in "The forsaken Maids Frollick or, A Farewell to fond Love," beginning "You Females all give ear,/To that which I shall declare" (Lord Crawford, Harvard, Roxburghe; reprinted in *RB* VII, 380), and "I met with a Iovial Beggar" in "An Excellent New Song Fitted for the Times," beginning "Let England now with me/Rejoice this day to see" (Pepys; reprinted in *PB* IV, 223).

All the broadsides cited in the preceding paragraph are clearly related to "The King's Delight," and they are all written in a single metrical pattern, despite some difference in arrangement and division of lines. But this stanza, typically eleven lines (syllabically 7.7.7 7.7.7 7.7.5.5.7, with 7-syllable lines rhyming in triplets), does not fit the music, which is, on the other hand, perfectly suited to the older ballad, "The Batchelors Delight," with its stanza 8.7.8.7.8.8.7.[3] I can offer no explanation of this situation except to suggest that another "King's Delight" came into being during the early years of Charles II but that the new music was not set down under that name. This is not persuasive, especially in the face of D'Urfey's remark, which certainly does not imply competition between an old and a new tune with the same name.

tion of a five-line refrain beginning "Once I lay with another Mans Wife." It is under this title that the tune of "The King's Delight" appears in Gay's *The Beggar's Opera*.

[2] I have no data on the second tune.

[3] Some musical texts repeat the final two bars, implying a repetition of the last line of each stanza.

The King's Jig,
or Winchester Wedding

Thomas D'Urfey's song "The Winchester Wedding, Set to the King's Jigg; a Country Dance," beginning "At Winchester was a Wedding,/the like was never seen," appears with the music in D'Urfey's *Several New Songs*, 1684, p. 2 (Fig. 266). It was reprinted in *180 Loyal Songs*, 1685,

and *Pills*, 1719–1720, I, 276, with inaccurate musical texts. The song had meantime been printed as a broadside (Pepys, Bagford, Douce, Lord Crawford, Roxburghe; reprinted in *RB* VII, 208), one issue of which (Harvard) contains the music.[1] The dance tune can be traced back at least to 1670, when it was included in the first edition of *Apollo's Banquet*, No. 91, as "The Irish Shagg."

The tune's first appearance in *The Dancing Master* is in the Supplement to the 6th ed., 1679 (probably added to the edition in the early 1680s); it is called "The King's Jigg," and the music is in common time.

---

[1] *The Songs of Thomas D'Urfey*, ed. C. L. Day, 1933, pp. 151–152, gives a full list of reprints of the song.

In 1698 (Second Part, 2d ed.) a new dance was introduced, using the same tune, now called "Winchester Wedding." In the eleventh edition, 1701, both dances appear, set to identical music. With the next edition, 1703, the compound time implicit in the original tune [2] is finally recognized: "The King's Jig" is in 9/4, "Winchester Wedding" in 9/8 time. With the edition of 1713 the older dance is dropped and the tune is now called by both names. It so appears in Walsh's *Compleat Country Dancing-Master*, 1718.

Humphry Salter's *Genteel Companion . . . for the Recorder* may have been the first to christen the tune after D'Urfey's song title. It is found among the unnumbered pages added to the 1683 edition, probably in the following year; the music, like that of the *Apollo's Banquet* version, is in 6/4 time, obscuring half the natural accents; but it is otherwise sound. In 1684 the tune was called "Winchester Wedding" on a broadside with music, "A New Song, In Praise of the Loyal Company of Stationers, who . . . obtain'd the first Charter of London," beginning "In London was such a Quarter,/The like was never known" (Bodleian Ashmole G.16 [173]; reprinted in *180 Loyal Songs*, p. 134).

Thereafter "Winchester Wedding" displaced "The King's Jig" as a broadside tune name. It was used in the following: "The Glory of the West, or, The Virgins of Taunton-Dean," 1685, beginning "In Lime began a Rebellion" (Wood 417 [144], Lord Crawford 659); in "Hey for Horn-Fair," beginning "At Charlton there was a fair" (Pepys; reprinted in *RB* VIII, 665); in "A Fairing for Young-Men and Maids" by Tobias Bowne, beginning "As Thomas and Mary did meet" (Pepys, Lord Crawford, Harvard, Roxburghe; reprinted in *RB* VII, 111); in "The Westminster Wedding," beginning "At Westminster was such a match" (Pepys IV, 105); in "Here, Here, Here is Pig and Pork," beginning "In Dublin was play'd such a Prank" (Pepys; reprinted in *PB* V, 68); and in "The Norfolk Stiff-Rump," 1692, beginning "In Norfolk there liveth a Yeoman" (Pepys V, 419).[3]

"Grist ground at Last," beginning "Give ear a while to my Ditty," has the tune direction "Give ear a while, &c. or, Winchester Wedding" (BM C.22.f.6, Lord Crawford, Harvard, Yale, Pepys; reprinted in *RB* VIII, 622). The first tune title does not seem to be associated with an

[2] D'Urfey printed the tune in 3/4 time, producing musical units of three and six bars. His practice is followed on broadsides and in songbooks, with the convenience of the singer doubtless in mind.

[3] The two ballads last cited are in stanzas of four and eight lines respectively. The tune, which is usually found with twelve-line stanzas, accommodates eight lines if the first strain is not repeated. I assume that the four-line form requires either two or three stanzas for each singing of the tune, depending on whether or not the first strain is repeated.

independent air, but the presence of the "Old Simon the King" burden implies that that tune could also be used for the ballad.

The tune was one of the most popular of those levied on in ballad operas, being used in no less than seventeen, and named for the title or the first line of D'Urfey's song. The following print the music: Walker's *The Quaker's Opera*, 1728; Hippisley's *Flora*, 1729; Ralph's *The Fashionable Lady*, 1730; Mitchell's *The Highland Fair*, 1731; *The Jovial Crew*, 1731; Fielding's *The Mock Doctor*, 1732 (music in 2d ed.); Drury's *The Devil of a Duke*, 1732; and Langford's *The Lover his own Rival*, 1736.

Labandala Shot

This sixteenth-century dance tune, doubtless of Continental origin, is found as "banda la shote galyarde" in Thomas Dallis's MS Lute Book, p. 14 (Fig. 267). A somewhat more florid setting appears without title in

the Marsh MS Lute Book, p. 368, and as "Galiard Labandala shotta" in Lord Middleton's MS Lute Book, fol. 22ᵛ. Although the Dallis text preserves the melodic line more carefully, the two other lute sets establish a forty-bar tune which also fits the ten-line stanza of ballads naming the tune.

By all odds the most popular piece sung to "Labandala Shot" was "A sorrowfull Sonet, made by M. George Mannington, at Cambridge Castle," beginning "I Waile in wo, I plunge in pain." Mannington was executed in 1576 and this "good-night" ballad was licensed in the same year. No copy of the broadside is extant, but it was reprinted in *A Handefull of Pleasant Delites*, 1584, ed. Rollins, p. 65. The most familiar imitation appears in Chapman, Jonson, and Marston's *Eastward Hoe*, 1605, V, v, beginning "In Cheapside famous for Gold & Plate," whence it is reprinted in altered form in *Wit and Drollery*, 1661, p. 100. An earlier parody is in the interlude *Misogonus*, II, v (of uncertain authorship and dating from c. 1560–1577). The opening line of the Mannington ballad is frequently quoted in Elizabethan and Jacobean drama, attesting to its continued popularity.[1]

Other ballads to the tune include D. Sterri[e]'s "A briefe sonet declaring the lamentation of Beckles . . . in Suffolk . . . burned with fire . . . 1586," beginning "My louing good neighbours, that comes to beholde" (Huntington, reprinted in Collmann, No. 87; BM Huth, reprinted in *A Collection of Seventy-Nine Black-Letter Ballads*, p. 78). Another is "A proper new ballad, devised vpon the theam I know not what . . . 1614," beginning "Who viewes the lyfe of mortall men" (*SB*, p. 50, *RB* VIII, xxvii***). Richard Johnson's *Golden Garland of Princely Pleasures*, 3d ed., 1620, contains "An excellent Song, entituled, A penny-worth of Wit," beginning "In ancient yeares as bookes expresse," a version of which is reprinted in *A Collection of Old Ballads*, 1723–1725, II, 215.

A curiosity is Thomas Deloney's "A New Song of King Edgar . . . depriued of a Lady . . . by a Knight of his Court," beginning "Whenas King Edgar did gouerne this land," which has the tune direction "To be sung in the old ancient sort, or else to the Tune of Labandalashot" (in his *Garland of Good Will*, 1631, reprinted in *Works*, ed. Mann, p. 305; a version is found also in *A Collection of Old Ballads* II, 25). The ballad consists of 9–10-syllable lines rhyming in couplets, with the burden "adowne, adowne, downe, down, down" after the first and "call him downe a" after the second line of each couplet. The singing direction implies a significant difference between old and new ways. The old way,

---

[1] See the extensive references in Professor Rollins's *Handefull*, pp. 118–121, and in his "Marginalia on Two Elizabethan Poetical Miscellanies," *J. Q. Adams Memorial Studies*, 1948, pp. 473–474.

for which no tune is suggested, may have been recitative in character, resembling the notation Deloney furnished in his *Strange Histories,* but the use of "Labandala shot" demands the omission of the burdens, without which the couplet pattern is substantially that of other ballads to the tune.[2]

A stage direction in the Latin university play *Hispanus* of 1596 (Bodleian MS Douce 234) names the tune as one of several from which a piper may choose; [3] and it is named as a tune for a mournful song in the anonymous comedy *Looke about you,* 1600, sig. F1.

No satisfactory explanation of the tune name has been advanced. T. W. Baldwin, in his *Shakspere's Five-Act Structure,* 1947, p. 433, suggested that it is "a transliteration of Greek." Earlier J. S. Farmer explained the *Misogonus* tune direction "Labondolose Hoto" as a rendering of *La bonne douloureuse hauteur,* "whence 'the extreme heights of sorrow' or 'doleful dumps' " (*Six Anonymous Plays,* 2d series, 1906, p. 381). R. W. Bond, thinking that it might be a "relic" of Italian players who appeared in Windsor and Reading in 1574, proposed the following: "(?La banda da Scozia, Lo bando lo ciotta, L'abbandonato ciotto [cripple], L'abbandono-scotto); or Spanish (El abbandonado soto [grove])?" (*Early Plays from the Italian,* 1911, p. 316). Thus far no Continental antecedents of the tune have been discovered, but in view of what we know about the history of many Tudor dance tunes, it seems probable that the origins of "Labandala shot" are to be sought in Italian, Spanish, or French sources.[4]

---

[2] Professor Rollins suggests a date of c. 1590 for Deloney's ballad. Another copy of the text, without tune direction or refrain, is in the Percy Folio MS (ed. Hales and Furnivall, III, 487). The refrain seems to be echoed in Ophelias's "You must sing, 'Down a-down, and you call him a-down-a,' " *Hamlet,* IV, v. The scrap sung by Mistress Quickly, "And down, down, adown-a, &c.," *Merry Wives,* I, iv, is too commonplace to be confidently associated with Deloney's "King Edgar" refrain.

[3] Quoted in *Shakespeare Jahrbuch,* XXXIV (1898), 300.

[4] John Ward discusses the tune in "Music for *A Handefull of Pleasant Delites,*" *JAMS,* X (1957), 173–174, and prints the Dallis setting fitted to the opening stanza of the Mannington ballad. Ward agrees that the source of the melody is probably in "Continental dance music of the 1550s and 60s."

Ladies of London

Thomas D'Urfey's song beginning "Ladies of London both wealthy and fair" appeared first in his *Compleat Collection,* 1687. Its popularity is striking, for most of the thirty-odd ballads to the tune were printed before the end of Richard Pocock's incumbency as licenser (1685–1688). The broadside version of the poem is "Advice to the Ladies of London, In the Choice of their Husbands. To an Excellent new Court Tune" (Pepys, Lord Crawford, Roxburghe; reprinted in *RB* III, 369), and although the term "Court Tune" is sometimes loosely used, it may be that we have here a cue to the immediate vogue of the song. It was reprinted with the music in *Pills,* 1719–1720, II, 8, but the tune had earlier appeared on a broadside of 1685–1688, "The Sorrowful Assembly: or, The Maidens Humble Petition to the Batchelors of London," beginning "Batchelors how could you prove so unkind" (Wood 417 [134]). The music is also found in *The Dancing Master,* 7th ed., 1686 (on the New Additional Sheet, c. 1688), and in subsequent editions; it is also in *Apollo's Banquet,* 5th ed., 1687, Part III, No. 13 (Fig. 268), called "Lon-

* Bb in original.

don Ladies," which is the title usually given the tune in ballad operas.

D'Urfey's piece inevitably inspired sequels and imitations. "An Answer to the Advice to the Ladies of London," beginning "As I was rambling near Temple-Bar" (Pepys IV, 86) was countered by "Advice to Young

Gentlemen; or, An Answer to the Ladies of London," beginning "All Jolly Blades that Inhabit the Town" (Pepys IV, 87, BM C.22.f.6 [27], Douce I, 2, Lord Crawford 40, Harvard).[1] A topical ballad on women's fashion exploited the popularity of the original broadside title: "Advice to the Maidens of London: to forsake their Fanatical Top-knots," beginning "Now you young Females that follows the Mode" (Pepys, Douce; reprinted in *BB* II, 934). And it gave rise to at least three others to the tune: "The Maidens Resolution; Or, An Answer to the Advice against Top-knots"; "The Women and Maidens Vindication of Top-knots"; and "The Weavers Request. Or, Their Just Complaint against the Rude Rabble, that revile against the Gentile Mode now in Fashion" (the three reprinted in *PB* IV, 18–28). A ballad to the tune of "London Top Knots," entitled "The Vindication of Top-Knots and Commodes," and beginning "The Fops and the Fools, like silly Night-Owls" (*BB* I, 122), is in the "Ladies of London" stanza pattern and may belong in this series.

A number of others to the tune are reprinted in *RB*. Here I shall cite only some of those that have not been reprinted: "The Sorrowful Wife: Or, Love in a Tub," beginning "As I was abroad one night with a friend" (Pepys IV, 116); "A New Ballad, called The Husbandmans Delight: or, A Song in the praise of Straw," beginning "[Com]e all ye Farmers, and listen a while" (Pepys IV, 317); "A Job for a Journeyman Joyner," beginning "Did you not hear of a Bricklayer of late" (Douce I, 106); "The Wealthy Grasier's Joys compleated," beginning "Prithee sweet Creature sit down by my side" (Pepys III, 168, Lord Crawford 1020, Harvard), and "An Answer to the Wealthy Grasier," beginning "Did you not hear of a Wedding of late?" (Pepys III, 172, Douce I, 5^v); "A New Western Ballad," beginning "A Farmer of Tanton-dean Town in the West" (Pepys IV, 125); "The Farmers Reformation," beginning "I have been such a bad Husband of late" (BM C.22.f.6 [118], Lord Crawford 581, Pepys II, 91, Harvard); "The Hasty Virgin," beginning "Mother I have a desire to wed" (Pepys III, 175); "The Contented Cuckold," beginning "There was a Beautiful Damsel of late" (BM C.22.f.6 [94], Lord Crawford 1120); "The Doctor and Beggar-Wench," beginning "There was a Doctor that lives in Barkshire" (Pepys III, 280, Lord Crawford 1126); and "The Kentish Frolick: or, The Tanner Betray'd," beginning "There was a Tanner that lived in Kent" (Douce I, 107).

D'Urfey is apparently the author of another song to the tune, which he printed among his others in the first two volumes of *Pills*, 1719–1720,

[1] The subject matter of this ballad is paralleled in D'Urfey's own "Advice to the Beaus" which is found only in *Pills*, 1719–1720, II, 10, but which one suspects to have been written earlier.

II, 14. It appeared on broadsides as "The Wanton Virgins Frighted," beginning "You that delight in a Jocular Song" (Lord Crawford 1425, Douce II, 239, III, 104ᵛ). It was reprinted as a single-sheet song, c. 1710, with the same music (BM H.1601 [539], Chetham 1578, Huntington, Harvard) and is later found with the tune direction "Ladies of London" in such miscellanies as *A Complete Collection of . . . English and Scotch Songs*, 1735–1736, III, 163. D'Urfey's poem was itself a reworking of an older piece, found in *Westminster Drollery*, 1672, II, 100, as "The Bathing Girls . . . To the common Galliard Tune," beginning "It was in June, and 'twas on Barnaby Bright too"; there is no prosodic similarity.

The tune is used in seven ballad operas. John Gay's *The Beggar's Opera* reprints the tune; Odingsells calls it "Ye Ladies of London" in his *Bays's Opera*, 1730; in the following it is cited as "London Ladies" or "Ladies of London": *The Court Legacy*, 1733; Arthur's *The Lucky Discovery*, 1737; Yarrow's *Love at First Sight*, 1742; *Court and Country*, 1743; *The Ragged Uproar*, c. 1754.

Lady, Lie Near Me

This tune is found in the first eight editions of *The Dancing Master*, 1651–1690 (1651, p. 92 = Fig. 269). In its earliest form it was apparently called "Laddy, lie near me," to judge by broadsides antedating the pub-

Original is unbarred.

lished tune; but different editions of the same ballad give both "Lady" and "Laddy" readings in tune title and refrain.

The primary ballad sung to the tune is "The Longing Shepherdesse or Laddy lye neere me," by R. G[uy?], beginning "All in the Moneth of May,/when all things blossome," to the tune of "Laddy lye neere me: or The Green Garter" (Manchester I, 28 [first half only]; Douce, Pepys, c. 1663–1674, reading "Lady" throughout; reprinted in *RB* VIII, 691, 865).[1] This is presumably the "Lady lie by me" in Thackeray's list of ballads in stock, c. 1689. The earliest edition must have antedated 1639, for in that year Francis Grove was licensed to publish "The courteous Shepherdesse . . . To the Tune of, Laddy lye neere me," beginning "Blith Lad, I prethee goe,/thou wilt deceive me" (Manchester II, 35, with Grove imprint; reprinted in *RB* VIII, xcii***). Both ballads are in the same dactylic meter; the twelve-line stanza of the former requires that both the first and second strain of the air be repeated, whereas the latter, with an eight-line stanza, requires a repetition of only the first strain.

A different tune "Laddie lay near me" is in William McGibbon's *Collection of Scotch Tunes*, IV, 116, in Oswald's *Caledonian Pocket Companion*, Book XII, and in Johnson's *Scots Musical Museum*, III, 226. The latter prints some harmless verses by Dr. Blacklock, followed by two stanzas of "Old Words," presumably furnished by Burns. This later Scotch tune will fit "Laddy lye near me," beginning "As I walked over hills, dales and high mountains," preserved in Ritson's *North Country Chorister*, 1802, and reprinted in his *Northern Garlands*, 1810. The piece has a refrain beginning "Near me, near me, laddy, lye near me," the second line of the couplet varying with each stanza.

The Lass of Cumberland

The names given to this tune are derived from a ballad of the 1670s, "[The Lass of] Cumberland. or, Love in Abundance," beginning "There was a Lass in Cumberland,/a bonny Lass of high degree," to the tune of "The Lass that comes to bed to me" (Douce; reprinted in *RB* VII, 464).[1] The refrain of the broadside supplies this name of the tune:

[1] I can offer no certain identification of "The Green Garter." Cambridge University Library MS Dd.3.18, fol. 23ᵛ, contains lute divisions upon "Green Garters," but the thematic material seems too brief to serve for "The Longing Shepherdesse." A tune entitled "Blew Petticoats or Green Garters" in *The Dancing Master*, 4th ed., 1670, p. 96, is rhythmically unsuited to the ballad.

[1] A later edition, entitled "Cumberland Nelly," has a different text after the two opening stanzas (Douce, Pepys; reprinted in *RB* VII, 463).

Oh! to bed to me, to bed to me,
the Lass that comes to bed to me;
Blith and bonny may she be,
the Lass that comes to bed to me.

Three stanzas of the ballad, with the music, appear in MS 30.G.20, p. 3 (c. 1680), in the Fitzwilliam Museum, Cambridge. A faithful version of the "Lass of Cumberland" text is found with the music in *Pills*, 1719–1720, IV, 133. The tune (Fig. 270) is printed twice in *180 Loyal Songs*,

270

1685, once as "There was a Lass of Cumberland," in association with the song "The Creditors Complaint against the Bankers," beginning "Bankers now are brittle Ware," p. 219; as "a new Tune" it is printed with "The Honour of Great York and Albany," beginning "The commons now are at a stand," p. 176.[2] The tune is called "To bed we'l go" in *Apollo's Banquet*, 5th ed., 1687, No. 113 (Fig. 271), and "to be[d] to me or The Northern lass" in *Youth's Delight on the Flagelet*, 9th ed., c. 1690.

An imitation of the original ballad, issued also in the 1670s, is "Cumberland Laddy; or, Willy and Nelly of the North," beginning "There was a Lad in Cumberland,/and he was born of high degree," to the tune of "The Lass that comes to Bed to me" (Douce; reprinted in *RB* VII, 465); the refrain supplies "Lad" for "Lass" and characterizes him as "brisk and lively" but otherwise follows the original. "The Northern Ladd . . . To the Tune of, There was a Lass in Cumberland," beginning "I am a Lass o'th North Country" (Lord Crawford, Harvard, Roxburghe; reprinted in *RB* VII, 171), also has a refrain in the original mold, the lad here being a "jovial Plowman."

Others to the tune include "The Maids Lamentation," beginning "My Love is gone alack a day," to the tune of "The Lass that comes to Bed to me, Or, Sawney is gone" (Lord Crawford 840, BM C.22.f.6 [63]);[3] another, to be sung "To its own proper Tune," but possessing the stanza

[2] This latter text is taken from a broadside of 1683 (Harvard), containing entirely different music to which no name is given.

[3] The second tune title may be the equivalent of "Sawney and Jockey," but I have not found a text which echoes the phrasing of the tune title.

271

pattern and refrain formula of "The Lass of Cumberland," is "An Excellent New Ballad, Intituled, Bide till you be married yet," beginning "When I was young, as you are now" (National Library of Scotland Ry III.a.10 [42]), with the burden:

> So bide you yet, so bide you yet,
> So bide till you be marri'd yet,
> The Half of that will serve you yet,
> If once that you were marri'd yet.

One other ballad, to the tune "To Bed to me," is noteworthy because it suggests a link with several pieces sung to "Nanny O." It is "The Yeomans Delight," beginning "There is a Lass whom I adore" (Pepys III, 169), with a refrain:

> For Katy, Katy, Katy O,
>   the love I bear to Katy O;
> All the world shall never know,
>   the love I bear to Katy O.

The identical refrain formula (substituting "Nanny" for "Katy") is found in "The Scotch Wooing of Willy and Nanny. To a pleasant new Tune: Or, Nanny O" (RB III, 408) and becomes the archetype of refrains in ballads sung to the latter tune. Because of the common refrain pattern we are led to suspect that "Nanny O" was, in the 1680s, another name for "The Lass of Cumberland" music, though one could wish for a stronger basis of proof. It is clear that in the eighteenth century "Nanny O," q.v., had its own tune.

Music of "The Lass of Cumberland" accommodates four octosyllabics. Since the usual stanza is eight such lines, a repetition of the tune is required for the second quatrain, which is ordinarily a refrain. The

Apollo's Banquet set does include a second strain, partially an embellishment of the first and perhaps added to give more substance to the violin arrangement. The second half of the ballad stanza could be sung to the added strain, but since it is not found in any version of the tune accompanied by words, I cannot vouch for its use in singing.

"The Cumberland Lass," beginning "In Cumberland there dwells a maid/Her charms are past compare," printed in *A Complete Collection of . . . English and Scotch Songs*, 1735–1736, I, 179, is in ballad meter and does not fit this tune.

Last Christmas 'Twas My Chance

A ballad with the rhyming title "The Pedler opening of his Packe, To know of Maydes what tis they lacke," is to the tune "Last Christmas 'twas my chance" and begins "Who is it will repaire" (Pepys; reprinted in *PG*, p. 116). Professor Rollins dated the Pepys copy c. 1620 but believed the ballad to be much earlier.

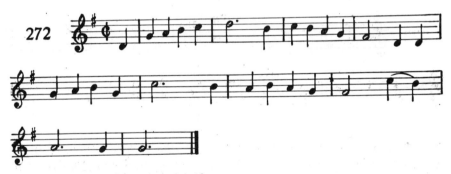

272

Key signature two sharps in original.

No contemporary version of the tune exists, but *Pills*, 1719–1720, V, 25, contains a song beginning "Last Christmas 'twas my chance," in the same distinctive four-and-a-half-line stanza pattern as in the ballad. The tune there printed (Fig. 272) has the earmarks of antiquity and may represent fairly faithfully the form in which it was sung a century earlier.

Lavender Green

This tune name is derived from the opening line of a ballad printed about 1675: "Diddle, Diddle. Or, The Kind Country Lovers," beginning "Lavenders green, didle, didle,/Lavenders blue," to the tune of "Lavender green" (Pepys, Euing, Douce, Lord Crawford, Roxburghe; reprinted in *RB* IV, 434). A posthumous edition of Ritson's *Gammer Gurton's Garland,* 1810, p. 46, includes "The Lady's Song in Leap Year," a chastened poem which suggests that elements of the old broadside survived through traditional circulation. It begins:

> Roses are red, diddle, diddle,
> Lavender's blue:
> If you will have me, diddle, diddle,
> I will have you.

I have found no seventeenth-century tune for "Lavender Green." The one tune associated with ballad remnants is perhaps a recovery from tradition, "Lavender's Blue" in E. F. Rimbault's *Nursery Rhymes,* c. 1846, p. 20 (Fig. 273). The three-stanza text and tune, transposed from

273

F to G, were reprinted in Walter Crane's *The Baby's Opera,* c. 1877, p. 15. For other appearances, see M. G. Quigley, *Index to Kindergarten Songs,* 1914. *The Oxford Dictionary of Nursery Rhymes,* ed. Iona and Peter Opie, 1951, No. 299, reprints Rimbault's text and four stanzas of the broadside; variants of the nursery form of the verses are cited, and the editors reproduce the sheet-music cover of a popular song which makes free use of tune and refrain: "Lavender Blue," 1948, beginning "Lavender blue dilly, dilly,/Lavender green," by Larry Morey and Eliot Daniel, written for the Walt Disney film, "So Dear to My Heart."

Lay By Your Pleading

This tune is known by a large number of names, including "Cyclops," "The Sword," "Love lies a-bleeding," "Law lies a-bleeding," "Lay by your pleading," "Ignoramus," "No Ignoramus juries now," and "The Loyal Conquest."

The original ballad sung to the tune is "Love Lies a Bleeding," beginning "Lay by your pleading/Love lies a bleeding," to the tune "The Cyclops" (Manchester, Euing; reprinted in *Merry Drollery*, 1661,[1] and *RB* VIII, 730). This is an attack on the Puritans, written c. 1653–1654, as a result of which the tune became "political" and was used with no other sort of ballad. I have found no information on "Cyclops" as a tune, but I suspect it to be connected with the dance. It may be significant that in its earliest appearance in print, in Jacob van Eyk's *Der Fluyten Lust-Hof,* Amsterdam, 1654, II, 41ᵛ, the tune is called "Ballet" (Fig. 274).

274

* Two variations follow in original.

"Law lies a Bleeding," 1659, beginning "Lay by your Pleading,/Law lies a bleeding," to the tune of "Love lies a bleeding" (Wood 401; reprinted in *RB* VIII, clxxxi*; see also xxxvi*), is an imitation and continuation of the original ballad, introducing current topical detail.[2]

[1] The *Drollery* title is "Love lies a bleeding: in imitation of Law lies a bleeding," but the imitation is, in fact, the other way around.

[2] A manuscript version of words and music, under the title "The Dominion of the Sword," and dated August 2, 1658, is reported by Thorn-Drury (see Brooks, "Rump Songs: an Index," notes 121, 21). The reprint in *Merry Drollery*, 1661, is titled "The Power of the Sword." The ballad is also found in BM MS Harl. 3991, fol. 51ᵛ, in *Rump*, 1662, in *A Loyal Garland*, 1686, and in *Loyal Songs*, 1731. It is printed with the music in *Pills*, 1719–1720, VI, 190.

From references here to the power of the sword comes the name of the tune in "Chipps of the Old Block . . . To the Tune of, The Sword," beginning "Now you by your good leave Sirs" (BM Thomason, dated Jan. 26, 1659/60, BM Luttrell II, 40, Wood 416 [36], Bagford III, 12, Harvard, MS date Jan. 30, 1659/60, Yale; reprinted in *Ratts Rhimed to Death* and *The Rump*, 1660, and *Loyal Songs*, 1731).

The tune was called into fullest play in the political warfare of the 1680s, but it was not forgotten meanwhile. It appeared as "Dours Catastrophe or Lawyers leave your Pleading" among the violin tunes appended to the 1665 edition of *The Dancing Master*. In an earlier and briefer supplement, c. 1662, No. 29 (Fig. 275), the tune is found with

only the first of these titles. Under the title "Love lies a bleeding" the tune entered the body of *The Dancing Master* with the 7th ed., 1686. In Shadwell's *Epsom Wells*, 1673, II, i, Clodpate sings "Lay by your pleading,/Law lies a bleeding, &c," which, though an "old Song," had not lost its savor for the country folk. *Mock Songs*, 1675, contains a parody of this song, beginning "Lay by your fighting,/Misses are inviting," in which politics are momentarily put by.

The ballads resume with "Ignoramus: An Excellent New Song," 1681, beginning "Since Reformation/With Whigs in Fashion," to the tune "Lay by your Pleading, Law lies a bleeding" (BM Luttrell, Bodleian Ashmole G.16, London Society of Antiquaries [Grant collection], Wood 417, Harvard, Yale, Huntington; reprinted in *Wit and Mirth*, 1682, in *180 Loyal Songs*, 1685, with music, and in *RB* V, 200). In the same year appeared "A New Ignoramus: Being the second New Song," beginning "Since Popish Plotters,/Join'd with Bogg-Trotters," to the tune "Law lyes a Bleeding" (BM 1875.d.6, Harvard, Yale, Huntington; reprinted in *Rome Rhym'd to Death*, 1683, and *RB* V, 202).

"The Loyal Conquest Or, Destruction of Treason," 1683, beginning "Now Loyal Tories/may Tryumph in Glories" (BM 1872.a.1, Harvard, Clark; reprinted in *180 Loyal Songs* and *RB* V, 321), contributes new names for the tune from its title and from the burden, which ends "No Ignoramus Jury's now/for Whigs but only hanging." Echoing the title is the tune direction, "The Loyal Conquest or Law lies a bleeding," associated with the broadside "Dr Oats last Farewell to England," beginning "Farewell to London,/To Trenchard, and Hamdan" (Harvard, Clark). "No Ignoramus Juries now" is the tune title in "The Whiggish Poet's Recantation," 1684, beginning "This is my Reformation,/and perfect Recantation" (Lord Crawford 1165, Clark; the copy in the British Museum, 1876.f.1 [26], is an undated issue with the title "A New Song of the Whiggish Poets Recantation"); it is also used for "Perjury Punish'd with equal Justice," beginning "All you that standeth near me" (Pepys; reprinted in *PB* III, 243).

The tune is called "Ignoramus; or, Lay by your Pleading" in "The Newcastle Associators," 1684, beginning "Lay by your Reason,/Truth's out of Season" (Harvard; reprinted in *180 Loyal Songs* and in *RB* V, 496).[3]

Stanza patterns vary widely among these ballads; some fit the tune without repetition of either strain, others require a repetition of both. Two stanzas of "Chipps of the Old Block" are needed to sing the tune once through. The music allows great metrical flexibility, and the syllabic count shows little uniformity from stanza to stanza within the same ballad; only the feminine ending of each line remains as a distinguishing constant.

Lay the Bent to the Bonny Broom

This tune is named for singing "A Noble Riddle wisele Expounded," beginning "There was a Lady of the North Country" (Euing, Wood E.25, Rawlinson, Pepys, Douce; reprinted in *RB* VIII, c***); the tune title derives from the burden of the broadside. The Euing copy was issued, c. 1658–1664, by Coles, Vere, and Gilbertson; the ballad was licensed to Coles, Vere, Wright, and Clark in 1675 (Wood, Rawlinson). It was an item in Thackeray's stock, c. 1689, and the Pepys copy has the im-

[3] In "A New Song. To the Tune of, Lay by your Pleading" (Harvard) the opening couplet is identical, but the ballad thereafter deals with events of 1689.

print of Thackeray and two partners of c. 1692, Elizabeth Millet and Alexander Milbourn. The Douce issue is a later one in roman letter. The broadside text is reprinted in *Pills*, 1719–1720, IV, 129, with a badly barred Dorian tune which gives every evidence of being traditional and not an art product (Fig. 276). Chappell (*PMOT* II, 531) printed the tune in 3/4 time, with lengthened notes for the first and third cadences which do less violence to the spirit of the original than his flatting the sixth and thereby destroying the modal character of the tune. Bronson's emendation in *The Traditional Tunes of the Child Ballads*, 1959–   , I, 4, preserves the *Pills* note values and follows Chappell's barring by reducing to 2/4 the measures containing the first and third cadences.

It is with "Riddles Wisely Expounded" that F. J. Child began *The English and Scottish Popular Ballads*, 1882–1898, and he showed the relationship of the story to a fifteenth-century verse dialogue between a maid and the devil. The broadside has romanticized the riddling contest by making the questioner a knight, whose hand the youngest daughter wins by answering his riddles. Both forms of the story have continued in tradition into the twentieth century in America, but modern survivals are rare in Great Britain.[1] Recent melodic tradition owes little to the *Pills* tune, as Bronson has shown.

The Leather Bottle

"A Pleasant new Song, in Praise of the Leather Bottell" was written by John Wade, a Restoration ballad maker of some prominence. It is to

[1] See T. P. Coffin, *The British Traditional Ballad in North America*, 1963, pp. 22–23, and Margaret Dean-Smith, *A Guide to English Folk Song Collections*, 1954, s.v. "Lay . . . broom." Among several recordings may be mentioned "The Devil's Nine Questions," sung by Mrs. Texas Gladden in 1941, LC Archive of American Folk Song, record 4A1.

the tune of "The Bottel-makers Delight," which may or may not be a name inspired by the sense of the ballad itself. It begins:

> God above that made all things,
>> the Heavens, the Earth, and all therein,
> The Ships that on the Sea do swim,
>> to keep Enemies out that now comes in:
> And let them do all what they can,
>> 'tis for the use and praise of man,
>>> And I wish in Heaven his soul may dwell
>>> That first devised the Leather Bottel.

The earliest extant edition was printed for Richard Burton (fl. 1641–1674) and is found in Wood E.25 (56);[1] later editions, usually entitled "A Song in Praise of the Leather Bottel," are in Pepys, Douce, Bagford, Roxburghe; reprinted in *RB* VI, 470. The entry in the Stationers' Register, 1678, is to Coles, Vere, Wright, and Clark, who distributed the issue represented by the Douce copy. The song was reprinted in *The New Academy of Complements*, 1671, *Wit and Drollery* and *Wit and Mirth*, 1682, and in *Pills*, all editions, 1719–1720, III, 246, with music (Fig. 277).

277

Wade's song showing the merits of the leather bottle over wooden cans, glasses, three-handled pots, and silver flagons invited the kind of imita-

---

[1] There is an allusion to the ballad in "Hey for our Town, But a Fig for Zommersetshire," also printed for Burton (Douce I, 96):

> Come, sing 's a merry catch, quo' Bob,
>> Quo' scraper, what the words?
> In praise o'th' Leather Bottel, quo' Bob,
>> For we'll be merry as lords.

tion and "answer" found in *Westminster Drollery*, 1672, II, 94 (reprinted in *RB* VI, 466): "In praise of the Black-Jack," beginning "Be your liquor small, or as thick as mudd," and with a burden:

> And I wish that his heires may never want Sack,
> That first devis'd the bonny black Jack.

Another version is in *Wit and Mirth*, 1682, and in *Pills* III, 249, beginning " 'Tis a pitiful thing that now adays, Sirs,/Our Poets turn Leathern Bottle praisers," and sung to the music of Wade's ballad.[2]

Both ballads are in stanzas of unequal length. In Wade's ballad the variation is from eight to sixteen lines, with some stanzas of eight, ten, twelve, and fourteen lines. Each of the musical phrases fits an octosyllabic couplet, and the architectonic shaping of the tune is so slight that any four-bar phrase may be repeated to allow for expansion of the text beyond the eight-line stanza which the music is designed to fit.[3]

Traditional survivals of the broadside text in Somerset and Oxfordshire are preserved in J. H. Dixon, *Ancient Poems, Ballads, and Songs of the Peasantry of England*, 1846, p. 208, and Alfred Williams, *Folk-Songs of the Upper Thames*, 1923, p. 244. A tune and two stanzas, noted by Cecil Sharp in Tewkesbury, 1908, are reprinted in *JFSS*, V (1914), 71. The tune is even more repetitious than that in *Pills*, to which it may be distantly related; the first stanza, describing a bottle made of "the old cow's hide," has no parallel in the broadside, but the second is related to the concluding stanza of the seventeenth-century text.

Let Caesar Live Long

This tune takes its name from the opening line, "Let Caesar live long, and his temper abide," of a broadside written during the lifetime of Charles II but apparently not published until after his death. It is titled "The True Loyalist; Or, The Obedient Servant"; the tune is named on the black-letter copy (Pepys; reprinted in *PB* III, 211); the music is

---

[2] It was probably this latter version that was registered as a ballad in 1675. The black jack was a large open-mouthed tankard coated outside with tar to give it its color. The balladist's chief argument in its favor is that with the jack one can be "Drunk in good time," whereas "the Bottle it runs as slow as my Rhime."

[3] Chappell (*PMOT* II, 513) saw signs of antiquity in the pronunciation of "bottle" required in Wade's ballad, and in the unequal length of stanzas.

printed on a roman-letter issue in Wood 417 (115).[1] With numerous variations in detail, the tune appears in *180 Loyal Songs*, 1685, p. 326 (Fig. 278), and the two opening stanzas of the ballad printed there are

278

also to be found, without music, in contemporary Garlands, as noted by Professor Rollins.[2]

"Let Caesar live long" was one of the most popular broadside tunes dating from the Restoration years. It is cited on some forty-five extant ballads, and only "Hey, boys, up go we" appears to have been used more often. Twenty-five ballads to the "Caesar" tune are in *PB*,[3] and most of

[1] The two issues of the broadside were licensed by Richard Pocock, who did not succeed Sir Roger L'Estrange until November, 1685 (see *PB* III, 210*n*.). Wood's MS date of 1686 has been canceled and 1683 substituted, perhaps to indicate what Wood thought to have been the date of composition. The ballad reference to twenty years of rule would suggest c. 1680 as a plausible date of origin, although the round figure may have been used with poetic license.

[2] Music on the broadside "Teague the Irish Soldier," 1691, is actually a garbled set of "Make your honors, Miss," although the tune direction is "Let Caesar Live long. or, Now, now the Fight's done" (Pepys; reprinted in *PB* VI, 134).

[3] In this count I do not include the ballad reprinted in *PB* III, 74, which derives its tune direction, "Let Caesar Live long," from the refrain of a ballad (*PB* III, 70) to the tune "Let Traytors plot on," q.v. The twelve-line stanza pattern of these two pieces contrasts sharply with the six-line anapestic tetrameter stanza of the ballads under discussion.

the others have been reprinted in *RB* or *BB*. The tune was a great favorite for political and military subjects, and its high tide of popularity came during the campaigns of 1689–1691, when more than half the ballads to the tune were issued.

An example of the attractiveness of the tune is suggested by the history of "The Clarret Drinkers Song," beginning "A Pox of the Fooling and Plotting of late." When the broadside version of this piece first appeared in 1680 (BM 1870.d.1 [124], Wood 417 [28], Lord Crawford 1004, Harvard, Yale), no tune was named on the sheet. It was set to anonymous music in *Choice Ayres and Songs,* Third Book, 1681, p. 28, reprinted in *Pills,* 1719–1720, III, 186. After the tune "Let Caesar live long" had become popular, an expanded version of the broadside was published, naming that tune (Roxburghe; reprinted in *RB* IV, 645).[4]

Although "Caesar" was a shopworn epithet for Charles II, a later ballad writer applied it to William III in "The Royal Character," c. 1696, beginning "Long live our Great Cesar, and long be his Reign," to the tune "Long Live our Great Cesar; Or, Now, now the Fight's done" (Pepys; reprinted in *PB* VII, 223). It may be that the first tune name indicates a new air, but I have found no music so titled, and the stanza form is that of the usual "Let Caesar live long" ballad. The same may be said of a song to the tune "Let Caesar rejoyce," beginning "Alphonzo, if you Sir,/Your Heart have resign'd," printed without music in *Pills* VI, 339.

A sheaf of ballads sung to "Let Caesar live long" (reprinted in *RB* VII, 756ff.) develop the old theme of a king's incognito visits among his subjects. Here the king is William of Orange, who is made to seem more human and less august than in the "great Caesar" role usually depicted by contemporary ballad writers. One of these, "The King and the Forrester" (*RB* VII, 763), deserves note because Ebsworth has erroneously assumed, in the absence of a tune direction, that it was sung to "Let Caesar live long." Its content justifies placing it in the series, but its quatrains do not fit the six-phrase tune.

Among the few ballads to the tune not reprinted, the following may be noted: "The Sorrowful Bride," beginning "I have now been Marry'd a Twelvemonth and more" (Pepys III, 244); "The Wanton Widows pleasant Mistake," beginning "A Buxom rich Widdow had late laid in Grave" (Pepys III, 306); "The Broken Vintner of London," beginning "A Vintner he from fair London would Ride" (Pepys IV, 291); "The Country Squire Deceiv'd," beginning "A Rich Country Squire, call'd up to the

---

[4] The author of the original song was John Oldham, in whose *Poems, and Translations,* 1683, it appeared, with the statement that it was written March 9, 1680. It is to be found also in *The Remains of Mr. Tho. Brown,* 1720, p. 11, but the attribution to Brown cannot be taken seriously. See H. F. Brooks, "A Bibliography of John Oldham," *Oxf. Bibliog. Soc. Proc.,* V (1936–1939), 19, 38.

Town" (Pepys IV, 361); and "The Frolicksome Bricklayer of Mile-End Town," 1693, beginning "Young Men shall be blam'd for their lewdness no more" (Pepys V, 166). "The Wheel-Wrights Huy-and-Cry after his Wife," beginning "How sad is my fate how unhappy my life," is to the tune of "Let Caesar Live Long, Or the Female Drummer" (Pepys IV, 115). I have no information on the second tune title.

Let Mary Live Long

This tune takes its name from the opening line of "The Loyal English Man's Wish For the Preservation of The King and Queen," 1692, a broadside containing an excellent version of the tune (Fig. 279) printed in the new "tied note" then coming into fashion (Lord Crawford, Pepys; reprinted in *PB* VI, 161). The tune is also found with the first three stanzas in *Pills,* 1719–1720, VI, 83, where the authorship of the words is credited to Anne Morcott. Two other broadsides to the tune contain meaningless music: "The Dissatisfied Subject," beginning "Behold in this Age" (BM

279

* F in original.

C.39.k.6 [24], reprinted in *OPB*, p. 62; Lord Crawford, Pepys, reprinted in *PB* VI, 218); and "King William Triumphant," beginning "Ye Iacobite Crew" (Pepys; reprinted in *PB* VI, 241).

The elaborate eleven-line stanza pattern and the highly ornamented tune are not the sort usually marked out for popular success. But "Let Mary live long" was instantly in vogue, and in less than a decade some twenty-five ballads called for the air. Professor Rollins reprinted sixteen ballads to the tune, most of which can be dated 1692–1693 (*PB* VI, *passim*); half a dozen more are found in the last volumes of *The Roxburghe Ballads*. In addition, "The Quaker's Wanton Wife," beginning "A Citizen's Wife I am, I declare it" (Pepys, Lord Crawford, BM C.39.k.6) was reprinted in *OPB*, p. 25.[1]

The following have apparently not been reprinted: "Labour in Vain," beginning "Young Women I pray/Be pleased to pity" (Pepys V, 168, Lord Crawford 1465); and a pair of related ballads, listing the tune as "Mary live long": "The Ladies of London's Petition . . . to the Parliament of old Women for Husbands," beginning "You Matrons all,/With humble Submission" (Lord Crawford 1412–1413, Harvard), and "The Young Mens Answer to the Ladies of London's Petition," beginning "To whom shall we go,/To make Application" (Douce II, 262ᵛ). A broadside of c. 1708 printed "for Mounsier de Garlick Pinch" and sung to "The King of Frances Lamentation" seems actually to have been meant for "Let Mary live long," for the eleven-line stanza is not casually to be duplicated; it is titled "England triumphant, or, the King of France in a violent Passion" and begins "Sir, Here's de express" (BM 1876.f.1 [42]).

"An Account of the Surrender of Bethune," beginning "Brave Boys, let us sing," and describing an event of 1710, is sung to the tune in *Political Merriment*, 1714. Drury's *The Mad Captain*, 1733, is the only ballad opera calling for the tune.

Let the Critics Adore

This tune takes its name from the first line of "Celia's Triumph, Or, Venus Dethron'd," a broadside licensed by Roger L'Estrange, May 8, 1678. Its opening stanza is:

> Let the Critticks adore,
> Their Old Venus no more,

[1] Later editions are found with the title "A pleasant Discourse of a Young Woman to her Husband the Quaker" (Harvard, BM 1871.e.9 [54]).

· 438 ·

280

She's a Gypsie,
Silly Mortals ne'r think,
That the Goddess will Drink
and be Tipsie.
None but Vulcan can abide her,
she's grown so Black of late,
In his Cole-hole he does hide her,
to secure her from fate:
All the Gods are stark mad,
for a Venus more fair,
And swear they'd be glad,
that my Celia were there.

The tune is named on the sheet "Let the Critticks adore, as it is Sung at the Play-house" (Lord Crawford 763, BM C.22.f.6 [35], Harvard).[1]

[1] Ebsworth (*RB* VII, 412) says that this ballad is sung to the tune of "Let the soldiers rejoice," but he overlooks both the evidence on the broadside itself and the total dissimilarity of stanza patterns.

At least two other ballads were sung to the tune. One is "Loves Tyranny: Or, Death more welcome then Disdain," beginning "Ah! how drousie's the Skies,/Now black Night does arise" (Lord Crawford, Harvard, Roxburghe; reprinted in *RB* VII, 413). The other is a broadside of 1682 which contains the music (Fig. 280): "Loyalty Triumphant: or, A Looking-Glass for Deceivers," beginning "Let the Whigs ne'r adore/Their old Grandees no more" (Huntington).

All these ballads are written in two-part stanzas, but only "Loyalty Triumphant" has a nine-line first section. The music to fit it is three phrases of five measures each, with the third phrase virtually a repetition of the second; eliminating this musical repetition adapts the tune perfectly to the other two ballads.

Let the Soldiers Rejoice

"Let the soldiers rejoice" is a song in the second act of *The Prophetess, or The History of Dioclesian*, 1690, a Purcell opera with libretto by Betterton.[1] At least two single-sheet editions with music brought the stage song intact to the public,[2] and it appeared also in Purcell's *The Vocal and Instrumental Musick of the Prophetess*, 1691, p. 33 (Fig. 281), and in *Pills*, 1719–1720, IV, 277. A harpsichord arrangement of "Let ye soldiers rejoyce" is in BM MS Add. 22099, fol. 8ᵛ, c. 1704–1707. The playhouse song with its air is in BM MS Add. 35043, fol. 5ᵛ; words alone are found in BM MS Lansdowne 852, fol. 175. The tune is called for in one ballad opera, *Love and Revenge*, c. 1729.

The playhouse text was twice expanded to broadside length and slanted toward the current Irish campaign. Probably the earlier of the two is "The Royal Conquest, or, The Happy Success against a Potent Enemy. As it was Sung in the Prophetess at the Queens Theatre. To a New Play-House Tune"; the sheet contains pied musical characters, part of which are stabs at the totally irrelevant "Hey, boys, up go we" (Harvard 25242.72 [244]). The other is "Royal Courage, Or, King William's Happy Success in Ireland. Tune is, Let the Soldiers Rejoyce"; the sheet contains

---

[1] Dryden may have had a hand in the songs, but the earliest single-sheet edition of "Let the soldiers rejoice" credits the words to "Mr. Batterton."

[2] "A New song sung in the Prophetess" is a small quarto engraved copy, probably of the early 1690s (BM C.180.a [2]); an issue of c. 1700, "A Song in Dioclesian Set by Mr. Henry Purcell," is of conventional folio size (BM H.1601 [278], Huntington).

281

Original is an octave lower.

music, not of the tune named, but of "Why are my eyes still flowing," to which the ballad cannot be sung (Pepys; reprinted in *PB* V, 203).[3] The first three stanzas of these broadsides are derived from the stage song; thereafter each balladist goes his independent way, but the titles are sufficient indication of the jubilant spirit induced by William's victory at the Boyne in July, 1690.

Of the eighteen or so ballads written to the tune in the last decade of the century, ten are to be found in *PB,* most of them capitalizing on the martial spirit of the original song, and several imitating its opening formula. One of these is "The Female Souldier: Or, The Virgin Volunteer," beginning "I Sing in the Fame/Of a pritty young Dame," a reworking of an old theme. In its more sentimental form, the damsel enlists to follow her soldier lover; here she is moved by patriotism but is discovered before she has tasted battle (Pepys; reprinted in *PB* VI, 302). Another on the same subject, and sung to the tune, is "The Woman Warrier," beginning "Let the Females attend," in which a young matron leaves her husband behind, crosses to Ireland and fights at the siege of Cork, where she is mortally wounded (Pepys, Lord Crawford, Harvard, Douce; reprinted in *BB* I, 323, and, with the music, in *Pills* V, 8). From this latter ballad comes "The Woman Warrier" as a tune name; it is cited for singing "The Constant Country-Man," beginning "Pritty Nancy my love,/

[3] Meaningless music is also found on the following broadsides: "The Loyal Wish" (Pepys V, 66; reprinted in *PB* V, 230); "The Church of Englands Wish" (Pepys V, 87; reprinted in *PB* VI, 19); and "The Loyal States-man . . . Tune of, The Sages of Old; or, Let the Souldiers Rejoyce" (Pepys V, 134; reprinted in *PB* VII, 130).

I adore thee above" (Pepys, Lord Crawford, Harvard, Roxburghe; reprinted in *RB* III, 551).

The following ballads sung to "Let the soldiers rejoice" have not been reprinted: "The Shepherds Petition to The Goddess of Beauty," beginning "Let my Celia prove kind,/Of a gentle soft mind" (BM C.22.f.6 [178], Lord Crawford 758); and "An Excellent new Ballad," a political parody beginning "Let the Soldiers rejoyce,/With a general Voice,/Since the Senate new Ho——nours decreed 'em," and reflecting the unpopularity of Stanhope, Sunderland, and Cadogan, probably near the end of Queen Anne's reign (Huntington).

One peculiarity of the stanza pattern in this group of ballads should be noted. Each half of the six-line stanza contains two anapestic dimeters followed by an anapestic tetrameter. But in some ballads the third line of each half stanza is a trimeter. This apparent lack of consistency is illustrated in line three of the original stage song, which in Purcell's published text is:

> and the Senate new honours decree 'em,

but in the expanded Pepys broadside reads:

> And the Senate new Honours and Glory decree 'em.

Both, however, can be sung to the music; the Purcell song devotes four beats in measures 6 and 7 to the first syllable of "honours," while the longer broadside line supplies syllables for each musical beat. Many ballads using the unexpanded line indicate the melisma with a dash:

> Since the Senate new Ho——nours decreed 'em.

The longer form of the line is sometimes achieved not through expansion but through repetition, as at the end of the first broadside stanza adapted from the song text:

> And so boldly, so boldly, so bravely did free 'em.

Let Traitors Plot On

This tune is named from the opening line of a song in Thomas D'Urfey's play *The Virtuous Wife*, 1680, Act I. The text of two stanzas and chorus appeared with music by Thomas Farmer in *Choice Ayres and Songs*, Third Book, 1681, p. 7 (Fig. 282), and without music in *Wit and*

282

Mirth, 1682; the first stanza is in D'Urfey's *New Collection of Songs,* 1683. In D'Urfey's play *Sir Barnaby Whigg,* 1681, IV, i, the title character sings a parody of the opening lines:

· 443 ·

Let the Roundheads Plot on,
Till at last they'r undone
By hurting their Brains to Decoy us.

The broadside version in eight stanzas is "The Loyal Protestant,"
beginning "Let Traytors Plot on till at last they'r undone,/By hurting
their braines to destroy us," to the tune "Let Traytors plot on" (Pepys;
reprinted in *PB* III, 70), probably issued in 1680. The refrain, beginning
"Let Caesar live long, let Caesar live long," is the source of the tune title
in another ballad of the same year, "Here Is Incouragement to Loyalty,"
beginning "You traytors be gone, for the Plot you thought on," to the
tune "Let Caesar Live long" (Pepys; reprinted in *PB* III, 74).[1]

Other ballads sung to the tune include "Gallantry All-a-Mode," begin-
ning "Let the Cinick Zealots,/Impose on Dull Sots," with refrain "Let
Bumpers go round . . ." (Roxburghe; reprinted in *RB* IV, 629), and
"Long lookt for is come at last," beginning "Now the Parliament Sits,
Traytors look to your Hits," to the tune "Let Bumpers go round" (Rox-
burghe; reprinted in *RB* IV, 194).

[Liberty's the Soul of Living]

This song appeared in D'Urfey's play *A Common-Wealth of Women*,
1686, III, i. A part of the song text was reprinted in the same year in
The Theater of Music, Third Book, p. 10, with music by Samuel Akeroyde (Fig. 283), and is in *Pills*, 1719–1720, II, 308. The original song,

283

---

[1] This is the only ballad to the tune "Let Caesar live long" which I have found
in the "Let Traitors plot on" stanza form of eight lines plus a refrain of four. From
the mid-1680s an entirely different tune, for a six-line anapestic tetrameter stanza,
is popular as "Let Caesar live long," q.v. It is named, not from D'Urfey's refrain
of 1680, but from the opening line of a new ballad. In both contexts "Caesar" is a
stock adulatory epithet for Charles II.

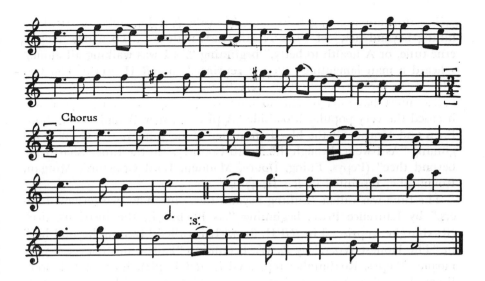

expanded to an eight-stanza dialogue between Liberty and Love, was issued as a broadside with the title "Love's Mighty Conquest . . . To a New Play-House Tune" (Pepys V, 201). Apparently no other broadsides were sung to Akeroyde's tune.

Lie Lulling Beyond Thee

This tune is found in the first eight editions of *The Dancing Master*, 1651–1690 (1651, p. 93=Fig. 284), where it is called "Lull me beyond thee" or "Lulling beyond thee."

Original a fourth higher and unbarred.

The tune apparently gets its name from the (varying) refrain, "till I lie lulling beyond her," of "The Northerne Turtle . . . To a new Northerne tune, or A health to betty," beginning "As I was walking all alone/ I heard a man lamenting" (Pepys; reprinted in *RB* II, 311).[1] The two editions in the Pepys collection were likely printed before 1640, and the ballad must have originated no later than 1624, for in that year was licensed the very popular broadside "A pleasant new Ballad to sing both Euen and Morne, Of the bloody murther of Sir John Barley-Corne," beginning "As I went through the North Country," to the tune "Shall I lye beyond thee" (Pepys, Euing, Douce, Madden, Lord Crawford, Morgan, Roxburghe; reprinted in *RB* II, 373).

The tune was called "Lulling beyond thee" in "The two feruent Louers," by Laurence Price, beginning "As Phebus in the lustrious aire" (Roxburghe; reprinted in *RB* II, 611).[2] It is called "Lulling beyond her" in "The Honest Woer," by R. W., beginning "Fairest mistris, cease your moane" (Pepys, Roxburghe; reprinted in *RB* I, 464). Both ballads were licensed in 1632. A publication of the previous year with the verse title "A constant Wife, a kinde Wife,/A louing Wife, and a fine Wife,/Which giues content vnto mans life," is to the tune "Lie lulling beyond thee" (Pepys; reprinted in *PB* II, 202). Later editions of the ballad have the tune title "Locks and Bolts do Hinder" (Manchester II, 15, Euing 41, Pepys IV, 82, Lord Crawford 1456, Harvard), suggested perhaps by a line in the ballad, "but doores and lockes do hinder." Its opening line, "Young men and maids . . ." becomes the name of the tune in Martin Parker's ballad of 1635, "The Lovers Ioy and Griefe," beginning "Among the nine, all Nymphes diuine" (Roxburghe; reprinted in *RB* I, 599; later editions, without Parker's initials, are in Pepys III, 345, Rawlinson 208, and Euing 187); and its refrain, "but locks and bolts doe hinder," is even more likely to be the basis of the tune title used both in later editions of "A constant Wife" and in Laurence Price's "Tis a wise Child that knows his own Father," beginning "Not long ago it chanced so" (Manchester II, 33), published c. 1635–1655.

[1] "A health to Betty" is an independent tune, q.v. The text of "The Northerne Turtle" appears as the second part of "The paire of Northerne Turtles," reprinted in *RB* II, 312. In the first part of this latter ballad the refrain is "which long lay lulling together."

[2] An alternative tune cited on this ballad is "The two louing Sisters," derived from a ballad of that name licensed in 1631 (*RB* III, 290), which was to be sung "To a pleasant new Tune," not now identifiable.

Light o' Love

Music for this tune is found in William Ballet's MS Lute Book, p. 103, as "lighttie loue ladyes" (Fig. 285), and in *Het Luitboek van Thysius,*

285

No. 382, as "Engelsche Volte"; both texts date from c. 1600. The tune is called "Light of Love" in *A Booke of New Lessons for the Cithern & Gittern,* 1652, in the contemporary Bedford Cittern MS, fol. 43A, and in *Musick's Delight on the Cithren,* 1666.

At least four ballads were sung to the tune, though there must have been others that have not survived. The earliest extant example, for instance, seems to be in answer to some lost ballad extolling the charm and allure of a wanton woman or "light o' love": "A very proper Dittie: to the tune of Lightie Loue," by Leonarde Gybson, whose title goes on to advise ladies to "leave lightie love . . . for fear of ill name." It begins "By force I am fixed my fancy to write," and its eight-line stanza requires a repetition of both musical strains (BM Huth; reprinted in *A Collection of Seventy-Nine Black-Letter Ballads,* 1867, p. 113).[1]

Other ballads to the tune include: Deloney's "Of the Lord Matreuers and Sir Thomas Gurney, being banished," beginning "Alas that euer that day we did see" (in his *Strange Histories,* 1602, and *Works,* ed. Mann,

[1] Chappell reprinted nine stanzas of the text in *PMOT* I, 224–225. The Stationers' Register lists "the comly behavyour for ladyes and gent[le]women" as an entry to Richard Jones, 1570–1571 (Rollins, *Anal. Index,* No. 331). Jones published the Gybson ballad, but Rollins does not associate it with the Register entry; the *STC* does. The date seems reasonable in any case.

p. 408); a ballad on the death of Francis Russell, second Earl of Bedford, 1585, "The poore people's complaynt," beginning "We goe to braue buildings of fayre bricke and stone" (Shirburn MS; reproduced in *SB*, p. 256; an imperfect printed copy, without imprint, is in Manchester II, 51); [2] and "A New Song . . . wooing of Queen Katherine, by . . . Owen Tudor, lately translated out of Welch," beginning "I salute thee sweet Princess with titles of Grace," to the tune "Light in leue Ladies," which appeared in Richard Johnson's *Golden Garland of Princely Pleasures*, 3d ed., 1620, 13th ed., 1690, and was reprinted in *A Collection of Old Ballads*, 1723–1725, III, 32; a broadside copy is Chetham 3050.[3]

Shakespeare alludes to the tune in *Two Gentlemen of Verona*, I, ii:

> Julia. Some love of yours hath writ to you in rhyme.
> Lucetta. That I might sing it, madam, to a tune.
> Give me a note; your ladyship can set.
> Jul. As little by such toys as may be possible.
> Best sing it to the tune of "Light o' love."
> Luc. It is too heavy for so light a tune.

And the byplay continues with elaborate puns on musical terms, beneath which is concealed the serious import of the scene, for the verses were addressed to Julia. Again, in *Much Ado About Nothing*, III, iv, the tune is the basis of swift but meaningful rhetorical sallies:

> Hero. Why, how now? Do you speak in the sick tune?
> Beatrice. I am out of all other tune, methinks.
> Margaret. Clap's into "Light o' love"; that goes without a burden. Do you sing it, and I'll dance it.
> Beat. Ye light o' love with your heels! Then, if your husband have stables enough, you'll see he shall lack no barns.
> Marg. O illegitimate construction! I scorn that with my heels.

The tune is also referred to in *Two Noble Kinsmen*, V, ii; in Fletcher's *The Wild Goose Chase*, IV, ii, the allusion is to the "light woman" connotation of the phrase. In *The Glasse of Mans Follie*, 1595, 1615, it is clear that the term has become a synonym of "greensleeves," for it is said of proper women that "they looke more Christian-like in small Ruffes, then Light of loue lookes in her great starched ruffs"; and later in the same work a poem describing the qualities of a Utopia quite unrealized in the present world devotes a couplet to her:

> Light of Loue is not so fine, but frames her selfe to thrift;
> And learnes good houswifery in time, frequenting no euill shift.

[2] The ballad was licensed to Yarrath James, Aug. 1, 1586 (Rollins, *Anal. Index*, No. 2138). The six-line stanza pattern requires a repetition of the second musical strain.

[3] In the eighteenth century Dicey republished the ballad with his customary historical introduction (Harvard, Harvard-Percy, Madden III, 874).

Lilliburlero

This is one of the most spirited and infectious tunes associated with the street ballad. While some circumstances surrounding the original words and music are shrouded in mystery, there can be no doubt of the popularity and influence of the song in 1688. Moreover, the large number of songs and ballads set to the tune over the next half century testifies to the vitality of this eminently singable melody and its power of evoking mass response. Bishop Burnet's *History of His Own Time*, 1724–1734 (ed. 1823, III, 319), gives a contemporary account of public response to the original song:

A foolish ballad was made at that time, treating the papists, and chiefly the Irish, in a very ridiculous manner, which had a burden, said to be Irish words, lero, lero, lilibulero, that made an impression on the army, that cannot be well imagined by those who saw it not. The whole army, and at last all people both in city and country, were singing it perpetually. And perhaps never had so slight a thing so great an effect.

Burnet was echoing the preface of *A Pill to Purge State-Melancholy*, 1715, pp. vii–viii, which pointed to the practical value of political songs:

There remains but one thing more to be said in behalf of this Collection, which is, that these sort of Songs have often been of the greatest use. An Instance of this we had at the late Glorious Revolution, in *Lilli-bo-lero;* which so perfectly struck in with the Humour of the People, that we feel some of the happy Consequences of it to this very day. And as that Ballad was highly instrumental in singing out a Bad Monarch, so many of these have been as successful in singing out a Bad M[iniste]r.

We do not know when or by whom the tune was composed. It is first found in Robert Carr's *The Delightful Companion*, 2d ed., 1686, sig. C3ᵛ, where it is untitled (Fig. 286). This instruction book for the recorder was engraved, and it is therefore likely that the tune would be found in the first edition, should a copy turn up.[1] An arrangement for virginals or harpsichord, entitled "A new Irish Tune" and subscribed "H. Purcell," is in *The Second Part of Musick's Hand-maid*, 1689, sig. E3ᵛ (reprinted in Purcell Society edition of *Works*, VI, 1895, 31), and it is on this evidence that the authorship of the tune has been popularly credited to

[1] As Chappell noted, the second edition is "corrected" but is not said to be enlarged; the tune appears near the middle of the book. Chappell's copy, now in the British Museum, is the unique survival of the work in any form. The page contains the MS addition "[Quick Step]" and, penciled in the margin, "Lilliburlero."

286

Original is a fourth higher.

Purcell. But he may merely have added the bass and filled in the harmonies to make a proper "lesson" for keyboard, much as William Byrd, Orlando Gibbons, and other Elizabethan composers arranged popular tunes for the virginals almost a century earlier.[2] Purcell used "Lilliburlero" as the ground of a Jig which he wrote as part of the incidental music for the anonymous play *The Gordian Knot Untied,* c. 1691 (printed in his *Ayres for the Theatre,* 1697; reprinted in *Works,* XX, 1916, 32). But this "quotation" of the tune has no bearing on authorship, for he made comparable use of a familiar air, "Cold and Raw," as the ground bass in a birthday ode to Queen Mary in 1692.

Whether Purcell composed or merely arranged the tune, it is clear that it was in print before the occurrence of events giving rise to the ballad from which the tune gets its name. In February, 1687, Richard Talbot, Earl of Tyrconnel, was made lord deputy of Ireland, and it was either at that time or upon his second visit the following year that he was ridiculed in the now famous piece of doggerel. Its opening stanza is as follows:

> Ho Brother Teague dost hear de Decree
>   Lilli burlero, bullen a la
> Dat we shall have a new deputie
>   Lilli burlero, bullen a la
> Lero, lero, lilli burlero
> Lilli burlero, bullen a la

[2] The fact that one piece is described as "set by Dr. Blow" suggests that the distinction between arrangements and original compositions was clearly felt. But Henry Playford's phraseology in the preface is ambiguous. The Second Part, he says, consists of "the newest Tunes and Grounds, Composed by our ablest Masters, Dr. *John Blow,* Mr. *Henry Purcell,* &c. the Impression being carefully Revised and Corrected by the said Mr. *Henry Purcell."* This description embraces composed tunes as well as ground basses invented for tunes already in being and leaves indecisive the argument for Purcell as composer of "A new Irish Tune," the melody of "Lilliburlero."

Lero, lero, lilli burlero
Lilli burlero, bullen a la.

I have seen no printed copy of the ballad earlier than one which Anthony
Wood dated in MS "Dec. 1688";[3] indeed, it would not have been safe
to publish the ballad until James II's departure from England during
that month. But it was circulating orally, as Bishop Burnet has testified,
and as we can see from a verse broadside, "An Epistle to Mr. Dryden.
Exeter Nov. 5, 1688," which begins "Dryden, thy Wit has catterwauld
too long,/Now *Lero, Lero,* is the only Song."

The broadside exists in several states. A black-letter issue without music
is "A New Song: To an Excellent Irish Tune, much in Request" (Pepys
IV, 312); among the other issues, all in roman letter, perhaps the earliest
is "A New Song," without tune direction but with music of "Cold and
Raw," which will scarcely fit the ballad (BM C.38.i.25 [3], Wood 417
[168], with MS date Dec. 1688).[4] Another version with the same title contains the tune (Fig. 287) in serviceable form (Lord Crawford 513, Harvard, Bodleian Firth; photographic reproduction in Sir Charles Firth's
edition of Macaulay's *History of England*, 1913, III, 1075). Still another
edition contains meaningless music (Pepys V, 33). The ballad was reprinted in *A Collection of the Newest . . . Poems . . . against Popery*,
1689 (on his copy Wood noted its publication "in the latter end of Dec.
1688"), in *The Muses Farewel to Popery and Slavery*, 1689, and in *Poems
on Affairs of State*, Second Part, 1697. Percy included it in his *Reliques*,
and it has more recently been reprinted in Crofton Croker's *The Historical Songs of Ireland*, 1841, p. 6, in Chappell's *PMOT* II, 572, and in
BB I, 370.

The authorship of the ballad has been attributed to Thomas Wharton,
first Marquess of Wharton, who was himself Lord Lieutenant of Ireland
during Queen Anne's reign. Wharton's claim rests chiefly on an account
in a pamphlet of 1711, which speaks of him as a man "who has so often
boasted himself upon his Talent for *Mischief, Invention, Lying,* and for
making a certain *Lilli bullero Song,* with which, if you will believe himself, he sung a deluded Prince out of Three Kingdoms."[5] If this does

3 The Bodleian Firth copy cited in the next sentence contains an ambiguous MS
note: "Made upon ye Irish upon Tyrconnells goeing Deputy thither. 25. Oct. 1688."
The date may refer to Talbot's movements, or to the composition of the ballad as
distinct from its publication or purchase.

4 The same music is to be found on another ballad intended to be sung to "Lilliburlero": "The Irish Lasses Letter; or, Her Earnest Request to Teague, her Dear-Joy,"
beginning "To my Dear-Joy this Letter I Write," sung "To an Excellent New tune"
(Wood 417 [166], with MS date Dec. 1688). Chappell theorizes that the printer had
not had time to prepare the proper musical types, but such discrepancies were common during this period. Furthermore, a good musical text had already appeared on a
broadside during the previous month, as I point out below.

287

not seem strong evidence for Wharton's authorship, it is at least more
plausible than the case for Lord Dorset, which Chappell exploded in
PMOT II, 569.

At least one broadside seems to have appeared with the music of "Lilliburlero" before that ballad itself was published, a paradox explained
by the availability of the tune, thanks to oral circulation of the original
ballad. "A New Song upon the Hogen Mogen's," beginning "D'ye hear
the News of the Dutch Dear Frank," is an engraved song sheet containing
the music of "Lilliburlero" and the Harvard copy has the MS date 17
Nov. 1688.[6] It was reprinted in *A Collection of the newest . . . Poems
. . . against Popery,* 1689, and in *Poems on Affairs of State,* 1704, III,
256. Its refrain "Hogen, Mogen, Hogen, Mogen, Sutterkin, Hogen, Her-
ring, Van Dunk" is clearly a rhythmic imitation of the original "Irish"
burden.

The tune of "Lilliburlero" is also found in *Apollo's Banquet,* 6th ed.,
1690, in *The Dancing Master,* commencing with the 8th ed., 1690, in
Dr. John Leyden's MS Lyra Viol Book (after 1690; G. F. Graham transcript, No. 70), in the Agnes Hume MS, 1704, No. 5, and in Walsh's
Compleat Country Dancing-Master, 1718. Thomas D'Urfey's *Choice Collection of New Songs and Ballads,* 1699, p. 4, contains "The National

[5] *A True Relation of the several Facts and Circumstances of the intended Riot and
Tumult on Queen Elizabeth's Birth-day,* 1711, p. 5.

[6] A variant issue, also containing the music, is a roman-letter broadside with the title
"A New Dutch Song," beginning "Dost hear the News that's of the Dutch Frank" (Harvard, National Lib. of Scotland). "Hogen Mogen" refers to *Hoogmogendheiden*—"High-
mightinesses"—the States-General of the Netherlands, a kind of constituent assembly.

Quarrel" set to the music,[7] and *Pills* reprints the air with this ballad (II, 76) and with two others (IV, 216,[8] V, 258). The tune is called for in twelve ballad operas, including the following which print the music: Gay's *The Beggar's Opera*, 1728; Phillips's *The Livery Rake*, 1733; Fielding's *Don Quixote in England*, 1734; and Langford's *The Lover his own Rival*, 1736. In *The Court Medley*, 1733, and *Court and Country*, 1743, the tune takes its name "The Modes of the Court" from the initial line of the *Beggar's Opera* song.

"The Irish-mens prayers to St. Patrick," beginning "O Broder Teague, and Teague my Roon," to the tune "The Countrey Farmer's now undone" (Pepys; reprinted in *PB* V, 25), contains a badly garbled musical score, with two passages of "Lilliburlero" interspersed among pied musical types. The tune cited is one of the names of "King James's Jig," to which the ballad can be sung; "Lilliburlero" fits the movement of the verses even better. The same jumbled music is printed on another broadside, "Romes Doctor" (Pepys; reprinted in *PB* IV, 291), but "The Two English Travellers" cited as the tune is required by the stanza pattern; and almost identical music is on the broadsheet of "The Royal Health" (Pepys; reprinted in *PB* IV, 177), which is properly sung to the tune "Come, Boys, Fill up a Bumper" named on the ballad.[9]

Among the large number of pieces set to "Lilliburlero" only a few can be singled out for special mention. Earliest among these is "The Second

---

[7] D'Urfey's ballad, beginning "Shone a Welch Runt, and Hans a Dutch Boor," is related to the broadside "Teague and Sawney," also sung to "Lilliburlero" (Lord Crawford, Wood 417, Pepys; reprinted in *PB* VI, 95). They both concern the surprise of rustics at seeing a windmill, and the first three stanzas of the broadside are echoed in D'Urfey's verses, with many variations in detail. D'Urfey's ballad lacks the pointed quality of the broadside, although its satire of national types is emphasized through the addition of Shone and Hans to the original pair. Professor Rollins dates the broadside 1691 or earlier; it is impossible to say when during the years 1688–1699 D'Urfey wrote his ballad, but it seems unlikely that it antedated "Teague and Sawney."

[8] This is "My Thing is my Own," beginning "I a tender young Maid have been courted by many." The four-line stanza is supplemented by a two-line burden which would have to be repeated to allow the entire tune to be sung. It had appeared early in the Restoration with the title "A New Ballad, called, Trap, Or, The Young Lass," to the tune of "Traps Delight: Or, I know what I know" (Wood E.25 [30], Pepys III, 17). The first tune name may be internally inspired; the second is derived from the burden of a ballad "Few Words are Best," to the tune "Ile tell you but so" (Euing, Manchester, Roxburghe; reprinted in *RB* I, 116). No music appears to have survived under any of these tune names.

[9] At least three other "Lilliburlero" ballads were issued with meaningless music: "The Protestants Delight," in praise of the Prince of Orange (Pepys; reprinted in *PB* IV, 142); "Teague and Sawney," discussed in note 7 above; and "Englands Hopes, Or, Look to't Teague," to the tune "Ise often for my Jeny strove, or, Lilli borlero" (Pepys; reprinted in *PB* V, 22).

Part of Lill-li burlero bullen a-la," 1688, beginning "There was an Old Prophesie found in a Bogg" (Wood 417 [172]), which continued the attack on Tyrconnel. Another with the same title begins "By Creist my dear Morish vat makes de sho' shad" (*A Second Collection of the Newest . . . Poems . . . against Popery and Slavery*, 1689, p. 20). Another ballad of 1688 is "The Reading Skirmish," beginning "We came into brave Reading by Night" (Wood E.25 [113], with MS date *"Decemb."*; Pepys, Bagford; reprinted in *BB* I, 373). Another on the same engagement between Irish troops of James II and soldiers of William of Orange is "Reading Fight," 1689, beginning "Dost hear, Brother Teague, how de Cause goes?" (Wood 417 [169]). "The True Protestant's Triumph; or, Lilli-Bolero in English," beginning "Come let's sing to the Honour and Praise," has a refrain appropriate to postrevolution days after the battle of the Boyne gave cause for optimism: "Mary, Mary, William and Mary; William and Mary, George and Ann" (Pepys, Roxburghe; reprinted in *RB* VII, 718).

The following ballads to the tune do not appear to have been reprinted: "West-Country Tom Tormented . . . by the News-Mongers of the Town," beginning "I am a Lad that's come to the Town" (Lord Crawford 545, Pepys IV, 322); "Faint Heart never won fair Lady," beginning "You that a fair Maids heart would obtain" (Pepys III, 21); "The False-hearted Glover," beginning "Pray now attend and listen a while" (BM C.22.f.6 [117], Pepys III, 92, Lord Crawford 1011, Douce I, 84ᵛ); and a ballad of 1715 on the attempt of "James III" to gain the throne: "Perkin Redivivus," beginning "The Papists and Tories do openly boast,/That the Pretender is now on the Coast" (BM 1871.e.9 [172]).

"The Protestant's Satisfaction . . . In the Birth of a young Prince," 1689, cites the tune as "Protestant Boys shall carry the day" (Pepys; reprinted in *PB* IV, 323), from the refrain of "The Valiant Soldier's Resolution to Conquer Tyrconnel and his Irish Crew. Tune of, Lilli burlero," found in *The Protestant Garland of Joy and Delight*, 1689, sig. A4ᵛ. In "Shinkin's Misfortune," beginning "Shinkin ap Shone was rob a creet House," the tune is named as "Teague and Sawney: or, Lilliburlero" (Lord Crawford 1051); the first name is derived from the title of a ballad discussed in note 7 above. "A New Song. Or, Englands Outcry against the late Lord Chancellor Jefferies," beginning "You Protestants all draw near to this place" (Harvard), names no tune, but the stanza fits the measure of "Lilliburlero," and the Irish echo "oh by me shoul" in the final stanza suggests that the writer might have had that tune in mind.

Many other songs to the tune, some of them separately issued as broadsides, can be found in such miscellanies as *Political Merriment*, 1714, *A Pill to Purge State-Melancholy*, 1715, and *A Collection of State Songs*, 1716, as well as the various editions of *Poems on Affairs of State*, 1697–

1716. Bickerstaffe used the air in his comic opera, *Love in a Village*, c. 1763.

The tune appears on such eighteenth-century song sheets as "The Iournalist Display'd," c. 1740 (BM G.316.d [122], Harvard), whose first stanza typifies both the vivacious meter and the satiric vigor bequeathed by the original ballad:

> Dear Friend, have y^u heard ye fantastical Chimes,
>   Ribbledum, Scribbledum, Fribbledum, Flash;
> As rung by the Iournalists, all of our times?
>   Satyrum, Traytorum, Treasondum, Trash;
> Popery! Slavery! Bribery! Knavery!
> Eruptions, Corruptions, & Some Body's, Fall;
> Pensions & Places, Removes & Disgraces
> And Something & Nothing & ye Divel & all.

The music of "Lilliburlero" is also used with a song variously called "Newcastle Ale" (Roxburghe III, 421, a late broadside, not reprinted in *RB;* reprinted in *The Duke of Gordon's Garland*, c. 1785, p. 7) and "Nottingham Ale" (Harvard, song sheet in Julian Marshall collection, partially reprinted by Chappell, *PMOT* II, 573–574, with the music), beginning "Fair [*or* When] Venus the Goddess of Beauty and Love." A MS commonplace book bound in with the British Museum copy of *The Vocal Enchantress*, 1783, contains the poem and identifies the author as "Mr. Saml. Gunthrope."

The familiar verses beginning "There was an old woman tossed up in a basket,/Seventeen times as high as the moon" have been customarily sung to "Lilliburlero" (see *Oxford Dictionary of Nursery Rhymes*, ed. Iona and Peter Opie, 1951, No. 545, for a discussion of variants and a list of reprints). The tune was traditionally associated with a Sussex whistling song (the whistling interludes being those passages employing the Irish refrain in the original "Lilliburlero"). It is "The Farmer's Old Wife," beginning "There was an old farmer in Sussex did dwell," which J. H. Dixon included in his *Ancient Poems, Ballads, and Songs*, 1846, p. 210, and which Child reprinted as "The Farmer's Curst Wife," No. 278 A. Frank Kidson noted (*Grove's Dictionary of Music and Musicians*, 1954, s.v. "Lilliburlero") that the tune served for "Protestant Boys," a song sung by Irish Orangemen in the late nineteenth and early twentieth centuries. During World War II, when the Allies occupied Rome in June, 1944, it was doubtless sheer exuberance that moved a group of Highland pipers to play "Lilliburlero" in St. Peter's Square, "gieing Popie a blaw." [10]

[10] Denis Johnston, *Nine Rivers from Jordan*, 1955, p. 294.

Loath to Depart

A tune called "Lothe to Departe" is preserved in Cambridge University MS Dd.2.11, fol. 9, in lute tablature of c. 1600. A keyboard arrangement by Giles Farnaby is found in *The Fitzwilliam Virginal Book* II, 317 (Fig. 288). The same air appears without title in the Euing Lute MS,

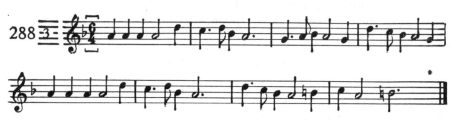

288

* Five sections of embellishment follow.

fols. 28, 31, c. 1600, and in a mid-seventeenth-century keyboard set in Paris Conservatoire MS Rés. 1186, fol. 57ᵛ. But a "Loath to depart" was any sort of farewell song, and it is clear that more than one tune went by this name. Its association with broadsides is through "A proper new ballett, intituled Rowlands god Sonne," beginning "Tell me Jhon why art thou soe sade," a ballad drama or jig which names the tune for singing all four parts (Bodleian MS Rawlinson Poet. 185, fol. 15ᵛ, probably taken from print; reproduced in *SB*, p. 354).[1] But the surviving tune, suitable for an octosyllabic quatrain, does not fit the elaborate eight-line stanza form of "Rowland's godson."

Two versions of a song called "loath to depart" appear without music in Cotgrave's *Wit's Interpreter*, 1655, beginning "Lie still [*or* near] my dear why dost thou rise"; it is in a six-line stanza with a hypermetrical fifth line which prevents its being sung to the tune.[2] Several other versions of the song exist with a regular fifth line which would allow the use of the "Loath to depart" music, though there is no clear reason to suppose that text and tune were ever intended to be joined.[3]

[1] The jig must be no later than 1592, for in that year the lost "Rowlandes godson moralized" was entered in the Stationers' Register.

[2] Chappell (*PMOT* I, 173), fitting the verse to the melody, suppressed the two final lines of the stanza.

[3] Texts include one in Harvard MS Eng. 686, p. 188, an early seventeenth-century commonplace-book version. The first stanza, beginning "Ah dear heart, why do you rise," was set by Orlando Gibbons in his *First Set of Madrigals and Mottets*, 1612 (re-

Allusions in the drama as early as Edwards's *Damon and Pithias,* 1571, sig. E1ᵛ, testify to the currency of "Loath to depart" as a type of song or the name of a specific tune. In Beaumont and Fletcher's *Wit at Several Weapons,* II, ii, Pompey hums the tune as he exits. An equivocal reference occurs in Middleton, Massinger, and Rowley's *The Old Law,* IV, i: "the old woman is loath to depart, she never sung other tune in her life." Davenant's *The Man's the Master,* 1669, III, i, names the song, but not without punning on its meaning.

Ravenscroft's *Deuteromelia,* 1609, includes a four-part round or canon whose music cannot have been a ballad tune, but whose words symbolize the sentiment of leave-taking and illustrate the generalized force of the tune name:

> Sing with thy mouth, sing with thy heart,
>   like faithfull friends, sing loath to depart,
> though friends together may not alwayes remaine,
>   yet loath to depart sing once againe.

A roughly contemporary copy is preserved also in Trinity College, Dublin, MS F.5.13, p. 68.

Although we can identify both words and music of "Loath to depart," we unhappily do not have music to fit the broadside text, or words for the music of c. 1600.

Logan Water

This tune, known as "The Liggan Waters," "Legon Water," and the like, with countless variations in the spelling of the river's name, is evidently associated with a song beginning "The Logan water is so deep," the name given to the tune in John Hippisley's ballad opera *Flora,* 1729. I have not found that poem. The origins of the tune must be looked for no later than the 1680s, for it is toward the end of that decade that ballads in profusion call for the tune. At least twenty broadsides name the

printed in *The English Madrigal School,* ed. E. H. Fellowes, vol. V, 1914). John Dowland, who may have written the poem, published a four-part setting of the two-stanza text, beginning "Sweet, stay awhile, why will you rise," in *A Pilgrimes Solace,* 1612. An anonymous set of the first stanza is in Elizabeth Rogers's Virginal Book (BM MS Add. 10337, fol. 20ᵛ, before 1656). The song is sometimes credited to John Donne, doubtless because some versions of the text include lines based on his poem "Break of Day." Charles F. Main, Jr., has a full discussion of these and other texts in his unpublished Harvard dissertation, An Early Stuart Manuscript Miscellany, 1953, pp. 894–898.

tune during the last years of the seventeenth century, but I have found no music for it earlier than the "Logan Water" in Alexander Stuart's compilation of *Musick for Allan Ramsay's Collection of Scots Songs,* c. 1725, p. 56 (Fig. 289). The tune also appears in Watts's *Musical Miscel-*

* The original adds a varied repeat of the tune.

lany, 1729–1731, VI, 58, where it is used for the Horatian imitation "Tell me, Hamilla, tell me why," a song which appeared without music but with the tune direction "Logan Water" in Ramsay's *Tea-Table Miscellany,* 1723, p. 57, and *The Hive,* c. 1733, III, 192. William Thomson printed an arrangement of the tune in his *Orpheus Caledonius,* 1733, II, No. 23, set to James Thomson's verses beginning "For ever, Fortune, wilt thou prove" (reprinted in Johnson's *Scots Musical Museum,* 1787–1803, I, 42, and Ritson's *Scotish Songs,* 1794, I, 37).

The tune was named in eight ballad operas; those printing the music are, in addition to *Flora:* Johnson's *The Village Opera,* 1729 (condensed into one act in Phillips's *The Chamber-maid,* 1730); Mitchell's *The Highland Fair* and Chetwood's *The Generous Free-Mason,* 1731; and *The Whim: or, The Miser's Retreat,* 1734. That the air was still in vogue after more than a century is suggested by its choice as one of the pieces arranged by Haydn for George Thomson's *Select Collection of Original Scottish Airs,* 1802, III, 16, set to Burns's verses beginning "O Logan sweetly didst thou glide."

Apparently the first broadside calling for the tune is "The Bonny Scotish Lad, and the Yielding Lass," which begins:

> Bonny Lass I love thee well,
>   bonny Lad I love thee better,
> Wilt thou put off thy Hose and Shoon,
>   and wend with me to Liggan Water?

The tune is named "The Liggan Waters," and the copy in Pepys V, 269, contains meaningless music (issues without music are in Lord Crawford, Harvard, Roxburghe; reprinted in *RB* III, 475). The imprints do not permit precise dating, but I suspect that a date of 1688 is not far wrong.

The siege of Londonderry in 1689 gave rise to at least seven new ballads that could be sung to the tune. The earliest of these appears to be "The Glory of London-Derry," beginning "Protestants chear up amain," to the tune of "The Leggan Water Or, Nanny Oh" (Pepys; reprinted in *PB* IV, 301). From the title of this ballad comes a new tune name, "London-Derry" or "Glory of London-Derry," with which "Liggan Water" or "Nanny O" is sometimes coupled in editions of other ballads in this series (reprinted in *PB* IV, 305, 309, 315, 332, 336, 351).[1]

Of the fifteen other ballads to "Logan Water" in the Pepys collection, nine are reprinted in *PB,* most of them relating to William III's military campaigns. Thus the victory at Cavan is celebrated (V, 89), as is the naval engagement at Beachy Head (V, 184) and the highly important battle of the Boyne (V, 187). Several reflect English attitudes toward Louis XIV, a symbol of Catholicism and of sympathy for the Jacobite cause (VI, 202, VII, 117), and one welcomes war with the French (V, 255). This last is "The Nations Joy for a War With Monsieur," beginning "Now England's Bloudy Flag's display'd," to the tune "Legin Water, or Round about the Hollow Tree," unusual in forsaking the customary octosyllabic quatrain of "Logan Water" ballads for an eight-line stanza in the same measure.[2]

"The Ladies Lamentation, Or, The Commanders last Farewel," beginning "In London liv'd a Squyre, where/He long enjoy'd a Lady fair," is a lament for the death of the commander in an unnamed battle, to the tune of "Loggan Water" (BM 1871.e.9 [93]); another issue names the tune as "Languishing Swain" for which see "He that loves best must suffer most" (Pepys; reprinted in *PB* VI, 207). "The Devonshire Boys Courage," beginning "Brave Devonshire Boys made haste away," is to the tune "The Devonshire Boys delight: Or, The Liggan waters" (Pepys, Euing, Lord Crawford, Roxburghe; reprinted in *RB* IV, 325); I have no

1 It is possible that "Londonderry" was the name of an independent tune, but we have no way to be sure of this without finding music so named. If it is another name for either "Logan Water" or "Nanny O," we should expect to find the kind of tune directions that exist. The fundamental ambiguity remains: when we find two tune names on a broadside, we cannot know, without further evidence, whether they refer to two distinct tunes or are two names for the same tune. Here we cannot say whether "Londonderry" is a separate tune, another name for "Logan Water," or another name for "Nanny O."

2 "Round about the Hollow Tree," for which the music is unknown, is cited as an alternative tune to "A Fig for France and Holland too" (also unknown) on a broadside of 1666, "Englands Royall Conquest," beginning "Rejoyce, Rejoyce, brave English boys" (Wood E.25 [55], Euing 101). This ballad has a stanza of eight octosyllabics, like the one cited above.

Some eighteenth-century texts set to "Logan Water" have an eight-line stanza pattern, with a second musical strain which varies but slightly from the original eight-bar melody.

information on the first tune title, although it appears to be internally inspired. "The Crafty Lass of the West . . . who Mortgag'd her Maiden-Head for a High-Crown'd Hat," beginning "Here is a Jest I do protest," to the tune "Liggan-Water," is one of those coarse pieces of hackwork that were the despair of Ebsworth, who heavily bowdlerized the text from a late Aldermary Church Yard issue (Pepys, Lord Crawford, Harvard, black-letter copies; Douce, Madden, Roxburghe; reprinted in *RB* VIII, 551).

The following ballads to the tune do not appear to have been reprinted: "The Country Travellers Advice . . . to Avoid . . . Drunkenness," beginning "Kind Travellers I pray attend" (Pepys II, 60); "A Dialogue Between Tom and Jack," beginning "Stout Tom and Jack from Cumberland" (Pepys IV, 359); "The Maiden's Melancholy Moan for the Loss of her Virginity," beginning "I was a fair young maid of late" (Pepys III, 68); and "The West-Country Squire," beginning "Early in the morning fair," to the tune of "Liggan Water. Or, Nanny Oh" (Pepys IV, 62). One other unreprinted broadside, containing meaningless music, is "Frollicksome Wager: or, the Ranting Gallants Ramble through the City," beginning "Behold! what Noise is this I hear," to the tune "Legan Water" (Pepys V, 199). It is in the usual "Logan Water" quatrain form, but the words "The Rant" are inserted between stanzas, suggesting that the burden of "The Rant," q.v., was to be sung as an interlude. This supposition is the more probable because three other ballads on the same subject were sung to that tune; the stanzas of the present broadside, however, do not fit the tune of "The Rant."

London Is a Fine Town

This tune is called "Watton town's end," "The Gowlin," and "London [or Oh London] is a fine [or brave] town." Several other tune names, such as "The button'd smock," have a more problematical relationship to the tune. Music is found in *The Dancing Master,* commencing with the 3d ed., 1665, p. 111 (Fig. 290), entitled "Watton Town's end." The tune is printed no less than seven times in the 1719–1720 edition of *Pills* (II, 150; IV, 40, 77, 179; V, 27, 139; VI, 144; all these texts are noticed below). Like many a dance tune, this air is circular, having no proper final cadence; the last note calls for a chord of the dominant which leads naturally back to the beginning of the tune. It is no surprise, then, to

find stanzas of eight and even twelve short lines set to a melody which encompasses only a quatrain.

"Watten Towns-end" is the title of a ballad which must have been in print very early in the seventeenth century, even though the extant editions, with Brooksby imprint, belong to the last quarter of the century. The tune direction is "Watten Towns end; Or, Lame Leg next the Wall," [1] and the ballad begins "As I came up by Arpendeen/and straight to Watten Town" (BM C.22.f.6 [223], Lord Crawford 91, Harvard). The refrain explains clearly enough the basis of the title and tune name:

> At Watten Towns end, at Watten Towns end
> At every Door, there stands a Whore,
> at Watten Towns end.

The early date of this ballad is established through the use of "Watton town's end" as the tune for "Turners dish of Lentten stuffe, or a Galymaufery," c. 1612, beginning "My Maisters all attend you,/if mirth you loue to heare" (Pepys; reprinted in *PG*, p. 31; Lord Crawford 841 is an issue of 1662). The tune is also used for the second part of "A merry new Ballad intituled:—The begger comes, the begger comes" (Shirburn MS; printed in *SB*, p. 140). A third ballad, with tune direction "See the golding, or Watton townes end," is Robert Guy's piece of c. 1626, "Sure my Nurse was a witch," beginning "In Londons Citty faire,/a merry Nurse doth dwell" (Pepys; reprinted in *PB* II, 65).[2]

A version of the ballad beginning "London is a fine town and a brave City" is in *Le Prince d'Amour*, 1660, p. 158. But echoes or parodies suggest that the song was known much earlier in the century. Nichols's

---

[1] I have no data on the second tune.

[2] The first tune title cited for singing Guy's ballad may be properly "See the gilding," derived from the opening line of "Cheapsides Triumphs" (*PB* II, 49), a ballad associated with the tune "See the building," q.v. Guy's ballad cannot, however, be sung to that complex and individualistic tune. A second possibility is that "See the golding" is related to D'Urfey's refrain "See the gowlin," cited later in the present discussion. Although I cannot demonstrate that the tune "London is a fine town" was called "See the golding" in the early seventeenth century, it is plausible to think that D'Urfey did not invent his refrain but adapted a phrase in current use. Still unexplained is whether Guy's tune title referred to gilding or to the daisy.

Progresses of King James, III, 73, contains a song in the same meter which dates from James I's visit to Cambridge in 1615:

> Now Cambridge is a merry Towne,
>   And Oxford is another;
> The Kinge was welcome to the one,
>   And fared well at the other.[3]

A broadside, "The Cities Loyaltie to their King," beginning "Why kept your Train-Bands such a stirre," has the refrain

> London is a brave Towne,
>   Yet I their cases pitty,
> Their Maior and some few Aldermen
>   Have cleane undone the City.

The copy among the Thomason Tracts bears the manuscript date Aug. 13, 1647 (other copies: Lord Crawford, Bodleian, Harvard, Huntington; reprinted in Wright's *Political Ballads,* p. 42, and Mackay's *Cavalier Songs,* p. 52).[4]

In Bodleian MS Ashmole 36–37, fol. 318, is an eighteen-stanza poem which is fuller and apparently earlier than the *Prince d'Amour* text. Its title, "Wattling-Streetes end," may be intended simply as a tune name; in any case it suggests a confusion between the famous Roman road and the tune name "Watton town's end," and it may be at least a presumptive link between the older tune and the song that was to give the air a new name. It begins "Att London there's a Mayor, and that same Mayor's a Lord." Its refrain is used in most of the later versions and revisions of the text:

> Oh London is a ffine towne, and a Gay Citty,
> Tis govern'd by the scarlett Gown give eare
>   unto my ditty.

Clearly indebted to the MS version is a text reprinted with the music (Fig. 291) in *Pills* IV, 40, which opens with the refrain; the first stanza proper begins "This City has a Mayor, this Mayor is a Lord." A broadside of c. 1685 titled "Londons Praise, Or, The Glory of the City," uses

---

[3] A copy entitled "On the Comoedians of Oxon & Cambridg" is in an early seventeenth-century commonplace book, Harvard MS Eng. 686, p. 53. Charles F. Main, Jr. (An Early Stuart Manuscript Miscellany, unpublished Harvard dissertation, 1953), has noted the appearance of the song also in Sir J. S. Hawkins's edition of George Ruggle's comedy, *Ignoramus,* 1787, p. xxxvii, and in *Inedited Poetical Miscellanies,* ed. W. C. Hazlitt and Henry Huth, 1870, sig. H8.

[4] Professor Rollins (*PB* III, 217) reprinted a passage from *The Parliament-kite,* July 20–27, 1648, p. 57, in which a quatrain is derived almost verbatim from the refrain of "The Cities Loyaltie."

291

the refrain, but its text is only generally related to the older forms. The tune is named "London is a brave Town"—the earlier pieces have no tune direction, except perhaps for the MS version—and the ballad begins "Of all the Songs that e're was pen'd" (Rawlinson, Pepys; reprinted in *PB* III, 218).[5]

Among the obvious parodies may be mentioned the following: "The Woman's Medley," beginning "O Woman is a fine thing so wondrous neat and pretty" (BM 1871.e.9 [115], imprint cropped, but probably c. 1700); a Dublin broadside of 1722, "Upon the Fringes, Commonly so call'd by the Vulgar," beginning "O Dublin is a fine Town,/and a Gallant City" (BM 839.m.23 [21]), concerning an equestrian statue of George I unveiled on August 1 of that year; and "The Champion's Defeat: Or, City Triumph" (Morgan 22a), which begins with the refrain:

> O London is a fine Town,
>   a true and gallant City;
> And sets aside Convention-Men:
>   come listen to my Ditty.

None of these list a tune, but the intention is clear enough from the text. The tune is named in "A New Ballad," 1726/27, beginning "My Lord M[ayo]r and his A[lderme]n and C[ommo]n C[ounci]l too" (Harvard, an eight-page pamphlet, part of which was reprinted in *British Journal*, March 18, 1727, and in Percival's *Walpole Ballads*, p. 10). And "The Suburbs is a fine Place belonging to the City" appears with the music in *Pills* V, 27.

One of the very popular ballads sung to the tune is a satiric piece found in *Wit and Drollery*, 1656, p. 116, beginning "A Begger got a baliff,/A baliff got a yeoman." The broadside version, usually titled "The Pope's Pedigree, or, the twineing of a Wheelband," begins "A Begger got a Beadle," and cites the tune as "London is a brave Town" (Lord Crawford, Euing, Harvard, Roxburghe; reprinted in *RB* IV, 101; an

---

[5] For later appearances of the words, see *PB* III, 217. An eighteenth-century single-sheet edition with music is called "The London Ditty," beginning "Oh London is a fine Town and a gallant City" (BM H.1601 [327], dated 1710?; Huntington, Harvard).

eighteenth-century edition is in Douce III, 77). The version in *Pills* III, 63, is printed with music of "The Friar and the Nun." [6]

Another ballad sung to "London is a Fine Town" is "The Religious Turncoat, or, a Late Jacobite Divine turned Williamite," beginning "I Lov'd no King in Forty One,/When Prelacy went down" (Lord Crawford, BM C.39.k.6, issues of 1693, reprinted in *OPB*, p. 103; BM C.20.f.2, BM 1876.f.1, Pepys, reprinted in *PB* VII, 25). An engraved song-sheet edition at Harvard containing music brings the text down to the time of George I; a broadside issue of c. 1715 with similar text but without music (BM 1871.e.9 [175]) is to be sung to "John Anderson my Joe." [7]

Other eighteenth-century pieces using the tune include: "A Ballad On Lord Pelham's Birth-Day, July 24, 1714," beginning "Come bring the Liquor hither" (Lord Crawford 234); "A New Ballad," beginning "The World's a frantick Whimsy, and B[ritai]n is a Farce," in *Political Merriment*, 1714; a piece on the Pretender, "The Right and True History of Perkin," beginning "Ye Whiggs, and eke you Tories give Ear to what I Sing," in *A Collection of State Songs*, 1716; and "A New Song upon a new Subject, to be sung or said as the Maggot Bites . . . by T. B., a Rum Duke," beginning "God Prosper long our king and Queen, and the wise Parliament," on liquor legislation being considered in 1736 (BM C.116.i.4 [23], [24]; after the tune name is the instruction: "You must sing the Chorus at the end of every Verse").

"The Masquerade Ballad" is a single-sheet song of c. 1720 beginning "O! a Masquerade's a fine Place,/for Ladies that are witty," and containing the music (BM H.1601 [345], Harvard). A considerably chaster song is "The Masquerade Garland," beginning "Come all ye sons of Adam," which appeared in such miscellanies as *The Hive*, 1725, III, 127 (in the 4th ed., c. 1733, III, 127, the tune is named), and with the air in Watts's *Musical Miscellany*, 1729–1731, III, 145, and *The Merry Musician*, c. 1731, III, 105. Another single-sheet song containing the music is "The Chimes of the Times," beginning "Ah! silly simple Town!/When will you e'er be wise" (Harvard), written "by the compiler of the Instructor, or the Art of Living Well."

Thomas D'Urfey wrote a "Scotch Song" beginning "A Broad as I was walking upon a Summer Day" for his play *Trick for Trick*, 1678,

---

[6] Another "pedigree" ballad, without tune direction but in the meter of "London is a fine town," is "The Parliaments Pedigree," beginning "No Pedigrees nor Projects/ Of after-times I tell" (*Rump*, 1662 [rpt. 1874], I, 24; other copies include Bodleian MS Ashmole 36–37, fol. 159, MS Ashmole 38, fol. 228, MS Rawl. Poet. 62, fol. 48, MS Douce 357, fol. 31, and BM MS Harl. 3511, fol. 10).

[7] "The Turn coat" is included in Samuel Butler's *Posthumous Works*, 2d ed., 1715, I, 220, along with a good many other pieces incorrectly attributed to him. For a related text, see "The Vicar of Bray."

II, i. No tune is named in the play, but the refrain contains the words "Ah see the Golin, my Jo, see the Golin," [8] from which came new names for the tune. The expanded broadside form is "To a New Play-house Tune: Or, See the Gowlin my Jo," and is titled "The Gowlin: Or, A Pleasant Fancy for the Spring" (Wood E.25 [134], an edition no later than 1679; other issues, naming the tune "See the Gowlin, &c.," are Lord Crawford 2, BM C.22.f.6 [120], Pepys III, 108; the first stanza is reprinted in *RB* IV, 657). Since D'Urfey printed the music of "London is a fine town" with the stage version of the song in *Pills* II, 150, we may suppose that it was originally sung to this tune. Another ballad employing the tune name is "Young Jemmy, Or, The Princely Shepherd," beginning "Young Jemmy was a Lad,/of Royal birth and Breeding," and sung "To a pleasant New Play-house Tune. Or, In Ianuary last, Or, The Gowlin" (Lord Crawford, Douce, Harvard, Roxburghe; reprinted in *RB* IV, 658).[9]

Two ballads reprinted in *Pills* use the music of "London is a fine town" in preference to the older tunes associated with each. One of these, beginning "Bonny Peggy Ramsey that any Man may see" (V, 139), must be a late reworking of the song that gave rise to the tune "Peg a Ramsey" before 1600. Similarly, "Cuckolds all," beginning "Not long ago as all alone I lay upon my Bed" (IV, 77), is the basis for the tune "Cuckolds all a-row," which had circulated at least since 1637, when the ballad was licensed. A third has connections which cannot be traced so confidently. It is "The Bonny Lass: Or, the Button'd Smock," beginning "Sit you merry Gallants,/For I can tell you News" (VI, 144). No earlier versions of this piece on the "Holland Smock" that's "button'd down before" seem to have survived, but "the Button'd Smocke" is the name given to the tune of "The Cuckowes Comendation," a broadside of c. 1615 (Pepys; reprinted in *PB* I, 97). The meter fits "London is a fine town," but we cannot be sure whether "Button'd Smocke" was the name of an independent tune (in which case D'Urfey would have been replacing an old "proper tune" with a more familiar one, as he did in the two instances just cited), or whether it is to be equated with "London is a fine town."

Still another *Pills* song to the tune is "Tottingham Frolick," beginning "As I came from Tottingham/Upon a Market-day" (IV, 179), a ballad which had appeared with the opening line "As I went to Totnam" in *Choyce Drollery*, 1656, p. 45, but without tune direction. A ballad entitled "The Lovers Pastime. or, Sport upon Sport under a Haycock,"

[8] *Golin* or *gowlin:* gowan, a Scotch word for daisy. The broadside explains it only as "The Gowlin is a yellow Flower/that grows upon the plains." Sexual symbolism is implicit in D'Urfey's refrain.

[9] The "Play-house Tune" was "Young Jemmy," q.v.

beginning "Abroad as I was walking in a Summer's day,"[10] is to the tune "As I went to Tatnum upon a Market-day" (Pepys V, 233, with meaningless music); but the stanza pattern is so widely at variance with that of "Tottingham Frolick" that the two could not possibly be sung to the same tune.

The history of "London is a fine town" would not be complete without a word on its use in the ballad operas. The tune is printed in Gay's *The Beggar's Opera*, 1728, in Fielding's *The Mock Doctor*, 1732, in Henry Carey's *The Honest Yorkshire-Man*, 1735 (music separately published, c. 1736), and it is called for in seven other operas.

Long Cold Nights

"Long cold Nights when Winter Froz 'em" is the opening line of "A New Scotch Song" in *Comes Amoris*, First Book, 1687, p. 37 (Fig. 292). The same tune, called "Long cold Nights," is in *Apollo's Banquet*, 5th ed., 1687, and the words are reprinted in *Compleat Academy of Complements*, 1705.

A broadside expanding the song text to seven stanzas is entitled "The Scotch Lasses Choice," and the opening line now ends with the word "Frozen"; the "pleasant New Scotch Tune" printed on the sheet is a badly garbled version of a different tune (Lord Crawford, BM C.39.k.6: reprinted in *OPB*, p. 68).

292

---

[10] There is no similarity to D'Urfey's "Gowlin" song after the opening line.

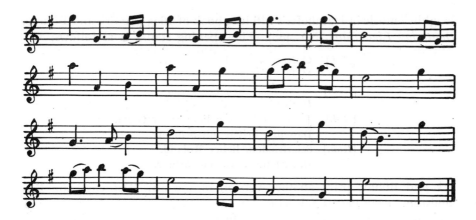

To the tune "In Cold Nights when Winter's Frozen" is sung "The Female Doctress, or Mother Midnights Cure for Barrenness in Women," beginning "All you Ladies that are Barren" (Pepys V, 417).

Lord Willoughby

This tune is known as "Lord Willoughby," "Lord Willoughby's March," "My Lord Willoughby's Welcome Home," "My Lord Willoughby's Tune," and "Brave Lord Willoughby." It is also found under the names "Rowland," "Soet Robbert," and "Soet soet Robbertgen," by which it seems to have first been known.

These latter associations evidently go back to a dramatic jig on Roland, Robert, Margaret, and the Sexton, which is preserved in a German text of 1599 (reprinted in C. R. Baskervill, *The Elizabethan Jig,* 1929, p. 491, with modern English translation on p. 220). Although no English original has survived, traces of sequels are present in a Stationers' Register entry for "the Second parte of the gigge betwene Rowland and the Sexton," Dec. 16, 1591, and perhaps in "the Thirde and last parte of Kempes Jigge," entered twelve days later.[1] The German text is coupled with the "Wil-

---

[1] Since Will Kempe, the actor, was well known for his connection with jigs, Baskervill thinks that this entry may refer to another Rowland jig, there being clearly more than one. He conjectures that Kempe may have introduced the Rowland jigs to the Continent when he visited the Low Countries in 1585 (pp. 107–109, 226). Baskervill also advances the belief (p. 231) that a Dutch translation of the lost jig must have been in existence to account for the "Soet Robbertgen" title associated with several versions of the tune. An alternative source of the Dutch title is offered by van Duyse. See note 3, below.

loughby" music in Hainhofer's MS lute book of 1603 (see Erk and Böhme, *Deutsches Liederhort*, No. 488). The opening stanza is as follows:

[*Rol.*] O Nachbar, lieber Robert,
Mein Herz ist voller Pein!
[*Rob.*] O Nachbar, lieber Roland,
Umb was mag das wol sein?
[*Rol.*] Johann Glöckner liebt mein Greta,
Dasselbig bringt mir Schmerz.
[*Rob.*] Sei zfrieden, lieber Roland,
Das ist noch wol ein Scherz.

Erk and Böhme print another version of the air, "Der englische Ro-landston," from Petrus Fabricius' MS Liederbuch, 1603. And the German composer Samuel Scheidt used the first strain of the tune for his in-strumental "Canzon à 5 voc. super O Nachbar Roland" in *Paduana, Galliarda, Couranta* . . . , 1621 (*Werke*, II–III, 47). A close variant of the melody is employed by Bach in the choral "Keinen hat Gott verlas-sen." [2]

The tune was popular in the Netherlands, usually named from a song beginning "Soet, soet Robbertjen," with which the air was used. Musical variants are preserved in *Het Luitboek van Thysius*, No. 78, a version of c. 1600, in Pieter van der Goes's *Den Druyventros der Amoureusheyt*, 1602, in Nicolas Vallet's *Secretum Musarum*, 1615, reissued in 1618 as *Le Secret des Muses*, in Adriaen Valerius's *Neder-Landtsche Gedenck-Clanck*, 1626, p. 83 (Fig. 293); and in Theodotus's *Het Paradijs*, 1621, 1648. The tune is also cited in Dutch songbooks without music, beginning with *Den Nieuwen Verbeterden Lust-hof*, 1602, 1607.[3]

The original English ballad to the tune is "Lord Willoughby; or, A true relation of a famous and bloody battel fought in Flanders," begin-ning "The fifteenth day of July,/with glittering spear and shield," to the tune of "Lord Willoughby" (Wood 401, Pepys, Lord Crawford, Bagford, Douce, Harvard, Roxburghe; reprinted in Percy's *Reliques* and in *RB* IV, 8). This recounts the bravery of Peregrine Bertie, Lord Willoughby of Eresby, who with fifteen hundred men is credited with defeating a Spanish army of forty thousand. The engagement is not named, but the ballad, for all its exaggeration, is evidently founded on some one of Willoughby's several successes in the Low Countries between 1585 and 1590 and was probably published during those years. It was popular

[2] For a fuller account of the sacred and secular, vocal and instrumental uses to which the "Willoughby" tune was put in Germany, see not only the extensive bibliography in Erk and Böhme but also the commentary in Johannes Bolte, *Die Singspiele der eng-lischen Komödianten und ihrer Nachfolger*, 1893, pp. 8–11, 167–169.

[3] Florimond van Duyse, *Het Oude Nederlandsche Lied*, 1903–1908, II, 1149ff., re-prints music from most of these sources and gives the words of "Soet, soet Robbertjen."

293

Original a fifth higher.

into the eighteenth century, as repeated publication attests; no surviving edition is earlier than the second quarter of the seventeenth century, and most copies are considerably later.

Which came first, the Willoughby ballad or the Rowland-Robert jig? Evidence is wanting for a categorical answer. It seems likely that our tune was initially "Rowland," from its association with the lost jig, and that it served as the tune for the ballad on Lord Willoughby and thus derived a second cluster of names. We do not know when the jig was written, performed, or printed, except that it must antedate the licensing of the "Second parte" in 1591. Moreover, "O Neighbor Roberte" is named as the tune for "A Pleasant New Sounge called the carmans Whistle," preserved in Bodleian MS Rawlinson Poet. 185, fol. 21, a commonplace book dated c. 1590.[4] If we cannot decide priority, it is none the less clear that the tune enjoyed Continental popularity under names derived from the jig or a related song, while in England the vogue of both jig and the Willoughby ballad is evident in tune names.

The music is found in Thomas Robinson's *Schoole of Musicke,* 1603, as "My Lord Willobies welcome home," arranged for lute. Other settings for the same instrument by John Dowland are in Folger MS 1610.1,

[4] The initial lines are quoted in *RB* VII, xiv. The text, beginning "In a pleasant morninge,/in the merrie month of May," is closer to "The Combers Whistle" (*RB* III, 564) than to the usual form of "The Carman's Whistle," though the two are textually related. Moreover, the latter ballad, which has its independent tune of the same name, q.v., lists "Lord Willoughby's March" as an alternative. In *PG,* p. 387, Rollins is in error when he states that "O Neighbor Roberte" and "The Carman's Whistle" are identical tunes, citing the Rawlinson poem as evidence. They are, rather, interchangeable.

294

* Followed in original by varied repeat of second strain and a 24-bar variation.

fol. 9ᵛ (Fig. 294), Wickhambrook Lute Book, fol. 12, Cambridge University MS Dd.2.11, fol. 58ᵛ, and in BM MS Egerton 2046, fol. 25; the latter manuscript has also a setting by William Byrd, fol. 33ᵛ, and one by Francis Cutting is in Cambridge MS Dd.5.78.3, fol. 28ᵛ. Anonymous divisions on the theme are in the Euing Lute MS, fol. 38, and a short setting is in the Richard Mynshall Lute MS, fol. 1. Byrd's virginal piece on the tune appears in his *My Ladye Nevells Booke,* 1591 (ed. Hilda Andrews, 1926, p. 186), in Will Forster's MS Virginal Book, 1624, p. 22, in Paris Conservatoire MS Rés. 1186, fol. 64ᵛ, and, with the title "Rowland," in *The Fitzwilliam Virginal Book* II, 190. An elaboration of the tune called "the second straine of o neighboure robart" in BM MS Add.

30485, fol. 115ᵛ, corresponds to the second section of Byrd's set in the Fitzwilliam and Nevell collections.

The tune is named "O neighbour Robert" in "The wonderfull example of God shewed vpon Iasper Coningham," a broadside published before 1600, beginning "It was a Scotchman,/a Scotchman lewd of life" (Lord Crawford 714; reprinted in *RB* III, 104; later editions are Lord Crawford 715, Manchester II, 45, Wood 401 [98], Wood 402 [56], Euing 399, Douce II, 258, Pepys II, 166, Roxburghe I, 470, Harvard).[5]

The tune is called "Lord Willoughby" in "Joyfull Newes for England," announcing the peace concluded with Holland and Denmark in 1654, and beginning "Now comfortable Tydings/is come unto England" (BM C.20.f.14; reprinted in *CP*, p. 342); it fits the tune, the refrain requiring a repetition of the second strain. "The Lord Willowbies March" is named for singing "Articles of agreement betwixt Prince Charles and the Parliament of Scotland," a ballad of 1650 beginning "The news from Scotland if you'l heare" (Manchester; reprinted in *CP*, p. 310), which has an elaborate thirteen-line stanza unsuited to the tune after the first quatrain. In two other ballads the tune is named "Brave Lord Willoughby": one is "A famous Sea-fight . . . September, 163[9]," by John Looks, beginning "[Giv]e ear you lusty Gallants/my purpose is to tell" (Manchester; reprinted in *PA*, p. 26); and the other, a ballad of 1649 with title shorn but with subtitle "A brief Relation of an Atheisticall creature," beginning "Good Christians all give eare awhile," to the tune of "Jesper Cunningame, or brave Lord Willoby" (Manchester; reprinted in *CP*, p. 278).

One final ballad deserves notice: "Newes good and new Too good to be true," published by John Trundle no later than 1625 and beginning "Now welcome neighbour Rowland" (Pepys; reprinted in *PG*, p. 217). This dialogue with jig elements is in the "Lord Willoughby" stanza, but I have no data on "Twenty pound a yeere," named as the tune on the broadside.

5 "Iasper Coningham" in turn becomes a name for the tune in "A wonder beyond mans expectation . . . 1631 . . . ," beginning "To England comes strange tidings" (Pepys; reprinted in *PG*, p. 387); and "The Wicked-mans Warning-piece," by T. L[anfiere?], beginning "Both old & young, both rich & poor" (Pepys II, 23).

Love Will Find Out the Way

This tune gets its name from the refrain of an early seventeenth-century ballad entitled "Truths Integrity, or, A Curious Northern Ditty called, Love will find out the Way," beginning "Over the Mountains/and under the waves" (Euing, Douce, Rawlinson, Roxburghe; reprinted in *RB* II, 639). The Roxburghe copy, printed for Francis Coles, must date from c. 1630, a possibility heightened by the August 9, 1633, entry in the Stationers' Register of "The Answere to Love will find out the way," a lost ballad (Rollins, *Anal. Index*, No. 81). The original ballad was re-entered in the Registers in 1656 (the Euing copy) and 1675 (Douce and Rawlinson issues). The broadside text is followed in *Pills*, 1719–1720, VI, 86; shorter versions are found in Ramsay's *Tea-Table Miscellany*, 1733, II, 178, in Percy's *Reliques*, and in Ritson's *English Songs*, 1783, I, 99, all beginning "Over the mountains,/And over the waves" but differing somewhat in detail.

Music of "Over the Mountaines" is found in *A Musicall Banquet*, 1651, Part I, No. 8 (Fig. 295), for lyra viol; in *A Booke of New Lessons*

Original an octave lower.

for the Cithern & Gittern, 1652, arranged for both instruments; in *Musicks Recreation on the Lyra Viol*, 1652; and in the coeval Bedford Cittern MS, fol. 4, and Trinity College, Cambridge, lute MS O.16.2, p. 135. In Forbes's *Cantus*, 1662, No. 48 (later eds., No. 45), the accompanying verses begin "Over the mountains and under the caves." The tune in *Musick's Delight on the Cithren*, 1666, No. 5, like the 1652 cittern air, is in common time, and the resulting three-measure phrases dislocate the familiar accents although the melodic line is not affected. *Pills* and Ritson's *English Songs* also reprint the music, but Johnson's *Scots Musical Museum* II, 157, gives five stanzas with a different tune. Chappell (*PMOT* I, 304) noted that the familiar air was in traditional circulation among Kentish hop pickers in the middle of the nineteenth century, and a quite similar tune was collected in Surrey at the beginning of the twentieth century (*JFSS,* I [1902], 205).

Other ballads sung to the tune include Robert Guy's "The Country-mans New Care away," beginning "If there were imployments" (Lord Crawford, Roxburghe; reprinted in *RB* I, 111). The Crawford copy, printed for Henry Gosson, is no later than 1640; it may be nearly a decade earlier if it is to be equated with "The Country mans Care away," which was licensed to Francis Coles in 1631 (Rollins, *Anal. Index,* No. 406), and if the two are not identical, the Crawford ballad was probably issued shortly after the piece for which the Stationers' Register entry was made.

Restoration pieces to the tune include "Strephon and Cloris; Or, The Coy Shepherd and Kind Shepherdess . . . To a pleasant New Play-house Tune; Or, Love will find out the way," a ballad of the 1670s beginning "Ah! Cloris awake,/it is all abroad day" (Lord Crawford, Wood E.25, Harvard, Roxburghe; reprinted in *RB* VI, 128; numerous later editions). The playhouse tune became known as "Ah! Chloris awake" and was used for a number of ballads; it is, then, an independent tune and its history is discussed under its own title. A second piece is R. Pilkington's "The Skilful Doctor; Or, The Compleat Mountebank," 1685, beginning "Come here you brave Gallants,/of Fame and Renown," to the tune "Over the Mountains" (Douce II, 201ᵛ, Pepys IV, 265).

The relationship between the tune of "Love will find out the way" and "Over hills and high mountains" is puzzling. The latter tune name is derived from the opening line of "The Wandring Maiden . . . To an excellent new Tune" (*BB* II, 572); and this ballad is so evidently a paraphrase of the earlier "Truths Integrity" that one is inclined to wonder whether the tune for it was indeed "new," or whether its description was merely a part of the advertiser's *dernier cri* psychology. We do not, at any rate, possess a tune called "Over hills and high mountains," although several late seventeenth-century ballads cite it for singing.[1]

[1] See, s.v. "Ah! Chloris awake," a brief discussion of some ballads naming the tune. Others will be found in *RB* VI, 124, 126. The following have apparently not been re-published: "The Dairy-Maids Mirth and Pastime on May-Day," beginning "Now the Season of Winter/doth his power resign" (Pepys III, 201); and "The Young-Mans Lamentation," beginning "Meeting's a pleasure,/but parting's a grief" (Douce II, 261ᵛ).

Four ballad operas use a tune called "On yonder(s) high mountain,"[2] for which no original words have been found; it bears a family likeness to the tune of "Love will find out the way," despite a good deal of difference in harmonic and melodic detail.

A Lovely Lass to a Friar Came

This tune is associated with a song inappropriately titled "The Fryar and the Nun"; the verses have nothing to do with a nun, and, to compound confusion, there is a tune "The Friar and the Nun" (q.v.) with its own history. Our piece begins:

> A lovely Lass to a Friar came,
>   to confess in the morning Early;
> In what my Dear was you to blame,
>   now tell to me Sincerely,
> I have done S^r what I dare not name,
>   with a Man that loves me Dearly.

Although it seems to stem from an older tradition, the earliest copy I have found is an engraved single-sheet edition (Fig. 296) conjecturally dated 1710 (BM H.1601 [26], Chetham 1408, Harvard).[1] It appeared also

296

[2] They are Ryan's *The Cobler's Opera*, 1729, *Momus turn'd Fabulist*, 1729, Lillo's *Silvia*, 1731, all with music; and Drury's *The Fancy'd Queen*, 1733, without music. Chappell (*PMOT* II, 682) used this music with one of the ballads calling for "Over hills and high mountains," but he recognized the lack of positive documentary evidence to link the two tunes.

[1] A three-stanza text doubtfully attributed to Rochester is reproduced in *The Common Muse*, ed. V. de Sola Pinto and A. E. Rodway, 1957, p. 297, from an unspecified

in Watts's *Musical Miscellany*, 1729–1731, VI, 177, and *The Convivial Songster*, c. 1782, p. 114. Another song to the same tune immediately follows it in the *Musical Miscellany* and is reprinted in *The Hive*, 4th ed., c. 1733, III, 177; it begins "How do they err, who throw their Love/ On Fate or Fortune wholly."

The tune appears as "The Old Fryer" in *The Dancing Master*, c. 1728, III, 44, and as "The Fryer and the Maid" in Walsh's *New Country Dancing-Master*, c. 1728, III, 157. As "A Lovely Lass to a Friar came," it was used in at least nine ballad operas, including Gay's *The Beggar's Opera*, 1728, and Odell's *The Patron*, 1729, which reprint the music. It was still in vogue in 1764, when it served as the tune for "If in the Courts your suit depend" in Act III of Kane O'Hara's comic opera, *Midas*.

Lumber Me

This strange tune title is associated with a ballad preserved in that notable Elizabethan collection of broadsides, *A Handefull of Pleasant Delites*, 1584 (ed. Rollins, p. 54), and on a leaf of another edition which may be as early as 1566. The piece is "A proper new Dity: Intituled Fie vpo[n] Loue and al his lawes," and its first stanza is as follows:

> Svch bitter fruict thy loue doth yeelde,
> Such broken sleepes, such hope vnsure,
> Thy call so oft hath me beguilde.
> That I vnneth can well indure:
> But crie (alas) as I haue cause,
> Fie vpon Loue and all his Lawes.

I am indebted to Mr. John Ward for the suggestion that "Lumber me" is a corruption of "L'homme armé," the name of a branle in vogue on the Continent during the second half of the sixteenth century. The music appears in Jan Fruytiers's *Ecclesiasticus*, 1565 (ed. D. F. Scheurleer, 1898, p. 95 [Fig. 297]), in Sebastian Vreedman's *Carminum . . . Liber Secundus*, 1569, fol. 16ᵛ, and twice in *Het Luitboek van Thysius*, compiled c. 1600, Nos. 8, 106. Mr. Ward found an untitled English set of the dance among some keyboard pieces at the end of Thomas Dallis's MS Lute Book (Trinity College, Dublin, MS D.3.30); for this portion of

and undated MS of the Duke of Portland, now deposited in Nottingham University Library.

297

Original is unbarred.

the MS he conjectures a date of c. 1570, thus lending strength to the belief that the tune was known in England at the time the *Handefull* ballad was published. Mr. Ward's edition of *The Dublin Virginal Manuscript*, 1954, contains the English set (No. 20), an edited version of the air designed to fit it to the *Handefull* verse, and a reprint of the Vreedman *"L'homarmé."*

Lusty Gallant

Two late sixteenth-century manuscript versions of "Lusty gallant" have been preserved. One is in William Ballet's Lute Book, p. 83 (Fig. 298); the other, with repetitions written out so that its adaptation to an eight-line stanza is evident, is an untitled setting in the Marsh Lute Book, p. 61.

There is ample evidence that the tune was current in the early years of Elizabeth's reign. A manuscript known to have been compiled by 1566, Bodleian MS Ashmole 48, contains two pieces calling for the tune (printed in *Songs and Ballads*, ed. Thomas Wright, pp. 183, 195). One, beginning "I rede howe that the marbell stone/Throwgholed ys by rany dropps," names the tune "Lusty gallant"; the other, beginning "When Troylus dwelt in Troy towne,/A man of nobell fame a," is sung to "Fayne

298

woold I fynd sum pretty thynge to geeve unto my lady." This name for the tune comes from the title and refrain of a ballad found in *A Handefull of Pleasant Delites,* 1584 (ed. Rollins, p. 57), called "A proper Song, Intituled: Fain wold I haue a pretie thing to give vnto my Ladie. To the tune of lustie Gallant." [1] The Troilus ballad was licensed in 1565–1566 (*Anal. Index,* No. 1124), but "A proper Song" must have been in print earlier, and was very likely included in the lost 1566 edition of the *Handefull.* The first stanza also serves as the refrain:

> Fain would I haue a pretie thing,
> to giue vnto my Ladie:
> I name no thing, nor I meane no thing,
> But as pretie a thing as may bee.

Two moralistic parodies were licensed in 1566–1567: "a fayne wolde I have a godly thynge to shewe vnto my ladye," and "fayne wolde I have a vertuous wyfe adourned with all modeste both mylde and meke of quyett lyf esteemynge chef hyr chastetye"; probably the ballad licensed Oct. 1, 1576, as "fayne would I haue and take no payne" was another of the same sort. These three have not survived. But *A Gorgeous Gallery of Gallant Inventions,* 1578 (ed. Rollins, p. 26), preserves a piece that was evidently a broadside: "A propper Dittie. To the tune of lusty Gallant,"

---

[1] Another version of this ballad is in Bodleian MS Rawlinson Poet. 108, fol. 44 (late 16th century), reprinted in *OEB,* p. 322. John Ward joins the opening lines of the *Handefull* text with the Marsh lute version in "Music for *A Handefull of Pleasant Delites,*" *JAMS,* X (1957), 169–170; on p. 176 he reproduces the Ballet notation in 2/4 time, to contrast it with the 6/4 measure of the Marsh setting. The Ballet air and the *Handefull* opening are also printed in Bruce Pattison, *Music and Poetry of the English Renaissance,* 1948, p. 169.

beginning "The glyttering showes of Floras dames/Delightes not so my carefull minde."

William Elderton wrote "A proper new Balad in praise of my Ladie Marques" (licensed 1568–1569), beginning "Ladies, I thinke you maruell that/I writ no mery report to you," to the tune "New lusty gallant" (BM Huth; reprinted in *A Collection of Seventy-Nine Black-Letter Ballads,* 1867, p. 14); the eight-line stanza fits the music we possess.

"Lusty Gallant" continued to be sung during the seventeenth century. It is used, for example, with "Londons Lotterie . . . for the good of Virginia," 1612, beginning "London, liue thou famous long" (Pepys; reprinted in C. H. Firth's *American Garland,* 1915, p. 17, and in *PB* I, 26). And it is also called for in "The sorrowfull complaint of Susan Higges," a good-night ballad of a murderess, beginning "To mourne for my offences,/and former passed sinnes" (Pepys; reprinted in *RB* II, 633).

"List lusty Gallants" is named as the tune for "A brave warlike Song," a ballad of c. 1626 on the Nine Worthies and the Seven Champions of Christendom (Pepys; reprinted in *PB* II, 57). It is possible that our "Lusty gallant" tune is meant here, for the ballad meter fits the tune; but the stanza of eight lines, plus a refrain of eight, would require the notes to be sung four times over. This is not inconceivable, but it is far more probable that a longer tune was intended.

Magina-Cree

This tune is named on a broadside licensed in 1633, "Good Admonition Or To al sorts of people this counsell I sing, That in each ones affaire, to take heed's a faire thing," beginning "To all christian people,/ this ditty belongs" (Pepys; reprinted in *PB* II, 240). The tune is named "Magina-cree."

Music is found in all editions of *The Dancing Master,* under various guises. In the 1651 edition, p. 20 (Fig. 299), it is "Mage on a Cree"; in 1670 it is "Mage on a Tree"; in 1721 it is "Madge on a tree: Or Margery Cree." Despite these efforts to make the title intelligible, only the basic idea of "Magpie in a tree" comes through with any clarity ("mag" and "Madge" are familiar names for magpie). I can offer no gloss on "Cree." The tune as arranged for violin can be sung to the ballad if a few notes are split to accommodate two syllables, an emendation frequently required in adapting an instrumental arrangement to vocal use. Miss Margaret Dean-Smith, in her facsimile edition of the 1651 *Dancing*

299

Original is unbarred.

Master, 1957, p. 20, notes that the dance coupled with the tune is a "progressive round, . . . generally regarded as one of the more ancient types displayed in the book."

Make Your Honors, Miss

In 1691 Thomas D'Urfey wrote a song beginning "Make your Honours Misse" for his play *Love for Money: Or, The Boarding School,* II, ii. It is found, with the music, in all editions of *Pills,* 1719–1720, II, 170, and without music in *The Compleat Academy of Complements,* 1705. The tune appeared in *Apollo's Banquet,* Second Book, 1691, and a badly garbled musical text was printed on a broadside of the same year, "Teague the Irish Soldier," along with a tune direction calling for "Let Caesar Live long. or, Now, now the Fight's done," to which it can be sung (*PB* VI, 134).

D'Urfey's stage song was expanded into a broadside entitled "An Excellent New Play-House Song, Called, Love for Money: Or, The Boarding School. To a New Play-House Tune," beginning "Make your Honours Miss, Tol, Tol" (Pepys V, 192, Lord Crawford 791, Harvard, all with meaningless music). The "Tol" refrain at the end of every line, occupying as many musical beats as the line itself, is evidently intended to be supplemented with pantomime as the dancing master passes gradually from commonplace instructions in posture and movement to the thinly veiled amatory *double-entendre* in which D'Urfey excelled. Another version of this ballad replaces the syllabic refrain with a line of verse, but without changing the tone of the ballad; it is called "The Modish Dancing-Master or, The Boarding School Miss. To a Pleasant Tune, call'd, A New Minuet" and begins "Make your Honors Miss, first to the Gentry here" (Pepys V, 435, with accurate music on the sheet [Fig. 300]).

· 479 ·

300

A satiric male adaptation of the original broadside is "The Fop Masters Instructions to All his Beau Schollars, that are desirous to commence Fops," to the tune of "Make your Honours Miss"; it begins "Cock up your Beaver Sir, Tol, tol, tol" (Pepys V, 429, with meaningless music). The tune may be referred to in "The Despairing Prodigal: or, The Happy Surprisall. To an Excellent New Tune, Sung at the Court, Call'd The Boarding School," beginning "Young men & Maids to these few lines give ear." The song is cast in a six-line stanza which fits the music reasonably well (Pepys IV, 313). Less certainly related, though the refrain is suggestive, is "The Fond Lovers Friendly Advice. To a Pleasant New Tune," beginning "Hi-ho, I've lost my Love, Toll la ra, Toll la ra ra" (Pepys V, 162, with corrupt music); the four-line stanza could be sung to the tune by omitting a repetition of the first strain.

An eighteenth-century slip song, "The Oxford Schollar," beginning "I Met a Man all on the way" (Morgan 22b), has a "toll" burden after the first, second, and fourth lines of its quatrain stanza and is almost certainly not intended to be sung to "Make your honors, Miss."

The tune was used in two ballad operas: Chetwood's *The Lover's Opera,* 1729, and Coffey's *The Boarding School,* 1733, both with music; Coffey calls the tune "Boarding School" and simply uses D'Urfey's original stage song.

Mall Peatly

This popular dance tune is found in D. P. Pers's Amsterdam songbook, *Bellerophon*, 1633. Called "Mal-Pedle," it employs common time in its first strain, while the second strain is in the equivalent of modern 6/4; English sets are in triple rhythm throughout. As "Old Marrinet, or Mal Peatly" it was included among the "Select New Tunes and Jiggs" at the end of the 1665 edition of *The Dancing Master,* and it appeared under this title in *Apollo's Banquet,* 1670, No. 92. With instructions for the dance it is found as "Moll Peatly" in *The Dancing Master* of 1670 and subsequent editions; "Moll Peatley the New way," appearing first in the eleventh edition, 1701, couples a new dance with the old tune. Thompson's *Compleat Collection of 200 Favourite Country Dances,* c. 1764, shows the air still flourishing, and Samuel Wesley arranged it as a rondo for pianoforte under the title "Moll Pately, A Celebrated Dance," c. 1810.

Thomas D'Urfey used an expanded form of the tune for a political mock-pastoral ballad "Gillian of Croyden," beginning "One holiday last Summer," which he published with the music in his *Choice Collection of New Songs and Ballads,* 1699, p. 2 (Fig. 301), and in all editions of *Pills,* 1719–1720, II, 46. (Song-sheet versions of the piece are in Harvard

and California.) At the commencement of Anne's reign, D'Urfey wrote a continuation of his ballad in the same measure, called "The Queen's Health: Or, New Gillian of Croydon," beginning "Fame loudly thro' Europe passes" (*Pills* I, 146, without music or tune direction; reprinted in *A Complete Collection of . . . English and Scotch Songs,* 1735–1736, I, 126, called "Gillian of Croydon" and without music). A ballad on the Old Pretender, "Perkin's Last Adventure," beginning "December last, in Frosty Weather," to the tune of "Mall Peatly, alias Gillian of Croydon," is in *A Collection of State Songs,* 1716, p. 116.

The tune was used in half a dozen ballad operas. In *Calista,* 1731, it is called "Moll Peakly," and in Gay's *Achilles* and Potter's *The Decoy,* 1733, it is "Moll Peatly." Ralph's *The Fashionable Lady,* 1730, Gataker's *The Jealous Clown,* 1730, and Lillo's *Silvia,* 1731, cite it as "Gillian of Croydon," exemplifying D'Urfey's frequent success in coupling a song to an old tune which thereafter took its name from his verses.

[Man Is for the Woman Made]

Peter Motteux wrote a song beginning "Man, man, man is for the Woman made," which was set to music by Henry Purcell and included in Thomas Scott's play *The Mock Marriage,* 1696, IV, ii. Words and

music appear in *Deliciae Musicae,* Third Book, 1696, p. 3 (Fig. 302), in all editions of *Pills,* 1719–1720, III, 222, and in *The Convivial Song-ster,* c. 1782, p. 18.

An expanded version of the song was published as a broadside with the title "The United Lovers . . . To a pleasant new Tune," but without music (Pepys V, 415). Despite the excellence of Purcell's melody, it was apparently not used for any other broadsides.

March, Boys

This tune takes its name from the refrain of a ballad celebrating the battle of the Boyne, July 1, 1690: "The Bogg-Trotters March . . . To an Excellent New Tune, Or, March Boys, March Boys, &c.," beginning "Old *James* with his Rascally Rabble of Rogues" (Lord Crawford 966, with meaningless music, Pepys V, 54, with sound musical score [Fig. 303]; text reprinted in *PB* V, 196). The refrain formula, whose details are changed in each stanza, runs as follows initially:

> March Boys, march Boys, merry, merry march, Boys,
>   *Teague's* but a Mushrom to a Man, Boys,
> See how they fly, how they run, how they dye,
>   whilest Conquering *William* leads us on, Boys.

The tune appears in *Apollo's Banquet,* 1693, as "A New Dance in the Play of *The Marriage-Hater match'd*" [by D'Urfey, 1692], reprinted in *OEPM,* ed. Wooldridge, II, 67. Music is found also in the Pepys copies of "The Young Damsels Courage and Conquest," beginning "A Souldier from Flanders he travell'd of late" (Pepys V, 172; with meaningless music in Lord Crawford 1078, BM C.39.k.6 [27]; reprinted in *OPB,* p. 70), as well as "The Merry Bag-Pipes," beginning "A Shepherd sat him under a Thorn" (Pepys V, 158; other copies, without music, include Lord Crawford, Bagford, Harvard, Roxburghe; reprinted with music in *Pills,* 1719–1720, IV, 136; bowdlerized reprint in *RB* VII, 326). The refrain of the latter ballad, "To thee, to thee, derry derry, to thee, &c.," is undoubtedly the source of the tune title "To thee, to thee" cited for "The Unconscionable Batchelors of Darby," a ballad in the same twelve-line stanza, beginning "You lovers of mirth attend a while" (Pepys, Lord Crawford, Roxburghe; reprinted in *RB* VII, 225, and *OPB,* p. 188).

"March, boys" is used for a handful of other ballads found in the

303

Pepys collection. Three topical pieces of 1692 have been reprinted by Professor Rollins: "France Out-witted," on the Duke of Richmond's return to England after being dismissed from his captaincy in the French army (*PB* VI, 157); "King William's Welcome to Holland" at the outset of his second military campaign (*PB* VI, 164; the original broadside contains meaningless music); and "The Glorious Victory," on the defeat of the French fleet at La Hogue (*PB* VI, 180). Four other ballads to the tune have not been reprinted: "London's New Cry: Or, The Dumpling Woman's Delight," beginning "Friends, I'm a gentlewoman born" (Pepys V, 422, Lord Crawford 400); "The Good Wives Humble Petition," beginning "Kind husband, the Comfort of my life" (Pepys IV, 75); "Robin the Plow-man's Courage," beginning "Stout Robin the Plow-man lov'd young Kate" (Pepys III, 305); and "The Bakers Lamentation," beginning "Good People I pray now pity my case" (Pepys V, 395, with meaningless music).

Mardyke

The music of "Mardike" is found among the violin tunes at the end of *The Dancing Master,* 3d ed., c. 1662, No. 43 (Fig. 304), 1665, No. 20,

304

in *Musick's Delight on the Cithren,* 1666, in *Apollo's Banquet,* 1670, in *Musicks Recreation on the Viol, Lyra-way,* 1682, and in *Pills,* 1719–1720, V, 65.

The tune takes its name from Mardyke, a fortress near the port of Dunkirk which was the scene of a British victory in October, 1657. A ballad on the subject, whose earliest extant edition is 1660, is called "Mardike: Or, The Soldiers Sonnet of his Sword. Sung to the Organ," beginning "When first Mardike was made a Prey" (Bagford I, 69). Later editions are titled "The Soldiers Fortune: or The Taking of Mardike" and are without tune direction (Lord Crawford, Euing, Douce, Harvard, Roxburghe; reprinted in *RB* VII, 651). The text is found in *Merry Drollery,* 1661, *Merry Drollery Complete,* 1670, *The Loyal Garland,* 1686, and *Pills,* a poor text with lines lost from almost every stanza.

Pepys alludes to the tune in his *Diary,* Feb. 4, 1660, and a more elaborate reference appears in D'Urfey's *The Fool Turn'd Critick,* 1678, II, ii, where a snatch of the final stanza is paraphrased:

Sir For[mal Ancient]. . . . this is a lewd Rogue, that gleans up all the fragments of cast Bawdy to make Songs A-la-mode, as he calls 'um: Sirrah can you sing the battle of *Mardike?*

1st Fid[ler]. No indeed Sir.

Sir For. I told you so—not sing the Battel of *Mardike?* Why thou ignorant Rogue, where hast thou bin bred?

(Sings)   And huffing, And puffing,
          And Snuffing, And Cuffing the Spaniard:
          Whose Brows have bin dy'd in a Tan-yard,
          Well got Fame, a Warriours Wife.

Old Wine[love]. O brave *Sir Formal.*

Sir For. Ah Sir, there's some matter in this now, an ill bred Raskal, not sing the Battle of *Mardike.* Here's Near a child in *Banbury* of 7 years old, but can Sing the Battle of *Mardike,* and has it readier then His Horn-book.

There seems to be no authority for attributing the ballad to Samuel Butler, despite the urgings of Ebsworth.

Maying Time

"The Maying-time" is named as an alternative tune to "[Let us to the] Warres againe" on a badly mutilated ballad of monthly predictions (Manchester I, 48), printed by John Hammond, c. 1650.[1] An earlier appearance of the tune title is in Richard Johnson's *Golden Garland of Princely Pleasures,* 3d ed., 1620 (13th ed., 1690), where "The Shepherd's Dialogue of Love between Willy and Cuddy," beginning "How now, Shepherd, what means that," is to be sung to "Maying time." The poem is found with music (Fig. 305) in the Leyden MS of 1639, fol. 11ᵛ (National Library of Scotland), in Forbes's *Cantus,* 1662, and in BM MS Add. 29481, fol. 10 (printed in *OEPM* I, 158); the same tune, called "The Willow Trie," [2] is in the Skene MS (published in *Ancient Scotish Melodies,* ed. William Dauney, p. 248). This air fits the Manchester fragment, though not without some division of notes to suit the octosyllabic measure.

Another tune called "May Time" or "Maying Time," preserved in John Playford's *Musicks Recreation on the Lyra Viol,* 1652, p. 1 (Fig. 306), and in his *A Booke of New Lessons for the Cithern & Gittern,* 1652,

---

[1] The air of "Let us to the wars again" has not survived. Ballads with such a tune direction (*CP,* pp. 96, 108) can, of course, be sung to "Maying time," an alternate tune; but the two are interchangeable, not identical. "Let us to the wars again" gets its name from the refrain of "Gallants, to Bohemia. . . . To a pleasant new Warlike tune," a ballad of c. 1632 (*PG,* p. 416).

[2] Percy prints a conflate text of Johnson's poem in the *Reliques,* calling it "The Willow Tree," from an occasional refrain in the poem.

305

306

Original is an octave lower.

has a quite different movement, but it could also serve the stanza pattern of broadside and poem.

"A modest Caroll for any of the Twelve dayes," beginning "A Dozen of good Points I'le give," found in *Good and True, Fresh and New, Christmas Carols,* 1642, is to the tune "In the merry Maying time." This carol could be sung to the music in Forbes's *Cantus,* but its tune name may be derived from the opening line "In this merry Maying time" of "A Pleasant Countrey Maying Song," c. 1625 (Pepys; reprinted in *PB* II, 9); the tune of that ballad is "The Popes Machina," which has not survived.

Merrily and Cheerily

This tune is in all editions of *The Dancing Master* (1651, p. 78=Fig. 307), called "Cherily and merrily" except in the second edition, 1652, p. 111, where it is named "Mister Webs Fancy." The more familiar tune

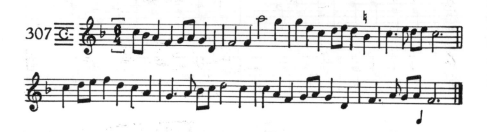

name comes from John Looks's ballad of 1641, "Keepe thy head on thy shoulders, And I will keepe mine. . . . To the tune of, Merrily and cherrily," beginning "Though Wentworths beheaded,/Should any Repyne" (Manchester; reprinted in *CP*, p. 127), with a refrain:

> Then merrily and cherrily
> Lets drink off our Beere,
> Let who as will run for it
> Wee will stay heere.

This ballad can be sung satisfactorily to the tune, requiring a repetition of the first strain in order that the second strain may be reserved for the refrain lines.

In S[amuel?] S[mithson?]'s "The Parliament Routed," 1653, beginning "Cheare up kind Countrey-men, be not dismayd," the tune is given as "Lucina, or, Merrily and Cherrily" (BM Thomason, Harvard; reprinted in Wright's *Political Ballads*, p. 126; Wilkins's *Political Ballads* I, 105; Mackay's *Cavalier Songs*, p. 102; and *RB* VIII, xlvii*, cxlv*). On "Lucina" see "The Beggar Boy"; "Merrily and Cherrily" fits the ballad with a repetition of each strain.

Methinks the Poor Town

Methinks the Poor Town Has Been Troubled Too Long is a poetical
miscellany of 1673 whose title derives from the opening of a poem by
Lord Dorset contained in the volume. His verses were set to music by
John Playford and appeared the same year in *Choice Songs and Ayres,*
p. 50 (Fig. 308), and were reprinted in every edition of *Pills*, 1719–1720,

* Normalization of cadences reflects their treatment in second edition, 1675
(except that the final one remained hypermetrical).

III, 172. This antipastoral states its aim in the first stanza:

> Methinks the poor Town has been troubled too long
> With Phillis and Cloris in every Song;
> By Fools, who, at once, can both Love and despair,
> And will never leave calling them cruel and fair:
> Which justly provokes me, in Rhime, to express
> The truth that I know of bonny Black Bess.

But only the name of the inamorata is fresh: the rest of the poem is
conventional encomium, set against a background of theatrical boxes
and pit.[1]

The tune, named from the entire first line of Dorset's song, is used for
at least two broadsides. One, containing on the sheet the licensing date
of June 24, 1685, is "The White-Chappel Maids Lamentation . . . upon

[1] *RB* IV, 90n., cites a contemporary parody beginning "Methinks this poor land has
been troubled too long," in which "Black Bess" is clearly identified as the Countess
of Dysart, second wife of the Duke of Lauderdale.

the Souldiers Departing to the Army," beginning "We Maids are undone, our sweet-hearts are flown" (Pepys III, 338). The other, which bears the initials of the licenser Roger L'Estrange and so is no later than 1685, is "The True Lovers Cruel Tragedy," beginning "Let True Lovers all our Fortunes Rehearse" (Pepys III, 351).

A ballad by John Wade, published c. 1675, is to the tune of "Bonny black Bess: Or, Digby"; it is "Tis Money that makes a Man," beginning "Oh what a Madness 'tis to borrow or lend" (Pepys, Wood E.25, Douce, Lord Crawford, Harvard, Roxburghe; reprinted in RB VI, 346). The ballad fits "Digby's farewell" without difficulty, but its eight eleven-syllable lines would require a repetition of Playford's first strain. It is indeed questionable whether "Bonny black Bess" is an allusion to the Dorset song.

The Milkmaids, or The Merry Milkmaids, or The Milking Pail

This fine dance tune is called "The milke maids" in Drexel MS 5612, p. 180 (New York Public Library, a seventeenth-century virginal set); an arrangement for lyra viol in Cambridge University MS Dd.6.48, fol. 14ᵛ (c. mid-seventeenth century), is "The merry merry milkmaids," a title used also in most editions of *The Dancing Master,* 1651–c. 1728 (1670, p. 71=Fig. 309); the version in *Musicks Recreation on the Viol, Lyra-way,* 1669, is "The merry Milk-Maid." The coeval virginal arrangement in Paris Conservatoire MS Rés. 1186, fol. 36, is entitled simply "A dance."

In 1634 Martin Parker wrote three ballads to the tune, all of them entered in the Stationers' Register and published by Thomas Lambert; the first two received the accolade of being sung by Maudlin, the milk-maid in Walton's *The Compleat Angler.* The first is "The Milke-maids Life . . . to a curious new tune called, The Milke-maids Dumps," beginning "You rurall goddesses,/that woods and fields possesse" (Roxburghe; reprinted in RB II, 116, and in Chappell, PMOT I, 295–296).[1]

---

[1] Parker's ditty was included in Henry Bold's *Latine Songs, with their English,* 1685, p. 70. Bold translates the refrain line "To carry the milking pail" as "Transvehunt Mulctrale." During the years 1685–1688, when Richard Pocock was licenser, there appeared another version of Parker's ballad which begins with his sixth stanza and con-

309

Original a fifth higher.

Parker's second piece was "Keep a good tongue in your head," beginning "I married a wife of late,/The more's my unhappy fate," to the tune "the Milkmaids" (Roxburghe; reprinted in *RB* III, 237; five stanzas are included in *PMOT* I, 298–299). His third, "Hold your hands honest men," to the tune of "Keep a good tongue &c.," is in the same measure and begins "I Haue as compleat a man,/as any poore woman can" (Roxburghe; reprinted in *RB* III, 243).

Thomas D'Urfey reworked Parker's "The Milke-maids Life" for his play *Don Quixote,* Part II, 1694, II, ii. It is in the same thirteen-line stanza, beginning "Ye Nymphs and Sylvan Gods," and incorporates the old refrain line "To carry the milking pail," but John Eccles provided fresh music which was printed in *The Songs to . . . Don Quixote,* Part the Second, 1694, p. 3 (Fig. 310). The song with Eccles's air is found in all editions of *Pills,* 1719–1720, I, 237, in early eighteenth-century single-sheet editions (BM H.1601 [545], BM G.316.f [124], Harvard, Huntington) and in *The Merry Musician,* c. 1729, II, 115. The popular broadside version is called "An Excellent New Play-House Song, Call'd The Bonny Milk-Maid" (Pepys V, 221, Lord Crawford 1376, with meaningless music), or "The Merry Milk-maids . . . To the Tune of, The

tinues with an independent text: "The Innocent Country Maids Delight. . . . Set to an Excellent Country Dance," beginning "Some lasses are nice and strange/That keep shop in the Exchange" (Lord Crawford, Douce, Harvard, Roxburghe; reprinted in *RB* VII, 27).

310

Milking-pail" (BM C.22.f.6 [151], Lord Crawford 1375; still other editions in Pepys III, 63, Lord Crawford 1377, and BM 1871.e.9 [23]—the latter an eighteenth-century slip song with the title "The Milking Pail. To its own proper Tune"). A continuation, "The Plowman's Praise . . . in Answer to the Bonny Milkmaid," is sometimes printed separately (Pepys V, 264, to the tune "The Bonny Milkmaid"; reprinted in *RB* VII, 288), sometimes included on the sheet with "The Merry Milk-maids."

"The Witty Lass of Lime-Street," beginning "Young Women and Lasses too" (Pepys V, 179), calls the tune "The Bonny Milk-maid," presumably after the title of the broadside version of D'Urfey's song. Three other late seventeenth-century ballads name the tune "The Milking-pail" from the refrain line of both Parker's and D'Urfey's verses; we therefore cannot know whether the old or the new tune was intended. These three are: "The Passionate Maid of Rochester," beginning "You pretty young Lasses all" (Pepys; reprinted in *PB* VII, 32); "The Conquer'd Lady: or, the Country Wooing," beginning "Young Nelly, my Heart's delight" (Pepys V, 216); and "The London Lasses Vindication," beginning "The Country Damsels boast" (Pepys V, 254).

Eccles's tune is found as "Milkin Pail" in *Youth's Delight on the Flagelet*, 11th ed., 1697, and in a setting for harpsichord, c. 1704–1707, entitled "Ye nymphs and syl" in BM MS Add. 22099, fol. 9ᵛ. A single-sheet song of c. 1720, "The Chief of Dairy-Maids, or The Green Gown," beginning "Of all the Maidens fair Who snuff the Morning Air" (BM I.530 [115], Harvard), uses the tune. And under the title "Ye Nymphs and Sylvan [*or* Sylvian] Gods," it appears in a dozen ballad operas, of which the following reprint the music: Coffey's *The Beggar's Wedding*, 1729; Chetwood's *The Lover's Opera*, 1729 (music in 3d ed., 1730); Odell's *The*

Patron, 1729; Gay's *Polly*, 1729; *The Jovial Crew*, 1731; and Field-ing's *The Mock Doctor*, 1732, and his *An Old Man taught Wisdom*, 1735. In *Momus turn'd Fabulist*, 1729, the air called "The merry Milk-Maids" is a different tune, beginning like Purcell's "Ah cruel bloody fate" but pursuing its own melodic and harmonic path after the first phrase.

Millfield

Music for this tune is preserved in the first ten editions of *The Dancing Master*, 1651–1698 (1651, p. 32 = Fig. 311).

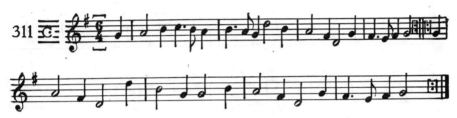

311

Original is unbarred.

William Elderton wrote "A new Ballad . . . Treason . . . against the young King of Scots [prevented by] one Andrewe Browne . . . the Kings Chamberlaine" to the tune of "Milfield, or els to Greensleeues"; it begins "Jesus God what a griefe is this,/that Princes subiects cannot be true" (London Society of Antiquaries [Lemon, *Catalogue*, No. 71]; re-printed in Percy's *Reliques* and in Child, No. 180, Appendix).[1] Elder-ton's ballad was licensed May 30, 1581, less than nine months after the first "Greensleeves" ballad was entered in the Stationers' Register. From the fact that "Milfield" is the first tune named, we may conclude that it was more familiar to his public than "Greensleeves," which had so lately come into vogue.

[1] An imperfect version of Elderton's ballad is in the Percy Folio MS (ed. Hales and Furnivall, II, 266). Another account of the same episode (based loosely on events of 1578, as Child has demonstrated), titled "Kinge James and Browne," is in the Percy Folio MS I, 135, and in Child, No. 180. This latter text, in ballad-meter quatrains, will not fit either of Elderton's tunes.

Mr. Lane's Maggot

This spirited tune appeared as "Mr. Lane's Magot" (i.e., "whim," "fancy") in *The Dancing Master*, commencing with the ninth edition, 1695, and as "The Ramble" in the Margaret Sinkler MS of 1710, fol. 27ᵛ (National Library of Scotland). *Thesaurus Musicus*, Fourth Book, 1695,

312

* A in original.

p. 3, contains "A Song made by Mr. D'Urfey upon a new Country Dance, called, Mr. Lanes Magget," beginning "Strike up drowsie Gut-Scrapers." The song was reprinted in *The Compleat Academy of Complements*, 1705, p. 121, and with music in *Pills*, 1719–1720, II, 218. D'Urfey's text was expanded into a broadside of the 1690s entitled "A new Song, call'd, The Richmond Recreation: or, The Royal Dance of Delight" (Pepys V, 408, with the music—Fig. 312).

Monsieur's Almain

The title of this dance tune recalls to us the old custom of naming a king's younger brother "Monsieur." The reference here is evidently to François, Duke of Anjou, and brother of Henri III of France. It may be assumed that the tune was in circulation before François's death in 1584. A Continental version of "Allemande Monsieur," c. 1600, is preserved in *Het Luitboek van Thysius*, No. 311 (Fig. 313); English settings include "mounsers almane" in the Wickhambrook Lute MS, c. 1595, fol. 17, and "Mounsieurs Almane" in the Welde Lute MS, c. 1600, fol. 14ᵛ. William

313

Byrd's keyboard pieces based on this tune are in *The Fitzwilliam Virginal Book* I, 234, 238. The first of these is found also in the Clement Matchett MS Virginal Book, 1612, No. 5 (ed. T. Dart, 1957), and Will Forster's MS Virginal Book, 1624, No. 42; the second Byrd arrangement appears also in his *My Ladye Nevells Booke*, 1591, No. 38, Forster, No. 60, and BM MS Add. 30485, fol. 92ᵛ. The tune is also used in Thomas Morley's *The First Book of Consort Lessons*, 1599, set for an ensemble consisting of treble and bass viol, cittern, pandore, lute, and flute (i.e., recorder). Slightly later is the setting by Daniell Batcheler in Robert Dowland's *Varietie of Lute Lessons*, 1610 (ed. Edgar Hunt, 1956, p. 41).

Thomas Deloney wrote "A ioyful new Ballad, Declaring the happie obtaining of the great Galleazzo," 1588, beginning "O Noble England,/ fall downe vpon thy knee," to the tune of "Mounseurs Almaigne" (BM C.18.e.2 [62]; reprinted in *RB* VI, 384, in Deloney's *Works*, ed. Mann,

p. 468, and in *Naval Songs and Ballads*, ed. C. H. Firth, 1908, p. 18). The ballad, licensed August 10, 1588, describes the capture of an enemy ship in the course of England's repulse of the Spanish Armada.

My Life and My Death

This tune takes its name from the opening line, "My Life, and my Death, are both in your pow'r," of a song which appeared in *The Theater of Music*, First Book, 1685, p. 32, with music by William Turner (Fig. 314). In the same year Thomas D'Urfey wrote a mock to the song, be-

ginning "My Life and My Death were once in your pow'r," and published it with Turner's music in his *Third Collection of New Songs*, p. 12. Both are to be found with the music in *Pills*, 1719–1720, III, 197, II, 56. The tune alone is in *Youth's Delight on the Flagelet*, 9th ed., c. 1690.[1]

[1] Meaningless music is contained on a broadside of about May, 1690, "A Dialogue between the French and Irish Officers," beginning "Oh Brother Taylor what shall we

The expanded broadside version of the original song is "Love and Constancy United," to the tune "My Life and my death," with a first line now reading "My life and my death lies both in your power" (Pepys III, 204). It was followed by "Alexis Loyalty . . . An Answer to My Life and my Death: To the same Tune," beginning "Thy Life and thy Death thou didst freely declare" (Pepys III, 180). Both ballads were licensed by Richard Pocock, who succeeded Sir Roger L'Estrange toward the end of 1685 and kept the office until shortly before the coronation of William and Mary. It is therefore puzzling that a ballad "On the Barbarous . . . Murder of the Earl of Essex," beginning "Attend and give Ear, good Christians to me," should bear the tune direction "My Life and my Death" (Pepys; reprinted in *PB* III, 92), dealing as it does with the death of Arthur Capel, Earl of Essex, on July 13, 1683. The ballad gives every evidence of having been written immediately after Essex' death, and before it became evident that he had slashed his own throat. But, as Professor Rollins has pointed out, the theory of murder continued to be popular; and it may be that the ballad represents a reissue of 1685 or after, when the tune named on the sheet was in circulation.

A dozen other ballads were sung to the tune, most of them issued during the reign of James II. Among these may be mentioned "The bad Husbands Reformation," beginning "I was a bad Husband, that had a good Trade," to the tune of "My Life and my Death; Or, The poor mans Counsellour" (Lord Crawford, BM C.22.f.6, Harvard; reprinted in *RB* VIII, 796).[2] To the same pair of tunes was sung "The wonderful Praise of a Good Husband," beginning "Dear Daughter, i'de have thee to take special care" (Lord Crawford, Pepys, Roxburghe; reprinted in *RB* VII, 147). "An Answer to the Praise of Good Husbands," to the tune "My life and my death," takes its first line from the refrain of its predecessor, "Good Husbands are Jewels far better than Gold" (Pepys V, 89). Others to the tune include the following, which have apparently not been reprinted: "The Distressed Damosel," beginning "Was ever poor Maiden so left in distress" (Pepys III, 5); "Robin's Delight," beginning "As Robin was riding one day to a Fair" (Pepys III, 202); and "The Country Damsels Resolution," beginning "A Beautiful Damsel, but Eighteen Years old" (Douce I, 34—with a MS addition to the tune title, "or Mogey's gone

now do" (Pepys; reprinted in *PB* V, 112). "The Modish London Life," which names "My Life and my Death" as well as "Now, now the Fight's done" as tunes for the ballad, actually contains an imperfect copy of the air Purcell wrote for the poem here expanded into a broadside beginning "Would you know how we meet o're our jolly full Bouls?" (Wood 417 [178], with the MS date Feb. 14, 1688).

2 "The poor Mans Councillor" is the title of a ballad to the tune of "The Poor Man's Comfort." A ballad by this title is sung to the tune of "Fair Angel of England," a name which comes from the first line of a ballad to the tune of "Bonny Sweet Robin," q.v.

over Seas with a Soldier," perhaps related to "Peggy's gone . . . ," q.v.). "The Dreaming Virgins Conceited happiness," beginning "I am a young Maiden so brisk and so gay" (Pepys III, 113), is probably to be dated c. 1685–1690; its stanza of eight anapestic tetrameter lines—six lines was usual—requires a repetition of the final musical strain.

"The two Unfortunate Lovers," beginning "O Where's my Rosinda? shall I never more," is sung to "My Life and my Death" in the original issue of c. 1688 (Pepys III, 350; reprinted in *PB* IV, 34). Another copy in the Pepys collection (V, 326) is titled "An Excellent New Song, Call'd, The Unkind Parents, Or, The Unfortunate Lovers . . . Tune of, Fond Boy." Still another issue, with a similar but not identical title, has the tune direction "Fond Boy, Or, Love's a Sweet Passion" (BM C.39.k.6 [33]; reprinted in *OPB*, p. 84). Other ballads to "My Life and my Death" may be found in *RB* VII, 46, and *PB* IV, 235, 264. In its heyday the tune was also coupled with "A Carrol for Christmas-day at Night" in *A Cabinet of Choice Jewels*, 1688, p. 7.

My Lodging Is on the Cold Ground,
or I Prithee, Love, Turn to Me

This tune, attributed to Matthew Locke,[1] is called "On the cold ground" in *The Dancing Master*, 1665, where it appears among the treble violin tunes at the end of the volume. It is in *Musick's Delight on the Cithren*, 1666, with the same title; and it is called "Prethe Love turn to me" in *Musicks Recreation on the Viol, Lyra-way*, 1669, and "I Prethee Love turn to me" in *Apollo's Banquet*, 1670, No. 138 (Fig. 315). The song is in Sir William Davenant's *The Rivals*, Act V, an adaptation of *The Two Noble Kinsmen* which Pepys saw in 1664, although it was not published until 1668. The first of Davenant's three stanzas is as follows:

> My lodging it is on the Cold ground,
> and very hard is my fare,
> But that which troubles me most, is
> the unkindness of my dear,

[1] Chappell (*PMOT* II, 526). I have been unable to discover Chappell's authority for the attribution, and Miss Rosamund E. M. Harding, the Matthew Locke bibliographer, has found no evidence to connect Locke with the tune.

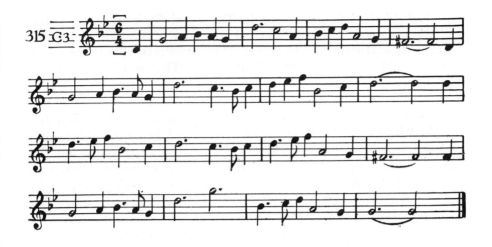

315 [G3.]

Yet still I cry, O turn Love,
    and I prethee Love turn to me,
For thou art the Man that I long for,
    and, alack what remedy.

The song was frequently reprinted. For example, it appears without music in *The New Academy of Complements*, 1669, *Merry Drollery Complete*, 1670, *Windsor Drollery*, 1671, *The Hive*, 1726, and *The Vocal Miscellany*, 1734. With new music (today known as "Believe me, if all those endearing young charms," from the words which Thomas Moore wrote to the tune) the song is found in *Vocal Music, or The Songster's Companion*, 1775, p. 18 (Fig. 316), in Domenico Corri's *Select Collection of*

316

the Most Admired Songs, c. 1779, in *The Vocal Enchantress,* 1783, and as "My Lodging" in several single-sheet issues of the late eighteenth century (BM, Huntington, Harvard). These later texts change the sex of the singer ("For thou art the only girl, love,/That is adored by me!") and otherwise sentimentalize the bedlamite qualities of the original.[2] A version of the later tune is coupled with verses beginning "I loe nae a laddie but ane" in Johnson's *Scots Musical Museum,* 1787–1803, III, 276, in Ritson's *Scotish Songs,* 1794, I, 187, and in George Thomson's *Original Scottish Airs,* 1805, IV, 185. In the two latter collections the tune name is given as "Happy Dick Dawson"; I have no information on its origin, but it is clearly related to "My lodging." During his years in London, Tommaso Giordani used the new tune of "My Lodging" (which he termed "The Mad Man's Song") for a larghetto movement in the third of his six concertos, op. 14, c. 1778; the theme-and-variation treatment for keyboard and three strings is singularly pedestrian.

Davenant's song was expanded into a broadside called "The Slighted Maid: or, The Pining Lover," to the tune "I prethee love turn to me" (Rawlinson 136, Euing 335, 336; later editions are in Lord Crawford, Roxburghe; reprinted in *RB* VII, 122). Davenant's stanzas are 2, 11, and 7 of the broadside, whose new opening stanza begins "Was ever Maiden so scorned,/by one that she loved so dear." The tune is referred to as "My lodging is on the cold ground" in "The Faithful Lovers Farwell," beginning "As I in a Meddow was walking" (Euing, Roxburghe; reprinted in

<hr>

[2] Nell Gwyn sang a parody of Davenant's song in James Howard's comedy *All Mistaken* when it was introduced in 1667. It begins:

> My lodging it is on the Cold Boards
> And wonderful hard is my fare,
> But that which Troubles me most is
> The Fatness of my Dear . . .

The personal allusion here is not, as Chappell thought (*PMOT* II, 785), a reference to the physique of her rival Moll Davis, who had appeared in Davenant's play; it is rather to the fat lover opposite whom she was playing in Howard's comedy (see J. H. Wilson, *Nell Gwyn, Royal Mistress,* 1952, pp. 71–73).

Another song which has been thought to be a parody may in reality have suggested to Davenant some of his refrain lines. "Women's Delight," which appeared first in *Merry Drollery,* 1661, I, 37, begins:

> There dwelt a maid in the Cunny-gate,
> And she was wondrous fair,
> And she would have an old man
> Was overgrown with hair;
> And ever she cry'd, O turn,
> O turn thee unto me,
> Thou hast the thing I have not,
> A little above the knee.

RB VII, 544); it is named as an alternative tune along with "Come Boyes fill us a Bumper" in "The Courtiers Health," beginning "Come boyes fill us a Bumper,/we'l make the Nation Roare" (Lord Crawford, Harvard, Roxburghe; reprinted in *RB* III, 631, V, 90), and as an alternative for "Come hither my own sweet Betty" [3] in "The Roaring Lad, and the Ranting Lass," beginning "I met with a Jovial Girl" (Rawlinson 87).

The tune is named "Turn Love" on at least three broadsides: "The crafty Young-Man," beginning "Once did I kiss a fair Lady" (Wood E.25 [41]); "The Lovers Pastime," beginning "An amorous pair of young Lovers" (Wood E.25 [90]); and "The Loyal Subjects Resolution," beginning "Brave English boyes come follow me" (Euing 161). It is "Turn Love, I prethee love turn to me" in "Wit bought at a Dear Rate," beginning "If all the World my mind did know" (Pepys, Lord Crawford, Harvard, Roxburghe; reprinted in *RB* VI, 478). And it is cited as "I prithee Love turn to me" in the following: "The Conceited Lover," beginning "Come Betty why art thou so bashful" (Wood E.25 [46]); "The English Seamans Resolution," beginning "I am an undaunted Seaman," with the alternative tune title "When this Old Cap was new," another name for "Old Simon the King" (Euing 106; reprinted in *Naval Songs and Ballads*, ed. C. H. Firth, 1908, p. 61); and "The Old Mans Complaint," beginning "O What a pittiful passion" (Roxburghe; reprinted in *RB* VIII, 197).[4]

Chappell has pointed out (*PMOT* II, 529) the gap of just over a century between the latest appearance of the original theater air and the first publication of the now universally familiar tune. It seems clear that the broadsides still used the old melody, for the new one bears all the marks of the second half of the eighteenth century. One ballad opera calls for "My Lodging it is on the cold Ground"—Breval's *The Rape of Helen*, 1737. Although it is printed without music, Breval's verse seems rhythmically to accord with the original tune.

---

[3] This tune is unknown to me.

[4] This last ballad has a refrain suggestive of the parody cited in note 2 above:

> For ever she cries, O turn, turn,
> I prethee now turn to me,
> She looks for the thing that I have not,
> O the cramp lies in my knee.

My Young Mary

This tune takes its name from "My young Mary do's mind the Dairy," the opening line of "The Happy Husbandman: Or, Country Innocence. To a pleasant New Court Tune" (Lord Crawford, Pepys, Euing, Harvard, Roxburghe; reprinted in *RB* VII, 29). It was published during the reign of James II. A ballad of 1689, with meaningless music, is to the tune of "My young Mary": "The English Painter For The French King's Picture," beginning "Wars and Arms, and loud Alarms" (Pepys; reprinted in *PB* V, 48). At least one other ballad calls for the tune, under the name of "My Maid Mary": "The Country Lass, Who left her Spinning-Wheel for a more pleasant Employment," beginning "Sweet fac'd Jenny receiv'd a Guinea" (Pepys III, 290, Lord Crawford 1100, BM C.22.f.6 [97]).

The tune is found as "My young Mary" in *Youth's Delight on the Flagelet,* 9th ed., c. 1690 (Fig. 317); eighteenth-century issues of the origi-

Original is an octave higher.

nal song, called "The Spinning Lass" and beginning "My Maid Mary she minds her Dairy," appear with the music in Walsh's *British Musical Miscellany,* 1734–1736, III, 43, and as single-sheet songs (BM G.316.e [84], Harvard). "My Maid Mary" is used in two ballad operas: Coffey's *The Merry Cobler,* 1735, with music, and Drury's *The Rival Milliners,* 1737.

Nancy Dawson

Nancy Dawson (c. 1730–1767) was a dancer who achieved great acclaim when in October, 1759, during a revival of Gay's *The Beggar's Opera,* the man who danced the hornpipe became ill and she took his place. Her popularity resulted in a long run for the ballad opera in Covent Garden and threatened Garrick's prestige at the rival Drury Lane. The music of the hornpipe was exploited on every hand. A ballad entitled "Nancy Dawson," attributed to George Alexander Stevens, was set to the tune (Fig. 318) and issued on single sheets (BM I.530 [114], Harvard, Califor-

nia, Huntington; reprinted in *Universal Magazine,* XXVII [Oct., 1760], 208). It gives as good an account as any of the dancer's sudden rise to fame.

> Of all the girls in our town,
> The black, the fair, the red, the brown,
> That prance and dance it up and down,
>   There's none like Nancy Dawson.
> Her easy mien, her shape so neat,
> She foots, she trips, she looks so sweet,
> Her very motion's so complete,
>   I die for Nancy Dawson.
>
> See how she comes to give surprise,
> With joy and pleasure in her eyes,

To give delight she always tries,
So means my Nancy Dawson;
Was there no task t'obstruct the way
No Shuter bold, nor House so gay,
A Bet of fifty Pounds I'd lay,
That I gain'd Nancy Dawson.

See how the Opera takes a run,
Exceeding Hamlet, Lear, and Lun,
Tho' in it there would be no fun,
Was it not for Nancy Dawson:
Though Beard and Brent charm every night
And Female Peachum's justly right,
And Filch and Lockit please the sight
'Tis kept up by Nancy Dawson.

See little Davy strut and puff
Pox on the Opera and such stuff
My House is never full enough,
A curse on Nancy Dawson:
Though Gxxxxxk he has had his day
And forc'd the Town his laws t'obey
Now Johnny Rich is come in play
With the help of Nancy Dawson.[1]

"Miss Dawson's New Hornpipe, as Perform'd at Drury Lane" was an arrangement of the tune for harpsichord, c. 1760 (BM H.1994.a [162], Huntington). The tune was also used in Rutherford's *Compleat Collection of 200 . . . Country Dances,* c. 1764, II, 13. It was introduced into Bickerstaffe's *Love in a Village,* 1763, I, x, as part of a medley beginning "I pray ye, gentles, list to me," and Kane O'Hara used it in his *Midas,* 1764, Act III, set to "The Gods were all call'd in to see."

Obvious parodies include "A Wolf in Sheep's Cloathing," beginning "Of all the Dunces in the Town/ . . . there's none like Doctor Squintum" (Harvard, single-sheet edition with music); "Zebra Rescued, or a Bridle for the Ass; by S. Wilks," beginning "Of all the Fools who've lately writ,/To show the Town they wanted Wit" (BM 1850.c.10 [80]); and "A New Song . . . Great News in the St. James's Chronicle," beginning "Of all the papers in the town,/The Brown, the White, the Whity-brown"

[1] Edward *Shuter,* the comedian, was currently enjoying the favors of Nancy Dawson. *Lun* was John Rich, the theatrical manager who was associated with Gay in the original production of *The Beggar's Opera* in 1728; he built and managed the Covent Garden Theatre and for many years produced annually a pantomime in which he appeared as Harlequin under his assumed name. John *Beard,* Rich's son-in-law and a celebrated tenor, was in the 1759 production of *The Beggar's Opera,* as was Charlotte *Brent,* who sang the role of Polly. *Little Davy* was, of course, Garrick.

(Harvard, Percy collection; the *Chronicle* was begun in 1761 and this slip song probably dates from shortly thereafter). The two latter broadsides are without music but name the tune as "Nancy Dawson."

The first strain of the tune is still used in "Here we go round the mulberry bush" and several other songs, including "I saw three ships a-sailing," which customarily employs a variant of the tune. On the latter, see Cecil Sharp, *English Folk-Carols*, 1911, No. 13, *Oxford Book of Carols*, 1928, Nos. 3 and 18, and *JEFDSS*, V (1946), 31–38.

Nanny O

This tune name originates in the refrain of "The Scotch Wooing of Willy and Nanny":

> It's Nanny, Nanny, Nanny O,
> The Love I bear to Nanny O,
>   all the World shall never know,
> The love I bear to Nanny O.

This ballad, issued 1685–1688, begins "As I went forth one Morning fair" and is sung "To a pleasant new Tune: Or, Nanny O" (Lord Crawford, Douce, Pepys, Roxburghe; reprinted in *RB* III, 408). The refrain was obviously derived from one found in a ballad to the tune of "The Lass of Cumberland," q.v., published during the same years, and it is very likely that originally both ballads were sung to the latter tune. But eighteenth-century song sheets and the ballad operas provide us with an independent "Nanny O" tune of a Scotch cast, whose origins I have not been able to trace earlier than about 1720. There is no doubt, however, of the vogue of "Nanny O" during the latter 1680s; our uncertainty is whether in those years "Nanny O" was another name for "The Lass of Cumberland" or whether the later tune had its beginning under the Stuarts.

The original ballad is followed by another to the same tune, "An Answer to Nanny O; Or, The Happy Agreement between . . . Willy & Nanny," with the same refrain formula (Lord Crawford, Douce, Roxburghe; reprinted in *RB* III, 411). The siege of Londonderry in 1689 gave rise to a handful of ballads which involve the tune: "The Glory of London-Derry," beginning "Protestants chear up amain," is to the tune of "The Leggan Water Or, Nanny Oh" (Pepys; reprinted in *PB* IV, 301), and others in the series give the tune as "London-Derry" or "The Glory of

London-Derry," with "Nanny O" usually added as an alternative (*PB* IV, 305, 309, 315, 332, 336, 351). The ballads of the Londonderry series are in quatrains without refrain and fit the tunes of "Logan Water" and "The Lass of Cumberland" (the latter air, though usually associated with eight-line stanzas, actually fits a four-line unit and is merely repeated for the second quatrain). The fact that the eighteenth-century music of "Nanny O" is for an eight-line stanza suggests that it was not the tune used for the Londonderry ballads. One ballad to "Liggan Water. Or, Nanny Oh" which has not been reprinted is also in quatrains without refrain: "The West-Country Squire," beginning "Early in the morning fair" (Pepys IV, 62).[1]

A piece on Queen Anne, published in 1714, copies the "Nanny O" refrain formula in ending each stanza after this manner:

> And all the World,
>   shall never, never, know
> The Love that I bear,
>   to my Nanny o.

It is "Song In Commemoration of Royal Nann," beginning "My Nan she was good,/My Nan she was Just" (BM 1876.f.1 [67]).

Allan Ramsay wrote a poem, "Nanny O," beginning "While some for pleasure pawn their Health,/'Twixt Lais and the Bagnio" (*Poems*, 1721), which he included in his *Tea-Table Miscellany*, 1723, p. 81; its burden is an adaptation of that in the original "Nanny O" ballad:

> My bonny, bonny Nanny-O,
> My lovely charming Nanny-O,
> I care not tho the World know
> How dearly I love Nanny-O.

Several editions of the song, entitled "My Nanny O," were issued as musical single sheets (BM G.305 [140], c. 1720; G.313 [72], c. 1735; G.316.f [63], c. 1750; several issues at Harvard). Alexander Stuart's *Musick for Allan Ramsay's Collection of Scots Songs*, c. 1725, p. 86, contains the tune (Fig. 319); the song was reprinted with music in Thomson's *Orpheus Caledonius*, 1725, No. 38, in Watts's *Musical Miscellany*, 1729–1731, III, 126, in Walsh's *British Musical Miscellany*, 1734–1736, II, 14, and in Johnson's *Scots Musical Museum*, 1787–1803, I, 89. The verses alone are in *The Vocal Miscellany*, 2d ed., 1734, p. 274. An imitation of Ramsay's poem is "A New Song, The Words by Mr. John D...s upon the loss of

[1] In the Douce copy of "The Shepherds Glory," sung to "True love rewarded with loyalty: Or, Flora Farewel" (II, 203), an additional tune direction has been written in: "'Tis Nanny Nanny Nanny O ye Love I bear &c," words derived from the "Nanny O" burden. This ballad is also in quatrains (reprinted in *RB* VI, 269).

319

his Mistress," beginning "Ye rural Swains who never knew,/Curst Lais or the Bagnio" (BM G.305 [307], Harvard, c. 1730). The chorus, following Ramsay's text, is "sung to the first part of the Tune & at the end of each Verse," repeating the instruction found with the *Orpheus Caledonius* music. Another song to the tune of "Nannio," entitled "Smirky Nan," is included in the 1740 edition of Ramsay's *Tea-Table Miscellany* IV, 377.

The tune was used in three ballad operas. It is "Nanny-O" in Mitchell's *The Highland Fair,* 1731; "Bonny Nanny O" in Coffey's *The Merry Cobler,* 1735; and "My Nanny-O" in Thomson's *The Disappointed Gallant,* 1738. Half a century later, William Shield's comic opera *Rosina,* 1782, Act II, used the music, calling it "Scots Tune," for a song beginning "When bidden to the Wake or Fair."

The New Bourrée

The earliest appearance of this tune I have encountered is in *A Collection of the Newest and Choicest Songs,* 1683, p. 12, where it is coupled with verses beginning "Fools for Women do sigh and Languish" (Fig. 320). An arrangement of the air called "Fools for Women. A Boree" is in Humphry Salter's *The Genteel Companion . . . for the Recorder,* 1683, among the unnumbered pages at the end, added probably in 1684. The melody is printed on sheets of "Cupids Tragedy," a broadside begin-

320

ning "Pritty Phillomel was so Charming,/so much sweetness grac'd each part," to the tune of "The new Bory; Or, Will you be a Man of Fashion" (BM C.22.f.6 [40], Douce I, 28ᵛ, 49, Lord Crawford 1022, Harvard). Another ballad sung to the tune is "The Dumb Lady, Or, No, no, not I I'le Answer," beginning "Underneath a little Mountain/where I us'd my self to walk," to the tune of "the Doubtful Virgin, or the new Borey, or Will you be a Man of Fashion" (Pepys, Lord Crawford, Douce, Harvard, Roxburghe; reprinted in *RB* IV, 352). The citation of "Will (i.e., Would) you be a Man of Fashion" enables us to date the two broadsides c. 1683 or after. But the "Bory" may have been known earlier, if we can assume it to be "The New Boxy," named for singing "The Subtil Girls well fitted," beginning "Prethee Cloris tell me how," found in *Westminster Drollery*, 1672, II, 3.

"New Bore," which began to appear in *The Dancing Master* with the eleventh edition, 1701, p. 253, is not suited to our ballads. In the same edition a still different tune is named "The New Bore" on p. 189 and "The Indian Queen," p. 267, and appears under the latter title in Walsh's *Compleat Country Dancing-Master*, 1718. The verse movement of eight trochaic lines alternating eight and seven syllables fits this tune, but not so smoothly as it does the earlier graceful melody.

A New Game at Cards

This tune takes its name from the title of a ballad licensed in 1656, beginning "You Gallants all that love to play,/At Cards to pass the time away," to "a pleasant new tune, Or, what you please" (Euing, Wood 401;

reprinted in *RB* VII, 615).[1] A manuscript version beginning "Youe gallants that desier to playe," without tune direction or music, is in BM MS Harl. 2127, fol. 23; another, with music (Fig. 321), beginning "You

321

gallants y[t] delight to play," is in Bodleian MS Ashmole 36–37, fol. 105 (partially printed in *RB* IV, 224, VII, 688).

An early Restoration successor to the original ballad, called "Win at first, lose at last; or, a New Game at Cards," beginning "Yee merry hearts that love to play/At Cards, see who hath wone the day," is to the tune of "Yee Gallants that delight to play" (Wood 401 [150]). This edition was issued by Francis Grove, who died in 1663, and it was written after the execution of the regicides in October, 1660. Later editions, sometimes subscribed with the initials of Laurence Price, were issued in 1680 and later (Pepys IV, 344, Harvard, Roxburghe; reprinted in *RB* VII, 685; another Pepys copy, II, 207, is dated 1692; a later reprint is in *Loyal Songs*, 1731, I, 242). A single-sheet edition of c. 1710, with music (Fig. 322), has the title "A New Game at Cards" (BM G.305 [247], Huntington, Harvard), while a broadside issue of c. 1720 with corrupt music is called

---

[1] "What you please" is an ambiguous tune direction. A melody bearing this name is found in *The Dancing Master*, commencing with the 3d ed., 1665, and in *Musick's Delight on the Cithren*, 1666; it is in 6/4 time, with movement more suitable to trochaic meter than to the iambics of the ballads cited below. With the addition of an introductory note, however, the music will serve for six lines of octosyllabics, or eight, if the second strain be repeated. Inasmuch as this tune seems to have had no further relation to the history of "A New Game at Cards," I have not concerned myself with it in the body of the discussion.

A long poem in ballad meter, "The Discovery: or, The Squire turnd Ferret," 1727, beginning "Most true it is, I dare to say," contains the tune direction "High Boys! up go we; Chevy Chase; Or what you please" (BM C.116.i.4 [30]). It can be sung to the second tune, or to the first (allowing two stanzas for the sixteen bars of "Hey, boys"); but the third tune designation is surely figurative and can have no relation to the *Dancing Master* tune.

322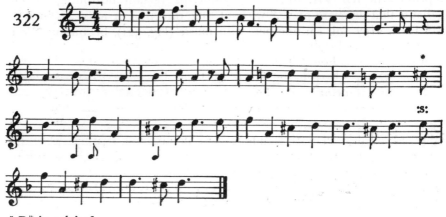

* D♯ in original.

"A Knave at the Bottom, The Dealer's sure of a Trump" (BM 112.f.44 [50]).[2]

In two ballads the tune name is "All you that do desire to play/At Cards, to pass the time away," paraphrasing the opening of the original "New Game at Cards." They are "No Money, no Friend," beginning "All you that freely spend your Coyn" (Pepys IV, 255, Harvard, Lord Crawford 58, BM C.22.f.6 [67]), and "Londons Drollery . . . the Pope and the Devil . . . 1680," beginning "All you that do desire to know/ The Mock Procession, how't did go" (Lord Crawford, Harvard, Roxburghe; reprinted in RB IV, 221)

The tune is cited as "A New Game at Cards" in "The Virgin Race," beginning "You that do desire to hear" (Pepys, Roxburghe; reprinted in RB VII, 84), and in "The Royal Match of Bear-Baiting," beginning "Old Lewis had a rugged Bear" (Pepys; reprinted in PB V, 176); the six-line stanza is octosyllabic throughout. The tune is similarly named in "Englands joys increased . . . coronation of James the Second," beginning "You Loyal-hearted English-men" (Pepys; reprinted in PB III, 149), and in "The Downfall of Popery," beginning "The Pope and his Agents strove of late" (Pepys; reprinted in PB IV, 72); in this pair of ballads the six-line stanza concludes with a decasyllabic line.

"Poor Robin's Dream . . . To a compleat Tune, well known by Musicians, and many others: Or, Game at Cards," beginning "How now good fellow, what all amort," was licensed in 1668 and appears in a

[2] An eight-stanza imitation written on the fall of Robert Walpole, 1741/42, is "Bob Booty's lost Deal, or, The Cards Shuffled fair at Last" (BM 1876.f.1 [126]; reprinted in RB VIII, 288, and in Walpole Ballads, ed. Percival, p. 178).

number of editions over the next century (Euing 285, Roxburghe III, 70, the original issue published by J. Clark; Pepys IV, 295, Euing 286, Lord Crawford 531, Roxburghe III, 895, Harvard, Bagford, late seventeenth-century editions; reprinted in *BB* II, 973). Among the eighteenth-century issues, a Bow Church Yard imprint names the tune "The new pack of Cards" (Roxburghe III, 472, Douce III, 76, Williams College); a Newcastle imprint in the Percy Portfolio (Harvard) is in a seven-line stanza beginning "How now my good Fellow, why now all alone." Another, with an eight-line stanza, is "The Poor Mans Prayer for Peace," c. 1685, beginning "Poor Englands sorrows this many a year," to the tune of "Game at Cards" (Lord Crawford, BM C.22.f.6, Harvard, Roxburghe; reprinted in *RB* VII, 753). "True Love will never decay," beginning "As I was wandring all alone," names its tune "Poor Robins Dream," and is in a seven-line stanza like most editions of the ballad with that title (Douce II, 226).

The two musical texts are not entirely unrelated, but the variation between them is greater than we normally find in specimens separated by half a century or so. Aside from the first cadence, which is on the dominant in the manuscript tune, on the tonic in the single sheet, there is sufficient congruence to enable us to view the two airs as different renderings of the same musical idea, not two independent melodies. The tunes fit the usual stanza pattern of six octosyllabics; the later form repeats the two final bars to accommodate a seventh line (found in "Win at first, lose at last" and several others), and a *dal segno* provides a further repetition of the same measures to accommodate an eight-line stanza (found in "The Poor Mans Prayer for Peace"). The original "New Game at Cards" of 1656, as well as "Englands joys increased" and "The Downfall of Popery," is in a six-line stanza with a hypermetrical last line which cannot be conveniently sung to either version of the tune. There may have been, then, still another melody whose currency extended through the second half of the seventeenth century. It is unusual to find four stanza patterns clustering about a single tune name and its congeners, especially when each pattern appears in several ballads and cannot be written off as whimsical.

The Nightingale

This was a very popular tune in the seventeenth century, not merely because of its lilting first strain, but also because of the bravura possibilities of the second half, in which the bird's song is imitated. Cittern arrangements are in Cambridge University MS Dd.14.24, fol. 19, in Bedford Cittern MS, fol. 16, and in *A Booke of New Lessons for the Cithern & Gittern,* 1652, No. 6. A setting for mandore is in the Skene MS (published in *Ancient Scotish Melodies,* ed. Dauney, p. 244). Two virginal pieces on the tune are in the New York Public Library Drexel MS 5612, pp. 147, 150; another pair are in Paris Conservatoire MS Rés. 1186, fols. 35ᵛ, 62ᵛ, the latter by Henry Loosemore. Still other keyboard sets are in Elizabeth Rogers's Virginal Book (BM MS Add. 10337, fol. 9) and in Christ Church MS 1236 (published in *The Contemporaries of Purcell,* ed. Fuller Maitland, 1921, VI, 7). It appears in *A Musicall Banquet,* 1651, No. 11 (Fig. 323), in *Musicks Recreation on the Lyra Viol,* 1652,

Original an octave lower.

p. 14, in Jacob van Eyk's *Der Fluyten Lust-Hof,* Amsterdam, 1654, I, 33ᵛ, called "Engels Nachtegaeltje," and another version at II, 33ᵛ, called "Den Nachtegael"; and it is in Thomas Greeting's *The Pleasant Companion . . . for the Flagelet,* 1673, No. 3.

It is astonishing that such a complex melody should appeal to a ballad writer. But Martin Parker used it for "The Wooing Lasse, and the Way-ward Lad," beginning "Vpon a Holy day,/When the Nimphs had leave to play" (Roxburghe; reprinted in *RB* III, 296). Two stanzas are reprinted with the music in *Pills*, 1719–1720, V, 86. The original ballad, which may have given rise to the tune, is "The Nightingale," beginning "You Gallants that resort/to Hide Parke or Totnam Court," sung "To a new and much affected Court Tune," entered in the Stationers' Register July 8, 1633 (Roxburghe; reprinted in *RB* II, 251). Ebsworth printed a fragmentary manuscript ballad written to the tune in his *Amanda Group of Bagford Poems*, 1880, p. 517.*

The ballad makers have dealt so freely with the rhythms of their own complex verse forms that the second part of the tune is difficult, and sometimes impossible, to fit to their words. The general congruence between words and music is such, however, as to make it certain that they were using the tune known to us.

In Odingsells' *Bays's Opera*, 1730, published without music, "The Nightingale" is named as Air 18 and the associated verse is rhythmically suited to the tune.

In recent times the tune has been rediscovered by Ottorino Respighi, who used it as a theme for one movement of his orchestral suite *Gli Uccelli*, 1927, composed as incidental music for Aristophanes's *The Birds*.

"The Nightingales Song," in an entirely different rhythmic pattern, is discussed under "Peg and the soldier," q.v.

No, No, Poor Suffering Heart

Henry Purcell wrote the music for a song beginning "No no, poor suff'ring Heart" in the second act of Dryden's *Cleomenes, The Spartan Heroe*, 1692. The music alone is in *Apollo's Banquet*, 7th ed., 1693. Words and music are found in *Comes Amoris*, Fourth Book, 1693, p. 1 (Fig. 324), in a contemporary single-sheet song edition (BM C.180.a [19]),

and in *Pills*, 1719–1720, VI, 89. In expanded form it was issued as a broadside with meaningless music, entitled "Cruel Celia: or, the Lover's Complaint . . . to an new Tune" (Pepys V, 302).

One other ballad was sung to the tune. It is "The Love-Sick Soldier," beginning "Why did the God of love wound a Commander" (Lord Crawford 1343, Pepys V, 213, BM C.39.k.6 [45], all with meaningless music; reprinted in *OPB*, p. 116).

Nobody Else Shall Plunder But I

This tune is called "No body shall plunder but I" in *A Booke of New Lessons for the Cithern & Gittern*, 1652, No. 35, and "None shall Plunder but I" in *A Musicall Banquet*, 1651, No. 18, lyra viol (Fig. 325), in *Musicks Recreation on the Lyra Viol*, 1652, p. 13, and in *Musick's Delight on the Cithren*, 1666, No. 26. Only the lyra-viol sets are of the correct length to accommodate an eleven-line stanza; the two cittern arrangements vary in detail and are corrupt in spots. All four musical texts are adapted to their instruments rather than to the demands of verse rhythms.

At least two ballads were sung to the tune. One, a badly mutilated fragment whose title may have been "Rupert and Maurice, their adieu

325

Original an octave lower.

to England," is concerned with the banishment in 1646 of the two princes, cousins of Charles II, after the siege of Oxford. It begins "Come Maurice my brother,/Let us go together" and is to the tune of "Plundering Jack, or, Nobody else shall plunder but I" (Manchester II, 27; reprinted in *RB* VIII, xxiii***).[1] The other ballad to the tune is Laurence Price's "The True-lovers Holidaies," beginning "My sweetest, my fairest,/my rarest, my dearest," which has an imitative refrain "that nobody else shall enjoy thee but I" (Pepys, Rawlinson, Lord Crawford, Harvard, Roxburghe; reprinted in *RB* VI, 73).[2]

[1] Presumably "Plundering Jack," a lost ballad, had a refrain "Nobody else shall plunder but I," the basis of the present tune title.

[2] In his *CP*, p. 55, Professor Rollins notes an advertisement in 1653 of "An excellent new Ballad, entituled *The life of a souldier* to the tune of *No body else shall plunder but I*, by Major General *Lambert*, together with an Appendix *de generatione hominum*, by Lieut. Gen. *Harrison*, a practitioner in that Science." This piece of obvious political propaganda is useful to us chiefly as an indication that the tune was known to the Commonwealth public.

Nonesuch, or À la Mode de France

This tune is called "Nonesuch" in *The Dancing Master*, where it appears in the first three editions, 1651–1665 (1651, p. 29=Fig. 326), and

326

Original is unbarred.

later in the "Second Part," beginning with the second edition, 1698. A statement of the tune in major is found with slight differences in all editions of *The Dancing Master* under the title "All a Mode de France" (1651, p. 49=Fig. 327). With the latter title it is found in *A Musicall Banquet*, 1651, No. 4; in *Musicks Recreation on the Lyra Viol*, 1652, p. 4; in *A Booke of New Lessons*, 1652, for cittern, No. 40, and gittern, No. 1; in *Musick's Delight on the Cithren*, 1666, No. 7; in *Youth's Delight on the Flagelet*, 9th ed., c. 1690; and in a mid-seventeenth-century lyra-viol manuscript in Cambridge University, Dd.6.48, fol. 13 (called "All the mode in ffrance").

The commoner tune name seems to have been derived from a ballad "The French Report," probably written in late 1642 or early 1643 while the Queen was in Holland raising money and troops for the prosecution of the Civil War. It begins "Me have of late been in England/Vere me have seen much sport," and each stanza closes with "a la mode de France." No broadside copy seems to have survived, but the verses were included in *Rump*, 1662, I, 27, and reprinted in *Loyal Songs*, 1731, I, 25. The eight-

327

Original is unbarred.

line stanza in ballad meter fits the tune, but we have only the refrain upon which to make any confident connection between words and music.

Northern Nancy

"The Map of Mock-begger Hall," c. 1635, beginning "I reade, in ancient times of yore," has the tune direction "It is not your Northerne Nanny; or, Sweet is the Lasse that Loves me" (Roxburghe; reprinted in *RB* II, 132).[1] Another edition, c. 1640, has the same pair of tune titles, but differs considerably in detail from the early issue; it is called "Mock-Beggers Hall" and begins "In ancient times when as plain dealing/Was most of all in fashion" (Roxburghe; reprinted in *RB* VI, 762). The refrain in both ballads gives rise to the tune name "Mock-Beggers Hall stands empty," cited for singing "The Ruined Lovers," beginning "Mars shall to Cupid now submit" (Euing 313, Douce II, 184ᵛ, an edition of c. 1670; later editions are Euing 314, Lord Crawford 798, Douce II, 187ᵛ, Harvard, Roxburghe; reprinted in *RB* VII, 411). Because two tunes are cited in the original ballads, it is impossible to know which is intended for "The Ruined Lovers."

I have not found "It is not your Northerne Nanny," either as a tune or as a line from a ballad. A tune which fits these ballads is in *The Dancing Master* as "Northern Nancy." It appears in G major—without key signature but with each F individually inflected—in the 4th–6th editions,

---

[1] On the second tune, see "Damask Rose."

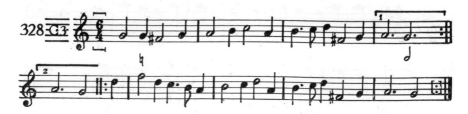

1670–1679 (1670, p. 146 = Fig. 328). In succeeding editions it is in G minor; the 7th–11th editions, 1686–1701, print the tune uniformly, but a slightly different version is found in the 12th–16th editions, 1703–1716, and further small changes occur in the 17th and 18th editions of the next decade. "Northern Nancy" is used in a single ballad opera—Gay's *Polly*, 1729, Air 31. The same tune, without key signature and almost identical with the first *Dancing Master* state, is found in Elizabeth Rogers's Virginal Book (BM MS Add. 10337, fol. 34ᵛ). This manuscript is thought to have been compiled before 1656, but a later hand has written the music for the tune, which is here called "The faithfull Brothers."

The use of "Northern Nancy" for these ballads is possible and even plausible, but the evidence for associating text and tune remains unsatisfactory. It is clear, however, that an early seventeenth-century tune called "Northern Nanny," q.v., cannot be used here because of the wide discrepancy between the complex fourteen-line stanza for which it is intended and the eight-line tetrameter stanza of the ballads we have discussed. "Northern Nanny" is the title of a ballad originating in the 1670s (see "In January last"), much too late to have any bearing upon the tune title "It is not your Northerne Nanny."

Northern Nanny

Richard Climsell's ballad "Pretty Nannie," to the tune of "Northern Nannie," was licensed Nov. 16, 1633 (Roxburghe; reprinted in *RB* II, 323). It has a complex fourteen-line stanza beginning "I Have a Loue so faire,/So constant, firme, and kind," and its refrain is:

> Pretty Nanny,
> My mistris of true constancy,
> I am thine owne, and shall be.

A poem of three stanzas closely related to 1, 2, and 7 of the Climsell broadside is found in an early seventeenth-century commonplace book,

Harvard MS Eng. 628, p. 314, and in the nearly contemporary Percy Folio MS (ed. Hales and Furnivall, I, 255). Since the tune appeared in the 1621 edition of Starter's *Friesche Lust-Hof*, p. 81 (Fig. 329), taking its title from

Original is unbarred.

the first two lines of the poem or ballad, it seems likely that the initial association was between tune and poem, and that the broadside was a later expansion. This supposition is the more probable since Climsell's activity as a ballad writer was confined almost entirely to the 1630s.

A ballad entitled "Northern Nanny" (Douce II, 163ᵛ) has no relation to the tune; it is a production of the 1670s to be sung to "In January Last," q.v., and has a different stanza pattern.

The tune title "It is not your Northerne Nanny" (for which see "Northern Nancy") is cited on a ballad having an eight-line stanza; it is therefore not interchangeable with "Northerne Nannie."

[The Norwich Loyal Litany]

"The Norwich Loyal Litany," beginning "Defend us from all Popish Plots," without tune direction, was issued by A. Banks in 1682 (Huntington, with MS date June 9, 1682; Bodleian Ashmole G.16 [182], Harvard). It was reprinted in *180 Loyal Songs*, 1685, p. 140 (with music), and in *RB* V, 187. Another issue of the same year, published by J. D[eacon?], was entitled "A New Song, being the Tories Imploration for Protection against the Whiggs, to an Excellent New Scotch Tune" (Harvard, with MS date Sept. 6, 1682; another issue, printed for W. D., 1682, is BM 1872.a.1 [95^v]).

Another song to the tune in *180 Loyal Songs*, p. 142, is "A Conventicle Litany," beginning "Let Baxter teach sedition," which had earlier appeared with the music in *A Dreadful Oration Deliver'd by that . . . Saint, Stephen Lobb*, 1683, sig. C3.

Doubtless because of its ballad-stanza quatrains, Ebsworth bracketed the tune title "Chevy Chase" with his reprint of the "Litany" in *RB;* but the music in *180 Loyal Songs* is quite different, resembling a hymn tune (Fig. 330).

330

* E in original.

Now at Last the Riddle Is Expounded

This tune takes its name from the opening line of "Treason Unmasqued, or Truth brought to Light," 1681, a political ballad in four stanzas without specific tune direction (Wood 417 [63], Harvard). Revised and expanded to ten stanzas in the same year, it appeared with a new title, "The Riddle of the Roundhead," and the tune was named "Now

331

at last the Riddle is Expounded" (BM Luttrell II, 180, Chetham 2705, Huntington, Harvard). This latter edition was reprinted, with the music, in *180 Loyal Songs,* 1685, p. 14 (Fig. 331).

Another ballad to the same tune is "The Loyal Sherifs of London and Middlesex. Upon their Election," 1682, beginning "Now at last the Matter is Dicided" (BM 1872.a.1 [44], BM C.38.i.25 [14], Wood 417 [110], Harvard; reprinted in *180 Loyal Songs,* p. 17, and *RB* V, 227); all copies of the broadside contain the music.

Now, Now Comes On the
Glorious Year

"Now, now, comes on the Glorious Year,/Britain has Hopes and France has Fear" is an act-song in D'Urfey's *The Modern Prophets,* 1709. It was issued as a single-sheet song with music (Fig. 332), entitled "A Song on the Ensuing Campaign" (BM H.1601 [315]), and was reprinted in *Pills,* 1719–1720, I, 27 (the music on p. 25). Words alone are found in such

332

miscellanies as *A Pill to Purge State-Melancholy*, 1715, and *The Merry Musician*, 1716.

Several roman-letter broadsides cite the tune, including: "England's Surprize; Or, The French King's Joy for the Duke of Marlborough's being turn'd out of Favour," c. 1712, beginning "What News is this flys up and down" (Lord Crawford 1271); "The Gentle Craft's Complaint," beginning "The jolly Shoemakers, 'tis said,/hath found a great Decay of Trade" (Douce, Madden, Chetham, Roxburghe; reprinted in *RB* VII, 35); "A New Song on St. George's Day: and to the Glorious Memory of Queen Anne," beginning "You that are loyal Churchmen smile" (BM 1876.f.1 [68]); and "An Excellent New Ballad, Entituled, Mar's Lament for his Rebellion" [1715], beginning "Noble Argyle when he went on" (Roxburghe; reprinted in *RB* VI, 621).

Upon the accession of George I, D'Urfey wrote another song to the tune, beginning "Britains, now let Joys increase," which was printed in *The Merry Musician* I, 172, and in *Pills* I, 25. And a host of songs to the tune are included in *Political Merriment*, 1714, *A Pill to Purge State-Melancholy*, 1715, *A Collection of State Songs*, 1716, and *Mughouse Diversion*, 1717. Some are obvious parodies of D'Urfey's stage song, as, for example, "The Glorious Year," by J. P., beginning "Now, now is come the Glorious Year,/When State-Betrayers only fear" (Lord Crawford 891; reprinted in *Political Merriment*, Part II, p. 1); "The Protestant Jubilee," beginning "Now comes on the Glorious Year,/Protestants Joy, and Papists Fear" (*A Collection of State Songs*, p. 135); and "Britain's Glory and Credit retriev'd," beginning "Now, Now, come on the glorious Days" (*Mughouse Diversion*, 5th ed., 1719, p. 47).[1] The tune is known also as

---

[1] "A Rare New Song Shewing the Bravery of . . . the Duke of Argile," beginning "Now, now comes on the glorious Year,/Britain's Hope, and France's Fear," clearly

"Guiscard" (*Political Merriment*, Part II, pp. 149, 162) from a ballad on Guiscard's attempted assassination of Robert Harley, Earl of Oxford (*ibid.*, p. 108); another tune title, "A Health to the Constitution" (*ibid.*, pp. 146, 162, 170; Part III, 1715, p. 45), derives from a song "A Health to the present Constitution," found with music in *The Merry Musician* I, 14.

Several songs in these collections, with no tune direction, have the distinctive 8.8.8.7.8.8.8.7 syllabic pattern of "Now, now comes on the glorious year" and were probably intended to be sung to that tune.

The tune is introduced into five ballad operas, all of which were published with music: Hippisley's *Flora*, 1729; Ralph's *The Fashionable Lady*, 1730; Chetwood's *The Lover's Opera*, 3d ed., 1730, and *The Generous Free-Mason*, 1731; and Lillo's *Silvia*, 1731.

Now, Now the Fight's Done

"Now, now the fight's done" was a song sung after the first act of Nathaniel Lee's *Theodosius*, 1680. It was included, with Purcell's tune (Fig. 333), in a musical supplement published with the play in the year of its production (reprinted in *Works*, Purcell Society edition, XXI, 127) and in 1681 was included in *Choice Ayres and Songs*, Third Book, p. 41. A manuscript version of the song with music has been preserved in Bodleian MS Mus. Sch. G.640 (39). The stage song was lengthened from three to twelve stanzas in its broadside form, issued as "Love's Conquest," to the tune of "Now, now the Fight's done, Or, Digbyes Farwell" (Pepys III, 105). The tune was a great success with the ballad audience, for during the next decade some two dozen ballads were written for it.

"A Congratulation on the Happy Discovery of the Hellish Fanatick Plot," beginning "Come now let's Rejoyce," appeared originally without the music (Huntington, with MS date July 26, 1681; Wood 417 [121], Bodleian Ashmole G.16 [109], Yale, Harvard); an issue of 1682, with badly barred music, is in Wood 417 (91); the ballad was reprinted with music in *180 Loyal Songs*, 1685, p. 62. Music is also found on the sheets of: "The Compleat Swearing-Master," 1682, beginning "Once on a time, the

draws on D'Urfey's song and is written in the same stanza. The tune cited, however, is "The Caping Trade" (National Lib. of Scotland Ry III.a.10 [86]), named from a ballad of that title, c. 1700, which is itself "To an excellent new Tune" or "To its own proper Tune," for which apparently no music has survived (Roxburghe III, 668, BM 1876.f.1 [32], Harvard).

333

Dr. did Swear" (Wood 276a [545], Harvard, Yale, Huntington; reprinted in *180 Loyal Songs*, p. 66); "Augusta's Restoration from Her City-Calenture," 1683, beginning "Augusta our fam'd Metropolitan Saint" (Harvard); and "Vienna's Triumph; With the Whigg's Lamentation For the Overthrow of the Turks," 1683, beginning "Now now's the Siege rais'd" (Roxburghe; reprinted in *RB* V, 359). Matthew Taubman printed the music with an imitative lyric "Now, now the Work's done" in his *An Heroick Poem . . . With Some choice Songs,* 1682, p. 10.[1] "The Newgate Salutation: or, A Dialogue between Sir W[illiam] W[aller] and Mrs. Cellier," beginning "Old Stories of State grow now out of date," to the tune of "The Fight is now ended," was issued without music (Huntington, with MS date June 25, 1681; BM 1872.a.1 [133], Bodleian Ashmole G.16 [95], Harvard), but the reprint in *180 Loyal Songs*, p. 108, contains the notes of the tune. "Now the Fight's done" is found without words in *Musicks Recreation on the Viol, Lyra-way,* 1682, p. 22.

At least eight other ballads to the tune of "Now, now the fight's done" are reprinted in *RB;* six are in *PB,* and another is in *PA.* Only a few of

---

[1] A ballad of 1688 with the same opening line is "England's happinesse or a health to the young Prince of Wales," sung to "Now, now the Fight's done," the details of which are noted in Rollins, *Analytical Index,* No. 696, from a copy owned by T. Pepys-Cockerell, Esq. Since this was on James III, the Old Pretender, it may have had nothing further in common with Taubman's poem.

these need be noted. "Cupids revenge," beginning "Now, now you blind boy I you clearly deny," is one of the few nonpolitical ballads sung to the tune (Harvard, Lord Crawford; reprinted in *RB* VIII, cxxxvi*); Ebsworth dates it c. 1673, but the syndicate issuing the ballad—Coles, Vere, Wright, Clark, Thackeray, and Passinger—had this membership only from about 1678 to 1680, and the tune title could not have been applied before 1680. Two ballads are written in stanzas of eight instead of the usual six lines. One of these is "Sad and Dreadful News," an account of Dorothy Winter-bottom's mortal struggle with the Devil in 1684, beginning "A Story most strange I shall to you declare," which lists "Packingtons Pound" as an alternate tune (Pepys; reprinted in *PA,* p. 216); the other is "Religion made a Cloak for Villany" (recalling "The Cloak's Knavery," a ballad sung to "From Hunger and Cold, or Packington's Pound," qq.v.), beginning "Let Tories Curse on and the Wiggs let them Rage" (Wood E.25, Lord Crawford, Roxburghe; reprinted in *RB* IV, 250). Both can be sung to "Now, now the fight's done" with a repetition of the last eight bars, a contingency indicated on the original *Theodosius* music. "The Merry Boys of Europe," beginning "I'le Drink of[f] my Bottle each night for my share," is in its broadside form sung to "Now, now the Fight's done" (Roxburghe; reprinted in *RB* V, 85), but it originally appeared in *Choice Ayres and Songs,* Third Book, 1681, p. 26, with a musical setting by John Reading.

The tune is named "Now, Now the Fights Done, and the Great God of War" in "The Whiggs Lamentation," 1681, beginning "Brave Colledge is Hang'd, the Chief of our hopes" (BM 1872.a.1 [70], Huntington; reprinted in *180 Loyal Songs,* p. 64). A song in George Stuart's *A Joco-Serious Discourse,* 1686, p. 64, beginning "Now, now the feat's done," is sung to "Now, now the Fight's done," as is "A Song, to be sung to the Merchant-Taylors on St. William's Day," beginning "The Taylor's a Man, come deny it who dare," in *The Honour of the Taylors; or, The Famous and Renowned History of Sir John Hawkwood, Knight,* 1687, p. 55. Perhaps the last ballad calling for the tune is an encomium to William III, after the discovery of an assassination plot in 1696: "The Royal Character," beginning "Long Live our Great Cesar, and long be his Reign," to the tune of "Long live our Great Cesar; Or, Now, now the Fight's done" (Pepys; reprinted in *PB* VII, 223). The first tune title appears to be internally inspired; it is probably coincidental that "Let Caesar live long," q.v., is a tune which would fit this stanza pattern.

Now the Spring Is Come

This tune takes its name from "Now the Spring is come, turn to thy Love," the opening line of "A Louers desire for his best beloued: or, Come away, come away, and doe not stay. To an excellent new Court Tune" (Roxburghe; reprinted in *RB* I, 617; the first six stanzas are in the Percy Folio MS, ed. Hales and Furnivall, III, 231). From the fact that the ballad was printed by the Assigns of Thomas Symcocke, we can assume that our extant text is no earlier than 1618, when Symcocke received his patent. To the tune of "Now the spring is come" is sung "Christmas Lamentation, For the losse of his Acquaintance, showing how he is forst to leave the Country, and come to London," beginning "Christmas is my name, farre have I gone" (Roxburghe; reprinted in *RB* I, 154). This copy, issued by Francis Coles, can be no earlier than 1624, when Coles's apprenticeship was concluded. In his *OEB*, p. 372, Professor Rollins printed a manuscript version of the ballad which he dated about 1624.

It does not contain the "yellow starch" stanza of the printed broadside; other alterations particularize an anti-Puritan tone which is general in the Roxburghe copy; and the manuscript contains no tune direction.[1]

The music is found in Elizabeth Rogers's Virginal Book (BM MS Add. 10337, fol. 22ᵛ, before 1656), a setting of the first stanza of "Now yᵉ springe is comne, turne to thy Loue." It is also in John Gamble's MS Commonplace Book, 1659, No. 60 (Fig. 334), with a six-stanza version of "Christmas is my name, far have I gone" which resembles the manuscript text more closely than that of the printed broadside. Reminiscent of "Now the spring is come," but without its distinctive two- and three-bar phrases, is the first strain of an early seventeenth-century Italian tune, "Fuggi fuggi fuggi da questo cielo" (*Acta Musicologica*, XX [1948], 49–50, 58), found in English sources as "ffuge" (Paris Conservatoire MS Rés. 1185, p. 331, mid-seventeenth century), "Fugga, Fugga, or the Italian Rant" (*A Booke of New Lessons for the Cithern & Gittern*, 1652, gittern section No. 6), and "Italian Rant" (*The Dancing Master*, supplement to 3d ed., c. 1662, No. 31, 1665, No. 14; and *Musicks Hand-maid*, 1678, No. 29).

Now the Tories That Glories

This tune is named from the first line, "Now the Tories that glory (*or* glories) in Royal Jemmy's return," of a song included in Matthew Taubman's *An Heroick Poem . . . With Some choice Songs*, 1682, p. 14. The music there is incorrectly barred, but on the broadside version of the same year, entitled "The Well-wishers to the Royal Family. To a New Play-house Tune" (Harvard, Bodleian Firth c.15 [19]), the barring is correct, but there are several errors of pitch or note value. The ballad was reprinted with extremely inaccurate musical score in *180 Loyal Songs*, 1685, p. 87; this text, rather than the broadside, seems to be the source of the reprint in *RB* V, 151. The air is found also in Humphry Salter's *The*

---

[1] From the references to yellow starch, Chappell (*PMOT* II, 464) concluded that the ballad must have been written before the 1615 execution of Mrs. Anne Turner for her complicity in the murder of Sir Thomas Overbury, for after her death the yellow starched ruff declined in vogue. An entry of 1586 in the Stationers' Register for "A northerne songe of Ile awaie" (Rollins, *Anal. Index*, No. 1969) may be a reference to the refrain, "Ile away, Ile away, Ile away, for here's no stay," of the final stanza of "Christmas Lamentation." A sixteenth-century date for this ballad would also suggest an equally early origin for "A Louers desire."

335

Genteel Companion . . . for the Recorder, 1683, p. 36, entitled "Now the Toryes the Gloryes," and in *Apollo's Banquet,* 5th ed., 1687, entitled "Now the Tories, &c. or, Royal James." One other broadside printing the music is "Justice Try[u]mphant," 1683, beginning "Now the Traytor, King-hater" (Clark; reprinted in *180 Loyal Songs,* p. 90, and in *RB* V, 339).

In 1682 Thomas D'Urfey wrote "The Whigg-Feast: A Scotch Ballad made to the Tune of a new and pleasant Scotch Dance," beginning "Woons! what noo is the matter?/Gud feth 'tis wondrous strange" (BM C.38.i.25 [9], Bodleian Ashmole G.16 [169] and Firth b.20 [92], Harvard, Yale; Huntington, with MS date April 24, 1682); the piece bore the title "A Scotch Sung [sic], sung at the Artillery Feast" [1] when D'Urfey included it with the music of "Now the Tories" in his *New Collection of Songs and Poems,* 1683, p. 74 (Fig. 335). Other ballads to the tune include "The Hunting of the Fox," 1682, beginning "Hey Jouler, Ringwood, and Towzer" (Harvard; reprinted in *180 Loyal Songs,* p. 363), and J. D.'s "Iter Boreale, or Tyburn in Mourning For the Loss of a Saint," 1682, beginning "Behold Great Heavens Protection" (Harvard, Huntington, Roxburghe; reprinted in *RB* V, 157).

[1] A Whig feast, scheduled for April 21, 1682, at Haberdashers' and Goldsmiths' Hall, was prohibited by order of council as seditious. The feast of the Artillery Company was held on April 20 at Merchant-Taylors' Hall. By Luttrell's account "the entertainment was very noble"—and presumably it was here that D'Urfey sang his freshly composed song against the Whigs. C. L. Day (*The Songs of Thomas D'Urfey,* p. 130) notes that D'Urfey's presence was alluded to in a newssheet of April 25.

Nutmegs and Ginger

This tune is found in Cambridge University MSS Dd.3.18, fol. 33, in lute tablature (Fig. 336), and in Dd.14.24, fol. 37, for cittern.

336

* Varied repeat in original.

With some difficulty the air can be made to fit the thirteen-line stanza of "A pleasant ballad of the mery miller's wooing of the Baker's daughter of Manchester," beginning "The miller, in his best array,/would needs a wooinge ride," to the tune "Nutmegs and ginger" (*SB,* p. 116). This piece, preserved only in MS, is no later than c. 1615 and may be the ballad registered in 1581 as "The Millers daughter of Mannchester" (Rollins, *Anal. Index,* No. 1765).

"The Miller would a wooing ride" is the tune named for singing Thomas Deloney's "How Wat Tiler and Iacke Straw, rebelled against king Richard the second" (*Works,* ed. Mann, p. 413) and "A new ballad of the Parrator and the Divell" (*SB*, p. 306); but these ballads are in octosyllabics and could therefore not be sung to the music of "Nutmegs and ginger."

O Fie! What Mean I, Foolish Maid?

A song beginning "Oh fye! what mean I, Foolish Maid" from John Crowne's *The Married Beau*, 1694, Act II, was reprinted as a broadside with the title "An Excellent New Song, Called, The Private Encounter" (Pepys, BM C.39.k.6; reprinted in *OPB*, p. 13); the tune is not named, and music on the sheets is meaningless. Music is, however, to be found on a single-sheet issue (Fig. 337), entitled "A Song in the last New Com-

337

edy call'd the Married Beau or the Curious Impertinent. Sung by Mr. Doggett & Sett by Mr. John Eccles" (Chetham 1391). It was reprinted with music in Eccles's *A Collection of Songs*, c. 1704, p. 35, and in all editions of *Pills*, 1719–1720, III, 243. The words are contained in *Wits*

Cabinet, c. 1700, p. 46, and *The Compleat Academy of Complements*, 1705, p. 162.

The tune was introduced into Lillo's *Silvia*, 1731, as "Alas! what mean I, foolish Maid?" and was called for in another ballad opera, *The Fox Uncas'd*, 1733 (published also as *The Wanton Countess*, 1733), for which no music has survived.

O How Happy's He

The music for this tune is found on a broadside "The Jovial Gallant: Or, The perfect Pleasure of a Private Life," beginning "Ah! how Happy's he,/Who's from Bus'ness free" (Pepys; reprinted in *PB* VII, 165). Rollins dates the ballad "1695?" but since it includes a toast to "King Williams good Success" it may have been written earlier in his reign.[1] A date of c. 1690 is further indicated by the fact that the same music appears, under the title "Oh! how happy's he!" in *Apollo's Banquet*, Second Book, 1691, No. 3 (Fig. 338). The first two stanzas of the ballad are reprinted

with the music in *Pills* (1707 and succeeding editions; 1719–1720, VI, 104), "The Words by Mr. Mumford [i.e., William Mountfort], Set by Mr. H. Purcell," and here the toast is to "Queen Anna's good success." An engraved single-sheet version of the ballad, probably printed in the 1690s, is among the pieces bound together as *Joyful Cuckoldom*, BM C.180.a (27). A parody beginning "Ah! how happy's he,/Lives from drink-

[1] Rollins's suggested date may have been influenced by the absence of any reference to Mary, who died in 1694.

ing free" is directed to the same music in *Pills*, 1714, V, 198; 1720, VI, 303.

Another broadside, sung "To the Tune of Oh! how happy's he, &c.," is "The Jacobite's Recantation," beginning "Gallants far and near,/Pray now listen here" (Pepys, with meaningless music; reprinted in *PB* VI, 2). Rollins assigns a date of June, 1691, to this ballad, which is an additional reason for conjecturing an earlier date than he has proposed for "The Jovial Gallant."

O Love! If E'er Thou'lt Ease a Heart

Pelham Humphrey composed the music to a stage song beginning "Oh Love! if e're thou'lt ease a Heart" for John Crowne's *Charles the Eighth*, 1672, Act IV. The words and music appeared in *Choice Songs and Ayres*, 1673, p. 19 (Fig. 339). An expanded version appeared on a

339

broadside without music as "The Tormented Lovers" (Lord Crawford, Harvard, Roxburghe; reprinted in *RB* VII, 408). The tune does not seem to have been used for other broadsides, but William Hicks's *London Drollery*, 1673, pp. 4, 116, contains two poems written as "a Mock to,

O Love if e're thoult ease a heart; And to that Tune," one beginning "O Bacchus if thoult ease a Soul," the other "O Mars, if e'er thou'lt ease a Blade."

O Man in Desperation

An entry in the Stationers' Register, August 15, 1586, for "A ballad begynnynge O man in desperation" (Rollins, *Anal. Index*, No. 1990) attests to an early, though perhaps not the original, state of this lost ballad. The tune taking its name from the opening line is used for several other sixteenth-century pieces which introduce us to additional names for the tune. On August 1, 1586, and again on the fifteenth (*Anal. Index*, Nos. 1682, 778), license was granted for a ballad which in surviving seventeenth-century editions is entitled "A Rare Example of a Vertuous Maid of [or in] Paris," beginning "It was a Ladies Daughter/ of Paris properly," to the tune of "O man of [or in] Desparation" (Euing, Pepys, Lord Crawford, Harvard, Roxburghe; reprinted in *RB* I, 35).[1] Two ballads sung to "The Ladies Daughter of Paris" will be noted below.

On Dec. 6, 1586, "A belman for England" was licensed (*Anal. Index*, No. 181), a contemporary copy of which is printed in *SB*, p. 36; it is "A proper new ballad intituled:—A Bell-man for England/night and day doth stand,/To ringe, in all men's hearinge,/'God's vengeance is at hand!' " to the tune of "O man in desperation" and beginning "Awake! Awake! Oh Englande!" (an early seventeenth-century edition is in Pepys I, 54).[2] This first line becomes the tune title in "The belman's good morrow," beginning "From sluggish sleep and slumber" (*SB*, p. 182, before 1615; another copy, c. 1616, is preserved in BM MS Add. 15225, fol. 45ᵛ, printed in *OPB*, p. 233); since this ballad was licensed Nov. 21, 1580, it follows that the source of its tune title was in circulation before that date, and hence that "O man in desperation" was then known as a tune.

[1] This ballad is alluded to in Beaumont's *The Knight of the Burning Pestle*, 1613, V, iii, and Glapthorne's *Wit in a Constable*, 1640, Act II. It survives in tradition as "The Romish Lady." For references to its widespread currency, see G. Malcolm Laws, *American Balladry from British Broadsides*, 1957, Q 32.

[2] A reworking of this ballad, with the same opening lines and the same tune title, was inspired by an eclipse of the sun in 1652 and continued to be popular through the rest of the century. Entitled "England's New Bell-Man," it is found in various editions in Wood E.25, Wood 401, Rawlinson, Pepys, Lord Crawford, Harvard, Bagford, Roxburghe; reprinted in *RB* IV, 467.

Two sixteenth-century references to the tune are worth mentioning. One is in the opening scene of Peele's *The Old Wives Tale,* 1595; the other occurs in a stage direction in an unpublished Latin university play, *Hispanus,* 1596, where the piper is given his choice of several tunes: "Dum ex aedibus exeat tibicinem iterum incipe vel hominem in desperatione vel Doctorem Faustum vel Doctorem Lopezzium vel Labandalashottum" (*Shakespeare Jahrbuch,* XXXIV [1898], 300).

Other ballads to "O man in desperation" include: Thomas Deloney's "A most ioyfull Songe . . . fourteen [traitors executed] . . . 20 & 21 of Sept. . . . 1586," beginning "Oh Englishmen with Romish harts, what Deuill doth bewitch you" (London Society of Antiquaries [Lemon, *Catalogue,* No. 83]; reprinted in Deloney's *Works,* ed. Mann, p. 460); "A . . . trewe Ballad . . . younge man . . . wrongfully hangd at . . . Bon in the lowe Countreyes . . . 1612 . . . ," beginning "The wondrous works of god above" (*SB,* p. 159); "The confession of a pænitent Sinner," beginning "Of Adams seed, poore sinner I," with a second tune title, "Some men for suddaine joyes doe weepe" (Roxburghe; reprinted in *RB* III, 168); [3] and "An excellent song made of the Successors of King Edward the Fourth," beginning "When as the king of England died" (Richard Johnson, *Crown Garland of Golden Roses,* 1659, ed. Chappell, 1845, p. 50; a contemporary text is in the Percy Folio MS [ed. Hales and Furnivall, III, 163]; eighteenth-century copies of this ballad, published by Dicey with his usual historical introduction, are in Madden III, 729, and Harvard).

Another ballad, beginning "Jerusalem, my happy home,/When shall I come to thee?" brings us to music which may be that of "O man in des-

[3] "Some men for sudden joys do weep" takes its name from the first line of a good-night ballad on the martyr John Careless, printed by Miles Coverdale in 1564 (see *OEB,* pp. 47ff., where it is collated with another sixteenth-century version of the ballad). No tune name has survived but several entries in the Stationers' Register (*Anal. Index,* Nos. 1302, 1303, 2456) attest its popularity well into the next century, and "Iohn Carelesse" is named as the tune for "A declaration of the death of Iohn Lewes, a . . . Hereticke . . . 1583" (*OEB,* p. 55). The first two lines of the John Careless ballad are echoed in *King Lear,* I, iv, and Thomas Heywood's *Rape of Lucrece* (*Dramatic Works,* ed. Pearson, V, 179). A further paraphrase is found in a manuscript addition to the British Museum copy of Thomas Ravenscroft's *Pammelia,* 1609, sig. A1v–A2, together with a stave of music in bass clef, which may be a harmonizing part and not the melodic line itself. The text runs:

> Late as I waked out of sleepe
> I harde a prety thinge
> some men for suddaine ioy do weepe,
> and some for sorrow singe
> fa la la

See a facsimile reproduction in Peter J. Seng, "An Early Tune for the Fool's Song in *King Lear,*" *Shakespeare Quarterly,* IX (1958), 585.

peration." The text is preserved in at least five versions, all with different titles. One, called simply "Another on the same subiect" (in *The Song of Mary The Mother of Christ*, 1601, p. 38), has no tune direction. Two others, "The zealous Querister's songe of Yorke" (*SB*, p. 170, from a manuscript copy made no later than 1615) and "The true description of the everlasting joys of Heaven" (Rawlinson 167, an edition of c. 1670, the second part of which is reprinted in *SB*), give the tune as "O man in desperation." A fourth, dating from c. 1616, is "A song mad[e] by F. B. P. To the Tune of Diana" (BM MS Add. 15225, fol. 36ᵛ; printed in *OEB*, p. 164). The fifth, c. 1624, entitled "The Queristers song of yorke in praise of heaven" (BM MS Add. 38599, fol. 133ᵛ; reproduced by H. E. Rollins, *PMLA*, XXXVIII [1923], 135), contains music but no tune direction (Fig. 340). Inasmuch as two tunes are named on other copies

340

Original is an octave lower and unbarred.

of this ballad, we cannot be sure whether the music is "O man in desperation," or "Diana," or is indeed a third air. Moreover, the musical notes, written in the old tenor clef, may represent an accompanying voice rather than the melodic line itself.[4] The music is presented with these reservations; and it should be added that to speak of "O man in desperation" and "Diana" as equivalent is merely to say that we do not have independent tunes for each, unmistakably named; this is not to say that they are two names for the same tune.[5]

[4] For a facsimile reproduction of the tune, see the frontispiece of Eleanor M. Brougham's *Corn from Olde Fieldes*, 1918.

[5] "Diana" is named from the opening line "Diana and her Darlings Deare" of "A new Sonnet, shewing how the Goddesse Diana transformed Acteon into the Shape of a Hart." This ballad was licensed as early as 1565–1566 (*Anal. Index*, No. 988), and extant copies show it to have been popular for two centuries. The earliest issue is to the tune of "Rogero" (Manchester I, 29; reprinted among the notes to *A Handefull of Pleasant Delites*, ed. Rollins, p. 93); other editions are "To a new Tune" or some variation of that ambiguous formula (Pepys, Bagford, Euing, Harvard, Roxburghe; reprinted in *RB* II, 520). Also to the tune of "Diana" is "The Lamentable Song of the Lord Wigmoore . . . and the fayre maid of Dunsmoore," in Richard Johnson's *Crown Garland of Golden Roses*, 1612, ed. Chappell, p. 14, reprinted in *RB* VI, 771; an eighteenth-century broadside issue is Lord Crawford 694. It is in quatrains of octosyllabics, whereas the ballad of "Diana" is in ballad-meter octaves.

At least two ballads were sung to "The Lady's daughter" or "The Lady's daughter of Paris," which we have seen derives from a ballad to the tune of "O man in desperation" and must therefore be congruent with that tune.[6] Thomas Deloney's "How King Henry the first had his children drowned," beginning "After our royall King,/had foild his foes in France" is to "the Ladies daughter" (*Works*, ed. Mann, p. 386; another version is in the Percy Folio MS III, 156); "Take Time, while Time is," beginning "Oh stay a while you lusty Lads," is to "The Ladies Daughter of Paris" (Roxburghe; reprinted in *RB* II, 559).

O Mother! Roger

This tune takes its name from the opening line "Oh Mother! Roger with his kisses/almost stops my Breath I vow!" of an anonymous song found in *The Loyal Garland*, 1686; with music it appears in *The Theater of Music*, Third Book, 1686, p. 25 (Fig. 341), and in all editions of *Pills*, 1719–1720, III, 202. The tune alone is in *The Dancing Master*, commencing with the 9th ed., 1695; the poem alone is reprinted in John Shirley's *The Triumph of Wit*, 2d ed., 1692. The broadside version, using only the first stanza of the song, is "Modesty Amazed . . . To an Excellent New Tune, much in request" (Pepys, Lord Crawford, Euing, Harvard, Roxburghe; reprinted in *RB* VIII, 201).

Some fifteen broadsides and garland poems were sung to the tune of "Oh Mother! Roger," most of them issued during the reign of James II and devoted to amatory rather than political topics. They include "The London Cuckold," beginning "A Trades-man hearing of the Story" (Pepys, Bagford, Lord Crawford, Harvard, Roxburghe; reprinted in *RB* VIII, 603) and "An Answer to the London Cuckold," beginning "I pray now listen to my Ditty" (Pepys IV, 123, only the first stanza of which is reprinted in *RB* VIII, 605). "The Cuckoldy Cook," beginning "Come listen to this pleasant Ditty," is to the tune of "The London Cuckold; or, Mother Roger" (Pepys V, 255).

Other ballads to the tune which have not been reprinted include: "The Trappand Cuckold-maker," beginning "There was of late a Cuckold-

---

6 A tune entitled "The Ladies Daughter" is preserved in Paris Conservatoire MS Rés. 1185, No. 120, a mid-seventeenth-century keyboard setting. It fits the ballads mentioned here. The tune had appeared earlier in Thomas Robinson's *The Schoole of Musicke*, 1603, sig. M2, as "Walking in a country towne," q.v.

341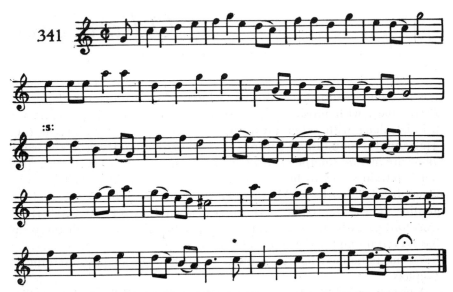

* Original contains sign :s: erroneously ending repetition one line short of entire refrain.

maker" (BM C.22.f.6 [185], Lord Crawford 1161, Harvard); "The Westminster Madams Lamentation," beginning "The Army now returns to London" (Pepys III, 339); "The Contention, between a Countryman & a Citizen, for a beauteous London Lass," beginning "There is a Lass of London City" (Pepys III, 255); and "The Old Mans Advice to Batchellors," beginning "If you would take a wife for pleasure" (Pepys IV, 104).

The tune is named for singing "A Carrol for Twelfth-Day" in *A Cabinet of Choice Jewels*, 1688, and for "A Merry Song to be sung at Christmas" in an eighteenth-century garland *Canterbury Tales [with] Witty Jests and Delightful Songs . . . by Chaucer, Jun.*, found in vol. III of Ritson's Penny Histories (Harvard). An earlier edition is among Pepys's Penny Merriments, vol. II, along with *The Country Garland*, 1687, which contains a song "True Love in its Purity" to the tune "Tell me Mother" (named from the burden of the original "Oh Mother! Roger" song).

"O Mother, Roger" was introduced into two ballad operas, Phillips's *The Mock Lawyer*, 1733, and Drury's *The Rival Milliners*, 1737. The former contains partial music at the end of the volume, but this tune is not one of those represented.

O Raree Show

A song which begins with the refrain "O raree show, O brave show" was introduced into Peter Motteux's interlude, *Europe's Revels for the Peace,* 1697, with music by John Eccles. In the following year it was printed along with other music by Eccles for the entertainment (Fig. 342), and it is found in all editions of *Pills,* 1719–1720, III, 312; the words alone are in *The Compleat Academy of Complements,* 1705, p. 153. Motteux's refrain seems to be echoed in a poem written by Ned Ward and issued in 1698: "O Raree-Show, O Pretty-Show: Or, The City Feast," beginning "On a Day of great Triumph, when Lord of the City" (Lord Crawford 968, Chetham, Harvard, Clark, Columbia). Although the poem has no refrain and makes no pretense of being a street song, it nevertheless seems to be modeled on Motteux's rather rough anapestic tetrameter couplets.

A parody called "O Raree Show, O Pritee Show. Will you see my Fine

343

Show," beginning "Here be De ver pritte Show, just come from Parry," is found on a broadside of about 1712 (BM Luttrell II, 155, Huntington, Roxburghe) and in several contemporary songsters, including *Political Merriment*, 1714, Part II, p. 17, which adds a second part. Ebsworth printed both parts from this source in *RB* VIII, 235. Another "Second Part," beginning "All loyal Men, come zee my vine rary Show," is in *A Collection of State Songs*, 1716, p. 151 (reprinted in *RB* VIII, 830).

"The Raree Show Ballad, or the English Missisippi" is a parody of c. 1720, which uses Motteux's refrain beginning "O Raree Show, O bravee Show, O pritee Show" to satirize the spectacle of a nation victimized by the Mississippi Bubble. A single-sheet issue of this ballad (Fig. 343) employs the first, third, and fourth strains of Eccles's music (BM G.305 [212], Huntington, Harvard). This abbreviated form of the tune appears in two ballad operas: Ralph's *The Fashionable Lady*, 1730 ("O rarée Show, O bravée Show"), and Kelly's *The Plot*, 1735 ("O rare Show"). The tune is loosely adapted to another "O Raree Show" sung in the Theobold-Galliard pantomime, *The Rape of Proserpine*, c. 1725 (single-sheet issues in BM G.306 [10], Harvard).

Eccles's four-strain song structure is all refrain except for the third section which incorporates the stanza, a series of intoned lines made distinctive by an octave drop at the end of each line. Music provides for a couplet, but the chant can easily be extended to accommodate the broadside quatrains of the 1712 parody.

Of All the Simple Things We Do

"The Mouse-Trap. Made to a comical new Tune in the Country Wake," beginning "Of all the simple Things we do,/To rub over a whimsical Life," was printed anonymously in *The Merry Musician,* 1716, I, 216 (Fig. 344). It was reprinted in *Pills,* 1719–1720, I, 249, among the

344

songs whose words were written by Thomas D'Urfey. No music was printed with Thomas Doggett's *The Country-Wake,* 1696, but the play introduces a country dance which is broken up by Old Hob. The tune printed in volume II of *The Dancing Master,* 3d ed., 1718, 255, is called "Old Hob: Or, the Mouse Trap." D'Urfey's text appears with music on several single-sheet issues, with title substantially as in *The Merry Musician* (BM H.1601 [326], Harvard, Huntington); it is reprinted as "Marriage" in Watts's *Musical Miscellany,* 1729–1731, V, 108, and is found without music in such poetical miscellanies as *The Hive,* 3d ed., 1726, I, 193.

A broadside of c. 1730 in the National Library of Scotland (Rosebery III.c.36 [122]) is a parody: "The Rake in Fetters: or, the Marriage Mouse Trap," beginning "Of all the simple Things I know"; the ballad contains neither tune direction nor music. Another parody is found in *Mughouse Diversion,* 1717, p. 24: "Tories greater Knaves than Fools," beginning "Of all the Fools that e'er was known," to the tune "Of all the simple Things we do." The music is printed without identification on a single-sheet song of c. 1720 entitled "The Constant Lovers. The Words by Mr. A. Bradley," beginning "As Strephon Wander'd 'midst the Dales" (BM H.1601 [8], Harvard, Huntington).

The tune was introduced into at least seven ballad operas, including the following which printed the music: Gay's *The Beggar's Opera,* 1728;

Odell's *The Patron*, 1729; Chetwood's *The Generous Free-Mason*, 1731; and Fielding's *An Old Man taught Wisdom*, 1735. In *Vanelia*, 1732, the tune name "Of all the foolish Things we do" may be a reference to the same air.

Of Noble Race Was Shinkin

This tune takes its name from the opening line of a song Thomas D'Urfey wrote for his play *The Richmond Heiress*, 1693, Act IV. It was evidently sung to the accompaniment of a Welsh harp, for which an antiphonal phrase is included in the music. The song is found in *Thesaurus Musicus*, First Book, 1693, p. 20 (Fig. 345), and in all edi-

345

tions of *Pills*, 1719–1720, II, 172. Several single-sheet issues with the music are found, the usual title being "A Song in the Play called the Richmond Heiress" (BM H.1601 [330], Harvard, Yale, Huntington). A manuscript version of D'Urfey's text is preserved in BM MS Harl. 2127, fol. 40.[1] The tune alone appears in *The Dancing Master*, commencing with the ninth edition, 1695.

D'Urfey used the air also for "The Authentick Letter of Marshal de Boufflers . . . on the late unfortunate . . . Battel . . . near Mons [Oct., 1709] . . . done into Metre, in broken English. Set to a famous Tune on the Welch Harp," beginning "Me send you, Sir, one Letter."

[1] For other appearances of the verses, see C. L. Day, *The Songs of Thomas D'Urfey*, 1933, pp. 150–151.

This appeared as a single-sheet song (Chetham 1522) and was reprinted in *The Merry Musician,* 1716, I, 49, and in *Pills* II, 140. A ballad on the Welsh, c. 1715, names the tune and takes account of the musical interludes within stanzas: "A Song to the Old Britons, on St. Taffy's Day," beginning "How are the Mighty fallen!" (Huntington, Clark). Another contemporary slip-song parody is "An Excellent new Ballad," beginning "Of doubtful Race was Georgy," a Jacobite piece (Huntington); others are found in *Mughouse Diversion,* 1717, p. 15; 5th ed., 1719, pp. 31, 32. The first anniversary of the defeat of the Excise Bill was celebrated with a ballad to the tune: "The Mayor and the Mob," beginning " 'Twas in the town of London" (BM 1876.f.1 [125]; reprinted in *A New Miscellany for 1734*).

A song beginning " 'Twas in the Land of Cyder," which has its own tune, "All in . . . ," q.v., is printed with the music of "Of noble race was Shinkin" in a single-sheet edition (BM G.305 [111], c. 1725) and in Watts's *Musical Miscellany,* 1729–1731, III, 47. Several songsters without music name this tune for the song: *The Vocal Miscellany,* 1734, p. 20; *The Musical Companion,* 1741, p. 245; and *The Merry Companion,* 2d ed., 1742, p. 284. Conversely, "Of noble race was Shinkin" was directed to be sung to " 'Twas in the land of Cyder" in *A Complete Collection of . . . English and Scotch Songs,* 1735–1736, IV, 61.

The air "Of a noble [*or* royal] race was Shenkin" was introduced into a dozen ballad operas, from Gay's *The Beggar's Opera,* 1728, to *Court and Country,* 1743; but only Gay's work reprints the music.

The Old Man's Wish

"The Old Man's Wish" was written by Dr. Walter Pope, astronomer, and author of "The Catholic Ballad" and other works. A broadside edition, beginning "If I live to grow old, (for I find I go down,)" and containing the music (Fig. 346), has a MS date of 13 Sept. 1684 (Clark; a variant issue in Harvard). The song made its appearance in a number of places in 1685, and imitations are numerous enough to attest its popularity. It is found in *The Theater of Music,* First Book, p. 50, with music attributed to Dr. John Blow. The verses alone are in *A Collection of Twenty Four Songs,* sig. C3. Words and music are also in *Two New Songs,* p. 3, and *180 Loyal Songs,* p. 234. In 1686 the song was reprinted in *The Second Book of the Pleasant Musical Companion,* 2d ed., Part II, No. 4. A number of single-sheet editions with music suggest its continued

346

popularity well into the eighteenth century (BM H.1601 [239], BM G.316.e [30], Huntington, Harvard, several issues). It was reprinted with music in all editions of *Pills*, 1719–1720, III, 16; in *The Convivial Songster*, c. 1782, p. 335; in Ritson's *English Songs*, 1783, and (words only) in *The Muses Delight*, 1754, p. 316. Music alone arranged for keyboard, c. 1700, is in Paris Conservatoire MS Rés. 1186 bis, Part I, p. 26. Several broadside editions of the poem without music but with the direction "To a Pleasant New Play-house Tune" were issued under the title "The Old Mans Wish" (Pepys, Douce, Roxburghe; reprinted in *RB* VI, 507); an edition entitled "Dr. Pope's Wish" appeared in 1693, "The only Correct and Finish'd Copy: never before Printed" (Wood 417 [183]); and a pamphlet issue of 1697 in twenty stanzas is entitled simply "The Wish."

Perhaps the earliest imitation of Pope's song is S. P.'s broadside "A New Song: or, The Old Womans Wish," 1684, which begins "Since Beauty now fails/And I find I decay," and calls for the tune of "The

Old Mans Wish" (Harvard, Huntington, Clark). This parody is vaguely similar in detail to two other pieces entitled "The Old Womans Wish," both found in *180 Loyal Songs*, 1685, pp. 235, 236, and both reprinted in *Pills* III, 19, 18: one, parodying Dr. Pope's poem almost line by line, begins "If I live to be old, which I never will own"; the other begins "When my hairs they grow hoary, & my cheeks they look pale."[1] A third piece to the tune in *180 Loyal Songs*, p. 237, is a political parody, "Jack Presbyters Wish," beginning "If the Whigs shall get up, and the Torys go down" (reprinted in *RB* IV, 648, without indication of source). In 1685 at least three other parodies were set to the tune. They include "The Young Bastards Wish, A Song To the Tune of the Old Mans Wish," beginning "If I live to be King, as the world knows I hope," a ballad on Monmouth (Lord Crawford 628, Harvard), and two associated pieces published by George Croom: "The Vertuous Young Maids Wish," beginning "I am a Young Maid,/And Daily am Taught" (Lord Crawford 560), and "The Vicious Young-Man's Wish," beginning "I'm a Lusty Young-Man,/And I'm vext with a Sprite," the latter to the tune of "The Old Womans Wish" (Clark). Still another parody is "The Pope's Wish," beginning "If I wear out of date, as I find I fall down," in *The Muses Farewel to Popery and Slavery*, 1689, p. 45, partially reprinted in *RB* IV, 313. And one which does not accept advanced years with the philosophical resignation of the original is "A New Song, Call'd, The Old Mans Wish: or his desire, for the Ladies sake, To be Young again," 1691, beginning "If I was young, as now I am old" (Pepys V, 186).

Others to the tune include: "An Answer to the Old Man's Wish: Containing the Young Lasses Longing to be Marry'd . . . to an Old Man rather than fail," beginning "O that I was now a Marry'd Wife" (Pepys V, 187); "The Taylor's Lamentation," beginning "I am a Taylor now in Distress" (Lord Crawford, Roxburghe; reprinted in *RB* VII, 474); "An Excellent New Song Call'd The Quakers Lamentation," 1692, beginning "Dear friends behold a Brother most sad" (Pepys V, 409); and "The Baker's Lamentation," beginning "Ah how I sigh! and how I moan" (Pepys V, 394).

The tune was introduced into two ballad operas of 1729: Odell's *The Patron* and Johnson's *The Village Opera*, with an altered and somewhat simplified second strain. In the latter the tune is called "If I live to grow Old."

---

[1] This song appears as "The Matron's Wish" in Alexander Smith's *The Musical Miscellany*, 1786, p. 102, set to a somewhat more florid eighteenth-century tune; the same music serves also for "The Old Man's Wish," which follows it.

Old Simon the King

The early form of this tune is found as "Simon the King" in *Musicks Recreation on the Lyra Viol,* 1652, p. 80 (Fig. 347). A closely related, but

Original is barred in 3/4.

nonetheless different, form is in *The Dancing Master,* commencing with the Supplement to the sixth edition, 1679; the tune is transferred to the body of the collection in the seventh edition, 1686. Elaborate variations are found in Humphry Salter's *Genteel Companion . . . for the Recorder,* 1683, p. 38, and *The Division-Violin,* 1685, No. 4. The tune is set as a keyboard lesson in *The Second Part of Musick's Hand-maid,* 1689, and in Paris Conservatoire MS Rés. 1186 bis, Part I, p. 23. A setting for violin is in *Apollo's Banquet,* 5th ed., 1687. The tune is called "Simon the King," more commonly "Old Simon the King."

Music (Fig. 348) is contained on a broadside of 1683: "The Whigs

* G in original.

laid open, or, An Honest Ballad of these sad Times," beginning "Now the Plotters & Plots are confounded," to "a Mery Tune, called Old Symon the King" (Harvard). The tune is also printed in *180 Loyal Songs*, 1685, p. 149, and four times in *Pills*, 1719–1720: II, 51, III, 143, IV, 47, and VI, 31.

Broadsides sung to the tune were registered as early as 1630, but the original ballad of "Old Simon the King" was probably known to Elizabethans, for *The Famous Historie of Fryer Bacon* (1629, sig. F3ᵛ) contains a quatrain paraphrasing the ballad, and the earliest editions of this chapbook, now lost, probably antedated Robert Greene's writing of *Friar Bacon and Friar Bungay*, c. 1591–1592.[1] The Percy Folio MS (ed. Hales and Furnivall, IV, 124) preserves a version of the ballad transcribed in the first half of the seventeenth century and beginning "In: an humor I was of late,/as many good fellowes bee." No printed broadside texts are extant, but the piece is found in *Wit and Mirth*, 3d ed., 1682, p. 46, and, with the first strain of the music, in *Pills* III, 143. The absence of the second half of the tune is conspicuous here, for the ballad is in twelve-line stanzas (each strain will accommodate only a quatrain), and the appended tag "Says Old Simon the King" is probably meant to stand for the usual quatrain refrain. This offers a problem, too, for it usually takes the following form (as found in several later ballads):

> Says Old Simon the King,
>   says Old Simon the King,
> With his thread-bare Cloaths, and his Mamsey Nose,
>   sing hey ding, ding, a ding ding.[2]

The hypermetrical third line is out of step with the 9/4 rhythm of the music, and suggests either that we have lost an important section of the tune or that the third bar of the refrain requires an added beat to

---

[1] Compare the chapbook quatrain:

> Lawyers they are sicke,
> And Fryers are ill at ease;
> But poore men they are drunke.
> And all is one disease.

with lines 9–12 of the Percy Folio ballad text:

> mine ostes was sicke of the mumpes,
> her mayd was ffisle att ease,
> mine host lay drunke in his dumpes;
> "they all had but one disease."

[2] In the Percy Folio MS the refrain runs on beyond the quatrain with further repetitions of the "hey ding" formula, but the precise wording is obscured by the scribe's "&c." and by mutilation of the manuscript. The third line reads: "with his ale-dropt hose, & his malmesy nose."

accommodate the four accents of the line. This latter possibility seems the more likely when we realize that the tune is sometimes barred in 3/4 time, sometimes in 6/4, as if the strong triple movement implicit in 9/4 were not always felt in the seventeenth century. It is singular, however, that no version of the tune exhibits the metrical irregularity needed to fit the refrain.

The original ballad is parodied in "The Breech Wash'd By a Friend to the Rump," a broadside of early 1660 beginning "In an humor of late I was/Ycleped a dolefull dump" (BM C.20.f.2 [35], Wood 416 [33], Bagford III, 11, BM Thomason, BM Luttrell II, 185, all without tune direction; reprinted in *Ratts Rhimed to Death*, 1660, *The Rump*, 1660 [with tune direction "Old Simon the King"], *Rump*, 1662, *Loyal Songs*, 1731, and Wright, *Political Ballads*, 1841, p. 198).

Perhaps the earliest ballad naming the tune is one licensed in 1630: "Ragged, and Torne, and True. Or, the poore mans Resol[u]tion, To the tune of Old Simon the King," beginning "I am a poor man, God knows" (Roxburghe; reprinted in *RB* II, 409); [3] from its title comes the most widespread of the several other names given to the tune. Among the ballads sung to "Ragged and torn and true" or "Ragged and torn" are two by Martin Parker, registered in 1632 and 1634 respectively: "Knauery in all Trades," beginning "As I was walking of late,/within the fields so faire" (Pepys; reprinted in *PG*, p. 410), and "A Messe of good Fellows," beginning "Well met my iouiall blades" (Roxburghe; reprinted in *RB* II, 143). Also to the tune are "The Souldiers delight in the North," c. 1640, beginning "Cvdie and Peggie together/Did meet in an evening late," to "The Northerne Diddle, or Raged and torne" (Manchester II, 32; cf. *RB* VIII, xxxiii***); [4] "The good Fellowes Complaint," beginning "[C]ome hither my jovall Blades" (Manchester; reprinted in *CP*, p. 209). A ballad by C. H., written about 1659–1660, has a verse title referring to Charles II:

> A Merry new song wherein you may view
> The drinking Healths of a Ioviall Crew,
> To 'thappie Return of the Figure of Two.
> The tune is, Ragged and torn and true.

It begins "I have beene a Traveller long" (Lord Crawford, Harvard, Roxburghe; reprinted in *RB* VI, 324). Several later ballads sung to "Ragged and torn" are in *RB*, vols. IV, VII, VIII.

[3] A reworking of the ballad is "An Item for honest men," signed S[amuel?] S[mithson?], beginning "O what a mad world is this," to the tune "Ragged and Torne," printed at the end of a pamphlet *The Man in the Moone*, 1657.

[4] "The Northern Diddle" is a tune name inspired by phraseology within the ballad; if it designated a new tune, none under that name has survived.

Martin Parker's "Well met Neighbour," beginning "Whither away good Neighbour," to the tune of "Ragged and Torne" (Euing, Roxburghe; reprinted in *RB* III, 98) has a burden "Oh! such a rogue would be hang'd" which becomes another name for the tune. Parker himself cited it as "O such a Rogue" for singing his "Have among you good Women," beginning "God morrow old father Starket" (Roxburghe; reprinted in *RB* I, 435), and it is "Such a Rouge would be hang'd" in Richard Climsell's "Joy and sorrow mixt together," beginning "Hang sorrow, let's cast away care" (Roxburghe; reprinted in *RB* I, 509); both are apparently products of the 1630s.

A song printed with the tune of "Old Simon the King" in *Pills* IV, 47, is "The Reformed Drinker," which has the burden "And ne'er be Drunk again" (reprinted in *A Complete Collection of . . . English and Scotch Songs*, 1735–1736, III, 173, in Ritson's *English Songs*, 1683, with the music, and in *RB* VI, 317). If we knew that it had been in circulation early in the seventeenth century, we might more confidently point to it as the source for "Ile nere be drunke againe," the tune named by Martin Parker for singing his "Times Alteration," beginning "When this Old Cap was new" (Pepys, Roxburghe; reprinted in *RB* II, 582; [5] Ritson reprinted the ballad in his *English Songs*, without the music but with the tune direction as in Parker's ballad). "When this Old Cap was new" is cited as a tune title in the following: "The praise of St. Davids day," beginning "Who list to read the deeds/By valiant Welshmen done" (Roxburghe; reprinted in *RB* II, 329); in "The Praise of our Country Barly-Brake," beginning "Both yong men, maids, and lads" (Roxburghe; reprinted in *RB* II, 386); and in "The English Seamans Resolution," beginning "I am an undaunted Seaman" (Euing 106), which has an additional tune title "I prethee, Love, turn to me," for which see "My lodging is on the cold ground."

"A True Character of Sundry Trades and Callings," beginning "Now Gentlemen sit you all merry," to the tune of "Old Simon the King" (BM C.22.f.6, Euing, Douce, Harvard, Bagford; reprinted in *Pills* IV, 49, and in *RB* VII, 17; a later edition in Roxburghe III, 592), gives rise to the second tune name in "The Naked-Truth; Or, A New Song without a Lye," beginning "Tho' Trading we find in the City," to the tune of "Old Simon the King: Or, The Character of sundry Trades and Callings" (Euing, Lord Crawford, Harvard, Roxburghe; reprinted in *RB* VII, 19). It may also be the source of yet another tune name, "All Trades," found on several ballads which contain the four-line refrain pattern.[6] Typical

---

[5] A copy of the ballad in BM MS Add. 38599, fol. 143, differing little from the printed version, is probably to be dated c. 1624. See *PMLA*, XXXVIII (1923), 134.

[6] "A True Character of Sundry Trades" also uses the refrain with its long third line and so seems a likelier source of the tune name "All Trades" than does Parker's earlier "Knauery in all Trades," which contains no hypermetrical line. See *RB* IV, 65ff.

of these is "The Doting Old Dad," beginning "There was a young Damsel of late" (Lord Crawford, Douce, Harvard, Roxburghe; reprinted in *RB* IV, 412); others are in *RB* IV, 66, 70.

"Grist ground at Last," beginning "Give ear a while to my Ditty,/ all you that intend to be merry," is a late seventeenth-century ballad containing the "Old Simon" refrain and evidently intended to be sung to that tune; the tune direction, "Give ear a while, &c. or, Winchester Wedding" (Lord Crawford, BM C.22.f.6, Harvard, Yale, Pepys; reprinted in *RB* VIII, 622), gives us a satisfactory alternate tune in "Winchester Wedding" (for which see "The King's Jig"), whereas the first tune named from the opening of the ballad may or may not refer to an independent melody.

"Old Simon the King" continued to be popular under its own name, despite the array of other names generated within balladry. Among later broadsides citing the original name of the tune may be mentioned "A General sale of Rebellious Houshold-stuff," beginning "Rebellion hath broken up House"; this was issued several times during the 1680s,[7] but its subject matter is drawn from the late years of the Commonwealth, when the ballad was probably originally written. It seems to have been allegorically useful to a later generation without any reworking of its contents, and we find it drawn upon again in the reign of Queen Anne, with the issuance of "An Excellent Old Ballad, made at the Restauration of K. Charles II, with a Second Part to the same Tune by a Modern Hand" (BM 1876.f.1 [55], dated 1711; another issue, BM 1850.c.10 [33], dated 1712). In all its states the ballad makes use of the "Simon" refrain, which in the last version begins "Says Old Simon the King,/And Young Simon the King . . ." An obvious parody in *The Muses Farewel to Popery and Slavery*, 1689, Supplement, p. 38, is "A Sale of old State Houshold-Stuff," beginning "The Government being resolv'd," with a refrain:

> Quoth J -- my the Bigotted K ---
> Quoth J -- my the Politick thing,
> With a thred-bare Oath,
> And a Catholick Troth,
> That never was worth a farthing.

[7] A 1682 edition is preserved in Bodleian Ashmole G.16 (195), BM 839.m.22 (16), Huntington, Harvard; reprinted in *180 Loyal Songs*, p. 149 (with music), and in Percy's *Reliques*. A 1685 text is in Library of Congress Broadside Portfolio 265 (20); the same issue may be represented by Wood 417 (154), whose indistinct date has been altered in MS to 1688 and its old-style equivalent, 1687, added. Still another issue, with the old title preceded by a new one, "Rebellion given over House-keeping," is in Pepys and Wood E.25, reprinted in *PB* IV, 4; its imprint, which includes the initials of Mary Coles (who succeeded her husband briefly after his death in 1680), suggests the early 1680s rather than the 1688 assigned by Professor Rollins.

And the appeal of the title is echoed in a ballad of 1689, "The Jesuites Market, Or, A General Sale of Popish Relicks," beginning "Last Sunday I met by chance" (Pepys; reprinted in *PB* IV, 128), also sung to "Old Simon the King."

"Newmarket; a Song sung to the King there," beginning "The Golden Age is come," was written by Thomas D'Urfey to the tune; it appeared in his *Several New Songs*, 1684, p. 6, with the music, and in the same year broadside issues were published, called "The New-market Song" (BM 1871.e.9 [75], Bodleian Ashmole G.15 [152], Harvard, Clark, the latter with MS date 16 Jan. 1684/3). The text alone was reprinted in *180 Loyal Songs* and in *RB* V, 144. The musical score in *Pills* II, 51, is sufficient for singing six of D'Urfey's quatrains, while the Clark sheet contains a complete melodic line for the twenty interlined stanzas, wrongly barred in 6/4 time and with elaborations more suited to instrument than voice.

The following ballads sung to "Old Simon the King" have apparently not been reprinted: "A New Wedding: or, The Marriage of Jenny, and Tommy," beginning "Jenny is a pretty young Lass" (Rawlinson 79); "A New Miracle or Dr. Nomans safe Return From the Grand Turks Court at Constantinople," beginning "All you that have formerly seen me" (Wood 417 [136], Wood 276b [82]; Clark, with MS date 16 Jan 1684/3); "The Lusty Friar of Dublin," beginning "There was an old Fryar of late" (Pepys III, 43); and a "Song" beginning "This making of Bastards great/And Dutchessing every Whore," found in BM MS Harl. 7319, p. 308.

The eighteenth-century popularity of "Old Simon the King" can be traced in an occasional ballad using the tune, such as "Whiggism laid Open," beginning "Now the Whigs and their Friends are confounded," written c. 1710 after the trial of Dr. Sacheverell (BM 1876.f.1 [53]), or in songs found in such topical miscellanies as *A Pill to Purge State-Melancholy*, 1715 ("Let's sing in the praise of French Wine," p. 151), and *Political Merriment* ("The Political Glass-Shop, Set up in Dublin," Part IV, 1715, 59). An old tale of the dyer who surprises his wife with a priest and dips him in a vat of green is told in "The Dyer of Roan [i.e., Rouen]," beginning "In good King Lewis's Land,/In a city of high degree," found in *The Hive*, 1725, III, 121, and with the music in Watts's *Musical Miscellany*, 1729–1731, III, 60. Allan Ramsay's *Tea-Table Miscellany*, 1733, II, 172, and *A Complete Collection of . . . English and Scotch Songs*, 1735–1736, II, 91, print a song beginning "Come here's to the nymph that I love" to the tune of "Auld Sir Symon the King."

Seven ballad operas call for the tune. In Gay's *The Beggar's Opera* it is "To old Sir Simon the King," and in Ryan's *The Cobler's Opera*, 1729, it is "And never be drunk again." It is "Old [*or* Auld] Sir Simon the

King" in the other five, which do not print the music. Joseph Reed's comic opera *Tom Jones,* 1769, Act II, introduced the tune—and most appropriately, since in Fielding's novel it was one of Squire Western's favorites.

The Old Wife She Sent
to the Miller Her Daughter

For the third part of his *Don Quixote,* 1696, III, ii, Thomas D'Urfey wrote a song "Sung by Mary yᵉ Buxom att her Wedding," beginning "The old wife she sent to the Miller her Daughter." It was printed in the *New Songs* to the play, 1696, fol. 10 (Fig. 349), and in all editions of

349

* Missing; emendation supplied from song sheet.

Pills, 1719–1720, I, 185. Single-sheet issues with the music bore the title "The Iolly Miller" (BM H.1601 [434], Harvard), used also in *Pills.* This spirited song, full of good-natured *double-entendre,* concludes with a (variable) refrain:

And all the Day long,
This, this was her Song,
Was ever Maiden so lericompoop'd.

A broadside without music, entitled "The Lusty Miller's Recreation
. . . To a pleasant New Tune," and beginning "The Good-Wife her
Daughter did send to the Miller," tells the same story of the miller
and the three daughters whom he "lericompoop'd" in turn, but its final
refrain line is softened to "Ay! marry Sir, there's a brave Miller indeed."
The surviving copies, all published by Philip Brooksby (Lord Crawford,
Euing, Douce, Roxburghe; reprinted in *RB* VIII, 618), were probably
issued after the play and are not to be considered the source of a re-
cooking by D'Urfey.[1]

The tune was used for such political ballads as "A Halter for Rebels, or
the Jacobites Downfall," beginning "A Junto of Knaves met at Paris
together," found in *A Collection of State Songs*, 1716, p. 40 (reprinted
in *RB* VIII, 825), with the refrain:

And all the Day long
This, this was their Song,
Dear Jemmy, dear Jemmy, depend on't, thou shalt be a King.

This is itself a parody of "A New Ballad. To a new Tune," beginning
"A Junto of Statesmen were late met together," in *Political Merriment*,
1714, p. 25 (reprinted in *RB* VIII, 824, with title and tune name supplied
from an unspecified source).

The tune was used in six ballad operas, including Odell's *The Patron*,
1729, and Drury's *The Devil of a Duke*, 1732, in which the music is
printed.

An Old Woman Poor and Blind

This tune takes its name from a ballad beginning "As I walk'd by an
Hospital,/I heard an old Woman cry," with a refrain:

And grant to me those Joys,
That belong to Woman-kind,

[1] "Maids, wives & widdows take heed of the miller's tole dish" (Rollins, *Anal. Index*,
No. 1636) was licensed March 12, 1656; though it may have been on the same subject,
I doubt that the Brooksby broadside is a later issue of this.

And the Fates above reward your Love,
To an old Woman Poor and Blind.

Two quite dissimilar tunes appear with copies of this text: one is on
a broadside of 1685 entitled "A Song" (Bodleian Ashmole G.15 [172],
Clark) and is found nowhere else (Fig. 350). In its final cadence and

its makeup of seven-measure phrases it seems old, but its rhythms are
those of the late seventeenth-century composer. The other tune is found
with the ballad, called "The Old Woman's Wish," in *Pills*, 1719–1720,
V, 29 (Fig. 351); its earliest appearance was in the 1707 edition of that
collection. Although later in point of time, it has a popular dance-tune
cast which suggests that it had not been recently composed; in any case,
it became the one known to the eighteenth century. It appears, though
without title, twice again in *Pills*: with "The Crafty Cracks of East-Smith-
Field," beginning "You Master Colours [i.e., Colliers] pray draw near,"

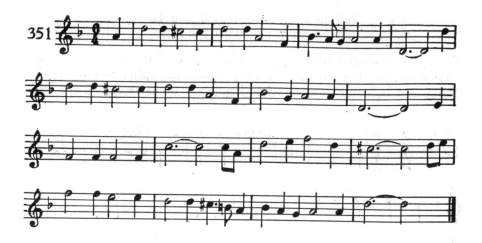

V, 22, and with "The Second Part of the Trader's Medly: Or, The Cries of London," beginning "Come buy my Greens and Flowers fine," VI, 124.[1] Two ballad operas using the tune make its identification unmistakable. Johnson's *The Village Opera*, 1729, reprints the air substantially as in *Pills*, calling it "An Old Woman Lame and Blind," and Ralph's *The Fashionable Lady*, 1730, Air 2, in a major key (Fig. 352), is called "An old Woman poor and blind."

Several early eighteenth-century broadsides are sung to the tune: "The Toothless Bride," 1705, beginning "You wanton Wives, that are grown Old" (Bagford; reprinted in *BB* I, 25); "The Debtford Plumb Cake," beginning "Come all you sweet lips, round me stand" (Bagford; reprinted in *BB* I, 71); "The Wedding Song of Gibbie and Marjorie; who were married in Edinburgh . . . 13th of June 1716; their Ages One Hundred and Sixty Years," beginning "Come all good People, give an Ear" (National Lib. of Scotland Ry III.c.36 [106]); and "A Dialogue between Jack and his Mother," c. 1720, beginning "Jack met his mother all alone" (Roxburghe III, 499, partially reprinted in Chappell, *PMOT* II, 552).

Also to the tune is a song "On Prince Eugene's routing the Turks," beginning "Here's a Health to the Great Eugene," concerning the Aus-

---

[1] "The Traders Medly: or the Crys of London" is found in *The Midship-Man's Garland*, c. 1694, p. 4, to the tune of "When Cold Winter storms are past" (reprinted in *BB* I, 115, and *A Century of Ballads*, ed. John Ashton, 1887, p. 71). A ballad with that beginning, bearing the title "The Scotch Lass Deceiv'd By her Bonny Lad Jockey. To a New Scotch Tune of Mr. Farmers" is found in Pepys V, 268, with the music (another copy, with meaningless music, is in BM C.39.k.6; reprinted in *OPB*, p. 7). Farmer's bravura tune can be fitted to "The Traders Medly" with some difficulty; but its existence establishes the fact, Ebsworth to the contrary notwithstanding, that "When cold winter storms are past" is not another name for the tune "An old woman poor and blind."

352

Transposed from key of C.

trian campaigns against the Turks, 1715–1718 (*A Collection of State Songs*, 1716, p. 146).

On the Bank of a Brook

This tune is named from the opening line "On the Bank of a Brook, as I sate fishing" of an anonymous song which in 1671 appeared without music in *A New Academy of Complements* and *Westminster Drollery*. With musical setting by John Banister it was included in *Choice Songs and Ayres*, 1673, p. 42 (Fig. 353). During the 1670s an expanded broadside version appeared under the title "The Happy Lovers Pastime," without music but with tune direction "On the Bank of a Brook" (Pepys

353

IV, 4, BM C.22.f.6 [121], Rawlinson 213; the first three stanzas are reprinted in *RB* VIII, xcv***).

At least one other broadside was sung to the tune: "A strange Encounter of two Lovers," beginning "Down in a Cypress Grove as I was lying" (Wood E.25 [147], Douce II, 211). A slightly indecent parody of the original song, to be sung "to that Tune," is in *Mock Songs*, 1675, p. 4.

Once I Loved a Maiden Fair

This tune, called "Maiden fair" or "Once I loved a maiden fair," is found in the first ten editions of *The Dancing Master*, 1651–1698 (1651, p. 47=Fig. 354), in *A Booke of New Lessons for the Cithern & Gittern*, 1652, in Playford's *Brief Introduction to the Skill of Music*, 1660 and suc-

354

Original is unbarred.

ceeding editions, in *Musick's Delight on the Cithren*, 1666, in Thomas Greeting's *Pleasant Companion . . . for the Flagelet*, 1673, in *Youth's Delight on the Flagelet*, 9th ed., c. 1690, and in *Apollo's Banquet*, 1670, *et seq.*

The tune takes its name from the opening line of a ballad licensed in 1629: "The Reuolted Louer . . . To a pleasant new tune" (Roxburghe; reprinted in *RB* II, 404). Patrick Cary, whose manuscript verse is dated 1651, wrote a song to the tune, beginning "Fayre-one! if thus kind you be,/Yett intend a slaughter" (*Trivial Poems,* ed. Scott, 1820, p. 3). In the comedy *The London Chanticleers,* 1659, Scene III, Ditty sings a ballad parodying "The Reuolted Louer." In D'Urfey's *The Fool Turn'd Critick,* 1678, IV, ii, "Maiden fair" is named as a fine old tune, as contrasted with the "lowsy lamentable" airs in current vogue.

Aston's *The Fool's Opera,* c. 1730, is the one ballad opera calling for the tune, but the printed copy contains no music.

One Night When All the Village Slept, or Martellus

This tune takes its names from a song by Sir Carr Scrope introduced into Nathaniel Lee's tragedy, *Mithridates, King of Pontus,* 1678, IV, i. A wretched contemporary setting by Louis Grabu was published in *Choice Ayres and Songs,* Third Book, 1681, p. 1 (Fig. 355). An ornate

but very singable air is provided for the text in Watts's *Musical Miscellany*, 1729–1731, II, 42 (Fig. 356), and in *The Merry Musician*, c.

1731, III, 166. Still another tune, entitled "One Night, when all the Village slept," is found in Lillo's ballad opera *Silvia*, 1731, Air 49 (Fig. 357). Yet a fourth, by James Oswald, was printed in *Gentleman's Maga-*

zine, XXV (Aug., 1755), 371, and reprinted in Ritson's *English Songs*, 1783, I, 69; a fifth is found in Edward Miller's *A Collection of New English Songs*, c. 1755, No. 3.[1] We are concerned here only with the

[1] The words of Scrope's song may be found also in *Tixall Poetry*, ed. Arthur Clifford, 1813, p. 185, from a late seventeenth-century MS; and in *The Hive*, 3d ed., 1727, II, 138.

first three tunes, of which the first is scarcely singable and the origins of the second and third are unknown. The second is in 6/8 time and the ballad-opera tune is in common time, but there are a few points of similarity to suggest that both may derive from a melody now lost to us.

Two broadside amplifications of Scrope's text have been preserved: one entitled "The Mournful Lovers Last Farewel. Or, Martellus and Selindra's fates," to the tune of "One night when all the Village slept, Or, Young Phæon" (Douce II, 157ᵛ), and "The Dying Lovers last Farwel: Or, the Tragical downfal of Martellus and Arminda," to the tune of "Stone walls cannot a Prison make. Or, Young Pheon" (Pepys III, 8, Lord Crawford 986, 987; reprinted in *A Collection of Old Ballads*, 1723–1725, III, 211).[2]

Two ballads which can be sung to "Martellus" name it as one of the suitable tunes: "Advice to Batchelors, or, The Married Mans Lamentation," beginning "You Batchelors that single are," to the tune of "Hey boys up go we; busie fame; Martellus; Or, Jenny Gin" (Pepys, Harvard, Roxburghe; reprinted in *RB* III, 376), and "The Unhappy Marriage, or, A Warning to Covetous Parents," beginning "Jenny she was a Wanton Girl," to the tune of "Jenny was a Wanton Lass; Or, Martellus" (Wood E.25 [76]). The "Jenny" tune title seems to be internally inspired and does not imply an independent melody.

Only Tell Her

This tune takes its name from the opening line of some verses by John Cutts, first published in his *Poetical Exercises*, 1687, p. 58. They appear with music in Robert King's *Songs for One Two and Three Voices*, c. 1690, p. ii. The song in its broadside form is entitled "The Modest Batchelor; And, The Beautiful Virgin. Sett to a Pleasant New Tune" and different music (Fig. 358) is printed on the sheet (Pepys III, 89). "Only tell her" is named as the tune for "The Frantick Shepherd:

2 "Stone Walls cannot a Prison make" is also named as the tune for a ballad "Written by J. Taylor, a Singer of Israel, Prisoner in the Kings Bench." Its title is "New Verses concerning the Plot, Londons Fire, & Godfreys Murder . . . ," 1680, and it begins "Give ear, O King, and Nobles all" (Harvard, Huntington, BM Luttrell; reprinted in *RB* IV, 153). I have found no tune so named; but see "When love with unconfined wings."

358

or, Floromello's Matchless Cruelty," beginning "Must I wear the wreath of willow" (Pepys V, 352, with meaningless music).

O'er Boggy

The Roxburghe collection contains an undated eighteenth-century broadside "To its own proper New Tune" called "An excellent new Song, lately composed, entituled I'le o're Bogie we him," beginning "All Batchelers and Lasses" (reprinted in *RB* VIII, 721, 871). The title comes from the refrain:

> I'll o're Bogie we my Love,
> I'll o're Bogie we him,
> And all my Kine had Sworn and said
> I'll o're Bogie we him.

Allan Ramsay wrote a version of "O'er Bogie" which has nothing in common with the broadside; its refrain begins "I Will awa' wi' my Love,/ I will awa' wi' her" (*Poems*, 1721; reprinted in *Tea-Table Miscellany*, 1723, p. 125); the tune is in Alexander Stuart's *Musick for Allan Ramsay's . . . Scots Songs*, c. 1725, p. 126 (Fig. 359). The Ramsay text, with refrain "I'll o'er Boggie, o'er Scroggie,/O'er Boggie wi'er . . ." appears with music in Thomson's *Orpheus Caledonius*, 1725, No. 47; Watts's *Musical Miscellany*, 1729–1731, V, 60; *The Merry Musician*, c. 1731, III, 11; and Johnson's *Scots Musical Museum*, 1787–1803, II, 175. Both refrain forms are to be found in the initial stanza of "an old silly song" which may or may not antedate Ramsay, and which Stenhouse reprints in his note to the *Museum* text. Stenhouse also calls attention to an early example of

359

the tune in Mrs. Crockat's MS music book of 1709, now presumed lost. The Julian Marshall collection at Harvard contains an early eighteenth-century engraved song sheet of "O'er Boggie" which closely follows the *Orpheus Caledonius* version.

The tune was used in at least five ballad operas, including Ramsay's *The Gentle Shepherd*, 1730 (music in 1786 ed.), Mitchell's *The Highland Fair*, 1731, and Gay's *Achilles*, 1733. In *The Cobler of Preston*, 1732, the tune is called "O're Scroggy, o're Boggy," from the songbook version of the refrain.

If Ebsworth's conjectured date of c. 1708 for the broadside be correct, Ramsay could have done no more than retouch a text already in circulation; it is more likely that the broadside dates from the 1720s, when the song was current in other media.

Over the Hills and Far Away

This tune takes its name from the refrain " 'Tis o'er the Hills, and far away [thrice],/The Wind has blown my Plad away" of "Jockey's Lamentation," a song beginning "Jockey met with Jenny fair." [1] Its earliest publication appears to be in *Pills*, 1706, IV, 99 (1719–1720, V, 316), with music (Fig. 360). A version in Scots dialect was reprinted in Allan Ramsay's *Tea-Table Miscellany*, 1733, II, 192, as an old song, and the

[1] The refrain is evidently a reworking and modernization of that in Child No. 2 A, reprinted from a broadside of c. 1670 with which it otherwise has no relationship:

My plaid awa, my plaid awa,
And ore the hill and far awa,
And far awa to Norrowa,
My plaid shall not be blown awa.

360

Ramsay text is the basis for that found with music in Johnson's *The Scots Musical Museum*, 1787–1803, I, 62. Another song to the tune found in the 1706 *Pills* is "The Recruiting Officer; Or, The Merry Volunteers," beginning "Hark! now the Drums beat up again," with "Over the hills and far away" occurring in the fourth and eighth line of every stanza (1719–1720, V, 319).[2]

As "My plaid away" the tune is found in the Margaret Sinkler MS, 1710, No. 18 (reversed). Its first appearance in *The Dancing Master* is in volume II, 2d ed., 1714, where it is called " 'Twas o'er the Hills." In Walsh's *Compleat Country Dancing-Master*, 1719, II, 74, it is "Over the Hills and far away." Under the same title the music is found with "The Queen of May. By Mr. W. Bedingfield" in Watts's *Musical Miscellany*, 1729–1731, III, 192, and in Walsh's *British Musical Miscellany*, 1734–1736, II, 65.

Music is printed on several eighteenth-century single-sheet songs, of which the earliest is D'Urfey's "The Hubble Bubbles," written in the speculative atmosphere surrounding the disastrous South Sea promotion. A number of editions exist, some beginning "Ye Circum and Uncircum-cis'd/come hear my Song, and be advis'd" (BM H.1601 [542], Harvard; an edition dated 1720, without music, is BM 1876.f.1 [90]); another version begins "Jews, Turks, and Christians, hear my Song" (Harvard, without music). Two Jacobite ballads from the '45 campaign appeared

---

[2] Farquhar's play *The Recruiting Officer*, which was first produced in April, 1706, uses the refrain and stanzas 10 and 12 of the *Pills* song. The latter may have been written shortly before the play or vice versa; but in any case it would appear that "Jockey's Lamentation" antedates Farquhar's play. Ebsworth (*RB* VIII, 292) traces "Jockey's Lamentation" to D'Urfey's comedy *The Campaigners*, 1698; he has evidently confused it with "Jockey was a dowdy Lad," which is in the play. I have not been able to discover any evidence that Peter Motteux had a hand in either song.

as single-sheet songs with music: "A Loyal Song. Sung by Mr. Beard at the Theatre Royal in Covent Garden," beginning "From Barren Caledonian Lands,/Where Famine uncontrould commands" (BM G.316.d [133], Harvard; another issue, without music, BM 1876.f.1 [133]); and "The Duke's Defeat of yᵉ Rebels," beginning "Come, my boys, let's drink and sing/Success to George our Sovereign King" (BM I.530 [32], Harvard). A roman-letter broadside on the coronation of Queen Anne, "The Scotch Lord's Welcome to England," begins "Come let us joyful Anthems raise"; the sheet contains no music, but the tune direction is "Over the Hills, and far away" (Lord Crawford 254).

The tune was introduced into ten ballad operas, of which the following contain the music: John Gay's *The Beggar's Opera*, 1728; Ralph's *The Fashionable Lady* and Cibber's *Patie and Peggy*, 1730; Coffey's *The Devil to Pay*, 1731; Kelly's *The Plot*, 1735. "The Original Medley Overture" composed by John Frederick Lampe for the pantomime *Columbine Courtezan*, 1735, includes the tune. And much later it was one of the melodies arranged by Haydn (to verses beginning "O how can my poor heart be glad") in George Thomson's *Select Collection of Original Scottish Airs*, 1805, IV, 161. The air may not be natively Scotch, but the Northern cast of the original words, and especially their "domestication" by Ramsay, must have contributed to the vogue of the song in Scotland. There the tune has persisted in tradition into recent times, for a version collected in 1906 is among the Gavin Greig MSS (reprinted with other eighteenth- and nineteenth-century analogues in B. H. Bronson, *The Traditional Tunes of the Child Ballads*, 1959–   , I, 14–16).

The Oxfordshire Tragedy

A late seventeenth-century broadside "The Constant Lady and False-hearted Squire . . . To a New Tune," beginning "Near Woodstock town in Oxfordshire,/as I walk'd forth to take the air" (Pepys V, 285; reprinted in *RB* VIII, 635) was known in eighteenth-century editions as "The Oxfordshire Tragedy: Or, The Death of Four Lovers" (Lord Crawford 865, Chetham 303, Douce III, 70ᵛ). Music for the broadside is preserved in several ballad operas: in Johnson's *The Village Opera*, 1729, Air 41 (Fig. 361), and Ryan's *The Cobler's Opera*, 1729, where it is named "Near Woodstock town in Oxfordshire"; in Lillo's *Silvia*, 1731, where it is "The Oxfordshire Tragedy"; and in Hippisley's *A Sequel to the Opera of*

361

Flora, 1732, without title. The tune is incorrectly barred, except in *The Village Opera.*

Another eighteenth-century piece was "The Oxfordshire Tragedy: Or, The Virgin's Advice," beginning "Young virgins fair, of beauty bright" (Williams College, Roxburghe; reprinted in *RB* VIII, 68, 175); it has no tune direction or stanza division, but its octosyllabics would allow it to be sung to the tune. *The Cruel Parents Garland,* n.d., contains "The Cruel Parents; or, The two faithful Lovers," beginning "My only Love my dearest Dear," to the tune of "The Oxfordshire Lady" (BM 11621.c.3 [34]); it too could be sung to the tune.[1]

Chappell tentatively associated the tune of "The Oxfordshire Tragedy" with two ballads whose tune direction is "As I went [*or* walkt] forth to take the air," since this phraseology corresponds to the second line of the "Oxfordshire" ballad. A stronger linkage, however, can be made with a seventeenth-century broadside, "True Love Rewarded with Loyalty," which begins "As I walk'd forth to take the Air" (*RB* VI, 260); this ballad is to be sung to "O hark, or Flora's Farewell," airs which have not survived.

Ebsworth (*RB* VIII, 629) erroneously associates the tune of "The Oxfordshire Tragedy" with "The Berkshire Tragedy, or the Wittam Miller," an eighteenth-century ballad having no tune direction. It is a close analogue of "The Oxford Girl," which perhaps explains Ebsworth's confusion. But "The Oxford Girl" and "The Oxfordshire Tragedy" are unrelated in either content or stanza pattern.

Packington's Pound

This is the most popular single tune associated with ballads before 1700. Its vogue began in the days of Queen Elizabeth, with whom Sir

---

[1] I have not found "The unfortunate Sailor's Garland," an eighteenth-century piece said to call for the tune of "The Oxfordshire Tragedy" (Chappell, *PMOT* I, 191).

John Pakington was a great favorite,[1] and at least one ballad and one version of the tune have been preserved from the sixteenth century. By the end of the next century more than a hundred ballads had employed the tune under one or another of its names (the next most popular being "Fortune my foe" with about ninety, and "Greensleeves," including its short form "Which nobody can deny," with about eighty). There was almost no letup in its popularity during the first half of the eighteenth century, and its disappearance on ballads coincides with the disappearance of tune titles generally. Although popular taste is notoriously whimsical, "Packington's Pound" is an excellent tune, easily singable, memorable without being monotonous. Like "Lilliburlero," it calls for a long stanza, but the anapestic rhythm is fluid and the movement rapid, even when the tune is sung slowly.

The earliest appearance of the music is in William Barley's *A New Booke of Tabliture*, 1596, Part II, sig. C4^v, where it is "Bockingtons Pound," set for the orpharion by Francis Cutting (Fig. 362). Keyboard arrangements are in *The Fitzwilliam Virginal Book* II, 234, in Paris Conservatoire MS Rés. 1186, fol. 101, and in Benjamin Cosyn's MS Virginal Book, p. 46. It is set for the lyra viol in Cambridge University MS Nn.6.36, fol. 21, and the melody appears in one Continental collection, J. J. Starter's *Friesche Lust-Hof*, 1621, p. 10 (Fig. 363). It is printed four times in *180 Loyal Songs* (Fig. 364), where thirteen ballads are sung to it, and five times in the 1719–1720 *Pills*, where it serves for twelve ballads and songs. Several broadsides contain the music: "The Praise of the Dairy-Maid," 1683, beginning "Let Wine turn a Spark, and Ale huff like a Hector" (Bodleian Ashmole G.15 [166]; reprinted with music in *The Second Book of the Pleasant Musical Companion*, 2d ed., 1686, Part II, No. 24; the words are found also in *180 Loyal Songs*, p. 58, and in *Pills* III, 6); "The Whigs hard Hea[rt for] The Cause of this hard Frost," 1683/84, beginning "Ye Whigs and Dissenters, I charge you attend," sung to the tune of "Oh London! Th'adst better have built new Bordello's" (Bodleian Ashmole G.15 [160], Clark; reprinted in *180 Loyal Songs*, p. 56,

---

[1] Other Packingtons have been suggested. J. F. R. Stainer (*Musical Times*, XLVII [1906], 243–244) advanced the name of an earlier Sir John Packington, great uncle of Queen Elizabeth's favorite; he died in 1560 and his name might have been associated with the tune title because he was instrumental in walling up the fourth side of the Inner Temple Gardens. W. H. Grattan Flood (*Musical Times*, LXVI [1925], 347) proposed the name of Thomas Paginton, a court musician at the coronation of Edward VI and Elizabeth, who lived until 1586 and was mentioned in contemporary livery warrants (see H. C. de Lafontaine, *The King's Musick*, 1909). Flood contended that the tune was composed by Paginton about 1560 and is properly referred to as "round," not "pound." The tune is, of course, not a round, even though it is so called on two broadsides noticed here.

362

and *RB* V, 461, where the tune is named "Packington's pound"); [2] "A New Song upon The Council of Six," 1689, beginning " 'Twere a Folly, if ever the Whiggs should endeavour" (Harvard); and "The Cloak's Knavery," beginning "Come buy my New Ballad," which is usually found with music of "From hunger and cold," q.v. (Roxburghe, a copy with engraved music, the text reprinted in *RB* IV, 605; in *Pills* III, 1, it is also coupled with music of "Packington's Pound").[3]

Perhaps the earliest broadside set to the tune is "A new ballade, shew-inge the cruell robberies and lewde lyfe of Phillip Collins alias Osburne . . . prest to death at newgate . . . 1597," beginning "There was a proud Banker, a theefe by his traide," to the tune of "Pagginton's rounde" (*SB,* p. 130). Since the Shirburn MS is believed to have been compiled from

2 "Oh London! . . ." is the refrain of Alexander Radcliffe's song upon the monu-ment erected in memory of the Great Fire. He included it in *The Ramble,* 1682, p. 45, and a copy of the song, called "Upon the Pyramid," is preserved in Harvard MS Eng. 636F, c. 1680, pp. 159–161. The version in *Pills* IV, 23, has the same title and is sung to the music of "Packington's Pound."

3 Portions of the air are found on the Pepys copy of "The Thankful Country Lass . . . Tune of, I am so sick of Love" (see "Aye, marry, and thank you too"), for which "Packington's Pound" could not possibly serve. The printer evidently took advantage of his customers' credulity in a period when so many ballad sheets con-tained meaningless music.

363

Original is unbarred.

broadsides by c. 1616, it is possible that this text represents a contemporary issue, although no license of the ballad appears in the Stationers' Register until 1631. No printed copies are known. The form of the tune name is identical in "The historie of the Prophet Ionas," c. 1615, beginning "Vnto the Prophet Ionas I read,/The word of the Lord secretly came" (Pepys; reprinted in *PG*, p. 66).

364

Original is a third higher.
* Original contains an excrescent quarter-note (E♭, i.e., G) following the cadence note.

Ben Jonson wrote a ballad to "Paggingtons Pound" which is sung by Nightingale in his *Bartholomew Fair,* 1614, III, v. It begins "My masters and friends, and good people draw neere/And looke to your purses, for that I doe say," and its refrain becomes important in the subsequent history of the tune:

> Youth, youth, thou hadst better bin staru'd by thy Nurse,
> Then liue to be hanged for cutting a purse.

The ballad, often called "The Cutpurse," was reprinted in *Wit and Drollery,* 1661, and in *Pills* IV, 20; an expanded version was published as an early Restoration broadside with the title "A Caveat for Cut-purses" (Roxburghe; reprinted in *RB* III, 492). "A Ballad on Sʳ Rob. Payton 1680," also called "Payton's fall," exists in several manuscript copies, one of which gives the tune as "Youth youth in Bartholmew faire," and the refrain "Oh Payton thou hadst better been hang'd at the Gallows . . ." suggests its relationship to Jonson's ballad (BM MS Harl. 7319, p. 113, BM MS Add. 23722, fol. 65, Bodleian MS Ashmole 36–37, fol. 299). "A Gentle Ballad call'd Lamentable Lory. 1684" names the tune "Youth, youth &c." in one copy and "Packingtons Pounde" in another (BM MS Harl. 7319, p. 331, BM MS Harl. 6914, fol. 40, Bodleian MS Ashmole 36–37, fol. 321). "Vox Clero, Lil-ly bur-le-ro, or, The Second Part of a merry New Ballad" [c. 1690], beginning "Canonical Black-Coats, like Birds of a Feather," is to the tune "Youth, youth, thou hadst &c." (Chetham 1156, Lord Crawford 203, Harvard, Yale, Huntington). And there are songs in *Folly in Print,* 1667, p. 101, *The Muses Farewel to Popery and Slavery,* 1689, Supplement, p. 6, and *Political Merriment,* 1714, p. 28, which name the tune from Jonson's refrain. A mutilated ballad of c. 1725 on medical ethics, doctors' charges, and the like, beginning "The Physicians of late/Held a Learned Debate," has as its tune title "You Cut Purses all, &c." (BM 1890.e.5 [241])—not merely a symbolic phrase, but also an echo of Jonson's closing stanza.

The tune of "4 able Phisitians are lately come down" is named for singing "Lady Fretchwell's Song of the Wives," beginning "You Scribblers that writt of Widdows and Maids" (BM MS Harl. 6913, p. 287, BM MS Harl. 7319, p. 193, the latter dated 1682). This tune title is derived from lines of "The Tunbridge Doctors":

> For from London-Town
> There's lately come down,
> Four Able Physicians
> That never wore Gown,

printed in *Pills* IV, 162, with music of "Packington's Pound"; the song, beginning "You Maidens and Wives,/And young Widows rejoyce," had appeared in *The New Academy of Complements*, 1669, and in *Wit and Drollery*, 1682, without music or tune direction.

Two other tune titles which may be related to "Packington's Pound" deserve notice. "A New Ballad, to the Tune of, Good People give ear, while a Story I tell,/Of Twenty black Tradesmen were brought up in Hell, &c., Or, Packington's Pound" was written during the 1680s and begins "To our once Loyal Town, is lately come down,/Such an Hodge-podge of Benchers, as never wore Gown" (BM C.20.f.2 [318], BM Luttrell II, 13, Lord Crawford 1197, Library of Congress). The poetical tune title here is drawn, as might be expected, from the opening lines of another ballad. Published before 1675, it is entitled "Here's twenty sworn brethren, Trades-men all . . . twenty several Callings that belong to Gentlemen Theeves," sung to "a pleasant new Tune" (Rawlinson 37); the ballad, without tune direction, is called "The Jovial Crew" in *Wit and Drollery*, 1682, p. 71. Although this piece could be sung to "Packington," evidence is lacking to tie it unmistakably to that tune. A more curious piece is "The Happy Return of the Old Dutch Miller," 1682, beginning "Good People of England, I hope you have had," to the tune of "The First" (Wood 417 [84], Wood 276a [549], Chetham 165, Lord Crawford 459, Harvard); this ballad was reprinted with the same tune direction in *180 Loyal Songs*, p. 257, but with music of "Hey, boys, up go we," which does not fit. It may be conjectured from the opening line and from the stanza pattern that the ballad was intended for "Packington's Pound"; a possible explanation of "The First" is suggested in the opening stanza, where "I am the Miller that was here before" implies a previous ballad.

Most of the fifteen or twenty alternative tunes named along with "Packington's Pound" on seventeenth-century broadsides are familiar enough; indeed, virtually every tune associated with anapestic tetrameter octaves can be found linked with "Packington." As we have seen, many of the alternative names are derivative and do not refer to independent tunes. One other such is found in Thomas Lanfiere's "A caveat for a bad husband Or, The Good Fellows Warning-Piece," beginning "Come all you good fellows wherever you dwell" (Rawlinson 155); the second tune name, "the World is grown hard," comes from the refrain of several stanzas of this ballad and probably does not refer to a new melody. Likewise "Timothy Dash the Scriveners Apprentice," which is the second tune named in "The Protestant Cuckold . . . how B. H. the Protestant-News-forger . . . caught his beloved Wife Ruth in ill Circumstances," 1681, is in reference to the man implicated in Benjamin Harris's cuckoldry and is probably not intended to be taken seriously as a tune name (Wood 417 [58], Lord Crawford 1175, Huntington, Harvard).[4] The second tune of

4 A facsimile of this ballad is in Worthington C. Ford, *The Boston Book Market*, *1679–1700*, 1917, facing p. 162.

"The Lawyers Demurrer Argued," 1681, is "The Round-Head Reviv'd" (BM 1872.a.1 [99ᵛ], Bodleian Ashmole G.16 [89], Huntington, Harvard), on which I have no information; it is probably the title of another ballad, but I have not encountered it.

There is almost no limit to the variety of subjects treated in "Packington's Pound" ballads, and because their number is overwhelming, it is unnecessary to swell this discussion with wholesale citations. Specimens are in all the great ballad collections; scarcely any of the songbooks of the late seventeenth and early eighteenth century fail to include political or amatory pieces to the tune; and modern reprints of broadsides are full of examples.

A half-dozen ballad operas introduce the tune, including Gay's *The Beggar's Opera*, 1728, Hippisley's *A Sequel to the Opera of Flora*, 1732, and Phillips's *The Mock Lawyer*, 1733, which reprint the music.

Peg a Ramsey, or Peggy Ramsey

This tune is found in William Ballet's Lute Book, p. 26 (Fig. 365); in Cambridge University MS Dd.6.48, fol. 13, for lyra viol, and in a viola

365

da gamba setting called "Pigges of Rumsey" in a seventeenth-century manuscript preserved in the Henry Watson music collection of the Manchester Free Reference Library. The Clement Matchett MS Virginal Book, 1612, No. 11 (ed. Thurston Dart, 1957, No. 7), is an arrangement of "Pegge Ramsey," a variant of the Bull keyboard setting in Paris Conservatoire MS Rés. 1186, fol. 122 (Fig. 366); another set of variations is in Paris MS Rés. 1185, No. 28. Some fragments of the tune occur in BM MS Add. 18936, fol. 58ᵛ (after 1612), in an untitled medley by William Cobbold, with the following words:

Little pegg of Ramsey
wᵗʰ yᵉ yellow hayre,

       & couldst thou greet if I were dead,
        marye would I feare. . . .

Another song, beginning "Bonny Peggy Ramsey that any Man may see,"
is printed in *Pills,* 1719–1720, V, 139, with the music of "London is a
fine town."

366

* Ten variations follow in the original.

Ballads to the tune include "An excellent merye songe of the freier and
the boye," beginning "In reading merry memoryes,/it was my chaunce
to finde" (*SB,* p. 153), which is probably taken from a late sixteenth-
century broadside, since the ballad was licensed in 1586, about the time
the compiler of the Shirburn MS is thought to have begun his transcriptions. "A merry jest of John Tomson, and Jakaman his wife," by M. L.,
beginning "When I was a Batchelour/I liv'd a merry life," also licensed
in 1586, is to the tune (Roxburghe, an edition of c. 1635, reprinted in
RB II, 137).[1] Burton's *Anatomy of Melancholy,* 1621 (ed. Floyd Dell and
Paul Jordan-Smith, 1927, p. 789), has an allusion to "Give me my yellow
hose again," a line from the burden of the ballad. Charles Blount's political squib of 1679, "The Sale of Esau's Birth-right: Or, The New Buckingham Ballad," beginning "A Wondrous Tale I will relate," is to the
tune of "The London Gentlewoman, or Little Peggey Ramsey" (Lord
Crawford, BM C.20.f.2, Wood 417, Bodleian Ashmole G.16, Harvard,
Huntington, Bagford; reprinted in *BB* II, 764).[2]

In *Twelfth Night,* II, iii, Sir Toby calls Malvolio a Peg-a-Ramsey in a
speech full of musical allusions. The seventeenth-century play *The Partiall Law,* II, iv, mentions "Peggy Ramsey" as a dance tune, and in a poem
"The Shepheards Holy-day" the tune is one of a number named as suitable for country dancing (*Wit's Recreations,* 1667, sig. U7–U7ᵛ). Despite
the fact that it had some seventeenth-century vogue, "Peg a Ramsey" does
not appear in *The Dancing Master,* an indication that its popularity had
waned by mid-century.

   [1] "When I was a Bachelor," arranged for voice by Harold Gregory, was published
in London in 1904. It uses the "Peg a Ramsey" music and three stanzas of the ballad.
A 1905 edition added a recitative opening with unrelated words and music (BM
H.1794.h [48], [50]).
   [2] For the first tune, see "The Hemp-dresser."

Peg and the Soldier, or
Peggy's Gone Over Sea with the Soldier

The tune "Peggie is over Ye Sie wi' ye Souldier" is found in the Skene MS (*Ancient Scotish Melodies,* ed. Dauney, p. 217), dating probably from the late seventeenth century (Fig. 367).

367

Tablature is unbarred and contains no time values. I have lowered pitch of Dauney's transcript a fourth and emended his disposition of notes in measures 7 and 8.

The tune takes its names from "A new Ballad of the Souldier and Peggy, To a new Northerne Tune," beginning "It was a brave Souldier/that long liv'd in warres" (Roxburghe, an edition of c. 1640, reprinted in *RB* II, 476; later copies are Euing 243, 244, Douce II, 208, 209ᵛ, Pepys IV, 151, Harvard). The tune is called "Peggy went over Sea with a Souldier" in Richard Climsell's "Constant, faire, and fine Betty," c. 1635, beginning "Now of my sweet Bettie" (Roxburghe; reprinted in *RB* I, 207).

To the tune of "Pegg and the Soldier" is sung "The Love-sick Blacksmith," beginning "Near Old Gravel-lane, a Widower does dwell" (Pepys V, 276). "The Nightingales Song; Or the Souldiers rare Musick," beginning "As I went forth/one Sun-shining day," is to the tune of "No, no, not I; or, Peggy and the Souldier" (Pepys; reprinted in *RB* VIII, clxx*; other editions in Douce II, 166ᵛ, Rawlinson 67).[1] At least two

[1] The first tune does not appear to have survived; it was also used for Richard Climsell's "A Warning for Maides" (*RB* III, 42), licensed in 1636. Both "The Souldier

black-letter ballads were sung to "The Nightingale's Song," though we cannot be sure whether one or both of the tunes named on the ballad of that title would have been used: "The Dairy Maid's Tragedy," beginning "As I through a Meadow one Morning did pass" (Pepys III, 320); and "An Answer to the Dairy Maid's Tragedy," beginning "The Dairy-maid's Tragedy when I beheld" (Pepys III, 321). Some eighteenth-century issues of "The Gosport Tragedy" include the tune direction "Peggy's gone over Sea"; others are without tune direction (Lord Crawford, Madden, Chetham, Harvard, Roxburghe; reprinted in *RB* VIII, 143, 173).

In all these ballads the stanza is an anapestic tetrameter quatrain, which distinguishes it from the irregular octave found in "The Valiant Trooper and pritty Peggy"; that ballad and its offshoots are discussed under "I live not where I love," q.v.

Peggy, I Must Love Thee

This air is first found in *Apollo's Banquet,* 5th ed., 1687, Part III, No. 5, as "A Scotch Tune in fashion" (Fig. 368). In *The Second Part of*

368

Musick's Hand-maid, 1689, sig. C1, a keyboard setting entitled "A New Scotch Tune" is credited to Henry Purcell. With the latter title it appears in *Apollo's Banquet,* 6th ed., 1690, and also in the Second Book of that work, 1691. In *Youth's Delight on the Flagelet,* 9th ed., c. 1690, the tune is called "Billy was as blith a lad" (no relation to "Willy was so blith a

and Peggy" and "The Nightingales Song" have survived in tradition on both sides of the water. For references to texts and tunes, see G. Malcolm Laws, *American Balladry from British Broadsides,* 1957, P 13, P 14.

Lad," *Choice Ayres,* 1676, p. 76). It appears untitled in all editions of *Pills,* 1719–1720, II, 148, III, 112. In the Margaret Sinkler MS, 1710, No. 32 (National Library of Scotland), it is called "Magie I most love thee," and in Alexander Stuart's compilation of *Musick for Allan Ramsay's Collection of Scots Songs,* c. 1725, p. 104, it is "Peggie I must love thee." This name of the tune is given for singing one of Ramsay's own poems in *The Tea-Table Miscellany,* 1723, p. 102, 1733, I, 56, beginning "As from a Rock past all Relief." This song is found with the music in Thomson's *Orpheus Caledonius,* 1725, No. 29, in Watts's *Musical Miscellany,* 1729–1731, II, 78, and in *Calliope, or English Harmony,* 1739–1746, I, 88; the words alone are in several poetical miscellanies.[1]

The tune appears without title on an engraved broadside, "A New song on the Calling of a free Parliament. January 15th. 1688/9," beginning "A Parliament with one Consent/is all the Cry O th' Nation" (Lord Crawford 994). It is not certain that any other broadside was sung to "Peggy I must love thee." The two *Pills* songs which use the tune had earlier been published in expanded form as broadsides, but the sheets contain ambiguous tune directions, and it may be that the coupling of tune to text in *Pills* is arbitrary. One is "The Scotch Lad's Moan. Or, Pretty Moggies Unkindness. To an excellent New Scotch Tune," beginning "A Lad o' th' Town that made his moan," issued 1685–1688 with corrupt musical text (Pepys, Lord Crawford, Harvard, Roxburghe; reprinted in *RB* VII, 364); this is an amplification of a three-stanza poem by Thomas D'Urfey, found in his *New Poems,* 1690, and in *Pills* II, 148. The other broadside, "Tom and Will. or, The Shepherds Sheepfold. To a Pleasant new Country Tune," beginning "Tom and Will were Shepherds Swains" (Douce, Pepys, Roxburghe; reprinted in *RB* VII, 257), is based upon a poem first printed anonymously in *Sportive Wit,* 1656, and subsequently attributed to Sidney Godolphin (d. 1643). It was reprinted in several drolleries before being included in the first volume of *Pills,* 1699 (1719–1720, III, 112).

Another after-the-fact association with the tune appears on the Roxburghe copy of "My Wife will be my master," where the printed tune direction "A Taylour is no man" is supplemented by a MS notation:

---

[1] It is possible that Ramsay worked over an older poem, for "A New Song . . . The Words by Mr. Ramondon, Senior," to the tune "Peggie I must love thee" (BM 1871.e.9 [179], without music), is no later than c. 1720, when Lewis Ramondon died or became inactive. Moreover, another poem in the *Tea-Table,* 1723, p. 143, 1733, I, 76, signed "C" (Robert Crawford?), is to the tune "Peggy, I must love thee," and lines 8 and 32 contain these words as a burden. There is the additional bit of evidence in the name given the music in the Sinkler MS, suggesting that a poem on Margaret (whence the names Maggie or Peggy) was in circulation by c. 1710.

"Tune Pigie I most love thee." The ballad can, in fact, be sung to the latter tune (Roxburghe, reprinted in *RB* VII, 188).[2]

"Peggy I must love thee" was introduced into three ballad operas, including *The Jovial Crew* and Mitchell's *The Highland Fair,* 1731, which print the music.

Pepper Is Black

This tune is found in *The Dancing Master,* 1651–1690, and in a mid-seventeenth-century keyboard setting entitled "Pepper" in Paris Conservatoire MS Rés. 1186, fol. 17 (Fig. 369). It was named by William

369

Elderton for singing "A Ballad intituled, Prepare ye to the plowe," beginning "Looke vp, my Lordes, and marke my wordes," licensed in 1569–1570 (BM Huth; reprinted in *A Collection of Seventy-Nine Black-Letter Ballads,* 1867, p. 174). "Pepper is black" is one of a number of dance tunes alluded to in Nashe's *Have With You to Saffron-Walden,* 1596, along with "Rogero," "Greensleeves," and "Peg a Ramsey."

Phil. Porter's Dream

"Porters Dream" is among the "Select New Tunes and Jiggs for the Treble-Violin" inserted at the end of *The Dancing Master,* 3d ed., c. 1662,

---

2 "A Tailor is a man," the usual form of the tune name, is used also for Laurence Price's "The Maydens of Londons brave adventures" (*RB* VII, 491), but no music appears to have survived for it.

370:3-

No. 54 (Fig. 370), 1665, No. 28. I have found no broadsides that call for
the tune, but a song in *Westminster Drollery,* 1672, II, 112, entitled "The
beneficial wedding," beginning "And I have a mind to be marry'd," is
directed to be sung to "Phil. Porters dreame" and fits the *Dancing Master*
music.

A different tune is "Phill. Porters Lamentation" found in Elizabeth
Rogers's MS Virginal Book (before 1656). "Phil. Porter's Farewel," a song
appearing first in *The Mysteries of Love and Eloquence,* 1658, is reprinted
in *Pills,* 1719–1720, IV, 4, with the music of "Chevy Chase." It cannot be
sung to the *Dancing Master* tune.

Phillida Flouts Me

An early seventeenth-century keyboard arrangement of "Filliday
floutes me" is found in Benjamin Cosyn's MS Virginal Book, p. 64 (published in *Twenty-five Pieces . . . from Benjamin Cosyn's Virginal Book,*
ed. Fuller-Maitland and Barclay Squire, 1923, p. 22). Another seventeenth-century set of keyboard variations is entitled "Phillida" in Paris
Conservatoire MS Rés. 1186, fol. 105ᵛ (Fig. 371). Thomas Jordan printed
an unembellished version of the tune (Fig. 372) to which he set two songs
in the civic pageant *London's Glory,* 1680.[1] The ballad whose burden

[1] The first is "The Protestants Exortation," the second "The plotting Papists
Litany." The latter is reprinted in *RB* IV, 211.

371

* Three variations follow in original.

372

gives the tune its name dates from c. 1600. An early edition preserved in the Shirburn MS is titled "A prettye sonnet of the disdainefull sheppeardesse," beginning "O what a plague is love!/how shall I beare it?" to the tune of "Dainty come thow to me" (*SB*, p. 297).[2] A broadside version of c. 1650, omitting six Shirburn stanzas and adding three new ones, is "Phillida flouts me. Or, the Country Lovers Complaint," to the tune of "Phillida flouts me" (Roxburghe; reprinted in *RB* VI, 461). A still different version is in Mennes and Smith's *Wit Restor'd*, 1658, p. 164, beginning "Oh! what a pain is love" and without tune direction. Eighteenth-century texts with music (Fig. 373) are found in single-sheet editions of "The Jealous Swain. To be Answer'd by Mr. A. Bradley" (BM G.305 [16], Harvard), along with Bradley's "Answer" to the same music (BM G.305 [17]). Both poems are in *The Hive*, 3d ed., 1727, II, 271, 274, without music, and in Watts's *Musical Miscellany*, 1729–1731, II, 132, 136, with music.[3] The "Answer" is reprinted in *RB* VI, 463.

[2] Ballads to this popular lost tune are uniformly in a different meter from those to "Phillida"; hence there appears to be a mistake in directing the Shirburn ballad to be sung to "Dainty come thou to me."

[3] Both eighteenth-century musical texts cited alter the earlier barring and shift the accents from two (6/4) to three (3/2) per measure.

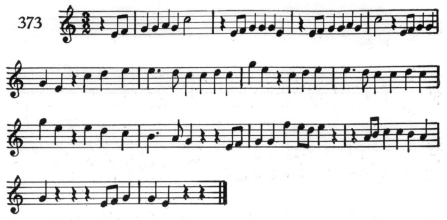

373

Transposed from key of D.

The tune is cited for singing a song beginning "Come to me pritty Lasse./and Harken to my Plainte" in the recently discovered jig *Michael and Frances* [1601] (C. J. Sisson, *Lost Plays of Shakespeare's Age*, 1936, p. 135). Johnson's *A Crown Garland of Golden Roses*, 1612 (ed. Chappell, 1842, p. 32), includes "A short and sweet sonnet . . . upon the death of Queene Elizabeth . . . To a new Tune, or Phillida flouts me"; it begins "Gone is Elizabeth,/Whom we have lov'd so deare," but its twenty-line stanza cannot be sung to "Phillida" (designed for twelve lines) without inordinate repetition of motifs already repeated. A ballad of c. 1625, called "No body loues mee," beginning "Now all my mony is gone, how should I swagger?" is directed to "Philliday" (Pepys; reprinted in *PB* II, 31); the second part, to "Dainty come thou to me," is an independent composition unrelated to the first part. Patrick Cary wrote a song to "Phillida flouts me," beginning "Ned! she that likes thee now" (*Trivial Poems* [1651], ed. Walter Scott, 1820, p. 37).

Four ballad operas call for the tune: Walker's *The Quaker's Opera*, 1728; *The Court Medley*, 1733; and, with a portion of the original ballad, Cibber's *Love in a Riddle*, 1729, and its one-act abridgment, *Damon and Phillida*.

Phyllis the Lovely

"Phillis the Lovely" is the tune named for singing "The Suffolk Comedy," an eighteenth-century three-part ballad beginning "You young men and maidens of beauty most bright" (Douce III, 88ᵛ, Harvard). Music (Fig. 374) is found on an engraved song sheet of "Phillis the

Lovely . . . set to a Trumpet Minuet of Mr. Handell's," c. 1720, the words by Mr. Kirkland beginning "Phillis the lovely, the charming and fair" (BM G.311 [12], Huntington; another edition, Harvard). Another song sung to the trumpet minuet begins "Thyrsis, afflicted with Love and Despair" (BM G.305 [41]). The tune is best known from its appearance as one of the movements in Handel's *Water Music*.

Pretty Parrot, Say, or Pretty Poll

"A Song translated from ye French. Set by Mr. [John] Freeman," beginning "Pretty Parrot, say when I was away," is a Harvard single-sheet song of c. 1705 with music (Fig. 375).[1] It was included in *Pills* in 1706 and in all later editions, with the music, 1719–1720, V, 279. The tune,

[1] Another engraved edition of about the same date is "Pretty Poll A Pleasant Dialogue between a Parret and his Master" (BM H.1601 [364], Huntington, Harvard).

375

called "Pretty Poll," is in the second volume of *The Dancing Master,* 2d ed., 1714, and of Walsh's *Compleat Country Dancing-Master,* 1719.

The music is also found with a political parody of c. 1706 issued as a single-sheet song, "The Paris Gazetteer A Dialogue between ye English & Paris Gazett," beginning "Paris Gazett say, tho tis not your way" (BM H.1601 [373], Huntington). D'Urfey wrote "The fond Keeper's Relapse" to the tune of "Pretty Poll," printed only in the final edition of *Pills* I, 162. A broadside without music is "The French Invasion," 1708, beginning "Have you heard of late,/How Affairs of State," to the tune of "Prety Parrot say" (Huntington).

The tune took a new lease on life when Gay introduced it into *The Beggar's Opera,* 1728. In that same year "A New Ballad inscribed to Polly Peachum" paid tribute to Gay's heroine and at the same time parodied both the original words and Gay's adaptation. Where the dramatic song began "Pretty Polly, say,/When I was away," the ballad opened "Pretty Polly say,/when did J[ohnn]y G[ay]" (BM C.116.i.4 [38]). It was followed by "An Answer to Polly Peachum's Ballad," beginning "Pray, Sir, who are you,/That thus dares to shew" (BM C.116.i.4 [40]). There was also "An Excellent New Ballad Inscrib'd to the Irish Polly Peachum," 1728, beginning "Since evr'y Scribbling Bays,/Fain would Sing thy Praise," the tune named "Pretty Polly Say" from Gay's opening line (BM 839.m.23 [167]). The tune is given the same name in Ward's *The Happy Lovers,* 1736, the only other ballad opera using Freeman's tasteful air. It is called "Pritty Polly, Says" in the first of two Walpole ballads printed together on a sheet; the title is "Admiral Vernon's Resolution," and the piece begins "Prithy Robin say, make no more delay" (Roxburghe; reprinted in *RB* VIII, 284).

[*Pretty Peggy Benson*]

A broadside issued by Philip Brooksby, probably in the last quarter of the seventeenth century, is "Oppertunity Lost, Or The Scotch Lover Defeated. . . . To a pleasant Northern tune," beginning "There was a Lass in our Town/Slea Willy Stenson" (Lord Crawford 1132, Harvard, BM C.22.f.6 [68]). No music is on the sheet. But a mid-eighteenth-century version of the ballad, called "Peggy Benson for the German Flute sung by Mr. Beard," beginning "There liv'd not far from our Town,/Slow Wally Stenson" (Harvard), was issued as an engraved song with music (Fig. 376). "Pretty Peggy Benson" is the burden of this song in which

376

"Slow Willy" is displaced by a miller whose wooing is more spirited. D'Urfey echoed the ballad in a song snatch containing the lines "Slow Will of Stenson" and "Oh! pretty Pegg of Benson," in *The Virtuous Wife*, 1680, Act I.

The Prince of Orange's Delight

Music for "The Prince of Orange's Delight" (Fig. 377) appears on a broadside of 1682, "The Tory Ballad on Their Royal Highnesses Return from Scotland," beginning "Room, room for Cavaliers, bring us more Wine" (Bodleian Ashmole G.16 [136ᵛ], Harvard, Yale, Huntington; reprinted without music in *180 Loyal Songs*, 1685, p. 268).[1] Nothing more

[1] An edition of the same year, without music, is titled "The Brimigham Ballad On Their Royal Highnesses Return from Scotland," and the tune named is "Monk's March," for which no music seems to have survived (BM C.38.i.25 [13], Lord Crawford 1032, Wood 417 [87]).

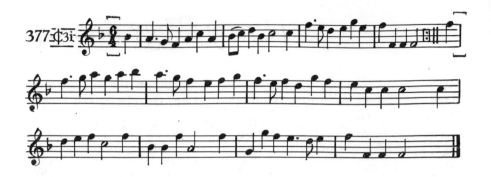

seems to have been heard of the tune until William of Orange was suddenly thrust into the foreground of public attention upon the death of James II. Very early in 1689 several ballads were written to the tune. Oddly enough, they are all in a stanza that fits but half the tune, and metrically they are quite unrelated to "Room, room for Cavaliers." But they can be sung to the 1682 tune; the music of a violin piece called "The Prince of Orange's Delight" in *Apollo's Banquet,* 5th ed., 1687, is in duple rather than triple meter and does not fit the verse.

These 1689 ballads include "Great Britains Delight, or, A Health to . . . the Prince of Orange" (Pepys; reprinted in *PB* IV, 42) and a slight reworking of it called "A New Song. To the Tune of, The Prince of Orange's Delight" by Richard Rigby (Pepys; reprinted in *PB* IV, 84). "A New Song Made in the Praise of the West of England" is to the tune of "The Protestant Prince; or, Vp the green Forrest" (Pepys; reprinted in *PB* IV, 80). The first tune name is not only an obvious reference to the Prince of Orange but is an echo of a phrase prominent in "Great Britains Delight"; on the second tune, see "Cupid's Trepan."

Princess Royal

This air, entitled "Iantha," is included among "The Tunes of the French Dances," a supplement to the third edition of *The Dancing Master,* c. 1662, No. 26 (Fig. 378). It is not in the 1665 supplement but is found twice in *Apollo's Banquet,* 1670, Nos. 176 ("Ianthae") and 200 ("La Princess Royal") and continues under the latter title in subsequent editions of that work. As "Princess Royal" the tune subsequently appeared in Thomas Greeting's *The Pleasant Companion . . . for the*

378

Flagelet, 2d ed., 1673, No. 35; and in *Musicks Hand-maid,* 1678, No. 56, a keyboard arrangement.

The only broadside use of the tune I have found is in "The Noble Prodigal," a medley calling for six airs. The section set to the tune of "Princess Royal" begins "Here's a health to him that may" (Lord Crawford, Harvard, Roxburghe; reprinted in *The Loyal Garland,* 5th ed., 1686, ed. Halliwell, 1851, p. 69, and in *RB* VI, 490).

"Princess Royal" is called for in two ballad operas printed without music—*Love and Revenge,* c. 1729, and *The Court Medley,* 1733—but from the stanza pattern it would appear that some other air was intended.[1]

Prithee, Friend, Leave Off This Thinking

"Prethy friend leave off this thinking" is the tune named for "Lex Talionis: or, London Revived" (BM Thomason; reprinted in *CP,* p. 185), a ballad which its original owner dated Sept. 3, 1647. The tune title is

[1] "Princes roaeyle," preserved in Jacob van Eyk's *Der Fluyten Lust-Hof,* Amsterdam, 1654, II, 10ᵛ, is unlike the English tune. It fits neither the broadside nor the ballad-opera stanza pattern.

379

evidently derived from the first line of a ballad which has not survived in any early seventeenth-century form. A brief drinking song beginning "Prethee friend leave off thy thinking" may be the text we seek, but its earliest extant version is in William Hicks's *Oxford Drollery,* 1671. It is, however, in the same stanza form as "Lex Talionis," and the late seventeenth-century music written for the song by Samuel Akeroyde (*Pills,* 1719–1720, IV, 79) will fit (Fig. 379). We still are in want of the original "Prithee friend" ballad and its tune.

Psalm 81

"A prayer, and also a thankesgiuing vnto God, for . . . Queene Elizabeth . . . this xvii. day of Nouember 1577. Made by I. Pit, minister," beginning "Be light, and glad, in God reioyce, which is our strength and ayd," is directed to be sung "as the foure score and one Psalme" (London Society of Antiquaries [Lemon, *Catalogue,* No. 68], Lord Crawford 165;

380

reprinted in Collier's *Broadside Black-Letter Ballads,* 1868, p. 16). Pitt's text follows Sternhold and Hopkins for the first quatrain; thereafter the ballad turns to praise of the Queen.

The "proper tune" for Psalm 81 is first found in *The Whole Booke of Psalmes,* 1562, p. 201 (Fig. 380). For a detailed account of the tune, see Maurice Frost, *English & Scottish Psalm & Hymn Tunes, c. 1543–1677,* 1953, p. 132.

Psalm 137

"A godly ditty or prayer . . . against all Traytours, Rebels, and papisticall enemies," beginning "Our liuyng God, to thee we cry,/Now tend vnto our playnt," is an Elizabethan religious ballad by John Awdely,

381

containing the following tune direction: "Syng this after the tune of the cxxxvij Psalme, which begins, When as we sat in Babilon; or such lyke" (BM Huth, c. 1569; reprinted in *A Collection of Seventy-Nine Black-Letter Ballads,* 1867, p. 121). The music is found in Sternhold and Hopkins, *The Whole Booke of Psalmes,* 1562, p. 350 (Fig. 381).[1]

---

[1] The tune appeared earlier in Sternhold's *One and Fiftie Psalmes of David,* Geneva, 1556, and was still acceptable when John Playford began to issue *The Whole Booke* in 1677. For further information on its history, see Maurice Frost, *English & Scottish Psalm & Hymn Tunes, c. 1543–1677,* 1953, p. 189.

The *branle* (Eng. *braul, brawl*) was a popular sixteenth-century dance featuring a sidewise motion. Though of Continental origin, it was taken up in England, along with the pavan, galliard, and courante. The dance movements, both as examples and as types, figure largely in Elizabethan keyboard literature.

A lost ballad, entered in the Stationers' Register for 1565–1566, is "the Cater bralles bothe Wytty and mery" (Rollins, *Anal. Index*, No. 265). An extant ballad found in *A Handefull of Pleasant Delites*, 1584, ed. Rollins, p. 25, is "The Historie of Diana and Acteon," beginning "Diana and her darlings deare/Walkt once as you shall heare," to the tune of "the Quarter Braules."

382

As "Quatre brant" the tune is preserved in *Carminum quae Chely vel Testudine canuntur, Liber primus,* 1549, fol. H1ᵛ, a work issued by Pierre Phalèse of Louvain. It is also to be found in Tielman Susato's *Danserye,* 1551, ed. F. J. Giesbert, 1936, I, 28 (Fig. 382), and in a setting of c. 1600 in *Het Luitboek van Thysius,* No. 412. That the tune was known also in England is confirmed by the presence of "Quarte bransle" in Folger MS 448.16, fol. 15ᵛ, dating from the 1570s.[1]

[1] A transcription of the Folger setting, fitted to the opening stanza of the Diana

Queen Dido, or Troy Town

This tune is variously known as "Queen Dido," "Troy town," "When Troy town," "When Troy town for ten years' wars," and "Æneas, wandering prince of Troy," all deriving from the old ballad of Dido and Aeneas first licensed as "the Wanderynge prynce" in 1564–1565. A moralization was licensed in 1568–1569 and the original ballad was re-entered several times during the following hundred years. Probably the earliest surviving version is "A proper new Ballad intituled The wandring Prince of Troye," beginning "When Troye towne for ten yeers' wars," to the tune of "Queene Dido," copied into the Shirburn MS no later than 1616 (*SB*, p. 276). The version in the Percy Folio MS, almost certainly copied from a broadside, is titled "Queen Dido" (printed in Percy's *Reliques*, 4th ed., 1794, *et seq.*). Among the many printed editions, those dating from the first half of the seventeenth century are Pepys I, 84, Wood 402 (3), Manchester I, 51. The Roxburghe copy reprinted in *RB* VI, 548, is but little later.

Imperfectly notated music for this ballad, together with the first eleven stanzas of the text, is preserved in the Shanne family commonplace book, BM MS Add. 38599, fol. 138ᵛ.[1] The same tune, set by John Wilson for 3 voices, is in *Select Ayres and Dialogues*, 1659, p. 94 (Fig. 383), in Wilson's *Cheerfull Ayres*, 1660, p. 2, and in *Catch that Catch Can*, 1667, p. 122. A version for solo voice and bass, c. 1650–1675, is in Edinburgh University Library MS Dc.1.69, p. 84. An anonymous keyboard arrangement entitled "Troy towne," dating from perhaps the middle of the seventeenth century, is preserved in Paris Conservatoire MS Rés. 1186, fol. 57ᵛ. The entire ballad is printed in *Pills*, 1719–1720, IV, 266, with a sound version of the tune which is closely followed in Gay's *Polly*, 1729. Coffey's *The Devil to Pay*, 1731, the only other ballad opera calling for "Troy Town," preserves the tune in an older chantlike rhythm. Ritson printed music for the ballad in his *English Songs*, 1783, evidently following *Pills*.[2]

ballad, appears in John Ward's "Music for *A Handefull of Pleasant Delites*," *JAMS*, X (1957), 159–160. I am indebted to Professor Ward for drawing my attention to the Phalèse occurrence of the tune.

[1] See Hyder E. Rollins, *PMLA*, XXXVIII (1923), 133ff. The ballad is found in a part of the MS that may be dated c. 1611; Rollins describes the transcript but does not print it or the musical score.

[2] Because the evidence seemed to indicate that the "Troy town" tune was written by Dr. John Wilson (it was of course only arranged by him), Wooldridge argued (*OEPM* I, 183) that it couldn't have been the original tune. He reprinted an arrangement of it but also included "When as the Greeks did enterprise" from Forbes's

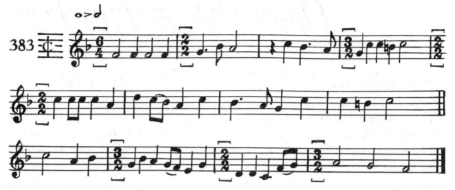

383

Original is in the key of G.

We may say of the two common names of the tune that "Queen Dido" held undisputed sway until about 1630. After that date it continued to be named on a few ballads, but "Troy town" is much more frequently encountered. Among those texts calling for "Queen Dido" are: "A new Ballad intituled A myrrour or lookinge glasse for all sinners," beginning "O mortall man, bedrencht in synne" (*SB*, p. 149); Thomas Deloney's "The Dutchesse of Suffolkes Calamitie," beginning "When God had taken for our sinne" (*Strange Histories*, 1602; reprinted in *Works*, ed. Mann, p. 389; Richard Johnson's *A Crown Garland of Golden Roses*, 1659, ed. Chappell, 1845, p. 20; several broadside editions are represented by the reprint in *RB* I, 288); [3] "The Spanish Tragedy," an early seventeenth-century broadside précis of Kyd's play, beginning "You that haue lost your former ioyes" (Roxburghe; reprinted in *RB* II, 454); and "A Looking-Glass for Ladies," a ballad on Penelope's constancy, beginning "When Greeks, and Trojans, fell at strife," to the tune of "Queen Dido: or, Troy Town" (Pepys, Lord Crawford, Rawlinson, Harvard, Roxburghe; reprinted in *RB* VI, 553). A mutilated copy of the ballad of St. George and the dragon, undoubtedly the earliest extant issue, beginning "[Of H]ectors deeds did Homer sing," names the tune as "Queene [Dido]," which fits the meter perfectly (Manchester II, 55; another edition, second part only, is in II, 42). Other editions name the tune as "Fly-

Cantus as being "more ancient in character than Wilson's." The discovery of Richard Shanne's early seventeenth-century notation of the tune obviates the need and destroys the validity of Wooldridge's hypothesis.

[3] Deloney's ballad is on Catherine Bertie (d. 1580), mother of Peregrine Bertie, Lord Willoughby, for whom a very popular ballad tune was named, q.v.

"Troy Town; Or, The Dutchess of Suffolk" is the tune direction in "The Mournful Subjects," on the death of Charles II (Pepys, Roxburghe; reprinted in *RB* II, 210, and again V, 527).

ing Fame" (for which see "Chevy Chase"), inappropriate for a six-line octosyllabic stanza.[4]

Of the eighteen or twenty ballads naming the tune as "Troy Town" only a few can be noticed. These include "The Sinners supplication," beginning "O Gratious God and heavenly King" (Roxburghe; reprinted in *RB* II, 498), a ballad of c. 1630 and probably the earliest using this name of the tune. "A Caroll for Christmas day," beginning "The glorious Son of Heaven is up," is sung to "Troy Towne" in *Good and True, Fresh and New, Christmas Carols*, 1642, sig. A2. "The Royal Wanderer," a ballad on Charles II, beginning "When ravishing Rebellion reignes," names the tune "The wandring Prince of Troy, or, Troy Town" (Euing 312). "The Fair Maid of Dunsmore's Lamentation," beginning "All you that ever heard the Name/of Wigmore that renowned Lord," is to "Troy Town" (Euing, Lord Crawford, Wood E.25, Bagford, Roxburghe; reprinted in *RB* VI, 767).[5]

Among late seventeenth-century ballads, I note only "A New Ballad of The Midwives Ghost . . . 1680," beginning "To speak of Murthers that have been," which names the tune "When Troy Town" (Douce, Pepys; reprinted in *PB* III, 33), and two pieces on the shooting of Thomas Thin (*or* Thyn), Feb. 12, 1682. The first is J. M.'s "Murther Unparalel'd," beginning "Come and assist my Trembling Pen" (Bodleian Ashmole G.15 [48], Huntington; another issue, with the title "The Matchless Murder," is in Wood E.25 and Roxburghe; reprinted in *RB* V, 111). This was followed almost immediately by "The Wonderful Discovery: Or, The Murtherers brought to light," beginning "Come listen all while that I sing," to "Troy Town, Or, A Warning for lewd livers" (Morgan 66).[6]

Eighteenth-century ballads include two to the tune of "When Troy Town for Ten Years Wars": "The Mourning Court," on the death of Queen Anne, beginning "With bleeding Heart and weeping Eyes" (BM 1876.f.1 [66]), and "A New Moral Song . . . wrote by Nat Withy . . . the Wandering Bard," beginning "You that would read or hear my Song" (BM 1872.a.1 [140]). Another ballad entitled "The Mourning Court," on the death of Prince George of Denmark, 1708, beginning "Come let us mourn for well we may," is to "Troy Town" (BM 1876.f.1 [44]). A song called "The Stroler, or a hard Fate, but good Fate at last," beginning "Young Perkin a poor wand'ring Knight," makes the imitation of the

4 Since the seven final stanzas are found in the Shirburn MS (*SB*, p. 96), the ballad must have been in print by 1616. The ballad has been reprinted in Percy's *Reliques* and in *RB* I, 380.

5 Chappell (*PMOT* I, 371) cited an entirely different ballad on the subject (see a note, s.v. "Diana's a nymph") as if it were merely another edition of "The Fair Maid."

6 The second tune name may be derived from "A Warning to all Lewd Livers" (*RB* III, 23), which is itself to the tune of "Sir Andrew Barton"; that ballad was in turn sung to "Come, follow my love," a tune which has not survived.

old Dido ballad explicit in the tune title: "Æneas Wand'ring Prince of Troy" (*A Collection of State Songs*, 1716, p. 107). "The Bowes Tragedy," beginning "Good Christian people pray attend," on an episode of 1714, shows us that "Queen Dido" had not been completely forsaken as a name for the tune (Harvard, reprinted in Ritson's *Yorkshire Garland*, 1788).

The Queen's Almain

The tune of "Queens Almayne" is named for singing John Barker's ballad licensed 1568–1569, "Of the horyble and woful destruccion of Ierusalem," beginning "An Emperour Vaspasian/Some tyme in Rome there was" (Huntington; reprinted in Collmann, No. 5; a mid-seventeenth century edition is Wood 401 [82]).

The Fitzwilliam Virginal Book II, 217, contains William Byrd's arrangement of the tune (Fig. 384); another keyboard set, which may date

384

Melodic line extracted from second section of Byrd's setting; original contains varied repeats of each strain.

from the middle of the seventeenth century, is preserved in Paris Conservatoire MS Rés. 1186, fol. 27.[1] The tune is found also in Dr. John Leyden's MS Lyra Viol Book (after 1690; G. F. Graham transcript, No.

[1] In a discussion of this MS, which is of English provenience, Mlle. M.-L. Pereyra, *Revue de Musicologie*, XI (1927), 211n., points out the correspondence between "The Queen's Almain" and a French carol "Une Jeune Fillette" which Eustache du Caurroy used as a theme for a three-voiced piece in his *Fantaisies*, 1610. For a transcription of this composition, see *An Anthology of Early French Organ Music*, ed. Joseph Bonnet, New York, 1942, p. 7.

47). Mabel Dolmetsch gives the figures of this almain, together with the Fitzwilliam tune, in her *Dances of England and France, 1450–1600*, 1949, pp. 150–151.

The Queen's Old Courtier

This tune is variously known as "An Old Courtier of the Queen," "The Queen's Courtier," "The Queen's Old Courtier," "The King's Old Courtier," "An Old Soldier of the Queen's," and "The Queen's Old Soldier." The music calls for the intoning of verses upon a single note, with the commonly found two-line burden set to a musical phrase suggesting a psalm chant.

The ballad giving the tune most of its names begins "[With] an old song made by an old aged [*or* ancient] pate," and its refrain is:

> Like an old courtier of the Queen's,
> And the Queen's old courtier.

In the second half of the poem "old" becomes "new" and "Queen's" becomes "King's," as the poet laments the decay of tradition after Elizabeth's death. It may be inferred, therefore, that the piece was written in the reign of James I, although no surviving copies are so old.[1] Of two manuscript texts, one and perhaps both antedate the Restoration: "The Old Courtier of the Queenes" is in Bodleian MS Ashmole 38, p. 113, and an untitled version is in John Gamble's MS Commonplace Book, 1659, No. 120. The poem is in *Le Prince d'Amour*, 1660, p. 161, with "Old Courtier" and "New Courtier" as separate titles of the two parts (reprinted in *RB* VI, 756). "An Old Song of an Old Courtier and a New" is in *An Antidote against Melancholy*, 1661, p. 14. Many later reprints of the song exist with varying titles; for example, it is in *A New Academy of Complements*, 1671, in *Wit and Drollery*, 1682, and *Wit and Mirth*, 3d ed., 1682; with music it is in all editions of *Pills*, 1719–1720, III, 271, in *The Convivial Songster*, c. 1782, and in Ritson's *English Songs*, 1783. An early eighteenth-century song-sheet edition with

---

[1] Pepys seems to have heard the ballad on June 16, 1668: "a song of the old courtier of Queen Elizabeth's, and how he was changed upon the coming in of the King, did please me mightily, and I did cause W. Hewer to write it out, 3s 6d." But the diarist did not listen very carefully: the ballad is not about the alteration of the courtier's manners, but rather the contrast between the father, wedded to tradition, and his son, whose manners and morals are "new-fangled."

carefully notated air (Fig. 385) is "The Old and New Courtier of the Queens" (BM H.1601 [498], Huntington, Harvard).

A reworking of the ballad by "T. Howard, Gent." to the tune of "The Queens Old Courtier" is "An Old Song of the Old Courtier of the Kings, with a New Song of a New Courtier of the Kings," c. 1670, beginning "An old Song made, of an Old aged pate." Here, despite the title, the contrast between old and new is carried out in alternate stanzas; the Queen has been eliminated (Pepys, Douce, Roxburghe; reprinted in *RB* VI, 758). A century later there appeared another reworking on a song sheet entitled "Moderation and Alteration," with a refrain "Moderation Moderation 'tis a wonderful Moderation," in which the key word is changed to "Alteration" in the last eight stanzas; and the music for the refrain is altered (BM G.809.c [70], Harvard, California).

That the original ballad was circulating before 1642 is suggested by the imitative form of the refrain in "Thankes to the Parliament," 1642. This piece, beginning "Come let us cheere our hearts with lusty wine," has a variable refrain after this pattern:

> Thanke the great Counsell of the King,
> And the Kings great Counsells.

This ballad is without tune direction, but it can obviously be sung to "The Queen's old courtier" (BM Thomason, BM Luttrell; reprinted in *CP*, p. 140). Another of the same sort, beginning "To make Charles a great King and give him no power," is entitled "Verses made in 1642 by N. N." in the manuscript version printed in *RB* VIII, lxii***; it appears without title in Bodleian MS Ashmole 36–37, fol. 67, and with the tune title "The Queens old Souldier" in *Rump*, 1662, I, 13, and *Loyal Songs*, 1731, I, 3. Its refrain is "The New Order of the Land, & the Lands new Order." Still another is "The Tub-Preacher," beginning "With face and fashion to be known," without tune direction but with refrain " 'Tis a new teacher about the town,/Oh the town, the towns new teacher" (*Sportive Wit,* 1656, p. 37; other versions, with different titles and some verbal differences, are in *Parnassus Biceps,* 1656, and *J. Cleaveland Revived,* 1659; reprinted in Mackay's *Cavalier Songs,* pp. 18, 61). The song has been credited to both Cleveland and Samuel Butler, but there is no authority for assigning it to either.

"The old soldier of the Queen's" is another name for the tune. It comes from the refrain "It was an old souldier of the Queens/Oh the Queens old souldier" associated with a song beginning "With an old mothy coat & a mamsey nose," which appears without tune direction in *Wit and Drollery* and *Merry Drollery,* 1661, and in *A New Academy of Complements,* 1671.[2] That it was in circulation before the Restoration is evidenced by two ballads of early 1660 which are to be sung to "An [*or* The] old soldier of the Queen's." One is "Saint George, and the Dragon, Anglice, Mercurius Poeticus," beginning "News, News:—Here's the Occurrences: and a new Mercurius" (BM Thomason, with MS date Feb. 28, 1659/60; Wood 416 [43], with MS date Feb. 1659, and Harvard, with MS date Feb. 27, 1659, both dates old style; reprinted in *Ratts Rhimed to Death* and *The Rump,* 1660; *Rump,* 1662; Wright, *Political Ballads,* p. 205; Mackay, *Cavalier Songs,* p. 133). The other is "A Free-Parliament-Letany," beginning "More Ballads;—here's a spick-&-span new Supplication" (BM Thomason and Harvard, with MS date March 17, 1659/60, Wood 416 [60], with MS date March, 1659; Bagford; reprinted in *The Rump,* 1660, *Rump,* 1662, *Wit and Mirth,* 3d ed., 1682, Wilkins, *Political Ballads* I, 125, and *RB* VII, 665). Both ballads are in the usual form, with four long lines to be chanted, followed by a sung refrain of two lines. Here the refrain ends "Libera nos Domine," suggesting a kinship with the host of litanies that appeared during the last months of the Commonwealth and again during the 1680s. Their distinguishing feature is the final refrain line (sometimes Anglicized to "Forever, good Lord, deliver us"), preceded by three or four long, often irregular, lines. A few were to be sung to "Cavalilly Man" or "When Jockey first the wars began," or "Which nobody can deny" (see "Greensleeves"), and many seem particularly well fitted for the latter tune.[3]

[2] A continuation, with a refrain ". . . a new Souldier of the Kings . . . ," reminiscent of the second part of "The Old Courtier," often accompanies the ballad of the old soldier. It begins: "With a new beard but lately trimmed."

A song in *Westminster Drollery,* 1672, II, 24, beginning "Of old Soldiers the Song you would heare," has the refrain "Like an old Soldier of the Queens/And the Queens Old Soldier." It was reprinted in *Wit and Drollery,* 1682, and with the music in *Pills* V, 217. Its rehearsal of Elizabethan military exploits suggests that it is a good deal older than its drollery appearances; it may antedate "With an old mothy coat," but either song could have been the source of the new tune name.

[3] The commonest stanza pattern is three lines of eleven syllables each, followed by the refrain. While this is admirably suited to the short form of "Greensleeves,"

But ordinarily no tune name appears on the ballad sheet; indeed, many litanies seem to be verse satires rather than songs for singing.

A humorous sketch of a conducted tour through Westminster Abbey is reprinted in *Pills* V, 220, directed to be sung to the tune of "Old Soldiers." The ballad, beginning "Here lies William de Valence," is a running account of the great who lie buried in the Abbey. What gives it point is a prefatory prose account of the apprentices and maidens who are gathered to see the sights; the margins contain their naïve comments, and the total effect is mildly dramatic. The piece appeared in *Sportive Wit*, 1656, *The Mysteries of Love and Eloquence*, 1658, and other miscellanies, but without any indication of a tune. The title of a late broadside edition of the piece suggests why *Pills* should have coupled it with "The Queen's old courtier" music: "The Tombs in Westminster Abbey. As Sung by Brother Popplewell in the manner of Chanting in a Cathedral" (Roxburghe; reprinted in *RB* VII, 268).[4] Since the stanza is rough ballad meter, rhyming *abcb*, it is clear that only the chanting portion of the tune can be used, and there is no reason to suppose that verse and music were coupled before the *Pills* editions, if indeed the piece had ever been intended for singing.

The tune was introduced into three ballad operas: Ralph's *The Fashionable Lady*, 1730, Fielding's *The Genuine Grub-Street Opera*, 1731, and his *Don Quixote in England*, 1734. Fielding's name for the tune in both productions was "The King's old Courtier," and the text of both songs is that which has continued in vogue with a different tune as "The Roast Beef of Old England," q.v.

this very pattern is found in "A New Litany," 1710, beginning "From the fine Roman Whore, or the Geneva Slut," to the tune of "An Old Courtier of the Queen" (Harvard). As we have seen, this latter tune calls for a two-line refrain; something of the effect could be achieved by singing the third long line and the Latin phrase to the refrain notes, leaving the first two lines of the stanza to be chanted, but the unity of the stanza is weakened. On the whole, I consider the 1710 ballad rather arbitrarily coupled to "An Old Courtier," and I am inclined to doubt that this tune was used for litanies, except for the two 1660 examples cited.

4 Brother Popplewell is an elusive figure on whom more information would be welcome. I can supply only one further scrap: "A Gallon a Day," c. 1775, a single-sheet song parodying "The Vicar of Bray," names him in the title as the singer who has made it a "favourite" (Harvard, BM G.309 [152]).

Quoth John to Joan

This tune takes its name from the opening line "Quoth John to Joan, wilt thou have me" of "The Clowns Courtship, a Song made and sung to the King at Windsor, to an excellent Scotch Tune." This piece by D'Urfey, printed in his *New Collection of Songs and Poems*, 1683, p. 48, appeared in two expanded broadside forms, one "The North Country lovers: Or: The plain Downright wooeing between John and Joan . . . as it was sung before the Court at Windsor," to the tune of "Quoth John to Joan" (Pepys IV, 24); the other, "The Country-man's Delight . . . John the Serving-Man, In his Courting of Joan the Dary-Maid," to "a New Play-House Tune: Or, Dolly and Molly" (Lord Crawford, Pepys, Harvard, Roxburghe; reprinted in *RB* III, 593).[1] With the "Scotch Tune," which does not quite fit, D'Urfey's song appears in every edition of *Pills,* 1719–1720, III, 114 (Fig. 386).

386

D'Urfey very probably made over an old song. His refrain, "I cannot come every day to woo," is an echo of "And every day I cannot come to woo," in *Taming of the Shrew,* II, i. A passage from a lost inter-

---

[1] "Dolly and Molly" is a tune derived from a ballad of the same name, directed to be sung to "Bacon and Beans," for which music has apparently not survived.

lude, *The Woer,* containing the line "I cannot come a woing euery day," is found in *The Arte of English Poesie,* 1589, ed. Willcock and Walker, 1936, p. 203. And an entry in the Stationers' Register of "John wooinge of Jone &c," Jan. 18, 1592, seems to point to an early ballad version, now lost, which D'Urfey may have recalled.

J. Stafford Smith, *Musica Antiqua,* 1812, I, 32, reprints from an un-identified sixteenth-century MS a single-stanza song "Joan qᵈ John when wyll this be," with the refrain D'Urfey was to use and a tune which, for all its irregularity, has a great deal in common with the *Pills* air.[2] The refrain is also found in "A wooing Song of a Yeoman of Kents Sonne" in Ravenscroft's *Melismata,* 1611, No. 22; the tune in common time bears marked harmonic resemblances to the beginning and end of the 6/4 air in *Pills.* The text, beginning "I haue house and land in Kent," is reprinted in *RB* VI, 591.

The Rant, or Give Ear

to a Frolicsome Ditty

This tune appears as "The Rant," altered on the engraved plate to read "The Ramble," in *Youth's Delight on the Flagelet,* 9th ed., c. 1690,

11th ed., 1697. In *Apollo's Banquet,* Second Book, 1691, it is called "The City Ramble." The same music, without tune direction (Fig. 387), is

---

[2] A version of the Smith song, with differing text beginning "John, quoth Joan, is there such haste," is printed in *The First Book of Elizabethan Songs,* ed. Peter Warlock,

found on a broadside of 1691, "An Excellent New Song, Entituled, A Hot Engagement Between A French Privateer, and an English Fire-Ship," beginning "I'm a Prize for a Captain to fall on" (Pepys V, 386, text reprinted in *PB* VI, 154). A different edition, entitled "A Fight Between An English Fire-Ship And A French Privatiere," has no music but contains the direction "Tune of, Give ear to my Frolicksome Ditty" (Lord Crawford 597). This latter tune title is derived from the first line of a ballad of the 1680s, "The Jolly Gentleman's Frolick: Or, The City Ramble . . . To a Pleasant New Tune" (Lord Crawford, Harvard, Pepys, Douce, Roxburghe; reprinted in *RB* VI, 513).[1] An early eighteenth-century single-sheet edition of "The Iolly Gentlemans Frolick" (Harvard, BM G.316.d [155]) reproduces the tune in the form usually found in the ballad operas (Fig. 388).

388

Original is in 6/4, key of Bb.

Two other ballads on the same subject, and presumably to the same tune, are "The Ranting Rambler," beginning "I pray now attend to this Ditty," to the tune of "The Rant, Dal, derra, rarra" (Bagford; reprinted in *BB* I, 205); and "Mark Noble's Frollick," beginning "One night at a very late hour," to the tune of "the New Rant" (Pepys, Harvard, Lord Crawford, Roxburghe; reprinted in *RB* VI, 510).[2]

The following ballads list the tune as "The Rant": "The Female Frollick," beginning "You Gallants of every Station,/give ear to a Frollicksome Song" (Pepys, reprinted in *PB* V, 292; copies entitled "The Female Highway Hector" are in Harvard and Lord Crawford, reprinted in *RB* VIII, ix*); and "The London Lasses Hue-and-Cry After Her Dearly Beloved Robin," beginning "Good People pray give your Attention" (Pepys III, 245, BM C.22.f.6 [140], Lord Crawford 460, Harvard). The following give the tune as "The City Ramble" and use the

---

1926, pp. 25–28. Warlock's source is a series of early seventeenth-century part books, BM MS Add. 17786–17791, in which [Richard] Nicholson is named as the composer.

[1] Later copies give the tune as "The Rant, Dal dera Rara."

[2] This ballad can be sung to "The Rant" but not to the tune of "New Rant" which is preserved in *A Booke of New Lessons for the Cithern & Gittern*, 1652, Part II, No. 21.

"Rant" stanza pattern with refrain: "An Excellent New Song, Call'd, Fox-Hall Frollick," beginning "The Potter a lusty young wooer" (Pepys V, 208); "An Excellent New Song, call'd The Baily of Hounslow," beginning "The Baily that now goes a Wooing" (Pepys V, 160); and two eighteenth-century broadsides both entitled "A New Summons to Horn-Fair," one beginning "Ye Cuckolds that dwell in the City" (BM 1876.f.1 [149*]), the other "You Sots that are joyn'd to a Woman" (BM 1871.e.9 [114]; BM 1876.f.1 [149] is another edition, with varying title). The tune is called "The City Rant" in "The Buxome Lass of Bread-street," beginning "I have been a Twelve-month at London" (Pepys III, 295), while "The Conceited Bell-man," beginning "The Bell-men that walk in the weather," is to the tune of "The Midnight Ramble, with the burden to it" (Pepys IV, 262).

The tune, in a more singable form than one encounters in seventeenth-century sources, was used for at least nine ballad operas, where it is usually entitled "Give ear to (or Have you heard of) a frolicksome ditty." In Gay's *The Beggar's Opera* it is set to verses beginning "How happy could I be with either," which becomes another name for the tune in "An Eligiaick Song. On the Death of . . . Mrs. Mary Wall . . . June, 1729" by H. Ware, beginning "Ye Beaus, who all Hear my sad Ditty" (BM 1890.e.5 [27], a Dublin broadside). The tune is cited under the same name in "A Fore-castle Song," beginning "Do you see, as a Sailor, I'll heave off/A bit of a song in my way" (George A. Stevens, *Songs, Comic and Satyrical,* 1772). Joseph Ritson printed a ballad by "George Knight, Shoemaker" entitled "The Hare-Skin," to the tune "Have you heard of a frolicsome ditty," in his *Bishopric Garland,* 1784, reprinted in *Northern Garlands,* 1810. "Give Ear to a Frolicksome Ditty" appears as a MS tune direction in the Douce copies of several broadsides alongside the printed tune name "Moggie's Jealousy" (for which, see "You London Lads").

Also sung to the tune is "Saddle to Rags," a ballad collected in Yorkshire, 1845, by J. H. Dixon and included in his *Ancient Poems, Ballads, and Songs of the Peasantry of England,* 1846. Though it had been in traditional circulation since the end of the eighteenth century, it is ultimately derived from print. Child gives it as "The Crafty Farmer" (No. 283) and establishes its origin in his headnote and his *a* and *b* texts. It has flourished widely in America as "The Yorkshire Bite," but is sung to different tunes. See further G. Malcolm Laws, *American Balladry from British Broadsides,* 1957, L 1.

Chappell has noted the kinship between "The Rant" and the tune found in *The Dancing Master,* 2d ed., 1652, called "Winifreds Knot, or Open the door to three." There it is unbarred; in editions of 1665 and after, the measure is 6/4; with the 1703 edition it is properly printed in 9/4 time. The ballad-opera tune is usually incorrectly barred in 6/4.

Red Bull

An early seventeenth-century ballad "To the tune of the new dance at the Red Bull Play-house" is entitled "A mad kinde of wooing, Or, a Dialogue betweene Will the simple, and Nan the subtill." Its twelve-line ballad-meter stanza begins "Sweet Nancie I doe loue thee deare/Beleeue me if thou can" (Pepys, Roxburghe; reprinted in *RB* II, 121). Although the connection is farfetched, a tune appearing in *The Dancing Master* from the 10th ed., 1698, as "The red Bull" will actually fit the ballad, provided each strain be repeated in turn. The music had appeared in *Apollo's Banquet*, 1670, No. 75, as "The Dam'sells Dance" (Fig. 389).

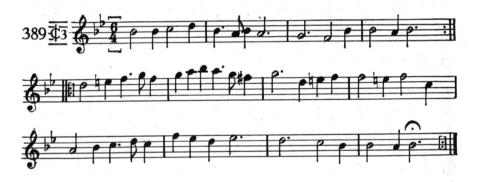

The Red Bull Theater itself was the headquarters of Killigrew's company at the Restoration but soon afterward ceased to be used. Coincidence, then, seems to play a large part in giving us a suggestively named tune which will fit a commonplace measure (but note that the stanza length is not equally commonplace).

Remember Ye Whigs

D'Urfey's song beginning "Remember ye Whigs what was formerly done" is best described in the title he prefixed to it in *Pills*, 1719–1720, I, 246: "Advice to the City, a famous Song, set to a Tune of Signior Opdar, so remarkable, that I had the Honour to Sing it with King Charles at Windsor; He holding one part of the Paper with Me." D'Urfey included the song in his *New Collection of Songs and Poems*, 1683, and it was reprinted in *180 Loyal Songs*, 1685; in neither volume is music printed with the song. Broadside versions had appeared in 1682, entitled "Advice to the City, or, the Whiggs Loyalty Explained. To an Excellent New Tune" (Wood 417 [94], without music; an engraved song sheet with the same title contains the Opdar music [Fig. 390]: Bodleian

Ashmole G.16 [105], Harvard, Huntington); still another issue is entitled "Advice to the City: Sung to the King at Windsor, to a Theorbo," without tune direction or music (BM 82.1.8 [38], Wood 276a [530], Bodleian Ashmole G.16 [210], Harvard, Yale; reprinted in *RB* V, 281, from an unspecified copy). As "Remember ye Wiggs" the tune is given in Humphry Salter's *Genteel Companion . . . for the Recorder*, 1683, p. 16.

The intricacy of the song suggests that Opdar set D'Urfey's words, not vice versa as his *Pills* title implies. Despite the honorable auspices that made the song memorable for D'Urfey, it seems not to have been a favorite, for it is included in only the final edition of *Pills*.

The Rich Merchant Man

This tune is called "The Merchant," "The Merchant Man," "The Merchant of Emden," "The Rich Merchantman," and "There was a Rich Merchant Man," from a ballad by Thomas Deloney which was licensed in 1594. Many seventeenth-century editions survive, usually with the title "A most sweet Song of an English Merchant, borne at Chichester. To an excellent new Tune"; the first line is "A Rich Merchant Man there was,/that was both grave and wise" (Wood 401, Pepys, Euing, Douce, Lord Crawford, Bagford, Harvard, Morgan, Roxburghe; reprinted in *RB* I, 320, and in Deloney's *Works,* ed. Mann, p. 485). The ballad stanza here consists of three poulter's-measure quatrains, the third of which is the burden. This pattern is followed generally in other ballads to the tune, but some are written in eight- or four-line stanzas, much as we find with "London is a fine town."

Despite the popularity of Deloney's ballad and the frequent use of the tune associated with it, no music has survived which can be confidently identified. A ballad by J. P., licensed in 1678, is titled "The Merchant-man and the Fidlers wife . . . To a Pleasant Northen Tune," and begins "It was a Rich Merchant man/That had both ship and all" (Pepys IV, 163); it is reprinted in *Pills,* 1719–1720, V, 77, with a tune that was more accurately given in editions of 1707 and 1712, III, 153 (Fig. 391). Despite the presence of echoic words in title and first line,

the ballad seems to me in no sense an imitation of Deloney. The only other basis for associating the music with our tune titles lies in the 6.6.8.6 quatrain of J. P.'s ballad, for the eight-bar melody fitting his words would also fit a quatrain of our "Rich Merchant Man" ballads. Although the tune is of popular cast and seems a good deal older than the last quarter of the seventeenth century, the evidence simply does not allow us to make a positive identification.[1] In the discussion that follows, this tenuousness between our tune names and the *Pills* music is assumed.

"The fearefull Judgement of almighty god, shewed vpon two sonnes who . . . murthered their . . . father," beginning "A heavy dolefull storye/I am abovt to wright," to the tune of "The Marchant of Emden or Crimson Velvet," was copied into the Shirburn MS by 1616 (*SB*, p. 164).[2] Another early ballad using the tune is "A dittie most excelent for euerie man to reade/that doth intend for to amende & to repent with speede," to the tune of "a rich marchant man or John come kiss me now," beginning "Whoe loveth to live in peace: & marketh euerie change." It is found in BM MS Add. 15225, fol. 56 (c. 1616), but it had been licensed as a broadside in 1564 after having appeared in *Tottel's Miscellany*, 1557. The tune titles must have been newly added in the manuscript version.[3]

Perhaps the most popular production associated with the tune is "An Excellent Ballad of George Barnwel," beginning "All youths of fair England," to the tune of "The Merchant" or "The Rich Merchant-Man" (Pepys, Bagford, Douce, Lord Crawford, Wood 401, Euing, Harvard, Roxburghe; reprinted in Percy's *Reliques* and in *RB* VIII, 61). This account of youth undone by a strumpet, the basis of Lillo's *London Merchant*, 1731, was licensed in 1624 and may well be older. From it came another name for the tune used on at least two ballads: "The Unfaithful Servant," beginning "Young Maidens all beware," to the tune of "The Rich Merchant-man: Or, George Barnwel" (Pepys; reprinted in *PB* III, 132), and an eighteenth-century ballad "The Cruel Lover: or, The Credulous Maid," beginning "Young Men, I pray attend," to the tune of "George Barnwell" (Harvard).

"Christ's Tears over Jerusalem," beginning "When Christ our Lord

[1] Chappell (*PMOT* I, 381) was concerned more with the disparity between tune length and stanza length than with the problem of identification. He suggested that only half the tune was preserved in *Pills*, or that there must have been another tune for the longer stanza form.

[2] The first part is in 16-line ballad-meter stanzas; the second part, naming only the first tune, has 8-line stanzas of the same measure. "Crimson Velvet," usually associated with a 20-line stanza of two quatrains and four triplets, does not fit. "The Merchant of Emden" takes its name from an allusion in Deloney's opening stanza to the place where the English merchant killed a man and was under sentence of execution. Another ballad using this form of the tune name is "The Cucking of a Scould," beginning "A Wedded wife there was," which Professor Rollins dated 1615 or earlier (Pepys; reprinted in *PG*, p. 72).

[3] No tune directions are contained in earlier manuscript copies: Bodleian MS Ashmole 48, fol. 37ᵛ, c. 1555–1565 (*Songs and Ballads*, ed. Wright, 1860, p. 57) and BM MS Sloane 1896, fol. 35ᵛ, c. 1576. Rollins included full collations in his edition of *Tottel's Miscellany*, 1928–1929, II, 302ff.

drew nigh/unto Jerusalem," to the tune of "The Merchant [Man]," has been attributed to Deloney (*Works*, ed. Mann, p. 497) on the ground that it may be the "Repent, England, Repent" of Deloney's named in Nashe's *Have With You to Saffron-Walden*. It was entered in the Stationers' Register in 1624 (probably a transfer) and again in 1675; surviving editions are late seventeenth century (Pepys, Rawlinson; reprinted in *RB* VII, 787). Several ballads to the tune are reprinted in *RB* and *BB*. A few others are worth noting here: "Englands Warning-Piece," beginning "Rouse up dull sinners all," was issued by Richard Burton about the middle of the century (Wood E.25 [127]); "Strange Newes from Brotherton," beginning "Oh wretched England mind," related a miraculous rain of wheat on Easter day, c. 1648 (Manchester; reprinted in *PA*, p. 40); "A Godly Ballad of the Just Man Job," which begins "Walking all alone,/No not long agone" (Pepys II, 62, Rawlinson 203, Lord Crawford 1239, Harvard), is a reworking of a ballad registered 1564–1565, the early form of which, in a different measure and without tune direction, is printed from MS in *OEB*, p. 209; "Treason Justly Punished," beginning "O Stay and lend an Ear," is an account of the execution of William Staley in 1678 (Harvard). The tune is called "There was a Rich Merchant Man" in "The Unnatural Mother . . . Sept. 1680. Drowned her self and two poor Babes in a Well," beginning "Attend good People all,/unto my Story strange" (Pepys; reprinted in *PB* III, 43).

"The Kentish Miracle," beginning "Take comfort Christians all," to the tune of "A Rich Merchant Man" (Pepys, Lord Crawford, Roxburghe; reprinted in *RB* VIII, 39), is the basis of another name for the tune, found in "The Ungrateful Son," beginning "Of an ungrateful Son,/ my purpose is to write," to the tune of "Kentish miracle" (Lord Crawford, Harvard, Bagford; reprinted in *BB* I, 443).

Finally, we should mention a four-quatrain song sung to "a rich Merchant man," beginning "Time was when thou a Kettle," in *The Famous Historie of Fryer Bacon*, 1629, sig. C2ᵛ; the earliest editions of the chapbook, now lost, probably antedate Greene's play, written c. 1591–1592.

The Roast Beef of Old England

Richard Leveridge, a celebrated eighteenth-century bass singer, wrote the music of this familiar song and some, at least, of its verses. A single-sheet edition, perhaps of the 1730s, is "A Song in Praise of Old English

Roast Beef. The Words and Musick by Mr. Leveridge," beginning "When mighty Roast Beef was the Englishmans Food" (Harvard), reprinted in Walsh's *British Musical Miscellany*, 1734–1736, III, 121 (Fig. 392). The words alone appeared in *A Complete Collection of . . . Eng-*

lish and Scotch Songs, 1735–1736, II, 5. A song sheet of about the same date with the original seven stanzas extended to eleven is "The Roast Beef Song by Mr. Leveridge. The Additional Verses by a Lady of Quality" (BM G.313 [135], Harvard). The song was frequently reprinted through the eighteenth century and has become a staple of Britain's national music.

The relation of Fielding to the song is not quite clear. His *Grub-Street Opera*, 1731, contains a two-stanza song, Air 45, to the tune of "The King's old Courtier." Except for a line in the second stanza and slight variation in the refrain, the text agrees with that credited to Leveridge. Fielding's *Don Quixote in England*, 1734, Air 5, reintroduces the same tune and opening stanza; a second stanza is not duplicated in Leveridge. In the absence of further evidence we may suppose that Fielding wrote his ballad-opera verses with "The Queen's old courtier" in mind (he follows faithfully the refrain pattern associated with that tune); and that Leveridge soon afterward grafted new verses onto Fielding's two stanzas and supplied a new air.

Among the parodies may be mentioned "A Song in Praise of Old English Brown Beer. The Words by Mr. Kirkland," beginning "When Humming Brown Beer was the Englishmans Tast" (BM G.316.f [113], Harvard), which is found also in *A Complete Collection*, 1735. Another on the same subject, to the tune of "Roast Beef," begins "When good queen Elizabeth, history's boast" and is found in Joseph Reed's comic opera version of *Tom Jones*, 1769, Act III. Political broadsides which name the tune either from Leveridge's title or from the first line of his song include: "Frederic of Prussia . . . By Mr. Lockman," c. 1743, beginning "While Britons securely their Blessings enjoy" (BM C.116.i.4 [117]); "Englands Scotch Friend. A New Song by Sawney McStuart," c. 1762, beginning "Now Peace it is finish'd it surely doth tend" (BM 1876.f.1 [168]); "The Grumblers of Great Britain . . . By a Grumble- tonian," 1762, beginning "Good People attend (if you can but spare Time)" (BM 1850.c.10 [77]); and a ballad on Tom Paine, "The Re- former of England," beginning "Come listen, good fellows, and a tale I'll relate" (BM 1871.e.9 [221]). "The Roast Beef Cantata," c. 1765, be- ginning "Twas at the Gate of Calais Hogarth tells" (Harvard, BM G.316 [146]), is a medley set to verses written by Theophilus Forest for Hogarth's famous work of 1749. The last strain is Leveridge's tune, but only the refrain lines are retained from the original song. A Napoleonic squib to the tune is "A Fig for the Grand Buonaparte," 1803, beginning "Since our Harry's and Ned's three to one we are told" (Harvard). This list could be multiplied, but it is sufficient to show the popularity of Leveridge's tune, especially during the second half of the eighteenth century when very few broadsides identified the music to which they were designed to be sung.

[Robin Hood and the Bishop of Hereford]

"The Bishop of Hereford," a late eighteenth-century song sheet, con- tains the music (Fig. 393) for the ballad beginning "Some they may

393

:s: :s:

talk of bold Robin Hood" (Harvard, BM G.311 [126]). Ritson reprinted the music from another engraved issue bearing the title "Robin Hood and the Bishop of Hereford" (*Robin Hood*, 1795, II, 150); Chappell's version of text and tune is drawn from still another, but earlier, song sheet, entitled "The Bishop of Hereford's entertainment by Robin Hood . . . in merry Barnsdale" and beginning "O some they will talk of brave Robin Hood" (*PMOT* II, 395).[1]

The simple but effective tune might serve for any of the other Robin Hood ballads written in quatrains, but our ability to trace such relationships is handicapped by the absence of tune directions on broadside and garland copies of "Robin Hood and the Bishop of Hereford" without music (see Child No. 144). A tune bearing strong harmonic and melodic relationship to that of the eighteenth-century song sheets is said to have been found by Rimbault on a flyleaf of a copy of *Parthenia*, c. 1613; he printed it as "Robin Hood and the Curtall Fryer" in Gutch's *Robin Hode*, II, 436 (Fig. 394). Rimbault's air will fit "The

394

Original is in key of A.

famous Battell betweene Robin Hood and the Curtall Fryer. To a new Northerne tune," beginning "In Summer time when leaues grow greene/ and flowers are fresh and gay" (Pepys I, 78, an early seventeenth-century copy; later issues are represented by the reprints in *RB* VIII, 521, and Child No. 123 B).[2]

[1] This copy, which I have been unable to trace, was the source of Rimbault's tune in Gutch's *Robin Hode*, 1847, II, 441.

[2] "In summer time," a much-cited broadside tune, is usually associated with octosyllabics and is therefore not derived from the "Curtal Friar" ballad. Nor is there any relation between that ballad and "King Edward the fourth, and a Tanner of Tamworth" (Roxburghe, reprinted in *RB* I, 531; Child No. 273), which begins "In Summer time when leaues grew greene,/and birds sitting on euery tree." "The Noble Fisherman: Or, Robin Hoods preferment," with almost identical first line, is to the tune of "In Summer time," q.v.

Robin Hood and the Stranger

Despite the antiquity of Robin Hood as a subject of balladry (an allusion to songs about him appears in *Piers Plowman*) the great majority of Child's Robin Hood examples—Nos. 117–154—come from the seventeenth or even eighteenth century. The Percy Folio MS, c. 1650, is an important source, but a number of texts are incomplete. The broadside versions, without which there would scarcely be a Robin Hood literature, seem to be revampings of received texts; black-letter survivals are probably outnumbered by eighteenth-century stall copies, and one cannot easily disagree with Child's general contempt for the heightened sensationalism and general deterioration achieved by the later ballad hacks. A specific case in point, Child feels, is the reworking of a group of Robin Hood ballads into a common five-line stanza form to fit them for singing to a single tune. The stanza is characterized by a metrically irregular ballad-meter quatrain into which a refrain "With a hey down, down, and a down" has been introduced after the first line; moreover, internal rhyme is present in the second tetrameter, and occasionally in the first as well. Whether one believes with Child that either or both characteristics of the stanza pattern may be a sign of revamping, it is a curious fact that our only music for a five-line stanza is "Arthur a Bland," found in *The Jovial Crew*, an anonymous ballad opera of 1731, Air 2 (Fig. 395); early seventeenth-century versions of the tune

395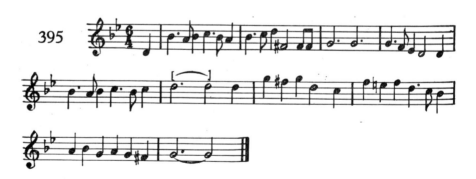

differing considerably in detail are designed for a verse quatrain (Cambridge University MS Dd.9.33, fol. 81ᵛ [bandora], and Will Forster's MS Virginal Book, p. 430, both called "Robin Hood," the former in minor

396

[Fig. 396], the latter in a major key).[1] One other significant feature of all three tunes is the triple rhythm which reflects the tendency of ballad meter to swell from iambics to anapests.

Arthur a Bland, who gives his name to the tune, appears as the outlaw's opponent in "Robin Hood and the Tanner . . . To the tune of Robin Hood and the Stranger" (*RB* VIII, 502; Child No. 126). The ballad begins:

> In Nottingham there lives a jolly tanner,
> > With a hey down down a down down
> His name is Arthur a Bland;
> There is nere a squire in Nottinghamshire
> Dare bid bold Arthur stand.

Also to the tune of "Arthur a Bland" are "Robin Hood and Little John," beginning "When Robin Hood was about twenty years old" (*RB* VIII, 504; Child No. 125; earlier than the text of either reprint is a black-letter edition of c. 1700 in Lord Crawford 1320; the ballad was licensed in 1624), and some editions of "Robin Hood and the Ranger," beginning "When Phoebus had melted the sickles of ice" (Child No. 131). "Robin Hood and the Tanner" is named as the tune for "The Launching of

---

1 The Forster set is printed in Thomas Tomkins, *Keyboard Music,* ed. S. Tuttle, *Musica Britannica,* V (1955), 139. Two other early versions of the tune are untrustworthy after the opening phrase. In Thomas Ravenscroft's *Pammelia,* 1609, it appears as one of three country dances arranged to be sung simultaneously, and the words to it begin "Robin Hood Robin Hood said little Iohn,/come dance before the Queen a." A piece by William Cobbold, after 1612, containing snatches of many songs, couples the opening bars of the melody with the words "Robin hood Robin hood, and little John,/they leand them to a tree" (BM MS Add. 18936, fol. 60).

the Strickland," by George Knight, a late piece reprinted in Ritson's *Bishopric Garland*, 1784, having the refrain "with a hey down, down and a dee"; an earlier ballad, "Long Lent 1685, Or a Vindication of the Feasts," beginning "Lent fourty Work dayes ever was," has the same tune direction, but the stanzas are eight lines without refrain (National Lib. of Scotland Ry III.a.10 [32]). It could be sung to the earlier form of the tune.

The ballad of "Robin Hood and the Stranger" has not survived,[2] but as a tune name it is found on several other ballads, including "Robin Hood and the Bishop," beginning "Come Gentlemen all, and listen a while" (*RB* II, 449; Child No. 143), "Robin Hood and the Beggar," by Thomas Robins, beginning "Come light and listen you Gentlemen all" (*RB* VIII, 517; Child No. 133), and an unrelated ballad, "The Jovial Lass: or Doll and Roger," beginning "As Roger did rise in the morning betimes" (Pepys III, 116). "Robin Hood and the Beggar" in turn becomes a name for the tune in Thomas Robins's "Robin Hood and the Butcher," beginning "Come all ye brave Gallants and listen a while" (*RB* VIII, 535; Child No. 122), his "Robin Hood's Chase," beginning "Come you gallants all, to you I do call" (*RB* VIII, 512; Child No. 146), and "Little John and the four Beggers," beginning "All you that delight to spend some time" (*RB* VIII, 497; Child No. 142 B).

Also sung to this tune is a political ballad of January, 1660, called "The Gang or the Nine Worthies," beginning "It was at the Birth of a Winters morn," with a five-line stanza, the "hey down" refrain line, and the tune direction "Robin Hood" (BM Thomason, BM Luttrell, Wood 416, Roxburghe; reprinted in *The Rump*, 1660, *Rump*, 1662, *Loyal Songs*, 1731, and *RB* VII, 658). Another ballad in *The Rump*, 1660, p. 62, without title or tune direction, but written in the distinctive stanza pattern, begins "We came from Scotland with a small force,/ With a hey down down a down a."

"Robin Hood newly reviv'd: to a Delightful New Tune," beginning "Come listen a while you Gentlemen all," is also in five-line stanzas (*RB* II, 426; Child No. 128); and to the tune of "Robin Hood reviv'd" are sung "A Famous Battle between Robin Hood, and Maid Marian," by S[amuel?] S[mithson?], beginning "A Bonny fine maid of a noble de-

[2] Ritson assigned this title to a ballad usually known as "Robin Hood newly reviv'd" (*RB* II, 426; Child No. 128); Child thought it might more probably be associated with an older version of "Robin Hood and Little John" (*RB* VIII, 504; Child No. 125). There are strangers in both ballads, to be sure; but it should be noted that a recurrent formula in Robin Hood ballads is the outlaw's meeting a stranger, fighting him without success, and inviting him to join the band. Hence the title cannot be easily restricted, and there is no reason to doubt that still another ballad adhering to the formula may have existed.

gree" (*RB* VIII, ciii***; Child No. 150), and the eighteenth-century
piece, "Capt. Hind's Progress and Ramble," beginning "There's many
a comical story you know" (Douce, Madden, Williams College, Harvard,
Roxburghe; reprinted in *RB* VII, 644).

"Robin Hood, Will. Scadlock and Little John," to the tune of "Robin
Hood; or, Hey down, down a down," seems from the second tune name to
be related to the ballads in five-line stanzas sung to "Robin Hood and
the Stranger," but surviving copies lack the refrain line and the internal
rhyme found in other ballads of this group (*RB* II, 432; Child No. 129).

Robinson's Almain

Thomas Deloney's ballad "The widdowes solace," beginning "Mourne
no more faire widdow,/teares are all in vaine," is directed to be sung "To
the tune of Robinsons Almaine" (Deloney's *Garland of Good Will*, 1631;
reprinted in *Works*, ed. Mann, p. 330). The tune direction is uncertain,
for Thomas Robinson published seven almains in his two collections.

Making the best fit with Deloney's verses is the almain which alone appears in both volumes of Robinson, *The Schoole of Musicke*, 1603, sig.
H2ᵛ (lute) and *New Citharen Lessons*, 1609, No. 19, and which is addi-
tionally found in a Continental manuscript of c. 1600, *Het Luitboek van*

Thysius, No. 319 (Fig. 397).[1] One or two of the other almains are awkwardly possible of adaptation, but more nearly suitable is "An Allmaine by Mr. Robinson" preserved in the cittern section of John Playford's *A Booke of New Lessons for the Cithern & Gittern,* 1652, No. 45.

Rogero

This tune is to be associated with the *Aria di Ruggiero,* from which it gets its name. The *Ruggiero* air was one of a number of sixteenth-century Italian ground basses upon which a singer could extemporize a descant when chanting epic poetry. The appearance of Ariosto's *Orlando Furioso* in 1532 apparently gave new impetus to the practice, and the *Ruggiero* formula, named from Canto 44, stanza 61, beginning "*Ruggier, qual sempre fui, tal esser voglio,*" was perhaps the most widely used. In instrumental pieces the air is occasionally found in the superius, but it is properly a series of bass notes with their implied harmony, upon which melody can be rather freely invented.[1]

The ballad tune "Rogero" is not the original Italian formula, but is a descant erected upon the *Ruggiero* bass, with which it harmonizes. A

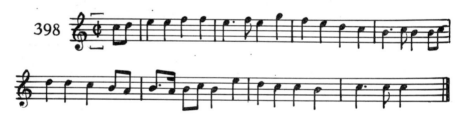

good version of the tune, set for cittern, is in Cambridge University MS Dd.4.23, fol. 23ᵛ (Fig. 398). Others are found in Thomas Dallis's MS Lute Book, 1583, p. 20, with "The Division of Rogero" on p. 21, in the Marsh MS Lute Book, c. 1590, p. 305, and in Cambridge MSS Dd.3.18, fol. 1

[1] The same conclusion was reached by Richard Newton, who reprinted the 1603 tablature in his article "Thomas Robinson and the Ballad Writers," *Lute Society Journal,* I, No. 4 (1958), 82–87.

[1] For a detailed study of the air in both vocal and instrumental music, see Alfred Einstein, "Die Aria di Ruggiero," *Sammelbände der Internationalen Musikgesellschaft,* XIII (1912), 444, and the same author's "Ancora sull' 'Aria di Ruggiero,'" *Rivista Musicale Italiana,* XLI (1937), 163. The melody is reprinted in Gustave Reese's *Music in the Renaissance,* 1954, p. 326.

(lute), and Dd.14.24, fol. 1 (cittern).[2] None of these settings retains the Italian bass; the tune has, in effect, become independent of its original generating force.[3] "Rogero" consists of four brief musical phrases, each with a loose cadence; this feature is important in giving the air such flexibility that it can be used for singing quatrains of ballad meter (8.6.8.6), trimeter (6.6.6.6) or poulter's measure (6.6.8.6). The latter form is found in the earliest ballads, whereas the most common stanza pattern is ballad-meter octave, which requires that the air be sung twice over.

The tune quite understandably is called "New Rogero" in three ballads of the 1580s. These include: one found in *A Handefull of Pleasant Delites*, 1584, ed. Rollins, p. 63, entitled "A faithfull vow of two constant Louers"; William Elderton's "The Lamentation of Follie," beginning "Alas what meaneth man,/with care and greedy paine" (Huntington, reprinted in Collmann, No. 43); and Arthur Bourcher's "A worthy Mirrour, wherein you may Marke, An excellent discourse of a breeding Larke," beginning "A Larke sometimes did breed" (London Society of Antiquaries, reprinted in *RB* III, 87; Huntington, reprinted in Collmann, No. 10; a seventeenth-century edition, tune "Rogero," in Roxburghe I, 464).

Two ballads to the tune of "Rogero" are found in the Shirburn MS, compiled from broadsides, 1585–1616: "A right Godly and Christiane a. b. c.," beginning "Arise, and walke from wickednesse," an acrostic ballad, the initial capitals of each stanza comprising the alphabet, to which extra stanzas have been added as a prayer for James I (*SB*, p. 43; an early seventeenth-century broadside print is in Roxburghe, reprinted in *RB* III, 160); [4] and "The torment of a Jealious minde," beginning "All

2 The last named MS is one of several part books for broken consort. The bass-viol part, Dd.5.20, fol. 1, contains a loose approximation of the *Ruggiero* ground. For a transcription of the two parts, see John Ward, "Music for *A Handefull of Pleasant Delites*," *JAMS*, X (1957), 173. Professor Ward has discussed a number of musical texts which antedate the appearance of "Rogero" as an English ballad tune and has quoted an interesting brief harmonization of "ruger" by Rychard Pyttyns (BM MS Royal App. 74, fol. 46v) dated no later than 1547–1548.

3 William Byrd used a part of the *Ruggiero* theme in the bass of "La Virginella," a five-voiced madrigal on Ariosto's words (*Psalmes, Sonets & Songs*, 1588), of which an English version, "The fair young virgin," appears in Nicholas Yonge's *Musica Transalpina*, 1588. See Byrd's *Collected Works*, ed. E. H. Fellowes, 1937–1950, XII, 124, XVI, 1, 8.

4 The first entry in the Stationers' Register, 1557–1558, is "a ballett called a Ryse and wake"; but Professor Rollins (*Anal. Index*, No. 93) believes this to refer to "Aryse and wak, for Cristis sake," in Bodleian MS Ashmole 48, printed in Thomas Wright's *Songs and Ballads*, 1860. It seems to have no connection with the Shirburn ballad or with "Rogero," no tune being named. Collier's "Arise and wake," printed in his *Extracts* I, 185, has been shown to be a fabrication made to fit two entries in the registers (*Anal. Index*, Nos. 93, 115); see Rollins, *MLN*, XXXIV (1919), 342.

such as lead a Jealous lyfe" (*SB*, p. 263). Thomas Deloney wrote "The valiant courage and policie of the Kentishmen with long tayles" to the tune (*Strange Histories*, 1602; reprinted in *Works*, ed. Mann, p. 383, and in Chappell, *PMOT* I, 94). Richard Johnson's *Crown Garland of Golden Roses*, 1612, ed. Chappell, 1842, p. 76, contains "A pleasant new sonnet, intituled, mine owne deare lady brave" to the tune, and his *Golden Garland of Princely Pleasures*, 3d ed., 1620, 13th ed., 1690, contains another, "A lamentable Song of Lady Elinor," beginning "In England lived once a Duke." The tune is also used for the mid-century religious piece, "A most Godly and Comfortable Ballad of the Glorious Resurrection," beginning "What faithful [*or* faithless] froward sinful man" (Pepys, Lord Crawford, Euing, Roxburghe; reprinted in *RB* I, 389).

"A new Sonnet, shewing how the Goddesse Diana transformed Acteon into the Shape of a Hart," beginning "Diana and her Darlings Deare/ went walking on a Day," names the tune "Rogero" only in the earliest extant broadside edition (Manchester I, 29, c. 1625; reprinted among the notes in *A Handefull*, ed. Rollins, p. 93);[5] other issues are to "a pleasant new Tune" or some variation of this formula (Pepys, Bagford, Euing, Harvard, Roxburghe; reprinted in *RB* II, 520).

"The Norfolk Gentleman his last Will and Testament," beginning "Now ponder well you parents dear," was originally sung to "Rogero" (Pepys, Bagford, Euing, Douce, Wood 401, Wood 402, Harvard, Lord Crawford, Roxburghe; reprinted in *RB* II, 216), but in the eighteenth century it had another tune to which it gave the name "The Children in the Wood." The ballad and its offshoots are noticed in more detail under that heading.

"A comfortable new Ballad of a Dreame of a Sinner" to the tune of "Rogero" begins "In slumbring sleepe I lay" (Pepys, Douce; reprinted in *PG*, p. 176). It was licensed in 1624, and its first line became a new name for the tune in a ballad of 1626, "Iohn Spenser . . . his life and repentance," by Thomas Dickerson, beginning "Kind hearted men, a while geue eare" (Pepys; reprinted in *PG*, p. 257), and another which was licensed in 1630, "The poore man payes for all," beginning "As I lay musing all alone" (Roxburghe; reprinted in *RB* II, 334). The disparity between the trimeter quatrain of the first and the ballad-meter octave of its two derivatives is indeed puzzling until one realizes that "Rogero" accommodates both meters (the octave requiring, of course, a complete repetition of the tune).

[5] The *Handefull* version is to the tune of "Quarter Braules," q.v.

Room for Company

This air derives one of its names from the title and opening lines of a broadside licensed in 1614: "Roome for Companie, heere comes Good Fellowes. To a pleasant new tune" (Pepys; reprinted in *PB* I, 52). Martin Parker's earliest ballad, c. 1624, in the same measure, is to the tune of "Roome for &c": "A Scourge for the Pope," beginning "Famous Brittany,/Giue thanks to God on high" (Pepys; reprinted in *OEB*, p. 189, and *PB* I, 219). "Roome for Company" is also the tune for "The fetching home of May," c. 1635, beginning "Now Pan leaves piping,/The Gods have done feasting" (Roxburghe; reprinted in *RB* III, 312). Versions of this ballad were reprinted in *An Antidote against Melancholy*, 1661, and in *Pills*, 1719–1720, IV, 26, where the title "The Green-Gown" is a polite euphemism for that amatory longing of so many ballad maidens in the spring.

Music printed with the *Pills* song is substantially the same as that found in *Musicks Recreation on the Lyra Viol*, 1652, p. 5 (Fig. 399), and

Original is an octave lower.

in a seventeenth-century lute tablature (Trinity College, Cambridge, MS O.16.2, p. 132), under the title "Roome for Cuckolds." This name may, indeed, be the original form and ". . . Company" its euphemistic doublet. The "Cuckold" title is named in the comedy *The London Chanticleers*, 1659, Scene III, as a song Ditty has in his pack. "Room for Cuckolds, here comes a Company" seems to be a proverbial catchphrase when used as subtitle of "Hey for Horn-Fair," c. 1685, a ballad on cuckoldry sung to "The Winchester Wedding" (for which see "The King's Jig").[1] A song in *Sportive Wit*, 1656, to "Room for Cuckolds" is "The Hunting of the Gods," beginning "Songs of Sonnets, and rusticall Roundelays." Other versions, often replacing "Sonnets" with "Shepherds," appear in the following: the Percy Folio MS (ed. Hales and Furnivall, III, 304); *Westminster Drollery*, 1672, II, 64; *Wit and Drollery*, 1682; *A Collection of Old Ballads*, 1723–1725, III, 198; *The Convivial Songster*, c. 1782; and Ritson's *English Songs*, 1783—the two latter with music. The fact that this song was about the hunting of the hare may explain the tune title "Hunt the Hare" associated with the music in Thompson's *Compleat Collection of 200 Favourite Country Dances*, c. 1780, IV, 52. A late eighteenth-century song sheet (Huntington, Harvard) bears the title "Hunting the Hare. The Words by Geo. Alexr. Stevens." It begins with the familiar "Songs of Shepherds in rustical Roundelays" and is only a shortened version of the drollery poem, with the familiar tune and minor textual variants.

The tune appears a second time in *Pills* VI, 136, with "Room for Gentlemen," beginning:

> Room for Gentlemen, here comes a Company,
> Room for Gentlemen, here comes my Lord-Mayor.

The four opening lines fit the tune and appear as a refrain throughout the song; but the five-line stanzas are not suited to the music. From an anecdote concerning Sir Thomas Myddelton (1550–1631), who was Lord Mayor of London in 1613, we learn that "having married a young wife in his old age, the famous song of *Room for cuckolds, here comes my lord mayor!* was invented on the occasion."[2] Though this song seems to have disappeared, it is possible that the refrain in the *Pills* song is an echo of the original.

With slight alteration the tune appears as "A Minuet" in Gay's *Achilles*, 1733. In two ballad operas without music, it is called for: in *The Footman*, 1732, it is cited as "Room for Cuckolds," and in Drury's *The Fancy'd Queen*, 1733, as "Pan leave Piping."

---

[1] A ballad entitled "Roome for Cuckolds" was issued in 1660, designed to be sung to "Cuckolds all a-row," q.v. Because of the difference in rhythmic patterns, it could not have been sung to the 1652 lyra-viol tune of "Roome for Cuckolds."

[2] Thomas Pennant, *Tours in Wales*, 1778–1781, II, 29.

Room, Room for a Rover

Thomas D'Urfey's song, "The Blackbird," beginning "Room, room, room for a Rover,/Yonder Town's so hot," first appeared in the 1700 edition of *Pills* (1719–1720, II, 204) and was reprinted without music in *Wits Cabinet,* c. 1700, p. 154. A song-sheet edition of c. 1705, entitled "Room for a Rover" (BM G.305 [211], Harvard, California), credits James Paisible with the music, "call'd yᵉ new Dance" (Fig. 400).[1]

Original is in 6/4.
* B in original.

A contemporary broadside using D'Urfey's entire first line as the tune title is "The Valliant English Seamans Call . . . to serve . . . against France and Spain," beginning "Come brave English Sailors" (Harvard). D'Urfey wrote another song to the tune, beginning "Whilst Content is wanting/In the World below," which he introduced into his comedy, *Wonders in the Sun,* 1706, Act IV. It is reprinted in *Pills* II, 206.

Two ballad operas of 1731 call for the tune, naming it "Room, Room for a Rover": *The Jovial Crew* and Lillo's *Silvia.*

1 On the sheet line 2 has been re-engraved to read "London is so Hot," but the original wording is faintly visible. Another edition, entitled "A Song the Words by Mr. D'urfey, to a Tune of Mr. Peasable's, call'd the new Dance; and exactly engrav'd by Tho: Cross" (Harvard), also reads "London."

Row Well, Ye Mariners

This tune is found in Thomas Robinson's *Schoole of Musicke*, 1603, in all editions of *The Dancing Master*, 1651–c. 1728 (1651, p. 102 = Fig. 401), and in *Pills*. The complex melody calls for a twelve-line stanza,

Original contains double bars but not repeat signs.

each quatrain of which is metrically distinctive, but all the sixteenth-century ballads naming the tune may be sung very smoothly to it.

"Roowe well ye marynors &c.," was licensed in 1565–1566; in the following year came "Roo well ye marynors moralyzed" (twice re-entered) and "stande faste ye marynours"; in 1567–1568 "Rowe well ye Christes marynours" and "Rowe well Godes marynours"; and in 1569–1570 "Rowe well ye marynours for those that loke bygge." None of these ballads have survived, but the entries in the Stationers' Register are evidence of the success of the original—and of the irresistible urge to appropriate its lilting lines to moralizing purposes.

A Handefull of Pleasant Delites, 1584, ed. Rollins, p. 22, contains a ballad to the tune, "A proper sonet, wherin the Louer dolefully sheweth his grief to his L. & requireth pity," which may well have been in the lost 1566 edition of that miscellany.[1] Three ballads now in the Huntington Library illustrate the use of the tune in the 1570s; they were all printed in J. P. Collier's *Old Ballads,* and more recently in Collmann, Nos. 75, 70, 69. The first is Thomas Preston's "A Lamentation from

[1] The Robinson lute setting of 1603 is transcribed and the first stanza of the ballad interlined in John Ward, "Music for *A Handefull of Pleasant Delites*," *JAMS*, X (1957), 158–159.

Rome," 1570, beginning "All you that newes would here"; another, on the execution of John Felton, May 15, 1570, is "A letter to Rome" by Steven Peele, beginning "Who keepes Saint Angell gates"; and the third is Ralph Norris's "A warning to London by the fall of Antwerp," beginning "The sturdy Oke at length," which may be dated after November, 1576, when the Low Country city fell. Still another ballad of about this time is "A Ballet, diclaring how euerye christian ought to prepare them selffe," beginning "Marche out, godes soldiours,/Youre enimies be sure at hand" (BM MS Cotton Vespasian A.xxv, fol. 150ᵛ [olim 159ᵛ], printed by K. Böddeker in *Jahrbuch für roman. und engl. Sprache*, N. F. II [1875], 347).

"Row well, ye mariners" is mentioned as a hanging tune in the anonymous comedy *Looke about you*, 1600, sig. F₁—evidence that there must have been other ballads to the air which have not survived.

The tune is found in *Pills*, 1719–1720, IV, 191, with a ballad "John and Joan," beginning "If't please you for to hear,/And listen a while what I shall tell." It is a piece of ribaldry which must have been circulating as a penny ballad during the Restoration, but I have not found a broadside edition. The last musical phrases are slightly altered to fit a fuller final quatrain; otherwise the tune has suffered almost no change in a century of use.

Royal and Fair

This tune takes its name from the opening line "Royal and fair, great Willy's dear Blessing," a thinly veiled political pastoral song which Thomas D'Urfey wrote for his comedy *Love for Money*, 1691, IV, iii. D'Urfey's two stanzas are found with music in all editions of *Pills*, 1719–1720, I, 314. For broadside publication the poem was lengthened to five stanzas and entitled "An Excellent New Song, Call'd; The Charmin Regent's Wish," as if it were a composition of Queen Mary. An issue with

402

Original is a fifth higher.
* Note is a half tone lower in original.

accurate music (Fig. 402) is Pepys V, 204 (text reprinted in *PB* VI, 22); another, with meaningless music, is Lord Crawford 1035.

At least one other broadside was sung to "Royal and Fair": "The Mournful Lover," beginning "Heavens look down and pity my crying" (Pepys V, 369, without music).

[The Royal Ball]

This tune is found on broadsides of "The Royal Ball: As it was perform'd in Masquerade by Two Seamen. . . . To an Excellent New Tune, Sung at Court." This expression of enthusiasm for King William and the fleet was written, as Professor Rollins reminds us, in 1690 before the disaster of Beachy Head on June 30, and begins "Since all the World's in

403

Original is a fourth higher.
* Note is a half tone higher in original.

Arms,/And full of loud Allarms" (Lord Crawford, BM C.39.k.6, Pepys; reprinted in *PB* V, 156, and *OPB,* p. 166). The typical theater tune, printed with only fair accuracy on the broadside (Fig. 403), apparently was not used for any other ballads. Its name here is therefore arbitrarily assigned.

Russell's Farewell

Lord William Russell was one of those implicated in the Rye House plot against Charles II and James, Duke of York, early in 1683. Although he pleaded not guilty and there seems to have been little ground for suspecting him, he was convicted of high treason and was executed July 21, 1683. A number of good-night ballads were written upon his death, including "Russel's Farewell," to the tune of "Oh, the Bonny Christ-Church Bells" (*RB* V, 324), and "The Lord Russell's Farewell," to the tune of "Tender Hearts of London City" (*RB* V, 326). We are presently concerned with yet a third, "The Lord Russels Last Farewel to the World," 1683, beginning "Farewel, farewel to Mortal Powers," a broadside written and published by James Dean, with music on the sheet (Harvard, Huntington, Wood 417; reprinted in *BB* II, 1002, and in *RB*

V, 691). The music is wrongly barred (in 6/4 time instead of 4/4) and contains several misprints; it is on the whole a serviceable tune (Fig. 404), but it lacks the memorable quality one would expect of a ditty ex-

No time signature in original; barred as 6/4.

ceeded in popularity only by "Packington's Pound," "Fortune my foe," "Greensleeves" and "Hey, boys, up go we." Under the name of "Russell's farewell" or "Johnson's farewell," the tune was used for fifty or more ballads during its twenty years of greatest vogue. Pepys acquired about forty of these broadsides, whether attracted by the tune itself or by the recurrent theme of execution in ballads naming the tune; thirty are reprinted in *PB,* and most of the rest are to be found in *BB* or *RB.*

In 1684 Dean wrote "Oates's Bug...Bug...Boarding-School, at Camberwell," to the tune of "My Lord Russels Farewell," beginning "Rouse, Rouse my lazy Mirmidons" (Harvard, Clark; reprinted without music in *180 Loyal Songs,* p. 328).[1] Another early piece to the tune is "The Sorrowful Lamentation of the Widdows of the West," beginning "Alas! we Widdows of the West,/whose Husbands did Rebell" (Lord Crawford 19, licensed by L'Estrange, containing corrupt music; Pepys II, 245, licensed by Richard Pocock, without music; reprinted in *RB* V, 724).

"Capt. Johnsons last Farewel," beginning "You noble Lords of high Degree," is to the tune of "Russel's Farewel" (Pepys, BM C.39.k.6, both with meaningless music; reprinted in *RB* VII, 742, and in *OPB,* p. 43; the copy in Roxburghe III, 786, an eighteenth-century issue, is not fol-

[1] Dean not only subscribed his name as author, but in the continuation of the title listed several of his other ballads, including "The Lord Russel's Farewell."

lowed by Ebsworth). It was based on the execution of Sir John Johnston, Dec. 23, 1690, for his minor part in the abduction of a thirteen-year-old heiress.[2] From this ballad come other names for the tune. It is "Sir John Johnson's Fare-well" in "The Charmed Lover; or a young Man that Courted a Welch Lady," beginning "As I was walking in the Fields" (Pepys V, 203). A handful of others name the tune "Johnsons Farewell," including: "The Dying Lamentation of Thomas Randal," 1696, beginning "Oh horred, horred is my Crime" (Harvard); "The Unhappy Tayler . . . Who Hang'd himself," 1699, beginning "Come all Rash Lovers pray draw near" (Harvard); "The Condemn'd Bridegroom . . . Executed . . . 9th of December, 1702 . . . in South-wark," beginning "You that have courted Women-kind" (BM 1871.e.9 [135]); "Fatal Love or, The Young Maiden's Tragedy," 1704, beginning "You Maidens who intend to wed" (Bagford; reprinted in *BB* I, 47); and "Councillor Layer's Last Farewell . . . executed for High-Treason, 17th of May, 1723," beginning "This Day I am ordain'd to die" (BM 1872.a.1 [166ᵛ]). Three others to the tune are reprinted in *PB,* including "Capt. Whitney's Confession . . . 1693," beginning "The fatal day is come at last" (Pepys; reprinted in *PB* VI, 322).

The end of Whitney's predatory career was celebrated in several other ballads, including "The Penitent Robber . . . Capt. James Whitney . . . his Execution . . . First of February, 1693," to the tune of "Russels last Farewel" (Pepys; reprinted in *PB* VI, 326), and "The Notorious Robbers Lamentation, or, Whitneys Sorrowful Ditty," to the tune of "Russels Farewel" (Pepys, Bagford; reprinted in *BB* II, 559). "Whitney's Dying Letter To his Mistriss that betray'd him," in the same eight-line stanza, is to the tune of "Whitney's Farewell" (Pepys; reprinted in *PB* VI, 316). This may be another name for "Russell's farewell," deriving from one of the foregoing ballads, but it is significant that "Whitney's Farewell" in the 1695 edition of *The Dancing Master,* p. 163, is an entirely different tune.[3]

[2] See *PB* V, 276–280, for a detailed account of the affair. Also to the tune of "Russell's Farewell" is "Captain Johnson's Love's Lamentation" (Pepys V, 6, with meaningless music; reprinted in *PB* V, 281). "Sir John Johnson's Farewel, by Jo. Hains," in the same meter, is printed in *Pills,* 1719–1720, VI, 202, with music of "Chevy Chase" (reprinted in *RB* VII, 744).

[3] Information given in *PB* III, 260, VI, 315, concerning the music of "Russell's farewell" and "Whitney's farewell" is subject to correction. The original of Professor Rollins's No. 211 (*PB* IV, 187) contains crudely engraved notation of "Hey, boys, up go we"; the broadside of No. 327 (*PB* V, 281) contains meaningless music. *The Dancing Master* tune is not a set of "Russell's farewell." Since "Whitney's farewell" is named as the tune of only one extant ballad, there can be no question of its displacing "Russell's farewell" as a name for the tune after 1693. Indeed, two-thirds of the *PB* pieces sung to "Russell's farewell" originated after the date of Whitney's execution.

Among the few ballads to "Russell's farewell" which appear not to have been reprinted the following may be mentioned: "Perjur'd Steward's Cruelty," beginning "In Wapping there did dwelt of late" (Pepys III, 377); "The Brave Boys of Bristol," beginning "Brave Bristol Boys, where e're you be," to the tune of "Hey Boys up go we; Jenny Gin; Busie Fame; Or, Russels Farewel" (Douce I, 19); and "Damons Triumph; or, Celia's Joy," beginning "My dearest dear could I relate," to the tune of "Russels Farewel: or, Jenny Gin" (Pepys III, 66).

Sabina

The song beginning "As on a day Sabina fell a sleepe" is found with music (Fig. 405) in BM MS Add. 24665, fol. 9ᵛ, 1615–1626 (the words printed in *Giles Earle His Booke,* ed. Peter Warlock, 1932, p. 17). The

405

Original is unbarred.

music, which is in the style of the early seventeenth-century lutenist school, requires a double repetition of the first four syllables of the third line in each stanza, and ballads sung to the tune print these repetitions

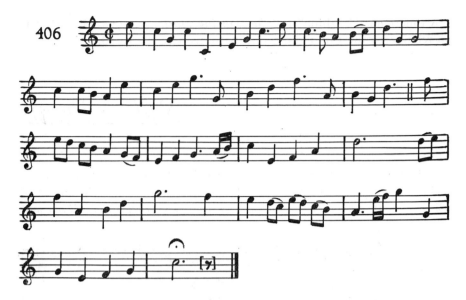

406

in extenso. A broadside version of the song is "Cvpids Covrtesie: in the wooing of fair Sabina. To a pleasant new Tune" (Lord Crawford, Rawlinson, Harvard, Roxburghe; reprinted in *RB* III, 645).[1] These copies are c. 1670; the ballad was registered in 1656, but it is evidently considerably older, for Laurence Price's "A Complete Gentle-woman," beginning "You Muses all your aide to mee assigne," to the tune of "Sabina," was registered in 1633 (Roxburghe; reprinted in *RB* I, 197), and the original ballad was very likely in print before that date.

An unknown hand reworked the Sabina verses, preserving much of the imagery but little of the original delicacy. Beginning "Sabina in the dead of night,/In restless slumbers wishing lay," the new song appeared in *The Banquet of Musick*, Third Book, 1689, p. 22, with music by Samuel Akeroyde (Fig. 406). The new tune and text were reprinted in all editions of *Pills*, 1719–1720, III, 209, and in *The Convivial Songster*, c. 1782, p. 82. The words are in *The Compleat Academy of Complements*, 1705, p. 127. Akeroyde's tune, called "Sabina in the dead of Night," was included in *Apollo's Banquet*, 6th ed., 1690, and it is printed erroneously on two broadsides of about the same date.[2]

[1] This ballad has no connection with the tune "Cupid's Courtesy," as metrical comparisons make clear.

[2] One is "[The] Old Cavalier. To an Excellent New Tune" (*PB* V, 305) for which the tune is properly "The Clear Cavalier," q.v.; the other is "A Dialogue Between A Master and his Maid," to the tune of "Aye, marry, and thank you too," q.v. The fact that the Akeroyde music was in type suggests that it must originally have been prepared for a broadside version of the *Banquet* song or some other piece for which the tune was suitable. But no such broadsides appear to have survived.

A tune named "Sabina" in *The Dancing Master,* c. 1728, III, 186, has no relation to the tunes and stanza patterns here discussed.

Sad as Death

This tune takes its name from the first line, "Sad as death at dead of night," of a song introduced into Lee's *Theodosius,* 1680, the music of which is contained in a supplement to the play (Fig. 407). Words and

music are also found in *The Newest Collection of the Choicest Songs,* 1683, p. 66. The song, expanded to ten stanzas, was issued as a broadside entitled "Repentance too Late," to the tune of "Sad as death: or, Parthenia unto Cloe cryed" (Pepys, Roxburghe; reprinted in *RB* VI, 52). On the second tune, see "Sitting by yonder river side."

The Sages of Old

This tune is named from the first line of a song introduced in a revival of D'Urfey's *The Virtuous Wife* a few years after its original production in 1679. An engraved single-sheet edition of c. 1690, called "A New Song" (Harvard), attributes the words to D'Urfey and the music to Thomas Tollet (Fig. 408). A violin setting of the tune appeared in

Cadence note in bars 7, 14, 21, and 28 should extend through an additional measure.

Apollo's Banquet, Second Book, 1691. The stage song was printed in all editions of *Pills,* but in 1719–1720, II, 17, the words were revised for fresh topicality, the title changed to "The Parallel," and the original tune now credited to John Eccles.

During the 1690s the poem was expanded to broadside length as "The Loyal States-man: Or, A Plain Discription of these Present Times. Tune of, The Sages of Old; or, Let the Souldiers Rejoyce" (Pepys; reprinted in *PB* VII, 130). The sheet contains meaningless music. The twelve-line stanza fits the music of Tollet, but Purcell's tune "Let the soldiers rejoice," q.v., is for a stanza of half the length.

D'Urfey's song was reprinted in such poetical miscellanies as *A Collection of Bacchanalian Songs*, 1729, p. 36, *The Hive*, 1725, III, 240, and Allan Ramsay's *Tea-Table Miscellany*, 1733, III, 353.[1] It appeared also as a single-sheet song, entitled "The true-hearted Englishman" (BM G.312 [113], c. 1765), with still different music.

St. George for England

This tune is known as "St. George," "St. George for England," "St. George and the Dragon," and "St. George for England and the Dragon." As we shall see, the tune is used for several ballads on St. George; but the narrative of his encounter with the dragon and his eventual marriage to the king of Egypt's daughter, in a different meter, is sung to "Queen Dido," q.v.

The oldest ballad to the present tune is "Saint Georges commendation to all Souldiers . . . with a memoriall of the Worthies . . . To a pleasant new tune," 1612, beginning "Why doe you boast of Arthur and his Knightes" (Pepys; reprinted in *PB* I, 43; the text in Percy's *Reliques* is inaccurate and in *RB* VI, 780 is incomplete). The ballad is actually a catalogue of Biblical, legendary, and historical adventurers, none of whom can surpass the English patron saint who slew the dragon, as the refrain declares:

> S. *George* for *England*, S. *Dennis* is for *France*,
> Sing *Hony soit qui mal y panse*.

The ballad was more than once reworked and the gallery of heroes freshened, but the basic formula remained unchanged. Later editions of the old ballad, beginning "Why should we boast/of Arthur and his Knights," are titled "An Excellent [*or* A New] Ballad of St. George and the Dragon" and some copies contain the tune direction "When Flying Fame" (Lord Crawford, Bagford, BM C.22.f.6, Douce, Roxburghe; reprinted in *RB*

---

[1] *The Hive*, 4th ed., c. 1733, III, 160, contains another song to the tune of "The Sages of Old," called "Hair of the same Dog" and beginning "If any so wise is,/That sack he despises"—a drinking song current at least since John Hilton's *Catch that Catch Can*, 1652, where it was printed as a round with entirely different music.

VI, 727). This version was widely anthologized, usually under the title "St. George for England." It is found in *The Mysteries of Love and Eloquence*, 1658, *Merry Drollery*, 1661, *An Antidote against Melancholy*, 1661, *Wit and Mirth*, 3d ed., 1682, *Wit and Drollery*, 1682, and with music in all editions of *Pills*, 1719–1720, III, 116. Another version, probably written during the 1650s, was subscribed S[amuel?] S[mithson?]; its title is the old refrain: "St. George for England, And St. Dennis for France . . ." and it begins "What need we brag or bost at all/Of Arthur or his Knights" (Wood 401 [118]).

A continuation of the old ballad, written by John Grubb, M. A., of Christ Church, Oxford, was issued in broadside form around the end of the seventeenth century (Morgan) and is found in *Pills* III, 315 (reprinted also in Percy's *Reliques* and in *RB* VIII, 771). Its stanzas, burlesquing the tone of the original ballad, conclude with the traditional refrain but are so swollen in length that they seem designed for recitation rather than singing.

One further imitation should be mentioned: "A New Ballad of King Edward and Jane Shore," 1671, beginning "Why should we boast of Lais and his Knights," to the tune of "St. George for England and the Dragon" (Roxburghe; a bowdlerized reprint in *RB* VIII, 423). It is found with the music in *Pills* IV, 272, and without music in *A Collection of Old Ballads*, 1723–1725, I, 153. As "Jane Shore, and King Edward" it is reprinted in Samuel Butler's *Posthumous Works*, 4th ed., 1732, p. 263.

Pepys in his diary for March 6, 1667, records that he has read "a ridiculous ballad, made in praise of the Duke of Albemarle, to the tune of St. George—the tune being printed." A copy of the ballad with the music (Fig. 409), one of the few broadsides to be so printed before about 1680, is preserved in the Luttrell Collection I, 101, of the British Museum (reprinted in *RB* VI, 730, without the music). It is entitled "A Heroical Song On . . . George [Monk] Duke of Albemarle . . . Made in August, 1666," and begins "King Arthur and his Men they valiant were and bold." The colophon bears the publication date of 1667; the name of John Playford as publisher helps to explain why the music was included. This "loyal" ballad has the refrain:

> Lord George was born in England, restor'd his Countryes Joy,
> Come let us sing Vive le Roy.

Somewhat indebted to this ballad is "Vive le Roy: Or London's Joy. A New Song on the Instalment of the present Lord Mayor of London," on Sir John Moore who took office in October, 1681. Beginning "You London Lads rejoyce, and cast away your care," it names the tune "St. George for England," and has the refrain:

Sir John He's for the King's Right, which Rebels wou'd destroy.
Vive, Vive, Vive le Roy.

Copies of the original are in Huntington, Wood 417, Harvard, BM 1872.a.1; reprinted in *RB* V, 276. The ballad was also reprinted in *180 Loyal Songs*, 1685, and more recently in Mackay's *Cavalier Songs*.

* Measures 1–12 incorrectly barred in original.

"Lancashire's Glory," beginning "Old England many Counties hath," is to the tune "St. George" (Rawlinson 134), but the eight-line ballad-meter stanza is too short to fit the tune, and the refrain does not follow the distinctive metrical pattern. The same ballad, with the title "Darbyshires Glory," is to the tune "I am a Jovial Batchellor" (Lord Crawford 965, Harvard), which is commonly used with this stanza form. The tune itself, however, has not survived.

Sawney and Jockey

This tune takes its name from a "Scotch Song" beginning "Twa bonny Lads were Sawney and Jockey" which Thomas D'Urfey wrote for his play *The Royalist*, 1682, III, iii. The song was reprinted in D'Urfey's

New Collection, 1683, and both words and music are found in the coeval Fitzwilliam Museum MS 30.G.20, p. 66, and in such eighteenth-century collections as *The Musical Entertainer*, 1737–1738, I, 59, in *Calliope, or English Harmony*, 1739–1746, I, 128, and in *Universal Musician*, c. 1738 (an unpaginated collection of engraved sheets). Single-sheet issues of about the same date bear the title "Jenny's Complaint" and exhibit some variation in text (BM G.316.f [42], Harvard). The tune alone is preserved in Thomas Greeting's *Pleasant Companion . . . for the Flagelet*, 1683, No. 77, and in Humphry Salter's *Genteel Companion . . . for the Recorder*, 1683, p. 22.

The broadside history of D'Urfey's song begins with a reprint of the playhouse text and tune, under the title "Jenneys Lamentation for the loss of Jocky or, A New Song in the Play called the Royalist" (Bodleian Ashmole G.15 [171], Wood 417 [86], with MS date March 1681/2). In expanded form it appeared in 1682 with music (Fig. 410) as "The Scotch Lasses Constancy: or, Jenny's Lamentation for the Death of Jockey" (Har-

vard, Huntington, Roxburghe; reprinted in *RB* V, 613; facsimile in *A Century of Broadside Elegies,* ed. J. W. Draper, 1928, p. 157), and in an undated edition without music, the title reading ". . . loss of Jockey" (BM C.22.f.6 [174], Lord Crawford 1217, Douce II, 190). Still another edition, without music, is called "Unfortunate Jockey, And mournful Jenny" (Pepys III, 359, 389, Roxburghe IV, 83, reprinted in *180 Loyal Songs,* 1685, p. 282).

The tune was used by Matthew Taubman in a section of his "Medley on the Association" beginning "Jockey away Man, Dee'l ha' me by the Lug" (*An Heroick Poem,* 1682, p. 4). The music is found both there and in the broadside publication of this poem, "Scotlands Good Wishes to His Royal Highness . . . To a New Tune," 1682 (BM C.38.i.25 [7]). Another ballad containing music is "The Rebel Captive," beginning "Three bony Lads were Sawny Cloud Hammilton" (Harvard; reprinted without music in *180 Loyal Songs,* whence the text found in *RB* V, 621).

Other ballads calling for the tune of "Sawney and Jockey" include: "The Loyalist. Setting Forth the Whigg in his own Colours," 1682, beginning "Come, fill it up, and give me a Brimmer Boy" (Bodleian Ashmole G.16 [143], Harvard); "A Message from Tory-Land To the Whig-Makers in Albian," by R. S., 1682, beginning "From Rome I am come, His Holyness sent me" (Huntington, Harvard); "All For Love, Or, The Happy Match," beginning "As Jockey and Jenny one evening were walking" (Lord Crawford 125, BM C.22.f.6 [28], Douce I, 4, Harvard); and "The Shepherds Unconstancy," beginning "Unfortunate Clea now e'ne broken-hearted" (Douce II, 205).

Sawney Will Never Be My Love Again

This tune takes its name from the refrain of a song which Thomas D'Urfey wrote for the third act of his comedy *The Virtuous Wife; or, Good Luck at Last,* performed in 1679 and published the following year. The song, beginning "Sawney was tall and of noble race," was printed in *Choice Ayres and Songs,* Third Book, 1681, p. 9 (facsimile in *The Songs of Thomas D'Urfey,* ed. C. L. Day, p. 103). No composer is named, but Chappell (*PMOT* II, 618) conjectured that Thomas Farmer, who supplied other music for the D'Urfey play, may have written this tuneful melody (Fig. 411). The first four lines of the song are sung in Edward Ravenscroft's *The London Cuckolds,* 1682, III, i. D'Urfey's poem is in *Wit and Drollery,* 1682, and in D'Urfey's *New Collection,* 1683; both

411

* E in original.

words and music are in every edition of *Pills*, 1719–1720, I, 316. As "A Scotch Song" it is preserved in Fitzwilliam Museum MS 30.G.20, p. 3, with accurate music. The tune is erroneously called "Sawney and Jockey" in *The Dancing Master*, 6th ed., 1679, Supplement (the mistake continues through the seventh and eighth editions, but with the ninth edition, 1695, the title becomes "Sawny was tall"), and in *Youth's Delight on the Flagelet*, 9th ed., c. 1690. It is "A Scotch Tune called Sawney" in *Musicks Recreation on the Viol, Lyra-way*, 1682, and "Sawney" in *Apollo's Banquet*, 5th ed., 1687.

D'Urfey's playhouse song, lengthened to ten stanzas, was issued as a broadside called "The Scottish Lasses Complaint for Sawney's Unkindness," to the tune of "Sawny will ne'r be my Love again" (Douce II, 206ᵛ). It was followed by "Jennies Answer to Sawny," beginning "When Sawny left me he had store of gilt," to the same tune (Lord Crawford, Harvard, Roxburghe; reprinted in *RB* VII, 15).

"Sawney" lent itself readily to political parody, and among the earliest targets of attack was Thomas Osborne, Lord Danby, after his impeachment. A ballad of c. 1680 lampoons him as "The Disloyal Favourite Or, The unfortunate States-Man," beginning "Tommy was a Lord of high renown" (Lord Crawford, Harvard, Roxburghe; reprinted in *RB* IV, 85). An answer written to the tune, with music on the sheet, satirizes Shaftesbury as "Tony" and is titled "The Loyal Feast . . . in Haberdashers Hall, on Friday the 21st of April 1682 . . . and how it was Defeated," beginning "Tony was small, but of Noble Race" (Harvard, Bodleian Ashmole G.16 [144], Yale, Huntington; reprinted with music in *180 Loyal Songs*, 1685, and without music in *RB* V, 148, VIII, 754). The bookseller

Nathaniel Thompson was credited with this ballad in one of the two rejoinders which quickly appeared: "The Coat of Arms of N. T. J. F. & R. L. An Answer to Thomson's Ballad call'd The Loyal Feast," beginning "Tory is small and of no good race." [1] Sixteen preliminary lines of poetry are to be sung "to what tune Thomson pleases, but let the rest be to his own Tune, Sawny will ne're be my Love again" (BM 1875.d.6 [20], Huntington, Bodleian Ashmole G.16 [49], Harvard). The other sequel is "An Answer To the Pamphlet called, The Loyal Feast . . . To the same Tune. Sauney will never be my Love again," 1682, beginning "Tories are Tools of the Irish Race" (Lord Crawford, BM 1876.f.1, Chetham, Harvard, Huntington; reprinted in *Rome Rhym'd to Death*, 1683, p. 95, and *RB* IV, 256, VIII, 755).

Others to the tune include: "The Poets Dream: Or, The . . . Complaint of the Land against Bayliffs and their Dogs," beginning "As I lay Slumbering in a Dream" (Pepys, dated 1679; Lord Crawford, BM 82.l.8, Harvard, Roxburghe; reprinted in *RB* VII, 11). The burden of this ballad—"And that's the cause that the Land Complains"—becomes another name for the tune of a broadside on an analogous subject, "The poor Peoples Complaint of the Unconscionable Brokers and Talley-Men," beginning "Will you hear how the rich do oppress the poor," to the tune of "This is the cause that the Land complains, or, Sawny will never be my love again" (Pepys; reprinted in *PB* III, 87). Also related to the "Poet's Dream" is "Poor Robins wonderful Vision," beginning "When drousie Orbs did begin to appear," with the refrain "Which alas makes the Nation sore complain" (BM C.22.f.6 [70], Lord Crawford 1291, Harvard). "The Sodomite, or the Venison Doctor," beginning "Listen (if you please) a while," is a libelous ballad on Oates and others (Clark, with MS date 13 Sept. 1684; reprinted in *180 Loyal Songs*, p. 197), and another to the tune is a ballad of c. 1689, "A King and No King: Or, King James's Wish," beginning "My Wretched Fate, I do declare" (Pepys; reprinted in *PB* IV, 165). Among nonpolitical ballads may be mentioned "The Bonny Lass of Bristol," beginning "There was a Lass her name was Nell" (Pepys III, 303), and "The Credulous Virgins complaint," beginning "Come hearken to me young Maidens all" (BM C.22.f.6 [107], Lord Crawford 246, Douce I, 40, Harvard). T. Robins's "The Scornful Maid and the Constant Young-Man," beginning "All hail, all hail, thou Lady gay" (Lord Crawford, Harvard, BM C.22.f.6, Douce; reprinted in *RB* VIII, 867) names the tune as "Sawney," along with two others for which music has not survived—"Times Changling I will never be" and "A Fig for France [and Holland too]."

[1] The initials are identified by Luttrell in the Huntington copy as standing for Nathaniel Thompson, John Farwell, and Roger L'Estrange—all Tories.

Allan Ramsay's poem "Corn Riggs are bon[n]y," beginning "My Patie is a lover gay," which he included in his *Tea-Table Miscellany*, 1733, II, 144, appears with the music of "Sawney" in his ballad opera, *The Gentle Shepherd*, 1729 (music in the 1786 edition), and in its English adaptation by Theophilus Cibber, *Patie and Peggy*, 1730. Words and music are in William Thomson's *Orpheus Caledonius*, 1733, II, No. 18, *Calliope, or English Harmony*, 1739–1746, I, 41, *Universal Harmony*, 1745, p. 43, Alexander Smith's *Musical Miscellany*, 1786, Johnson's *Scots Musical Museum*, 1787–1803, I, 94, and in several single-sheet editions (e.g., BM G.310 [86]).[2] The tune is introduced into several ballad operas under the name of "Corn riggs are bonny": Mitchell's *The Highland Fair*, 1731, Phillips's *The Livery Rake*, 1733, Coffey's *The Merry Cobler*, 1735, and *The Whim* (MS of 1741, Huntington Library). As "Sawney was tall" it appears in Chetwood's *The Lover's Opera*, Gay's *Polly*, and Johnson's *The Village Opera*, 1729, Phillips's one-act condensation of the latter, *The Chamber-maid*, 1730, and Coffey's *The Devil to Pay*, 1731. Evidently the popularity of Ramsay's song was responsible for the alteration of the tune name in later ballad operas.

The Scotch Haymakers

This tune is associated with a song which Thomas D'Urfey contributed to Thomas Scott's play *The Mock-Marriage*, 1696, Act III. It begins " 'Twas within a Furlong of Edinbrough Town," and the tune is sometimes given that name. Henry Purcell wrote the music for two other songs in the play, and contemporary reprints include his name; this song is not so credited. It is, however, listed in the Purcell bibliography in *Grove's Dictionary of Music and Musicians*, 5th ed., 1954, VI, 1012, and is doubtfully admitted to the canon in the Purcell Society edition (*Works*,

[2] Although the origin of the tune is clear, the popularity of Ramsay's song has led to attempts to claim tune and all for Scotland. Thus James C. Dick writes (*Notes on Scottish Song by Robert Burns*, 1908, p. 90): "To controvert the English origin it may be stated that from a tune, *New Cornrigges* in *Blaikie's MS.*, 1692, it is evident that there existed in Scotland some other tune of the name." His argument is that the name "New Cornrigges" implies an earlier "Cornrigges" tune, a logical inference which is not always borne out by the facts of tune naming. The chief weakness in his claim, however, is that much of the lost Blaikie MS is (as can be seen from a nineteenth-century partial transcript now preserved in the Dundee Free Library) eighteenth century in origin, despite the 1692 date found in the MS. The "New Cornrigges" tune is not (nor does Dick claim it to be) a version of "Sawney."

412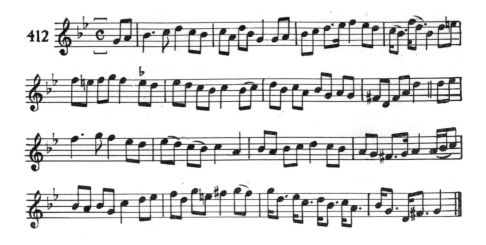

XX, 1916, 115). More conclusive attribution appears in the title of a contemporary engraved single-sheet edition of the ditty: "A Scotch Song in the Mock Marriage Sung by the Girl Set by Mr. Charles Powell and exactly engrav'd by Tho: Cross" (Harvard). Miss E. N. Backus's *Catalogue of Music in the Huntington Library* queries Jeremiah Clarke as the composer, probably on the authority of an early eighteenth-century harpsichord setting by "Clarke" of " 'Twas within a furlong" (BM MS Add. 22099, fol. 9). Of the three possibilities, Charles Powell seems to have the strongest claim, especially since the wording of the song-sheet title suggests that it was published when the play was fresh in the minds of the London audience.

It appears, with other songs from the play, in *Deliciae Musicae,* Third Book, 1696, p. 2 (Fig. 412), in another single-sheet edition called "Scotch Song" (BM G.312 [51]), and in all editions of *Pills,* 1719–1720, I, 326. The tune is in *The Second Part of the Dancing Master,* 1696 (2d ed., 1698), whence it entered the eleventh and succeeding editions of *The Dancing Master.* The song was widely reprinted during the eighteenth century, appearing in such miscellanies as *The Hive,* 3d ed., 1727, II, 240, and, with music, in *The Convivial Songster,* c. 1782, p. 286.[1]

The stage song was expanded from three to six stanzas and issued as

[1] For further information on the later currency of the playhouse song, see *The Songs of Thomas D'Urfey,* ed. C. L. Day, 1933, p. 149. A sentimentalized adaptation of D'Urfey's text, with different music, is found in Alexander Smith's *The Musical Miscellany,* Perth, 1786, p. 272, beginning " 'Twas within a mile of Edinburgh town." The same words and music are in Johnson's *Scots Musical Museum,* 1787–1803, I, 49, and in a single-sheet edition of c. 1800 which credits the music to "Mr. Oswald." James Hook wrote "Within a mile of Edinburgh" for *Harlequin and Faustus,* produced in 1793 (BM G.295 [13]); Stenhouse was thus led to credit Hook with the *Museum* tune.

a broadside with meaningless music: "The Scotch Hay-Makers: Or, Crafty Jockey's Courtship To Coy Jenny of Edenborough" (Pepys V, 266, Lord Crawford 1221). It was followed by "An Answer to the Scotch Hay-Makers," beginning "Attend young lasses all of Edenborough Town," to the tune of "Twas within a furlong of Edenborough Town," again with meaningless music (Pepys V, 260, Lord Crawford 154). Within the next few years some eighteen or twenty other ballads were written to the tune, usually called "The Scotch Haymakers" from the title of the original broadside. At least three were issued in 1696: "Sir John Friend and Sir William Perkins Last Farwell to the World . . . Executed . . . 3d. of April, 1696," beginning "The Riddle is Expounded, the Plot is very plain" (Chetham 53, with mutilated title; Pepys; reprinted in *PB* VII, 215); "The Young Farmer's Answer to his Sweet-heart Nanny, who . . . complained . . . of a Troublesome Maiden-head," beginning "What's this my dearest Nanny, that fain would be a bride" (Roxburghe; reprinted in *RB* VIII, 207); [2] and "An Excellent New Song, Called, Rare News for the Female Sex," beginning "As I of late was walking by a Country Bakers door" (Pepys III, 184, V, 426).[3]

The following ballads to the tune have apparently not been reprinted: "A Copy of Verses of a Baker and a Mealman," beginning "In Blackman-street there dwelt Sir a Baker of renown" (Pepys III, 72); "The Cuckold's Calamity," beginning "Hear my lamentation, good People, now I pray" (Pepys V, 256); "The Dorset-shire Lovers," beginning "Passing through a Meadow, young John and [*or* did] Joany meet" (Lord Crawford 995, Harvard); "The Dorset-shire Wedding," beginning "John and Joan sat talking beneath the Mirtle-tree" (Morgan 37); "Pecunia's Departure," beginning "We have lost a Lady belov'd of Rich and Poor" (Pepys IV, 325); "True Love Indeed," beginning "Come hither my dear Betty, and sit thou down by me" (Pepys III, 26); "Truth in Mourning," beginning "Conscience, for a fancy, rambl'd forth to find" (Pepys II, 52); "The Jolly Cheese-Monger," beginning "Here's a pleasant Ditty I'll Sing you, if you please" (Pepys III, 67, Morgan 43); and "The Slighted Virgin," beginning "Come you lusty Lovers and hear a pleasant Jest" (Pepys III, 69).

The tune, usually called " 'Twas within a Furlong," was used in eight

[2] The ballad to which this is an answer, and which must have received prior publication, is "The Maulsters Daughter of Malborough," beginning "Mother let me Marry, I long to be a Bride" (Pepys III, 70, Lord Crawford 823), also sung to "The Scotch Hay-Makers."

[3] The burden "Now e'ery Lass that means to pass must all be punched this Year" makes clear the relationship between this ballad and an undated continuation, "The Young Damsels Lamentation . . . against the late Punching," beginning "Here's a Lamentation that's spread abroad of late" (Pepys III, 287), also to the tune.

ballad operas, of which the following print the music: Chetwood's *The Lover's Opera,* Gay's *Polly,* and Johnson's *The Village Opera,* 1729; the one-act condensation of the latter, Phillips's *The Chamber-maid,* 1730; and Coffey's *The Devil to Pay,* 1731.

The Scotch Wedding

The song from which the various names of this tune are drawn is "The Blythsome Wedding," the opening lines and refrain of which are:

> Fy let us all to the Briddel,
> for there will be Lilting there,
> For Jockie's to be marry'd to Maggie,
> the Lass with the Gauden Hair.

The song was apparently first published in James Watson's *Choice Collection of . . . Scots Poems,* 1706–1711, Part I, p. 8. A single-sheet version entitled "(The Scotch Wedding) or the Lass with the Golden Hair," beginning "Now Jockey and Moggy are ready," was issued in London about 1710 (BM H.1601 [317], Huntington, Chetham 1386, Harvard = Fig. 413) and was reprinted with that title in *Pills,* 1714, V, 279, 1719–1720, VI, 350, and in *The Merry Musician,* 1716, I, 211. Music is oftener found in 6/8 than in the correct 9/8 barring. A broadside version of "The Blythsome Wedding. To its own proper Tune" is in the National Library of Scotland (Rosebery III.c.36 [128], without music). Allan Ramsay included it as an old song, with the title "The blythsom Bridal," in his *Tea-Table Miscellany,* 1723, p. 165, and words and music under

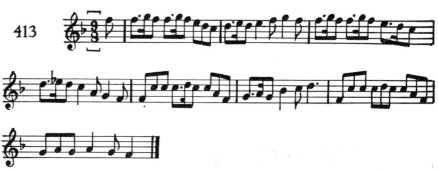

413

Original time signature and barring are 6/8.

that title are to be found in William Thomson's *Orpheus Caledonius,* 1725, No. 36, and in Johnson's *Scots Musical Museum,* 1787–1803, I, 58. A reprint of Watson's text is in *The Poems of the Sempills of Beltrees,* ed. James Paterson, 1849, p. 67; the claims of Sir William Scott and Francis Sempill to the authorship of the song are there resolved in favor of the latter, but the argument is not conclusive.

Several broadsides were written to the tune. In "The High Church Lovers . . . to be Married by Dr. Sacheverel," 1710, beginning "Young Lovers pray be of good Chear," the tune is called "Golden Hair" (BM 1872.a.1 [158ᵛ]). Another of the same date is "Jack Presbiter's Triumphant Rejoycing . . . at the Rebuilding of the Old Doctor Burgess's Meeting," beginning "Dear Brethren do ye hear how fine," to the tune of "The Scotch Wedding: Or, Jocky is to be married to Moggy the Lass with a Golden Hair" (BM 1876.f.1 [46]). A slightly different ballad on the same subject is "The Dissenters Triumph," beginning "Dear Sisters, come see you how fine," to the tune of "The Scotch Wedding" (*A Collection of Poems, for and against Dr. Sacheverell,* 1711, Part 4, p. 14; *Tory Pills to Purge Whig Melancholy,* 2d ed., 1715, p. 55). An imitation of the original song is "The Munster Wedding," 1722, beginning "Oh! there was a jovial Wedding, a jovial Wedding I trow," to the tune of "Sawny's to be Married to Moggy" (BM 839.m.23 [14]).

A version of the tune, called "And the Kirk would let me be" (perhaps an earlier title than "The Scotch Wedding" and its congeners), is in Alexander Stuart's *Musick for Allan Ramsay's . . . Scots Songs,* c. 1725, p. 42. Ramsay had cited "The Kirk wad let me be" as the tune for the second half of "The Satyr's Comick Project," in *Poems,* 1721 (Scottish Text Soc. ed., 1945, pp. 192–193), for "Slighted Nansy," an "old" song in his *Tea-Table Miscellany,* 1723, p. 40, and for a song in the ballad-opera version of his *The Gentle Shepherd,* 1729. "An the Kirk wad let me be" is found as an air with bass in William McGibbon's *Scots Tunes,* Book I, 1742, p. 18. For the "kirk" verses giving this title to the tune, see David Herd, *Scottish Songs,* 1776, II, 224, and *Songs from David Herd's Manuscripts,* ed. Hans Hecht, 1904, pp. 119, 290.

The tune was introduced into five ballad operas under five different names. In Theophilus Cibber's *Patie and Peggy,* 1730, it is "The blithsome Bridal"; in *Lord Blunder's Confession,* 1733, "Fie, let us all to the Wedding"; in *The Sturdy Beggars,* 1733, "Fie, let's awa to the Bridal"; in *The Wedding,* 1734, "Come, let us all to the Wedding"; and in Brooke's *Jack the Gyant Queller,* 1749, "Hye let's away to the Wedding." Only the first named contains the music.

"The Scotch Wedding" is the title of two late eighteenth-century broadsides which are not to be confused with the genuine Scotch piece here discussed. One is to the tune of "In January last," the other to "Jenny gin," qq.v.; the iambic rhythmic patterns of both serve to distinguish them from the anapestics of the earlier song and its offshoots.

See the Building

This sophisticated tune takes its name from "A Well-wishing to a place of Pleasure," directed to be sung to "an excellent new tune" and beginning "See the building,/where whilest my mistris liued in,/was pleasures essence" (Pepys, Roxburghe; reprinted in *RB* III, 57). The poem, with considerable variation of text, is in the Percy Folio MS (ed. Hales and Furnivall, IV, 1); in *Giles Earle His Booke, 1615–1626,* ed. Peter Warlock, 1932, p. 103 (the original, BM MS Add. 24665, fol. 75ᵛ, contains empty musical staves); and in Thomas Smith's MS songbook of 1637, collated in Warlock.

A ballad on the reburnishing of a famous cross in 1626, "Cheapsides Triumphs," begins "See the guilding/Of Cheapsides famous building/the glorious Crosse" and is to the tune of "the Building" (Pepys; reprinted in *PB* II, 49). Another of about the same date, which names the tune "See the building," is "A delicate new Song, Entituled, Sweet-heart, I loue thee," beginning "Sweet-heart I loue thee/And deeme no Lasse aboue thee/in all this City" (Pepys; reprinted in *PB* II, 71). And still another, on the sheet with "A Well-wishing" and in the same distinctive stanza pattern, is manifestly intended for the tune; it is "An inconstant Female," beginning "Louing mortall,/In loue I here exhort all/in that estate" (Pepys, Roxburghe; reprinted in *RB* III, 60). Phineas Fletcher named "See the building" as the tune for singing his paraphrase of Psalm 137 published in 1633 (Giles and Phineas Fletcher, *Poetical Works,* ed. F. S. Boas, 1908–1909, II, 252). And a solemn parody of "A Well-wishing" was sung in the fourth act of William Heming's *The Jewes Tragedy),* 1662 (ed. H. A. Cohn, 1913, p. 53).

Music entitled either "The Building(s)" or "See the Building" is generally adequate, although no tune has been set down in conjunction with a song text, and therefore detailed adjustments are required to fit the small but persistent verbal irregularities. Perhaps the best version is a relatively unadorned virginal set of c. 1600–1625 in Christ Church MS 431, fol. 4ᵛ (Fig. 414). Two others are in Priscilla Bunbury's MS Virginal Book, Nos. 21, 30, dating perhaps from the 1640s. Of uncertain

date within the seventeenth century is the lute accompaniment, expertly conceived but not often melodic, in Trinity College, Cambridge, MS O.16.2, p. 136. A viola da gamba tablature probably of the second half of the century is ascribed to R[ichard] S[umarte] in a manuscript preserved in the Henry Watson Music Collection of the Manchester Free Reference Library. The sole printed exemplar I have discovered is a cittern set in the early Playford tutor, *A Booke of New Lessons for the Cithern & Gittern,* 1652, No. 53.

The broadside texts of "A Well-wishing" require a repetition of the first strain of "See the Building," whereas all the other pieces associated with the tune use the first strain only once; even the MS texts of "A Well-wishing" exemplify the shorter stanza form with the elimination of lines 7–12 of each broadside stanza.

Sefautian's Farewell

Giovanni Grossi (1653–1697) was an Italian male soprano who entered the papal chapel in 1675 and later had a notable operatic career in both Italy and England. After his success in the role of Siface (Syphax) in a revival of Cavalli's *Scipione Africano* at Venice in 1678, he was universally known as Siface. He spent part of the next decade in London, and we have the testimony of John Evelyn's *Diary* (April 19, 1687) that he sang at Pepys's house, though his connection with the theater and

415

with James II's chapel is doubtless of greater moment. The public acclaim which attended him must explain the inspiration for a ballad written in 1688 upon his return to Italy. It is "Sefautian's Farewel: or, Fair Silvia's Matchless Cruelty. To an Excellent New Tune: Or, Sefautian's Farewel," beginning "Hope Farewel, adieu to all Pleasure" (Pepys, Wood 417; reprinted in *RB* III, 414).[1] Music appears on the sheet (Fig. 415) and is found also with "An Answer to Sefautians Farewell . . . To the same Tune," beginning "My Sefautian, art thou Deceased" (Wood 417 [160]; another edition, without music, is in Euing, Lord Crawford, Roxburghe; reprinted in *RB* III, 416). The tune is found as "Sefauchi's Farwell" arranged for virginals in *The Second Part of Musick's Hand-maid,* 1689, sig. E4ᵛ, and as "Cefachio's Farewel" in *Apollo's Banquet,* 6th ed., 1690. The appearance of Purcell's name in the former arrangement raises the question whether he composed the tune or merely set it, as does his signature on "Lilliburlero" in the same volume. Both tunes were in print before the publication of *Musick's Hand-maid,* and

[1] Another edition, without music, may be a Scottish imprint; at any rate, Siface is not mentioned in either title or tune direction: "Hope farewel, Adieu to all pleasure, or Silvia's Matchless Cruelty," to the tune of "Hail great Sir" (National Lib. of Scotland Ry III.a.10 [51]). I have no information on the tune named.

only in that work is Purcell's name subscribed. For reasons which I have advanced in the discussion of the other tune, the issue cannot be decided conclusively.

Half a dozen other ballads were written to the tune. Those bearing the name "Sefautian's Farewell" include: "The Perjur'd Swain," beginning "As I rang'd for my Recreation" (Pepys IV, 60, Lord Crawford 99, BM C.22.f.6 [162]); "The True Protestants Contemplation," beginning "Let all men God's Mercies admire" (Pepys; reprinted in *PB* VI, 237); and "England's Pride," beginning "Pride's a reigning Sin of this Nation" (Lord Crawford; reprinted in *RB* VIII, 18, 801). In the following the tune is named "Hope (*or* Hope's) Farewell" from the opening line of the original ballad: "The French King's Vision," c. 1689, beginning "On the Fourteenth day of October" (Pepys; reprinted in *PB* V, 52); "The Two Faithful Lover's Tragedy," beginning "In London liv'd a Crafty old Miser" (Harvard, Lord Crawford, BM C.22.f.6; reprinted in *A Century of Ballads,* ed. John Ashton, 1887, p. 106); and "The Royal Funeral . . . of Mary, Queen of England . . . Fifth of March, 1695," beginning "Here I write a sorrowful Ditty" (Pepys; reprinted in *PB* VII, 71). "Celia's Conquest," beginning "Let others prepare for brisk Wars and Alarms," is to be sung "To an excellent new Court Tune: Or, Hope Farewell" (Harvard, with meaningless music); the "Court Tune" is evidently that by Bernard Berenclow found with a brief version of the text in *Comes Amoris,* Third Book, 1689, p. 2. Finally, *Pills,* 1719–1720, VI, 345, contains a short lyric beginning "Fates I defie, I defie your Advances" to the tune "Hopes farewel," printed without music.

Sellenger's Round,
or The Beginning of the World

This famous sixteenth-century dance tune is found in William Ballet's MS Lute Book, p. 101, in Cambridge University MS Dd.3.18, fol. 5 (lute), and, as "Brande d'Angleterre" in *Het Luitboek van Thysius,* No. 389. William Byrd's variations include a statement of the tune in *The Fitzwilliam Virginal Book* I, 248 (Fig. 416), and also in his *My Ladye Nevells Booke,* No. 37. A seventeenth-century virginal set without title is in Paris Conservatoire MS Rés. 1186, fol. 78; another

416

keyboard arrangement is contained in *Musicks Hand-maid*, 1678, No. 10. The roughly coeval Bedford Cittern MS contains two settings, and one for lute is in Trinity College, Cambridge, MS O.16.2, p. 128. The air is in *The Dancing Master*, 1665–1690, with directions for the dance.

The origin of the tune is unknown, though it has been supposed that the name was originally "St. Leger's round." [1] The explanation of "The Beginning of the World" in Thomas Tomkis's comedy *Lingua*, 1607, III, vii, is of course facetious:

Ana[mnestes]. By the same token the first tune the planets plaied, I remember *Venus* the treble ran sweet diuision vpon *Saturne* the base. The first tune they plaied was *Sellengers* round, in memory wherof euer since, it hath beene called the beginning of the world.

References to the tune under one name or the other abound in literature of the sixteenth and seventeenth centuries. Thus in *Bacchus Bountie* by "Philip Foulface," 1593, 1595, allusion is made to "the old hop about, commonly called Sellengars round." And in Thomas Morley's *A Plaine and Easie Introduction to Practicall Musicke*, 1597, a student is taken to task for imitating the opening of "Sellenger's Round" in one of his compositions. In the first act of Thomas Heywood's *A Woman Killed with Kindness*, acted 1603, the company has a hard time picking a dance tune, some preferring "Rogero," others "John, come kiss me now," "The

[1] W. H. Grattan Flood, in his *History of Irish Music*, 1905, p. 159, and in *TLS*, Sept. 29, 1921, p. 628, argues for the Irish origin of the tune and for the derivation of its name from Sir Anthony St. Leger, who held three appointments as lord deputy of Ireland between 1540 and 1556.

cushion dance," "Tom Tyler," "The hunting of the fox," "The Hay,"
or "Put on your smock a Monday"; finally they agree on "Sellenger's
Round." In many another allusion (see Chappell, *PMOT* I, 70) the
tune is thought of as an air for dancing, in the spirit of John Cleveland's

> Who should he but hear, our organs once sound,
> Could scarce keep his hoof from Sellenger's round.[2]

But it was also used for songs and ballads, even from an early date. For
in John Pickering's interlude *Horestes*, 1567, sig. B2ᵛ, a song beginning
"Farre well adew, that courtlycke lyfe,/To warre we tend to gowe," is
to the tune of "haue ouer yᵉ water to floride or selengers round." Richard
Johnson's *Crown Garland of Golden Roses*, 1612 (ed. Chappell, 1842,
p. 68) contains "A new sonnet of a knight and a faire virgin," a version
of the loathly lady tale sung to the tune of "Selengers round." Perhaps the
earliest extant broadside calling for the tune is William Hockom's "The
Beggers Intrusion, Or the worlds Illusion," c. 1628, beginning "A Begger
of late most poore in estate" (Pepys; reprinted in *PB* II, 95).

Other broadsides to the tune include "The Great Boobee," licensed
1656, beginning "My friend, if you will understand," which was "to a
pleasant new Tune ['The Great Booby,' q.v.], or, Salengers Round"
(Pepys, Euing, Douce, Roxburghe; reprinted in *RB* VII, 273). Another,
which must have appeared about the same date, is found in Mennes
and Smith's *Wit Restor'd*, 1658, p. 168, as "To the Tune of The beginning of the World. R. P. Delight," beginning "O Mother, chave bin a
batchelour." Extant broadside copies, dating from after the Restoration,
are titled "The Merry Wooing of Robin & Joan the West-Country Lovers," and the tune direction is "The beginning of the World, or Sellingers
Round, or Great Boobe" (Pepys, Roxburghe; reprinted in *RB* VII, 308).

Another mid-century ballad to "Sallengers round" is "Hey for our
Town, But a Fig for Zommerset-shire," beginning "In Winter time when
flowers do fade" (Douce I, 96), which is in answer to a ballad extant only
in late seventeenth-century copies: "The West-Country Delight: Or, Hey
for Zommerset-Shire," beginning "In Summer time when flowers do
spring," to the tune of "O how they did Firk it: Or, Salengers round"
(Douce II, 242ᵛ, 247; reprinted in *Pills*, 1719–1720, IV, 122, with the music
of the first tune, for which see "Under the Greenwood Tree"). Still
another ballad to this pair of tunes is "The Fair Maid of Islington; or
The London Vintner Over-reach'd" (*BB* I, 410).[3]

[2] *Poems*, 1653, reprinted in *Minor Poets of the Caroline Period*, ed. George Saints-
bury, 1921, III, 75.

[3] "The Fair Lass of Islington," *Pills* V, 46, is a version of "The Fair Maid" text, but
the fine modal tune accompanying it is not related to either of those named on the
broadside. "The bailiff's daughter of Islington" is an independent text and tune, q.v.

"A Ballad on Queen Elizabeth," beginning "I [*or* I'll] tell you all both great and small," is in *Choyce Drollery,* 1656, to the tune of "Sallengers round"; under other titles, but usually without tune direction, it was reprinted in Hicks's *London Drollery,* 1673, and in Henry Bold's *Latine Songs, with their English,* 1685. The English and Latin texts are both found in *Pills* VI, 233, coupled with a tune by Samuel Akeroyde which was used also for "The Great Boobee," V, 94; it is unsuitable for either ballad.[4]

A carol "For St. John's day," beginning "In honour of St. John we thus/do keep good Christian fare," is directed to be sung to the tune in *New Carolls,* 1661, sig. A7. An eighteenth-century burlesque, "Captain Dill upon Hogg-back," 1710, to "the Old Tune of Sallengar's Round," opens its frothy text "At the first beginning of Sallengar's Round, the Man leap'd into the Moon" (Harvard).

Ballads sung to "Sellenger's Round" are uniformly in ballad-stanza octaves and call for sixteen bars of music, omitting a repetition of the final section of the second strain found in the Byrd arrangements. The tune itself is circular, like many other dance tunes; it not only ends on the chord of the dominant, thus forcing a return to the beginning, but much of its second strain pivots around the key of the dominant in such a way as to make its tonality uncertain. It must rank, however, as one of the most melodious of all dance tunes borrowed for ballad singing, and the only wonder is that its popularity was not greater in the late seventeenth century.

Resembling "Sellenger's Round" in melodic contour, but set in stately common-time rhythm, is the hymn tune of Melchior Teschner to verses by Valerius Herberger beginning "Valet will ich dir geben." It appeared in *Ein andächtiges Gebet . . . ,* Leipzig, 1615 (see Johannes Zahn, *Die Melodien der deutschen evangelischen Kirchenlieder,* 1889–1893, No. 5404a). It is best known today in English-speaking countries as the tune of "All glory, laud, and honour/To Thee, Redeemer, King" (*Hymns, Ancient and Modern,* 1950, No. 98). Bach drew on Teschner's melody for a *St. John's Passion* chorale, "In meines Herzens Grunde, dein Nam' und Kreuz allein" (Bach Ges. Ed. XII.1, 95), and he also set the tune with its original words (*The Four-Part Chorals of J. S. Bach,* ed. C. S. Terry, 1929, Nos. 324 and 325). For some of this information I am indebted to Margaret Dean-Smith, *JEFDSS,* VI (1950), 30.

[4] The tune appears a third time in *Pills,* at IV, 96, where it is attributed to Akeroyde; it fits the words there printed, but they are not in the meter of "Sellenger's Round" ballads.

Shackley Hay, or To All You Ladies Now at Land

Although it may originally have been a dance tune, "Shackley hay" appears to derive from a place name prominently featured in a ballad licensed March 16, 1613: "A most excellent Song of the loue of young Palmus, and faire Sheldra," beginning "Young Palmus was a Ferriman,/Whom Sheldra faire did loue," to the tune of "Shackley-hay" (Pepys, Euing, Lord Crawford, Bagford, Douce, Roxburghe; reprinted in *RB* III, 6). The first stanza of the ballad has been copied from the original broadside issue in BM MS Add. 38599, fol. 140, where an excellent version of the air has been set down (Fig. 417). Only through the

Original a fifth lower and unbarred.

preservation of this early seventeenth-century musical text can we see how integral was the "fa la" refrain following the sixth and eighth lines of each stanza. A considerably later arrangement for mandore, in 6/8 rather than common time, is found in the Skene MS; Chappell printed it, but since it did not seem to demand a repetition of the second strain Chappell suppressed the "fa la" refrain throughout.[1] That the tune was sometimes

[1] An ambiguous setting of "Shackerley Hay" in unbarred tablature without time values is in the seventeenth-century Bedford Cittern MS.

sung without the repetition is shown by the existence of drollery songs and at least one broadside in seven-line stanzas.

The full ten-line stanza form is found in William Meash's ballad of 1614, "Leanders loue to loyall Hero. To the tune of Shackley hay," beginning "Two famous Louers once there was" (Pepys, reprinted in *PG*, p. 49); a copy without title, tune direction, or author's name is in the Percy Folio MS (ed. Hales and Furnivall, III, 295). Another ballad to the tune is "The Knitters Jobb," beginning "Within the Town of Walton fair," with a seven-line stanza (Douce, Lord Crawford, Harvard, Roxburghe; reprinted in *RB* VII, 331).

A number of drollery songs call for the tune, naming it "Shackle de hay": "The Politick Wedding" is in William Hicks's *London Drollery*, 1673, p. 69; "A Song on the Declensions" is in *Westminster Drollery*, 1671, I, 40, and in Hicks's *Grammatical Drollery*, 1682, p. 62, where "My Mistress is all the Genders," p. 56, and "My Mistress understands all the Cases," p. 58, are also found; the two latter had appeared in Hicks's *Oxford Drollery*, 1671, pp. 26, 29.

An entry in the Stationers' Register for Dec. 30, 1664, is for "The Noble seamans complaint to the Ladies at Land, to ye tune of Shackerley Hay" (Rollins, *Anal. Index*, No. 1960). On the following January 2, Pepys noted in his *Diary*: "to my Lord Bruncker's, by appointment, in the Piazza, in Covent Garden; where I occasioned much mirth with a ballet I brought with me, made from the seamen at sea to their ladies in town; saying Sir W. Pen, Sir G. Ascue, and Sir J. Lawson made them." The ballad was actually written by Charles Sackville (then Lord Buckhurst and afterward Earl of Dorset), but copies of the original issue of 1664 seem not to have survived.[2] Perhaps the oldest copy of the poem is an eleven-stanza version preserved in a manuscript of the era of Charles II (BM MS Harl. 3991, printed in *Seventeenth Century Lyrics*, ed. N. Ault, 2d ed., 1950, p. 348). But the chief vogue of the song came in the eighteenth century, when it was repeatedly issued as a single sheet and was included in many poetical miscellanies (with and without music), along with a host of parodies and imitations. The Stationers' Register entry makes it clear that the ballad was originally sung to "Shackley hay,"

---

[2] The belief that Dorset wrote the ballad in June, 1665, "the night before the engagement," was popularized by a reference in the dedicatory epistle of Prior's *Poems on Several Occasions*, 1718 (ed. A. R. Waller, 1905, p. xvi) and furthered by such a title as the following: "Written at Sea, by the late Earl of Dorset, in the first Dutch War, the Evening before a bloody Sea-fight" (*The Hive*, 4th ed., 1733, II, 154). The statement in Pepys's *Diary* establishes an earlier date, which the Stationers' Register entry confirms. The mystery of Pepys's not having retained his copy of the original broadside may be explained by the fact that he did not begin systematically to collect ballads until the next decade.

418

but most commentators have assumed that its tune was a new one. The several forms of the eighteenth-century air can be seen, however, to have developed from the original tune.

The earliest version with music (Fig. 418) seems to be a single-sheet song of c. 1707 entitled "A Ballad by yᵉ late Ld Dorset when at Sea, never before Printed," beginning "To you fair Ladys now at Land" (BM G.305 [180], Chetham 1875; another issue, omitting from the title "late" and the three last words, BM H.1601 [428], Harvard). This was reprinted in *Pills*, 1714, V, 168, 1719–1720, VI, 272, and also in *The Merry Musician*, 1716, I, 39. The music is in 3/4 time, with bizarre accentuation resulting when phrases of 3⅓ or 4⅔ measures are repeated. Meantime another tune variant, fitted to a song beginning "Well I'll say that . . ." in *Pills* (1700, II, 268; 1719–1720, IV, 222), retains the common time of "Shackley hay" and some of its refrain pattern but otherwise looks forward to the later form of the tune (Fig. 419). It is more truly an example of the transitional state than are the versions in 3/4 time, even though the latter contain most of the melodic shifts which the old air was to undergo. The shift was completed with the early ballad operas: Mottley and Cooke's *Penelope*, 1728, prints the tune "To all you Ladys" in common time but with some uncertainty of note values; in the following year, Gay's *Polly* air is awkward at the outset but in the second strain agrees with the virtually final form in Coffey's *The Beggars' Wedding*. In Ryan's *The Cobler's Opera*, 1729, Air 7 (Fig. 420), the familiar tune is fully evolved. Music is also printed in Chetwood's *The Lover's Opera* (ed. of 1730), in *Robin Hood*, 1730, and in *The Jovial Crew*, 1731, and the tune is called for in ten other ballad operas whose printed editions contain no music. The air is printed with a parody, "To you, fair Ladies, now in Town," in Watts's *Musical*

419

Miscellany, 1729–1731, III, 90, and in *The Merry Musician,* c. 1731, III, 107; and it is found with "Let others sing of flames and darts" in *The Convivial Songster,* c. 1782, p. 273.

The number of songs sung to "To you fair [*or* To all you] Ladies now at Land" is legion. A great many may be found in such topical anthologies as *Political Merriment, A Collection of State Songs, A Pill to Purge State-Melancholy,* and *Mughouse Diversion,* some of them citing the tune name "To you, Dear Ormond," derived from the opening line of a parody on the Jacobite James Butler, second Duke of Ormonde. *The Hive,* II, 3d ed., 1727, contains half a dozen pieces constituting an exchange of poetical epistles between a prisoner in Marshalsea and another in Newgate. Pope wrote "The Court Ballad," 1717, to the tune; it begins "To one fair Lady out of court" (see *Poems,* Twickenham edition, VI, 1954, 180). Attributed to Pope but evidently spurious is "News from Court," beginning "Ye Ladies Fair who live remote," which circulated as a broadside dated 1719 (Chetham 65). Others to the tune, picked

420

Original a fourth higher.

almost at random from a large number, include: "The Soldiers Lamentation For the Loss of their General," 1712, on the downfall of Marlborough (BM 162.m.70 [12], Chetham 119); "The Ladies Skreen, A New Ballad," c. 1728, beginning "Let P[ultene]y speak, or Caleb write" (BM C.116.i.4 [42], Harvard; another issue, BM C.20.f.2 [316], Huntington, lacking first half of title); and such parodies as "A Pastoral Letter," c. 1718, beginning "To all the Clergy in this Land/Eleven Bishops write" (BM 1876.f.1 [83], Huntington, Harvard) and "The Fate of Courtezans And Their Enamerato's," 1735, beginning "To you, fair Nymphs of Venus' Train" (BM 1876.f.1 [109]).

The Shaking of the Sheets

A very inaccurately notated version of "the shakinge of the sheetes" is preserved in William Ballet's MS Lute Book, p. 84; it can be roughly cast into fourteen-measure form to accommodate, if uneasily, the seven-line stanza associated with the tune name (Fig. 421). William Byrd's fantasia

421

on "Ut.re.my.fa.sol.la" (Paris Conservatoire MS Rés. 1122, p. 1, printed in Forty-five Pieces for Keyboard Instruments, ed. S. Tuttle, 1939, p. 86, and Byrd, Collected Works, ed. E. H. Fellowes, 1937–1950, XX, 130) quotes motifs from "The shaking of the sheets" in the fourth variation.

A different tune is found in The Dancing Master, 1651–1690 (1651, p. 3=Fig. 422) under the title "The Night piece, or (The shaking of the Sheets)"; in some editions only the first title appears. The dance tune, with a threefold repetition of its second strain written out in 1651, appears in 1670 with only the two four-bar phrases of thematic material and the usual repeat signs. B. H. Bronson, who reproduces both the Ballet and the 1651 Playford tunes in *The Traditional Tunes of the Child Ballads,* 1959–   , I, 361, shrewdly guesses that the long form of the dance air is a typographical device to fill out the line. Neither a sixteen- nor a twenty-bar tune is suitable for the seven-line stanza. Chappell repeated the seventh line to form an eight-line stanza vaguely adaptable to the sixteen-bar tune, but it seems doubtful that words and music were intended for each other.

Original is unbarred and is a fifth higher, without key signature.

The ballad which appears to have given the tune its name, but which may have been written to a dance tune already known, is Thomas Hill's "A dolfull daunce & song of death Entituled: the shakeing of the sheetes," beginning "Canne you dance the shakinge of the sheetes/a daunce that everie man must dooe." This ballad was licensed in 1568–1569 (Rollins, *Anal. Index,* No. 480), but the earliest surviving version is in BM MS Add. 15225, fol. 15, c. 1616. It is the only copy containing Hill's name and is without tune direction. Printed editions, in which the second half of the title is altered to "Dance after my Pipe," direct the singing "To a pleasant new tune" (Wood 402, Wood 401, Pepys, Rawlinson, Harvard, Lord Crawford, Roxburghe; reprinted in *RB* III, 184).

"The Shaking of the Sheets" is named as the tune for "The Old Abbot and King Olfrey," beginning "In old times past there was a king we read" (Douce, Pepys; reprinted in *RB* VI, 753). An early seventeenth-century ballad with the tune direction "Death's dance" cannot be sung to the William Ballet tune but might be intended for the *Dancing Master* version, each half of which suffices for a stanza of the ballad. It is "An excellent new Ditty: Or, Which proveth that women the best Warriors be," beginning "Old Beelzebub, merry/disposed to be" (Roxburghe; reprinted in *RB* I, 331).

"Dance after my pipe" is alluded to as the name of a tune in Fletcher's *A Wife for a Month,* III, iii, and as a catchphrase in Webster and Dekker's *Westward Ho!,* II, i. The manuscript play *Misogonus,* II, iv (of uncertain authorship), and Heywood's *A Woman Killed with Kindness,* I, i, refer to "The shaking of the sheets" as a country dance. In *The Meeting of Gallants at an Ordinarie,* 1604, a young man who was exposed to the plague "daunced the shaking of one sheete within fewe daies after." Although the phrase could refer to rigor mortis, it was far more commonly a euphemism for intercourse, as used in Dekker's *The Shoemakers' Holiday,* V, v, Fletcher's *The Mad Lovers,* IV, ii, Massinger's *The City Madam,* II, i, and Marston's *The Insatiate Countess,* Act II.

Shall I Wrestle in Despair

This tune name is a corruption of "Shall I, wasting in despair,/Die because a woman's fair," the opening of a poem by George Wither. It was first published in his *Fidelia,* 1615, and later appeared in the pirated *Workes,* 1620, and in *Faire Virtue,* 1622. The poem may have been written before 1610, for a passage in Beaumont's *Knight of the Burning Pestle,* II, viii, "Why, an if she be, what care I?" seems to echo the refrain of Wither's song. A much expanded version, retaining four of Wither's five stanzas, was issued as a broadside c. 1615: "A new Song of a Young mans opinion, of the difference betweene good and bad Women. To a pleasant new tune," beginning "Shall I wrestling in dispaire" (Pepys; reprinted in *PB* I, 61). Another expanded text, of eight stanzas, is found in Richard Johnson's *Golden Garland of Princely Pleasures,* 3d ed., 1620, called "The Shepheards resolution. To the tune of the yong mans opinion." A stanza-for-stanza parody, employing images which are the converse of Wither's, is found in *A Description of Love. . . . And Also Mast. Johnsons Answere to Master Withers,* first issued c. 1618 (reprinted from 5th ed., 1625, in Ben Jonson's *Works,* ed. Herford and Simpson, 1925–1952, VIII, 439; and from 6th ed., 1629, in *The Poetry of George Wither,* ed. F. Sidgwick, 1902, I, 145, where Wither's original poem may also be found, I, 138; Richard Johnson has been suggested as the author of the parody). The Percy Folio MS (ed.

Hales and Furnivall, II, 50) contains a four-stanza version of Wither's poem.

A six-stanza text (comprising stanzas 1,2,3,7,8,9 of the broadside) is preserved with music (Fig. 423) in the Leyden MS of 1639, fol. 17^v,

423

Original is unbarred.

National Library of Scotland; its first stanza begins "Sall I wrastling in despair die because a woman is fair." The first four stanzas of the broadside are coupled with the same tune in another early seventeenth-century version, MS 1018, fol. 12, in St. Michael's College, Tenbury. A fresh setting of Wither's text by "Mr. King" is in *Pills*, 1719–1720, IV, 120. Other musical treatments are in *London Magazine*, XXVII (Feb., 1758), 92, and in a single-sheet issue of c. 1780, "What care I for whom she be. Sung by Mr. Vernon" (BM G.311 [123], Harvard).

Other ballads, designed to be sung to the early seventeenth-century setting, include two which call the tune "Shall I wrastle in despair": "This Maide would giue tenne Shillings for a Kisse," c. 1615, beginning "You young men all take pitty on me" (Pepys; reprinted in *PG*, p. 79), and a broadside of c. 1625 shorn of its title, but with the subtitle "The vnfortunate Gallant gull'd at London," beginning "From Cornwal mount to London faire" (Pepys; reprinted in *PB* I, 238). "Jone is as good as my Lady," c. 1620, beginning "Shall I here reherse the story," is to the tune of "What care I how faire she be," a name derived from Wither's refrain (Pepys; reprinted in *PB* I, 158).

She Got Money By't,
or Fourpence Halfpenny Farthing

This tune is found in *The Dancing Master*, 7th ed., 1686 (New Additional Sheet, c. 1688, p. 5) and in the body of succeeding editions as "The Jockey"; with the fifteenth edition, 1713, it becomes "Four Pence halfpeny Farthing, or The Jockey," and under the latter titles is found also in Walsh's *Compleat Country Dancing-Master*, 1718. A slightly more singable version of the tune, called "She got Money by th' Bargain," is introduced into two ballad operas, Hippisley's *Flora*, 1729, Air 7 (Fig. 424), and Langford's *The Lover his own Rival*, 1736. Scotch settings in-

clude "She gote Money by it" in the Agnes Hume MS, 1704, and "Money in both yʳ pockets" in Dr. John Leyden's MS Lyra Viol Book, after 1690 (the latter preserved in the nineteenth-century G. F. Graham transcript, No. 14).

About 1629 Martin Parker wrote a ballad whose title and refrain were "Fourepence halfepenney Farthing" (see the discussion s.v. "A health to Betty"). In the 1680s a handful of new ballads took up Parker's catchphrase and added another, which seems to have appeared first in "The Lady of Pleasure, or, the London Misses Frolick . . . To a Pleasant New Play-House Tune," beginning "There was a Lass in London Town," with a refrain:

> She got money by't, she got money by't,
>   she got money by th' bargain;
> she got money by't, she got money by't,
>   four-pence-half-penny Farthing.

The ballad appeared c. 1682–1685 (BM C.22.f.6, Lord Crawford, Harvard, Douce; reprinted in *RB* VIII, 710). This was followed by "London Miss well fitted, or, an answer To the Four-pence-Halfpenny Farthing," beginning "The London Miss was Ranting fine," to the tune of "Four pence-Half penny Farthing," and with a refrain beginning "Now she got nothing by't" (Pepys III, 238). Others with analogous burdens include: "Mony makes the Mare to go," beginning "Tis Money makes the Mare to go," with tune title as in the ballad just cited, and a refrain beginning "If he gets money by't" (Pepys IV, 257, Harvard); and "The Extravagant Gallants Resolution," beginning "Room for a Blade that spares no Gold," with a refrain " 'Twas he the money got . . ." in the first stanzas, shifting to "But I'll the mony spend . . ." (Pepys IV, 249), the tune named "She got Mony by't or four pence half-peny farthing."

Others to the tune of "She got money by't" include: "The Nine Maidens Fury to the Hartford-Shire Man," beginning "There was a young-man liv'd of late" (Pepys III, 275), followed by "The Hartford-shire Mans Fears of the Maidens Furies. It being an Answer to the Nine Maidens Attempt in Gelding the Young-man," beginning "I wonder that this Age is grown" (Pepys III, 276); "A New Summons to Green-Goose-Fair," beginning "Young Men and Maidens all arow" (Pepys III, 278); and "The Unfortunate Damsel," beginning "In Debtford liv'd a Bonny Lass," to the tune of "My Child must have a Father. Or, She got money by 't" (Pepys; reprinted in *PB* III, 274).[1]

Other ballads citing the tune as "Four-pence-half-penny-Farthing" include: "The London Taylors Misfortune," beginning "A Damsel came to London Town" (Douce, Lord Crawford; reprinted in *RB* VII, 470); "The Couragious Gallant," beginning "Away with Cupids idle Darts" (BM C.22.f.6 [102], Lord Crawford 159, Harvard); "The Green sickness cured," beginning "Here's for Jenny a tempting Guinney" (Wood 417 [177]); and "The London Lady or, Wise and Wanton," 1689, beginning "There liv'd a Lass in London Town," with a refrain "She liv'd by her Witts . . ." (Pepys III, 41).[2]

[1] "My Child must have a Father" is another name for the tune "Daniel Cooper," q.v.
[2] This last ballad names "Tom the Taylor" as an alternative tune, for which see "Daniel Cooper."

The tune is named "He got Mony by't" in "A new Ballad. Truth needs no Vindication. 1686," beginning "If devout Paulet Mary/Had been crafty as Sarah" (BM MS Harl. 7319, p. 467), but the six-line stanza fits only half the tune.

She Lay All Naked in Her Bed

This tune name is derived from the first line of a song which appeared in *Wit and Drollery,* 1656, and in *Merry Drollery Complete,* 1691. A musical setting by John Wilson is coupled with an abridged version of the text in a pre-1660 Bodleian collection, MS Mus.b.1, fol. 134 (Fig. 425).

A broadside version, "Loves Fancy, Or, The Young-mans Dream," beginning "She lay naked in her Bed/and I my self lay by" (Wood E.25 [88]), is directed to be sung to "The Hay-makers march," which may or may not be the same as "The Haymakers," q.v., but is almost certainly not Wilson's tune. The Wood sheet anticipates by up to a dozen years the edition entered in the Stationers' Register in 1675 (Rollins, *Anal. Index,* No. 1564). The first line of this ballad became in turn the tune name given for singing "Loves Mistery: Or, A parcel of clouded Waggery," beginning "All in the merry Month of May,/the prime time of the Year" (Roxburghe, partially reprinted in *RB* VII, 322). Another broadside, "The distracted damsel Or the mad Maids Morris," beginning "Fair Coelia in her Frantick Fits," is to the tune of "She lay all naked in her bed, or the mad Mans Morris" (Rawlinson 145).[1] Likewise, a piece in *Mock Songs,* 1675, called "The Gadding Gallant," is to be sung to "She lay all naked in her bed." In the same meter and perhaps related to this tune is Laurence Price's "The dainty Damsels Dream," beginning "As I lay on my lovely bead [sic]," to the tune "As she lay sleeping in her bed" (Roxburghe; reprinted in *RB* VII, 102). Wilson's music could have served for all these pieces, but we cannot establish its currency beyond the original association with "She lay all naked" verses. Neither can we be assured of the identity of the broadside tune, "The Hay-makers march."

The Shepherd's Daughter

This tune appears in all save the first edition of *The Dancing Master* (1652, p. 83=Fig. 426), usually called "Parson upon Dorothy" or "Par-

426

son[s] and Dorothy," but in the 1670–1690 editions called "The Shepherd's Daughter." Under the former name the tune is also found in three ballad operas: *Momus turn'd Fabulist* and Gay's *Polly,* 1729, and Lillo's *Silvia,* 1731.

The traditional ballad known as "The Knight and Shepherd's Daughter" (Child No. 110), licensed as a broadside in 1624 and again in 1656, is preserved in an edition representing the second of these entries and published by Gilbertson: "The beautifull Shepherdesse of Arcadia," beginning "There was a Shepherd's Daughter/came triping on the way"

[1] "The Mad-mans Morrice" is a broadside by Humphrey Crouch "To a pleasant new tune" whose identity cannot be traced (*RB* II, 154).

(Roxburghe III, 160).[1] This issue and another of not much later date (Douce I, 11ᵛ, 14) bear the tune title "The Shepheards Delight"; in issues of c. 1700 the tune is called "The Shepherd's Daughter" (Lord Crawford, Douce, Chetham, Roxburghe; reprinted in *RB* III, 451). The stanza is a ballad-meter quatrain with a burden "Sing trang dil do lee"; music in *The Dancing Master* and the ballad operas, however, is designed for a six-line or (with each strain repeated) a twelve-line stanza in this meter, and there is no provision for a refrain. It may be doubted, then, that the tune as we have it was used for singing the ballad. Chappell "adapted" the tune by eliminating the second strain which nearly or completely repeats the first, and adding a two-bar coda for the refrain (*PMOT* I, 127). This reconstruction, while it has no textual validity, is probably sound: as the tune passed from ballads to country-dance sets, a two-bar refrain would almost certainly have been discarded, in order to allow the conventional four-bar phrases to flow unimpeded.

"The forsaken Damosel: Or, The Deluded Maid," beginning "Abroad as I of late did walk," is to the tune "A Shepherds daughter once there was" (Rawlinson 24). The tune name may be a paraphrase of the opening line of "The Beautiful Shepherdess"; except for the absence of a refrain line here, the stanza patterns are identical.

The earlier tune name, "The Shepherd's Delight," is found as the title of two ballads whose metrical patterns are so widely at variance with the measure of "The Beautiful Shepherdess of Arcadia" that neither can be seriously considered as a source of the tune title.[2]

Most of Child's traditional texts of "The Knight and Shepherd's Daughter" lack a refrain, but as B. H. Bronson shows (*The Traditional Tunes of the Child Ballads*, 1959– , II, 535), "*every* copy collected *with* its tune has strong elements of refrain." A Somerset version which Cecil Sharp included in his *One Hundred English Folksongs*, 1916, p. 6, supplements the ballad quatrains with a burden "Line twine the willow dee," phonetically reminiscent of the "Sing trang dil do lee" of the seventeenth-century broadside; the two-bar tag at the end of the tune is characteristic of several Sharp recoveries in which the last line of each stanza is repeated or a single-line burden appended.

[1] Stanza five of the ballad is sung by Crack in Richard Brome's comedy *The City Wit*, 1653, II, ii.

[2] One is in a twelve-line stanza which is the equivalent of six anapestic tetrameters (see "Bonny Sweet Robin"); the other is in iambic tetrameter octaves (see "Frog Galliard").

Sick, Sick

This tune takes its name from the refrain:

> Syck sicke & totowe sike
> & sicke & like to die
> The sikest nighte that euer I abode
> god lord haue mercy on me

of William Asheton's ballad on Captain Car, found in the late sixteenth-century BM MS Cotton Vespasian A.xxv, fol. 178, olim 187 (published by K. Böddeker in *Jahrbuch für roman. und engl. Sprache*, N. F. III [1876], 126, and in Child, No. 178). A Stationers' Register entry "sick sick &c" of March 24, 1579, may refer to this ballad or to the lost moralization entered on June 19 of the same year: "sicke sicke ingraue I would I were for griefe to see this wicked world yat will not mend I feare" (Rollins, *Anal. Index,* Nos. 2442, 2443).

To the tune of "Sicke and sicke" William Elderton wrote "A newe Ballade, declaryng the daungerous shootyng of the Gunne at the Courte," beginning "The seuentene daie of Iulie laste, at euenyng toward night," with imitative refrain:

> Weepe, weepe, still I weepe, and shall doe till I dye:
> To thinke vpon the Gun was shot, at court so dangerously.

Despite the fact that on August 10, 1579, Edward White was fined 12d for printing it and its circulation was surely not encouraged, the ballad escaped destruction, for a copy is extant in the library of the London Society of Antiquaries (Lemon, *Catalogue,* No. 72; a reprint is in the *Harleian Miscellany* X, 272).[1]

The refrain of Elderton's ballad establishes the source of "Weep, weep," named as the tune for W. M.'s "The Lamentation of Englande . . . Fraunces Throgmorton . . . executed . . . the tenth day of July last past. 1584," beginning "With brinishe teares and sobbing sighes,/I Englande pine in paine" (Lord Crawford; reprinted in J. P. Collier's *Broadside Black-Letter Ballads,* 1868, p. 21). To the same tune Deloney wrote "A proper new Ballad breefely declaring the Death . . . of 14. most wicked Traitors . . . the 20. and 21. of September. 1586," beginning "Reioyce in hart good people all,/sing praise to God on hye" (Lord Crawford; reprinted in Collier, p. 36, and in Deloney's *Works,* ed. Mann, p. 464).

---

[1] See Arber's *Transcript of the Stationers' Register,* II, 850, and Hyder E. Rollins, "William Elderton: Elizabethan Actor and Ballad-Writer," *SP,* XVII (1920), 223.

A fragment of the "Captain Car" refrain is quoted in the anonymous play *Looke about you,* 1600, sig. G2, and a paraphrase of the refrain is sung in Nashe's *Summer's Last Will and Testament,* sig. H1, of the same year. A reference to "the sick tune" in *Much Ado about Nothing,* III, iv, is to an unrelated melody which Wooldridge reprints erroneously in connection with "Sick, sick" (*OEPM* I, 74).

The tune of "Sicke sicke and very sicke" is preserved in Antony Holborne's *Cittharn Schoole,* 1597, sig. D3 (Fig. 427) and in Cambridge Uni-

427

* Variations upon the air follow in the original.

versity MS Dd.4.23, fol. 6, also in cittern tablature. Both sets are for a ballad quatrain. Elderton's ballad requires a repetition of the tune for the refrain; the other two, containing an eight-line stanza plus a quatrain of refrain, require a double repetition of the melody.

Since Celia's My Foe

This tune, called also "Celia's my foe," takes its name from the opening line of a song by Thomas Duffett printed in his *New Poems, Songs, Prologues and Epilogues,* 1676, p. 1, under the ambiguous title "Song to the Irish Tune." In the same year it appeared in *A New Collection of the Choicest Songs* and with an anonymous musical setting in *Choice Ayres, Songs, and Dialogues,* p. 77 (Fig. 428). It is found also in *The Wits Academy,* 1677, and *Wit and Drollery,* 1682. In expanded form it was issued as a broadside called "Amintor's lamentation for Celia's unkindness . . . To a delicate New Tune: Or, Since Celias my foe" (Wood E.25, Lord Crawford, Rawlinson, Douce, Harvard, Roxburghe; reprinted in *RB* III, 386, and *OPB,* p. 205). This was followed by "Celia's answer to Amintor's lamentation," beginning "Tis better then so,/Tho' you force me to go" (Douce, Rawlinson; reprinted in *RB* III, 389). Another pair

of ballads to the tune are "The Forc'd Marriage. Or, Unfortunate Celia,"
by W. P[ope], beginning "To what great distress/without hopes of re-
dress" (Wood E.25, Lord Crawford, Euing, Douce, Harvard, Roxburghe;
reprinted in *RB* VIII, 190), and "An Answer To the forc'd Marrige:
Or, the old mans vindication," beginning "Since Celia's a Whore,/I'le
abide her no more" (Lord Crawford, Harvard, Rawlinson; reprinted in
RB VIII, 192).

Other ballads to the tune include Lawrence White's "The happy greeting of Iohn and Betty," beginning "Come sit down my dear,/until I declare" (Wood E.25 [138], Rawlinson 96); "The Deceived Virgin . . . a
New Song Sung at Windsor: By B. G.," 1684, beginning "Come Hither
all you,/Who to Love never knew" (Chetham 279); "Cupid's Master-
Piece," beginning "God Cupid's unkind/Since my Soul he confin'd" (BM
C.22.f.6 [39], Lord Crawford 427, Rawlinson 73, Harvard); and "A Song
on the Confession and Dying Words of William Stevenson . . . executed
at Durham . . . 26th of August, 1727," beginning "Good Lord! I'm undone, thy Face I would shun" (Harvard, Chetham 258).

Chetwood's *The Lover's Opera,* 1730, contains an air entitled "Since
Celia's my Foe," but it is actually a version of the Scotch tune "Loch-
aber," associated with a song by Allan Ramsay (*Poems,* 1728, in *Works,*
ed. Burns Martin and J. W. Oliver, 1953, II, 281; words and music in
William Thomson's *Orpheus Caledonius,* 1733, II, No. 20, in Johnson's
Scots Musical Museum, 1787–1803, I, 96, &c.).[1]

[1] For a note on the Scotch origin of the tune, see *The Bunting Collection of Irish
Folk Music and Songs,* Part VI, pp. 32ff., in *JIFSS,* XXVIII–XXIX [1939, for 1932]).
Chappell (*RB* III, 384) follows Bunting's *Ancient Music of Ireland,* 1840, p. 69, in
claiming "Lochaber" as the composition of Miles Reilly, an Irish harpist born in 1635.

Sing, Sing Whilst We Trip It

In the second act of Purcell's opera *The Fairy Queen*, 1692, Mrs. Ayliff sang the highly ornamented "Sing, sing whilst we trip it, trip, trip it,/ trip trip it upon the Green." It was included in *Some Select Songs . . . in the Fairy Queen,* p. 3, published in the same year (Fig. 429), and the

* Misprinted 6/4 in original.

tune alone was included in *Apollo's Banquet,* 7th ed., 1693. A printed broadside edition with music is "An Excellent new Song, Call'd The Fairy Queen, or, The merry Companions" (Lord Crawford, BM C.39.k.6; reprinted in *OPB,* p. 51; the copy in Pepys V, 157, contains meaningless music). An engraved song-sheet edition has the title "A Song in the New Opera call'd, The Faiery Queen. Sung by Mrs. Aliff" (BM C.180.a [15]). Words and music are to be found in every edition of *Pills,* 1719–1720, III, 298. No other broadsides were sung to the tune.

Sing Tantara Rara

The "tantara rara" refrain was attached to at least three different tunes, each adapted to a different stanzaic pattern. "Which nobody can

* E in original; emendation from 1714 *Pills*.

deny," the short form of "Greensleeves," q.v., is sung with a stanza of three anapestic tetrameter lines plus refrain, which in one ballad is:

> Sing Tantara rara Boys hey, Boys hey,
> sing Tantara rara Boys hey.[1]

Another example is in *Pills*, 1719–1720, V, 270, where the "Which nobody" refrain appears, except that the last stanza employs the "tantara" formula above with "Whores all, Whores all."

An anonymous tune (Fig. 430) found in all editions of *Pills* with the

[1] "Epithalamium . . . 1689. To the Tune of, Lulla by baby, &c." (*PB* IV, 206).

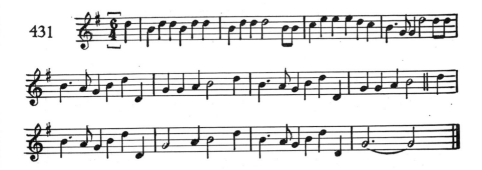

song "You mad caps of England who merry wou'd make" (III, 281), serves for a four-line stanza plus a refrain formula:

> Sing Tanta, ra, ra, ra, ra, ra Boys,
> Tanta ra, ra, ra, ra, ra Boys,
> Tanta ra, ra, ra, ra, ra Boys drink, Boys drink.

But in succeeding stanzas the refrain is written in the old way, scarcely singable without some alteration in the tune:

> Sing Tanta ra, ra, &c. Wear Horns, wear Horns,
> Sing Tanta ra, ra, &c. Wear Horns.

Five ballad operas, all without music, seem to call for this *Pills* tune. In Fielding's *The Genuine Grub-Street Opera*, 1731, and Drury's *The Rival Milliners*, 1737, it is called "Ye [You] Madcaps of England"; in *The Beggar's Pantomime*, 1736, the final "Song and Chorus" displays no tune title but contains the "Sing tantara rara" refrain. Others naming the tune are Peterson's *The Raree Show*, 1739, and Ayres's *Sancho at Court*, 1742, the latter using the name "Tantarara Rogues all." It is perhaps to this tune that a Dublin broadside of c. 1730 was sung: "A New Ballad On the Game of Bragg," beginning "Ye Belles and ye Beaus for a moment attend," with the refrain "Sing Tanta-ra-ra-ra Bragg All, &c." (BM 1890.e.5 [35], without tune direction or music).

The third tune, composed by William Defesch, was made popular through "The Masquerade Song Sung by Mr. Beard at Ranelagh," beginning "Ye Medley of Mortals that make up this Throng" (Fig. 431). This was issued as a single-sheet song (BM G.305 [174], Harvard, Huntington) and was published in *Universal Magazine*, July, 1749, in *Gentleman's Magazine*, August, 1749, and was reprinted in *Muses Delight*, 1754. Its pattern consists of four anapestic tetrameters, plus refrain:

Sing Tantararara Masks all, Masks all,
Sing Tantararara Masks all.[2]

George Alexander Stevens's *Songs, Comic and Satyrical,* 1772, contains
several pieces written to the tune, which he identifies as "Masks all" (pp.
42, 81, 186) or "Ye medley of mortals" (p. 220) or "Sing Tantararara
Toast all" (p. 124, the tune named for the refrain of this song). Others
include: a song by Garrick, "All in the wrong," c. 1750, beginning "Ye
Critics above, and ye Critics below" (BM G.316.f [118]); a song of c. 1787
entitled "Cox-Heath Camp," beginning "Adieu to dear London the gay
Folks all cry" (BM G.306 [91]); and a piece by H. Howard, c. 1762, without music or tune direction, called "The Pe[as]e Soup Makers," beginning "Of late we have heard of a Laird in high Station," with the characteristic refrain pattern "Sing Tantararara Cooks all, Cooks all . . ."
(BM 1850.c.10 [78]).

Sir Eglamore

This tune, which is very closely akin to "The Friar in the well," had
its vogue in the second half of the seventeenth century, although the ballad from which it is named is much earlier. "Sir Eglamore" was originally "set downe . . . verbatim" but without title by Samuel Rowlands
in his *Melancholie Knight,* 1615, sig. E2. A slightly longer version, called
"Courage Crowned with Conquest . . . To a pleasant new Tune," appeared on broadsides, of which the earliest extant edition is dated 1672
(Pepys, Bagford, Lord Crawford, Rawlinson, Harvard, Roxburghe; reprinted in *RB* III, 607; the Euing 53 copy is about ten years later). It
had meantime been printed in several miscellanies, including *Wit and
Drollery,* 1656, and *Antidote against Melancholy* and *Merry Drollery,*
1661. Probably the earliest version of the tune, c. 1650–1675, is that which
appears with bass accompaniment and the first stanza of the ballad in
Edinburgh University Library MS Dc.1.69, fol. 114ᵛ reversed (Fig. 432).
This form of the air is also found in *The Second Book of the Pleasant
Musical Companion,* 2d ed., 1686, Part II, No. 20, in a setting for three
voices with the full ballad text. The same melodic line and text appear
in every edition of *Pills,* 1719–1720, III, 293.

---

[2] Some copies contain the tune direction "Sing tantararara Fools all," implying that
Defesch's melody had been previously used for another song. And this supposition is
strengthened by the presence of the Masquerade song in *Thesaurus Musicus,* fol. 140,
a collection of single-sheet songs provisionally dated 1743.

A parody "Sir Eglamor and the Dragon. Or, A Relation how Generall George Monk slew a most cruell Dragon February 11. 1659[/60]" to the tune of "Sir Eglamor" is in customary quatrain form but without the burden required after the first, second, and fourth lines of each stanza (*The Rump*, 1660, reprinted in *Rump*, 1662, and *Loyal Songs*, 1731). Other ballads to the tune include: "Ignoramus-Justice: or, The English-Laws turn'd into a Gin, To let Knaves Out, and keep Honest Men In," 1682 (BM C.38.i.25, Wood 417, Huntington, Clark; reprinted in *180 Loyal Songs*, 1685, p. 276, with the music, and in *RB* V, 78); and "Truth Tryumphant, Over Perjury Rampant. On the Tryal of the Salamanca Doctor [Titus Oates] . . . May the 8th. and 9th. 1685" (Lord Crawford 1125; reprinted in *180 Loyal Songs*, p. 279).

The close relationship to the *Dancing Master* tune of "The Friar in the well" is most evident in the first strain of the *180 Loyal Songs* "Sir Eglamore" and the second strain of the Edinburgh MS version and its congeners.

Sitting by Yonder River Side

This tune is named for the first line of a "Song Made by a Gent." and sung in the third act of Aphra Behn's comedy *Sir Patient Fancy*, 1678. With music by Thomas Farmer it appears in *Choice Ayres & Songs*, Second Book, 1679, p. 35 (Fig. 433). The air alone is in *Musicks Recreation on the Viol, Lyra-way*, 1682, p. 21; the words alone are in Henry Bold's

433

Latine Songs, with their English, 1685, p. 56, and *The Hive*, 3d ed., 1727, II, 145.

The expanded broadside version, called "Parthenia's Complaint," is "To a New Tune much in Request: Or, Sitting beyond a River side" (Lord Crawford, Euing, Douce, Harvard, Roxburghe; reprinted in *RB* VI, 47). It was followed by "Amintor's Answer to Parthenia's Complaint," beginning "Under a pleasant Willow shade," to the same tune (Lord Crawford, Douce, Wood E.25, Harvard, Pepys, BM C.22.f.6; reprinted in *RB* VI, 50).

Another ballad to the tune is "Repentance too Late," beginning "Sad as death at dead of night," to the tune of "Sad as death [q.v.]: or, Parthenia unto Cloe cryed" (Pepys, Roxburghe; reprinted in *RB* VI, 52). The alternative tune title is a paraphrase of "Parthenia thus to Cloe cry'd," the second line of the original playhouse song.

Smiling Phyllis

A broadside of c. 1680, "Charming Phillis. Or, The Disloyal Lover," begins "Smiling Phill[i]s has an Air,/so oblieging all Men Love her" and is to be sung to "Smiling Phillis" (Douce I, 24). The song from which the broadside is expanded had originally appeared, with music by Thomas Farmer, in *Choice Ayres & Songs*, Second Book, 1679, p. 38 (Fig. 434). The words are also in *Wit and Drollery*, 1682, John Shirley's *The Complete Courtier*, 1683, and with the music in *Pills*, 1719–1720, IV, 281.

434

* E♮ in bass.

"Happy is the Countrey life, Or, Smiling Phillis" is given as the tune direction for "The Country Mans Delight. Or, The Happy Joyes of a Countrey Life," beginning "Happy is the Countrey life,/bless'd with content, & health, and ease" (Pepys, Roxburghe; reprinted in *RB* V, 564).[1] Farmer's "Smiling Phillis" music does not fit this ballad, for the six-line stanza would require only three-quarters of the tune, and the rhythmic patterns of verse and music are at cross purposes. The broadside is, however, an expansion of a song first published in *Choice Ayres and Songs,*

435

Fourth Book, 1683, p. 36, with music by James Hart which does fit (Fig. 435). The tune of "Happy is the country life" was included in Humphry

[1] The Roxburghe copy "To a pleasant new tune" has the title "The Country Innocence" and is without imprint. The Pepys copy, licensed by Pocock, was issued 1685–1688.

Salter's *The Genteel Companion . . . for the Recorder,* 1683, and the original song was reprinted in *Pills* IV, 288, and Watts's *Musical Miscellany,* 1729–1731, VI, 44.

A Soldier and a Sailor

This tune takes its origin from a song beginning "A Souldier and a Sailor,/A Tinker, and a Tailor," the music by John Eccles, sung in the third act of Congreve's *Love for Love,* 1695. It was reprinted with the tune in *Thesaurus Musicus,* Fourth Book, 1695, p. 27 (Fig. 436), and in a number of contemporary single-sheet issues (BM G.315 [42], G.316.d [17], H.1601 [51], California). Words and music are in all editions of *Pills,* 1719–1720, III, 220, and in such other collections as *British Melody,* 1739, No. 12. The verses are in many poetical miscellanies, including *The Compleat Academy of Complements,* 1705, p. 161, and *The Hive,* 4th ed., c. 1733, III, 265. The tune alone is in *The Dancing Master,* commencing with the Second Part, 1696 (and in the body of 11th ed., 1701, *et seq.*); it is also in *Youth's Delight on the Flagelet,* 11th ed., 1697.[1]

The text, lengthened from three to six stanzas, was issued as a broadside called "Buxom Joan of Lymas's Love to a Jolly Sailer: or, The Maiden's Choice: Being Love for Love again. To an excellent new Play-house Tune," containing meaningless music (Pepys, Lord Crawford, BM C.39.k.6; reprinted in *OPB,* p. 154). An eighteenth-century edition, to a "Pleasant New Tune" but without music, is "A Soldier and a Saylor Or Buxom Joan" (Harvard, BM 1871.e.9 [51], with cropped title).

Other ballads to the tune include: "The Lusty Lad of London," beginning "Come listen to this Ditty" (Lord Crawford, Pepys, BM C.39.k.6; reprinted in *OPB,* p. 91); "The French Satyre," beginning "In fair and pleasant Weather" (Pepys; reprinted in *PB* VII, 53); "The Saint turn'd Sinner," beginning "You Friends to Reformation" (Bagford; reprinted in *BB* I, 30; a version of the text is in *Pills* VI, 215, to music printed at p. 213); and "The Battle Royal," 1698, beginning "A Dean and Prebendary" (Lord Crawford 1010, *Pills* VI, 213, with music; text alone in *The Hive,* 1725, III, 100).

[1] For a note on several contemporary MS copies of the tune, see *Songs from the Restoration Theater,* ed. Willard Thorp, 1934, p. 117. Thorp reprints in facsimile (p. 67) the version containing a canonic bass accompaniment which Sir John Hawkins had included in his *History of Music,* 1776, V, 65.

436

* Preceded in the original by two half-measure rests.
** Two-measure rest in original omitted here.

Political parodies to the tune are found in *Tory Pills to Purge Whig Melancholy*, 2d ed., 1715, p. 59, and *Political Merriment*, Part III, 1715, p. 6. "The Competition. Occasion'd by the Success of the Beggar's Opera" depicts the rivalry between the two leading Italian singers of the day, Faustina and Cuzzoni, in a song to the tune printed in *The Hive*, 4th ed., III, 167.

Eccles's tune was introduced into Gay's *The Beggar's Opera*, 1728, Phillips's *The Mock Lawyer*, 1733, and six other ballad operas, but the music is found only in the two named.

Some Say the Papists Had a Plot

This tune takes its name from the opening line of a broadside entitled "A New Song, Being the Tories Tryumph . . . to a New Theatre Tune," 1682 (Harvard, Huntington, Yale, Bodleian Ashmole G.16 [77]). It was

437

Original is a fourth higher.

reprinted with music in *180 Loyal Songs*, 1685, p. 212 (Fig. 437), along with another to the tune which had also been previously published as a broadside: "A New Narrative of the Old Plot, being A New Ballad," 1683 (BM 1872.a.1 [124ᵛ], Bodleian Ashmole G.16 [85], Lord Crawford 1327, Chetham 81, Huntington, Clark, Harvard; a 1684 edition in Ashmole G.16 [138], Clark and Harvard).

Other ballads to the tune include: "A new Song between Whig and Tory," 1683, beginning "What Chear poor foul mouth'd Whig what Chear?" (Chetham 306); "Jack Presbiter," 1690, beginning "Jack Presbyter pricks up his Ears" (BM 1871.e.9 [90]); and "The Wounded Lover," beginning "Mythinks I feel fresh bleeding wounds," to the tune of "Some say there was a Papist plot; or, Jenny Gin" (Pepys III, 381).

Sound a Charge

I have not found a ballad from which the tune name "Sound a Charge" could be derived. About 1660, however, a ballad was published that calls for the tune. It is T. R.'s "The Royall Subjects Joy" (Euing, Roxburghe; reprinted in *RB* VII, 678), which has the following distinctive stanza form:

You Loyall Subjects all
sing for joy, sing for joy;

> Good news here's at *White-Hall,*
>   *sing for joy.*
> A second *Charles* is come,
> Though heavy news to some,
> Let them say no more but mum,
>   *sing for joy, sing for joy.*

Another is "Touch and go; or, The French Taylor finely Trapann'd," c. 1670, beginning "A Tayler in the Strand,/Touch and go, touch and go," to the tune "Sound a Charge, Sound a Charge" (Rawlinson; reprinted in *RB* VII, 486). Its stanza contains four rather than three lines upon the *b* rhyme.

I have found no music entitled "Sound a Charge." *The Dancing Master,* 1701 *et seq.,* contains a tune "Touch and Go" whose rhythms are unsatisfactory for singing either ballad. Several other pieces cast in the mold of "The Royall Subjects Joy" give us names of still other tunes which do not seem to have survived: "Captain Kid's Farewel to the Seas," c. 1701, is to the tune of "Coming down" (Lord Crawford 843, reprinted in C. H. Firth's *Naval Songs and Ballads,* 1908, p. 134); and a D'Urfey poem "The Moderator's Dream" is to "Chimney Sweep" (*Pills,* 1719-1720, II, 182, without music).[1] There is, however, in *Pills,* 1714, V, 117,

438

1719-1720, VI, 251, an amorous song beginning "A Young Man and a Maid, put in all, put in all," which contains music (Fig. 438) suitable to

[1] In 1701, the year Captain Kidd was executed, a chimney sweep named Jack Hall was hanged for burglary. His exploits were the subject of a traditional song collected by Cecil Sharp (*Folk Songs from Somerset,* 4th series, 1908, p. 20); its concluding line, "O but never a word said I coming down," suggests a possible link between the lost tunes "Chimney Sweep" and "Coming down."

all these ballads save the hypermetrical "Touch and go." The same air is found in *The Dancing Master,* II, 2d ed., 1714, 121, entitled "Put in All." Although we cannot be sure that this tune was used for the seventeenth-century pieces, a strange bit of evidence strengthens the possibility. "Londons farwell to ye parliament," a manuscript ballad of c. 1642 in the hand of Henry Lawes and attributed to him, is coupled with an unnamed air (Fig. 439) clearly related to the eighteenth-century "Put in

439

all." The first stanza, a variant form interlining the music, shows the close metrical similarity to the ballads just cited:

> farwell to ye parlyament
>   with a Hey with a Hey,
> far well to ye parliament
>   with a Hoe,
> your dear delight ye Cittye,
> whose wants have made us witty
> & a figg for ye close Comittee
>   with a Hey tronony nony noe.[2]

Except for the length of the closing line here (in the text of the ballad the line contains an additional "nony"), the structure is congruent with that of the other pieces under discussion. The difference is reflected in the final phrases of the two tunes. It should be noted that the refrain tags of "Londons farwell" are preserved intact in a group of late seventeenth-century political ballads cited under "I am the Duke of Norfolk,"

---

[2] BM MS Add. 32343, fol. 11. The entire text on fol. 12 has been printed in Willa McClung Evans, *Henry Lawes: Musician and Friend of Poets,* 1941, pp. 223–226. She accepts the British Museum Catalogue of Manuscript Music attribution of words and music to Lawes; they are obviously in his autograph but I strongly doubt that he was their creator. Her date of 1659 is not sustained by a careful reading of the ballad, whose topical allusions are to persons and events prominent at the very beginning of the civil war.

q.v.; because those pieces have a stanza body of four lines rather than five, they cannot be sung to the tune Lawes has recorded. With the omission of measure 6, however, the tune would fit those ballads better than does "I am the Duke of Norfolk."

The stanza pattern of "The Royall Subjects Joy" is also found in the more recent ballad "Sam Hall," with a fine traditional tune. It lies, however, outside the scope of our discussion.[3]

The Spanish Gipsies

This tune, called "The Spanish Gipsy [*or* Gipsies]," is found in every edition of *The Dancing Master* (1651, p. 23=Fig. 440), and in *Musick's*

Original is unbarred.

Delight on the Cithren, 1666, No. 35. In the third volume of *The Dancing Master,* c. 1728, 145, there is an additional appearance of the tune under the name "Fairy Queen." Paris Conservatoire MS Rés. 1186, fol. 36, contains a mid-seventeenth-century keyboard setting of the tune.

The tune may have received its name from Middleton and Rowley's play *The Spanish Gipsie,* acted in 1623; at any rate, a song sung by gipsies

[3] For an illuminating study of the roots of this ballad and associated texts and tunes, see Bertrand H. Bronson, "Samuel Hall's Family Tree," *California Folklore,* I (1942), 47–64.

441

(Act III) beginning "Come follow your Leader follow,/Our Convoy be Mars and Apollo" fits the tune, and its opening formula seems to have been often appropriated in songs specifically calling for the tune. The most influential of these is the broadside "The Fairy Queene," beginning "Come follow follow me,/You Fairy Elves that be" (Manchester I, 13). The publisher was Edward Wright, who was active from 1611–1653, and the ballad may be dated, at a guess, about 1625. The verses may be found in Bodleian MS Ashmole 36–37, fol. 187; in a pamphlet of 1635 by R. S. entitled *A Description of the King and Queene of Fayries*, in *The Mysteries of Love and Eloquence*, 1658, in Percy's *Reliques*, and with modernized form of the tune in Watts's *Musical Miscellany*, 1729–1731, II, 22 (Fig. 441), and in Ritson's *English Songs*, 1783, II, 157. In addition, the Harvard, Huntington, and British Museum libraries contain several eighteenth-century single-sheet issues of the song.

To the tune of "The Spanish Ipsie" is "The braue English Iipsie," beginning "Come follow, follow all" (Roxburghe; reprinted in *RB* III, 329); since this was an issue of John Trundle, it is to be dated no later than 1626. Martin Parker's "The three merry Coblers," beginning "Come follow follow me,/toth' Alehouse weele march all three," is an interesting imitation, licensed in 1634 (Roxburghe; reprinted in *RB* II, 587). The anonymous "Cuckolds Haven," licensed in 1638, begins "Come, Neighbours, follow me,/that Cuckollized be" and names the tune (Roxburghe; reprinted in *RB* I, 148). *Good and True, Fresh and New, Christmas Carols*, 1642, sig. B2, contains a "merry Caroll" beginning "Come follow follow me,/Those that Good fellowes be," set to "The Spanish Gipsies." And an eighteenth-century imitation, without tune direction but in the unmistakable pattern with echoes of the "Fairy Queene" broadside, is

"The New Fairies: or, the Fellow-Craft's Song," beginning "Come all ye Elves that be/Come follow, follow me," in *A Curious Collection of . . . Songs in Honour of Masonry*, 1731, p. 1.

The tune was introduced into seven ballad operas. It is called "Come follow, follow me" in Hawker's *The Wedding*, 1729, Odingsells' *Bays's Opera* and Ralph's *The Fashionable Lady*, 1730, Potter's *The Decoy*, 1733, and Brooke's *Jack the Gyant Queller*, 1749. In Gay's *Achilles*, 1733, it is "Fairy Elves," and in *Court and Country*, 1743, it is "The Fairy Song."

The Spanish Lady

This tune takes its name from Thomas Deloney's ballad "The Spanish Ladies Loue to an English Gentleman," beginning "Will you heare a Spanish Lady/how she wooed an Englishman" (*Garland of Good Will*, 1631, reprinted in *Works*, ed. Mann, p. 375). Although no extant broadside copies are earlier than c. 1660, the ballad was registered in 1603 and probably was written at least a decade earlier; many editions reflect its popularity to the end of the eighteenth century. Seventeenth-century copies are usually "To a Pleasant New Tune," while some later issues are to "Flying Fame," doubtless a printer's haphazard choice inappropriate to the complex meter of the Deloney ballad. Copies are to be found in all the large ballad collections, and reprints may be seen in Percy's *Reliques*, in *RB* VI, 655, and in *OPB*, p. 219.

The opening of the ballad is quoted in Edward Sharpham's *Cupids Whirligig*, 1607, sig. H2ᵛ, and Aphra Behn's *The Rover*, Part II, 1681,

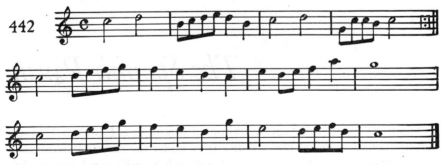

442

Dauney transcript is in key of D.

443

II, i. Brome's *The Northern Lass*, 1632, II, ii, contains an allusion to the Spanish Lady's jointure; in Rowley's *A Match at Midnight*, 1633, V, i, "Will [you] heare a Noble Prittaine" begins a scrap of parody with a slight Welsh accent. An eighteenth-century curiosity is Thomas Hull's *The Spanish Lady, a Musical Entertainment, in two acts; Founded on the Plan of the Old Ballad*, 1765. The ballad itself is printed at the end of the libretto text.

Music for "The Spanish Ladie" is found in the Skene MS, printed in William Dauney, *Ancient Scotish Melodies*, 1838, p. 242 (Fig. 442), and in Walker's *The Quaker's Opera*, 1728, Air 23 (Fig. 443). Another ballad opera, *The Jovial Crew*, 1731, gives the tune title as "Did you not hear of a Spanish Lady." The Skene air is in common time, whereas the version in both ballad operas is in 3/4; melodically too there is such great divergence between the tunes that only distant cousinship can be seen. Both, however, fit the measure of the ballad.

Another to the tune of "The Spanish Lady" is "The Westminster Wedding or, Carltons Epithalamium," beginning "Will you hear a German Princesse,/how she chous'd an English Lord" (Douce; reprinted in *RB* VII, 230), an account of the notorious Mary Moders, who passing herself off as a German heiress made a bigamous marriage with John Carleton.

The Spanish Pavan

Despite its name, this tune is Italian in origin. It is found in Fabritio Caroso's *Il Ballarino*, 1581, as a dance tune under the name "Pauaniglia." Sets of keyboard variations were made by such Spanish musicians as An-

tonio de Cabezón (d. 1566) in his *Obras de música,* 1578, where the theme
is called "El pavana italiana" (reprinted in *Hispaniae schola musica sacra,*
ed. Felipe Pedrell, 1894–1898, VII, 73), and Alonso de Mudarra in his *Tres
libros de música en cifra,* 1546 (ed. Emilio Pujol, 1949, p. 22). In England
the tune, uniformly known as "The Spanish pavan," began to be popular
toward the end of the sixteenth century. It appears in the following: the
Wickhambrook Lute MS, c. 1595, fol. 14ᵛ; William Ballet's MS Lute
Book, p. 112; Antony Holborne's *Cittharn Schoole,* 1597, sig. C2ᵛ;
Thomas Robinson's *Schoole of Musicke,* 1603, sig. L2ᵛ; BM MS Egerton
2046, fol. 10ᵛ; and BM MS Add. 31392, fol. 25ᵛ (the two latter arrangements, in lute tablature, are by Alfonso Ferrabosco and Francis Pilkington). Virginal settings are in Paris Conservatoire MSS Rés. 1186, fol. 117,
and Rés. 1186 bis, Part II, p. 6, in *The Fitzwilliam Virginal Book* II, 131,
arr. John Bull (Fig. 444), and in Christ Church MS 437, fol. 3. Other

444

* Seven additional sections not transcribed.

musical texts are found in *A Booke of New Lessons for the Cithern &
Gittern,* 1652, in the Skene MS (William Dauney, *Ancient Scotish Melodies,* 1838, p. 21, entitled "I Loue my Loue for Loue Again," but measures 9ff. are "Spanish pavan"), and in several Cambridge University MSS:
Dd.4.23, fol. 26 (cittern); Dd.2.11, fol. 66ᵛ; Dd.3.18, fol. 14ᵛ; Dd.9.33, fol.
82ᵛ; and Add. 3056, fol. 20ᵛ (all lute). A sampling of the numerous seventeenth-century Dutch settings of "Pavane d'Espagne" is contained in
Florimond van Duyse's *Het Oude Nederlandsche Lied,* 1903–1908, I,
610ff. Mabel Dolmetsch, *Dances of Spain and Italy from 1400 to 1600,*
1954, pp. 90–108, describes the dance, reprints Caroso's music, and is

authority for the statement that the dance "goes at a lively pace, unlike the solemn processional pavan."

Perhaps the earliest ballad sung to this dance tune is "A most excellent and famous Ditty of Sampson Iudge of Israel," beginning "When Sampson was a tall yong man." It was registered in 1586, but the two extant editions cannot be earlier than c. 1620 (Pepys, Roxburghe; reprinted in *RB* II, 460). Here and in other ballads to the tune, the stanza is in eight lines, octosyllabic except for lines 4 and 8, which are six and three syllables respectively. Anthony Munday's *Banquet of Daintie Conceits,* 1588, sig. E1ᵛ, contains a song beginning "Two freends that had a stocke of Corne," to be sung "to the note of the Spanish Pavin." Other ballads to the tune include: "A merry Discourse betweene Norfolke Thomas and Sisly Standtoo't his Wife," by Ed[ward] Ford, beginning "To London is mad Thomas come" (Roxburghe, probably the issue licensed in 1638; reprinted in *RB* II, 170); "A Monstrous shape . . . a female creature [with] . . . a head like a swine," beginning "Of horned Vulcan I haue heard" (Wood 401, with MS date 1640; reprinted in *PG,* p. 451); "An excellent new Medley," beginning "When Philomel begins to sing" (Pepys, Roxburghe; reprinted in *RB* I, 57); and "The Daughters Complaint, to her mother, for a Husband," beginning "As I walkt forth upon a day," to the tune of "The Spanish paving, or the Lovers Dream; or, Martin Parkers Medly" (Douce I, 52, 66ᵛ).

This last tune title recalls two medleys written by Martin Parker, both in the measure of "The Spanish pavan," but with the tune direction "Tarleton's Medley." No ballad of that title is known, but on metrical grounds one may conjecture that if it were found it would fit "The Spanish pavan" and might name that tune. Parker's ballads are "A new Medley, or, A Messe of All-together," beginning "Strange news is come from Hounslo heath" (Roxburghe; reprinted in *RB* II, 240), and "An Excellent Medley Which you may admire at (without offence) For euery line speaks a contrary sense," beginning "In Summer time when folks make Hay" (Pepys, Lord Crawford, Euing, Harvard, Roxburghe; reprinted in *RB* I, 52). In the same distinctive stanza pattern is "Englands Gentle Admonition," by Thomas Robins, beginning "Good People all I pray draw near," to the tune of "Poor Toms Progress: Or, John Dory sould his ambling Nag for Kick-shaws" (Roxburghe; reprinted in *RB* IV, 477). I have not identified either tune name (the second cannot be another name for the tune "John Dory"); in the want of further evidence it is sufficient to say that the ballad could be sung to "The Spanish pavan"; or if not, then to tunes which are its metrical equivalent.

One further use of the tune may be pointed out. In *Good and True, Fresh and New, Christmas Carols,* 1642, sig. A7ᵛ, it is used for singing a "merry Caroll" beginning "Cast care away, tis Holyday,/This is no time to work, but play."

References to "The Spanish pavan" abound in Elizabethan and Jacobean literature. In Dekker's *Old Fortunatus*, 1600, III, i, "la pauyne Hispanola" is mentioned and presumably danced; in John Ford's *The Lady's Trial*, 1639, II, i, the tune is whistled, and in his *'Tis Pity She's a Whore*, 1633, I, ii, the dance is mentioned. The jestbook *Robin Good-fellow*, Part II, 1628 (ed. Collier, 1841, p. 34), refers to "The Spanish Pavan" as a ballad tune. In *Eastward Hoe*, 1605, II, ii, Quicksilver sings a parody on "When Samson was a tall young man," presumably to its proper tune.

The Spinning Wheel

This tune, used for some twenty broadsides, takes its name from "The Bonny Scot: Or, the Yielding Lass. To an Excellent New Tune," beginning "As I sate at my Spinning-Wheel" (Pepys, Douce, Bagford; reprinted in *BB* I, 19). It was followed by "An Answer to the Bonny Scot," beginning "Behold, I pray, what's come to pass," to the tune of "The Spinning-wheel" (Lord Crawford, Douce, Harvard, Roxburghe; reprinted in *RB* III, 399). Both ballads were licensed by Richard Pocock (1685–1688). The original piece was included in every edition of *Pills*, 1719–1720, III, 88, with music, the most accurate notation of which is 1714, I, 113 (Fig. 445); and a somewhat altered version of the tune (Fig. 446) appears on an engraved song-sheet edition of "The Spin-

445

Original is in key of B♭.

446

ning Lass," c. 1740 (BM I.600 [118], Harvard).[1] Allan Ramsay included the verses in his *Tea-Table Miscellany*, 1733, II, 187, as "The Loving Lass and Spinning-Wheel."

Thomas D'Urfey wrote a more literary poem, beginning "Upon a sunshine summer's day," on the theme of the maiden finally persuaded to turn away from her spinning wheel to the arms of a lover. It appeared without music in his *New Collection of Songs and Poems*, 1683, p. 78; in early *Pills* editions it immediately follows "As I sat at my Spinning-Wheel" and is directed to be sung to the music of the latter; in the 1719–1720 edition the two songs are in different volumes (D'Urfey's at II, 176) and the tune is separately printed for each. Although the song may have antedated the "Bonny Scot" ballad, D'Urfey apparently accepted the ballad tune for his verses. The commonplace tetrameter form of both makes this possible, though D'Urfey's eight-line stanza requires a repetition of the final four bars of the tune.[2]

Of the numerous late seventeenth-century broadsides to the tune, seven are reprinted in *PB*, others in *RB* and *BB*. "A Ready Cure for Vneasie Minds," beginning "Kind Countrymen, Attention give," names the tune "As I sat at my Spinning-Wheele" (Pepys; reprinted in *PB* VII, 176). The following, apparently not reprinted, all cite the tune as "The Spinning Wheel": "The City Rambler," beginning "I pray now listen to this song" (Pepys IV, 334); "Kates Hue-and-Cry after Her Maidenhead," beginning "Good people all I pray draw nigh" (Pepys III, 76); "Joans sorrowful Lamentation to Roger," beginning "As Jone was

---

[1] A short form of the text was recovered in 1935 from an Indiana singer who had learned it from his father in Carlisle; unfortunately the music is not reproduced (*JAF*, LVII [1944], 283).

[2] With a different tune, D'Urfey's text is found on an early eighteenth-century song-sheet called "The Spinning Wheel" (Harvard), reprinted in *The Merry Musician*, c. 1733, IV, 109. Words alone are reprinted in *Wit's Cabinet*, 15th ed., 1731, p. 124. A poem in *The Hive*, 1732, IV, 57, beginning "As, on a sun-shine summer's day," is not D'Urfey's, nor is it in his stanza form.

walking o're the Green" (Pepys III, 292, Lord Crawford 126); "Nell's Courtship," beginning "As bonny Nell went to the Mill" (Pepys IV, 67); "The Mothers Kindness," beginning "Come listen now dear Daughter Joan" (Pepys IV, 212); "The Young Seaman's Misfortune," beginning "You loyal Lovers far and near" (Pepys IV, 224); "The Quaker's Wives Lamentation For the Loss of Her Husbands Jewels," beginning "Oh Wretched Woman that I am" (Pepys III, 302); and "The Unfortunate Fencer," beginning "You that delight in merriment" (Pepys IV, 358, BM C.22.f.6 [196], Lord Crawford 1427, Harvard).

A still different tune found in the ballad operas is called "As I sat at my Spinning Wheel" in Lillo's *Silvia*, 1731, and "Spinning-Wheel" in Coffey's *The Merry Cobler*, 1735. In *The Jovial Crew*, 1731, it is named "Still I turn'd my Wheel about," paraphrasing the refrain of D'Urfey's song.

State and Ambition

This tune takes its name from the opening line "State and Ambition, alas! will deceive ye,/There's no solid Joy but the Blessing of Love," of Thomas D'Urfey's "To Sylvia; a Song set to a New Playhouse Tune," first published in *A Collection of the Newest and Choicest Songs*, 1683, p. 6, with an unsuitable tune of Farmer's which actually belongs to verses beginning "I Will Love I know not who" (*ibid.*, p. 3). Corrupt versions of the proper "State and ambition" air appear with D'Urfey's poem in his *Several New Songs*, 1684, p. 10, and in *180 Loyal Songs*, 1685, p. 92; a much better musical score is in *Pills*, 1719–1720, II, 34. The tune is also found among the unnumbered pages at the end of Humphry Salter's *Genteel Companion . . . for the Recorder*, 1683, and in *Apollo's Banquet*, 5th ed., 1687. An expanded form of D'Urfey's verses was issued as a broadside entitled "State & Ambition. A New Song at the Dukes Theatre," 1684 (Harvard), with a good musical text (Fig. 447); an undated edition, with incomplete and inaccurate musical text, is found in Wood 417 (147); still another edition contains the music of "I never saw a face till now," to which the verse is unsuited (Pepys V, 404; reprinted in *RB* V, 561).

A moralistic parody of D'Urfey's song is "The Protestant Father's Advice To His Ambitious Son," beginning "State and Ambition, alas, will deceive you,/there's no solid Joy but in Blessings above" (Lord Crawford, BM C.39.k.6; reprinted in *RB* VIII, clix*, and in *OPB*, p. 159).

447

* G in original.

The tune of "State and Ambition" is used also for "A New made Medley Compos'd out of sundry Songs," beginning "State and Ambition, all Joy to great Caesar" (Pepys V, 411, with meaningless music; early eighteenth-century song-sheet editions with accurate score in BM H.1601 [407], Harvard, Huntington; reprinted in *Pills* V, 11, and in *RB* VIII, clxi*).

Some fifteen other ballads were sung to the tune. Three are in *180 Loyal Songs*, pp. 94, 271, 273, and several others are reprinted in *RB*. The following have apparently not been reprinted: "The Royal General or the Camp at Putney Heath," 1684, beginning "Now the great Monarch of England's bright Splendor" (Bodleian Ashmole G.15 [184], Clark, Harvard); another of the same year, "Sr. Thomas Armstrong's Last Farewell to the World," beginning "Adue to the pleasure of murther and whoring" (BM 1875.d.6 [8], Harvard); "Loves Unlimited Power," licensed June 6, 1685, beginning "The passions of Love are too great and too cruel" (Pepys III, 215); "The Seaman's Joyful Return; being an Answer to the Seamans Doleful Farewell,"[1] 1685, beginning

[1] The ballad to which this was the answer is reprinted in *RB* VII, 549, VIII, 780.

"Wellcome my dearest with joy now I see thee" (Pepys IV, 179); and "Content and Rich; Or, the Glass of Vain Glory," beginning "Promotion's a Trifle, a vanishing Vapour" (Pepys II, 26). An edition of "True Love Unvail'd, Or, The Coy Lady Over-come at last," beginning "Down in a Valley where Nymphs are a playing," is "To a Rare New Tune, Or, The French Minnim" [2] (Lord Crawford 322, Douce II, 138ᵛ [with MS addition to tune direction: "State & Ambition"], II, 227, Harvard). A reworking of the ballad (Douce II, 231), licensed by Richard Pocock, 1685–1688, is directed to be sung to "State and Ambition"; its title is altered to "True Love Revealed . . . ," its opening line begins "Down in a Meadow . . . ," and the seduction scene of the old ballad is now preceded by a recital of marriage vows.

The tune was introduced into one ballad opera—Phillips's *The Stage-Mutineers*, 1733, printed without music.

Step Stately

This tune is in the first ten editions of *The Dancing Master*, 1651–1698 (1651, p. 100=Fig. 448), in *A Musicall Banquet*, 1651, in *Musicks*

Original is unbarred.

Recreation on the Lyra Viol, 1652, in *A Booke of New Lessons for the Cithern & Gittern*, 1652, and in Playford's *A Brief Introduction to the Skill of Music*, 3d ed., 1660.

A song to the tune in *Westminster Drollery*, 1671, I, 37, is "A late and true story of a furious Scold, served in her kind," beginning "Was ever man so vex'd with a Trull/As I poor Anthony since I was wed." It was

[2] I have no information on this tune.

reprinted in *Wit and Drollery,* 1682, without tune direction; in *Pills,* 1719–1720, IV, 154, music is printed which is not "Step stately" but which fits the ballad more smoothly than does the older tune. There are several reworkings of the story on broadsides. One of them, to a "New Play-House Tune" which may be the music in *Pills,* is "The Scoulding Wife, or, The Poor Mans Lamentation of his bad Market in his chusing him a Wife," 1689, beginning "Was there ever any Man so plaug'd with a Trul" (Pepys IV, 136). Another is "Poor Anthony's Complaint . . . against his miseries of marriage . . . with a scolding Wife," beginning "Was ever man so vext with a Wife," to the tune of "Tom the Taylor, the Journey-man Shoomaker, or Billy and Molly" (Pepys IV, 121).[1] Both broadsides retain the eight-line stanza form of the original drollery piece. But "Couragious Anthony," beginning "Was ever poor Man so perplext with a Trull," recasts the verse in quatrains of anapestic tetrameters to fit the rhythms of "The two English Travellers," a lost tune to which it is set (Pepys IV, 146).

The "Poor Anthony" ballads appear, then, to ignore the old relationship between the drollery song and the tune "Step stately," despite the fact that *The Dancing Master* continued to print the tune until the end of the century. Miss Margaret Dean-Smith, in her edition of the 1651 *English Dancing Master,* 1957, p. 84, observes that although Playford's tune is "dull," the dance "is one of the most beautiful" in the collection.

Still I'm Wishing, Still Desiring

The song beginning "Still I'm wishing, still desiring" is one of several pieces in the Purcell-Betterton opera *The Prophetess,* 1690, V, i, that were turned into broadsides for street circulation. The original song is contained in Purcell's *Vocal and Instrumental Musick of the Prophetess,* 1691, p. 138 (Fig. 449), and in *Pills,* 1719–1720, IV, 262. An engraved song-sheet issue of the 1690s is found in the British Museum collection known as *Joyful Cuckoldom* (C.180.a [5]). The broadside issue, expanding the text from two to nine stanzas, is entitled "The Contented Lovers, or Dioclesions Wish . . . To an Excellent New Play-

[1] On these tune titles, see "Daniel Cooper." The Euing copy of "Poor Anthony's Complaint" lists the first tune as "Cold and Raw," for which see "Stingo."

449-31-

House Tune, Sung at the Opera" (Pepys V, 232, with meaningless music).
The tune does not seem to have been used for singing other broadsides.
A violin version of the air, called "Still I'm wishing, &c.," appears on
an additional sheet in *Apollo's Banquet*, Second Book, 1691.

Stingo, or Oil of Barley,
or Cold and Raw

This tune is called for in ballads of the first half of the seventeenth
century, but the earliest musical texts appear in *The Dancing Master*,
1651–1686 (1651, p. 10=Fig. 450), and *A Booke of New Lessons for the
Cithern & Gittern*, 1652, as "Stingo, Or the Oyle of Barly." John Hilton
used the tune in the third part of "A Northern Catch," in his *Catch that*

· 687 ·

450

Original is in G minor and unbarred.

Catch Can, 1652, and the melody as altered by Hilton is almost exactly the form later popularized as "Cold and Raw." [1]

Early seventeenth-century ballads refer to the tune under various names. It is "Stingo" to which "The little Barly-Corne" is sung; this ballad, beginning "Come, and doe not musing stand" (Roxburghe; reprinted in *RB* II, 29), celebrates the virtues of barley and alcohol generally, and from topical references can be dated in the second quarter of the century. "The willy [i.e., wily], witty, neat, and pritty, Damsell," c. 1649, beginning "Not long agone,/Walking alone," is to the tune of "The Oyle of Barly" (Manchester; reprinted in *CP,* p. 292). A pair of ballads give rise to still other tunes. "The Countrey Lasse," by M[artin] P[arker], beginning "Although I am a countrey lasse," is "To a daintie new Note, which if you cannot hit,/There's another tune will as well fit./To the tune of, The mother beguild daughter" (Pepys, Roxburghe; reprinted in *RB* I, 165). Although "The Mother beguiled the Daughter" is a different tune, the "daintie new Note" may have been "Stingo," for a version of this ballad appears in all editions of *Pills* with the later "Cold and Raw" music (1719–1720, II, 167). The rivalry between Martin Parker and Laurence Price, who often answered each other's ballads, resulted in one

[1] Hilton's piece was retained in editions of *Catch that Catch Can* through 1667 and in Playford's enlarged edition of 1673 entitled *The Musical Companion.* It begins "Ise goe with thee my sweet Peggy, my Honny," and the section sung to "Stingo" music has the following words, which may echo a song originally associated with the tune:

> Thou and I will foot it Joe,
>   fa, la, la, la, la, la,
> And what w'eel doe neene shall know,
>   but taste the Juce of Barly,
> Wee'l sport all night for our delight,
>   and home in the morning early.

451

by the latter author to the tune of the former's "The Countrey Lasse."
It is "Good Ale for my money. The Good-fellowes resolution of strong
Ale,/That cures his nose from looking pale" (Roxburghe; reprinted in
RB I, 412), whose refrain is:

> I cannot go home, nor I will not go home,
>   It's long of the oyle of barley;
> I'll tarry all night for my delight,
>   And go home in the morning early.

This is perhaps indirectly the source of Hilton's words for his catch.
The final line of the refrain gives rise to yet another tune title, which
appears as "Goe home in the Morning Early" in a Manchester ballad,
"The Anabaptists out of order," whose beginning is defective (reprinted
in *CP*, p. 175).

Chappell (*PMOT* I, 308–309) reprints a song from *Merry Drollery*,
1661, with the music, although no tune direction is given in the original.
Entitled "A cup of old Stingo," it celebrates strong ale—"Stingo" per-

· 689 ·

sists even today in Great Britain as a brand name—and it does fit the tune. For our purposes, the song serves chiefly to assure us that the tune title and its association with ale were a commonplace of the middle of the seventeenth century.

"Cold and Raw" superseded "Stingo" as a name for the tune, thanks to the popularity of "The last New Scotch Song," beginning "Could and Raw the North did blow," in *Comes Amoris,* Second Book, 1688, p. 16 (Fig. 451). Thomas D'Urfey acknowledged authorship of the words by including them in his *New Poems,* 1690. Meanwhile both the new text and the old air had quickly become influential. The tune appears twice— the music identical but the dances different—in *The Dancing Master* ("A New Addition," c. 1689, to the 7th ed., 1686, as "The Juice of Barly," p. 2, and "Cold and Raw," p. 6).[2] A ballad dated 1689 (Pepys V, 247, and Bagford I, 96) prints the musical score of "Cold and Raw," though, as is often the case, that tune does not fit the ballad.[3] The tune appears in tablature form in *Youth's Delight on the Flagelet,* 9th ed., c. 1690.

A number of ballads to the tune were licensed by Richard Pocock, and are therefore issues of 1685–1688. They include a broadside version of D'Urfey's poem: "The Northern Ditty, To an excellent New Scotch Tune, of Cold and Raw the North did blow" (Madden, with the music; Euing, Harvard, Roxburghe; reprinted in *RB* VII, 233; later editions in Douce II, 168, III, 70, and Chetham 91). Several sequels were immediately generated: "An Answer to Cold and Raw," beginning "Riding down a narrow lane,/two or three hours after" (BM C.22.f.6 [30]; reprinted in *RB* VII, 234); "A Third Merry Ditty of Cold and Raw," beginning "Cold and Raw you can't forget,/the Maid that sold the Barley" (Lord Crawford, Harvard, BM C.22.f.6; reprinted in *RB* VII, 235); and "Rogers Renown: Or, The Fourth and Last Merry Ditty of Cold and Raw," beginning "Roger did a letter send/of late to London City" (Douce; reprinted in *RB* VII, 236).

Before the end of James II's reign still others were published: "The Downright Wooing of Honest John & Betty," by E. W., beginning "Well met my pritty Betty/happy be our Meeting" (Lord Crawford 1262, Douce I, 63, Harvard, BM C.22.f.6 [113]); "The London Jilts lamentation Or, A Hue-and-Cry after a fine Lac'd Smock," beginning "Here is wonder-

[2] Both dances appear in the eighth edition, 1690; in the ninth edition, 1695, the tune is called "Cold and Raw," but the dance directions are those formerly printed with "Juice of Barly." In the seventeenth edition, 1721, the dance originally associated with "Cold and Raw" replaces that of "Juice of Barly," used in all intermediate editions. Minor changes in the music take place from early to late editions.

[3] The broadside is a ballad version of "Why are my eyes still flowing," which has its own tune. Garbled versions of "Cold and Raw" appear on two other Pepys broadsides (V, 191, 334) and a good musical text is coupled with the words of "Lilliburlero" in BM C.38.i.25 (3) and Wood 417 (168); the latter copy bears the MS date "Dec. 1688."

ful strange News" (Douce I, 116, Lord Crawford 503); "The Wealthy Farmers Choice," beginning "Near a pleasant shady Grove,/in prime of Summer Weather" (Douce, BM C.39.k.6; reprinted in *OPB*, p. 142); "The Miserable Mountebank," beginning "In a Market town of late,/a Mountebank was balling" (Lord Crawford 633). "The Lusty Fryer of Flanders . . . [who] got Thirty Nuns with Child in three Weeks time," beginning "Not long ago from hence I went,/to travel into Flanders," is dated 1688 in the Douce and Pepys copies; the Roxburghe copy, undated, with cropped imprint, is reprinted in bowdlerized fashion in *RB* VII, 232, VIII, 715. "The States-Man's Almanack," beginning "The Talk up and down,/In Country and Town" occurs in BM MS Harl. 7319, p. 590, dated 1688, and a printed broadside version is in Library of Congress, Lord Crawford 1106 (erroneously dated 1683), and Chetham 1149; it was reprinted in *The Muses Farewel to Popery and Slavery*, 1689, Supplement, together with a parody, "The State-Holder: or, the Prince's Almanack . . . a Counterpart to the States-Man's Almanack," and is later found in *Poems on Affairs of State*, 1704, III, 159.[4] One further ballad is dated 1689: "The Poor Contented Cuckold," beginning "Was e'er man so unfortunate" (Pepys IV, 133).

This tune-of-all-work is attached to a D'Urfey ballad usually sung to "The Hemp-dresser": "Roger's Delight: or, The West-Country Christning," beginning "When Sol had left his weary Teams" (black-letter copies in Pepys and BM C.22.f.6; *RB* VII, 210, reprints from an eighteenth-century edition without tune title). This version is found in *A Complete Collection of . . . English and Scotch Songs*, 1735–1736, III, 136, as well as another with the usual first line: "The sun had loos'd his weary team," I, 124; "Cold and Raw" is given as the tune for each.

In 1692 Purcell used "Cold and Raw" as a ground bass for verses beginning "May her blest example chase/Vice in troops out of the land" in Sir Charles Sedley's birthday ode for Queen Mary (Purcell Society edition of the *Works*, XXIV, 1926, 19–21).[5] This deliberate musical quotation of a popular air was Purcell's retaliation at the Queen's taste. A familiar anecdote recounted in Hawkins's *History of Music*, 1776, IV, 6, relates Her Majesty's impatience with several of Purcell's songs, sung to her by Mrs. Arabella Hunt and Mr. Gostling, with Purcell at the harpsichord.

4 "The States-Man's Almanack" and its parody are in a six-line stanza (with a syllabic pattern of 5.5.9 or 6.6.9) which fills but half the tune of "Cold and Raw." They can, of course, be sung to the tune if two stanzas are considered as a verse unit.

5 Preceding the soprano solo is a full announcement of "Cold and Raw" by the bass and continuo in unison, and it is followed by a ritornello in which strings and continuo repeat the soprano air, again with the "Cold and Raw" ground prominent.

At length the queen beginning to grow tired, asked Mrs. Hunt if she could not sing the old Scots ballad "Cold and Raw," Mrs. Hunt answered yes, and sung it to her lute. Purcell was all the while sitting at the harpsichord unemployed, and not a little nettled at the queen's preference of a vulgar ballad to his music; but seeing her majesty delighted with this tune, he determined that she should hear it upon another occasion . . .

The tune appears three times in *Pills:* with D'Urfey's words "Cold and Raw the North did blow," in all editions, 1719–1720, II, 167; with "The Country Lass," beginning "What tho' I am a Country Lass,/A lofty mind I bear *a,*" IV, 152 (this song is ordinarily sung to its own tune—see s.v. "The Country Lass"); and with "An Old Ballad new Reviv'd: Or, A little of tone with t'other," beginning "A Young Man late, that lack'd a Mate," 1707, 1712, III, 224. The latter piece is derived from a song in *Merry Drollery,* 1661, in which every stanza ends "A little o'th' t'on with t'other." D'Urfey used this refrain in a song beginning "A Beau dress'd fine met Miss divine," to which he gave the title "A little of one with t'other; A New Song, to the Scotch Tune of Cold and Raw," *Pills,* 1719–1720, II, 169.[6]

In the eighteenth century the music is to be found in Walsh's *Compleat Country Dancing-Master,* 1718. It was used in thirteen ballad operas, including the following which print the music: Gay's *The Beggar's Opera,* 1728, Fielding's *Don Quixote in England,* 1734, and *The Whim: or The Miser's Retreat,* 1734. It appears twice in Kane O'Hara's comic opera *Midas,* 1764. In James Johnson's *Scots Musical Museum* II, 147, is a version of "Cold and Raw" of which Robert Burns noted, "The chorus of this is old; the two stanzas are mine." (*Notes on Scottish Song by Robert Burns,* ed. Dick, 1908, p. 28. Dick adds that the earliest record of the tune in Scotland is in McGibbon's *Scots Tunes,* 1755, where it is called "Up in the morning early," from the second line of D'Urfey's song.)

---

[6] This refrain appears in a seventeenth-century broadside, "The New Courtier, To an Excellent New Court Tune," beginning "I Prethee Moll,/Be not so dull" (Pepys III, 49). Its stanza, printed as twelve lines, will fit "Cold and Raw," though it is doubtful that it was written with that tune in mind. The refrain becomes a tune title in "Hey ho, for a Husband," beginning "You maidens that are fair and young," to the tune of "Ile warrant thee boy she's right, Or, a little o' th tone with 'tother" (Pepys IV, 9). This ballad is also of the same measure as "Cold and Raw," but it does not seem justifiable to equate the two tune titles. On "Ile warrant thee boy" see s.v. "Drive the cold winter away."

Strawberry Leaves Make Maidens Fair

"A mery new Iigge. Or, the pleasant wooing betwixt Kit and Pegge," beginning "Well met faire Maid,/my chiefest ioy," is to the tune of "Strawberry leaues make Maidens faire" (Pepys, Roxburghe; reprinted in *RB* II, 101). This early seventeenth-century dialogue by Valentine Hamdulton is in a stanza of eight short lines equivalent to an octosyllabic quatrain. Contemporary music which will fit a stanza of twice that length is found in BM MS Add. 17786, fol. 15, as a five-voiced in-

452

Original is unbarred.

strumental piece entitled "Strawberry leaues." The melody is obtained from the superius part, supplemented in bars 7–8 by the medius notes where there are rests in the superius. The resultant tune is a nicely flowing air of popular cast (Fig. 452).

Sweet, If You Love Me

"The Helpless Maidens Call to the Batchellors," 1691, beginning "Sweet if thou Lov'st me come away," is a broadside with music (Pepys V, 195). Its continuation, "A New Song, Call'd The Batchellor's Answer to the Helpless Maiden," beginning "Love I am ready at your call," is of the same year and contains identical music (Pepys V, 196). The tune (Fig. 453) is a version in minor of that found in major in the eighteenth

453

Original is a fourth higher.

century. It is used, for example, in a single-sheet song of c. 1720, "A Dialogue between Sly and Lovett. Sung at Fielding's Booth at Bartholomew Fair," beginning "Sweet if you love me, smiling turn" (BM I.530 [149], Harvard).[1] A slightly different version of the tune is found in

454

two ballad operas, Ralph's *The Fashionable Lady*, 1730, Air 58 (Fig. 454), as "Sweet if you love me come away," and in Phillips's *The Livery Rake*, 1733, as "Sweet, if you love me." *The Female Rake*, 1736 (reissued as *The Woman of Taste*, 1738), and *The Sharpers*, 1740, also call

[1] The text of this song is printed in *The Vocal Miscellany*, 2d ed., 1734, I, 1, with the tune direction "Sweet if you love me come away."

for the tune but do not print the music. Later in the century the tune was introduced into the comic opera *The Golden Pippin*, 1773, Act I. The original ballad, with its repetitions and its sudden stop four bars from the end, fixed a pattern followed by all the songs mentioned. The tune itself may be said to have been refined during the early decades of the eighteenth century, but its eventual form, for all its grace, has not quite the strength of the original.

Sweet, Use Your Time

Thomas D'Urfey's song "Kingston Church," beginning "Sweet use your time, abuse your time/no longer, but be wise," was first published without music in his *New Collection of Songs and Poems*, 1683, p. 15. It appears with an anonymous musical setting of about the same date in Fitzwilliam Museum MS 30.G.20, p. 67 (Fig. 455). D'Urfey's two stanzas

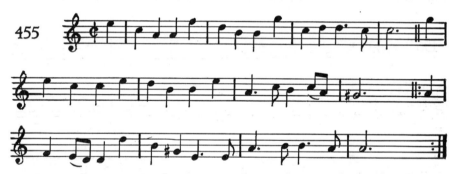

455

Original is a fourth higher.

were expanded for broadside issuance as "A Word in Season: or, Now or Never," to the tune of "Sweet use your time, &c." (Lord Crawford, Harvard, Pepys, Roxburghe; reprinted in *RB* VI, 140). The Crawford *Catalogue* notes that the music is "probably by Tom Farmer" but offers no evidence. Farmer collaborated with D'Urfey on many songs, half a dozen of which were in the 1683 collection (only one with music).

Tangier March

The British occupation of Tangier from 1662 to 1684 brought that strategic North African outpost into prominence at home, especially in the years just before its abandonment, when this tune achieved a brief vogue. Music of "Tangier March" is printed in *180 Loyal Songs*, 1685, where three ballads are set to the tune. It is also found in *Apollo's Banquet*, 5th ed., 1687.

Perhaps the earliest broadside naming the tune is "Londons Joy and Tryumph, On the Installment of Sir William Pritchard Lord Mayor," 1682, beginning "Let the Whigs revile,/The Tories Smile" (Huntington; reprinted in *180 Loyal Songs*, p .112). "A new Song on the old Plot," beginning "Let the Whigs repine, and all combine," is in *180 Loyal Songs*, p. 110 (whence the text of *RB* V, 455), but must have circulated as a broadside in 1682 or 1683; for in the latter year appeared "The Whigs in Mourning," beginning "Let the snarling Whig/Ne'r look so big," to the tune of "Let the Whigs repine, and all combine" (Harvard) and with the music of "Tangier March" on the sheet (Fig. 456).

456

* E in original.

One other broadside to the tune is "Tangiers Lamentation, On the . . . Blowing-up of the Town, Castle and Citadel, November the 5th," 1683, beginning "Let the Moors repine,/Their hopes resign" (Clark; reprinted in *180 Loyal Songs*, p. 114, whence the text of *RB* V, 474).

The stanza pattern requires repetition of the first musical phrase, not the last, as is erroneously indicated in *180 Loyal Songs*.

Tell Me, Jenny

The two-stanza song beginning "Tell me Jenny, tell me roundly" is found with air and bass in *A Collection of the Newest and Choicest Songs*, 1683, p. 1, and *Choice Ayres and Songs*, Fifth Book, 1684, p. 27. The verses were reprinted in *Wit and Mirth*, 3d ed., 1684, p. 137, and *The Compleat Academy of Complements*, 1705. Words and music are in all editions of *Pills*, 1719–1720, III, 259.

No less than three broadside expansions of the original song have been preserved. The texts all begin with the original poem, and only with the third stanza does their individuality emerge. Perhaps the earliest is "Coy Jenny, and Constant Jemmy," with no tune direction;

457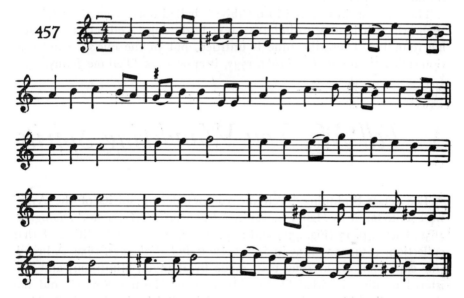

its third stanza begins "Prithee Jenny, don't despise me" (Pepys, Roxburghe; reprinted in *RB* III, 541; a condensed version in *180 Loyal Songs*, p. 290, without music, names the tune). Another, which from the imprint can be no later than 1684, is "Come to it at last," to the tune of "tell me Jenny," with third stanza beginning "Prithee Jenny, don't deny me" (Lord Crawford, Harvard, Roxburghe; reprinted in *RB* III, 537). The third is "The Love Sports of Wanton Jemmy and Simpering Jenny," to the tune of "Tell me Jenny," with third stanza beginning "Prithee Jenny, why so fretful?" (BM C.22.f.6 [143], Douce II, 140, Lord Crawford 1108).

Still other ballads on this amorous pair call for the tune: "Love put to it's Shifts: Or, The Merry Meeting of Jemmy and Jenny," beginning "On a time as I was walking" (Pepys IV, 34), and "Couragious Jemmy's Resolution, or, An Answer to Coy Jenny's Reply," beginning "Jenny when I was most Loyal," to the tune of "Jenny tell me Roundly" (Roxburghe; reprinted in *RB* III, 544).

The original song must have been immediately popular, for two ballads to the tune are dated 1683. One of these, a broadside containing a good copy of the music (Fig. 457), is "Monmouth's Return; Or, The Mistaken Whiggs," beginning "Now the Rash Imputing Torys," to the tune of "Tell me Jenny &c." (National Lib. of Scotland, Harvard, Huntington, Clark, Yale). A second is "George the Glover, and Grace the Bone-Lace-maker," beginning "Come my Grace come sit thee by me," without music but with the tune direction "Tell me Jenny tell me roundly" (Pepys III, 227).

The tune was introduced into Cibber's ballad opera *Love in a Riddle*, 1729, where it is sung to imitative text beginning "Tell me, Philly, tell me roundly." There the tune is untitled, but in the one-act condensation called *Damon and Phillida*, 1732, it appears as "Tell me Jenny."

Tell Me, You Wandering Spirits

The verses beginning "Tell me you wandering spirits of the Ayre" were set to music by Henry Lawes in *Select Musicall Ayres, and Dialogues*, 1652, Part 1, p. 17 (Fig. 458) and appeared in the second edition of that collection, 1653, as well as in *Select Ayres and Dialogues*, 1659. A broadside expansion of the song text, made by S[amuel] S[mithson] and registered in 1656, is titled "Loves Mistresse or Natures Rarity" and has the tune direction "Tell me you wandring Spirits in the Aire" (Manchester I, 25; later editions in Pepys III, 12, Wood E.25 [79], Rawlinson 66).

Other ballads to the tune include "The mournfull Shepherdesse of Arcadiah," beginning "Assist me Muses with your power divine" (Manchester I, 21), subscribed A. S. and published about the time of Smithson's ballad. Another is "Loves Wound, And Loves Cure," beginning "Amintas loved Cloris that fair one," to the tune of "The Wandring Spirits in the Air" (Rawlinson 158, Pepys III, 114, Wood E.25 [137], Douce I, 135).

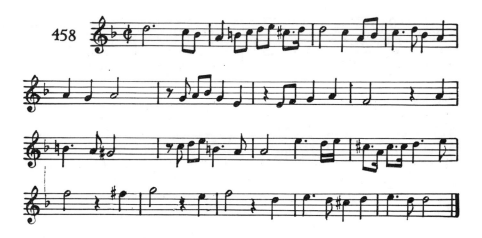

458

Lawes's music is in the academic song style of the mid-seventeenth century, with such freedom from the ordinary square-cut phrasal development that one is surprised to see it adopted as a broadside tune. It is clear, however, that the ballad writers were sensitive to the requirements of the music, for they took care to provide a repetition of syllables, following the pattern in the original song.

Tender Hearts of London City

On March 10, 1683, the stationer Jonah Deacon registered the broadside "Loves lamentable Tragedy . . . To a Pleasant New Play-house Tune," beginning "Tender hearts of London City,/now be mov'd with grief and pitty." At least two Deacon issues have survived, one (Fig. 459) with good musical text (Pepys III, 352, Lord Crawford 1110, Douce I, 124[v], Roxburghe IV, 21) and another with meaningless musical characters (BM C.22.f.6 [82[v]], Roxburghe II, 272[v], II, 437[v]). A later edition without music is in Douce II, 138. The ballad was reprinted in *RB* VI, 80.[1]

[1] It is to be found also in *A Collection of Old Ballads*, 1723–1725, II, 232, with the tune title "In the West of Devonshire," derived from the opening line of "The Devonshire Nymph," a ballad to the tune of "Tender Hearts of London City" contained in the same collection, I, 227, whence it was reprinted in *RB* VI, 96. Another ballad to the tune of "Tender Hearts" is "True Love Exalted," with a similar beginning, "In the West in Devonshire" (Pepys, BM C.22.f.6, Harvard, Lord Crawford; reprinted in *RB* VI, 93).

459

Two sequels were written to the ballad: "Loves Unspeakable Passion: Or, The Youngman's Answer to Tender hearts of London City," licensed June 12, 1684 (Lord Crawford, Douce, Harvard, Roxburghe; reprinted in *RB* VI, 83), and "The True Lovers Ghost" (Lord Crawford, Douce, Harvard, Roxburghe; reprinted in *RB* VI, 85).

Another broadside printing the music is "The Lord Russels Farewel, Who was Beheaded for High-Treason . . . July 21st. 1683," beginning "Pride the bane of humane creatures," to the tune of "Tender hearts of London City" (Lord Crawford, Harvard, Pepys; reprinted in *RB* V, 326).[2] "Love and Loyalty," beginning "Susan, I this letter send thee," is properly directed to the tune, but music contained on the sheet is actually "Cavalilly man," q.v., which does not fit (Pepys, Douce, Lord Crawford, Roxburghe; reprinted in *RB* VII, 497).

The popularity of "Tender hearts" as a tune is reflected in its use with fifteen or more broadsides, including: "The Dutchess of Monmouth's Lamentation For the Loss of Her Duke," 1683, beginning "Loyal Hearts of London City" (BM 1876.f.1; reprinted in *RB* V, 640); "True Love Rewarded with Cruelty," an account of the death in July, 1683, of Mary Story, a jilted lover (Lord Crawford, Roxburghe; reprinted in *BB* II, 949); and "The tender Citizens," beginning "Young mens hearts of London City," published before the end of 1684 (Pepys III, 251, Douce II,

---

[2] The very popular tune of "Russell's farewell," q.v., takes its rise not from this ballad in five-line stanzas, but from "The Lord Russels Last Farewel to the World," in ballad-meter octaves.

217^v). The following broadside to the tune seems not to have been re-printed: "The Faithful Lovers: or, Tommy and Bettys Declarations," beginning "Tommy and his Love were walking" (Douce I, 73^v, Harvard, Lord Crawford 1208). A handful of others will be found in *RB* and *BB*.

Then, Then to the Duke,

Let's Fill Up the Glass

A ballad with this tune on the sheet (Fig. 460) is entitled "A New-Years Gift for the Whigs" and begins "Great Souls that are free from

Faction, rejoyce" (Lord Crawford 466, Bodleian Ashmole G.16 [129], Clark). The Clark copy contains the MS date "30 Dec. 1684" inscribed by Narcissus Luttrell, its original possessor. I have no information on the source of the tune name, but "Then then to the Duke let's fill up the Glass" sounds like the beginning of a refrain. The tune was apparently not cited for singing other broadsides.

There Is One Black and Sullen Hour

This tune, called also "Sullen hour" or "Black and Sullen hour," is named from the opening line of a song in D'Urfey's comedy *The Banditti*, 1686, I, i. In the same year it appeared in a setting by Samuel Akeroyde in *The Theater of Music*, Third Book, p. 6 (Fig. 461), re-

461

printed in all editions of *Pills*, 1719–1720, IV, 256. The tune is also found in *Youth's Delight on the Flagelet*, 9th ed., c. 1690. An expanded form of the text was issued as a broadside with the title "Beauties Cruelty: Or, The Passionate Lover. . . . To a New Play-House Tune" (Pepys; reprinted in *RB* IV, 414; other issues in BM C.22.f.6, Lord Crawford, Euing, Douce); it was licensed by Richard Pocock, 1685–1688, as were four others to the tune. One of these was reprinted in *RB* IV, 416, another in *BB* II, 539; two others apparently have not been reprinted: "The Painted Ladies Rambles," beginning "A Youthful Damsel fair and bright" (Pepys III, 203), and "The Seven London Lasses Lamentations For the Loss of Simon," beginning "Simon the Salter, fine and trim" (Pepys III, 335).

Also to the tune is "Romes Cruelty: Or, The Earl of Essex Barbarously

Murthered in the Tower" (Pepys; reprinted in *PB* III, 96), a ballad clearly written soon after Arthur Capel, Earl of Essex, virtually decapitated himself with a razor, July 13, 1683. One cannot be sure that an edition was published immediately, when popular sentiment favored the thesis of murder as set forth in detail on the broadside. The broadside could, however, scarcely have contained the tune direction "There is one Black and Sullen Hour" three years before D'Urfey's play. Professor Rollins (*PB* III, 90–91) quoted MS notes of Anthony Wood to the effect that the murder theory was again in the public consciousness after the revolution, aided by a pamphlet which circulated in London and Oxford late in 1688. It is not unreasonable, then, to suppose that the unique copy of "Romes Cruelty" with Brooksby's imprint is a reissue.

Matthew Taubman, one of London's pageant writers, used the tune for a song in *London's Yearly Jubilee*, 1686. Two songs which name the tune as "[The] Sullen Hour" appear in *The True Lover's Garland*, 1687.

Thomas, You Cannot

This tune takes its name from the burden of a ribald song beginning "Thomas: vntyed his points apace," preserved in the Percy Folio MS (ed. Hales and Furnivall, IV, 116). The music is found in Paris Conservatoire MS Rés. 1186, fols. 18ᵛ, 71ᵛ, as "Thomas you cannot"; in *A Booke of New Lessons for the Cithern & Gittern*, 1652, and in *Musick's Delight on the Cithren*, 1666, as "Thomas I cannot"; in *The Dancing Master* as "Thomas you Cannot," editions of 1670–1686 (1670, p. 93= Fig. 462), and as "Tumas I cannot; Or, Tom Trusty," Volume II, 3d ed., 1718, 4th ed., 1728. The tune is introduced into thirteen ballad operas under the name of "Thomas I cannot" or "Sir Thomas I cannot," including the following which print the music: Gay's *The Beggar's Opera*, 1728; Chetwood's *The Generous Free-Mason*, 1731; Fielding's *The Mock Doctor*, 2d ed., 1732, and his *An Old Man taught Wisdom*, 1735; and Langford's *The Lover his own Rival*, 1736.

The earliest extant broadside to the tune of "Thomas you cannot" seems to be "A New-yeeres-gift for the Pope," c. 1624, of which only the first part has been preserved (Pepys; reprinted in *PG*, p. 170). The song in the Percy Folio MS may not be much older. Another blackletter ballad to the tune is "Honesty is Honesty, Come off of my Mother, Sirrah!" beginning "Upon a certain day when Mars/and Venus met

462 ¢3

together" (Rawlinson 60),[1] the refrain of which furnished the tune title "Come off my Mother Sirrah, Sirrah" to two ballads of the second half of the seventeenth century: "The Married Mans complaint," beginning "Was ever poor man mistaken so" (Douce II, 150), and "The Married wives complaint," beginning "I am a poor Married Wife God knows" (Douce II, 144ᵛ).

A song beginning "Come, my Molly, let us be jolly," to the tune of "Thomas I cannot" is in William Hicks's *Grammatical Drollery*, 1682, p. 75, and in *A Complete Collection of . . . English and Scotch Songs,* 1735–1736, IV, 14. *Political Merriment,* Part IV, 1715, p. 63, contains "A New Ballad on the Pretender's Coming" to the same tune. And it is also used for a song in *Perseus and Andromeda,* 1728, p. 11, beginning "In London Town there liv'd, well known," a song also issued in single-sheet form c. 1730 (BM G.305 [10]). Another song sheet with the music is "The Footman's Holy-day. The Words by Mr. Arthur Bradley," beginning "Come Jenny come Molly come Kitty come Dolly" (BM H.1601 [81], c. 1720; Harvard). Chappell (*PMOT* I, 337) printed the opening stanza of yet another eighteenth-century song to the tune, found in W. R. Chetwood's *A General History of the Stage,* 1749, p. 182.

[1] The first five stanzas were printed in *National Ballad and Song,* ed. J. S. Farmer, 1897, I, 35, from Bodleian MS Rawl. Poet. 1335, fol. 31ᵛ. A version of six stanzas, only two of which are in the printed broadside, may be found in a commonplace book of c. 1625–1635, Harvard MS Eng. 686, p. 82. Neither manuscript text contains a tune direction.

Three Travelers

"The Jovial Companions, or, The Three Merry Travellors . . . To an excellent North-Country Tune," beginning "There was three Travellers, Travellers three," has survived in a broadside edition of 1690 or after, though the song is doubtless considerably older (Bagford; reprinted in *BB* I, 51). It is reprinted in *Pills*, 1719–1720, VI, 177, with the tune (Fig. 463). A late seventeenth-century copy of "A new Ditty to an

old Tune of three Travellers," beginning "Ile show you a [sic] Captains of Aubrey Vere," is in BM MS Harl. 6913, p. 321. Both ballads are in couplets with an interlaced refrain, in which line 2 of each stanza is "With a hey down, ho down, Lanktre down derry" or "With a hey ho Langledown Dilly," and line 4 is "Without ever a stiver of Money" or "Who has never a penny of Mony." [1]

Through the Wood, Laddy

A song on the battle of Worcester, written by John Tatham for his comedy *The Scots Figgaries*, 1652, Act V, may lead us to the earliest manifestations of this tune. The song, beginning "Cam lend, lend y'ar lugs Joes, an Ise speeke a song," is without tune indication; the reprint in *Rump*, 1662, I, 248, adds not only an eleventh stanza but also a tune direction "Through the Wood Lady." Music for that tune may not have

[1] "Never a Penny of Money" and "Without ever a penny of Money" are tune titles used in connection with ballads of quite different metrical pattern. See "The Crossed Couple."

464

* A 16-measure variation follows in original.

survived; but a number of eighteenth-century settings of "Through the wood, laddy" are preserved, and they fit the anapestic tetrameter quatrain of Tatham's song, although musically they seem no earlier than the last quarter of the seventeenth century.

Allan Ramsay may have reworked an older piece for his song "Throw the Wood Laddie," beginning "O Sandy, why leaves thou thy Nelly to mourn?" (*Tea-Table Miscellany*, 1723, p. 85). The tune is in Alexander Stuart's *Musick for Allan Ramsay's . . . Scots Songs*, c. 1725, p. 90 (Fig. 464). The second volume of the *Tea-Table* (ed. 1733, II, 179) contains a song—not by Ramsay—to the tune of "Thro' the wood laddie," beginning "As early I walk'd, on the first of sweet may." Several single-sheet editions titled "Through the Wood Laddy" had appeared from c. 1720, the text beginning "As early I walk'd on the first day of May" (BM G.306 [48], Huntington, Harvard). The song-sheet music and text are found in William Thomson's *Orpheus Caledonius*, 1725, No. 4, Watts's *Musical Miscellany*, 1729–1731, II, 116, and Walsh's *British Musical Miscellany*, 1734–1736, III, 113. The tune is joined with Ramsay's poem in Johnson's *Scots Musical Museum*, 1787–1803, II, 161,[1] and Graham's *Songs of Scotland*, 1848–1849, III, 56.

The tune is introduced into three ballad operas, including Gay's *Polly*, 1729, and Ralph's *The Fashionable Lady*, 1730, which reprint the music.

[1] The *Museum* also reprints, II, 162, "The Original words of Thro' the Wood, Laddie," but these are of recent composition. See James Glen, *Early Scottish Melodies*, 1900, p. 110. A single-sheet song of about 1765 unites Ramsay's poem with music by Michael Arne (BM G.310 [232], Harvard, Huntington; see also *London Magazine*, XXXIV [1765], 426).

Thursday in the Morn

The great naval victory at La Hogue, May 19–23, 1692, in which the English and Dutch fleets routed the French and set fire to a dozen enemy ships, was celebrated in a number of ballads. One which begins "Thursday in the Morn the Ides [*or* nineteenth] of May" is no better than the four reprinted in *PB* VI, 179–196, but its century of popularity under various titles justifies some notice. As "Admiral Russel's Scowering The French Fleet: or, The Battle at Sea," 1695 (Harvard), it was issued as a broadside with music (Fig. 465); a 1694 edition at Harvard, its heading

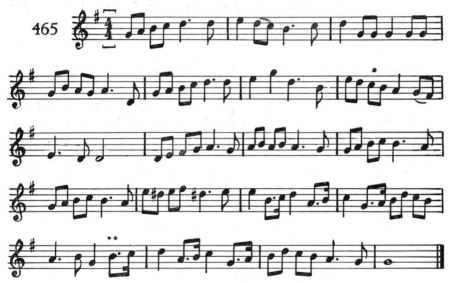

465

Original is a fourth higher.
* These two eighth notes are one step higher in original; emended from 1694 edition.
** Whole tone lower in original.

shorn down to its subtitle "The Battel at Sea," contains imperfect music. A short version of the text accompanies the tune in *Pills*, 1719–1720, IV, 333, where Samuel Akeroyde is credited as the composer. Other musical miscellanies reprinting the song include *Clio and Euterpe*, 1759–1762, I, 76, *The Convivial Songster*, c. 1782, p. 316, and Ritson's *English Songs*, 1783, II, 181. A number of song-sheet editions were published during the eighteenth century, usually with the title "Russells Triumph" (BM G.312 [84], BM H.1994.b [85], Harvard). In *The Midshipman's Garland*, n.d., p. 7, the ballad bears the original broadside title (reprinted in *BB* I, 119, and in *Naval Songs and Ballads*, ed. C. H. Firth, 1908, p. 119). A roman-letter broadside version without imprint or music is called "The Gallant Sea-Fight" (BM 1871.e.9 [94]).

Also sung to the tune of "Thursday in the Morn" is "The Valliant Admiral," an account of Sir John Leake's raising of famine at Barcelona after capturing French provision ships in 1708 (reprinted by Firth, p. 156, from *The Seafaring Garland*, n.d.).

[Tobacco Is an Indian Weed]

Among the host of poems devoted to the pleasurable or baleful effects of tobacco, one has retained its popularity over more than two centuries. It has been ascribed to George Wither, though on no very reliable evidence; it exists in several forms, differing chiefly in the opening stanza, but also revealing the shifts in language as the verb associated with tobacco is first "drink," then "take," and eventually "smoke." The only tune that can be associated with this medley of texts appears in *Pills*, all editions, 1719–1720, III, 291 (Fig. 466).[1]

Perhaps the earliest form of the song is that found in a seventeenth-century commonplace book, BM MS Add. 22603, fols. 34^v–35:

UPON TAKINGE OF TOBACCO. A MEDITATION.

Why should you so much despise
So good so graue an exercise,
As earely and late to meditate
So thinke then drinke Tobacco.

The earthen pipe so lilly white
Shewes y^t thou art a mortall wight
Tis even such, broke with a touch,
This thinke then drinke Tobacco.

[1] Chappell (*PMOT* II, 563–564) follows Rimbault's *A Little Book of Songs and Ballads*, 1851, p. 170, in noting that a broadside of 1670 contains the music. I have been unable to locate the broadside, whose title Rimbault gives as "Tobacco is an Indian Weed."

466

Original is a fourth higher.

    When yᵉ smoke ascends on high
      Then thinke thou seest yᵉ Vanity
    Of wor[l]dly stuffe gon with a puffe,
      This thinke, then drinke Tobacco.

    When yᵉ Pipe's all foule within
      Thinke how thy soul's defyld with sin
    To be purg'd with fire, it doth require,
      This thinke then drinke Tobacco.

    Lastly the Ashes left behind
      Doe dayly serue to moue thy mind
    That to ashes and dust, returne thou must,
      This thinke, then drinke Tobacco.[2]

A four-stanza version of these verses, with minor verbal differences, is printed in *The Marrow of Complements*, 1655, p. 176, under the title "Meditations on Tobacco." This latter miscellany is evidently the source of the seventeenth-century copy in *The Bannatyne Manuscript*, ed. W. Tod Ritchie, 1928–1934, IV, 330.

Another text, beginning "The Indian weed withered quite/Greene at noone, cut down at night," appeared as the last of thirty-one epigrams in Thomas Jenner's *The Soules Solace*, 1626. The poem is not signed, as are the others in this volume, but the following is appended:

    Answered by *G. W.* thus,
    Thus thinke, drinke no Tobacco.

An early seventeenth-century commonplace book version of the 1626 text is preserved in Harvard MS Eng. 686, p. 113: "Observations in the vse of Tobacco"; a variant appears in Rimbault's *A Little Book* as from the (unlocated) 1670 broadside. Another variant is found in a pamphlet of 1672, *Two Broad-Sides against Tobacco*, p. 30, where the initials of

---

[2] Substantially this text appears with Wither's initials in J. P. Collier's spurious manuscript which purported to be from the time of James I. It was printed by Rimbault, *A Little Book*, p. 226, and reprinted in *Notes and Queries*, 2d ser., I (1856), 378, and in Chappell, *PMOT* II, 563.

the 1626 end-note are expanded into Wither's name.[3] A slightly altered beginning, "Tobacco that is withered quite/Grown in the morning, cut down at night," is found in the text printed in *Merry Drollery*, 1661, I, 16.

A manuscript "Ballad upon Tobacco," beginning "Tobacco is but an Indian Weed," is preserved at the end of Pepys's ballad collection, V, 436. It was probably copied from a broadside, and, except for the transposition of the third and fourth stanzas, it agrees almost verbatim with the text printed in *Pills*. This was the form generally reprinted during the next century and a half. Samuel Wesley wrote "A 3 Part Song" to the text, making no use of the *Pills* tune (BM I.66o.e [384], with Wesley's signature and the date "Sunday June 22 1800" engraved on the sheet; see also a copy in BM MS Add. 31764, fol. 17). Dr. Charles Hague also made a fresh musical setting for the Rev. James Plumptre's *Collection of Songs*, 1805, p. 112. Seven Dials presses continued to issue the text during the nineteenth century (cf. a copy "Tobacco" in BM C.116.i.1 [195], and another edition from Jennings of Fleet Street, "Human Mortality; or Tobacco an Indian Weed," in a Harvard portfolio, 25242.7*, p. 48).

The Rev. Ralph Erskine's "Smoking Spiritualized," consisting of the old song in the "This Indian weed now wither'd quite" version, followed by "a new Addition to it or Improvement of it," was published in *An Elegy . . .* , 1739, p. 23, in his *Sermons, and Other Practical Works*, 1764–1765, II, 662, and in later editions of his *Gospel Sonnets*. Erskine's dreary verses were reprinted in *Notes and Queries*, 2d ser., I (1856), 258, in the course of an extensive correspondence on "Tobacco is an Indian weed" spread through its pages from March through May, 1856.[4]

Tom a Bedlam

Music of "Tom of Bedlam" is preserved in a lute manuscript of c. 1613–1616, BM MS Add. 38539, fol. 14. As "Tom a Bedlam" it ap-

---

[3] The same text, entitled "A religious use of taking Tobacco" and ascribed to Robert Wisedome, is found in a mid-seventeenth-century commonplace book in Trinity College, Dublin (MS G.2.21, pp. 459–460). Norman Ault accepts the attribution, identifies the author as the Robert Wisdom who was archdeacon of Ely (d. 1568), and includes the Dublin text in his *Elizabethan Lyrics*, 3d ed., 1949, p. 56. Ault's identification, however, does not seem conclusive enough to establish it as a sixteenth-century poem.

[4] For a discussion of the Harvard manuscript text and other important versions of the song, see Charles F. Main, Jr., An Early Stuart Manuscript Miscellany, unpublished Harvard dissertation, 1953, pp. 148–149, 689–699.

pears in a virginal arrangement in Drexel MS 5612, p. 159, and it is the setting (Fig. 467) for "I am a Rogue and a stout one" in John Gamble's MS Commonplace Book, 1659, No. 64 (both in New York Public

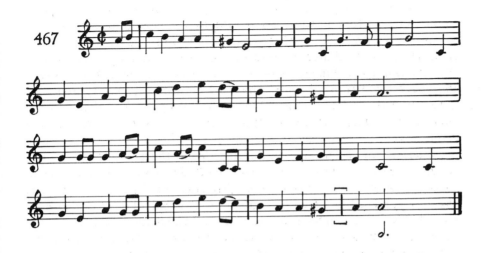

467

Library). An indifferent version of the tune is in *Musick's Delight on the Cithren*, 1666, No. 33. The first strain appears twice in *Pills*, 1719–1720, associated with drollery songs requiring the entire tune. One is "Mad Maudlin, To find out Tom of Bedlam" (IV, 189), on the same subject as a "Tom of Bedlam" beginning "From forth the Elizian feilds" in *Wit and Drollery*, 1656, p. 126. The other is "On Doctor G. formerly Master of St. Paul's School" (IV, 263), an account of the floggings administered by Alexander Gill, high master of the school, 1635–1640.[1]

In Ben Jonson's *The Devil is an Asse*, V, ii, Pug says "Your best songs *Thom o' Bet'lem.*" This is an ambiguous allusion, for the title is commonly found in seventeenth-century songs, and the likeliest candidates cannot usually be traced to a date earlier than their appearance in Restoration drolleries.[2] We can be sure, however, that the tune was used with several ballads of the first half of the century, and we are fortunate to have one and perhaps two versions of the tune from the time of

[1] It had originally appeared without tune direction or music in *The Loves of Hero and Leander . . . with . . . other choice Pieces of Drollery*, 1651, p. 54. A modification of the poem, in a five-line stanza, fitting only the first strain of the tune, was printed in *Mock Songs*, 1675, p. 108, as "On a whipping School-master," to the tune of "Old Tom a Bedlam."

[2] On other ballads called "Tom of Bedlam," "Mad Tom," or "New Mad Tom of Bedlam," see the discussion under "Gray's Inn Masque." Most of the texts mentioned there and here have been reprinted, with elaborate notes, in *Loving Mad Tom: Bedlamite Verses of the XVI and XVII Centuries*, ed. Jack Lindsay, 1927.

James I. The earliest broadside to the tune of "Tom of Bedlam" is "The cunning Northerne Begger," beginning "I am a lusty beggar," licensed in 1634 (Manchester, Euing, Roxburghe; reprinted in *RB* I, 137). Typical of the spate of political ballads which anticipated the Restoration and were popular in both broadside and songster form are two of 1659/60 to the tune: "A New Ballade, To an Old Tune," beginning "Make room for an honest Red-coat" (BM Thomason, BM Luttrell, Wood 416, Bagford, Harvard, Roxburghe; reprinted in *Ratts Rhimed to Death* and *The Rump*, 1660, *Rump*, 1662, *180 Loyal Songs*, 1685, *Loyal Songs*, 1731, and *RB* VII, 648); and "The Cock-Crowing at the Approach of a Free-Parliament," beginning "More Wine Boy; To be sober," to the tune of "Mad Tom of Bedlam" (Wood 416 [49], *The Rump, Rump,* and *Loyal Songs*).

"A Relation of a Quaker," beginning "All in the Land of Essex," was published first as a broadside in 1659 (BM Thomason); in its original form and in *Ratts* it is without tune direction, but in *The Rump*, p. 6, the tune is named as "Tom of Bedlam." [3] This ballad gave rise to both tune names found on a broadside of c. 1681: "The Saint turn'd Curtezan," beginning "All in the Zealous City," to the tune of "The Quakers Ballad: or, All in the Land of Essex" (Huntington, with MS date April 13, 1681; Wood 417 [65], BM C.38.i.25 [8], Lord Crawford 39, Harvard, Yale). Also to the tune of "All in the Land of Essex" is "Worcester Dumb-Bells," *temp.* Queen Anne, beginning "I sing the famous City" (Harvard, Morgan 21).

Bishop Richard Corbet's familiar song beginning "Am I mad, O noble Festus" is usually found without tune direction, but in *An Antidote against Melancholy*, 1661, p. 35, "Tom a Bedlam" is indicated for singing, and the verses fit that tune.[4]

[3] The ballad is there titled "News from Colchester," as also in Bodleian MS Ashmole 36–37, fol. 88, and in Sir John Denham's *Poems and Translations*, 1668. In *Merry Drollery*, 1661, and *Wit and Mirth*, 3d ed., 1682, the title is "The Colchester Quaker." The ballad is included in John Cleveland's *Works*, 1687, and in *Loyal Songs*, 1731. Other copies are in Bodleian MS Rawl. Poet. 147, p. 183, and BM MS Harl. 3991, fol. 49ᵛ. This sordid tale of buggery, aimed at Quaker hypocrisy, was based on a notorious event of c. 1653, and is more probably the work of Denham than of Cleveland. The opening lines of the ballad are imitated in a later song, beginning "All in the land of cider," for which see the tune of that name.

[4] This satire on Puritanism at Cambridge was probably composed between 1633, when Laud became Archbishop of Canterbury, and 1635, the year of Corbet's death. Its earliest printed version is in *A Brief Dialogue between Zelopit . . . and Superstition . . . Composed by Owen Dogerell*, 1642, sig. A4, followed by its appearance in Corbet's *Certain Elegant Poems*, 1647, p. 66. It is found also in *Le Prince d'Amour*, 1660, *Merry Drollery*, 1661, *Rump*, 1662, *Wit and Mirth*, 3d ed., 1682, and *Loyal Songs*, 1731. A copy is in the Percy Folio MS (ed. Hales and Furnivall, III, 269), but the chief source for the *Reliques* text was the 1672 edition of Corbet's *Poems*. Other manuscript

Le Prince d'Amour, 1660, contains two songs entitled "Tom of Bedlam" which fit the tune. The older of these, beginning "From the Hag and hungry goblin" (p. 167), had been recorded, without music, in Giles Earle's songbook, 1615–1626 (BM MS Add. 24665, ed. Peter Warlock, 1932, p. 97); it was reprinted in *Westminster Drollery,* 1672, II, 17, as "Tom of Bedlam; and to that Tune," and in *Wit and Drollery,* 1682, p. 149, without tune direction. The other begins "From the top of high Caucasus" (p. 164) and was included among the bedlamite songs in the *Reliques.* "The Oakerman," beginning "The star that shines by daylight," names the tune "Tom of Bedlam" (*Westminster Drollery* II, 21, *Wit and Drollery,* p. 153). Without tune direction but in the same stanza pattern is "Loving Mad Tom," beginning "I'll bark against the dogstar," in *Wit and Drollery,* p. 184.[5]

Two other pieces seem, from their metrics, to be intended for the tune. They are "The zealous Puritan. 1639," beginning "My Brethren all attend/And list to my relation" (*Merry Drollery, Rump, Loyal Songs;* a copy is in Bodleian MS Ashmole 36–37, fol. 100; reprinted in *An American Garland,* ed. C. H. Firth, p. 25); and Sir Francis Wortley's "Mad Tom a Bedlams desires of Peace: or his Benedicities for distracted Englands restauration to her wits again," 1648, beginning "Poor Tom hath been imprison'd" (BM Thomason, Lord Crawford 1003, Harvard; reprinted in Wright's *Political Ballads,* p. 101).

"The Poets News-years-gift: or, A Pleasant Poem in praise of Old Sack," beginning "Come hither, learned Sisters," is a broadside of c. 1675 to the tune of "The Jovial Tinker, or Tom a Bedlam" (Douce II, 180). The first tune takes its name from "A pleasant new Songe of a iouiall Tinker," beginning "There was a iouiall Tinker/dwelt in the towne of Thurbie" (Pepys; reprinted in *PB* I, 104). This ballad, published c. 1616, is to the tune of "Fly Brasse," on which I have no information. But among the imitations of "The Jovial Tinker" Rollins cites "I am a Rogue and a stout one," which, in John Gamble's commonplace book of 1659, is coupled to the tune of "Tom a Bedlam," lending some weight to the possibility that "The Jovial Tinker" and "Fly Brass" may be other names for "Tom a Bedlam." [6]

copies include the following in the British Museum: MS Sloane 1446, fol. 11v, MS Harl. 3991, fol. 60v, MS Egerton 923, fol. 12.

[5] It had appeared earlier in *The New Academy of Complements,* 1671, No. 317. Refurbished as "I'll sail upon the dog star" it was introduced into D'Urfey's *A Fool's Preferment,* 1688, Act IV, with a bravura setting by Purcell (supplement to the play, p. 10).

[6] "The iouiall Tinker" is also named as the tune for "The famous Ratketcher," c. 1615, beginning "There was a rare Rat-catcher" (Pepys; reprinted in *PG,* p. 60; see also *SB,* p. 94).

Tom Tinker

In C. T.'s *Laugh and lie Downe: or, The worldes Folly,* 1605 (reprinted in *The Works of Cyril Tourneur,* ed. Allardyce Nicoll, 1930, p. 280), there

Original is unbarred.

is an allusion to a ballad of "Whilom I was," sung to the tune of "Tom Tinker." That ballad is lost, unless it be echoed in "When that I was," the clown's song at the end of *Twelfth Night.* A "Tom Tinker" tune

Original is a fourth higher.

has, however, been preserved in the first ten editions of *The Dancing Master*, 1651–1698 (1651, p. 88 = Fig. 468). A different tune is found with a late version of a wittily indecent ballad, beginning "Tom Tinker's my true love, and I am his Dear," *Pills*, 1719–1720, VI, 265 (Fig. 469). The *Pills* music is also found in late editions of *The Dancing Master* and in Gay's *The Beggar's Opera,* the only ballad opera calling for the air.

[A Tory, a Whig, and a Moderate Man]

"The Moderate Man," beginning "A Tory a Whigg & a Moderate Man," appears in a two-stanza engraved song-sheet edition of 1710 (Fig. 470), "ye words by Mr. D'urfey to a pretty French Tune" (Harvard; another copy is in a collection of engraved sheets entitled *Musa et Musica,*

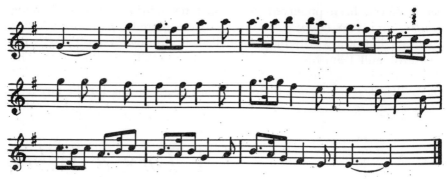

* C♯ confirmed from flute version on sheet.

BM H.82 [1]). Undated song-sheet issues, for which the provisional date of "1705?" may be too early, are found in BM G.306 (43), BM H.1601 (32), and Huntington. A four-stanza broadside version of 1713 without music is entitled "The Country Courtship, or, The Maiden's Choice. . . . To a pretty French Tune" (BM 1876.f.1 [65]). In the 1714 edition of *Pills* V, 321, the text contains three stanzas and the air is described as "a French Tune." The edition of 1719–1720, I, 7, uses the 1710 text of two stanzas and the music is credited to "the famous Signior [Arcangelo] Corelli."

Trenchmore

"Trenchmore" was a lively dance tune in vogue from the middle of the sixteenth century. Fantasias for lute found in Folger MS 448.16, fol. 10, dating from the 1560s, and in Cambridge University MS Dd.3.18, fol. 12ᵛ (by John Johnson, who died c. 1595) give no satisfactory reading of the tune. The late seventeenth-century setting by Denis Gaultier preserved in Jane Pickering's Lute Book (BM MS Egerton 2046, fol. 51ᵛ) is useful only for the first half of the tune; a fragment is in the Bedford Cittern MS, fol. 43ᵛ. More useful are the texts in the Marsh Lute Book, c. 1590, p. 139, and in Paris Conservatoire MS Rés. 1186, fol. 32, the latter a seventeenth-century set of keyboard variations.

Among the printed sources, the earliest versions of the tune are probably those in Thomas Ravenscroft's *Deuteromelia*, 1609, set to two songs, "Tomorrow the Fox will come to towne" (No. 20), and "Willy prethe goe to bed" (No. 21). The latter is also preserved in *Pills*, eds. of 1699–1714, I, 51, with the music. Perhaps the best version of the tune is in *The Dancing Master*, 2d ed., 1652, *et seq.*, set to a longways dance (1652, p. 103=Fig. 471).

471

Original is unbarred.

References to "Trenchmore" in Renaissance literature uniformly speak of it as a dance. As early as 1564 it is named as part of the stock in trade of a mountebank (William Bullein, *A Dialogve bothe pleasaunte and pietifull . . . against the fever Pestilence,* reprinted in Early English Text Society, Extra Series 52, 1888, p. 94). Therapeutic qualities of the vigorous measure are suggested in Song 6 of Thomas Weelkes's *Ayeres or Phantasticke Spirites,* 1608:

> Fill the pipe once more,
> My braines daunce trenchmore.
> It is headdy,
> I am geeddy;
> My head and braines,
> Backe and raines,
> Jointes and vaines,
> From all paines
> It doth well purge and make cleane.

In Lodowick Barry's play *Ram-Alley,* III, i, Justice Tutchin says: "Well I shall catch him in a narrow roome,/Where neither of vs can flinch; If I do,/Ile make him dance a trenchmoore to my sword." Selden, in his *Table-Talk* (ed. Frederick Pollock, 1927, pp. 64–65), contrasts the court of Elizabeth with that of Charles I as symbolized by the dance: "Att a Solemne dancing, first you have the grave measures, then the Corantoes & the Galliards, & all this is kept upp wᵗʰ ceremony, att length they fall to Trenchmore, & so to the Cushion-Dance . . . In King James time things were pretty well[.] But in K Charles time there has binn nothing but Trenchmore & the Cushion dance, Omnium gatherum, totty polly, hoyte come toyte."

The tune does not seem to have been used for singing any sixteenth-

or seventeenth-century ballads. A broadside entitled "The West-Country Jigg: Or, A Trenchmore Galliard" is to "a Merry Scotch Tune, Or, Up with Aley Aley," q.v. (*RB* VII, 343), and "Trenchmore" in the title suggests merely fast, tripping rhythm. "A New Ballad" beginning "What do Members now ail,/To the King to turn Tail," printed in *Poems on Affairs of State*, 1704, III, 139 (2d ed., 1716, III, 124), is to the tune of "Trenchmore," but it cannot be sung easily to the *Dancing Master* air.

[*'Twas Early One Morning*]

Thomas D'Urfey wrote the song beginning " 'Twas early one morning, the Cock had just Crow'd" for the first part of his comedy *Don Quixote*, 1694, Act IV. It appears among the *Songs* of the play published in the same year, p. 27, with a musical setting by John Eccles (Fig. 472) and was reprinted in *Pills*, 1719–1720, I, 228. The three stanzas sung in the

theater were anonymously expanded to seven and issued as a broadside entitled "The Complaining Bridgroom: or, Roger's Repentance after Marriage" (Pepys V, 237, without music). Eccles's tune does not seem to have been used for any other broadside.

'Twas When the Seas Were Roaring

The song beginning " 'Twas when the seas were roaring" was sung in John Gay's *The What D'ye Call It: A Tragi-Comi-Pastoral Farce*, 1715, II, viii. With music attributed to Handel it appeared in a host of musical miscellanies, beginning with *The Merry Musician*, 1716, I, 297 (Fig. 473), and including Watts's *Musical Miscellany*, 1729–1731, II, 94, *British Melody*, 1739, No. 58, *Calliope, or English Harmony*, 1739–1746, I, 168, *Universal Harmony*, 1745, p. 54, *Muses Delight*, 1754, p. 176, and Ritson's *English Songs*, 1783 (1813, III, 36).[1] Several song-sheet editions have survived (BM H.1601 [427], BM G.305 [59], Chetham 1871, Harvard). The tune, called "Chloe's Farwel," is found in the second volume of *The Dancing Master*, 3d ed., 1718, p. 321, and in Walsh's *Compleat Country Dancing-Master*, 1719, II, 342. The popularity of the tune after the first quarter of the century seems to have been stimulated by its inclusion in

[1] Ritson's collection contains also a later setting of the song by William Jackson of Exeter.

473

Gay's *The Beggar's Opera* and in seven other ballad operas whose printed texts name the air but do not reprint the music.

Several political songs to the tune imitate Gay's verses. A broadside of c. 1716 called "A New Song" begins "When Faction loud was Roaring" (Douce IV, 21**; another version is in Bodleian MS Rawl. Poet. 207, p. 106). "The Pretender's Flight" is "In Imitation of a new Song sung at the Playhouse in the Comick Tragick Farce, or, what d'ye call it," and begins " 'Twas when the Seas were roaring/With Blasts of Northern Wind" (*A Collection of State Songs*, 1716, p. 125, *Mughouse Diversion*, 1717, p. 30). Another parody, beginning "Twas when the Winds was blowing," is in the 1719 edition of *Mughouse Diversion*, p. 40.

Several eighteenth-century editions of "A Famous Sea-Fight between Captain Ward and the Rainbow," beginning "Strike up, you lusty Gallants," are directed to be sung to " 'Twas when the seas were roaring" (Roxburghe III, 654, Harvard, Yale).[2] The music is found with other texts on song sheets, as for example "The Dying Virgins Farewel," beginning "Beneath a shady Bower,/close by a Crystal Brook," an early eighteenth-century production (Harvard); and "Sir John Barleycorn," beginning "There was four Men Came out of the North" (Harvard), a mid-century issue.

[2] The tune named on earlier editions of the ballad (it was licensed in 1609) is "Captain Ward," which does not appear to have survived. The ballad is reprinted in *RB* VI, 426.

'Twas When the Sheep Were Shearing

The song beginning " 'Twas when the Sheep were shearing" was introduced into D'Urfey's opera *Cinthia and Endimion*, 1697, III, i. It is found with the music in all editions of *Pills*, 1719–1720, I, 318 (Fig. 474).

An imperfect version of the tune, named for the first line, is included in *Youth's Delight on the Flagelet*, 11th ed., 1697. A broadside edition of the same year is "An Excellent New Playhouse Song Call'd, The West-Country Fairing, Or, Dicks Present to Doll Under the Barly Mow," without tune direction or music (Harvard); it is the soundest of the three texts.

The Two Entire Lovers

This tune by Moses Snow is found in *The Banquet of Musick*, First Book, 1688, p. 3 (Fig. 475), set to a song beginning "I Lov'd you dearly

475

once, 'tis true,/but now thank Heav'n I'm free." A broadside of about the same time called "The Two Entire Lovers . . . To an Excellent New Ayre" begins similarly but expands the song to eight stanzas; meaningless music is on the ballad sheets (Pepys, Lord Crawford; reprinted in *RB* VIII, 687). From this broadside comes the tune title, "The Two Entire Lovers," cited for the singing of "The Shepherd's Ingenuity: Or, The Praise of the Green Gown," beginning "Amongst the pleasant shady Bowers," in the same stanza form (Lord Crawford, Douce, Roxburghe; reprinted in *RB* VIII, 689).

Under and Over

This tune is found as "A man had 3 sones" in Drexel MS 5612, p. 148, New York Public Library (Fig. 476), and an untitled keyboard set is in Paris Conservatoire MS Rés. 1186, fol. 70^v. The air is in all editions of *The Dancing Master* except the first, titled "Under and Over." The first strain is little more than a version in minor of "Joan's ale is new"; after

476

the first eight bars, however, the resemblance ceases and the two tunes imply verse patterns that are not interchangeable.

The original ballad giving the tune its name is "A New little Northren Song called, Vnder and ouer, ouer and vnder . . . To a pretty new Northern tune," beginning "As I abroad was walking,/I heard two louers talking" (Pepys; reprinted in *PB* II, 208). The eight-line stanza is supplemented by a variable refrain based on the following formula:

> For vnder and ouer, ouer and vnder,
> vnder and ouer agen,
> quoth shee sweet heart I loue thee,
> as maydens should love men.

This ballad was published about 1631, in which year Laurence Price's "Rocke the Cradle John" was licensed. It begins "There was a country Gallant,/that wasted had his talent" and the tune direction is "Ouer and vnder" (Roxburghe; reprinted in *RB* VII, 162; a Pepys copy, issued by the same publisher, has the title "Children after the rate of 24 in a yeare"); its stanza pattern is exceptional in having twelve lines plus a refrain.[1]

Others naming the tune "Ouer and Vnder" include: Martin Parker's "A good throw for three Maiden-heads," beginning "Three maides did

[1] "Rock the Cradle sweet Iohn" is named as the tune for "Choice of Inuentions, Or Seuerall sorts of the figure of three," beginning "There were three men of Gotam" (*RB* I, 105). Its stanza of twelve lines plus a refrain of eight is evidently intended for another tune; its metrical pattern differs too from that of "Under and over." From the refrain of "Choice of Inuentions" is derived the tune name "There was a Ewe had three Lambes," cited for Robert Guy's ballad of 1632, "It is bad Iesting with a Halter" (Pepys; reprinted in *PG*, p. 394); it has an eight-line refrain following stanzas of eight, twelve, and sixteen lines.

make a meeting" (Pepys; reprinted in *PG*, p. 380); "The Times abuses: or, Muld Sacke his grievances briefly exprest," beginning "Attend my Masters and give eare" (Roxburghe; reprinted in *RB* II, 576)—Mulled Sack being a familiar London character of the early seventeenth century. "Vnder and ouer" is the tune name given for singing "Rocke the Babie Joane," a ballad of 1632 beginning "A Young man in our Parish" (Pepys; reprinted in *PB* II, 214). Another piece metrically suited to the tune and containing an "under and over" refrain is "A Songe of a Journey," beginning "Of late as I was journinge/All in a pleasant morninge," found in a mid-seventeenth-century commonplace book, BM MS Add. 22603, fol. 54^v, without music or tune direction.

Under the Greenwood Tree

The original ballad giving rise to this tune is "The West-Country Delight: Or, Hey for Zommerset-Shire," beginning "In Summer time when flowers do spring,/and Birds sit on a Tree," to the tune of "O how they did Firk it: Or, Salengers round" (Douce II, 242^v and 247 [variant issues]; reprinted with the music in *Pills*, 1719–1720, IV, 122). The broadsides, issued by Philip Brooksby, are no earlier than 1670, but words and unbarred music are also found in Bodleian MS Ashmole 36–37, fol. 294^v (Fig. 477), for which Chappell (*PMOT* II, 541) suggests a date not long after 1634. The refrain, subject to considerable variation (see the *Pills* version), is:

> Oh how they did jerk it,
> Caper and ferk it,
>   under the Green-wood Tree.

477

An answer to the ballad is "Hey for our Town, But a Fig for Zommerset-shire," beginning "In Winter time when flowers do fade/And Birds forsake the tree," to the tune of "Sallengers round" (Douce I, 96), with a refrain "Oh, how they did swill it,/Slabber and Bill it/Under the Holly-bush tree." This ballad, issued by R. Burton, who flourished 1641–1674, also implies a pre-Commonwealth date for "The West-Country Delight"; and the use of "Sellenger's Round" in the answer suggests that the new tune was not familiar. A ballad published in the mid-1670s and fitting either tune is "She is bound but won't Obey," beginning "I am a poor married man truly," to the tune of "The West-Country-delight" (Wood E.25, Rawlinson; reprinted in *RB* VII, 429, VIII, clxix*). Here the tune name is obviously derived from the title of the original ballad.

Other ballads to the tune are: "The Fair Maid of Islington; or The London Vintner Over-reach'd," beginning "There was a fair maid at Islington," to "Sellengers Round; or, Caper and ferk it" (Pepys, BM C.22.f.6, Douce, Lord Crawford, Roxburghe, Bagford; reprinted in *BB* I, 410; a variant version of the same ballad is in *Pills* V, 46, beginning "There was a Lass of Islington," but the tune is different and accommodates only half the eight-line stanza); "The Beggars Song, Both in City and Country," beginning "In Summertime when Men make hay," to "Oh, how they did Firk it, Caper and Jerk it, under the Greenwood Tree" (Pepys IV, 250); "The Jolly Widdower: or, A Warning for Batchelors," beginning "Young men and Batchelors, pray attend," to the tune "Caper and jerk it" (Pepys IV, 102).

The tune, called "Caper and jerk it," is used with "A Carrol for New-Years-day" in *A Cabinet of Choice Jewels,* 1688, and with "A delightful Song in honor of Whitsontide" in *Canterbury Tales by Chaucer, Junior,* 1687 (Pepys's Penny Merriments, vol. II; an eighteenth-century edition is in Ritson's Penny Histories, vol. III). As "Firk it and jerk it" it is used for a song beginning "My husband spends his time abroad" in another garland, *John & his Mistress* (Pepys's Penny Merriments, vol. I; a later edition is in Ritson, vol. IV).

A ballad of the 1680s which echoes the refrain and which is metrically compatible with the tune is "The Mistery Discovered; or, Frollick upon Frollick," beginning "Come let us be Frollick and Gay," to the (internally inspired) tune "Come let us be Frollick" (Lord Crawford, Roxburghe; reprinted in *RB* VII, 323). A song in *The Hive,* 4th ed., c. 1733, III, 260, to "Greenwood Tree" is "A Wife the greatest Curse."

"The Zealous Lover," issued in the 1670s and beginning "Come prethy Love let me prepare," is to the tune "Underneath the Green wood Tree" (Lord Crawford, Euing, Harvard, Roxburghe; reprinted in *RB* VII, 451), but its uniform octosyllabic lines do not fit the tune easily at all points. A ballad in the same meter and to the tune of "The Zealous Lover, or, A Fig for France" is "[The] Jeering Lover: or, A new way of Wooing," beginning "As through St. Albones I did pass" (Douce II, 260).[1]

A Compendious Book of Godly and Spiritual Songs, 1567, ed. A. F. Mitchell, 1897, pp. 204ff., contains a song in the meter of "Under the Greenwood Tree" which includes that phrase in its refrain:

> The Paip, that Pagane full of pryde,
> He hes vs blindit lang,
> For quhair the blind the blind dois gyde,
> Na wounder baith ga wrang;
> Lyke Prince and King, he led the Regne,
> Of all Iniquitie:
> Hay trix, tryme go trix, vnder the grene [wod tré].

Professor H. E. Rollins has noted that this is based on a secular ballad whose first stanza was quoted in Thomas Deloney's *Gentle Craft,* Part II, c. 1598 (*Works,* ed. Mann, p. 176), beginning "The Primrose in the greene Forrest,/the Violets they be gay," and ending "With hey tricksie, trim goe tricksie,/vnder the greenewood tree." [2] No firm line can be drawn between the "Primrose" ballad and "The West-Country Delight"; the coincidences are perhaps of the order found in "Robin Hood and the Monk" (Child No. 119), in which line 8 is "Vnder the grene-wode tre" and the ballad opens "In somer, when the shawes be sheyne."

The tune of "Under the Greenwood Tree" is found in *The Dancing*

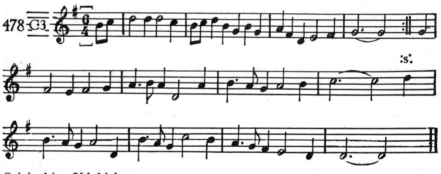

Original is a fifth higher.

---

[1] Ebsworth calls attention to the latter ballad in *RB* VII, 452, but misreads the title as "Young Lover." The tune "A Fig for France [and Holland too]" has apparently not survived.

[2] "Concerning Bodleian MS. Ashmole 48," *MLN,* XXXIV (June, 1919), 340–351. The "Primrose" ballad was registered in 1563–1564 and it is No. 76 of the Ashmole MS, into which four stanzas of another ballad have been inserted; "the telescoping of the two ballads," Rollins noted, "has played havoc with the refrain."

Master, supplement to the sixth edition, 1679. Through the next two editions it appears in common time. Meanwhile, in the seventh edition, 1686, a second version in 6/4 time is included among the additional tunes, No. 21, entitled "Oh! how they frisk it! or Leathern Apron" (Fig. 478). Beginning with the ninth edition, 1695, it appears in 6/4 time, with the original title. It is also found in Walsh's *Compleat Country Dancing-Master,* 1718. It was named in at least fourteen ballad operas, including the following which print the music: Ryan's *The Cobler's Opera,* 1729; *Momus turn'd Fabulist,* 1729; Johnson's *The Village Opera,* 1729; Coffey's *The Devil to Pay,* 1731; *The Jovial Crew,* 1731; Drury's *The Devil of a Duke,* 1732; and Potter's *The Decoy,* 1733.

Up Tails All

This tune is preserved in *The Fitzwilliam Virginal Book* II, 360, in an arrangement by Giles Farnaby. It is also included in *The Dancing Master,* 1651–1690 (1651, p. 97 = Fig. 479), with some variation between

479

Original is unbarred.

the musical text of the first and of later editions. Since none of these settings is designed for singing, it is impossible to tell the precise divisions that would be made in the half notes of the virginal text and of the 1651 *Dancing Master* text. The later dance tune version approximates a vocal treatment, but none of the ballads naming the tune can be sung to it without further editing.

What may be a reworking of an old text is a song found in *Pills,* 1719–1720, IV, 176, beginning "Fly merry News among the Crews,/That love to hear of Jests," in an eight-line stanza culminating in the burden "At Up-tails all." This requires a repetition of the tune but is rhythmically suitable.[1] Two broadsides from the end of the Commonwealth years call for the tune. One is "A Psalme Sung By the People before the Bone-Fires . . . on the 11th of February [1659/60]," beginning "Come lets take the Rump" (Wood 416 [40], BM Thomason, BM Luttrell); the other is "A Vindication of the Rump," beginning "Full many a Ballad hath been penn'd" (BM Luttrell). Both were reprinted in *Ratts Rhimed to Death,* 1660, *The Rump,* 1660, *Rump,* 1662, and *Loyal Songs,* 1731. The stanza patterns of the two ballads differ widely, and neither fits the music. Indeed, it seems likely that the tune name was just sufficiently in harmony with the rump imagery of the ballads to make it a part of the jest rather than a serious designation to be followed in singing.

Allusions to "Up tails all" suggest that it was primarily a dance tune. But such a passage as that in Sharpham's *The Fleire,* 1607, III, i, in which it is said of a woman that "she eurie day sings *Iohn for the King,*[2] and at *Vp tailes all,* shees perfect," would suggest that a ballad and/or a tune "Up tails all" was sung, were it not for the persistent *double-entendre* of the passage which makes the tune name primarily a play on words.

Robert Herrick wrote an engaging lyric entitled "Up tailes all" (*Poetical Works,* ed. L. C. Martin, 1956, p. 247) and five other poems in the same meter; they do not fit our tune, however, for they are in six-line stanzas made up of units which are syllabically 5.5.8 or 6.6.9. Chappell (*PMOT* II, 773) cites the six poems and erroneously concludes that the tune was a favorite of Herrick's. In truth, his "Up tailes all" suggests only an interest in the proverbial phrase; the metrical pattern is commonly encountered in songs and poems of the period.

Up with Aley, Aley

This tune, called also "Up goes Aley," takes its name from a refrain which may have appeared first in a ballad of c. 1675 called "The New Corant; Or the merry wooing of Jonney and Jenny," beginning "Here is a new fine ditty/If you will but draw near" (Pepys III, 293, Wood E.25 [14]). The refrain is:

[1] The *Pills* song is printed with music of "The Friar and the Nun," to which it can be sung with only slight emendation of note values. Evidently the tune of "Up tails all" had fallen into disuse, while the old text had been rejuvenated and coupled with a tune of equal age but of superior durability.

[2] The lost ballad of "John for the king To the tune of Hey Downe derrye" was registered in 1603 (Rollins, *Anal. Index,* No. 1297).

Then up goes aly aly
     up goes Mary & Nan
Johnney was courting of Jenny
     and so they went merrily on.

Other ballads to the tune, all containing some paraphrase of the "aley" refrain, include: "A Tory in a Whig's Coat," 1682, beginning "What! still ye Whigs uneasie!" to "an Old Scotch Tune, Up with Ayley, &c." (Huntington, Harvard, Bodleian; reprinted with music in *180 Loyal Songs,* p. 117); "The West Country Jigg, or, A Trenchmore Galliard," beginning "Jack's a naughty Boy/for calling his Mother Wh---" (Euing, Lord Crawford, Harvard, Roxburghe; reprinted in *RB* VII, 343); and an early eighteenth-century ballad without tune direction or title but with a headpiece paraphrasing Dryden: "She put her hand upon his Scull/With this prophetick Blessing, Be Thou Dull &c.," beginning "Ye Coblers and Taylors draw near" (Harvard). The original form of the burden is found in a song "The Game Cock Conquer'd" in *The Unconstant Moggy's Garland,* c. 1765, p. 4.

The jig tune found in *180 Loyal Songs* (Fig. 480) closely resembles the "Up goes Ely" in *The Dancing Master,* c. 1728, III, 54, and in Walsh's

Original is a fourth higher.
* Emended from G (i.e., C in original).

481

New Country Dancing-Master, c. 1728, III, 87. A slightly different form is printed as "Up with Aily" in the twelfth through seventeenth editions of *The Dancing Master,* 1703–1721 (1703, p. 343 = Fig. 481), and this form of the tune is used in a single-sheet song of c. 1740, "We're gayly yet. Sung by Mr. Beard," beginning "We're gayly yet & we're gayly yet," with eight bars in 6/8 time preceding the *Dancing Master* tune in 9/8 time (BM I.530 [170], Harvard). This latter song is found also in *Thesaurus Musicus,* c. 1743, fol. 11, in Herd's *Scots Songs,* 1769, in *The Convivial Songster,* c. 1782, p. 276, and in Alexander Smith's *The Musical Miscellany,* 1786, p. 288.

Upon a Summer's Day

This tune is called "Upon a Summers Day" in the first three editions of *The Dancing Master,* 1651–1665 (1651, p. 1 = Fig. 482), and in *Musick's Delight on the Cithren,* 1666; it is called "The Garland, or a Summers day" in editions of *The Dancing Master,* 1670–1690. A seventeenth-century keyboard setting called "one a sumers day" in Christ Church MS 437, fol. 8, is in 9/4 time, although not so barred.

The tune apparently gets its name from "The Maid a bathing," a song in *Merry Drollery,* 1661, beginning "Upon a Summers day,/'Bout middle of the morn," but it may also be related to a broadside of c. 1630, "A pleasant new Court Song, Betweene a yong Courtier, and a Countrey Lasse. To a new Court Tune," beginning "Vpon a Summers time,/in the middle of the morne" (Pepys, Roxburghe; reprinted in *RB* I, 80).

In three broadsides the tune is called "Upon a summer['s] time": "Seldome Cleanly," by Laurence Price, beginning "Draw near you coun-

482

Original is a fourth higher and unbarred.

try girls" (Euing, Roxburghe; reprinted in *RB* II, 514); "The Discourse betweene a Souldier and his Loue," beginning "My dearest deare adue" (Pepys; reprinted in *PB* II, 254); and Charles Records's "The Good-Fellowes Advice," beginning "Farewell good company,/now I must leave you all" (Roxburghe; reprinted in *RB* III, 261). "I Smell a Rat. To the tune of, Vpon a Summer tide. Or, The Seminary Priest" begins "I Traueld farre to finde" (Pepys; reprinted in *PB* II, 140).[1]

Upon St. David's Day

March 1 has long been dear to the hearts of Welshmen, and is celebrated as St. David's Day. A ballad of c. 1660, titled "England's Pleasant May-Flower, or, Charles the Second, as we say, Came home the twenty-ninth of May," is directed to be sung to the tune "Upon Saint Davids Day" (Euing; reprinted in *RB* VIII, xxx*). It begins "Why should we speak of Cesar's Acts" and the double ballad stanza has as its customary closing line "the twenty-ninth of May," in allusion to the king's birthday, but more particularly the day in 1660 on which Charles II "came home" and the monarchy was restored.

[1] I have no information on "The Seminary Priest," though it is probably an interchangeable tune named from a lost ballad. It is used also for singing "A Pleasant new Ballad you here may behold, How the Devill, though subtle, was guld by a Scold" (Rawlinson, Roxburghe; reprinted in *RB* II, 367).

The origin of the tune is obscure, but it must have been in vogue before 1660. It may get its name from "The Welsh-Mens Glory, Or, The
Famous Victories of the Ancient Britains Obtain'd upon St. David's
Day," a ballad with stanza pattern like that of the Charles II panegyric,
and with a burden "Upon St. David's Day." Unhappily, this piece has no
tune direction, and extant copies are from late in the seventeenth century
(Bagford, Bodleian Ashmole G.15; reprinted in *BB* II, 847). No contemporary tune seems to have survived, but a "St. David's Day" to which
the ballads might be sung is in the second volume of *The Dancing*

Master, 2d ed., 1714, *et seq.* (Fig. 483), and in Walsh's *Compleat Country
Dancing-Master*, 1719, II, 37. The relationship between dance tune and
ballad texts is not advanced with confidence.

The Usurer's Daughter

This tune takes its name from a ballad apparently lost. But its sequel
has been preserved, with corrupt music on the sheet (Fig. 484): "The
Usurers Daughters Reply, Or, Floramellas Answer to Phaon. To a
Pleasant New Play-House Tune," beginning "Now young tempting
Phaon you shall have your prey" (Lord Crawford 913, BM C.39.k.6 [15],
text reprinted in *OPB*, p. 39). This ballad, licensed by Sir Roger
L'Estrange, was printed before the end of 1685, as was another with the

484

same imperfect music: "The Windsor Gallant Courting the Country Farmers Daughter," beginning "Let my Fairest Virgin prove most kind to me," to "a New Tune played at the Court; or, The Usurers Daughter" (Pepys III, 279). A third ballad to the tune, dating from the reign of James II, is "The Unfeigned Lover," beginning "Cease my pretty Nancy do not thou bewail" (Pepys IV, 169).

Valiant Jockey's Marched Away

"Valiant Jockey" or "Valiant Jockey's march'd away" is a tune named from the opening line of a song written by Thomas D'Urfey upon the occasion of the battle of Killiecrankie, July 27, 1689. In his *New Poems*, 1690, p. 183, D'Urfey prefaced the song with a statement that it was "sung to the Queen at Kensington," and that the verses were "made to a pretty New Scotch Tune." Words and music appear in *Pills*, 1719–1720, II, 228. The poem was expanded from two to seven stanzas and issued as a broadside entitled "The Maiden-Warrier . . . To an Excellent New Tune" (Pepys, Lord Crawford, Euing, Harvard, Roxburghe; reprinted in *RB* VII, 737). The tune, called "Valiant Jockey," is in *Youth's Delight on the Flagelet*, 9th ed., c. 1690, in *Apollo's Banquet*, Second Book, 1691, No. 6 (Fig. 485), and in *The Dancing Master*, 9th ed., 1695. A manuscript version of "Vallent Jockie" was recorded in Dr. John Leyden's Lyra Viol Book, after 1690 (G. F. Graham transcript, No. 40).

At least two broadsides to the tune contain corrupt or meaningless music: "The Courtly Triumph," beginning "Let us all rejoyce amain" (Pepys; reprinted in *PB* V, 249), and "The New Loyal Health," be-

ginning "Let each jovial Heart rejoyce" (Pepys; reprinted in *PB* V, 252), both written in September, 1690, upon King William's return from the Irish wars. Other ballads on the campaigns of 1690 and 1691 citing the tune include "The Glorious Conquest . . . of Cork [and] Kings-sale," beginning "Here is joyfull News come o'er" (Douce I, 88) and several others which have been reprinted in *RB* III, 522, and *PB* V, 145, 210, VI, 39, 98, 113. "The Perjur'd Youth," beginning "Let falsehearted Lovers now" (Pepys; reprinted in *PB* V, 296), is a ballad of c. 1690 dealing not with national affairs but with the retribution overtaking a youth who had hoped his neck would be broken if he proved false to his beloved.

The tune, which is not especially attractive, seems to owe its brief popularity to the Scotch vogue then at its height. Except for "The New Loyal Health," all the ballads require a repetition of the first strain. The distinguishing feature of the prosody is the internal rhyme in the first and third lines of the final quatrain (sometimes printed as six lines, with the rhyming halves printed as separate lines).

The Vicar and Moses

To a tune whose beginning is like that of a hobbyhorse dance "Jolly Roger Twangdillo" (*Pills*, 1719–1720, I, 19) D'Urfey wrote a ballad called "The Yeoman of Kent," beginning "In Kent I hear, there lately did dwell/Long George, a Yeoman by trade" (*Pills* I, 126). This music (Fig. 486), with the addition of two bars for a "Tol de rol" refrain, is used

486

for two distinct songs entitled "The Vicar and Moses."[1] Both were current in the last quarter of the eighteenth century and priority is uncertain. Though verbally quite different throughout, they both tell the humorous-grotesque story of a vicar and his clerk Moses who in their cups set about burying a child of the parish on a rainy night.

The more poetically ingenious of the two songs begins "There was once,—it is said,/When,—'tis out of my head" (BM 1872.a.1 [124*]). A single-sheet edition with music, conjecturally dated c. 1775 (BM G.312 [141], Huntington, California), attributes the "Original Words" to "G. A. S. Esqr.," who is usually identified as George Alexander Stevens. Words and music are reprinted in *The Convivial Songster*, c. 1782, p. 234, but the piece is not in Stevens's *Songs, Comic and Satyrical*, 1772, perhaps because it was written subsequently.

The second, beginning "At the Sign of the horse, old Spintext of course," is on song sheets of c. 1780 (BM G.306 [136], Harvard, California; an edition in Huntington is dated 1784). The song appears in Alexander Smith's *The Musical Miscellany*, 1786, p. 12, and on several broadsides without music (BM 1872.a.1 [124], Roxburghe III, 875), including one edition which ascribes the words to Stevens (Roxburghe III, 313). Ebsworth, who listed the Roxburghe copies without reprinting them (*RB* VIII, 184), credited the authorship to John Allbutt, about 1777.

Two early nineteenth-century broadsides were sung to "Vicar and Moses": "A Relish for Old Nick," a ballad on Napoleon's threatened invasion of England, beginning "Arm Neighbours at length" (Harvard), and "The Witty Ale Wife," 1812, beginning "At the sign of the Lion" (London Society of Antiquaries [cf. Lemon, *Catalogue*, p. 156]). Another

---

[1] A closely variant tune is used with a song by Richard Estcourt on Marlborough's victories, c. 1708–1710, beginning "You tell me Dick you've lately read,/that we are beaten in Spain," found in single-sheet issues (BM G.314 [33], Harvard) and in *Pills*, 1719–1720, VI, 331. On the Harvard song sheet, whose heading is simply "The Words by Mr. Estcourt," the entire tune is repeated for the refrain "With a fal la la . . ." A second tune, very similar to the first, is also on the sheet, with a two-bar "fal la" refrain. Another issue with music, "Britain's Jubilee" (Harvard), contains the *Pills* tune and the full "fal la" refrain.

late piece, with a burden "The Recorder for ever Huzza," is "A Song" beginning "Good People draw near, a story you'll hear" (Harvard).

The Vicar of Bray

The proverbial Vicar of Bray, who changed his political opinions with the times but preserved his ruling principle, which was to remain Vicar of Bray, was a legend in the seventeenth century. But not until the time of George I was a song written to commemorate this amiable paragon of adaptability.[1] The earliest copies of the words I have found are in

* F♯ on song sheet. Corrected from measure 12.
** Second strain repetition written out in full on song sheet.

Walsh's *British Musical Miscellany*, 1734–1736, I, 30, and in song sheets of about the same date (BM H.1994.b [44], Harvard, Huntington), where the tune used is "O Bessy Bell and Mary Gray" (Fig. 487), popularized in Gay's *The Beggar's Opera*. It begins "In good King Charles's golden days,/When loyalty no harm meant," but on broadsides without music

[1] The song, tracing the Vicar's views from the reign of Charles II to George I, is said to have been written "by an officer in Colonel Fuller's regiment in the reign of K. George the First" (John Nichols, *Select Collection of Poems*, 1780–1782, VIII, 234n.). The search for a historical original has proved fruitless, especially the attempt to connect the turncoat with Simon Aleyn, a sixteenth-century holder of the office.

the opening is usually "In Charles the Second's Golden Days [*or* Reign]" (BM 1871.e.9 [186], Morgan 24, Lord Crawford 644).

Another version of the ballad, printed in *London Magazine,* V (January, 1736), 37, has a new opening stanza, beginning:

> Of Bray the vicar long I've been
> And many a test and trial
> I've stood, and various changes seen,
> Yet never prov'd disloyal. . . .

Its second stanza begins the familiar royal procession in slightly variant verbiage: "In Charles the second's jovial days,/When loy'lty had no harm in't." A most interesting detail is that the tune cited for singing is "the Turncoat," a likely reference to a ballad of 1693 sung to "London is a Fine Town," q.v., and entitled "The Religious Turncoat" (in one version simply "The Turncoat"). That ballad of "a Late Jacobite Divine turned Williamite" is a clear prototype of "The Vicar of Bray," tracing an unlocalized cleric's allegiances from '41 through a half century of doctrinal shifts. And its tune will serve for singing this version of "The Vicar of Bray."

Yet another tune, found in Walker's *The Quaker's Opera,* 1728, as "Country Garden," [2] and brought to world-wide popularity in the twentieth century through Percy Grainger's settings, became standard for "The Vicar of Bray." It is found on song-sheet editions (Fig. 488) as early as c. 1740 (Harvard) and in such musical miscellanies as *The Convivial Songster,* c. 1782, p. 238, and Ritson's *English Songs,* 1783 (1813, III, 272). The same music is found in such imitations as "A Gallon a Day. The Favourite Parody on the Vicar of Bray, with the original Tune as Sung by Brother Popplewell," [3] c. 1775, beginning "In Charles the Second's merry Days" (BM G.309 [152], Harvard), reprinted in *The Convivial Songster,* p. 182.

Other pieces written to the tune include: "A New Song," beginning "In good King G[eor]ge's golden days," with MS date 1779 (BM 1850.c.10 [69i]); "The Priest's Confession," beginning "I am a Parson orthodox" (BM 1871.f.16), a Jacobite ballad of c. 1745; "The Loyalist. Sung . . . on Monday, January 28, 1793," beginning "When Britain first her fair domain" (Harvard); and "A New Song on Parker . . . head of the Mutiny at Sheerness," c. 1797, beginning "I will not

---

[2] The music, untitled, appears also at the end of Phillips's *The Mock Lawyer,* 1733, No. 11. The air is cited in Fielding's *The Grub-Street Opera,* 1731, but no music is in the printed edition.

[3] Could this be the same Popplewell referred to in a ballad on "The Tombs in Westminster Abbey," chanted to the music of "The Queen's old courtier," q.v. (*RB* VII, 268)?

488

Chorus

sing in Parker's praise" (*Naval Songs and Ballads,* ed. C. H. Firth, 1908, p. 281).

In the nineteenth century the tune was used for "The Neglected Tar," by "a Gentleman of Liverpool," popularized through its inclusion in the Rev. James Plumptre's *Collection of Songs,* 1805, p. 88. The tune was introduced into a burlesque pantomime by Tom Taylor and others, *William Tell,* 1856, p. 7. And Charles Mackay wrote his song "The Wintry Winds" to it (*Poetical Works,* 1876, p. 574).

Vive le Roi

This tune takes its name from the burden of a song beginning "What though the Zealotts pull down the Prelates," found with music in BM MS Add. 11608, fol. 53ᵛ, dated 1656–1659 (Fig. 489). The words were reprinted in *Rump,* 1662, I, 145, and *Loyal Songs,* 1731, I, 102.[1] The

[1] The text is also found in Chappell, *PMOT* II, 430, and in Mackay's *Cavalier Songs,* p. 27. In the latter the tune is erroneously named "Love lies a-bleeding," doubtless because that tune immediately follows "Vive le Roi" in Chappell.

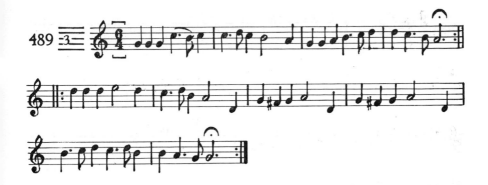

489

tune "Vive le Roy" had originally appeared in *A Booke of New Lessons for the Cithern & Gittern*, 1652; Playford later used it in such other collections as *Musicks Recreation on the Viol, Lyra-way*, 1661, and in *Musick's Delight on the Cithren*, 1666.

One other ballad was sung to the tune: "Englands Honour and Londons Glory, with the manner of proclaiming Charles the Second King of England this eight[h] of May, 1660," beginning "Come hither, friends, and listen unto me," and containing the "Vive le Roy" burden at the end of each stanza (Euing 97).

Walking in a Country Town

A lute arrangement of "Walking in a country towne" appears in Thomas Robinson's *The Schoole of Musicke*, 1603, sig. M2 (Fig. 490). No broadsides call for that tune, nor have I found a song with such an opening line; the air is introduced only conjecturally into the present discussion.[1] A ballad of the first quarter of the seventeenth century, "The two Le[ice]stersheire Louers. to the tune of, and yet my thinkes I loue thee," begins "Walking in a meddow greene," and its stanza fits the Robinson music (Roxburghe; reprinted in *RB* II, 598). I have not traced the tune title of this ballad, although it may be derived from "For still me thinkes I loue thee," a line in stanza 2 of "The Northamp-

[1] Any identification must be all the more tentative because a mid-seventeenth-century virginal set of the tune in Paris Conservatoire MS Rés. 1185, No. 120, is entitled "The Ladies Daughter." For ballads associated with this tune name, see "O Man in Desperation."

490

ton-shire Louer," a ballad of c. 1615 in the same stanza pattern (*PB* I, 73).[2]

The Leicestershire ballad contains the burden "upon the meddow brow," which becomes a tune name on several ballads. The earliest of these, licensed in 1618, is "I would you neuer had said so," beginning "Two louing Friends once meeting" (Pepys; reprinted in *PB* I, 123). Another, entered in 1631, is "Death['s] Dance," beginning "If Death would come and shew his face," to the tune of "O no, no, no, not yet, or the meddow brow" (Pepys, Roxburghe; reprinted in *RB* I, 283).[3] A third is Bishop Richard Corbet's "A proper new Ballad . . . The Fairies farewel, or God a Mercy Will, to be sung or whistled, to the tune of the Medow Brow by the learned, by the unlearned to the tune of Fortune," beginning "Farewell rewards and Fairies." This was written during the reign of James I but first published in Corbet's *Certain Elegant Poems*, 1647, p. 47 (reprinted in his *Poemata Stromata*, 1648, p. 91, with an additional stanza; found also in Percy's *Reliques* and in *Seventeenth Century Lyrics*, ed. Norman Ault, 2d ed., 1950, p. 24). The assignment of an eight-line ballad-meter stanza to the tune of "Fortune" is at first sight grotesque; but the ballad can be sung to it with division of some notes to produce a completely undignified jiggy effect—doubtless part of Corbet's humorous intention.

[2] Its tune is "Falero lero lo," for which no music has survived.
[3] On the first tune, which has not survived, see "I'll never love thee more."

Walsingham

This tune is found in William Barley's *A New Booke of Tabliture*, 1596, sig. D2, arranged for orpharion by Francis Cutting, in Antony Holborne's *The Cittharn Schoole*, 1597, sig. C3ᵛ, as a lesson for lyra viol in William Corkine's *The Second Booke of Ayres*, 1612, sig. H1ᵛ, and in Cambridge University MS Dd.5.20, fol. 19, the latter published in *Jacobean Consort Music*, ed. Dart and Coates, *Musica Britannica*, IX, 1955, 200. Settings for lute are found in Cambridge University MSS Dd.2.11, fols. 82ᵛ (Dowland), 96 (Cutting), 96ᵛ (Collard), 98 (John Johnson); Dd.5.78.3, fols. 12 (Holborne), 37 (Dowland), 50ᵛ (Cutting); Dd.9.33, fols. 21 and 26ᵛ (anon.), 67ᵛ (Dowland). The Euing lute MS contains a Cutting set, fol. 43ᵛ; a Collard arrangement is in the Welde lute MS, fol. 9ᵛ; and anonymous versions are in BM MS Add. 15118, fol. 32ᵛ, and in the Wickhambrook lute MS, fol. 17. *The Fitzwilliam Virginal Book* contains two settings: one by Dr. John Bull, a copy of which is in Benjamin Cosyn's MS Virginal Book, No. 52, Christ Church MS 1113, No. 92, and Paris Conservatoire MS Rés. 1185, No. 58; another by William Byrd, found also in his *My Ladye Nevells Booke*, No. 31, in Will Forster's MS Virginal Book, No. 12, and in BM MS Add. 30486, fol. 2. A version of the tune is found in D. R. Camphuysen's *Stichtelyche Rymen*, 1647, p. 100, set to a song beginning " 'S menschen sterven, in sich selven."

One other version of the tune, probably contemporary with the earliest printed copies, is reproduced from the Shirburn MS in *SB*, pp. 245–246 (Fig. 491). The air and bass are there coupled with "Mr.

Original is unbarred.

Attowel's Jigge," for the first six stanzas of which "Walsingham" serves. The jig opens "As I went to Walsingham,/to the shrine, with speede," but after five lines the Walsingham ballad is abruptly dropped. The piece was licensed in 1595, and a copy of the original edition in the Pepys collection is reprinted in *PG*, p. 2, under the title "Frauncis new Jigge."

The ballad which has given the tune its names exists in several forms. A version beginning "As yo^w cam from that holly land, of Wall-syngham," found in Huntington Library MS HM 198, I, iv, has been partially printed in *PB* II, 22. Variant forms of this text appear in the Percy Folio MS (ed. Hales and Furnivall, III, 471) and in Deloney's *Garland of Good Will*, 1631 (in *Works*, ed. Mann, p. 365). Mann thought the ballad to be from Deloney's pen, except for the first stanza, which he considered traditional. A contemporary transcript in Bodleian MS Rawl. Poet. 85, fol. 123 (printed in *Elizabethan Lyrics*, ed. Norman Ault, 3d ed., 1949, pp. 282–284) is subscribed "Sr W. R." Agnes M. C. Latham in her *Poems of Sir Walter Ralegh*, 1951, p. 121, accepts the ascription and dates the poem c. 1592, contemporaneous with the last books of Raleigh's *Cynthia*. A broadside reworking of the ballad in "The contented Couckould," c. 1625, provides a more modern framework for the story of the man seeking his beloved and discoursing on the frailty and faithfulness of women. The old ballad is lavishly paraphrased in the first part, which begins "Com hither thou seaman braue/sir what do you require"; an added second part brings the husband from Newcastle to London, where he finds his wife and is reconciled.[1]

The opening quatrain of the Walsingham ballad is sung by Merrythought in Beaumont's *The Knight of the Burning Pestle*, II, viii; in Rowley's *A Match at Midnight*, I, i, the Welshman Randall sings a quatrain of paraphrase beginning "Did her not see her true Loves,/As her came from London." There are references to teaching birds to whistle or sing "Walsingham" in Beaumont and Fletcher's *The Honest Man's Fortune*, V, iii, in John Phillips's translation of *Don Quixote*, 1687, p. 278, and in Dryden's *Limberham*, I, i.

Ophelia's song, "How should I your true love know from another one?" (*Hamlet*, IV, v) recalls the "Walsingham" lines "How should I know your true love/That have met many a one," but the parallel extends no further. The melody usually associated with the Shakespeare song is untitled in Gay's *The Beggar's Opera*, Act II, Air 14 (in Chetwood's *Generous Free-Mason*, 1731, it is called "You'll think ere many Days ensue," from the opening line of Gay's song); the tune has both

---

[1] The ballad (Pepys; reprinted in *PB* II, 24) is to be sung "To a very pleasant new Tune," but the meter is unsuitable for "Walsingham." Some of the same subject matter is found in the song "Came you not from Newcastle" in Percy Folio MS I, 253. Professor Rollins has pointed out the distinctive features of "The contented cuckold" that reflect its indebtedness to traditional rather than broadside sources; what he says is less true of the second part, where a seventeenth-century balladmaker's hand is evident.

melodic and harmonic affinities with "Walsingham," but the iambic verse lines of the ballad-opera songs begin on unaccented notes, and two bars of music are added at the end to provide for a "Twang dang dillo dee" refrain.

In the British Museum copy of William Slatyer's *Psalmes, or Songs of Sion*, 1642, "Walsingham" has been written in as the tune for singing Psalm 11, p. 4, and Psalm 114, p. 31. A tune resembling "Walsingham," but in duple rather than triple rhythm, is used with Colley Cibber's "The Blind Boy" in Walsh's *British Musical Miscellany*, 1734–1736, I, 84.

The Wanton Wife

"Wanton Wife" is the tune named for "The second part of the Widdow of Watling-streete and her three Daughters," beginning "The beautifull widdow of Watling streete" (Shirburn MS, printed in *SB*, p. 16; BM Huth, reprinted in *A Collection of Seventy-Nine Black-Letter Ballads*, 1867, p. 162; Pepys, Roxburghe, reprinted in *RB* VIII, 10). The Shirburn copy is probably transcribed from the original edition, licensed in 1597; the printed copy in the Huth collection is a Pavier

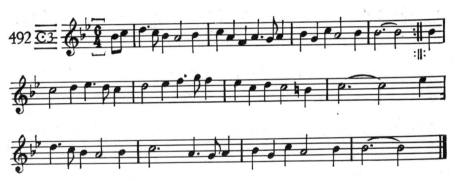

Original is a third higher.

imprint of 1600–1625. The first part of the ballad, in different meter, is to be sung to "Bragandary," a lost tune.

"Wanton Wife" may take its name from "Wanton Wife of Westminster," a lost ballad registered in 1597. This fuller form is found as a tune title for a ballad of c. 1626, "Nobody his Counsaile to chuse a

Wife," beginning "Let Young men giue eare/vnto that I reherse" (Pepys; reprinted in *PG,* p. 263). "The Wanton Wife" is also named as the tune for "A new Ballad; Declaring the Excellent Parable of the Prodigal Child," licensed in 1656 and beginning "There was a grave man, both wealthy & wise" (Pepys, Euing, Harvard, Roxburghe; reprinted in *RB* II, 393).

All three of these ballads are in a stanza metrically equivalent to "Packington's Pound." I have found no contemporary tune which might serve. But the Additional Sheet bound in with *The Dancing Master,* 7th ed., 1686, contains a tune named "Hayn's Jigg, or The Wanton Wife." I doubt that this is the tune we seek, but it can be used for singing these ballads if the notes of each cadence are divided to accommodate the syllables of even-numbered lines (Fig. 492).

The Waterman's Dance

In *The Merry Musician,* 1716, I, 74–75, is a song "The Country Sheep-shearing: Made to the Water-man's Dance by Mr. D'Urfey," beginning "Jenny, and Molly, and Dolly" (Fig. 493). Words and music are

also found in *Pills,* 1719–1720, II, 68, and in song-sheet editions of c. 1720 with the same title (BM H.1601 [223], Harvard, Yale, Huntington). The circular tune in 9/4 time seems ideally suited for country dancing, but I have not found it in dance books.

"The Waterman's Delight," named as a tune for singing several ballads of the second half of the seventeenth century, has not been found; but the octave of ballad meter, or poulter's measure, is so different rhythmically from the twelve-line stanzas of D'Urfey's song that the dance tune cannot be equated with the earlier tune name. Several ballads sung to "The Waterman's Delight," including one bearing that title, have been reprinted in *BB* I, 257, II, 578, 581, 955, and unpublished ballads to the tune are Rawlinson 216 and 217.

Watkins's Ale

Keyboard arrangements of this tune are preserved in *The Fitzwilliam Virginal Book* II, 236 (Fig. 494), and in Will Forster's MS Virginal Book,

494

Original is a third higher and contains varied repetition of each strain.

p. 460. The Welde MS Lute Book, fol. 8, contains a setting. Unbarred accompanying parts for a mixed consort are in Cambridge University MSS Dd. 5.20, fol. 7 (bass viol) and Dd.5.21, fol. 6ᵛ (treble recorder) under the name "Mother B. A.," but the latter MS calls it "Mother W. Ale" in the table of contents.

The tune takes its name from a ballad of c. 1590, "A ditty delightfull of mother Watkins ale, A warning well wayed, though counted a tale," beginning "There was a maid this other day,/And she would needs go forth to play" (BM Huth; reprinted in *A Collection of Seventy-Nine Black-Letter Ballads*, 1867, p. 251). This piece of good-natured bawdry was attacked in the prefatory letter to Munday and Chettle's *Gerileon of England*, Part 2, 1592, sig. A4, in which T. N. (thought to be Chettle) professed to wonder what printer "would bee so impudent to print such odious and lasciuious ribauldrie, as Watkins Ale, The Carmans Whistle, and sundrie such other." The phrase "Watkins's ale" is, of course, a transparent euphemism comparable to the carman's whistle and the Northumberland bagpipes—all relating to the sexual act.

Contemporary with the ballad is a manuscript piece, "A new ballad of mother watkins ale," beginning "As watkins walked by the way,/he met a las and made her stay," which may be intended for the same tune (Bodleian MS Rawlinson Poet. 185, fol. 14^v; cf. *RB* VII, xiv).

We All to Conquering Beauty Bow

This tune is named from the opening line of a poem by Thomas D'Urfey which first appeared, without music, in his *New Collection of Songs and Poems,* 1683. In 1685 it was included in his *Third Collection of New Songs,* with music by Dr. John Blow (Fig. 495). It was also re-

495

printed in *Pills,* 1719–1720, II, 36. A broadside version, licensed by Pocock, 1685–1688, "To an excellent new Air" but without the music, is titled "The Conquering Virgin: or, The Maiden Triumph" (BM C.39.k.6; reprinted in *OPB,* p. 4).

"The Lovesick Shepherd Cured," beginning "Tell me, O Shepherd, why so sad" (Pepys V, 330, with meaningless music) was to be sung either to this tune or to "I never saw a Face till now," q.v.

Welladay

Music for "Welladay" is preserved in a mid-seventeenth-century set of keyboard variations in Paris Conservatoire MS Rés. 1186, fol. 25 (Fig. 496).[1] A tune of this name was known as early as 1569–1570, for an entry

496

The first two of twelve sections.

under that date in the Stationers' Register licensed Thomas Colwell to print a ballad by William Elderton, "a newe wel a Daye as playne master papeste as Dunstable waye" (Rollins, *Anal. Index,* No. 1911), beginning "Amonge manye newes reported of late" (BM Huth; reprinted in *A Collection of Seventy-Nine Black-Letter Ballads,* 1867, p. 1).[2]

The first important ballad sung to "Welladay" is "A lamentable Dittie composed vpon the death of Robert Lord Deuereux late Earle of Essex, who was beheaded in the Tower of London, vpon Ashwednesday in the morning," 1601, beginning "Sweet Englands pride is gone/welladay welladay" (Huntington; reprinted in Collmann, No. 37, perhaps the earliest

[1] At fol. 118 of the same manuscript is a short "Welladay" unrelated to the other setting.

[2] An even earlier entry is for license to print "the secounde well a daye generaly Rede and then Juge indefferently &c" in 1566–1567 (Arber, *Transcript* I, 330). Although the fee was the usual fourpence required for entering a ballad, Rollins does not include the item in his *Analytical Index,* evidently not considering it to refer to a ballad.

issue); copies of later issues (Manchester, Pepys, Wood 401, Lord Crawford, Euing, Bagford, Roxburghe; reprinted in *RB* I, 564) are usually
on the same sheet with another ballad on the same subject to the tune of
"Essex last goodnight," q.v. The earliest copies are dated 1603 (the ballad
was licensed on May 18 of that year), but Rollins (*Anal. Index,* No. 1401)
shows that the ballad was in existence within two days after Essex's
execution.

Another ballad of 1603, "A new song . . . King James his Proclama-
tion, upon the 24. of March . . . in . . . London," beginning "Sweet
England Reioyce and sing,/Louingly: louingly," is sung to the tune,
here called "Englands pride is gone," from the opening line of the
Essex ballad (Harvard). Other ballads fashioned in the tone of the Essex
ballad include: "Sir Walter Rauleigh his lamentation: Who was beheaded . . . the 29. of October. 1618," beginning "Courteous kind
Gallants all,/pittie me, pittie me" (Pepys; reprinted in *PG,* p. 89); "No
naturall Mother, but a Monster . . . hang'd . . . 11. of December,
1633," by Martin Parker, beginning "Like to a dying Swan,/pensiuely,
pensiuely" (Manchester; reprinted in *PG,* p. 425); "The true manner of
the life and Death of Sir Thomas Wentworth . . . beheaded the 12 . . .
of May, 1641," by Laurence Price, beginning "Country men list to mee/
patiently patiently" (BM C.20.f.2; reprinted in *CP,* p. 120); and the
fragmentary "King Charles His Speech, and last Farewell to the World
. . . Ianuary 30. 1648," beginning "Faire Englands joy is fled,/Weladay,
weladay" (Manchester; reprinted in *RB* VIII, xc***, and *CP,* p. 233).

Others to the tune are the following: "Murther vnmasked, or Barne-
viles base Conspiracie against his owne Country," beginning "All you
that Christians be/vsefully, vsefully" (Pepys; reprinted in *PG,* p. 104);
"A Looking glasse for Corne-hoorders," beginning "Of wonders strange
that was /euer heard, euer heard" (Pepys; reprinted in *PG,* p. 370); "The
Arraignment of the Divel, for stealing away President Bradshaw," beginning "If you'l hear news that's ill,/Gentlemen, Gentlemen" (BM
Thomason, Harvard, both dated in MS Nov. 7, 1659; Wood 416; reprinted in *The Rump,* 1660, *Loyal Songs,* 1731, Wright, *Political Ballads,*
1841, and Mackay, *Cavalier Songs,* 1863). Richard Johnson's *Crown
Garland of Golden Roses,* 1659, ed. Chappell, 1845, contains "The
Princely song of the six queens that were married to Henry the Eighth,"
beginning "When England fame did ring,/Royally, royally," to the tune
of "Welladay." It is also cited in *New Carrolls,* 1661, with a song "For
Candlemas day," beginning "Christmas hath made an end,/Welladay,
welladay" (reprinted in *Seventeenth Century Lyrics,* ed. N. Ault, 2d ed.,
1950, p. 337).

Wert Thou More Fairer
Than Thou Art

This tune name is derived from the opening line of a song by Thomas Stanley, published in his *Poems*, 1651. The appearance of several vocal settings within the decade makes it impossible for us to know which is intended when the tune is named on broadsides. Music by Dr. John Wilson is in *Select Musicall Ayres, and Dialogues,* 1652, Part I, p. 26 (Fig. 497). A second edition in the following year includes both Wilson's

setting (Part I, p. 23) and one by William Webb (Part III, p. 22=Fig. 498). *Select Ayres and Dialogues,* 1659, p. 27, contains a fine version by Henry Lawes (Fig. 499); still different music appears in John Gamble's MS Commonplace Book, 1659, p. 212 (Fig. 500). The setting by Giovanni Gastoldi in *Synopsis of Vocal Music,* 1680, p. 110, found also in Forbes's *Cantus,* 3d ed., 1682, sig. L4ᵛ, is too late to concern us here.

498 C⅓

A broadside of c. 1675 calling for the tune is "Loves Tide: or, A Farewel to Folly," beginning "How cool and temperate am I grown," to the tune of "Wert thou more fairer, &c. Or, Lusty Bacchus" (Douce I, 134). This ballad had originally been licensed in 1649, before the publication of "Wert thou more fairer," and it is doubtful that copies of this lost edition contained the 1675 tune direction. The poem of which the broadside is an expansion appears with music by Henry Lawes in *Select Musicall Ayres, and Dialogues,* 1652, Part I, p. 11, in later editions of that work, and in Gamble's MS, p. 266. I have no information on "Lusty Bacchus," except that it is named as the tune of a ballad licensed in 1656,[1] in which the eight-line octosyllabic stanza is at variance with the six-line stanza of "Loves Tide" but corresponds with the stanza form of most ballads containing the tune direction "Love's tide."

A ballad issued by William Gilbertson, who died in 1665, is to the tune of "Loves ride, or, Wert thou more fairer": "The Virgins Constancy," beginning "Hard hap had I, poor harmless Maid" (Douce II, 272, Lord Crawford 480, Harvard). The first tune title is evidently intended to be "Love's tide." The ambiguity facing us here, as elsewhere, is whether this ballad was to be sung to Lawes's setting of "How cool and temperate" or to some one of the settings of "Wert thou more fairer" issued during the

[1] It is "You pretty little Ladies will do so," beginning "Forth walking in the Summers time" (Pepys IV, 12, Douce II, 266, Rawlinson 55).

1650s.[2] "The honest Maidens Loyalty," beginning "Most early in a morning fair," is also to "Wert thou more fairer" (Lord Crawford 821, BM C.22.f.6 [125], Manchester I, 34, Yale, Harvard), as is "The happy Adventure, or the witty Lady: A story," in Thomas Jordan's *A Royal Arbor*, 1664, p. 63; both are in six-line stanzas.

Several ballads licensed in 1656 were to be sung to "Love's tide": Laurence Price's "The Famous Flower of Serving-Men," beginning "You beauteous Ladies great and small," to "a delicate new Tune, or Flora farewel, Summer Time, or Love's Tide" (Euing 111, Douce I, 83ᵛ, Wood E.25 [75], Pepys III, 142; reprinted in Child, No. 106; roman-letter editions in Douce III, 30ᵛ, Lord Crawford, Roxburghe; reprinted in *RB* VI, 567); and "The Maids Revenge upon Cupid and Venus," beginning "You Maids and Widows all a row," to the tune of "Loves Tyde, or, Flora Farewel," also by Price (Roxburghe; reprinted in *RB* VII, 104). Another entered in 1656 is "If you Love me tell me so," beginning "A fierce Dispute of late there was" (Rawlinson 53; a later edition, entitled "Loves Fierce Dispute," is in BM 1871.e.9 [46]). From this ballad comes another name for the tune, found in Charles Hammond's

---

[2] An edition of "The Virgins Constancy" (Pepys IV, 55) issued after 1665 alters the tune direction to "Amarillis," q.v.

500

"Times Darling," beginning "You Lovers [all] where ere you be," to the tune of "If you love me tell me so, Or, Loves Tide" (Douce, Manchester, Pepys, Bagford; reprinted in *BB* II, 523), and in T. J.'s "The Love-Sick young man, and Witty maid," beginning "All you that Loyal Lovers are," to the tune of "wert thou more fairer than thou art, Or, the skilful Doctor, Or, If you love me tell me so" (Douce II, 137).[3]

A ballad of the 1680s whose metrics are anapestic rather than iambic is directed to be sung to "Loves Tide: Or, At home would I be in my own Country." It is "The Lancashire-Lovers: or, The merry Wooing of Thomas and Betty," beginning "My Betty thou knowst I have courted thee long" (Douce; reprinted in *RB* VII, ix*). On the second tune, see "I would I were in my own country."

What If a Day

"What if a day, or a month, or a year," a two-stanza song thought to have been written by Campion, appeared first in print at the end of an anonymous Scottish comedy *Philotus*, 1603.[1] Specifically attributed

[3] The second tune title may be derived from "The Skilful Doctor of Gloucestershire" (*RB* VIII, 570), sung to the lost tune "Beds Making."

[1] The poem is found in substantially the same form in several manuscripts of earlier date: BM MS Lansdowne 241, fol. 49 (John Sanderson's diary, under an entry for 1592); Bodleian MSS Rawlinson Poet. 112, fol. 9, and 148, fol. 10v (both from the 1590s), the latter published in Norman Ault's *Elizabethan Lyrics*, 3d ed., 1949, p. 156; and a fourth in Cambridge University MS Kk.5.30, fol. 82v. For further discussion of manuscript and printed copies, see Ault as well as A. E. H. Swaen, *Modern Philology*, IV (1907), 397, V (1908), 383, the latter corrected in Campion's *Works*, ed. P. Vivian, 1909, pp. 377–378. Additional observations are in *Giles Earle his Booke*, ed. Peter Warlock, 1932, pp. 124–125, 134ff. The Rawlinson MSS attribute the poem to the "E. of E."

501

Original is unbarred.

to Campion, it is found in Richard Alison's *An Howres Recreation in Musicke,* 1606, p. 17, with music unlike the settings to be mentioned presently. Four stanzas were copied into the Shirburn MS not long after 1600 (*SB,* p. 239) and three stanzas are found in BM MS Add. 6704, fol. 163, a commonplace book of the Wigley family (reproduced in *Reliquiae Antiquae,* ed. Wright and Halliwell-Phillipps, 1845, II, 123). Richard Johnson's *The Golden Garland of Princely Pleasures,* 3d ed., 1620, 13th ed., c. 1690, also contains the poem.

Words and music are in Alexander Gill's *Logonomia Anglica,* 1619, p. 140 (Fig. 501), at the end of a discussion on Campion; in BM MS Add. 24665, fol. 25ᵛ, compiled in 1615–1626 and containing a second version in eight stanzas (texts reprinted in *Giles Earle his Booke,* pp. 34, 89); in Forbes's *Cantus,* 1662 *et seq.,* No. 17; and also in Trinity College, Dublin, MS F.5.13, p. 37. Two-stanza texts with music are preserved in the secular addenda to the Scottish Metrical Psalter, compiled by Thomas Wood, c. 1600–1650 (University of Edinburgh MS La.III.483, fol. 189) and in the late seventeenth-century Keith Book (Edinburgh MS La.III.491, p. 12). Music alone is in the following: Jane Pickering's Lute Book (BM MS Egerton 2046, fol. 19); in Cambridge University MSS Dd.4.23, fol. 32 (cittern) and Dd.9.33, fol. 62ᵛ (lute); in Thomas Robinson's *New Citharen Lessons,* 1609, No. 45; in the Skene MS, arranged for mandore (printed in *Ancient Scotish Melodies,* ed. Dauney, 1838, p. 246); and in a viola da gamba MS of c. 1660 in the Henry Watson collection of the Manchester Free Reference Library. Thomas Tomkins's virginal setting is in Drexel MS 5612, p. 70 (New York Public Library), and another, attributed to R. Creigton, is in Paris Conservatoire MS Rés. 1186, fol. 15, along with a fragment of the same tune at fol. 14.

The tune also appears in several Dutch songbooks, including: J. J.

Starter's *Friesche Lust-Hof*, 1621, p. 77; Adriaen Valerius's *Neder-Landtsche Gedenck-Clanck*, 1626, p. 247, called "Comedianten dans"; and Camphuysen's *Stichtelyche Rymen*, 1647, p. 146, called "Essex Lamentatie of Wat if a day &c." Other references to the tune are detailed in F. van Duyse's *Het Oude Nederlandsche Lied*, 1903–1908, II, 1787ff.[2]

The song, altered and amplified, exists in a number of broadside editions under the title "A Friends aduice: In an excellent Ditty, concerning the variable changes in this world. To a pleasant new tune." The ballad was licensed in 1624 and the earliest edition, printed by Thomas Symcocke assignees at about that date, is found in the Roxburghe collection (reprinted in *RB* I, 348). Other early copies include a Gosson imprint (Pepys I, 52) and a Francis Coles issue (Douce I, 74ᵛ); an edition by Coles, Vere, and Wright, 1663–1674, is not uncommon (Rawlinson 199, Roxburghe III, 908, Lord Crawford 1268, Harvard).

The tune is not named for singing other ballads, but a MS note in the British Museum copy of Slatyer's *Psalmes, or Songs of Sion*, 1642, p. 36, indicates that the tune was thought appropriate for singing Psalm 126.

What Shall I Do to Show
How Much I Love Her?

This tune takes its name from the opening of a song in the third act of Purcell and Betterton's *The Prophetess*, 1690. In the next year Purcell's *The . . . Musick of the Prophetess*, p. 67, included the song (Fig. 502), which was reprinted in *Pills*, 1719–1720, IV, 234. The air is in *Apollo's Banquet*, Second Book, 1691. The poem, by Betterton or Dryden, was a favorite in miscellanies for a century.[1]

No broadside version of the stage song is extant, but Purcell's tune

---

[2] A. E. H. Swaen, "De Engelsche Stemmen in Valerius' *Gedenck-Clanck*," *Neophilologus*, XXX (1946), 80, adds very slightly to van Duyse's list. In citing Philip Rosseter's *A Booke of Ayres*, 1601, however, he has mistaken Campion's "What is a day, what is a year" for "What if a day."

[1] See *The Songs of John Dryden*, ed. C. L. Day, 1932, pp. 168–169, for detailed references.

502

was used for several ballads. It was evidently intended for singing "An Answer to What shall I do to show how much I love her," beginning "Whence comes the Voice that makes this Lamentation"; the broadside contains meaningless music and the direction "To an excellent new Play-house Tune" (Pepys V, 243). Four others name the tune: "The Ruined Lover," beginning "There was of late a young Beautiful Lady" (Pepys III, 369); "The Love-Sick Lady," beginning "Near a fair Fountain a Damsel sat weeping" (Pepys, Lord Crawford, Roxburghe; reprinted in *RB* VII, 735); "The Valiant Soldiers last Farewell," beginning "Farewell Lucretia, my amorous Jewel" (Pepys V, 280, with meaningless music; Lord Crawford 384, Harvard); and "The Taylor's Wanton Wife of Wapping," beginning "Here I will give you a perfect Relation" (Lord Crawford, Harvard, Roxburghe; reprinted in *RB* VII, 484).

The tune was used in two ballad operas: Gay's *The Beggar's Opera*, 1728, and (without music) *The Jew Decoy'd*, 1733.

When Aurelia First I Courted

This tune takes its name from the opening line of a song printed in
Hicks's *Oxford Drollery,* 1671, and in *Windsor Drollery,* 1672. With
music by Pelham Humphrey it is found in *Choice Songs and Ayres,* 1673,
p. 11 (Fig. 503), and in later editions of that work. It is reprinted in

Pills, 1719–1720, IV, 248, and a manuscript version is preserved in the
Keith Book (University of Edinburgh MS La.III.491, p. 60). The verses
continued to appear in eighteenth-century collections such as *The Hive,*
1725, III, 19, and, with new music by Dieupart, in Watts's *Musical
Miscellany,* 1729–1731, V, 164. Watson's *Choice Collection of . . . Scots
Poems,* Part III, 1711, p. 87, contains the drollery poem under the title
"On the Lady Cast[lemai]n."

A broadside of the 1680s, "The Redeemed Captive," beginning "Surely
now I'm out of danger," is to the tune "When Aurelia first was" and
can be sung to Humphrey's music (Lord Crawford, Euing, Roxburghe,
Harvard, Bagford; reprinted in *BB* II, 549, and *OPB,* p. 199). On "The
Repriev'd Captive," which is a tune title associated with ballads sharing
the eight-line trochaic stanza and internal rhyme (ll. 5 and 7) of "The
Redeemed Captive," see the discussion under "The Doubting Virgin."

When Cannons Are Roaring

A song in Forbes's *Cantus,* 1662, No. 38 (Fig. 504), beginning "Brave Mars begins to rouse," has a refrain which is the source of the tune title:

> When cannons are roaring,
>   and bullets are flying
> He that would honor win,
>   must not fear dying.

504

Original is unbarred.

Like many others in Forbes's collection, this song was known from early in the century; indeed, the three extant ballads calling for the tune all antedate the songbook.[1] The earliest of these is "A Statute for Swearers and Drunkards," issued c. 1624, beginning "You that in wicked wayes/long time haue ranged" (Pepys; reprinted in *PG,* p. 190). Another is Laurence Price's "Newes from Hollands Leager," describing the destruction of Mrs. Holland's brothel in 1632; it begins "You that desire newes,/list to my story" and names the tune "Canons are roaring" (Pepys; reprinted in *PG,* p. 400). A third to the tune is "The Loyal Subjects hearty Wishes to King Charles the Second," by J. P., a ballad of 1660 beginning "True Subjects all rejoyce/after long sadness" (BM

[1] James Shirley's *The Schoole of Complement,* 1631, II, i, quotes the first two lines of the refrain, as Professor Rollins noted in *PG,* p. 189.

C.120.h.4 [1]; reprinted in Mackay's *Cavalier Songs*, p. 236, and *RB* VIII, xli*).

The tune in Forbes's *Cantus* calls for a stanza of eight lines and a refrain of four, as is found in Price's ballad. Stanzas of the other two broadsides contain an additional quatrain, requiring each strain to be repeated (for a more monotonous effect, the first strain can be doubly repeated, saving the refrain bars for the final quatrain of each stanza). The tune name "The Cannons roar" is to be associated with "Hark the thundering cannons roar," q.v.

When First Amintas Sued for a Kiss

D'Urfey's song, beginning "When first Amintor sued for a kiss," is found in his *Compleat Collection*, 1687, p. 5. In the same year it was included in *Comes Amoris*, First Book, p. 9, and *The Theater of Music*, Fourth Book, p. 50, with music described as "a Scotch Tune. Set by Mr. Henry Purcell" (Fig. 505). It was reprinted with the tune in all edi-

* In original, repetition is written out in full. Accidental in measure 4 appears only in the repeat.

tions of *Pills*, and in the 1719–1720 edition it is followed (I, 336) by "A Mock to the foregoing Song," which D'Urfey had originally printed in his *New Poems,* 1690, p. 80. The air, entitled "When first Amintas sued for a kiss," is in *Youth's Delight on the Flagelet,* 9th ed., c. 1690.

A broadside expanding D'Urfey's original song to five stanzas is titled "Charming Amintas: or, The Yielding Virgin. To a Pleasant New Tune" (Harvard, Lord Crawford 1295, BM C.22.f.6 [36], Douce I, 50ᵛ). Music on the sheets is meaningless, but the Purcell set is evidently intended to be used for singing the ballad.

When First the Scottish Wars Began

An imperfect version of this tune, entitled "The Scottish Warr," is found in a lyra-viol arrangement in the mid-seventeenth-century Cambridge University MS Dd.6.48, fol. 21ᵛ. Its shortcomings are remedied in the excellent setting called "Coll. Middleton's March" in *Apollo's Banquet,* 1670, No. 37 (Fig. 506). The original ballad to which it was

506

sung is "Jockies Lamentation, Whose seditious work was the loss of his Country, and his Kirk," by S[amuel?] S[mithson?], licensed in 1657 to Francis Grove. A copy with the Grove imprint is in Wood 401 (152). The ballad, which is "To a stately new Scottish Tune," begins "When first the Scottish wars began/The English man did lead the van." Five of the ten stanzas were reprinted in *Merry Drollery,* 1661, I, 89, under the title "The Scotch War," whence the name of the tune in the Cambridge manuscript (reprinted also in *Rump*, 1662, I, 228, and *Loyal Songs*, 1731, I, 58). Other copies of the broadside are in Pepys and Bagford collections, reprinted in *BB* I, 331.[1]

A broadside of 1660 to the tune of "When first the Scottish Wars began" is "Iter Boreale, the Second Part . . . Voting King Charls the Second home . . . By T. H. a Person of Quality," beginning "Good people all hark to my Call" (Harvard, Bagford; reprinted in *RB* VII, 670). A variant issue bears the title "The Noble Progresse . . . the Lord Generall Monks Political Proceedings . . . Vote for his Sacred Majesty" (BM C.120.h.4 [2]; reprinted in Wilkins's *Political Ballads* I, 153, and Mackay's *Cavalier Songs*, p. 223).

When I Have Often Heard
Young Maids Complaining

The song "When I have often heard young Maids complaining" is found in the third act of Purcell's *Fairy Queen*, 1692. It was printed in *Some Select Songs* from the opera, issued in the same year, p. 7 (Fig. 507).

---

[1] H. F. Brooks, "Rump Songs: an Index," *Oxford Bibliog. Society Proceedings* . . . , V (1936–1939), 304, note 179, lists several manuscript copies of the piece, including one headed "The Scotch Cronick. Feb. 20th 1656."

A printed broadside issue with music has the title "An Excellent New Song, Called, The Politick Lady. Sung at the Play-House, in a New Play much in Request. To an Excellent New Tune" (Lord Crawford 1310). An engraved song-sheet issue is in BM C.180.a (16). Words and music are in *Pills*, 1719–1720, VI, 155. The tune alone is in *The First Book of Apollo's Banquet*, 7th ed., 1693. No other broadsides make use of the tune.

When Love with Unconfined Wings

Richard Lovelace's best-known poem, "To Althea, from Prison," written in 1642 and published in his *Lucasta*, 1649, has been levied upon for several tune titles. But the only extant music to which these tune names might refer does not seem completely satisfactory as a source. Dr. John Wilson's setting of Lovelace's opening stanza was published in *Select Ayres and Dialogues*, 1659, p. 97 (Fig. 508), and in Wilson's *Cheerfull Ayres*, 1660, p. 10. But a broadside licensed in 1656, "The Pensive Prisoners Apology," beginning "Love with unconfined wings," borrows considerably from Lovelace's poem, and the tune direction, identical with the opening line, implies that a tune of this name was available no later than the date of registry.[1] A further objection to accepting Wil-

---

[1] Two issues of this ballad have survived: one without imprint (Roxburghe; reprinted in *RB* III, 179); the other, in an imprint of c. 1675, with a second tune title "No, no, no, no, not yet" (BM C.22.f.6 [161], Lord Crawford 780, Pepys II, 80, Harvard). This is a lost tune, on which see further s.v. "I'll never love thee more."

508

son's air as a tune used for ballads is that other tune names are, as we shall see, drawn from parts of Lovelace's poem which Wilson did not set. It is idle to deny that, once the first stanza was set, the rest of the poem could be sung to the music; but it seems far more likely that an air in popular style, doubtless antedating Wilson's rather academic setting, is to be posited for the uses to which the tune was put. Unhappily, only Wilson's music has been preserved, and the following discussion may be irrelevant to it.

"The Charming Eccho," beginning "As I was walking all alone,/one evening fair and clear," is to the tune of "Oh love with unconfined Wings; Or, Young Pheon" (Pepys III, 187; another issue, Douce I, 47ᵛ, adds "Busie Fame" as an alternative tune title and gives the first tune as "Oh love *whose* . . ."). Another in the same ballad meter, but in quatrains instead of the usual octaves, is "The Lamentation of Dell's Mistris," beginning "Dell's Mistris dear, with Carret hair," to the tune of "The little Fishes in the Deep, knows no such liberty," a title drawn from the end of Lovelace's second stanza (Pepys III, 333).

"Stone Walls cannot a Prison make," Lovelace's most familiar line, is named as the tune for two other ballads. These are John Taylor's "New Verses concerning the Plot, Londons Fire, & Godfreys Murder," 1680, beginning "Give ear, O King, and Nobles all" (Harvard, Huntington, BM C.20.f.2, BM Luttrell; reprinted in *RB* IV, 153); and another of about the same date, "The Dying Lovers last Farwel," beginning "One night when all the Village slept," to the tune of "Stone walls cannot a Prison make. Or, Young Pheon" (Pepys III, 8, Lord Crawford 986; reprinted in *A Collection of Old Ballads,* 1723–1725, III, 211).[2]

---

[2] On the latter ballad, see "One night when all the village slept" for another edition with differing tune direction.

[*When Maids Live to Thirty*]

"No Prophecy like a True one: being A New Play-house Song, sung in the *Cornish Comedy*," is a broadside version, with meaningless music, of a song in George Powell's play of 1696, II, i. It begins "When Maids live to Thirty, yet never repented," and is "To a Pleasant New Tune" (Morgan 57). The song, with music by Jeremiah Clarke (Fig. 509), was

issued in single-sheet form about 1698 (BM H.1601 [486], Huntington, Harvard) and appeared also in *Pills*, 1719–1720, V, 98. No other broadsides seem to have been sung to the tune.

[*When My Kids and Lambs I Treated*]

An anonymous two-stanza poem beginning "When my Kids and Lambs I treated" is set to music by Samuel Akeroyde in *The Theater of Music*, Third Book, 1686, p. 40 (Fig. 510). A broadside text expands the poem

510

* Written out in full in original.

to seven stanzas as "The Languishing Shepherd," with meaningless music on the sheet (Lord Crawford, BM C.39.k.6, reprinted in *OPB*, p. 11). Apparently no other broadsides made use of Akeroyde's tune.

When the King Enjoys His Own Again

Martin Parker's most famous ballad is "The King enjoyes his own again," written to bolster the fortunes of Charles I and a Cavalier cause that was seriously pressed in the several campaigns of 1643.[1] Beginning "What Booker can Prognosticat[e]?/or speak of our Kingdoms present state?" the balladeer sets himself up as the equal of Booker, Dade, Pond, Swallow, and other almanac makers and astrologers, and proceeds to

[1] Parker's name does not appear on the ballad, though he was usually scrupulous in signing his work; it would have been dangerous for author or printer to have been openly associated with the ballad during the civil war. The identification rests on a passage in *The Gossips Feast or, Morrall Tales*, 1647, p. 5: "Gammer Gowty Legs replyed, by my faith *Martin Parker* never got a fairer Brat, no, not when he pend that sweet Ballad, *When the King injoyes his own again.*" The date is established roughly by the lines in the ballad, "Full forty years the royal crown/hath been his father's and his own," and by a manuscript version of the ballad mentioned below.

predict the ultimate victory of the king and his return to power. No exactly contemporary issues of the ballad seem to have survived,[2] but the absence of imprints on extant copies (Lord Crawford 1266, BM 1876.f.1 [3], Roxburghe; reprinted in *RB* VII, 682) suggests that they were issued before the Restoration. The Crawford copy directs the ballad "To be joyfully sung with its own proper sweet Tune." A copy bearing the imprint of Francis Grove (d. 1663) is entitled "Englands Great Prognosticator, Foretelling when England shall enjoy a settled peace," and names the tune "When the King injoyes his own again" (Euing 96). One of the earliest states of the ballad is "The kinge enioyes his righ[ts againe]," a four-stanza text beginning "What Booker can prognosticate," preserved in the Percy Folio MS (ed. Hales and Furnivall, II, 24). The burden follows the phrasing of the title; no tune is named. A text of six stanzas, the first four substantially as in the Percy version and on broadsides, is to be found in BM MS Add. 22603, fol. 17^{v}: "On the Prognosticators of the yeare 1644," beginning "Though Booker doth prognosticate/Concerninge this o[u]r k[ing]d[om']s state," without tune direction. This version, evidently written before the end of 1643, has a burden echoing the common form of the tune title, whereas in the broadsides it is "When the king comes home in peace again." [3]

Perhaps the earliest printed version of the tune is the lyra-viol set in John Playford's *A Musicall Banquet,* 1651. In the next year it was included in two other Playford publications, *Musicks Recreation on the Lyra Viol* and *A Booke of New Lessons for the Cithern & Gittern.* Another lyra-viol set is in Cambridge University MS Dd.6.48, fol. 22^{v}; contemporary keyboard arrangements are found in Paris Conservatoire MS Rés. 1185, p. 252, and in Elizabeth Rogers's Virginal Book (BM MS Add. 10337, fol. 5^{v}=Fig. 511). The tune is reprinted in *Musick's Delight on the Cithren,* 1666, and in *180 Loyal Songs,* 1685, p. 186. In the third volume of *The Dancing Master,* c. 1728, the tune appears as "The Restoration of King Charles." Chappell (*PMOT* II, 435) believed that the tune was originally called "Marry me, marry me, quoth the bonny lass," on the ground that the tune bears that name in the Skene MS (printed in Dauney, *Ancient Scotish Melodies,* 1838, p. 239). But the resemblance to "When the King enjoys his own" is more rhythmical than melodic, and except for the first strain the two tunes have little in com-

[2] A slightly variant text, entitled "Upon Defacing of Whitehall," is printed by Ebsworth (*RB* VII, 633) as though it were a contemporary exemplar. He cites no source, and search has not revealed a copy with this title.

[3] The ballad is reprinted in *The Loyal Garland,* 5th ed., 1686, and in *A Collection of Loyal Songs,* 1750. Ritson's text in his *Ancient Songs,* 1790, p. 229, is a composite of these two versions. His music I have not traced, but I observe that it is wrongly barred throughout.

511

mon. The Skene tune, moreover, is of different length and does not fit Parker's ballad. Ebsworth followed Chappell's tentative suggestion without reservation, to the extent of supplying the "Marry me" tune title in brackets in *RB* VII, 633, 682. Elements of both strains may be seen more clearly in John Dowland's arrangement of "Mistris Whittes thinge" preserved in the Wickhambrook Lute Book, c. 1595, fol. 15 (Yale).

Among the numerous ballads sung to "When the King enjoys his own again," the earliest include "The World Is Turned Upside Down," beginning "Listen to me and you shall hear," with MS date April 8, 1646 (BM Thomason; reprinted in *CP*, p. 161), and "A new Ballad, called a Review of the Rebellion, in three parts. To the tune of, When the King injoyes his Rights againe," beginning "Britaines awake from your six yeares dreame," with MS date June 15, 1647 (BM Thomason; reprinted in Wright's *Political Ballads*, p. 13). After the death of Charles I, the tune became identified with the fortunes of his son, as in a ballad describing his escape from Worcester in September, 1651: "The last Newes from France . . . the King of Scots . . . conveyed away by a young Gentleman in womans apparrell," with its refrain "And the King himself did wait on me" (Euing 181, a contemporary edition; later issues in Pepys, Douce, Roxburghe; reprinted in *RB* VII, 635, and in A. M. Broadley's *The Royal Miracle*, 1912, p. 213).

The tune was again in vogue at the Restoration, being designated for such ballads as: "General Monks Welcome . . . to Whitehall," by G. Ticwhit, beginning "All ye Heroes of the Land" (Harvard, Wood 416 [52]); "The Glory of these Nations . . . King Charles's Royall progresse . . . to . . . Westminster the 29. of May last," beginning "Wher's those that did Prognosticate" (BM C.120.h.4 [5]; reprinted in *RB* VIII, xxxvii*, in Wright's *Political Ballads*, p. 223, and Mackay's *Cavalier Songs*, p. 217); "Englands Joyfull Holiday . . . 23. of April. [1661]," beginning "Come brave England, be of good cheare" (Wood 401 [28ᵛ, 27]); "The Loyal Subjects Exultation for the Coronation of King Charls the Second," beginning "What Writers could Prognosticate," to the tune of "When the King comes home in Peace again" (Euing 158); and "A Countrey Song, intituled, The Restoration," beginning "Come, come away,/To the Temple and pray," in half stanzas, without tune direction but with the refrain "And the King enjoyes his own again" (BM Thomason, with MS date May, 1661; reprinted in Wright, p. 265, Mackay, p. 248, and *RB* VIII, xxvi*).

Later seventeenth-century broadsides include one on the events of August, 1666, entitled "More News from the Fleet . . . against the Dutch," beginning "Of English Acts I intend to write" (Rawlinson 118b), and two political pieces of the 1680s: "An Excellent New Song of The Unfortunate Whig's," 1682, beginning "The Whigs are but small, and of no good Race" (Wood 417, Roxburghe; reprinted in *RB* V, 140; the parody of "Sawney was tall and of noble race" does not extend beyond the opening line), and "The Christian Conquest," a ballad on the overthrow of the Turks at Vienna, September, 1683, beginning "Good people all sing and rejoyce" (Roxburghe; reprinted in *RB* V, 372). Another political squib, no broadside version of which has survived, is "Monarchy Tryumphant, or the fatal fall of Rebels," beginning "Whigs are now such precious things," printed with "When the King" music in *180 Loyal Songs*, p. 186.

In the eighteenth century the tune continued in use. A broadside of 1711 tells the old story of "The Royal Martyr: Or, The Bloody Tragedy of King Charles the First," but the final stanza brings the ballad up to date: "Then let Us pray for Royal Anne" (Harvard). Another of the same year is "A New Ballad, shewing All shall be well One Hundred Years hence," beginning "Sad Times! sad Times! are coming on" (Harvard). "Peace and Dunkirk; being an Excellent New Song upon the Surrender of Dunkirk to General Hill," 1712, beginning "Spight of Dutch Friends and English Foes," modifies the refrain in deference to the ruling Queen (BM 1850.c.10 [13], Harvard). One other broadside deserving mention is "Sobieskia," beginning "Let Brittons bravely dare,/Now fear a Civil War," a piece soliciting sympathy for the Old Pretender upon his marriage to Maria Sobieski in 1719 (BM 1876.f.1 [85]). Several ballads on George I were written to the tune and may be found in such songsters as *Political Merriment*, 1714, *A Pill to Purge State-Melancholy*, 1715, and *A Collection of State Songs*, 1716. And *A Collection of Loyal Songs*, 1750, contains not only Parker's ballad but also three other songs to the tune, pp. 24, 65, 69.

A curiosity showing the persistence of the tune into the nineteenth century is a slip song of 1820, sympathic to Queen Caroline at a time when she was trying to establish her royal status: "The Queen Shall enjoy her own again," beginning "Spite of Detraction, Fraud, and Spleen," to the tune of "The King shall enjoy his own again" (BM 1871.f.16).

When the Stormy Winds Do Blow

The history of this tune name begins with a ballad by Martin Parker, "Saylors for my money. A new Ditty composed in the praise of Saylors and Sea affaires . . . To the tune of the Iouiall Cobler" (Pepys I, 420; reprinted in *RB* VI, 797, without indication of source). The opening line is "Countrie men of England" and the burden is "How ere the winde doth blow"; no music for "The jovial cobler" has survived under that name. A later version of the ballad, somewhat reworked, has a refrain from which our tune takes its name. It is titled "Neptunes raging fury, or, The Gallant Sea-mens Sufferings . . . To the Tune of, When the Stormy Windes doe blow" and begins "You Gentle men of England/ That lives at home at ease"; the earliest edition of this state, with a Richard Burton imprint, is signed J. P. (Euing 239; reprinted in Ritson's *English Songs*, 1783, II, 130). A number of late seventeenth- and early eighteenth-century editions are extant (Pepys, Bagford, Lord Crawford, Douce, Harvard, Roxburghe; reprinted in *RB* VI, 432).[1]

A shorter form of the text is found on song sheets with music, c. 1735 (Fig. 512), as "The Valiant Sailor" (BM G.316.f [140], Harvard).[2] A somewhat different tune, badly printed, is in *180 Loyal Songs*, 1685, p. 192, set to a ballad "The History of Whiggism," beginning "You Calvinists of England," which had appeared separately as a broadside in 1684 (Bodleian Ashmole G.16 [135]).

Other ballads to the tune include "The Valiant Seamans Congratulation to his sacred Majesty King Charls the second," beginning "Great Charles, your English Seamen/upon our bended knee"; it can be sung to "Let us drink and sing, and merrily troul the bowl. Or, The stormy

[1] Comparable to Parker's ballad in subject matter, and of about the same date, but without verbal parallels and in a different metrical scheme, is "The praise of Sailors . . . with their hard fortunes," beginning "As I lay musing in my bed,/full warm and well at ease" (Pepys, Euing, Rawlinson, Douce; reprinted in *RB* VIII, lxxxi*). No tune is named for singing.

[2] Several other single-sheet editions were published during the eighteenth century, from one of which Halliwell-Phillipps took the text of "The Valiant Sailors" for *The Early Naval Ballads of England*, 1841, p. 34. Others are represented by BM G.314 (109) and H.1601.b (34), both c. 1780.

512

winds do blow. Or, Hey Ho, my Hony" (Euing 368; reprinted in *Naval Songs and Ballads,* ed. C. H. Firth, 1908, p. 53), but since it contains the refrain "When the stormy winds do blow," it was probably written with that tune primarily in mind.[3] A recruiting ballad of the early 1660s is "Englands Valour and Hollands Terrour," beginning "Brave Loyal Hearted Englishmen," to the tune "The stormy winds do blow" (Euing 103); another of the same decade is propaganda against the French and Dutch, despite its title: "The Worlds Wonder! or, The Prophetical Fish. . . . taken by Fisher-men . . . near China, in . . . 1664," beginning "[I]le tell you of a Wonder,/that lately hath been Shewn" (Douce; reprinted in *PA,* p. 152). Another to the tune is "The Valiant Virgin; Or, Phillip and Mary," beginning "To every faithful Lover/that's constant to her dear," an example of that large class of "female sailor" ballads (Lord Crawford, Harvard, Roxburghe; reprinted in *RB* VII, 546). "Englands Welcome to King William," probably written in April, 1691, begins "You Nobles Here of England" and names the tune "When the Stormy Wind does Blow" (Pepys; reprinted in *PB* VI, 66).

[3] I have no information on the first tune name. For the third tune, see "Come hither, my own sweet duck."

Where's My Shepherd?

A complex of interconnected ballads from the years 1685–1688 (most of them licensed by Richard Pocock) gives us several tune names which we may associate with a single surviving melody. Music is found only in the Wood 417 (152) copy of "Cupids Victory over the Virgins Heart," beginning "Where's my Shepherd (my love) Hey-ho," sung "To a Pleasant New Play-Tune; Or, Where is my Shepherd" (Fig. 513). Other

513

copies, without music, are "To a Pleasant New Play-Tune; Or, The Maids a Washing themselves" (Pepys, Douce, Euing, Lord Crawford, Roxburghe; reprinted in *RB* III, 554), and presumably the "Play-Tune" is the rather florid music of the Wood broadside. "The Maids a Washing themselves" is a tune name evidently drawn from the central situation of "The Devonshire Damsels Frollick. Being An Account of nine or ten fair Maidens; who went one Evening lately, to wash themselves in a pleasant River, where they were discovered by several Young men . . . who took away their Gowns and Petticoats . . ." That ballad begins "Tom and William with Ned and Ben" and is to be sung "To a Pleasant new Play-House Tune; or, wher's my Shepherd?" (Pepys, Euing, Lord Crawford, Douce, Roxburghe; reprinted in *RB* IV, 438).[1] Music con-

---

[1] Ebsworth also reprinted the broadside in his edition of *Choyce Drollery*, 1876, Appendix, p. 342. An earlier version of the story, in different meter, is preserved in "The Bathing Girles: to the common Galliard tune," beginning "It was in June, and

tained on the sheets is unhappily meaningless, thus preventing us from knowing whether the "Play-House Tune" was an independent melody or was identical with "Where's my Shepherd?" To explain the combination of tune names on these three ballads, we may, however, surmise that "Cupids Victory" with music was the first to be published, followed by "The Devonshire Damsels Frollick" and then by editions of "Cupids Victory" which name "The Maids a Washing themselves" as a tune title.

"Where's my Shepherd?" is cited in one other ballad (as an alternative to "A fig for France, or, The Country Farmer"); [2] it is "The Loving Mistress, and The Wanton Clerk," beginning "A Lawyer in our Town did dwell" (Pepys III, 164).

"The Maids a Washing Themselves" is named as the tune for "The Discontented Bride," beginning "Will the Baker a Wooing went" (Pepys IV, 119). And "The Maids a Washing" is also found on two broadsides: "Dicks Loyalty To his True Love Nancy," beginning "Dick resolved to Court young Nan" (Pepys III, 182, Douce I, 64^v), and "The Wanton wenches of Wiltshire," beginning "Now young Batchelors all draw near" (Lord Crawford, Roxburghe; reprinted in *RB* VIII, 651). Two other tune names seem to be offshoots of the ballad title: "The Devonshire Frollick" is the tune for "Wit Out-witted, Or, The Cheater Cheated," beginning "Iohn and Jone in one House did dwell" (Douce II, 255), and it is named (along with "The Country Farmer") for singing "The Welch Wedding," beginning "Now sweet Shinny wilt thou be wed" (Pepys IV, 109, BM C.22.f.6 [203], Lord Crawford 903, Douce II, 244). Two other ballads have the tune direction "The Country Farmer. Or, The Devonshire Damosels": "A Warning and good Counsel to the Weavers," beginning "You Gentlemen all come listen a while" (Pepys; reprinted in *PB* IV, 30), and "The Young-Man & Maidens Fore-cast," beginning "I'll tell you a Jest of a Provident lass" (Pepys IV, 371, Lord Crawford 588, Harvard, BM C.22.f.6 [210]; reprinted in *A Century of Ballads,* ed. John Ashton, 1887, p. 326). All these ballads are in an eight-line stanza, with several metrical patterns varying from eight to eleven syllables to the line, but they can all be sung to the tune. If we accept the evidence that "The Devonshire Damsels Frollick" was sung to "Where's my Shepherd?" it follows that the derivative tune names mentioned in this paragraph should all be related to the music we possess.

'twas on Barnaby Bright, too" (*Westminster Drollery,* 1672, II, 100), but galliards are too numerous for us to single out one which might go with the song. Still another version of the "bathing girls" story is found in the broadside "The Kentish Frolick," to the tune of "Let Mary live long" (Pepys; reprinted in *RB* VIII, 548).

[2] The tune of "A fig for France" has not survived. On "The Country Farmer," see "King James's Jig."

While I Gaze on
Chloris Trembling

An anonymous song beginning "Whilst I gaze on Cloe trembling" appears in *The Banquet of Musick,* Third Book, 1689, p. 6, with music by Overbury (Fig. 514). The two stanzas, slightly altered in details, were

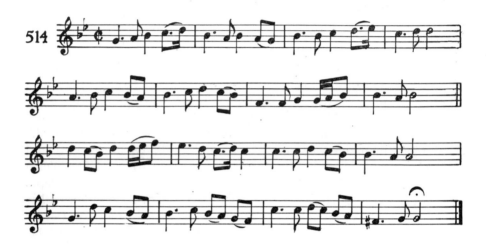

514

published as a broadside, "The Jealous Lover's Complaint," beginning "While I gaze on Cloris trembling," to the tune of "While I lay gazing" (Lord Crawford, BM C.39.k.6; reprinted in *OPB,* p. 79). Search has not revealed verses beginning "While I lay gazing," or a tune of that name; possibly Overbury's music is intended, inasmuch as the broadside was issued in the last years of the century, presumably after the appearance of the songbook.

No other broadsides were set to the tune. Eighteenth-century engraved editions of the original song, with an added stanza and new music (Fig. 515), were published as "Cloe's Admirer. . . . The Words by a Parson of Quality," c. 1720 (BM H.1601 [482], Huntington, Harvard). Entitled "The Lukewarm Lover," the song was reprinted in Watts's *Musical Miscellany,* 1729–1731, II, 76, where an elaborated version of the song-sheet air is credited to Lewis Ramondon. The Ramondon music was called for in ten ballad operas, including the follow-

515

ing, whose printed editions contain his tune: Gay's *Polly*, 1729, Ralph's *The Fashionable Lady*, 1730, Coffey's *The Devil to Pay* and Lillo's *Silvia*, 1731, and Phillips's *The Mock Lawyer*, 1733.

A fresh setting of "The Lukewarm Lover" by James Oswald is in *Calliope, or English Harmony*, 1739–1746, II, 182, and in a single-sheet edition of c. 1750 (BM G.316.a [56]).

Who List to Lead a Soldier's Life

"Who list to lead a soldier's life" is named as a tune for singing several ballads. Judging by metrical schemes, there must have been more than one tune, but none have survived under this name. The closest approximation is "Souldiers life" or "The Souldiers Life," an air preserved in every edition of *The Dancing Master*, 1651–c. 1728 (1651, p. 65=Fig. 516), and in *A Booke of New Lessons for the Cithern & Gittern*, 1652. This same tune is found in several seventeenth-century keyboard versions. As "The Souldiers delight," it is in Elizabeth Rogers's Virginal Book (BM MS Add. 10337, fol. 18ᵛ). As "Ye Souldiours dance" it forms one movement of William Byrd's programmatic suite "The Battle" in Paris Conservatoire MS Rés. 1186, fol. 99 (printed in Byrd's *My Ladye Nevells Booke*, ed. Hilda Andrews, 1926, p. 39; an interpolation, since the Nevell MS does not contain the movement). Transcripts of the piece from both the Rogers and Paris manuscripts are in the New York Public Library MS Drexel 5609, pp. 25, 67 (the former printed in

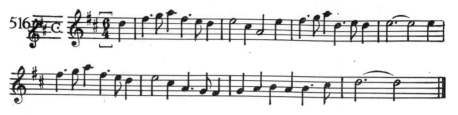

Original is unbarred.

Byrd's *Forty-five Pieces for Keyboard Instruments,* ed. S. Tuttle, 1939, p. 112). E. H. Fellowes included both versions of the movement in his edition of Byrd's *Collected Works,* 1937–1950, XVIII, 126, 127.

The tune is suitable for a ballad-meter quatrain and, with repetition, will serve for the eight-line stanzas of "The Joyfull Peace, concluded betweene . . . Denmarke and . . . Sweden," 1613, beginning "The Lord of Hosts hath blest no Land," to the tune of "Who list to lead a Soldiers life" (Pepys; reprinted in *PG,* p. 45). Two other ballads in the same meter naming the tune are in Richard Johnson's *Golden Garland of Princely Pleasures,* 3d ed., 1620, 13th ed., 1690: "A Song of an English Knight . . . afterward made Duke of Suffolk," beginning "Eighth Henry ruling in this Land," and "A Song of the life and death of King Richard the Third," beginning "In England once there raign'd a King" (the latter also found in an eighteenth-century Dicey broadside edition, Madden II, 476, Harvard); the two were reprinted in *A Collection of Old Ballads,* 1723–1725, III, 64, 50.

A ballad by Thomas Deloney, "Of the Imprisonment of King Edward the second," beginning "When Isabell faire Englands Queene/In wofull warres had victorious beene," calls for the tune, but its ten-line octosyllabic stanza will not fit the "Souldiers life" music (*Strange Histories,* 1602; reprinted in *Works,* ed. Mann, p. 402). Likewise "Goe too, goe too, you Britaines all," an eight-line song in octosyllabics, sung by a harper to the tune of "Who list to lead a Souldiers life" in Peele's *Edward I,* 1593 (ed. W. W. Greg, Malone Society, 1911, ll. 497ff.) does not fit the music before us.

I have encountered no ballads sung to "Souldiers life." At least two, however, call for "The soldier's delight," and one of them, in double ballad stanza with anapests replacing iambs, can be sung to the tune. It is "The Country-Maids Delight . . . a . . . song in praise of a Plowman," beginning "You young-men and Maids that in Country doth dwell," and is directed to be sung to "the souldiers delight; Or, the seamans adieu to his dear"[1] (Wood E.25; reprinted in *RB* VII, 818). Less well adapted to the tune is "Of A Maid that was deep in Love, With a Souldier brave and bold Sir," beginning "When first this Couple fell in Love," to be sung to "the Souldiers delight" (Lord Crawford 1302).[2] The twelve-line stanza, alternating eight and seven syllables, would require two repetitions of the tune for each stanza, and the fit is ungainly.

As Chappell observed (*PMOT* I, 144), our "Souldiers life" tune is but another version of "Tomorrow is St. Valentine's Day," known to us from Ophelia's singing;[3] the tune is found in Walker's *Quaker's Opera*, 1728, Ryan's *The Cobler's Opera*, 1729, and is named in three other ballad operas. In all editions of *Pills*, 1719–1720, IV, 43, it is coupled with verses from Heywood's *The Rape of Lucrece*, 1630, beginning "Arise, arise, my Juggy, my Puggy." "Souldiers life" also resembles a traditional tune of "Lord Thomas and Fair Eleanor" which has survived into the twentieth century.[4]

[*Who Liveth So Merry*
in All This Land]

In 1557–1558 John Wally and Mrs. Toy licensed a ballad "who lyve so mery and make suche sporte as thay yat be of the pooreste sorte" (Rollins, *Anal. Index*, No. 2948). No contemporary text has survived, nor do any broadside editions seem to be extant. But the lines of the Stationers' Register entry are found in the eighth stanza of a song be-

---

[1] The second tune is named from a ballad so titled (*RB* VII, 524). The quatrains of "The seaman's adieu" suggest that its tune ("I'le go to Sir Richard," which has not been found) would require complete repetition, as would "Souldiers life," to fit "The Country-Maids Delight."

[2] This is a later edition of "The famous Woman-Drummer," sung to the lost tune of "Wet and Weary" (*RB* VII, 730).

[3] Rollins, *Anal. Index*, No. 2120, queries the possibility that a lost ballad licensed in 1591, ". . . Twoo stamering lovers . . . pleasant meetinge on Sainct Valentines daie," might be the basis of Shakespeare's verses.

[4] See *JFSS*, II (1905), 105ff.

517

Original is unbarred.

ginning "Who liueth so merry in all this land" in Thomas Ravenscroft's *Deuteromelia,* 1609, No. 18 (Fig. 517). A text without music or tune title is in *Wit and Drollery,* 1682, p. 252, and with music in early editions of *Pills,* 1699–1714, I, 49.

The central thought of the song as paraphrased in the couplet—

> Who can sing so merry a note,
> As he that cannot change a groat?—

is sung in Edwards's *Damon and Pithias,* 1571, and in Nashe's *Summer's Last Will and Testament,* 1600, and is quoted in Heywood's *Proverbs.* Another echo occurs in Richard Barnfield's "The Shepherd's Content" in *The Affectionate Shepherd,* 1594:

> For who sings commonly so merry a Noate,
> As he that cannot chop or change a groate.

[Who's the Fool Now?]

"Martyn said to his man, whoe is the foole nowe" was licensed in 1588 to Thomas Orwin. Although no broadside copies have survived, the song was included among the "Freemens Songs of 4. Voices" in Thomas Ravenscroft's *Deuteromelia,* 1609, No. 16 (Fig. 518). It is also found in Forbes's *Cantus,* 1662 ed. only, No. 55, and in *Pills,* 1699–1714, I, 47. An anonymous arrangement of the tune is in *The Fitzwilliam Virginal Book* II, 275. The refrain line is referred to in Dekker's *Old Fortunatus,* sig. C1ᵛ, where Shadow describes fops who overdress, "onely to make other Ideots laugh, and wisemen to crie who's the foole now?" The opening of the song is quoted in Anthony Brewer's *Love-sick King,* Act III, and in Dryden's *Sir Martin Mar-All,* IV, i, as Professor Rollins has noted (*Anal. Index,* No. 1681).

518

Original is unbarred.

The tune name at the head of this discussion is arbitrarily assigned and might equally well have been "Martin said to his man," the title of the Fitzwilliam set.

Whoop! Do Me No Harm, Good Man

This melodious jig tune is found in William Corkine's *Ayres*, 1610, sig. F1ᵛ, among the lyra-viol lessons at the end of the volume. A keyboard setting of about the same date, entitled "Hoope do me no," is in BM MS Add. 30486, fol. 21 (Fig. 519); others are in Christ Church MS 431, fol. 2ᵛ (see Orlando Gibbons, *Complete Keyboard Works*, ed. M. H. Glyn, 1925, II, 3), and Paris Conservatoire MS Rés. 1186 bis, Part II, p. 35. An arrangement for viola da gamba by Richard Sumarte, c. 1660, is preserved in a manuscript in the Henry Watson music collection of the Manchester Free Reference Library.[1]

The tune is evidently named from the refrain of a lost ballad antedating Corkine's collection. The refrain is twice quoted in *The Winter's Tale*, IV, iv, 199–201, so that we know it was familiar to Shakespeare before 1611. The earliest text calling for the tune is "A proper new

[1] The manuscript, without pressmark, has the following spine title: "A Miscellaneous Collection of Music for Viol-da-gamba by various Composers. MS. circa 1660. Translated into ordinary notation by Henry Watson, 1909." The manuscript has been interleaved with modern music paper, but Watson's "translations" extend only to p. 15. A separate volume contains a transcription of the whole, prepared under the supervision of Dr. T. Lea Southgate c. 1913. A copy of the tablature manuscript is BM MS Add. 39556; BM MS Add. 38783 is a copy of the Southgate text.

519

ballad to the tune of whoope do me no harme good man or the Cleane
contrary way wᶜʰ you please as your voyce and the tune Can best agree,"
beginning "There was an old lad Rode on an old pad vnto an old lasse
a wooing" (BM MS Add. 15891, fol. 245ᵛ; printed in John Fry's *Pieces
of Ancient Poetry,* 1814, p. 21; other copies are in Bodleian MS Rawlinson Poet. 160, fol. 162, in Harvard MS Eng. 628, p. 319, and in *Wit and
Drollery,* 1656, p. 92, without tune direction).[2] This ballad, concerning
the intrigues between Robert Carr, Earl of Somerset, and the Countess

[2] The one surviving tune of "The clean contrary way," q.v., is designed for a
double ballad-meter stanza and will not fit "There was an old lad." There must have
been an early seventeenth-century tune of the name to which the ballad could be
sung; it would fit also "A merry new catch of all Trades," beginning "All Trades
are not alike in show," to the tune of "The cleane Contrary way" (Pepys; reprinted
in *PG,* p. 196), a ballad in quatrains with the final line repeated.

Dekker and Webster's *Northward Ho!,* 1607, V, i, contains two snatches making a
stanza which is probably an echo of a still older song:

> Ile make him do a thing worse than this,
>   Come loue me where as I lay. . . .
> He shall father a child is none of his,
>   O the cleane contrary way.

The same pattern with interlaced refrain is found in *Merry Drollery,* 1661, I, 95,
and with variations in *Wit and Mirth,* 3d ed., 1682, p. 17:

> It was a man, and a jolly old man,
>   Come love me whereas I lay,
> And he would marry a fair young wife
>   The clean contrary way.

A song beginning "Come heare, lady muses, and help mee to sing" contains the double
refrain with a repetition of the final line (*Poems and Songs relating to George Villiers,
Duke of Buckingham,* ed. F. W. Fairholt, Percy Society, 1850, p. 10).

of Essex, was written after the death of Sir Thomas Overbury in 1613 and before the execution of Mrs. Turner and her confederates in 1615. Another early seventeenth-century piece written to the tune begins "Our eagle is flowne to a place yet vnknown/To meet with the Phoenix of Spaine" (Bodleian MS Rawl. Poet. 160, fol. 176ᵛ); it deals humorously with the spectacle of England suddenly rolling in wealth and may have been written in 1623 when Prince Charles set out for Madrid to woo the Spanish Infanta. Yet another from the same manuscript (fol. 191ᵛ) is "A Proper new song made Of those that Comenc'd the King being at Cambridg[e]. 1624," beginning "When yᵉ King came of late wᵗʰ his peers of state" (another copy is in BM MS Add. 22603, fol. 53).

I have found but two printed ballads naming the tune directly. One of these is "A merry Ballad of a rich Maid that had 18. seuerall Suitors," c. 1625, beginning "I am a young lasse, and my time doth so passe,/That of late I did long for to marry" (Pepys; reprinted in *PB* I, 243). The other, entitled "The Golden Age: Or, An Age of plaine-dealing. To a pleasant new Court tune: Or, Whoope doe me no harme good man," c. 1622 (Pepys; reprinted in *PB* I, 208), begins as follows:

> Come grant me, come lend me
>   your listning eares:
> The golden Age now againe
>   plainely appeares,
> Carowse away sorrow,
>   and fling away feares,
> Leaue your wife wealthy,
> Shee'l neuer shead teares:
>   Oh this is a golden Age,
>   Oh this is a Iouiall Age.

This ballad may have been preceded by "The siluer Age, or, The World turned backward. To a pleasant new Court tune," licensed in November, 1621, and beginning "My Lady Pecunia/is a faire creature" (Pepys; reprinted in *PB* I, 202). It was followed by Laurence Price's "The Honest Age," beginning "You Poets that write of the ages that's past" (Pepys; reprinted in *PG*, p. 406) and Martin Parker's "The wiuing age," beginning "The Maidens of London are now in despaire," both to the tune of "The Golden age" (Pepys; reprinted in *PG*, p. 235). "The Wiuing Age" became in turn the tune for singing three ballads: "The cunning Age," by John Cart, beginning "Good morrow, kind Gossip, why whither so fast" (Pepys; reprinted in *PG*, p. 239), "The Cooper of Norfolk," beginning "Attend, my Masters, and listen well" (Pepys, Douce, Euing, Lord Crawford, Roxburghe; reprinted in *RB* I, 99),[3] and "I tell you,

[3] An Elizabethan account of the brewer who meant to cuckold a cooper and was himself properly served is found, in a different stanza pattern and to the tune of "In Somer time," in *A Collection of Seventy-Nine Black-Letter Ballads*, 1867, p. 60.

John Iarret, you'l breake," beginning "Pray gentle Iohn Iarret, give eare to my words" (Pepys; reprinted in *PG*, p. 337). And "The Golden Age" is named as the tune for I. D.'s "Doctor Do-good's Directions," beginning "If any are infected, give audience awhile" (Roxburghe; reprinted in *RB* I, 234). "The Cheating Age . . . To a pleasant new tune," beginning "From olde famous Lincolne that's seated so hye" (Pepys; reprinted in *PG*, p. 244), is in the same stanza form and was undoubtedly intended to be sung to the same tune as the others in the "Age" series.

It should be noted, however, that the stanza of "The Golden Age" and its congeners is too long to fit the tune of "Whoop! do me no harm" without adjustment. The fourth and eighth lines require a division of the cadence notes, and the burden in lines 9 and 10 requires a double repetition of the final musical phrase. Both stratagems are awkward, the latter especially so. It is possible, of course, that the "new Court tune" was genuinely adapted to the verses, and that "Whoop" was merely a serviceable approximation. Or there may have been another version of "Whoop" which has not survived.

A song "Of Jonny and Jinny" in *Westminster Drollery*, 1672, II, 72, with the following opening stanza, fits the usual "Whoop" meter and was probably intended for that tune:

> The pretty sweet Jinny sate on a hill,
> Where Jonny the swain her see,
> He tun'd his quill, and sung to her still,
> Whoop, Jinny, come down to me.

Sir Frederick Bridge's vocal arrangement of the song is found in the modern transcript of the Watson manuscript mentioned earlier, and in BM MS Add. 38783, fol. 107^v.

The tune, called "Oh doe me no harme good man," is named for singing a song beginning "You roaring Boyes, and sturdy Theeues,/you Pimpes, and Aples-squires," in *The Famous Historie of Fryer Bacon*, 1629, sig. D4^v. Since the initial editions of this chapbook, now lost, probably antedate Robert Greene's play, *The Honourable Historie of frier Bacon, and frier Bongay*, 1594 (written c. 1591–1592), the tune may have been in vogue earlier than we can demonstrate positively.

Why Are My Eyes Still Flowing?

This tune takes its name from the opening line of a song by Thomas D'Urfey, "set to a famous Italian Ayre," but printed without music in his *Compleat Collection*, 1687, p. 24. In the same year the music, "A New Italian Ground," appeared in *Apollo's Banquet*, 5th ed., Part III, No. 42 (Fig. 520). D'Urfey's verses were reprinted in John Shirley's *The*

Triumph of Wit, 2d ed., 1692, p. 142, in *The Compleat Academy of Complements*, 1705, p. 156, and with music in *Pills*, 1719–1720, II, 198.

An expanded broadside version, licensed by Richard Pocock and therefore no later than 1688, is "The Constant Lover: Or, Celia's Glory exprest to the Life . . . sung after the Italian manner . . . To a pleasant new Tune of, Why are my Eyes still flow——ing" (Lord Crawford 1341, BM C.22.f.6 [93]). The florid music is found on another broadside which uses the two stanzas of D'Urfey's song and then diverges from "The Constant Lover"; dated 1688, it is titled "The Happy Lovers, or, Caelia won by Aminta's Loyalty" (Wood 417 [161]). A 1689 edition with the same title contains music which is actually "Cold and Raw" (Pepys V,

247; an undated impression is in Bagford, reprinted in *BB* I, 89). A good copy of the tune is found on another broadside of 1689, "The Young Squires Conquest," beginning "By all the Powers, I love you so" (Pepys V, 227).[1] In *Youth's Delight on the Flagelet,* 9th ed., c. 1690, the tune appears with the title "Why are my eyes or The eunuttch song," suggesting that our air or an alternative one was associated with the singing of a castrato, novel but not unknown to the London scene. A corrupt version of the tune is printed on two Pepysian broadsides: "Royal Courage," whose proper tune is indicated as "Let the Soldiers Rejoyce" (V, 65), and "The Languishing Lass," a ballad of 1689 to the tune of "I am So sick of Love," on which see "Aye, marry, and thank you too" (V, 306).

Some fifteen songs and ballads were sung to the tune, most of them written in an irregular eight-line stanza with separate syllables for almost every note in ornamented passages. An exception is "The Coy Damosel Conquered," imitating the original pattern, and beginning "With many Glasses flow——ing" (Pepys III, 296).

"An Excellent New Song; or, A True Touch of the Times . . . to . . . James the Second," beginning "King James the First was a Gallant King," is to the tune of "The Loyal Health; or, Why are my Eyes still Flowing" (Euing; reprinted in *RB* VII, 707; a later edition, bringing the account down to William III, is in BM C.22.f.6 [32] and Harvard).[2] Two other ballads of early 1689 bearing the title "A New Touch of the Times, Or, The Nation's Consent, For a Free Parliament" have different texts but both are to be sung to "Why are my Eyes still flowing" (*PB* IV, 107, 112). It is possible that the tune "The touch of the times" derives its name from the first of these three ballads. It is named on more than twenty broadsides, the earliest of which were issued during the reign of James II. No music has survived under this name, and we can only speculate as to whether "The touch of the times" became another name for the tune "Why are my eyes still flowing."

"The Protestants of Englands Prayers," 1689, beginning "The Truble in this Kingdom puts us to a stand," is to the tune of "The English Travellers, or, Why are my Eyes still Flowing" (Pepys; reprinted in *PB* IV, 312). The first tune, usually cited as "The two English travelers," is associated with anapestic tetrameter quatrains rather than the eight-line stanza of irregular meter found here. Its popularity can be judged

---

[1] The text of this ballad, based on a D'Urfey song, could be sung to the printed music. The song with a new tune by Samuel Akeroyde was printed in D'Urfey's *Third Collection of New Songs,* 1685, and was reprinted in *Pills* II, 40.

[2] On the first tune, see "At the foot of a willow."

from the existence of more than twenty broadsides naming the tune for singing, but unhappily the music has not been preserved.[3]

Other ballads to the tune of "Why are my eyes still flowing" are reprinted in *PB* IV, 198, V, 192, and *RB* III, 508, 635, IV, 405, VI, 349, 535, VII, 710. It is named also as the tune for a song beginning "Pourquoy mon Coeur toûjours fidelle" in Abel Boyer's *The Complete French-Master*, 1694, No. 10. And the first strain of the music is introduced into Gay's *The Beggar's Opera*, 1728.

Wigmore's Galliard

This dance tune is found in William Ballet's MS Lute Book, p. 112 (Fig. 521). A number of Elizabethan ballads were sung to it, the earliest

521

of which is probably "A famous dittie of the ioyful receauing of the Queens . . . majestie . . . Nouember, 1584," beginning "The twelfe day of Nouember last/Elizabeth our noble Queen" (BM Huth; reprinted in *A Collection of Seventy-Nine Black-Letter Ballads*, 1867, p. 182). "A most excellent new Dittie . . . wise sentences of Salomon," beginning "Those that will run a Vertuous race," was licensed in 1586, but the

[3] One ballad sung to "The Two English Travellers" is printed with meaningless music combined with scraps of "Lilliburlero": "Romes Doctor," c. 1689, reprinted in *PB* IV, 291.

earliest copy dates c. 1600 or soon after (Huntington; reprinted in Collmann, No. 84). The ballad continued to be popular under the title of "Solomons Sentences" (Pepys, Bagford, Euing, Lord Crawford, Roxburghe; reprinted in *RB* II, 539), and in some copies another ballad called "Solomons Sacrifice" is printed on the sheet, in different meter and "to a new tune."

Also to the tune of "Wigmor's Galliard" is "A right excellent and godly new Ballad . . . vncertainetye of this present lyfe," beginning "All carefull Christians, marke my Song" (*SB*, p. 40). This ballad, licensed in 1591, has a refrain beginning "The glasse doth run," from which is derived the tune name cited in "And [sic] louer's lamentable complaint . . . to take heede of women," beginning "Come! come! come! come! What shall I say" (*SB*, p. 81).

Deloney named "Wygmors Galliard" for singing his "How King Henry the second crowning his Sonne king of England, in his owne lifetime, was by him most grieuously vexed with warres," beginning "You parents whose affection fond" (*Strange Histories*, 1602, in *Works*, ed. Mann, p. 394). Other ballads naming the tune include two licensed in 1624: "A most excellent Ditty, called Collins Conceit," beginning "Conceits of sundry sorts there are" (Pepys; reprinted in *PG*, p. 179), and "An Hundred Godly Lessons," beginning "My children dear mark well my words" (Euing 143, an edition of c. 1675; later copies naming the tune "Dying Christians Exhortation" are in Pepys, Bagford, Lord Crawford, Roxburghe; reprinted in *RB* I, 428). "A Warning for all Murderers," beginning "Give eare unto my story true," is another production of the first quarter of the century (Roxburghe; reprinted in *RB* III, 137).

The tune is named for singing the solemn verses beginning "The Well this man for refuge tooke,/the World dooth represent" in Anthony Munday's *Banquet of Daintie Conceits*, 1588, sig. H4. It is also used with "A Caroll for Saint Stevens day," beginning "I Thinke none here but they have heard," in *Good and True, Fresh and New, Christmas Carols*, 1642, sig. A4ᵛ.

The music fits an octosyllabic quatrain, but the usual stanza found with the tune is in eight lines, requiring a repetition of the entire air. One of the Shirburn ballads is in a six-line stanza, the final couplet of which can be sung to a repetition of the last eight bars. Several of the seventeenth-century texts are written in ballad meter, and the alternate short lines fit the music somewhat awkwardly. If we possessed a version of the tune arranged for singing, we might find it readily adaptable to varying line lengths; the instrumental arrangement avoids the vacuum of long notes through skillful ornamentation, but in the absence of variants with which to compare the Ballet lute set, we cannot be sure when a running passage is ornament and when it is integral.

William and Margaret

The ballad of "Fair Margaret and Sweet William" was known before the production of Beaumont's *The Knight of the Burning Pestle*, c. 1611, in which Merrythought twice sings passages from it. The more important of these is the quatrain in Act II, Scene viii:

> When it was growne to darke midnight,
>   And all were fast asleepe,
> In came *Margarets* grimely Ghost,
>   And stood at *Williams* feete.

The oldest extant copy of the entire ballad is "Fair Margaret's Misfortune, or, Sweet William's Frightful Dreams on his Wedding Night: With the sudden Death and Burial of those Noble Lovers. To an Excellent New Tune," beginning "As it fell out on a long Summer's Day,/ two Lovers they sat on a Hill." This roman-letter broadside, issued by Sarah Bates early in the eighteenth century, is preserved in Douce I, 72 (reprinted in Percy's *Reliques* and in Child No. 74 A).[1] Later editions from Aldermary Church Yard are in Douce and Roxburghe collections (reprinted in *RB* VI, 641). The ballad has survived in traditional circulation and is very popular in America, where details of the story have often been much changed, though affinities with Child A are usually evident. See Tristram P. Coffin, *The British Traditional Ballad in North America*, rev. ed., 1963, pp. 70–72.

The dominant eighteenth-century form of the text is found on a late black-letter broadside called "William and Margaret, an old Ballad," which begins "When all was wrapt in dark Mid-night." The sheet contains an interesting tune in recitativo style (Fig. 522), supplemented by the printed note: "This Ballad will sing to the Tunes of Montrose's Lilt, Rothes's Lament, or the Isle of Kell" (BM 1876.f.1 [107], reprinted in *RB* III, 671).[2] To the sheet is affixed a halfpenny tax stamp, enabling

1 Child, following Chappell, noted that Sarah Bates was publishing "about 1685." She was almost certainly the wife of the publisher Charles Bates and continued the business after his death, which was well after 1700, perhaps as late as 1715. She is known to have been active in 1719–1720 (Plomer).

2 On "Montrose's Lilt," see "I'll never love thee more." "Rothes's Lament" is one of two tunes named for singing a song beginning "As Silvia in a Forrest lay" in Allan

522

us to assign a date of 1711 or later; the BM *Catalogue of Printed Music* conjectures 1723.[3]

"'William and Margaret,'" says Child, "is simply 'Fair Margaret and Sweet William' rewritten in what used to be called an elegant style." It quickly became popular—not always in the form it had had on the black-letter broadside, for a competing version soon appeared with very slight changes beyond the opening stanza. This was the work of a young Scotsman David Mallet, who passed off his text as founded on fact and inspired by the stanza in *The Knight of the Burning Pestle.* Scholars are now generally agreed in giving precedence to the black-letter text and crediting Mallet only with the merest touching up, but there is no doubt of the popularity of the verses. They appeared unsigned in Aaron Hill's *The Plain Dealer,* No. 36, July 24, 1724, and quickly passed into such poetical miscellanies as *The Hive,* 2d ed., 1724, I, 169; signed with Mallet's initials the poem appears in Ramsay's *Tea-Table Miscellany,* 1733, II, 148.[4] "William and Margaret. An old

Ramsay's *Tea-Table Miscellany,* 1723, p. 119. I have no information on "The Isle of Kell."

[3] Chappell, in *RB* III, 668, argues for a date during the reign of Queen Anne. The tax, he notes, was an impost on newspapers, and ballads were soon exempted from its provisions. It is true that stamps are seldom found on ballads, but in the very portfolio containing the "William and Margaret" under discussion, the piece numbered 109 is a broadside dated 1735 on which is an identical tax stamp. The conjectured dating of the BM "William and Margaret" sheet seems therefore conservative.

[4] A manuscript note in the BM copy of this edition states that Mallet wrote his ballad "while he was Janitor of the High School of Edinb." When the poem entered the *Tea-Table* is not easy to say, for some early editions have disappeared entirely. A cursory search reveals the poem, with Mallet's initials, in a Dublin edition of 1729.

The *Plain Dealer* text, which Hill said he found in a Garland in a form which needed retouching, begins as follows:

> When Hope lay hush'd in silent Night,
> And Woe was wrapp'd in Sleep,

Scotch Ballad with the Original Scotch Tune" appeared in William Thomson's *Orpheus Caledonius*, 1725, No.49; but despite the claims of the subtitle, the text is Mallet's and the tune is "I'll never love thee more," the "Montrose's Lilt" cited as an alternate air for singing the black-letter "William and Margaret." [5]

The musical setting most commonly found in the eighteenth century began to appear on single sheets about 1725 (Fig. 523), sometimes with

523

Mallet's verses, sometimes with the older text beginning "Now all was wrapt in dark midnight" (BM H.1601 [521], BM G.316.f [95], Harvard, Chetham 1472). This tune was reprinted in Watts's *Musical Miscellany*, 1729–1731, II, 84, with variant first line, " 'Twas at the silent midnight Hour." It is this air which is found in Johnson's *The Village Opera*, 1729, as "Margaret's Ghost," and in Coffey's *The Devil to Pay*, 1731, as "When all was wrapt." In Ritson's *Scotish Songs*, 1794, II, 204, the ballad appears with Mallet's own amended beginning, " 'Twas at the silent solemn hour,/When night and morning meet," and with the tune in major mode.

> In glided Marg'ret's pale-ey'd Ghost,
> And stood at William's Feet.

The *Tea-Table* text may be Mallet's original version:

> 'Twas at the fearful midnight hour,
> When all were fast asleep . . .

Mallet's "final" text, appearing in his *Poems*, begins:

> 'Twas in the silent solemn hour,
> When night and morning meet . . .

5 In Thomson's 1733 edition the subtitle was dropped.

A Dublin broadside of c. 1725 without music is "Margaret and William, A Ballad," beginning "Now all was wrapt in dark Mid-Night" (BM 839.m.23 [115]), and the tune named is "Fair Rosamond," for which see "Chevy Chase." [6]

Among parodies of the eighteenth-century text the following may be mentioned: "Watty and Madge. In Imitation of William and Margaret," beginning " 'Twas at the shining mid-day hour," in *The Tea-Table Miscellany*, 1740, IV, 333. A satirical broadside of c. 1756 on the Newcastle administration, "Wonder upon Wonder; or the Cocoa Tree's Answer to the Surrey Oak," beginning " 'Twas in the Dark and dead of Night,/ Hard by St. James Square," is to the tune of "William and Margaret" (Harvard, BM 1875.d.6 [14], BM 1876.f.1 [159 and 160]).

[Willow, Willow]

In *Othello*, IV, iii, Desdemona sings some fragments of a willow song beginning "The poor soul sat sighing [*or* singing] by a sycamore tree" and adapted to a feminine character. There are a number of such songs in Elizabethan literature,[1] but those antedating the production of Shakespeare's play in 1604 have little in common with the verses sung there, except for a general similarity of the "Willow, willow" refrain.

Two broadsides of the first half of the seventeenth century do seem, however, to preserve a text from which Shakespeare worked. One is "A Louers complaint being forsaken of his Loue," beginning "A Poore soule sat sighing under a Sicamore tree" (Pepys I, 358, an edition printed for the unidentifiable "I. W."; reprinted in Percy's *Reliques*); the other has a variant title, "The Complaint of a Lover forsaken of his Love," and the first line replaces "under" with "by" (Roxburghe I, 54; printed by M. P. for Edward Wright, who flourished 1611–1656; reprinted in *RB* I, 171). Both issues call for the ballad to be sung "To a pleasant new Tune." A third text, with eight instead of the twenty-three broadside stanzas, is in BM MS Add. 15117, fol. 18, "after 1614," among

---

[6] For a detailed discussion of backgrounds, reprints, imitations, and musical settings, see Frederick Dinsdale's edition of *Ballads and Songs by David Mallet*, 1857, supplemented and corrected by A. E. H. Swaen, "Fair Margaret and Sweet William," *Archiv*, CXXXVI (1917), 40–71.

[1] See a discussion in *A Gorgeous Gallery of Gallant Inventions*, ed. Hyder E. Rollins, 1926, p. 189.

524

* In the MS, the first and second notes are E.

a group of songs with lute accompaniment. The burdens here are fuller than in *Othello* or the broadside texts, doubtless because the musical score requires greater explicitness. The anapestic tetrameter couplets forming the body of each stanza are metrically identical in all versions of the song. This is one of the finest Renaissance airs to be associated with Shakespeare's songs; it is regularly used in contemporary performances of the play and has become part of the standard repertoire of Shakespearean music (Fig. 524).[2] The song did not disappear from broadside literature until the nineteenth century. A very late exemplar in the Harvard library is a slip ballad in three stanzas, entitled "The Willow" and beginning "A poor soul sat sighing beneath a tall tree." No tune is named.

[2] For a complete transcription and a discussion of the inadequacies of earlier renderings, see John P. Cutts, "A Reconsideration of the Willow Song," *JAMS*, X (1957), 14–24. A facsimile of the manuscript song forms the frontispiece of C. F. Tucker Brooke's *The Shakespeare Songs*, 1929.

A lute setting of the 1570s, "All of grene willowe," is in Folger MS
448.16, fol. 19 (facsimile in *Shakespeare Quarterly*, IX [1958], 420), and
another version, called "All a greane willowe," is in the Thomas Dallis
MS Lute Book, 1583, p. 25 (the air is transcribed in *OEPM* I, 110).
Neither one fits the broadside text or the Shakespearean adaptation, but
the melody belongs to the Elizabethan song tradition, and the titles show
an affinity to customary refrain patterns; were the refrains explicitly disposed in extant song texts, we could doubtless demonstrate the relationship.

A version of the broadside poem was set afresh by Pelham Humphrey,
perhaps in the 1660s; it was included in John Stafford Smith's *Musica
Antiqua*, 1812, II, 171, from an unspecified source (reprinted in *OEPM*
I, 108). A form of the Humphrey tune is coupled with a parody beginning
"A Poor Soul sate sighing near a Ginger-bread Stall" in *The Second Book
of the Pleasant Musical Companion*, 1686, Part II, No. 17 (Fig. 525). E. F.
Rimbault printed a version of the song in his *Musical Illustrations of*

Percy's Reliques, 1850, p. 9, from a "MS volume of old songs and ballads, dated 1668," which he possessed but which cannot now be traced. Still another version of the Humphrey tune is used with a poem by Nicholas Rowe, "Ah Willow," beginning "To the brook and the willow that heard him complain," found in Ritson's *English Songs,* 1783 (1813, III, 25).

Wilson's Wild

"Wilson's wild," a fast and rhythmical dance tune, is found in several lute manuscripts of the late sixteenth and early seventeenth centuries: Folger MS 1601.1, fol. 3 (Fig. 526); William Ballet's MS Lute Book,

526

Original contains varied repeat of each strain.

p. 112; Cambridge University MS Dd.2.11, fol. 68ᵛ. It is set as a cittern piece in Cambridge University MS Dd.4.23, fol. 6, in the Bedford Cittern MS, fol. 7, in *A Booke of New Lessons for the Cithern & Gittern,* 1652, and in *Musick's Delight on the Cithren,* 1666. An anonymous keyboard setting is in Paris Conservatoire MS Rés. 1186, fol. 17, and New

York Public Library MS Drexel 5609, p. 103; the tune is named but music is wanting in Will Forster's MS Virginal Book, 1624, p. 70. William Byrd gave the title "Wolseys Wilde" to his arrangement in *The Fitzwilliam Virginal Book* II, 184.

I have found but one ballad calling for "Wilsons wilde": Thomas Deloney's "The Queenes visiting of the Campe at Tilsburie with her entertainment there," 1588, beginning "Within the yeare of Christ our Lord/a thousand and fiue hundreth full,/And eightie eight by just record." A copy in the British Museum, C.18.e.2, fol. 64, has been reprinted in *RB* VI, 390, and in Deloney's *Works,* ed. Mann, p. 474. The ballad is in a ten-line stanza, beginning and ending with an octosyllabic quatrain; the middle of the stanza is made up of a pair of nine-syllable lines, and the ballad fits the tune neatly.

Three ballads of the 1580s are to be sung to "Wilsons tune" or "Wilsons new tune," but their eight- or twelve-line stanzas in ballad meter do not fit "Wilson's wild." They are: "A godly and good example" (*OEB,* p. 245); "A proper newe Ballad . . . Traytors . . . executed . . . September, 1586" (London Society of Antiquaries [Lemon, *Catalogue,* No. 84]); and Deloney's "A proper new sonet declaring the lamentation of Beckles" (*A Collection of Seventy-Nine Black-Letter Ballads,* 1867, p. 81, and Mann, p. 457).

With a Fading

In Beaumont's *The Knight of the Burning Pestle,* IV, i, the Citizen's Wife says, "I will haue him dance *Fading; Fading* is a fine Iigge Ile assure you Gentlemen." E. W. Naylor, in his *Shakespeare and Music,* rev. ed., 1931, p. 82, identifies "fading" with "Rincce Fadda," an Irish country dance. In *The Winter's Tale,* IV, iv, a servant describes the ballad wares of Autolycus as including love songs with "delicate burdens of dildos and fadings"—a bit of irony, surely, for if those words seemed meaningless to the innocent, they were, nonetheless, indelicately and equivocally used in ballad refrains.

"With a fading" became a refrain tag and so a tune name. In James Shirley's *The Bird in a Cage,* 1633, IV, i, Morello extemporizes a song beginning "What other is the world then a Ball" in which "With a Fading" is a refrain with *double-entendre.* It is a nonsense burden in "The Clowns Song," beginning "The Courtier scorns us Country-Clowns," in *Sportive Wit,* 1656 (an earlier commonplace-book version, *temp.* Charles I, is in Harvard MS Eng. 686, p. 150; the verses were reprinted in *Oxford Drollery,* 1671, and with the music and three additional stanzas in *Pills,* 1719–1720, IV, 99).[1] "With a fadding" (the word is rhymed with "gadding") is cited as the tune for "The merry Forrester," a broadside of c. 1630 by Robert Guy with refrain tags all ending "kisses" or "kissing" (Pepys; reprinted in *PB* II, 153). And Thomas Jordan named the tune for a song beginning "Let's Drink and Droll and Dance and Sing" in his civic pageant *London Triumphant,* 1672, p. 13.

Another name for the tune came from its association with "The Pudding," beginning "From twelve years old, I oft have been told/A Pudding it was a delicate bit." This song is without tune direction in *Wit and Mirth,* 3d ed., 1682, p. 18, but in *Pills* III, 72 (Fig. 527), and *The*

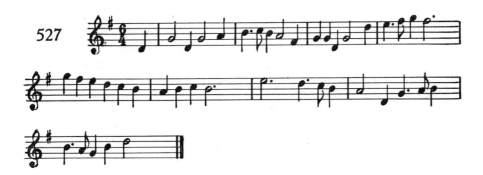

527

Convivial Songster, c. 1782, p. 68, it appears with the music of "With a fading." The "pudding" refrain is used with the same suggestive effect possessed by the "fading" burden. "The Passionate Damsel," a ballad of 1685–1688, beginning "I am a young Maid of Beauty bright," names its tune "The Vertue of the Pudding" (Lord Crawford 561, BM C.22.f.6 [159], Douce II, 176, Harvard). Half a dozen political ballads centering around William of Orange were written to the tune of "The (*or* A) Pudding," the most important being "A New Song of an Orange, To that excellent Old Tune of a Pudding, &c.," 1688, beginning "Good People come buy/The Fruit that I Cry" (Harvard; variant issues are in Pepys; reprinted in *PB* III, 334, and with date of 1689 in Wood 417 [162]). An engraved song-sheet issue (Harvard, Clark), without date or tune direction, contains "With a fading" music (Fig. 528). A variant of this ballad with identical opening stanzas is "The Rare Vertue of an Orange; Or, Popery purged and expelled out of the Nation. To the Tune of, The

---

[1] The first stanza was set as a three-voice catch by a Mr. White in *Catch that Catch Can,* 1667, p. 79. White's music has no relation to the popular tune in *Pills.*

528

Pudding" (Pepys; reprinted in *PB* III, 337). Still another is "The Orange," beginning "Good people I pray/Throw the Orange away" (Lord Crawford 449, Harvard, Yale, Texas).[2] And a fourth is "The Famous Orange: Or, an Excellent Antidote against Romish Poison," beginning "There's none can express,/Your great Happiness" (Pepys; reprinted in *PB* IV, 50). All these texts use the "Orange" refrain as an obvious play on words, but the political effect was significant in helping to popularize William in the eyes of a vast public. A few other ballads of 1689–1692 continued to name the tune "The Pudding," but "The (*or* An) Orange" quickly outstripped it and was used for some twenty-odd ballads.[3]

Among the ballads using the new "Orange" name for the tune, the following may be mentioned: three related pieces on the doubling of the excise tax in December, 1690, two taking the part of the poor on whom the levy falls, "The Brewers Benefit" and "The Bountifull Brewers: Who pays the King's Taxes out of the Poor Mens Purses" (*PB* V, 270, 266), and "The Brewers Answer" defending the trade (*PB* V, 274). Another is "The Country-Mans Kalender . . . Predictions for . . . 1692" (*BB* I, 186). The tune was still popular in 1702, when it was used for "Great Brittain's Joy . . . Queen Ann's being . . . Proclaim'd" (*PB* VII, 309). The following broadsides sung to "An Orange" or "The Orange" have apparently not been reprinted: "The Handsome Maid of Milkstreet," beginning "I am a young Maid that now am afraid" (Pepys III, 289); "The Bloody Battle at Billingsgate . . . between . . . Doll

[2] This, like "A New Song of an Orange," was reprinted in *A Collection of the Newest . . . Poems . . . against Popery*, 1689, and *Poems on Affairs of State*, 1697.

[3] Other "Pudding" ballads include "The Protestant Court of England . . . Coronation of K. William III. and Q. Mary II" (*PB* IV, 255); another edition, entitled "The Court of England. Or, The Preparation for the Happy Coronation . . . ," 1689 (BM Luttrell III, 144, Bodleian Ashmole G.16 [204]), was reprinted with the music in Watts's *Musical Miscellany*, 1729–1731, III, 36. For additional ballads to the tune, see *PB* V, 29, VI, 35, 172.

and Kate," beginning "One morning of late, hard by Billingsgate" (Pepys IV, 289); "A New Song, call'd The Bakers Frollick," beginning "I'le Sing you a Song and a true one indeed" (Pepys V, 207); "The Complaint of All the She-Traders . . . against the City Cheats," beginning "A Curse of your Shams, ye Coffee-house Dames" (Pepys V, 405); "A New Copy of Verses, Containing A Catalogue of Taylors," 1691, beginning "Young lasses draw near, good news you shall hear" (Pepys V, 433, with meaningless music); "The Jolly Porters," beginning "I pray now attend to what I have penn'd" (Pepys IV, 292); "A Market for young Men . . . where young beautiful Virgins and graz'd Widows are to be sold for Clip'd Money," beginning "You single Men all whose Money is small" (Pepys III, 250, IV, 234, Douce II, 153ᵛ); and "The Maidens Frolicksome Undertaking To Press Twenty Taylors," beginning "Late near Temple-Bar, a Frollick we hear" (Pepys IV, 276–277).[4]

Two ballads having the stanza of "With a fading" (a tetrameter quatrain plus a four-syllable refrain tag) are probably to be identified with this tune. One is "The New Compos'd Medley; or, The true Vertue of the Hop-Sack," 1685–1688, beginning "I pray draw near, and you shall hear," to the tune of "With a hop-sack" (Pepys IV, 369);[5] the other is "The Princely Scuffle," a ballad of c. 1690, beginning "All you that pass by, I pray you draw nigh," and without tune direction (Pepys; reprinted in *PB* V, 315).

Woe Is Me

James Paisible, a singer and court musician during the latter years of the seventeenth century, was also a composer of instrumental music, chiefly for the theater. His compositions for two flutes (i.e., recorders) contributed to *Thesaurus Musicus* include a Hornpipe (Second Book, 1694, pp. 38–39) to which D'Urfey wrote "A Scotch Song," beginning "Waa is me what mun I do,/drinking Waters I may rue," which appeared in

[4] A loose paraphrase of this last ballad, "The Maidens Frollick," beginning "Of late near the Strand we well understand," and reducing the number of tailors to fourteen, is reprinted in *RB* III, 402, with an answer at p. 405. A nineteenth-century slip-song version entitled "Female Pressgang," without tune direction, was printed by Pitts in Seven Dials (Harvard).

[5] "The New Broach't Heresie, or, the French Prophets Miraculous Predictions," beginning "A Crasie Brain Crew, does daily pursue," is a roman-letter ballad to the tune of "An Orange," with a burden "In a Hop-sack" (Morgan 68).

529

* Written out in full in original.

the same work, Third Book, 1695, p. 30 (Fig. 529). The tune, taking its title from D'Urfey's opening line, was introduced into *The Dancing Master*, Second Part, 1696. D'Urfey's text, expanded to four stanzas, was issued as a broadside without music, entitled "The Scotch Lover's Complaint . . . To a new Tune, much in Request" (Pepys V, 356). Two stanzas appear with music in *Pills*, 1719–1720, I, 53. The melody has pace and spirit but lacks the musical wit abounding in hornpipes by Purcell. The elaborate seventeen-line stanza (printed as nineteen in *Pills*) marks the verse as a solo piece not likely to prove popular as a street song.

Woodicock

This dance tune is found in Cambridge University MSS Dd.5.20, fol. 33^v, as divisions for bass viol (printed in *Jacobean Consort Music*, ed. Dart and Coates, *Musica Britannica*, IX, 1955, 200), and Nn.6.36, fol. 2^v, arranged for lyra viol; in *The Fitzwilliam Virginal Book* II, 138, in a setting by Giles Farnaby; in Starter's *Friesche Lust-Hof*, 1621, p. 99, as "Drinck-Liedeken," and Valerius's *Neder-Landtsche Gedenck-Clanck*, 1626, p. 198, as "Engels Woddecot, *ofte:* Datonen eens van drincken spraeck" (Fig. 530). Other Low Country settings from 1631 to 1649 un-

der the latter title or "Amarilletje mijn vriendin" are given in van Duyse, *Het Oude Nederlandsche Lied*, 1903–1908, II, 1106. A set of variations on the tune is preserved in a viola da gamba MS of c. 1660 in the Henry Watson collection, Manchester Free Reference Library (a copy of the tablature is in BM MS Add. 39566, transcribed in staff notation in BM MS Add. 38783). "Woodicock" appears in the first eight editions of *The Dancing Master*, 1651–1690; from the fourth edition it is named "Woodicock, or The Green Man."

An early seventeenth-century broadside, "A proper new Ballad, shewing a merrie iest of one Ieamie of Woodicock Hill, and his wife," beginning "One Iemie there was that dwelt in a towne," is to "a new tune, called Woodicocks Hill" (Bodleian Firth c.23 [109ᵛ]; a rotograph copy in H. E. Rollins's MS Copy-book, Harvard 25254.24.19F, fol. 24). The tune name is apparently derived from the lines "Iemie he hied to woodicock hill,/for there his businesse lay truly," though a secondary significance of woodcock=cuckold is strongly suggested by the ballad narrative. Another ballad in the same six-line stanza pattern is "The second part of Jeamye," to the tune of "Gigg-a-gogge, or Woddycocke" (*SB*, p. 189).[1] This is not a sequel of the Firth broadside, for here the protagonist is unmarried; but the *double-entendre* of "hey nonnie nonnie" is found in both pieces.

None of the extant "Woodicock" tune variants is completely satisfactory. Most lack an initial anacrusis; the *Gedenck-Clanck* possesses this but requires a division of some half notes to accommodate the anapests irregularly occurring in both ballads.

[1] On the first tune, see "Jig a jog-goo."

Would You Be a Man of Fashion?

This tune takes its name from the opening line of an anonymous song in *Choice Ayres and Songs,* Fifth Book, 1684, p. 14, with music by Capt. Simon Pack.[1] It was undoubtedly written earlier, for in 1683 an amplified form of the song with Pack's music had been issued as a broadside entitled "The Compleat Citt: or, The Man of Fashion" (Lord Crawford, Bodleian Ashmole G.16, BM C.39.k.6; reprinted in *RB* IV, 349, and *OPB,* p. 112). Words and music of the ballad were reprinted in *180 Loyal Songs,* 1685, p. 163; the original one-stanza song is found with the music in *Pills,* 1719–1720, V, 154. Another broadside containing the music is "A New way to play an Old Game," 1683 (Fig. 531), beginning "Have you heard of Forty-One Sir" (Bodleian Ashmole G.16 [104], Harvard, Clark; reprinted in *180 Loyal Songs,* p. 165).[2]

Meaningless music is found on a parody of January, 1689, "A Man in Favour, Or, The way to Preferment," beginning "Would you be a Man in Favour" (BM C.38.i.25 [1], BM C.39.k.6 [42], reprinted in *OPB,* p. 110; Pepys, reprinted in *PB* IV, 132; Wood 417 [171]). This is an expansion of "A New Song," in two stanzas, beginning "Wou'd you bee a man off Favour," issued as an engraved song sheet with its own tune (Harvard, two copies, one with MS date Oct. 26, 1688; Lord Crawford 1372); the text was reprinted in several political miscellanies (see *PB* IV, 131).

Other broadsides to the tune include: "Popery Pickled," 1689, beginning "Would you have a new Play Acted" (Library of Congress, Broadside Portfolio 266, No. 5; reprinted in *A Second Collection of the Newest . . . Poems . . . against Popery,* 1689, p. 19, and *Poems on Affairs of State,* 1704, III, 315); "Cupids Tragedy," beginning "Pritty Phillomel was so Charming," to the tune of "The new Bory; Or, Will you be a Man of Fashion," with music of the former on the sheet (BM C.22.f.6 [40], Douce I, 28[v], 49, Lord Crawford 1022, Harvard); and "The Dumb Lady," beginning "Underneath a little Mountain," to the tune of "the Doubtful Virgin; Or, the new Borey; or Will you be a Man of Fashion" (Harvard, Douce, Pepys, Roxburghe; reprinted in *RB* IV, 352). Two others offer

---

[1] This was Pack's most famous song. As a musical amateur he wrote a good deal for the theater and is by no means a negligible figure in the period. For a detailed account of the man and his work, see Willard Thorp, *Songs from the Restoration,* 1934, pp. 99–102.

[2] Still another topical song to the tune is found in *180 Loyal Songs,* p. 167, and probably represents a reprint from a broadside now lost: "The Poor Spanish Souldier's Complaint," beginning "Will you be a Reformado,/Will you lead a Hellish life?"

531

* G♯ on original sheet.

the alternative tune of "Doubting Virgin": "The Hasty Wedding," beginning "Sitting with my Dearest Dear" (*RB* VII, 203), and "Doubtful Robin," beginning "Dearest Nanny prithee tell me" (*RB* IV, 376).

In BM MS Harl. 7319 are two other contemporary parodies, one "A new Way to Honour," beginning "Wou'd you be a Man of Honour" (p. 598), the other "The true way to Honour," beginning "Wou'd you, Sir, Attain that Honour" (p. 619).

Would You Know How We Meet

"A new Catch," beginning "Would you know how we meet o're our jolly full Bowls?" with music by Henry Purcell and words by Thomas Otway, first appeared in *The Theater of Music*, Second Book, 1685, p. 19 (Fig. 532). In the next year it was included in *The Second Book of the Pleasant Musical Companion*, which went through ten editions by the 1740s.

Expanded to nine stanzas, the song was issued as a broadside under the title "The Modish London Life; or, The Merry Meeting. To an excellent New Tune. Or, My Life and my Death. Or, Now, now the

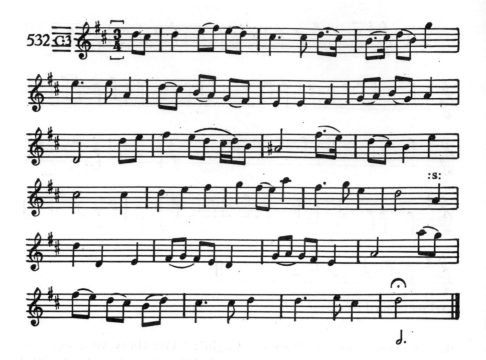

532

:s:

Fight's done," with a corrupt version of Purcell's music on the sheet (Wood 417 [178]).[1] The stanzas of six anapestic tetrameters can also be sung to the two tunes named. Purcell's air, designed as a three-voice catch, is sufficiently melodious to be sung as a solo composition. "News from the West," a ballad of 1685–1688, beginning "Come listen all you who to mirth are inclin'd" (Bodleian Ashmole G.15 [163]), is designed to be sung "To a New Tune, Or The Delights of the Bottle, Or, Would you know how we Drink." Perhaps this last may refer to Purcell's tune; unidentified music on the sheet may be that of the "New Tune."

Wully and Georgy

"A Scotch Song Sung at Tunbridge Set to Musick by Mr. Ackroyd" (Fig. 533), beginning "Wully and Georgy now beath are gean," was issued

[1] The broadside was licensed by Richard Pocock (1685–1688). Wood's annotation on the sheet: "Bought at Oxon for a new Ballad 14. Feb. 1688[/89]" implies that it was not actually fresh merchandise at that time.

533

Phrasing added by editor.

as an engraved song sheet, c. 1700 (Bagford; text reprinted in *BB* I, 94).
Words and music are in all editions of *Pills*, 1719–1720, III, 297. As
"Woolly and Georgey" the tune was added to *The Dancing Master* commencing with the eleventh edition, 1701. The first line of the song serves
as the tune name in Johnson's *The Village Opera*, 1729, and in the one-
act condensation, Phillips's *The Chamber-maid*, 1730.

Ye Commons and Peers

Jonathan Swift seems to have written the poem beginning "Ye Commons and Peers,/Pray lend me your Ears" upon the battle of Audenarde,
July 11, 1708.[1] It was published in *Poetical Miscellanies*, Sixth Part,
1709, and in the same year it appeared in *Pills* IV, 331, with music
by Richard Leveridge which eventually became the standard tune named
for the opening line (Fig. 534). Words and music were reprinted in *The
Merry Musician*, 1716, I, 259, and in *Pills*, 1719–1720, VI, 1. The text
is to be found in such miscellanies as *A Pill to Purge State-Melancholy*,
1715, and *The Hive*, 1732, IV, 219.

Four early broadside issues deserve special mention, since they were
apparently published before Leveridge's tune became well known. An

[1] The piece has also been ascribed to Congreve and Prior; Harold Williams, though
holding Swift's authorship in doubt, included the poem among attributed works in
his edition of the *Poems*.

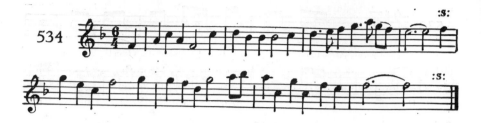

534

edition in thirteen stanzas, "Jack Frenchman's Lamentation. An Excellent
New Song," with tune title "I'll tell thee Dick, &c.," was issued by John
Morphew in 1708 (Harvard; a second Morphew edition of the same date
is in Bodleian Firth b.21 [64]; reprinted in *Poems of Jonathan Swift,* ed.
Harold Williams, 1937, III, 1078–1080). Another edition, without date
or imprint, has the same title and tune direction (BM 12350.m.18 [3]).
Still another edition with the same title contains fourteen stanzas and
has the tune direction "I'll tell the[e] Dick, &c. Or, Who can but love a
Seaman" (BM 1876.f.1 [40]). Another fourteen-stanza edition bears the
title "Jack French-Man's Defeat" (Bagford; reprinted in *BB* I, 386)
and is to be sung to "There was a Fair Maid in the North-Country, Came
Triping over the Plain," a tune on which I have no information. Of
the tunes named in other editions, I have been unable to discover "Who
can but love a Seaman"; and "I'll tell thee, Dick" does not fit the distinctive six-line stanza. An engraved song sheet of c. 1710 or earlier,
entitled "A Ballad on the Battle of Audenarde" (Harvard), contains
music which is actually "Ladies of London," rhythmically compatible
but of a length to accommodate two stanzas of the poem.

"Ye Commons and Peers" was popular enough to be introduced into
nine ballad operas, and Leveridge's tune is printed in those containing
music: Johnson's *The Village Opera,* 1729, Phillips's one-act condensation, *The Chamber-maid,* 1730, and Fabian's *Trick for Trick,* 1735.

The original verses were imitated in "A New Ballad, Occasion'd by
the Pretenders Declaration," 1722, beginning "Ye Commons and Peers,/
Ye've heard with your Ears" (Harvard, a Dublin imprint), and "The
Secret Committee. A New Ballad," beginning "Ye Commons and Peers,/
Come prick up your Ears" (BM 1850.c.10 [69c], with MS date April 13,
1742). Of the many other eighteenth-century broadsides which call for
the tune, only a sampling can be noted. The six-line stanza pattern was
a great favorite in political miscellanies of the period, and doubtless
many ballads without tune direction were intended for the tune. The
following citations, however, specifically designate the tune "Ye Commons
and Peers" or some variation of the phrase: a ballad written c. 1709 after
the fall of Tournay is "The Glorious Campaign," beginning "Alack and

a Day/Poor Monsieur they say" (Harvard); "An Irish Ballad, upon the Rev^d Mr. Francis Higgins his Tryal . . . in Dublin" begins "At a Sessions of late,/There arose a Debate" (BM 1876.f.1 [56]); another is J. P.'s "To Robert Earl of Oxford . . . on his Excess of Mirth, at the Proclaiming of . . . King George," beginning "I Thought to have sent/My due Compliment" (BM 1871.e.9 [147], reprinted in *Political Merriment*, Part II, 1714, p. 154). The tune is named "Ye Commoners and Peers" in "The Lecturers Combat," 1720, beginning "No sooner there came,/From Kingston on Thame" (BM 1850.c.10 [56]). Two Dublin ballads are "The Alderman's Guide," beginning "Kind Heav'n has granted/At last what we wanted" (BM 839.m.23 [111]), and "An Excellent new Ballad . . . Pothecary was catch'd in Bed with . . . 2 Sisters," beginning "An Apothecary Cloathed in Black" (BM 839.m.23 [145]). "A Sequel to Britannia Excisa," beginning "Good People draw near,/To my Ballad give Ear," is to "Ye Commons and Peers" (BM C.116.i.4 [19], undated; another edition is in BM 162.n.71, a pamphlet of 1733); the ballad to which it is the answer is "Britannia Excisa: Britain Excis'd," 1733, directed "To be Sung in Time, and to some Tune"—doubtless that of the sequel (BM C.116.i.4 [18], Harvard; reprinted in Percival's *Walpole Ballads*, p. 63). "Swaddling John's Address to the Publick," beginning "All People draw near;/Cit, Rustick, and Peer," gives the three opening lines of the Swiftian poem as the name of the tune (BM 1890.e.5 [162], an imprint of Dublin, 1748).

The Yellow-Haired Laddy

This tune is named on a broadside issued by Philip Brooksby, who was one of the important figures in the ballad publishing fraternity from 1670 until at least 1695. The title is "The Country-mans care in choosing a Wife . . . Tune of, I'le have one I love &c. Or, The Yellow hair'd Laddy," and it begins "I am a brisk Youngster,/and fain would be Wed" (Pepys, Lord Crawford, Douce, Harvard, Yale, Roxburghe; reprinted in *RB* III, 597). The first tune name derives from the ballad's refrain, "Then I'le have one I love,/though I live the less while."

I have found no seventeenth-century ballad of "The Yellow-haired Laddy" which might be the source of the other tune name. But a song of Allan Ramsay's beginning "In April when Primroses paint the sweet Plain" appears in his *Poems*, 1721, and in *The Tea-Table Miscellany*, 1723, with the title "The Yellow-hair'd Laddie." Alexander Stuart's

535

Musick for Allan Ramsay's Collection of Scots Songs, c. 1725, p. 84, includes a tune by this name (Fig. 535), and it is found with Ramsay's poem in a number of song-sheet issues (BM H.1601 [259], BM G.309 [92]; Harvard, several editions), and in such collections as William Thomson's *Orpheus Caledonius,* 1725, No. 7, Walsh's *British Musical Miscellany,* 1734–1736, IV, 78, *Calliope, or English Harmony,* 1739–1746, I, 72, Domenico Corri's *Select Collection of . . . Songs,* c. 1779, III, 93, Alexander Smith's *Musical Miscellany,* 1786, p. 282; Johnson's *Scots Musical Museum,* 1787–1803, II, 127, and Ritson's *Scotish Songs,* 1794, I, 13. Another *Tea-Table* song, the anonymous "Ye Shepherds and Nymphs that adorn the gay Plain," is directed to be sung to "The yellow hair'd Laddie," and words and music are coupled in a single-sheet edition (BM G.316.f [117]), in Watts's *Musical Miscellany,* 1729–1731, I, 106, in *The Merry Musician,* c. 1729, II, 132, and in Ritson I, 76. The tune, sometimes called "Yellow-hair'd Lady," is used in five ballad operas, including Cibber's *Patie and Peggy,* 1730, *The Jovial Crew,* 1731, and Phillips's *The Mock Lawyer,* 1733. "Ye Shepherds and Nymphs" in Gay's *Achilles,* 1733, is a different tune. Still other music appears on a late eighteenth-century song sheet, "The Yellow Hair'd Laddie As Now Sung by Miss Wright at Vauxhall" (Huntington, BM 1994.a [186]).

We cannot be sure whether the tune named on the seventeenth-century broadside is the same as the "Yellow-haired Laddy" which evidently owes much of its popularity to Ramsay. Musically the air has affinities with a quantity of synthetic Scotch songs made in London during the closing years of the century. But in the absence of any trace of the tune itself before the 1720s, we cannot confidently associate it with the broadside, even though the two are a good fit. Perhaps the missing link between the centuries is "The auld yellow hair'd Laddie," beginning "The yellow hair'd Laddie sat down on yon brae," which Ramsay included in the 1733 edition of the *Tea-Table* II, 201, as if it were his own song, but which may be simply an old piece brushed up.[1]

[*You I Love by All That's True*]

An anonymous poem beginning "You I love, by all that's true" was set to music by Charles Taylor in *Choice Ayres and Songs,* Fourth Book, 1683, p. 53 (Fig. 536). Words and music were reprinted in *A Collection of Twenty Four Songs,* 1685, sig. B2, and in *Pills,* 1719–1720, V, 336. The

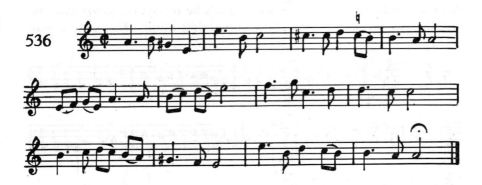

536

words were reprinted in *180 Loyal Songs,* 1685, p. 321, and *The Hive,* 3d ed., 1726, I, 43.

During the years 1685–1688 the song was twice reworked and expanded to fill a broadside. "The Wounded Lover's Lamentation to Silvia," beginning "You I love, (by Jove) I do," incorporates the song into the opening stanzas of the ballad and directs that it be sung "To an Excellent New Tune, Sung at Court" (Lord Crawford, BM C.22.f.6, Douce; reprinted in *RB* VII, 202). The other broadside, with similar tune direction, is entitled "The London Lads Lamentation to Cupid"; it begins "Cloes Face is Heav'n to me" and its three final stanzas comprise a

[1] In Johnson's *Scots Musical Museum* II, 128, it immediately follows the familiar tune which accompanies Ramsay's "In April," and is clearly intended to be sung to that tune. In the *Tea-Table* "The auld yellow hair'd Laddie" appeared without tune direction.

version of the original song (Pepys, Douce, Euing, Lord Crawford, Roxburghe; reprinted in *RB* VII, 109). Presumably the court tune was Taylor's.

You London Lads Be Merry,

or Moggie's Jealousy

On June 1, 1684, Jonah Deacon received a license to publish "A new song of Moggie's jelousie, or Jockie's vindication." Two editions of this ballad survive, with titles following the Stationers' Register entry, and both are to be sung to "You London Lads be merry; or, Woo't thou be wilfull still my Joe." [1] One issue, containing music (Fig. 537), begins

537

Original barred as 3/4; no time signature.

"Where art thou ganging my Moggy" (Huntington, Harvard); the other, without music, begins "There was an a bonny young Lad" but, with the second stanza, takes up the text of the other issue (Pepys, Douce, Roxburghe; reprinted in *RB* VI, 171). Luttrell's MS date of Nov. 20, 1682, on the Huntington copy may be in error, or the earlier issue may not have been licensed. The identity of the jig tune on the broadside is established by the presence of variant music (printed in 6/4 time, thus

[1] On the second tune name, see Ebsworth's discussion in *RB* IV, 543–544, which suggests a possible derivation but does not lead us to an air with this title.

obscuring the essential 9/4 rhythm) in *180 Loyal Songs*, 1685, p. 160, where it is called "Ye London Lads be merry." This same collection contains (p. 162) a song beginning "Ye London lads be merry/your Parliament friends are gone" which is apparently the source of the tune title; I have been unable to trace the verses to any earlier appearance than in *120 Loyal Songs*, 1684, and no broadside copy seems to have been preserved, although it is likely that it was originally so printed.[2]

At least two ballads name the tune "There was an a bonny young Lad," from the opening line of "Moggie's Jealousy." The first is "The Merciful Father," an account of the Duke of Monmouth's return to favor, and hence it is to be dated late in 1683; it begins "You Gallants of Country and City" (Pepys; reprinted in *RB* V, 641). Another is "The Faithful Shepherd," beginning "When Tommy became first a Lover" (Lord Crawford, Douce, Roxburghe; reprinted in *RB* VI, 174).

"Moggie's Jealousy" must have been an instant success, for within three weeks of its registry Deacon entered two other ballads which were to be sung to the tune of "Moggie's Jealousie." "The Surprizd Shepherdess," licensed on June 10, 1684, begins "There was an a bonny young Lass," echoing the opening of the earlier ballad (Douce II, 198^v, Lord Crawford 1121, Pepys III, 199, BM C.22.f.6 [184], Harvard). "The Crafty Miss," beginning "There was an Excise-man so fine" (Pepys, Lord Crawford, Douce, BM C.22.f.6, Roxburghe; reprinted in *RB* VIII, 553), was licensed on June 19, and its title became another name by which the tune was known. Thus "The West-Country Wedding," beginning "Now listen and be not mistaken," is sung to "The Crafty Miss, Or, Moggies Jealousie" (Pepys IV, 108), and "The Scotch Souldiers Kindness," a ballad of the following year, beginning "Scotch Jemmy, and Jockey, and Sawny," gave the tune direction simply as "The Crafty Miss" (Lord Crawford, Harvard, Roxburghe; reprinted in *RB* VIII, 472).

A dozen other ballads of an amatory cast were sung to "Moggie's

[2] This ballad, written on the occasion of the convening of Parliament in Oxford, March, 1681, was reprinted in *RB* V, 24, probably from one of the *Loyal Songs* volumes, though Ebsworth specifies no source. A contemporary manuscript copy, without title or tune direction, beginning "Ye Loondon Ladds be sorrey/youre Parliament frinds are gain," is in Bodleian Ashmole G.16 (155), and a modern transcript of another seventeenth-century manuscript copy may be found in Harvard MS Eng. 633, p. 120. Still other texts are in BM MS Harl. 6913, p. 205, and MS Harl. 6914, p. 19. The version in *120 Loyal Songs* is to the tune "You Yorkshire Lads be merry," on which I have no information; the first line reads ". . . merry" but in the first-line index it is ". . . sorry." It seems likely that the latter form was the original.

A parody of c. 1683, "You Loyal Lads be merry,/For Perkin that State Buffoon," is in *120 Loyal Songs* and *180 Loyal Songs*. Ebsworth's reprint in *RB* V, 470, is evidently from one of these collections, but his reading of the first line is ". . . sorry."

Jealousy."[3] Some of these will be found in *RB,* vols. VII and VIII. The following do not seem to have been reprinted: "The Debtford Wedding," beginning "At Debtford there was such a Wedding,/the like before never was known" (Douce I, 54); "The West-Country Revell," beginning "All you that in mirth do delight" (Douce II, 257ᵛ); "John the Glover, and Jane his Servant," beginning "O Jane, come and sit thee down by me" (Douce I, 103ᵛ); "The Countrey Clerk," beginning "There was an Attorney of Lincoln" (Pepys III, 264); "Invincible Love," beginning "My Dearest come hither to me" (Pepys III, 147); "Roger and Mary," beginning "As Roger and Mary were toyling" (Douce II, 186, Harvard, Lord Crawford 134 and 135, BM C.22.f.6 [72]); and "The Shepherds Complaint," beginning "Oh Cupid thou now art too cruel" (Douce II, 202, Pepys III, 217, Lord Crawford 931, BM C.22.f.6 [177]; another edition, Lord Crawford 930, Harvard).

Young Jemmy

The history of this tune begins with Aphra Behn's poem on Monmouth, "Young Jemmey was a Lad/Of Royal Birth and Breeding," which was circulating by 1681 and was printed among pieces by other authors in Joan Philips's *Female Poems on Several Occasions,* 2d ed., 1682. In the same year it appeared in *Wit and Mirth,* 3d ed., p. 98, and in 1684 Mrs. Behn included it in her *Poems upon Several Occasions.* A broadside version expanding the original four stanzas to ten is "Young Jemmy, Or, The Princely Shepherd," sung "To a pleasant New Play-house Tune. Or, In Ianuary last, Or, The Gowlin" (Lord Crawford, Douce, Harvard, Roxburghe; reprinted in *RB* IV, 658).[1]

Another ballad related to Mrs. Behn's text exists in two editions, one entitled "Young Jemmy. An Excellent New Ballad. To an Excellent New Tune," 1681 (BM 82.l.8 [62], Harvard, Huntington), the other, without

---

[3] No alternative tunes are named on this group of ballads, but Douce copies contain manuscript notes of other tunes which seemed preferable or more familiar. These include "Give ear to a Frolicksome Ditty" (i.e., "The Rant"), "Collins Complaint" (i.e., a name for "Grim King of the Ghosts" to which Nicholas Rowe's familiar poem was set), and "O so ungrateful a Creature" (a common tune of the late seventeenth century for which no satisfactory music has been preserved).

[1] On the second and third tunes, see "In January last" and "London is a fine town." The "Play-house Tune" immediately took its name from the broadside title or first line.

date, called "Englands Darling, Or Great Britains Joy . . . on that Noble Prince James Duke of Monmouth," to the tune of "Young Jemmy, or Philander" (Pepys, Euing, Lord Crawford, Harvard, Yale, Roxburghe; reprinted in *RB* IV, 503). It begins "Young Jemmy is a Lad/That's Royally descended," and while echoing occasional formulas of the original poem, it is more pointedly political. The sympathy with Monmouth, "hated of none but Papist and Tory," is unmistakable.

In honor of the other James—Duke of York—Matthew Taubman imitated the broadside text in a song "Old Jemmy," beginning "Old Jemmy is a Lad,/right lawfully descended," which he published with music (Fig. 538) in his *An Heroick Poem . . . With Some choice Songs,*

1682, p. 11. In the previous year his text had been expanded from four stanzas to ten and issued as a broadside: "Old Jemmy. An Excellent New Ballad," to the tune of "Young Jemmy" (BM Luttrell, Wood 276a, Wood 417, Huntington, Harvard; reprinted in *RB* IV, 667); the ten-stanza text appears in *180 Loyal Songs,* 1685, p. 20, with the music.[2]

The tune is also found in *The Dancing Master,* 6th ed., 1679, Supplement, p. 21, and in the body of the seventh and succeeding editions. It is in Humphry Salter's *The Genteel Companion . . . for the Recorder,* 1683, p. 19, in Thomas Greeting's *The Pleasant Companion . . . for the Flagelet,* 1683, No. 74, and in *Apollo's Banquet,* 5th ed., 1687. D'Urfey set his eight-line "Immortal Lovers" to the music in his *New Collection of Songs and Poems,* 1683, p. 9. The tune is named and the music re-

2 "Old Jemmy" became another name for the tune in "A New Song on the Arrival of Prince George And his Intermarriage with the Lady Ann," 1683, beginning "Prince George at last is come" (Manchester I, 4, Clark; reprinted in *180 Loyal Songs,* p. 23).

printed in a broadside "Tom-Son his Repetition to his Wife; Bewailing his present state," beginning "Will you hear of Tom'sons Dream," presumably on the vicissitudes of the stationer Nathaniel Thompson (Wood 417 [151], Lord Crawford 1355).

At least seven other broadsides were sung to the tune of "Young Jemmy." They include: "Jemmy & Anthony," 1682, beginning "Monmouth is a Brave Lad,/The like's not in our City" (Roxburghe; reprinted in *RB* V, 169); "The Triumph at an End, Or, The Tyranness Defeated," beginning "How bright art thou whose Starry eyes," to the tune of "How bright art thou &c. Or, Young Jamey" (Lord Crawford, Roxburghe; reprinted in *RB* VI, 76); [3] "The Protestants Wish for King William's Good Success in Ireland," 1690, beginning "Brave William is a Lad/Of Warlike Loyns Descended" (Pepys; reprinted in *PB* V, 149); and "The West Country Nymph," beginning "Come all you Maidens fair/and listen to my Ditty" (Douce, Lord Crawford, Roxburghe; reprinted in *RB* VI, 441). The following have apparently not been reprinted: "The Loyal Seamans Happy Return," beginning "No longer will I grieve" (Pepys IV, 170), and "The Farewel, and Sorrowful Lamentation of Mr. William Gregg . . . Executed for High-Treason . . . 28th of April, 1708," beginning "Oh! Mr. William Gregg/What mean you by this deed," to the tune of "Young Jemmy was a Lad: or, Monmouth's fall" (Morgan 19).[4] A ballad of 1689 called "The Soldiers Glory," beginning "Fie sluggish Country Man," names the tune "Old Jemmy is a Lad, of Royal Birth and Breeding," scrambling the beginnings of Taubman's and Mrs. Behn's songs (Pepys; reprinted in *PB* IV, 343).

The "German Gentleman" who wrote *A View of London and Westminster,* 2d ed., 1725, noted that contemporary sympathy for the Pretender was openly expressed without interference, and that in Cranburn-Alley "a Fellow stands eternally bawling out his *Pye-Corner* Pastorals in behalf of *Dear Jemmy, Lovely Jemmy,* &c." (p. 10). None of those pieces have come down to us in print, and we can only speculate whether they were sung to the tune of "Young Jemmy." That the tune was kept alive we do know, however, from its use in ballad operas, from Johnson's *The Village Opera,* 1729, *Love and Revenge,* c. 1729, and Odingsells' *Bays's Opera,* 1730, to Wilder's *The Gentleman Gardiner,* 1751, the latter based on *The Village Opera.*

[3] I have found no music for "How bright art thou." The piece, written in ballad-meter octaves, cannot easily be sung to "Young Jemmy," a tune perfectly suited to the 6.7.6.7.8.6.8.6 stanza usually associated with it.

[4] I have not found "Monmouth's fall" as the title of a ballad or the name of a tune. "Monmouth's Downfal" is a ballad of 1685 sung to "Hark the thundering cannons roar," q.v., written in a stanza pattern not congruent with that of "Young Jemmy."

Young Phaon

This tune takes its name from the opening "Young Phaon strove the bliss to taste/But Sappho still deny'd" of a song which first appeared in Charles Davenant's *Circe*, 1677, IV, ii. With music by John Banister it was reprinted in *Choice Ayres & Songs*, Second Book, 1679, p. 10 (Fig. 539), and in *Pills*, 1719–1720, IV, 287. The words are found in *The Art of Courtship*, 1686, sig. A8, and *The Aviary*, c. 1750, p. 652. Banister's

tune is also in *Youth's Delight on the Flagelet*, 9th ed., c. 1690, and in Dr. John Leyden's MS Lyra Viol Book of about the same date (G. F. Graham transcript, No. 44).

The song was expanded from two to twelve stanzas in a broadside entitled "Loves Conquest, or, Take her in the Humour. . . . To a New Pleasant Tune, Or, Amoret and Phillis" (Douce I, 128; the sheet contains the added MS tune direction: "Hy boys up go Wee"). The "New Pleasant Tune" is evidently Banister's, and "Amoret and Phillis," q.v., is Nicholas Staggins's air which appeared in the 1679 collection a few pages before Banister's song.[1]

A ballad of c. 1679–1680 unrelated to "Loves Conquest" is "The Con-

[1] Both the broadside and the *Art of Courtship* version begin "Young Pheon strove the bliss to taste,/but Strapho still deny'd," and the latter also names the tune "Amoret and Phillis." In an undated eighteenth-century edition of *The Art of Courtship* issued by the Petticoat Lane bookseller L. How, the names in the opening lines are respectively Strephon and Phæon, the latter now feminine.

stant Lovers Mortal Mistake," beginning "Young Phaon sate upon the brink/to view the silver stream." Its tune title "Young Phaon" is apparently not drawn from the opening line but is named for the lines already associated with Banister's tune (Lord Crawford, Harvard, Roxburghe; reprinted in *RB* III, 557).

Some fifteen other broadsides call for "Young Phaon," and, because of the commonness of the double ballad-meter stanza, the tune is often named along with older and perhaps more familiar airs. Thus in "The Subtle Damosels Advice" it is an alternative to "Jenny Gin," "The fair one let me in," or "Busie Fame" (BM C.22.f.6 [182], Lord Crawford 417). "The Amorous Petitioner" can be sung to "Cloris full of harmless thought, Young Phaon, Busie Fame, or the Lanthorn Horns grow dimn" (Pepys III, 109). "Popery Unvail'd," beginning "Hold fast thy Sword and Scepter Charles/sad times are coming on," is to "Young Pheon" (Douce II, 174ᵛ), and "Loyalty unfeigned," beginning "Hold fast thy Sword & Scepter Charles/sad Times may else come on," but thereafter exhibiting no verbal parallels to "Popery Unvail'd," has the tune direction "Busie Fame, Young Pheon, or, The Fathers Exhortation" (Lord Crawford, Harvard, Roxburghe; reprinted in *RB* IV, 640).[2]

A late seventeenth-century edition of "Flora's Departure," beginning "Dame Flora in her rich Array," is to "Young Phaon: Or, Busie Fame" (Roxburghe; reprinted in *RB* VI, 103); an eighteenth-century issue with the same title but a variant opening line, "Fair Flora beautiful and gay," is to the tune "Wheel of Fortune," for which I have found no music (Yale). "The Charming Eccho," beginning "As I was walking all alone,/ one Evening fair and clear," can be sung to "Oh love whose unconfined Wings; Or, Busie Fame: Or, Young Pheon" (Douce I, 47ᵛ, Pepys III, 187); for the first tune, see "When love with . . ."

"The Mournful Lovers Last Farewel," beginning "One night when all the Village slept," is to be sung to the tune named for the first line, q.v., or to "Young Phæon" (Douce II, 157ᵛ). A final ballad with multiple tune directions is "Unfortunate Strephon," 1685, beginning "Long Sporting on the flowery plain"; it can be sung to its own tune, named for the first line, or to "Young Strephon fain the Bliss would Tast" (i.e., "Young Phaon"), or to "Jenny Ginn" (Pepys III, 383).

Among broadsides naming only "Young Phaon," the following are worth noting simply because they do not seem to have been reprinted: "The Shepherds Joy Renewed," beginning "Come mourn with me ye Shepherds all" (Pepys IV, 53), and "Strephons Complaint For the Death of his Daphne . . . Sung at Winchester the 24th . . . September, 1684.

---

[2] A ballad "Father's exhortacon" was registered in 1675 but no copies seem to have survived. I have not found a tune of this name. "Hold fast . . ." became a broadside tune name with its own music, q.v.

by a Lady of Honour, named E. G.," beginning "What art thou fled unto thy Bed/Of Earth for want of me" (BM 1876.f.1 [25], Bodleian Ashmole G.15 [170], Clark).

Your Humble Servant, Madam

This tune takes its name from the title and burden of "Your humble Servant Madam . . . To a very fine Northern Tune," a ballad issued by William Gilbertson c. 1662, beginning "I am a Blade,/That from an old Trade,/Have taken out a new one" (Douce, Roxburghe; reprinted in *RB* III, 576). Of the two sequels, "The Ladyes Vindication: Being the Womens Answer, to Your humble Servant Madame. To the same Tune,"

beginning "The city has,/No Knave so base," is also a Gilbertson imprint, and the one known copy contains a MS date of 1662 (Roxburghe; reprinted in *RB* III, 582). The other was doubtless issued contemporaneously, though the extant copies are from the next decade; it is "The Counterfeit Court Lady: or, An Answer to, Your Humble Servant Madam," beginning "I am a Lass/That doth surpass" (Euing, Harvard, Yale, Roxburghe; reprinted in *RB* III, 579). Here the tune is named "Your Humble servant Madam," as it is on one other ballad of the 1670s, "The Cuckolds Dream," beginning "When Flora with rich Tapestry" (Wood E.25 [82], Rawlinson 89).

I have found no contemporary music for "Your humble servant, madam." The original ballad is, however, parodied in Isaac Bickerstaffe's comic opera, *Love in a Village,* 1763, p. 22, where the second section of a medley is a footman's song beginning "Behold a Blade who knows his trade,/In chamber, Hall, or Entry" (Fig. 540). The tune will fit the broadsides of the previous century, and since the opera music is a pastiche of popular and "composed" song tunes, it is possible that the medley air has some historical basis, even though no traces of seventeenth-century origin remain. In *RB* III, 575, Chappell suggested that the broadsides might have been sung to a seventeenth-century dance tune "Have at thy coat, old woman," q.v. There is, to be sure, a resemblance between the beginning of the dance tune and the initial phrase of the second strain of the opera air. Beyond that, however, the two tunes are unlike, and the dance tune will not fit the meter of the broadsides.

INDEX OF AUTHORS, COMPOSERS, PUBLISHERS, AND
COLLECTORS OF BALLADS AND BALLAD TUNES

Rachmaninov, Sergey, 217
Raleigh, Sir Walter, 121, 742, 748
Ralph, James, 152, 157, 168, 169, 175, 418, 482, 523, 539, 554, 563, 594, 677, 694, 706, 773
Ramondon, Lewis, 19, 55, 574, 772–773
Ramsay, Allan, xxxi, 33–34, 52, 71, 124, 134, 135, 154, 213, 222, 236, 247, 253, 254, 273, 282, 357, 367, 377, 402, 458, 472, 506–507, 550, 560–562, 563, 574, 628, 635, 638–639, 662, 706, 786–787, 788, 803–804, 805
Ravenscroft, Edward, 180
Ravenscroft, Thomas, 28, 165, 326, 398–399, 457, 534, 596, 609, 716
Rawlins, Thomas, 229
Raymund, John, 349
Reading, John, 318–319, 525
Records, Charles, 95, 731
Reed, Joseph, 551, 605
Respighi, Ottorino, 513
Rich, Barnabe, 271
Richardson, Samuel, 94
Rigby, Richard, 209, 582
Rimbault, E. F., 29, 30–31, 127, 237, 247, 264, 341, 386, 428, 607, 708, 709, 790–791
Ritson, Joseph, x, xxxi, 16, 28, 29, 33, 68, 71, 105, 107–108, 120, 171, 187, 197, 222, 246, 253–254, 264, 281, 298, 326, 348, 369, 402, 428, 458, 472, 473, 500, 537, 543, 548, 558, 590, 591, 598, 610, 616, 676, 707, 737, 768, 787, 791, 804
Robins, Thomas, 73, 117, 337, 400, 610, 680
Robinson, Thomas, 57, 60, 72, 80, 243, 258, 293, 323, 396, 469, 536, 611–612, 618, 679, 739–740, 753
Rochester, Earl of, 20, 105, 474–475
Rogers, Elizabeth, xix, 32, 95, 206, 209, 214, 331, 457, 512, 518, 527, 576, 765, 773
Rollins, Hyder, x, xxv, xxix, xxx, xxxi, 10–11, 37, 42, 79, 93, 97, 99, 139, 144, 158, 195–196, 234, 324, 359–360, 362, 363, 371, 420, 427, 435, 438, 447, 453, 497, 515, 526, 530, 531, 703, 726, 742, 747, 797
Rosseter, Philip, 35, 754
Rowe, Nicholas, 281–282, 808
Rowlands, Samuel, 130, 666

Rowley, William, 58, 129, 163, 228–229, 457, 675–676, 742
Russell, D., 282
Rutherford, David, 303, 407, 504
Ryan, Lacy, 124, 169, 179, 334, 386, 474, 550, 563, 649, 650, 727, 775

Sackville, Charles, 344, 489–490, 648
Salter, Humphry, 4, 23, 66, 67, 134, 217, 279, 285, 287, 306, 321, 344, 380, 382, 404, 417, 507, 545, 601, 631, 669–670, 683, 809
Sanderson, John, 752
Scarlatti, Domenico, 217
Scheidt, Samuel, 228
Schmid, Bernhard, 43
Scott, Samuel, 178
Scott, Thomas, 482, 635
Scrope, Sir Carr, 19, 557–558
Sedley, Sir Charles (1639?–1701), 12, 254, 335, 376, 691
Sedley, Sir Charles (18th c.), 334
Selden, John, xxix–xxx
Sempill, Francis, 207, 213
Settle, Elkanah, xvi, 359
Shadwell, Thomas, 1, 12, 25, 63, 67, 111, 170, 220, 430
Shakespeare, William, 61, 79, 86, 120, 125, 237, 260, 270–271, 302, 325, 346, 392, 411, 420, 448, 534, 571, 595, 661, 714, 742, 788–790
Shanne, Richard, 587, 588
Sharpham, Edward, 677, 728
Sheeles, John, 24
Shield, William, 507
Shirley, John, 215, 228, 255–256, 271, 536, 668, 757, 781, 792
Sime, David, 335
Simpson, Thomas, 60
Sinkler, Margaret, 494, 562, 574
Skelton, John, 241
Slatyer, William, 11, 36, 142, 205, 215, 743, 754
Smith, Alexander, 55, 213, 254, 335, 544, 636, 730, 735, 804
Smith, James, xxxiii, 273–274, 400, 577, 645
Smith, Robert, 62, 181–183, 184, 220–222, 384
Smith, Thomas, 640

INDEX OF TITLES, FIRST LINES, TUNE NAMES, AND REFRAINS OF BALLADS

Tune names are printed in italics. Titles, first lines, and refrains are printed in roman type, titles being enclosed in double, refrains in single quotation marks.

· 826 ·

As I was ranging the forest of fancy, 93
As I was upon the way, 26
As I was walking all alone I heard a man lamenting, 446
As I was walking all alone one evening fair and clear, 78, 762, 812
As I was walking forth I chanced for to see, 9
As I was walking forth of late, 292
As I was walking in the fields, 623
As I was walking in the shade, 172
As I was walking of late, 547
As I was walking over a plain, 347
As I was walking through Hyde Park as I used to do, 415
As I was walking under a grove, 373
As I was wandering all alone, 122, 511
As I was wandering on the way, 189
As I went forth one morning fair, 505
As I went forth one summer's day, 58
As I went forth one sunshining day, 572
As I went forth to take the air, 22, 564
As I went forth to view the plain, 55
As I went forth to view the spring upon a morning early, 54, 55
As I went forth to view the spring which Flora had adorned, 55, 154, 391
As I went through the north country, 446
As I went to Tottenham, 465
As I went to Tottenham upon a market day, 466
As I went to Walsingham, 741
As it fell on a holy day, 399, 400
As it fell out on a long summer's day, 785
As it fell out one Whitsunday, 403
As Jenny Crack and I, 366
As Jenny sat under a sycamore tree, 379
As Joan was walking o'er the green, 682–683
As Jockey and Jenny one evening were walking, 632
As Johnny met Jenny a-going to play, 379
As Johnny met Jenny on a summer's day, 378
As May in all her youthful dress, 21–22
As May in all her youthful dress, 21
As May was in her youthful dress, 22
As on a day Sabina fell asleep, 624
As on a sunshine summer's day, 682
As Phoebus in the lustrous air, 446

As Robin was riding one day to a fair, 497
As Roger and Mary were toiling, 808
As Roger did rise in the morning betimes, 610
As she lay sleeping in her bed, 658
As Strephon did unfold his flocks, 213
As Strephon wandered 'midst the dales, 540
As Sylvia in a forest lay, 785
As Thomas and Mary did meet, 417
As through Saint Albans I did pass, 726
As Tom met Roger upon the road, 307
As two men was walking down by the seaside, 224, 360
As walking forth to view the plain, 55
As Watkins walked by the way, 746
As you came from that holy land of Walsingham, 742
'Ash and the oak and the ivy tree, The,' 353
Assist me Apollo and help my conceit, 132
Assist me muses with your power divine, 698
Assist me some good sprite, 333
At a sessions of late, 803
At Charlton there was a fair, 417
At Deptford there was such a wedding, 808
At home would I be in my own country, 353, 752
At length the seaman he came home, 162
At London there's a mayor, 462
At night when all souls were asleep, 213
At Rome there is a terrible rout, 276, 278
At the first beginning of Sellenger's round, 646
At the foot of a willow, 23–25, 782
At the foot of a willow, 23
At the sign of the horse, 735
At the sign of the lion, 735
'At up tails all,' 727
'At Watton town's end at Watton town's end,' 461
At Westminster was such a match, 417
At Winchester was a wedding, 416
Attend and give ear good Christians to me, 497
Attend and you shall hear, 333
Attend good people all, 604
Attend good people lay by scoffs and scorns, 228

Come buy my new ballet, 244
Come cease your songs of cuckold's row, 146
Come cheer up my lads let us haste to the main, 301
Come cheer up my lads 'tis to glory we steer, 299
Come cheer up your hearts, 222
Come come away to the temple and pray, 767
Come come beloved Londoners, 179
Come come come come what shall I say, 784
Come come my brave gold, 199
Come cut again the game's not done, 348
Come fill it up and give me a brimmer boy, 632
Come follow follow all, 676
Come follow follow me, 677
Come follow follow me those that good fellows be, 676
Come follow follow me to the alehouse we'll march all three, 676
Come follow follow me you fairy elves that be, 676
Come follow my love, 365, 374, 589
Come follow your leader follow, 676
Come Frances come make haste, 226
Come free Britons let's all rejoice, 92
Come friend if thy leisure permit thee to stay, 62
Come friends and unto me draw near, 329
Come from the temple away to the bed, 38, 65
Come from the temple to the bed, 38
Come gallants and listen unto me a while, 220
Come gallants and welcome partake of my cheer, 409
Come gentle herdman sit with me, 258
Come gentlemen all and listen a while, 610
Come grant me come lend me, 779
Come hearken to me whilst the truth I do write, 131
Come hearken to me young maidens all, 634
Come here lady muses and help me to sing, 778
Come here you brave gallants, 473

Come here's to the nymph that I love, 550
Come hither all you who to love never knew, 662
Come hither friends and listen unto me, 739
Come hither learned sisters, 713
Come hither mine host come hither, 291
Come hither my dear Betty, 637
Come hither my jovial blades, 547
Come hither my own sweet Betty, 501
Come hither my own sweet duck, 116–119, 133, 367, 769
Come hither my own sweet duck, 116
Come hither my pretty Sue, 26
Come hither the merriest of all the nine, 44
Come hither thou seaman brave, 742
Come hither to me and I will declare, 143
Come hither Topham come, 333
Come hither you merriest of all the land, 45
Come hostess fill the pot, 291
Come Jack let's drink a pot of ale, 348
Come Jenny come Molly come Kitty come Dolly, 704
Come join hand in hand, 300
Come jolly Bacchus god of wine, 92
Come let us all to the wedding, 639
Come let us be frolic, 725
Come let us be frolic and gay, 725
Come let us cheer our hearts with lusty wine, 592
Come let us joyful anthems raise, 563
Come let us leave the town, xvi
Come let us merry be brave boys, 212
Come let us mourn for well we may, 589
Come let us prepare, 235
Come let us prepare, 235
'Come let's dally shall I shall I,' 190
Come let's sing to the honor and praise, 454
Come let's take the Rump, 728
Come let's to the tavern, 185
Come light and listen you gentlemen all, 610
Come listen a while and here I will relate, 172
Come listen a while and I here will unfold, 409
Come listen a while and I will relate, 408

· 841 ·

Cuckolds all awry, 147
'Cuckolds all of a row,' 147
"Cuckolds' Haven," 676
"Cuckoldy Cook, The," 536
"Cuckoo's Commendation, The," 465
Cuddy and Peggy together did meet, 547
"Cumberland Laddie," 425
"Cumberland Lass, The," 427
"Cumberland Nelly," 424
"Cunning Age, The," 779
"Cunning Northern Beggar, The," 712
"Cup of Old Stingo, A," 689
Cupid leave thy tyrannizing, 45
"Cupid Turned Tinker," 236
"Cupid's Conquest," 22
Cupid's courtesy, 145, 147–151, 625
"Cupid's Courtesy," 147, 625
"Cupid's Cure," 148
"Cupid's Delight," 338
"Cupid's Kindness to Constant Corydon,"
  93
"Cupid's Masterpiece," 662
"Cupid's Power," 63
Cupid's revenge, 525
"Cupid's Revenge," 346
"Cupid's Tragedy," 507, 798
Cupid's trepan, 151–153, 582
"Cupid's Trepan," 151
"Cupid's Triumph," 148
"Cupid's Victory over the Virgin's Heart,"
  770–771
Curse of your shams, A, 795
Curse on blind Cupid his name I do hate,
  A, 187
Curse on the zealous and ignorant crew,
  A, 200
Cushion dance, The, 644–645
"Cutpurse, The," 568
Cyclops, The, 429

"Daemon Lover, The," 369–370
Dagon's fall, 371
"Dagon's Fall," 5
Dainty come thou to me, 15, 16, 577, 578
"Dainty Damsel's Dream, The," 658
"Dairymaid's Tragedy, The," 573
"Dairymaid's Tragedy, An Answer to
  the," 573
Dairymaid's tragedy when I beheld, The,
  573

"Dairymaids' Mirth and Pastime, The,"
  473
Damask rose, The, 153–155, 391, 517
Damask rose nor lily fair, The, 153
Dame Flora in her rich array, 812
Dame of honor, The, 155–157
"Dame of Honor or Hospitality, The,"
  155
Damon and Pythias, 157–159
'Damon my friend is judged to die,' 158
"Damon's Triumph," 624
"Damosel's Hard Shift for a Husband,
  The," 221
"Damosel's Tragedy, The," 94
Damsel came to London town, A, 656
Damsel fair complete and fine, A, 374
Damsel I'm told, A, 152
Damsel I'm told of delicate mold, A, 152
Damsel with a knight lived of late, A, 234
Damsel's dance, The, 599
Dance after my pipe, 653
"Dance after My Pipe," 652
Dancing hobbyhorses, The, 310
"Danea Welcometh Home Her Lord Dio-
  phon," 195
Danger is over, The, 159–160
Danger is over is over is over, 159
Daniel Cooper, 74, 160–163, 656, 686
"Daniel Cooper," 161, 381
Daniel Cooper and his man, 161
Daphne, 163–164
Dargason, 165–166
"Darksome Cell," 264
"Daughter's Complaint, The," 680
Dean and prebendary, A, 670
Dear brethren do ye hear how fine, 639
Dear Catholic brother, 166–168
Dear Catholic brother are you come from
  the wars, 166
Dear daughter I'd have thee to take spe-
  cial care, 62, 497
Dear friend have you heard the fantasti-
  cal chimes, 455
Dear friends behold a brother most sad,
  544
Dear Gill I ne'er thought until last night,
  408
Dear Jack if you mean, 235
Dear Jockey, 390
Dear Jockey's gone to the wood, 390
Dear Mother I reckon to marry, 209

· 842 ·

From barren Caledonian lands, 563
From Cornwall mount to London fair, 654
From counsels of six where treason prevails, 88
From forth the Elysian fields, 711
From hunger and cold, 111, 244–245, 525, 566
From infallible Rome once more I am come, 393
From Jesuitical polls who proudly expose, 132
From Oberon in fairyland, 204
From old famous Lincoln that's seated so high, 780
From Rome I am come, 632
From Rumps that do rule against custom and laws, 275
"From Sir Roger Martin to Duke of Monmouth," 291
From sluggish sleep and slumber, 533
From the fine Roman whore, 594
From the hag and hungry goblin, 713
From the tap in the guts of the honorable stump, 88
From the top of high Caucasus, 713
From twelve years old I oft have been told, 793
Fugga fugga, 527
Fuggi fuggi fuggi da questo cielo, 527
"Full Description of These Times, A," 408
Full many a ballad hath been penned, 628

Gaberlunzie man, The, 246–247
"Gaberlunzie Man, The," 246, 247
"Gadding Gallant, The," 658
Gaillarde du comte Essex, 207
Gallant esquire named before, The, 295
Gallant lady gay as she was walking, A, 148
Gallant once did woo a lass, A, 283
"Gallant seafight, The," 708
"Gallant's Worthy Commendation of the Mug, The," 410
"Gallantry à la Mode," 444
Gallants far and near, 532
"Gallants of the Times, The," 45
"Gallants to Bohemia," 486
Galliard chi passa, 102
Galliard Essex, 207

Galliard Labandala shotta, 419
"Gallon a Day, A," 594, 737
Game at cards, 510, 511
"Gamecock Conquered, The," 729
"Gang or the Nine Worthies, The," 610
Garden green, 11
Gardener brisk and brave, A, 26
Garland, The, 730
Gather your rosebuds, 104, 247–248, 370
Gelding of the devil, The, 248–250
"Gelding of the Devil, The," 248
"General Feilding's Answer to the Duchess of Cleveland's Memorial," 156
General Monk hath advanced himself, 309
General Monk sailed through the Gunfleet, 309
General Monk was a nobleman, 309
General Monk's march, 309
General Monk's right march, 309
"General Monk's Welcome to Whitehall," 766
"General Sale of Rebellious Household-stuff, A," 549
"General Summons to Assemble at Horn Fair, A," 147
"Generous Lover, The," 211
Gentil madonna, 261
"Gentle Ballad Called Lamentable Lory, A," 568
"Gentle Craft's Complaint, The," 522
"Gentleman That Lately Lived, A," 370
"Geordie," 136
George Barnwell, 603
"George Barnwell, An Excellent Ballad of," 603
"George the Glover and Grace the Bonelace Maker," 698
Gerard's mistress, 250–252
Gerhard, 251
Gigg a gogge, 797
Gilderoy, 109, 252–254, 301
"Gilderoy," 253
Gilderoy was a bonny boy, 252–253
"Gilderoy's Last Farewell," 253
Gillian of Croydon, 482
"Gillian of Croydon," 481, 482
"Gipsies' Song, The," 42
Give ear a while, 417, 549
Give ear a while to my ditty, 417, 549
Give ear a while unto my song, 212, 381
Give ear O king and nobles all, 559, 762

· 867 ·

My love and I'll be married, 374
My love he was as brave a man, 253
My love is gone alackaday, 425
My love is on the brackish sea, 381
My loving friend I do commend, 204
My loving good neighbors that comes to behold, 419
My maid Mary, 502
My maid Mary she minds her dairy, 502
'My maidenhead will not load me,' 155
My maidenhead will not o'erload me, 155
My masters all attend you, 461
My masters and friends and good people draw near, 568
"My Mind to Me a Kingdom Is," 364
"My Mistress Is All the Genders," 648
My mistress is to Bulling (i.e., Boulogne) gone, 276
"My Mistress Understands All the Cases," 648
My mother's ay glowrin o'er me, 298
My muse arise and truth then tell, 58
My name is honest Harry, 292
My name is Tom of all trades, 42
My name it is Bougel a Boy, 74
My Nan she was good, 506
My Nanny O, 507
"My Nanny O," 506
My noble friends give ear, 332
My only love my dearest dear, 564
My passion is as mustard strong, 104
My Patie is a lover gay, 635
'My plaid awa my plaid awa,' 561
My plaid away, 562
My pockets begar were lined very well, 408
My pretty Betty I now must leave thee, 338
My pretty little rogue, 149
My pretty little rogue, 149
My Robin is to the greenwood gone, 59–64
My Savoy lord why dost thou frown on me, 228
My Sefautian art thou deceased, 642
My shepherd's unkind, 2
My son if you reckon to wed, 280
My sweetest my fairest my rarest my dearest, 515
"My Thing Is My Own," 453
My wife she is dumb, 334
"My Wife Will Be My Master," 574

My wretched fate I do declare, 634
My young Mary, 502
My young Mary does mind the dairy, 502
"Mystery Discovered, The," 725

Nachtegael, Den, 512
"Naked Truth, The," 548
Nancy, 14
Nancy Dawson, 503–505
"Nancy Dawson," 503
"Nancy's Ghost," 53
Nanny O, 426, 459, 460, 505–507
"Nanny O," 506
"Nanny O, An Answer to," 505
"Nation's Joy for a War with Monsieur, The," 459
Nation's sins are many fold, The, 156
"National Quarrel, The," 452–453
"Nature's Wonder," 16
Near a fair fountain a damsel sat weeping, 755
Near a pleasant shady grove, 691
'Near me near me laddie lie near me,' 424
Near old Gravel Lane, 572
Near to a fountain all alone, 296
Near Woodstock town in Oxfordshire, 563
Near Woodstock town in Oxfordshire, 563
Ned she that likes thee now, 578
"Neglected Tar, The," 738
"Nell's Courtship," 683
"Nell's Humble Petition," 26
"Nelly's Constancy, An Excellent New Song Called," 296
"Neptune's Raging Fury," 768
Never a penny of money, 144, 705
Never love thee more, 355
Never will I wed a girl that's coy, 354
"New and True Ballad of the Poet's Complaint, A," 331
"New Ballad, A" (Abigail Hill), 99
"New Ballad, A" (Junto), 552
"New Ballad, A" (Monmouth), 348
"New Ballad, A" (My lord mayor), 463
"New Ballad, A" (Queen Elizabeth), 410
"New Ballad, A" (The world's a frantic), 464
"New Ballad, A" (To our once loyal town), 569
"New Ballad, A" (What do members now), 718

Now now the work's done, 524
Now now the zealots all must droop, 306
Now now too weak alas I find our cause, 75
Now now you blind boy, 525
Now now you Tories pray give o'er, 307
Now now's the siege raised, 524
Now O now I needs must part, 242, 244
Now of my sweet Betty, 572
Now our bloody fight is over, 191
Now Pan leaves piping, 615
Now peace it is finished, 606
Now ponder well, 103–105
Now ponder well you parents dear, 103, 614
'Now she got nothing by't,' 656
Now sweet Shinny wilt thou be wed, 409, 771
Now that love's holiday is come, 350
Now the fatal fight is over, 191
Now the fatal fight is over, 191
Now the fight is over, 191
Now the fight's done, 524
Now the great monarch of England's bright splendor, 684
Now the Parliament sits, 444
Now the plotters and plots are confounded, 546
Now the rash imputing Tories, 698
Now the Rump is confounded, 199
Now the season of winter, 473
Now the spring is come, 526–527
Now the spring is come, 526–527
Now the Tories that glories, 527–528
Now the Tories that glory (glories), 527
Now the traitor king-hater, 528
Now the tyrant hath stolen, 62, 63, 183
Now the tyrant has stolen my dearest away, 62, 63
Now the Whigs and their friends are confounded, 550
Now to my true lover Betty, 404
Now Tom if Suckling were alive, 349
Now we are met in a knot let's take t'other pot, 193
Now we see the fight is over, 191
Now welcome neighbor Rowland, 471
Now would I give my life to see, 356
Now you by your good leave sirs, 430
Now you young females that follows the mode, 422

Now young bachelors all draw near, 771
Now young tempting Phaon you shall have your prey, 732
Nutmegs and ginger, 529–530

O a masquerade's a fine place, 464
O Bacchus if thou'lt ease a soul, 533
O Bessy Bell and Mary Gray, 736
"O Bessy Bell and Mary Gray," 298
O Birkenhead how hast thy tired thy muse, 310
O brave house, 210, 211
O broder Teague and Teague my roon, 408, 453
O brother Taylor what shall we now do, 496
O Chloris awake, 2
O Chloris awake, 2
O come my own dear let's dally a while, 144
O cruel bloody fate, 5, 6
O Cupid thou now art too cruel, 808
O dear lady Elizabeth which art our queen, 410
O do me no harm good man, 780
O do not do not kill me yet, 197
'O do not do not kill me yet,' 197
O doctor now repent since at the last, 76
O don't you remember a long time ago, 103
O Dublin is a fine town and a gallant city, 463
O Englishmen with Romish hearts, 534
"O Fain Would I Marry," 199
O fain would I wive, 199
O fie upon Cupid's skill, 219
O fie what mean I foolish maid, 530–531
O fie what mean I foolish maid, 530
O gracious God and heavenly King, 589
O gracious God look down upon, 121
"O Gramercy Penny," 263
O hark, 564
O hone O hone, 232–235, 267
'O hone O hone,' 233
O horrid horrid is my crime, 623
O how can I be merry or glad, 314–315
O how can I be merry or glad, 314
O how can my poor heart be glad, 563
O how happy's he, 531–532
O how I dote upon that lass, 92
O how I sigh, 221

O what a madness 'tis to borrow or lend, 490
O what a pain is love, 577
O what a pain it is, 149
O what a pitiful passion, 501
O what a plague is love, 577
O where am I now, 231
O where's my Rosinda shall I never more, 498
O who would fix his eyes upon, 108
O why am I always perplexed in mind, 319
O woman is a fine thing, 463
O wretched England mind, 604
O wretched man that lovest earthly things, 284
O wretched woman that I am, 683
O yes O yes O yes I cry, 297
"Oakerman, The," 713
"Oates Threshed in the Counter," 286
"Oates Well Threshed," 88, 274
"Oates's Bug . . . Bug . . . Boarding-school," 622
"Obsequy of Fair Phillida, The," 215
"Observations in the Use of Tobacco," 709
Ods bodikins ch'ill work no more, 348
Ods whirlikins what mun che do, 350
O'er boggy, 560–561
"O'er Boggy," 560
O'er scroggy o'er boggy, 561
Of a constant young seaman a story I'll tell, 3
"Of a Maid That Was Deep in Love," 775
Of a rich counselor I write, 343
Of a royal race was Shinkin, 542
Of a worthy Dublin drapier, 16
Of a worthy London prentice, 13
Of Adam's seed poor sinner I, 534
'Of ah ah ah my love's dead,' 182
Of all sorts of callings that in England be, 379
Of all spendthrifts in this land, 117
'Of all the caps that ever I see,' 45
Of all the curst plagues, 358
Of all the dunces in the town, 504
Of all the foolish things we do, 541
Of all the fools that e'er was known, 540
Of all the fools who've lately writ, 504
Of all the girls in our town, 503

Of all the maidens fair who snuff the morning air, 492
Of all the papers in the town, 504
Of all the professions that ever were named, 111
Of all the recreations which attend, 18, 377
Of all the sciences under (beneath) the sun, 275
Of all the simple things I know, 540
Of all the simple things we do, 540–541
Of all the simple things we do, 540
Of all the songs that e'er was penned, 463
Of all the trades that ever I see, 273, 275
Of an ungrateful son my purpose is to write, 604
Of Bray the vicar long I've been, 737
Of doubtful race was Georgy, 542
Of English acts I intend to write, 767
Of fire fire fire I sing, 372
Of Hector's deeds did Homer sing, 588
Of Herod's bloody reign, 372
Of horned Vulcan I have heard, 680
"Of Johnny and Jenny," 780
"Of King Edward II Being Poisoned," 316
Of late as I was journeying, 724
Of late did I hear a young damsel complain, 151
Of late I did hear a young man domineer, 152
Of late I did hear of a wooing, 321
Of late I did walk in a pleasant fair day, 186
Of late I heard a ditty, 256
Of late in the north a fine frolic did pass, 186
Of late it was my chance to walk, 203
Of late near the Strand, 795
Of late we have heard of a laird in high station, 666
Of late we hear in Devonshire, 347
Of Mandeville I do not tell, 349, 351
Of noble race was Shinkin, 12, 541–542
"Of Noble Race Was Shinkin," 542
Of old soldiers the song you would hear, 593
Of quarrels and changes and changelings I sing, 167
"Of the Downfall of One Part of the Mitre Tavern," 377

When Flora with rich tapestry, 813
When flying fame, 97, 628
When God had taken for our sin, 588
When good Queen Elizabeth history's boast, 605
When Greeks and Trojans fell at strife, 588
When honest redcoats leave cutting of throats, 193
When honesty first was in vogue, 188
When hope lay hushed in silent night, 786
When Humber in his wrathful rage, 364
When humming brown beer was the Englishman's taste, 605
When I had seen this Virgin's end, 58
'When I have no want of money,' 144
When I have often heard young maids complaining, 760–761
When I have often heard young maids complaining, 760
"When I Was a Bachelor," 571
When I was a bachelor I lived a merry life, 571
When I was a dame of honor, 157
'When I was a dame of honor,' 156
'When I was a man of honor,' 157
When I was young and handsome too, 73
When I was young as you are now, 426
When I went early in the spring, 296
When Isabel fair England's queen, 774
When it was grown to dark midnight, 785
When James in Scotland first began, 98
When Jesus Christ was twelve years old, 270
"When Joan's Ale Was New," 388
When Jockey first the wars began, 275, 593
When Jockey first the wars began, 88
"When John's Sail Was New," 388
"When Jones's Ale Was New," 388
When love with unconfined wings, 559, 761–762
When maids live to thirty, 763
When maids live to thirty, 763
When mighty roast beef was the Englishman's food, 605
When my hairs they grow hoary and my cheeks they look pale, 544
When my kids and lambs I treated, 763–764

When my kids and lambs I treated, 763
When of late I sought my bed, 34
When Philomel begins to sing, 680
When Phoebus addressed (had dressed) his course to the west, 197
When Phoebus did rest, 197
When Phoebus did rest, 197
When Phoebus had melted the sickles of ice, 609
When Phoebus had run, 3
When Phoebus with her glittering beams, 212
When Phoebus with his beams, 16
When ravishing rebellion reigns, 589
When Robin Hood was about twenty years old, 609
When Samson was a tall young man, 680, 681
When Sawney left me, 633
When Sol could cast no light, 149
When Sol did cast no light, 151
When Sol did cast no light, 149
When Sol had left his weary teams, 303, 691
When Sol will cast no light, 149
When Sol will cast no light, 149
When Sol with golden rays, 149
When stout young Jemmy went abroad, 308
When summer comes the swains on Tweed, 71
When that I was, 714
When the kine had given a pailful, 192
When the kine had given a pailful, 192
When the king came of late with his peers of state, 779
When the king comes home in peace again, 767
'When the king comes home in peace again,' 765
When the king enjoys his own again, 764–768
'When the king enjoys his own again,' 765
When the king enjoys his rights again, 766
When the king leaves off Sally and holds to the queen, 132
When the plot I first invented, 371
When the stormy winds do blow, 117, 768–769
'When the stormy winds do blow,' 769

You blades of the north, 379
You bold undaunted souls attend, 108
You bonny boon blades, 185
You Calvinists of England, 768
You cowed-hearted (coward-hearted) citizens, 147
You cruel parents most severe, 343
You cutpurses all, 568
You dainty dames so finely framed, 369
You dames I say that climb the mount, 196
You female trepanners I pray you draw near, 221
You females all give ear, 415
You friends to reformation, 670
You gallant ladies all, 233
You gallants all I pray draw near, 241
You gallants all that love to play, 508
You gallants of country and city, 807
You gallants of every station, 597
You gallants that delight to play, 509
You gallants that desire to play, 509
You gallants that resort, 513
You gentlemen all come listen a while, 409, 771
You gentlemen of England that lives at home at ease, 768
You gods and goddesses that rules in Helicon, 251
You horned fumbling cuckolds, 147
You I love by all that's true, 805–806
You I love by all that's true, 805
You I love by Jove I do, 805
You ladies draw near, 220
You ladies falsely deemed, 158
You limber ladies that appear, 18
You London dames whose passing fames, 42
You London lads be merry, 598, 806–808
You London lads rejoice, 629
You lordings cast off your weeds of woe, 196
You lovers all where e'er you be, 752
You lovers most loyal where e'er you be, 408
You lovers of mirth attend a while, 483
You lovers that have been false-hearted, 209
You loyal lads be merry, 807
You loyal lovers all help me to moan, 234
You loyal lovers attend to my ditty, 94

You loyal lovers far and near, 683
You loyal lovers that are distant, 336
You loyal subjects all, 672
You loyal young damosels, 221
You loyal-hearted Englishmen, 510
You lusty young bachelors, 360
You madcaps of England, 665
You madcaps of England who merry would make, 665
You maidens all that would be wise, 163
You maidens and wives and young widows rejoice, 568
You maidens that are fair and young, 199, 692
You maidens who intend to wed, 623
You maidens wild that were beguiled, 163
You maids and widows all a-row, 751
You maids that live in London town, 162
You master colliers pray draw near, 553
You matrons all with humble submission, 438
You merchants rich farmers and graziers, 209
You muses all your aid to me assign, 625
You noble lords of high degree, 622
You noble minds and famous martial wights, 226
You nobles and peers of the kingdom, 209
You nobles here of England, 769
You Norfolk freeholders whose generous hearts, 174
You parents whose affection fond, 784
You peers of this nation pray never rebel, 186
You poets that write of the ages that's past, 779
You Presbyters now relent, 321
You pretty ladies all, 155
"You Pretty Little Ladies Will Do So," 750
You pretty little young men all, 155
You pretty maidens all, 234
You pretty maidens all I pray give ear, 234
You pretty maidens listen well, 374
You pretty maids where e'er you are, 29
You pretty young lasses all, 492
You Protestants all draw near to this place, 454
You roaring boys and sturdy thieves, 780

About the Author

Claude M. Simpson, who holds both arts and music degrees from Southern Methodist University, received the Ph.D. from Harvard, and is presently Professor of English at Stanford University. He is the author of numerous books and articles on music, and has brought out editions of classical and folk music. In the field of literature, he collaborated with Allan Nevins on *An American Reader* (1941) and with Leon Edel, T. H. Johnson, and Sherman Paul on *Masters of American Literature* (1959).

The typeface used for the text of this book is Baskerville, with Garamond as display. The book is printed by letterpress on 55# Warren's 1854 Plate and bound in Columbia's Bayside Vellum and Spindrift. The endpapers are Schlosser Multicolor. It was manufactured by Quinn & Boden Company, Inc., Rahway, N.J.